PERSONNEL MANAGEMENT

PERSONNEL MANAGEMENT

JOBS, PEOPLE, AND LOGIC

R. DENNIS MIDDLEMIST

Oklahoma State University

MICHAEL A. HITT

Oklahoma State University

CHARLES R. GREER

Oklahoma State University

Prentice-Hall, Inc., Englewood Cliffs, New Jersey 07632

Library of Congress Cataloging in Publication Data

MIDDLEMIST, R. DENNIS.
  Personnel management.

  Includes bibliographies and index.
    1. Personnel management.   I. Hitt, Michael A.
II. Greer, Charles R.   III. Title.
HF5549.M466   1983   658.3   82-16487
ISBN 0-13-659003-9

Editorial/production supervision and
    interior design: Richard C. Laveglia
Cover design: Suzanne Behnke
Manufacturing buyer: Ed O'Dougherty
Cover photos courtesy of Shell Oil Company

Printed in the United States of America

10 9 8 7 6 5 4 3 2 1

ISBN 0-13-659003-9

Prentice-Hall International, Inc., *London*
Prentice-Hall of Australia Pty. Limited, *Sydney*
Editora Prentice-Hall do Brasil, Ltda., *Rio de Janeiro*
Prentice-Hall Canada Inc., *Toronto*
Prentice-Hall of India Private Limited, *New Delhi*
Prentice-Hall of Japan, Inc., *Tokyo*
Prentice-Hall of Southeast Asia Pte. Ltd., *Singapore*
Whitehall Books Limited, *Wellington, New Zealand*

To the parents who still nurture us—Arteen, George, and Floreine—we love you.

To those dear to me and still present,—Alva and Elrey (Dad and Mom) and Perry (little brother), and to a dear one who is no longer present—Don (big brother). Thank you for all you have given me.

To my family—Liz, Stacy, and John and parents Fern and Thornton

CONTENTS

HIRING FOR PERFORMANCE   83

5 The Logic of Selection   85

6 Human Resource Planning and Recruiting   98

7 Selection Tools   126

8   Selecting Managers and Professionals   158

THREE
TRAINING FOR PERFORMANCE   177

9   The Logic of Training   179

MOTIVATING AND COMPENSATING PERFORMANCE 241

13 Motivation   257

14 Compensating Jobs   276

15 Performance Appraisal: Compensating People   302

16 Incentives and Benefits   330

FIVE
MAINTAINING AN
EFFECTIVE WORK FORCE   355

17 Equal Employment Opportunity   357

18 Labor Relations   382

19 Occupational Safety and Health   415

20 Discipline   436

COMPLEX ISSUES   453

21 Organization Change: Individual and Organization Development   455

22 Quality of Life: Work, Living, and Retiring   484

23 Personnel Management and the Future   504

Glossary   517

Index   537

PREFACE

The organization of managerial systems to utilize human resources most effectively is one of management's most challenging responsibilities. The systematic process of managing human resources is called personnel management. The field of personnel management is becoming increasingly more important to organizations at the same time that it is growing in sophistication of technique. It is no longer possible to manage human resources effectively unless managers study, understand, and develop their skills in applying these techniques. It is for this purpose that we have designed this textbook. We feel that this text is a superior learning aid for classroom instruction that can provide *understanding* as well as exposure to personnel management techniques and applications.

Learning can be a difficult and uncertain task. It is especially perplexing when a field is replete with a variety of activities and techniques and involves the uncertainties of human nature as does personnel management. Traditionally, personnel management texts have focused on wide-ranging surveys of personnel management activities and techniques. These sometimes have been emphasized as being performed mainly by personnel specialists. With such an approach, the students quickly become less able to separate one technique from another, because although they know *what* an interview is and *what* job evaluation is, they can only guess at *why* the techniques are performed in particular ways.

In other places, we would refer to such learning as the trial and error method. That is, by exposing students to available techniques, they will later, through trial and error applications, begin to understand when one technique has an advantage over another. Eventually, the student manager will begin to establish a rationale that pulls together the loosely related techniques and to manage the organization's human resources effectively.

However, learning about personnel management does not need to be disorganized if we recognize that learning always involves a cognitive process in which the individual tries to create a rational framework that integrates seemingly isolated events. We have become accustomed first to presenting the events and then allowing students to create the rationale. A more effective learning process is one in which the rationale is already present and events can quickly be understood and readily integrated into their proper relationships. This is the process used in *Personnel Management: Jobs, People, and Logic*, namely, presenting logical frameworks that can be used to integrate and understand not only *what* personnel techniques are but *why* they need to be performed in particular ways. Hence the inclusion of the term "logic" in the title and our attention to the nature of "logical thinking" in the first chapter of the text.

The logic of personnel management is a *logic of managing*, not a logic of the nature of people. The logic is in determining whether one selection tool or another is best for the situation, whether the compensation scheme is sound, and so forth. These problems involve certain rationales that managers can use to apply personnel management techniques correctly.

Some may readily see that other logics can be developed for relating various techniques. We admit this; we have no corner on such rationales. However, the rationales we present in selection, training, motivation, and compensation follow a consistent logic. By at least presenting one simple rationale, the students' ability to understand more complex techniques is enhanced.

The logic chapters are not intended to do more than present one of the frameworks from which students can progress to a better understanding of personnel management activities. The chapters that follow each logic, then, contain a more complete survey of related techniques that can be evaluated and probed for understanding and potential applications. Certainly we feel that learning (as opposed to human nature) can be, and should be, a logical process.

Although the primary distinction of this text is the inclusion of appropriate logics, we have included certain other features that should enhance the learning process. A major feature is an opening interview in each chapter with a personnel specialist, manager, or employee regarding the subject matter in the chapter. These are more than simple interest features. In most cases, they illustrate a practitioner's philosophy or approach. In some cases, they identify certain problems that can be solved by logical application of personnel management techinques. They nearly always give a practical viewpoint and disallow an academic stiffness that might interfere with students' willingness to explore the material.

The book also includes substantial review of the research literature and current issues. Learning objectives are provided and related review questions help students to focus their studies. Finally, cases are provided to allow students to practice what they have learned from chapter concepts. We hope that these features make the study of personnel management one of the students' major learning experiences.

We would like to thank the many people who have contributed to our efforts in this work. The following people and organizations who provided chapter interviews were especially kind. Despite busy schedules, they were interested in the project and interested in students' education in personnel management. We gratefully acknowledge their contributions.

Ron Chilcott of Capital Records
John Devine of Xerox Corporation
Carolyn England of Macklanburg-Duncan Company
Dennis R. Cash of Texas-New Mexico Power Company
Douglas W. Pelino of Xerox Corporation
Joe Shepela of Hewlett-Packard Company
Mike Hornbuckle of American Tourister
Jim Rogers of NCR Microelectronics
Jane Kurtiss of Massachusetts Mutual Life Insurance
Judy Mason-Mertz of Xerox Corporation
Lewis Lash of Eastern Airlines
Wayne Wright of Texas Instruments
Fred Brown of GTE Sylvania
Norman L. Holton of Food Process Workers' Union
Betty Meyers of Texize Chemicals
Bob Klevin of Woodward Govenor Company
Richard Christenson of Thomas & Betts Company
H. Peter Perkins of Hewlett-Packard Company
James Grimaldi of Equibank
Wayne Smith of Phillips Petroleum Company
Roy Carney of KPNW Radio
Elise Dunphy of The Coca-Cola Company

We also are grateful to Richard Dutton, University of South Florida, Prof. Charles T. Maxey, University of Southern California, and Professor Mitchell S. Novitt who reviewed the manuscript and whose insightful comments led to consistent improvements of the text. We sincerely appreciate their efforts. We also appreciate the efforts of the many Prentice-Hall employees who helped obtain interviews.

Finally, no work is ever completed without the support of colleagues and secretarial assistance. Our colleagues at Oklahoma State University and Colorado State University have been most helpful and are appreciated. Also, Irene B. Larson and Jan Kuhnen provided excellent secretarial services and often aided in locating necessary reference material. We sincerely appreciate their patience and assistance. We would also like to acknowledge the assistance of Mary Anne Dorland and Jerry Scott. Finally, we would like to acknowledge Doris Stokes who compiled the glossary and provided other assistance.

PERSONNEL MANAGEMENT

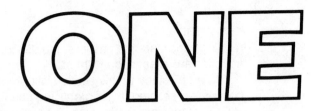

INTRODUCTION TO PERSONNEL MANAGEMENT

This book has two common threads. First, personnel management activities are not the exclusive responsibility of "personnel managers." To be sure, personnel managers perform a distinct set of organizational activities such as selecting, training, and developing the human resources of organizations. However, every manager, regardless of his or her specialized areas of activity, shares responsibilities for personnel management.

Second, the more complex issues in personnel management can be understood best by beginning with a simple, *logical* framework and developing understanding from there. With a few logical premises, complex relationships can be understood with ease. The purpose of the chapters in this first section, then, is to present these viewpoints and some of the basic personnel management tools that you will use throughout your study and application of personnel management concepts.

Chapter 1 introduces the three relationships in personnel management: organizations, jobs, and people. Relationships involving people rarely seem to be perfectly logical, but they should be examined and studied in a rational or logical manner. The notion of logic and the plan for presentation of concepts complete the topics in Chapter 1. Chapter 2 presents some fundamental considerations in the operation of personnel departments and examines recent data regarding career opportunities in the field. Even if you do not plan a career in personnel management, it is necessary to understand how personnel departments affect you and your employees.

Chapter 3 concerns the fundamental nature of job design, an activity that widely affects most other personnel management responsibilities. The proper selection, training, compensation, and motivation of employees depends heavily on the manner in which jobs are designed. Three other activities with similar wide-ranging effects are job analysis, job description, and job specification. These three activities are examined in Chapter 4.

Careful study of this section will prepare you for the personnel management concepts presented in the remaining chapters of this text as well as enhance your skills in managing human resources in organizations.

1

PERSONNEL MANAGEMENT: THE LOGIC OF ORGANIZATIONS, JOBS, AND PEOPLE

LEARNING OBJECTIVES

After reading this chapter, you should be able to

1. Define the term personnel management.
2. Describe some personnel management activities.
3. Discuss the responsibilities of line managers in performing personnel management activities.
4. Define personnel management logic.
5. Discuss the three central elements in personnel management relationships.

It is sometimes difficult to examine and study a management topic because we are unfamiliar with the general nature of that topic. To help develop an understanding of personnel management activities, we interviewed a personnel manager who shared some of his views with us.

Ron Chilcott is a corporation employee manager with Capitol Records and works in Capitol's Hollywood, California, office. This office employs between five hundred and six hundred people. He received his B.S. degree from Shenandoah University in Virginia, and he has three and a half years of experience in personnel work.

Interviewer: Briefly, what does the job "personnel manager" involve?

Ron Chilcott: The most basic activities are recruiting, interviewing, and selecting employees. However, the responsibilities go far beyond these basics. In part, what we do is perform a watchdog function for the corporation, trying to create the most effective working ambience for employees. For employees to be happy and productive, they must be well trained, well treated, and well respected by their managers. It is the personnel manager's duty to work with managers, to see that managers are professionally skilled in their interactions with employees.

Interviewer: Can you expand on this a little? In what ways does a personnel manager help the organization in its relationship with people?

Ron Chilcott: The personnel manager provides a channel for communication and counseling that meets a variety of needs: career guidance, manager-employee conflicts, personal problems that affect employee performance, and so on. It is the personnel manager's responsibility to train other managers to handle these problems as well.

Interviewer: Can you tell me one or two things your company does to improve the relationship between people and their jobs?

Ron Chilcott: Actually we do a lot of things, like occasionally providing baseball or concert tickets or letting employees take time off, occasionally, for doing things that are important to them personally. But the most important thing we do is with our job descriptions. Our job descriptions are written in a way that does not confine an employee to only one or two rather routine duties. Our jobs are defined in ways that allow employees who show a capacity and willingness for more responsibility to take on more challenging tasks. In this way, employees grow with their jobs and find them exciting and fulfilling.

Interviewer: Besides yourself, what other people are key elements in a successful program of personnel management?

Ron Chilcott: Successful personnel management is the result of activities by the entire management staff. It cannot be a thing that is done only once in a while or only by a personnel manager. Line managers are in daily contact with employees and are truly responsible for creating and establishing the feelings an employee has for the company, his job, and himself as a worker.

INTRODUCTION

The success of modern organizations is heavily dependent upon the contributions made by employees as they perform the various tasks to which they are assigned. Organizations tend to be successful when employees are satisfied and productive in performing their tasks. However, they are less successful when employees are less satisfied and productive in their task performances. This conclusion is obvious to most organizational managers, but the way in which managers should go about managing so that employees are satisfied and productive is not so obvious.

The subject of this book is the process of managing people, and their tasks, in organizations. This process is referred to as personnel management. The term personnel refers to "persons employed in various tasks and organizations." The term management commonly refers to "the integration and coordination of all resources in order to move effectively toward desired objectives."[1] This leads us to the definition of personnel management, which emphasizes the human resource.

Personnel management: the integration and coordination of human resources in order to move effectively toward desired objectives.

Personnel management activities, then, are those managerial processes that relate people (employees) to their various jobs and to the organization that employs them. This viewpoint is consistent with Ron Chilcott's and represents a current approach to personnel management. Personnel management activities include

1. Planning, designing, and evaluating employees' jobs, relating some jobs to other jobs, and determining how many people are needed to staff the jobs.
2. Recruiting, selecting, training, developing, and motivating employees to perform the jobs effectively.
3. Providing satisfactory relationships between the organization and people (employees) through fringe benefits, labor relations, and quality-of-work-life programs.

LEARNING ABOUT PERSONNEL MANAGEMENT

Any authors of a book designed for learning must ask themselves, "What does the reader need to learn about the subject?" The answer to this question largely determines both the content of the book and the manner in which it is presented. This book presents material in a manner somewhat different from the typical personnel management text.

There are three basic answers to the question just raised. First, we might conclude, as others have, that the reader needs to learn *what* personnel managers do. Second, we might conclude that the reader needs to learn *why* personnel managers do what they do. Third, and more correctly, we might conclude that the reader should learn both *what* personnel managers do and *why*. The third conclusion underlies the presentation of material in this book. As you discover that certain things are common personnel management processes, you should ask, "Why?" To understand why we feel this is the best approach for learning about the subject, we need to examine the who, what, where, and why of personnel management.

Who Performs Personnel Activities?

We often think of personnel activities as tasks that are performed by personnel managers. This viewpoint, although somewhat narrow, is generally accurate. Especially in medium- to large-sized organizations, responsibility for many personnel management activities is centralized within a personnel department. As shown in Figure 1-1, personnel activities are typically organized as a staff function. We examine the nature of personnel departments and their organization more completely in Chapter 2.

Staff activities are those that support the primary functions of an organization (e.g., production, marketing) but that have only an indirect impact on the organization's outputs. Staff activities often carry no direct authority over the primary functions. Therefore, managers of staff activities typically act in an advisory capacity, offering their expertise to other departments that are under little obligation to follow the advice.

This viewpoint is limited in two respects. First, personnel managers often have a great deal of authority over hiring practices, compensation policies, labor relations

Figure 1-1

Typical Organization Structure for Personnel Department

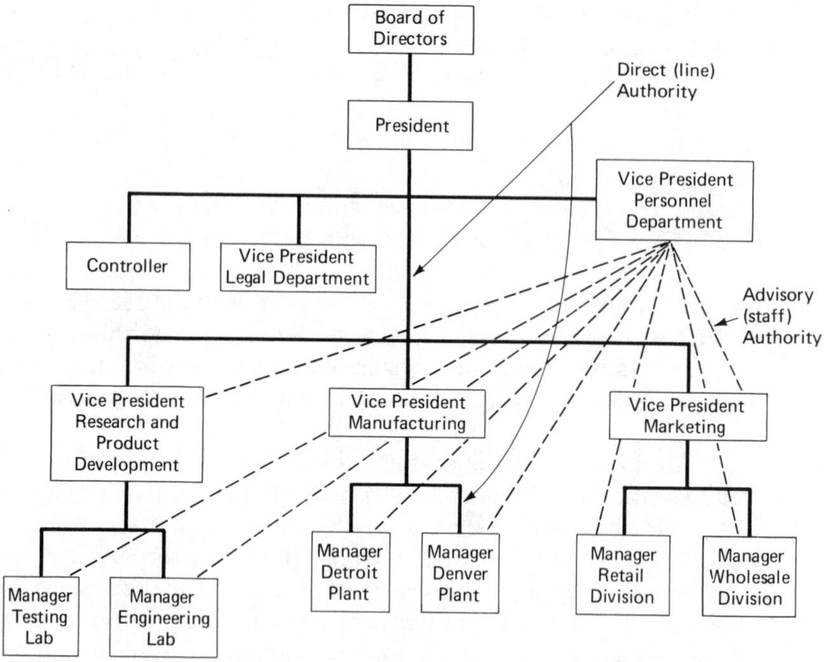

programs, and other important organizational employee-related activities. In some organizations, personnel activities are hardly staff activities, and the personnel department may be organized with direct line or functional authority. Second, if we think of personnel activities as being performed only by personnel managers (or departments), we overlook the many organizations that have no personnel departments but must still perform the same personnel activities.

We might also overlook the important personnel activities performed by every manager in the organization. Personnel activities are performed, to some extent, by every organizational manager. As Ron Chilcott described it, successful personnel management is the result of activities by the entire management staff. Line managers are in daily contact with employees and are truly responsible for creating and establishing the feelings that employees have for the company, their jobs, and themselves as employees.

Therefore, we can conclude that, while personnel managers and specialists need a high level of expertise in personnel activities, all managers must at least be familiar with the logic underlying those activities. Production managers or marketing managers who understand the logic will be more effective in their interactions with employees. They will be more likely to make effective hiring, salary, promotion, and training decisions. It is also more likely that their employees will be satisfied and productive.

What Are Personnel Activities?

Most people have a limited knowledge of the kinds of activities that make up the personnel management function. We may have applied for jobs at organizations in which our first contact was with the personnel department. We also may have had certain interactions with the personnel department in an organization for which we worked. These contacts and interactions may lead us to believe that personnel departments help a person to fill out a job application blank, administer selection tests, fill out W-2 forms, or explain company insurance programs.

To be sure, these activities are often performed by personnel departments, but they hardly represent the wide variety of activities that constitute personnel management. Virtually any activity that has the purpose of improving the relationships between employees and their jobs, or between employees and the organization, or between the organization and employee jobs is truly a personnel activity. Thus determining the correct method for performing a job is as much a personnel activity as is administering a retirement program. More completely, personnel management activities include

1. Designing organizational tasks to be compatible with organizational and individual needs.
2. Analyzing jobs to gather information that can be used for selection, training, and compensation purposes.
3. Planning for the organization's needs for various types of employees.
4. Recruiting and selecting skilled or trainable employees.

5. Integrating employees into the organizational environment.
6. Training and developing employee skills.
7. Ensuring that employees are motivated properly.
8. Determining and administering systematic and fair compensation programs.
9. Administering personnel programs required by law such as equal employment opportunity, occupational safety, and health programs.
10. Interacting with employee unions.
11. Administering fair disciplinary programs.
12. Preparing employees for organizational changes that result from dynamic societal forces.
13. Designing and administering employee benefits, such as insurance and retirement programs.
14. Helping the organization to develop and change as necessary to meet societal demands.

Where Are Personnel Activities Performed?

Formalized personnel departments are found in nearly all large organizations (public and private) and most medium-sized organizations but in very few small organizations. Formalization of personnel activities requires that specialists be hired, office space purchased, and so on. Therefore, formalization has a cost that smaller organizations can rarely afford. Yet, despite the lack of formalization, personnel management activities must be performed in every organization regardless of size.

The need to perform personnel management activities does not depend on whether the organization is a government agency or a private business or on the organization's size. It also does not depend on whether one is managing a group of accountants, engineers, sales people, or assembly workers. Personnel management activities are required whenever people are employed to perform organizational tasks. Thus these activities are performed in all types of organizations, in all areas, and at all levels within these organizations.

Why Are Personnel Activities Performed in Certain Ways?

The important "why" question is *not,* "Why are personnel activities performed?" but, rather, "Why are personnel activities performed in certain ways?" The answer to the first question tells us that organization effectiveness depends on integrating individuals into their jobs and the organization. But it does not tell us *how* to achieve the integration.

Achieving integration among people, their jobs, and the organization depends on the ability to know why one particular personnel activity is more appropriate than another. The ability to determine logically, for instance, whether one employee with certain skills is better suited to perform clerical tasks than another employee with different skills is fundamental and essential to management. This talent allows us to design effective personnel management activities whether we are in a large or small organization, or in a public or private organization, and whether we manage accountants or assembly-line workers.

To return to our initial discussion, then, this text focuses on learning not only what personnel managers do but also on the *logic* they must use in doing those things correctly. Personnel activities are performed in different ways in different situations, but knowledge of how to do them correctly follows similar logic processes in almost all situations.

THE GENERAL LOGIC OF PERSONNEL MANAGEMENT

From our preceding discussion, we can conclude that

1. Personnel management activities are performed not only by personnel managers and departments but by all managers of employees.
2. Personnel management activities must be performed in all organizations be they large or small, public or private.
3. Since formalized personnel departments are found mostly in larger organizations, to study only "what" they do would not be useful for many managers, especially in smaller organizations.
4. Since most organizations tend to perform personnel activities somewhat differently, there must be certain thoughts or "logical processes" that lead to their choices of what to do.

Thus we believe that the study of personnel management involves the development of a "way of thinking" rather than a simple memorizing of a series of management techniques that might, or might not, be applied correctly. We refer to this as logical thinking.

Logical thinking: finding valid or justifiable relationships between one idea, or set of ideas, and another.[2]

To think is not always to think logically. Our thinking processes are often at the mercy of our biases, values, and attitudes. For instance, we may believe that women are better suited than men to raise children. Thus we may conclude that it is "logical" for the wife to be given custody of any children in the event of a divorce. It does not take much analysis to determine that some husbands are better suited than their wives to raise children. What is truly logical, in this example, is for the parent-child relationship to be investigated on a case-by-case basis. The logical process would then involve evaluating the custody decision in terms of the needs of the children and the abilities of the parents. The relationship between the children's needs and the parents' abilities can then be established. In some cases, the mother might be the proper custodian, in other cases the father. Still in other cases, parental custodianship might be shared or divided in different ways according to the various needs of the children.

From this example, we can see that the important elements in logical thinking involve

1. Determining the ideas, or sets of ideas, about which we wish to determine their true relationships;
2. Gathering the facts that bear on the ideas and their relationships; and
3. Putting the facts together in order to conclude what the relationships are.[3]

Logic in Personnel Management

This book is based on the premise that the effective management of people involves logical thinking. By this we do not mean that people always behave logically; that is, an employee may sometimes behave illogically. For example, an employee may get into a physical fight with a co-worker, or operate a machine unsafely and lose a finger. Both are illogical behaviors.

What we do mean is that there are underlying, systematic relationships that *tend* to govern the relationships between a personnel management action and employee needs, behaviors, and performances in organizations. Logical thinking involves understanding these relationships and adjusting personnel actions accordingly. By logical, we also imply that the fundamental skill leading to effective personnel management is that of "thinking through" an action rather than blindly applying supposed "principles."

To illustrate, assume that a manager needs to hire someone to operate a telephone switchboard. What should the manager do to assure that the person hired will be able to perform effectively in that job? The manager may know that a large auto manufacturer gives a certain psychological test to switchboard operators, and only those who "pass" the test are considered for the job. Should the manager use the same test to help decide who the new switchboard operator should be? We can readily see that "what's good for General Motors" is not necessarily "what's good for the manager." To determine whom to hire, the manager needs to find the valid relationship between the job (operating the switchboard) and the employee (switchboard operator). That is, the manager needs, first, to think logically and, second, to apply the proper managerial action. (We return to the selection problem in Chapter 5.)

Elements and Relationships in Personnel Management

Personnal management logic and activities revolve around three central elements and the relationships between them. As illustrated in Figure 1-2, these are (1) the organization, (2) the jobs or tasks to be performed in the organization, and (3) the people employed to perform those tasks.

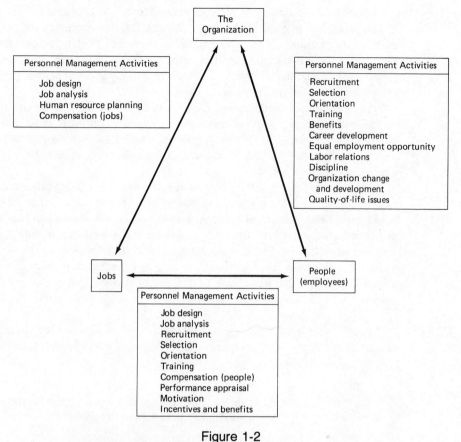

Figure 1-2

Central Elements and Activities in Personnel Management

THE ORGANIZATION.   Organizations are the first consideration in determining effective personnel management activities. This is not to say that people or jobs are less important; rather, it is simply that we can begin a logical analysis by thinking first about organizational considerations.

Organization: a social institution, composed of logically arranged task activities and persons with established patterns of interactions, having been developed to achieve specific goals.[4]

The reason for beginning our personnel management logic with organizations becomes clear when we examine the definition of organizations. Organizations are basically developed to achieve some specific goal or goals. For most organizations, the goals relate to the products or services manufactured or provided to the general public. For example, the goals of the larger automobile manufacturer relate closely to the manufacture of automobiles. The goals of a municipal hospital relate closely to providing a variety of health care services. Without these goals, there is no reason to have created the organization. Further, if the organization cannot meet the product or service goals effectively, it may cease to exist.

Thus personnel management logic must first consider the organization's goals, and the evaluation of personnel management effectiveness must be judged against the achievement of those goals. We must ask the question, "Given the particular organization's goals, how can human resources be used effectively within the organization to help achieve those goals?"

One final point is worth noting in our discussion here. Organizations vary widely in their goals and in the various resources available to achieve them. Therefore, we should expect that personnel management activities will vary also. The hospital will need approaches somewhat different from those of the large automobile manufacturer. Large organizations will need approaches somewhat different from those of small organizations. However, all organizations need to consider their goals. A similar logic process is used, but that logic leads to differences in personnel activities due to organizational goal and resource differences.

JOBS.   The second element to consider in personnel management is that of jobs. As shown in Figure 1-2, jobs constitute an important link between the organization and its employees.

Job: a specific arrangement of tasks, duties, and responsibilities that must be performed in order for the organization to achieve its goals.

Generally, the products and services provided by organizations and the complex society in which they operate necessitate that the larger work of providing products and services be broken into a series of smaller tasks. For example, it is much more feasible to manufacture and market automobiles by having specialized jobs such as "fender assembly," "wheel alignment," "body painting," "sales position," "public relations," and so on than by having people do a little of all the tasks. Because of the enormous number of tasks to be performed, it would hardly be possible for a single person to master them all. The same holds true in hospitals where there might be "emergency treatment," "registration," "maternity care," "brain surgery," "respiratory treatment," and so on.

When the larger work of providing the organization's products or services is reduced to a series of smaller tasks, duties, and responsibilities, we refer to it as job specialization. Personnel management logic is, at this time, concerned with "which arrangements and task groupings will be most effective?" This question can only be answered by attention to both the organizational goals and the needs and abilities of the people who will eventually perform the jobs.

PEOPLE.   The final element in the model is people. Although we consider this element last, it is as important as the others. Certainly tasks cannot be performed without people; and if tasks are not performed, goals cannot be achieved. As Figure 1-2 illustrates, the three elements are woven together in mutual relationships, each affected by the others and each affecting the others.

Personnel management, as stated earlier, is concerned with the proper integration and coordination of people (employees) to move effectively toward desired organizational goals. Personnel management logic, at this point, is concerned with "How can we arrange the organization and the job to utilize best the skills of employees?" or conversely, "How can we best develop the skills of employees to meet the organizational and job requirements?"

Relationships: Organizations, Jobs, and People

As shown in Figure 1-2, personnel management activities are performed to improve three relationships: (1) between organizations and jobs, (2) between jobs and people, and (3) between people and the organization. While we do not want to define these activities precisely at this point, we should note that the association between those relationships and certain personnel management activities is not always clear. For example, job design activities have primary effects on both organization-to-job relationships and job-to-people relationships.

With this thought in mind, we can see, in Figure 1-2, major personnel management activities and the relationships they primarily affect. These activities, and the logic underlying their uses, constitute the major content of this book.

PLAN FOR THE BOOK

We have, until now, been focusing on the question, "What does the reader need to learn about personnel management?" Obviously, we feel that the reader needs to know both what personnel management activities are and the logic used to apply them to specific organizations. This has determined the content and presentation style for the book.

However, there are a large number of activities and logics in the personnel management field. We also need to consider the order in which the topics should be presented. Several orders may make sense. For example, we could deal with one set of relationships at a time (e.g., organization to people, organization to jobs, jobs to people) and examine the activities and their logics. However, since some activities pertain to more than one relationship, there would be an excess of redundancy, and the logic would be less clear.

A second possibility, and the one we have chosen, is to present personnel management activities and their underlying logic in an employee-time sequence. Employee-time sequence refers to the natural, systematic order in which the employee moves into, through, and out of the organization. The employee-time sequence is illustrated in Figure 1-3.

It must be understood that the employee-time sequence is a useful one for presenting material in an orderly fashion. To follow a typical employee's development within the organization is a useful learning approach. However, in existing organizations, these personnel activities occur simultaneously and continually. Employees are constantly entering and leaving organizations. Therefore, managers must be preparing some jobs at the same time they are training employees in other jobs, at the same time they are determining salary systems, and so on. Our choice of presenting topics in an employee-time sequence is simply a pedagogical tool that helps us organize the material. It is not meant to imply that one activity is important only at one time and thereaf-

Figure 1-3

Employee-Time Sequence of Personnel Management Activities

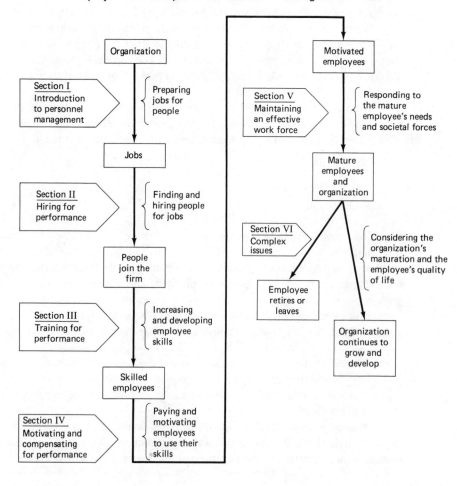

ter unimportant. Many activities, as you will see, continue to be applied throughout the employee's association with the organization.

Section I. Introduction to Personnel Management

The employee-time sequence begins when the organization sets its goals and begins to break the total work of the organization into an appropriate array of more specialized jobs. These jobs contain tasks, duties, and responsibilities that must be performed by people. Managers must be able to establish jobs that are matched logically to the organization's goals and that are prepared logically in anticipation of the needs and skills of the people who will be employed in the jobs. They must also assemble information about the jobs that can be used later to determine the types of skills new employees should have, the types and amount of training necessary, the levels of pay that should be provided, and the likely career paths along which employees can progress.

Chapter 2, Personnel Departments and People, reviews the nature and organization of personnel departments and career opportunities for personnel management specialists. Chapter 3, Job Design and the Nature of People, discusses the preparation of jobs and the process of matching jobs to organizational and human needs. Chapter 4, Job Analysis and Its Uses, presents the process of gathering job information and the logic governing its uses in other personnel management activities. These are important chapters in that job design and job analysis will be incorporated frequently throughout the text.

Section II. Hiring for Performance

The second phase of the employee-time sequence occurs when managers determine the numbers and types of employees needed to staff the jobs. Job information is used to determine the skills needed for various job activities (tasks, duties, and responsibilities). Information regarding the skills possessed by job applicants allows managers to match them correctly to appropriate jobs.

Chapter 5, The Logic of Selection, presents the rationale of the relationship between job requirements and human skills that leads to specific personnel management activities. Chapter 6, Human Resource Planning and Recruiting, discusses the process of determining the numbers and types of employees needed and how to locate prospective employees. Chapter 7, Selection Tools, demonstrates the use of various processes for determining employee skills. Chapter 8, Selecting Managers and Professionals, discusses unique factors associated with the selection of professional employees.

Section III. Training for Performance

The employee-time sequence continues when certain job applicants are finally hired for specific jobs. Perfect matches between jobs and people are difficult to obtain in the selection process. However, managers who know job skill requirements (through job analysis) and existing employee skills (from selection tools) should be able to design programs that can correct skill deficiencies. They may also look at employee growth and enhance existing skills so that employees can progress into higher-skilled jobs.

Chapter 9, The Logic of Training, discusses the rationale governing the "training" relationships among jobs, people, and organizations. Chapter 10, Orientation and Training, presents the process of attitude and skill development. Chapter 11, Career and Management Development, speaks to unique issues of skill development of all employees with emphasis on managerial jobs.

Section IV. Motivating and Compensating for Performance

We continue our employee-time sequence by recognizing that even skilled employees may not be productive unless they are motivated and satisfied with the compensation received for performing their jobs. Of course, managers should consider motivation and compensation when the job is designed initially (remember the discussion on the simultaneous performance of personnel management activities). However, as employees become highly skilled and more tenured members of the organization, we need to make compensation adjustments and maintain enthusiasm in jobs that may have become more routine for them.

Chapter 12, The Logic of Motivation and Compensation, explores the rationale of motivational aspects of job to employee relationships and the economic aspects of jobs, people, and organizational relationships. Chapter 13, Motivation, examines concepts of motivation. Chapter 14, Compensating Jobs, discusses the manner in which compensation is partially determined by job characteristics, and Chapter 15, Performance Appraisal: Compensating People, describes the manner in which compensation also depends on individual employee characteristics. Chapter 16, Incentives and Benefits, completes the motivation-compensation discussion by examining the unique programs that supplement basic salary arrangements.

Section V. Maintaining an Effective Work Force

The employee-time sequence becomes less clear at this point, but we now present many issues that have important impacts on experienced employees following their initial adjustments to the organization but preceding their retirement or resignation. This long period in the organization-job-people relationship may be dominated by concerns about one's career growth, employment opportunities, labor union activities, and occasional disciplinary problems. Organizations must attend to these issues to maintain an effective work force.

Chapter 17, Equal Employment Opportunity, explores organizational and societal issues associated with meaningful career development for potential and existing employees who are considered an occupational minority. Chapter 18, Labor Relations, examines the impact of unionization. Chapter 19, Occupational Safety and Health, describes the legal issues of providing safe, healthful work environments and personnel programs that promote such environments. Chapter 20, Discipline, discusses the purpose and use of disciplinary programs.

Section VI. Complex Issues

The employee-time sequence ends, in the textbook sense, when we con~
bilities of leaving the firm, though the firm continues on and perhaps unuc̣ g̣__
changes in response to social forces. We expand this discussion by considering the
larger aspect of employee-organization relationships that is referred to as quality of
life.

Chapter 21, Organization Change: Individual and Organization Development,
examines the organization in a dynamic society, how it changes and develops in a continuing cycle, and how these changes affect organization, job, and people relationships. Chapter 22, Quality of Life: Working, Living, and Retiring, explores current
social considerations and their large impacts on employee expectations of organizations regarding work, leisure, and postemployment activities. Finally, Chapter 23,
Personnel Management and the Future, presents a cautious, but optimistic, look at the
likely course of personnel management activities in the emerging society and organizations of the future.

SUMMARY

This book concerns the process of integrating and coordinating human resources to
move effectively toward desired objectives. This process is called personnel management. Personnel management activities generally include designing and evaluating
jobs; finding, selecting, training, and developing employees for jobs; and determining
motivation and compensation systems to enhance job performance. These activities
also include consideration of areas that grow in importance as employees settle into
their careers, namely, fringe benefits, equal employment opportunities, labor union relationships, and organizational growth and quality-of-life issues.

This book presents a survey of typical personnel management programs, but it
does not simply describe these programs. Because organizations vary widely in terms
of their goals, available resources, and resulting job arrangements, each organization
must design personnel management activities in accordance with the unique aspects of
the organization. This requires that managers understand the logic that underlies
three important relationships: organization to jobs, jobs to people, and people to organizations. This book describes the relevant logic associated with personnel management activities that should enable the reader to acquire substantial insight as the
activities are described.

We have noted that personnel management activities must be performed by all
managers. This includes those who manage assembly workers, accountants, engineers,
and so on as well as specialists within personnel management departments. Hence we
do not hold the view that the reader wants to know how personnel departments function; rather, we believe that the reader wants to know how to manage human resources effectively within an organization. Our study begins by first considering the
dimensions of a job and how the tasks, duties, and responsibilities are designed and

prepared for the person who will perform that job. The importance of properly prepared jobs and the collection of information about those jobs is emphasized throughout the text as we examine other personnel management activities.

Finally, as you begin to enhance your personnel management skills, you may wonder if it is really worth the effort. Certainly, it requires a great deal of concentration and time to understand personnel management activities. Ron Chilcott of Capitol Records was asked about this effort and the benefits that might derive from it.

INTERVIEW WRAP-UP

It is imperative to provide good relationships between the organization, its jobs, and its employees. Good employee-job-company relationships cut down on employee turnover and, therefore, recruitment and training costs. Additionally, an employee should feel confident about his organization, that it has his interests in mind and will try to meet his professional and career needs. An employee who has an unpleasant experience working for a company with poor personnel management activities is bound to express that to people with whom he or she comes into contact. This affects the company's image. Finally, it is imperative that the effort for good employee-job-company relationships come from the bottom to the top as well as from the top to the bottom of the organization. —Ron Chilcott, corporation employee manager, Capitol Records.

REVIEW QUESTIONS

1. What is meant by the term personnel management?
2. Describe two or three personnel management activities; explain the mutual responsibilities of line managers and personnel managers in performing them.
3. Why is it important to understand the logic of personnel management?
4. What are the three central elements in personnel management?
5. At what point should the study of personnel management logic begin? Why?

KEY CONCEPTS

Employee	Organization
Job	Personnel management
Line authority	Personnel manager
Logic	Staff authority

CASE

THE AVERAGE SALARY

Joyce Thompson was distressed. She had been with Acme Paint Manufacturing for three years. She had graduated from Hickory College with a major in personnel management and had been fortunate to find this job. She had started as assistant to the head of purchasing but, by being persistent, had convinced Sarah Buckley to transfer her to the personnel department. Sarah, the director of human resources (the official title of the department), had been very good in training Joyce for her responsibilities, and this was the first assignment that Joyce had tackled on her own. She felt that it was important to impress Sarah with her decision-making skills and to make sure that her report was what Sarah wanted.

The assignment seemed simple enough. Sarah had said, "Joyce, some of our executives are concerned that our salary structure for the plant workers just isn't doing what it should be doing. Some of the employees are complaining that it isn't enough and we're losing some of them to other companies around town. Also, the union has complained that some of its members have reported concerns with the structure itself—not that it's too low, but that some jobs have been misrated. Now I don't know exactly what the problem is, but I'd like you to take a stab at finding that out. Do a survey, look at evaluations for all our plant jobs, and so on. Find out what is wrong with our salaries and tell me. See if you can't have something for me in about a month."

Joyce went home that night and thought about the assignment. She thought to herself, "Now what was it that Sarah said? . . . Oh, yes, we're losing some of our plant people to other companies because our salaries are too low. Now it seems that I should find out what these other companies are paying so that we can make our pay equally attractive. Yes, that seems logical; then our employees won't be so anxious to leave."

The following morning Joyce pulled the files on all the major plant jobs and discovered there were some twenty-four different classifications, ranging from $3.50 to $12.00 per hour. She wrote down the title for each job and its rate and then began to design a questionnaire that she could send to other companies to find out how much they were paying their plant employees.

Subsequently, she called local firms, and although several refused, she was able to identify twelve that would provide her with average hourly rates—if she would provide them a summary of her findings. She agreed to this and sent them the questionnaire, which listed all the job titles in which she was interested.

She was surprised to find, when the questionnaires were returned, that most of them were incomplete. As she called to find out why, she discovered that nobody had jobs like "mixer" or "dye" operator. It took a lot of encouragement on her part, but she was able to convince four of these other companies to go ahead and send her their lists of plant employees and average hourly rates, arguing that the important thing was simply to find out what the average plant employee earned.

Finally, Joyce determined that the average rate for all plant employees (in the four companies) was $7.58 with a range for low-paying jobs of $3.75 to high-paying jobs of $17.23 per hour. Since Acme's average salary for plant employees was $6.83, she decided that Acme's pay was probably about 75 cents an hour too low in the middle jobs and 25 cents and $5.23 an hour too low in the lower and higher jobs, respectively. By drawing a trend line for Acme's twenty-four plant jobs, she was able to determine exactly how much to increase each job to become competitive with the local job market.

Sarah had returned her report with the following comment: "Joyce, this just isn't sufficient. I'm not sure that every job we have is paid too little. Some are probably paid too much. Also, I'm not convinced that our highest-paid plant job is as demanding or skilled as those in the other companies. Our objective isn't to pay exactly what other companies pay. It's to pay the right amount depending on the nature of the job and to reduce the number of complaints. Now check with some of our people and find out what we should be doing."

CASE QUESTIONS

1. What was wrong with Joyce's "logic"?

2. If Joyce's solution produces a salary structure equivalent to the average plant salary in the area, is this desirable? Why or why not?

3. If you were Joyce, where might you start your analysis of the salary problem? Why?

NOTES

[1]M. Hitt, D. Middlemist, and R. Mathis, *Effective Management* (St. Paul: West, 1979), p. 5.

[2]K. Albrecht, *Brain Power* (Englewood Cliffs, N.J.: Prentice-Hall, 1980), p. 160.

[3]Ibid., p. 162.

[4]A. Bedian, *Organizations: Theory and Analysis* (Hinsdale, Ill.: Dryden Press, 1980), p. 4.

2

PERSONNEL DEPARTMENTS AND PEOPLE

LEARNING OBJECTIVES

After reading this chapter, you should be able to

1. Describe five common managerial activities.
2. Define and discuss three types of authority in organizations.
3. Explain three distinct organizational structures.
4. Describe factors that affect the authority, functions, and structure of personnel departments.
5. Describe career opportunities in personnel management.

It is sometimes difficult to visualize how an organization can structure its personnel activities so as to achieve coordinated manpower efforts. To help us gain some insights into this matter, we visited Xerox Corporation, at its Mid-Atlantic Region offices. There we spoke with John Devine, the director of personnel for this region, which includes the states of Ohio, Pennsylvania, North and South Carolina, Georgia, and Virginia. Mr. Devine has been with Xerox for fifteen years and is well acquainted with its personnel function and policies.

Interviewer: In what ways do personnel activities affect people who are in the middle of their careers?

John Devine: First, we must recognize that Personnel affects the career development of all employees, not only those in midcareer, but newer and older employees as well. It is an ongoing process involving the efforts of all managers. Managers are trained by personnel specialists to conduct performance appraisal and career counseling sessions with their employees. Through these sessions and other formal training programs, Personnel can guide and influence employee career progress in the well-defined Xerox structure. Specifically, midcareer counseling may emphasize enrichment of one's job at the current level or a managerial development program involving a series of training activities leading to a managerial assignment.

Interviewer: Please comment on the importance to Xerox of career development, equal employment opportunity, labor relations, and discipline.

John Devine: First, career development is very important here at Xerox. It is expected by employees, and Personnel is expected to provide the framework for it. Hiring and training new employees is expensive; it is better to keep what you have. One key to retention is to provide career opportunities and development. The company is presently involved with a program at the University of Southern California concerning long-service career studies and is developing training programs for situational leadership to improve career development.

Second, equal employment opportunity is perhaps one of the biggest driving forces in Personnel today, not only here at Xerox but throughout industry. The issues are subtle and hard to pin down, but the pressures are strong. Xerox is very active in government contracts and is quite sensitive to this issue. In this regard, Xerox hired an affirmative action specialist and conducted affirmative action seminars for managers who are on the front line of this activity. The issue of equal employment opportunity has been confronted and, we feel, successfully so.

Third, Xerox's philosophy in labor relations is one of an open-door policy. Employees are encouraged to challenge issues through the structure, including the next higher level and above.

Finally, Xerox has a well-defined corrective action process. If a problem relates to skill deficiencies, we authorize additional training. If it is a behavior problem, say, absenteeism, we issue a formal warning, and the employee then undergoes a probationary period. An employee of eight or more years' service cannot be fired without the chairman's approval. Personnel specialists and other line managers are willing, and trained, to work with employees, and termination is used only as a last resort.

INTRODUCTION

We have viewed personnel functions as consisting of activities performed by all managers throughout an organization. This is a correct view, as each manager must be concerned about job design and job analysis and hiring, training, compensating, and motivating employees. However, as we examine the diversity of these activities, it is easy to see that no manager can be an expert in all of them and still perform effectively the regular tasks of planning, organizing, directing, and controlling. Therefore, it is common practice to establish an organizational unit with the responsibility of organizing and coordinating personnel activities.

As our discussion with John Devine, director of personnel of the Mid-Atlantic Division of Xerox illustrates, the task of personnel specialists is complex and challenging. This complexity may require a variety of people trained in various skills. In our brief interview, Mr. Devine mentioned training specialists, career development specialists, and an affirmative action officer. Xerox's well-defined organizational structure contains many more positions for other types of personnel specialists as well.

The purpose of this chapter is to acquaint the reader with the personnel department—how it functions within the organization and how it manages its "people responsibilities"—and career opportunities in personnel management.

ORGANIZATIONS AND MANAGERS

Organizations have been defined as a collection of individuals formed for some meaningful purpose and having a distinct structure.[1] An organization, then, is a system composed of various parts (employees, supervisors, departments, functions, goals, etc.) that are designed to interact in cooperative effort to achieve its purpose. To see how personnel management activities "fit" into the organization, it is useful to review several basic features of organizational systems.

Managerial Activities

In nearly every organization, managerial activities can be classified broadly as planning, organizing, staffing, directing, and controlling.

PLANNING ACTIVITIES. Planning activities consist of forecasting and anticipating future events and preparing the organization to deal with them effectively. Planning is a major managerial responsibility regardless of a manager's specific area of specialization. That is, a production manager must plan with regard to raw materials, production schedules, inventory capacity, customer demand, *and* the need for employees with specific skills. Similarly, a marketing manager must plan with regard to production capacities, inventory capacity, delivery times, customer demands, product costs, *and* the need for employees with specific skills. In short, planning activities are performed by all managers, and human resource planning is included for every manager.

ORGANIZING ACTIVITIES. One of the more obvious differences among organizations is the way in which they are organized. Organizing involves the creation of specializations and departmental units and coordination so that necessary operations can be conducted effectively. Typically, this involves the creation of specialized jobs and departmental units as well as coordination. This usually requires the creation of a structure (seen in organization charts), lines of communication, and authority and responsibility relationships. In each case, this affects the nature of employee tasks, duties, and responsibility, and personnel consequences must be considered.

STAFFING ACTIVITIES.   Staffing refers to the selection and training of the needed employees. These activities are often confused as being the only activities that are a personnel management function. However, we have seen previously that staffing activities are not the sole role of personnel specialists, nor are they performed only by those specialists. All managers share in staffing activities.

DIRECTING ACTIVITIES.   The managerial process of guiding employees, supervising their activities, and leading them to effective performance is called directing. Each manager performs directing activities in a slightly different way (e.g., some use more discipline, some are more autocratic, and some provide more counseling and training). However, in each case directing involves interaction between supervisors and subordinates and thus includes an element of personnel management.

CONTROLLING ACTIVITIES.   Reviewing, measuring, and evaluating performance for the purpose of correcting problems and achieving goals are activities of control. Through control activities, managers can adjust plans, reorganize, restaff and retrain, and provide better direction for employees. Relative to personnel, managers must set performance standards, measure and review employee performances, and plan for correcting performance problems.

In a sense, every managerial activity involves an aspect of personnel management. Conversely, if an organization employs personnel management specialists, their activities will be similar to those of other managers. That is, personnel managers must also plan, organize, staff, direct, and control. As Mr. Devine stated, personnel managers at Xerox influence both the structure of the organization and the careers and efforts of all managers.

Authority Relationships

A second feature that is basic to organizational functioning is the nature of authority relationships among employees. Authority refers to the "right" of one person to take action in planning, organizing, staffing, directing, and controlling the activities of another. In organizations, authority is given differentially to various levels of managers and employees and normally is confined to issues related directly to organizational performance. Authority in organizations rests with the position (e.g., vice president, manager of production, inventory clerk) rather than with an individual. It is an important means of accomplishing coordination, since it enables a manager simultaneously to plan, organize, direct, and control the activities of several subordinates, thereby coordinating their activities.

Closer inspection of the manner in which organizational authority is distributed formally reveals that authority between organizational members differs not only in the amount each has but also in its characteristic content or type. The three most common types are line authority, functional authority, and staff authority.

LINE AUTHORITY.   Line activities are those involved directly in fulfilling the primary mission of the organization.[2] Such activities include manufacturing operations, marketing operations, engineering, and applied research activities. The authority given managers and employees in these activities is called line authority and normally contains primary decision rights and the right to discipline and reward subordinates. It is also limited in scope to those immediate subordinates in the manager's unit. That is, a line manager can issue a direct task-related command to a subordinate in the work unit and expect compliance, and failure to comply may yield a disciplinary action by the manager, which is part of his or her authority; however, the line manager could not exercise the same authority over an employee in a different department.

FUNCTIONAL AUTHORITY.   The term function as used in organizations refers to a specialized set of activities. For example, marketing is, in addition to being a line activity, a function, as it consists of a narrow set of specialized activities. However, functional authority is quite different from line authority. This is most obvious in functions that are not also line operations. For example, the controller position in an organization is not often a line position. Normally, the controller function involves setting budgets, monitoring cash flow, analyzing investment opportunities, and so on. Because such activities require highly specialized training, the controller needs authority to make the decisions in areas in which he or she is an expert. That is, few line managers are qualified to make these decisions, so the controller must have the final authority to do so, even if the decision problem is one involving line activities. Thus the production manager cannot make a decision to build and equip a new production plant. The controller will have this authority since it is an investment problem. We can also see that Mr. Devine has functional authority in such activities as labor relations and equal employment opportunity.

In summary, functional authority is not limited to the manager's own unit. It carries throughout the organization. However, it usually carries no disciplinary or reward power relative to other units and is constrained to only those decisions involving the specialized function. We should note that some positions carry both line and functional authority, and most managers have the power to discipline and reward subordinates in their own unit, whether it is a line or a functional position.

STAFF AUTHORITY.   The term staff authority is sometimes confusing to individuals when they are first learning about organizations and management. This is because staff positions rarely have much formal authority. Staff positions are like functional positions in that they usually involve highly specialized activities that are not related directly to the organization's primary mission. Normally, staff positions are viewed as an advisory or counseling service available to others who need periodic assistance in the specialized activity in which the staff has expertise. Normally, these activities are such that the line manager needs to retain the final decision power, but in which he or she lacks the expertise to make effective decisions without the advice of the staff expert. For example, most line managers must be finally responsible for deciding which of several applicants to hire as new employees. However, the manager may lack the expertise for designing, administering, and evaluating selection tools. Thus a personnel specialist serves as advisor, designing, administering, and interpreting selection measures, thereby enabling the line manager to make a better selection decision. Mr. Devine has indicated a number of activities for which he has staff authority, including performance appraisal and career counseling.

Organizational Structure

Broadly conceived, the organizational structure consists of the division of various activities among units and individuals, the division of necessary authority to accomplish the activities, and the coordination mechanisms (e.g., communication lines) that allow the system to function effectively. The two most common types of organization structure are the line structure and the line-staff structure. A less common, but important, type is the matrix structure.

LINE ORGANIZATION STRUCTURE.   The line structure is one that emphasizes line authority throughout the organization and that has no staff or functional positions. In this manner, the authority and responsibility of each employee is clear and distinct; that is, each employee has only one supervisor, and there are no specialists to issue conflicting (or confirming) directions. This is an especially common structure for small businesses that are unable to afford the advantages of specialized employees such as personnel managers, attorneys, and public relations officers.

LINE-STAFF ORGANIZATION STRUCTURE.   The line-staff structure is similar to the line structure, except that staff positions have been created. This occurs normally as the organization grows in size or complexity. Such growth increases the affordability and necessity for having experts who can keep pace with the developments in the specialized areas and provide advice and assistance to the line managers. A line-staff structure appears in Figure 2-1.

MATRIX ORGANIZATION STRUCTURE.   The matrix structure is an attempt to create both functional and line authority relationships. This is unusual because having authority in both line and functional positions often leads to conflicting orders or di-

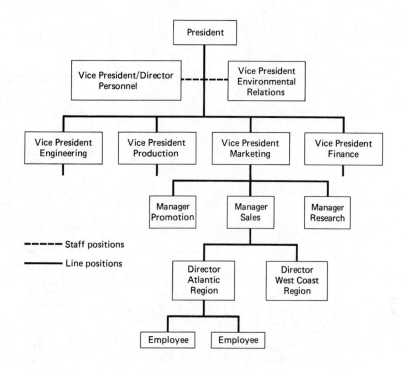

Figure 2-1

Typical Line-Staff Organization Structure

rections. That is, the subordinate may be unsure whether to follow the instructions given by the line manager or those given by the functional manager. This structure usually arises when either the customer product or market or the technology of operations becomes extremely complex. Because of this complexity, it may be more important to ensure that the specialist's advice is not ignored than to guarantee that the line manager has unchallengeable authority. This structure is illustrated in Figure 2-2.

Companies such as General Electric and organizations such as NASA have found that these structures can lead to participative decisions made possible by cooperation between the staff or functional managers and the product or project managers. In Figure 2-2, product or project managers create horizontal coordination between functional areas such as production and marketing. However, such a structure imposes a dual line of authority for subordinates; therefore, a great deal of interpersonal skill is required of the various managers. Patience, consideration, teamwork, and participation are essential if the structure is to be effective.[3]

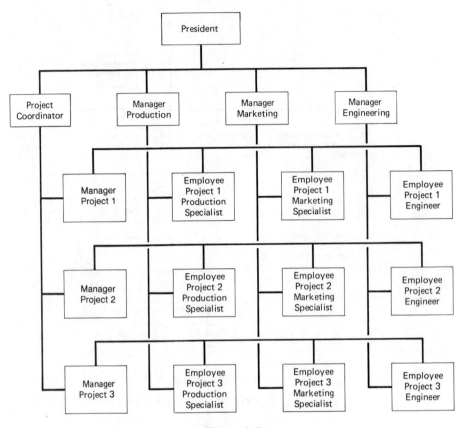

Figure 2-2

Typical Matrix Organization Structure

PERSONNEL DEPARTMENTS

While we have emphasized that personnel activities are included in every manager's responsibilities, most larger organization structures have well-defined personnel departments. Many smaller organizations, as well, have at least one individual whose primary duty involves the coordination of personnel management activities. The role of personnel departments has become increasingly important to organizations, due in part to a more educated and sophisticated work force, in part to increasing governmental regulation,[4] and in part to economic and technological growth.

Although personnel departments have become increasingly important to organizations, they differ considerably from organization to organization. These differences reflect the variations in the nature of resources, environments, and markets in which the organizations operate. These factors must be considered when the organization decides to establish a personnel department.

Size

While all organizations must conduct personnel activities, smaller organizations typically carry these out without resorting to the establishment of a specialized personnel management department. In fact, surveys of organizations have suggested that the average number of full-time personnel specialists per 100 organization employees is only 0.75. That is, organizations, on average, tend to have 133 employees before the need to have one full-time personnel specialist is justified.[5] Prior to gaining sufficient size, personnel activities are either shared by managers, or one manager (or executive secretary) may be given centralized responsibility for this function in addition to his or her normal duties. In extremely small organizations (less than 20 employees), the personnel responsibility is often retained by the owner-manager.

Conversely, we can see from the surveys that larger organizations may have a large personnel department. For example, organizations having 5,000 employees would have an average of 37 to 38 personnel specialists (.0075 $\times$ 5,000). We should recognize that these are average figures and that there may be considerable variation between similarly sized organizations in the exact size of their personnel departments.

Authority of Personnel Departments

The personnel department is typically seen in organizational charts, such as Figure 2-1, as a staff function carrying only staff authority (e.g., advisory). In part, this is a reflection of the difficulty associated with centralizing an activity that is, in reality, decentralized among all managers. Creating a personnel department is a response to the need for specialized expertise, for coordinating personnel decisions, and so on. However, final decision power must rest with the line manager for many types of personnel decisions (e.g., selection).

The view of personnel management as a staff position, however, does not reflect with accuracy the nature of the personnel department's authority in many organizations. The exact nature of authority granted to a personnel department depends on two factors.

1. The objectives set for the personnel department by top management.
2. The specific personnel activity being considered.

When top management views personnel as an integral part of the successful management of the organization, the personnel manager is likely to be a central figure in the organization's plans and objectives.[6] This management viewpoint places the personnel department as a staff position, but one that is located close to the chief executive officer (CEO). The personnel manager in this organization acts as a consultant to the CEO. Such a relationship forces the personnel manager to know the organization's total business needs and to exert an active influence on the design, development, and implementation of programs that permeate the organization and make the use of human resources more effective.[7] Line managers are likely to perceive the strategically placed personnel department as being much more than an advisory or staff function.

   Furthermore, we cannot make a consistent assessment of the personnel department's authority, since that authority typically varies from one personnel activity to another. The personnel manager may have staff authority in certain selection and training activities and functional and even line authority with regard to others. For example, he or she may have sole functional authority in equal employment opportunity decisions, design of training and orientation programs, and the implementation of fringe benefits. He or she may have line authority on grievance matters, acting as the next higher level to which an employee grievance is referred. He or she may decide unilaterally grievance matters, administering penalties to employees or overriding a manager's initial decision. Thus we can conclude that the personnel manager's authority is a mixture of line, functional, and staff authority, which often extends beyond the personnel department into other organizational units.[8] This conclusion is consistent with John Devine's description of the Xerox view of personnel management.

Functions and Structure of Personnel Departments

The structure of personnel departments depends on the top management view, the size of the organization, and the types of functions centralized in the department. Traditionally, the personnel department coordinated a few basic functions, including human resource planning, recruitment and selection, wage and salary administration, training, and labor relations. Given the rapid changes in our society and the growing importance of personnel management activities, these functions have increased considerably. A recent survey of personnel managers and professionals sheds light on the increased functions and responsibilities of personnel departments. According to this survey, personnel professionals now perform a number of additional important activities. These may include problem solving, consultation with operating managers, participation in designing and implementing corporate policy, evaluation and development of middle- and top-level managers, and contribution to the design of organizational structures and objectives.[9]

   The variety of functions performed by personnel departments is also affected by governmental regulations. Many changes in governmental laws and regulations require organizations to reevaluate their personnel departments, sometimes adding responsibilities or restructuring the department so as to facilitate compliance with new legislation. For example, the Equal Employment Opportunity Act and the Occupational Safety and Health Act have added important responsibilities to the personnel department's activities. Some organizations are more affected by these acts than are others, and these differences are reflected in the structures of their personnel departments. While it is impossible to present the "average" or "ideal" structure for a personnel department, one possibility is presented in Figure 2-3. This hypothetical structure reflects many of the personnel management activities and responsibilities that have been identified in our discussion.

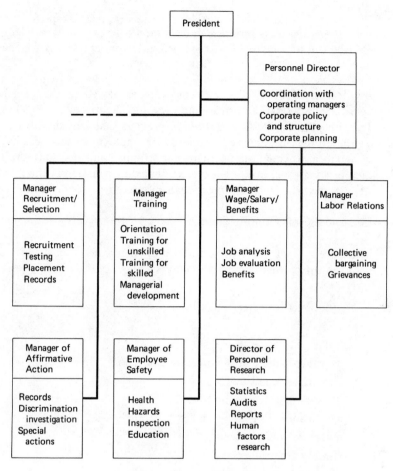

Figure 2-3

Structure and Activities for a Modern Personnel Department

CAREERS IN PERSONNEL MANAGEMENT

From the preceding discussion, one could surmise that the career opportunities for personnel managers and professionals are both varied and growing. The size of personnel department budgets and the number of staff employed by them is growing. This is a direct result of the increasing importance of personnel activities and an increase in the number of functions and services expected from the personnel department.[10] The *Occupational Outlook Handbook,* 1980–1981 edition, of the Bureau of Labor Statistics contains the following commentary:

The number of personnel and labor relations workers is expected to grow faster than the average for all occupations through the 1980s, as employers, increasingly aware of the benefits to be derived from good labor-management relations, continue to support sound, capably staffed employee relations programs.[11]

As of 1978, 405,000 persons were employed in the personnel management field—about 300,000 in private industry and slightly over 100,000 in public services. The *Occupational Outlook Handbook* predicts that growth also will be influenced by legislation that has imposed standards for employment practices in occupational safety and health, equal employment opportunity, and pensions. As employers review their existing programs, it is expected that they will modify their procedures and take steps to raise the level of professionalism in their personnel departments.[12]

Personnel Staff Opportunities

There are a great many opportunities for personnel management careers. Although not exhaustive, the following list suggests many of the possibilities:

Personnel recruiter/interviewer

Job analyst

Salary and wage specialist

Equal employment opportunity counselor

Training specialist

Employee benefits administrator

Occupational safety specialist

Labor relations officer

Testing design specialist

Personnel researcher

Human resource and organizational planner

While there is expected to be an increasing opportunity for careers in personnel management, it is difficult to specify the exact steps that one should take to enter this field. Given the trend toward professionalism in the field, we suspect that most entry-level positions are made available to college graduates. Approximately two hundred colleges offer undergraduate majors and thirty schools offer graduate education in personnel management. Further, some organizations provide entry-level positions to college graduates with majors in liberal education fields.[13] Although a college degree is useful, it may not guarantee that one will be able to find an opening without considerable effort. There is also a growing supply of individuals seeking entrance to the field, and competition for available positions may be stiff. General information on careers and opportunities in personnel management can be obtained from the American Society for Personnel Administration, 30 Park Drive, Berea, Ohio 44017.

Table 2-1

Median and Average Salaries for Selected
Personnel Specialists

	Annual Salary
Private industry[1]	
Personnel research manager	$29,940[1]
Labor relations manager	29,580[1]
Training and organization development manager	28,564[1]
Compensation and benefits manager	28,000[1]
Affirmative action (EEO) manager	27,000[1]
Plant training manager	26,936[1]
Employee benefits manager	24,810[1]
Personnel manager	23,600[1]
Employment manager	23,100[1]
Job analyst	22,600[1]
Safety specialist	22,250[1]
Wage and salary administrator	22,100[2]
Managerial and professional recruiter	21,575[1]
Employment interviewer (managerial)	17,000[1]
Employment interviewer (clerical)	15,122[1]
Public organizations (federal)[2]	
Mediator	33,892[2]
Personnel management specialist	24,174[2]
Employee development specialist	23,796[2]
Position classifier	22,777[2]
Occupational analyst	22,578[2]
Salary and wage administrator	21,843[2]
Staffing specialist	21,447[2]

[1]Median salary as reported by S. Langer "Personnel Salaries: A Survey, Part I," *Personnel Journal* (1980), 983–987.
[2]Average salary as reported in *Occupational Outlook Handbook*, 1980–81 ed. (Washington, D.C.: U.S. Department of Labor, Bureau of Labor Statistics, March 1980), pp. 127–129.

Salary Outlook in Personnel

Recent research, sponsored by the *Personnel Journal,* reveals wide variation in the salaries of personnel management professions. The higher-paid personnel professional is described as working for a merchandising firm with over 10,000 employees. He or she is probably located in the New York area, has a graduate degree, and has over fifteen years of experience. This individual earns in excess of $135,000 annually. However, the average for personnel managers across the country is lower.[14] A 1979 survey by an executive search firm found that the annual salaries of senior human resource executives and personnel executives averages between $52,000 and $79,000 depending on job responsibilities.[15] The lowest-paid personnel specialist is described as a personnel clerk working in a southwestern state, employed by an educational institution, not having a college degree, and with less than three years of experience. This individual's salary is less than $10,000 per year.[16]

The salary of a personnel professional is influenced by the nature of his or her specialization, the type of employer (manufacturing, nonmanufacturing, public organization), geographic location, the size of the employer, and the individual's level of education and length of experience. Given that we understand the large number of factors that can influence and cause the salaries of personnel professionals to vary widely, we can cautiously examine the average salaries for a number of personnel specializations. Table 2-1 presents a sample of personnel jobs and their average salaries.

As seen in Table 2-1, the salaries of experienced personnel specialists and managers is competitive with other professional occupations. Again, we emphasize the importance of a college education if one is preparing for a career in the field of personnel management. Not only does this make entrance into the job market more likely, but it also influences one's salary. For instance, the *Personnel Journal* reports that the median income of experienced personnel managers is $35,470 for those with a B.A. or B.S. degree and $37,858 for those having a graduate degree.[17]

SUMMARY

In this chapter, we have discussed the nature of personnel departments and how they operate in organizations. This discussion has been delayed so that students will not gain the impression that personnel activities are the exclusive domain of personnel departments. All managers perform personnel management activities.

However, this chapter reveals that personnel managers (managers of formal personnel departments) also engage in the usual managerial activities: planning, organizing, staffing, directing, and controlling. The authority of personnel managers depends on a number of factors, but it is commonly a mixture of staff and functional with regard to other departments and certainly a type of line authority over employees within the personnel department. Thus the personnel department is normally established as a staff unit, serving as an advisory or counseling service to other organizational divisions.

It is not unusual to find that the actual authority granted to personnel departments and managers is much more than staff or advisory. When top management views personnel as an integral part of successful organization management, the personnel department and manager became centrally involved in the total organizational objectives and plans. The personnel manager then reports directly to the CEO and becomes involved in problem-solving consultation, designing and implementing corporate policy, evaluating and developing executive talent, and designing the organization's structure. Furthermore, personnel departments are likely to have functional authority for administering programs mandated by governmental legislation (e.g., EEO, OSHA, ERISA).

Career opportunities in personnel management are varied and are expected to grow through the 1980s because of the increasing importance of personnel activities. In most instances, these opportunities will require a college education, but ample rewards are available for those seeking the challenges offered by a career in personnel management.

INTERVIEW WRAP-UP

Overall, the role of personnel at Xerox is both well structured and realistic. We ensure the viability of human resources by working indirectly but very actively through management and the corporate structure. —John Devine, director of personnel for Mid-Atlantic Region, Xerox Corporation.

WHAT MANAGERS SHOULD DO REGARDING PERSONNEL MANAGEMENT ACTIVITIES

1. Managers should determine if the size of their organization warrants creation of a specialized personnel management position.
2. Managers must consider the importance of personnel activities when planning, organizing, staffing, directing, and controlling.
3. Managers must understand the nature of various authority relationships in the organization. They can avoid confusion and conflict by agreeing that personnel managers should have functional authority over some matters (e.g., administering benefit programs) but staff authority in other matters (e.g., selection).

REVIEW QUESTIONS

1. What are five common managerial activities, and how do these figure in the personnel manager's job?
2. What are the differences and similarities among line, functional, and staff authority?
3. What type of authority is typically granted to personnel departments and managers? Why?
4. What factors are increasing career opportunities in personnel management?
5. Describe the major forces that affect career entrance and salary level in personnel management.

KEY CONCEPTS

Career opportunities in personnel   Matrix organization structure
Controlling activities   Organizing activities
Directing activities   Personnel department
Functional authority   Planning activities
Line authority   Staff authority
Line organization structure   Staffing activities
Line-staff organization structure

CASE

WHO HAS THE AUTHORITY?

John MacDonald shifted uncomfortably in his chair. Marvin Stenson had just turned in his resignation and was now angrily explaining his reasons. Although John had been the bank president for several years and had suffered the verbal abuse of angry employees before, it was still one of his least liked jobs. This particular exit interview was especially difficult because Marvin was one of his most valued managers and he could not be dissuaded from quitting.

Marvin's anger was directed toward Bev Kayson, John's administrative secretary. Bev was also an extremely valuable employee who had been with the bank for twelve years. She knew the business and was responsible for legal filings, customer relations, and personnel administration and acted as John's "right-hand man." John knew that Bev irritated some of the unit managers occasionally, but he also felt that much of this was male resentment of the wide-ranging authority Bev exercised. In fact, if John had to choose between Marvin and Bev, which is the way Marvin had put it, he would choose Bev every time. Still, Marvin's anger was justified.

Plainview Bank and Trust, a small bank located in the Midwest, employs seventy-five persons and offers a full range of services. John and Marvin had started to work for the bank at the same time, fifteen years ago, when there were just a few employees. But the bank had grown rapidly, due in part to the original owner's aggressiveness. It had been an exciting period, with opportunities readily available both in terms of salary and promotion and in increasingly challenging job responsibilities. John's education and success as a loan officer led to his promotion to the bank presidency when the owner sold his interests to an investment group. Marvin, with less educational background, had been promoted to unit manager for one of the three consumer loan groups and had been in that position for several years.

Originally, the owner had handled all personnel decisions, selecting employees by using "good people judgment" and hand training every loan and collection officer, since he considered these two positions the most critical in the bank's operations. When he left, John MacDonald fell heir to these responsibilities. However, he soon found that he lacked the judgment capabilities and was inept at training new employees. Also, his work load prevented him from spending much time with new employees. He decided that Bev, who had been the executive secretary for the previous owner, should assume the selection and training responsibilities.

While Bev was respected by most employees, she was not particularly well liked. Her manner caused people to perceive her as "talking down to them." She rarely mingled socially with other employees and was autocratic in her decisions. The particular incident that had caused Marvin to turn in his resignation was the culmination of what he viewed as a series of poor decisions by Bev.

Last week one of Marvin's loan officers resigned to accept a position with a competing bank. Marvin felt that he could have kept this loan officer by offering a salary increase and went to see Bev. She refused to allow Marvin to make the offer, and since salary increases needed her approval, Marvin was unable to offer the increase. Then this week, Marvin had interviewed several persons for the vacant loan officer position. He wanted to hire Fred Sandoval, an experienced loan officer. But this would have required making a higher salary offer than usual.

Bev, who had also interviewed all the applicants, did not like Fred. She thought he was "an obnoxious bore." She told Marvin he could hire Fred if he wanted to, but he could not offer more than the salary posted for the job, $1,200 a month. Marvin steamed out of her office and that night typed his letter of resignation.

CASE QUESTIONS

1. Describe the personnel function and authority relationships in this bank that have led to Marvin Stenson's problem.

2. How are personnel activities handled in this case? Is this consistent with your knowledge of how personnel activities are normally handled throughout an organization?

3. If you were John MacDonald, what would you do to solve this problem?

NOTES

[1] R. D. Middlemist and M. A. Hitt, *Organizational Behavior: Applied Concepts* (Chicago: Science Research Associates, 1981), p. 9.

[2] M. A. Hitt, R. D. Middlemist, and R. L. Mathis, *Effective Management* (St. Paul: West, 1979), p. 187.

[3] K. Knight, "Matrix Organization: A Review," *Journal of Management Studies*, 13 (1976), 113.

[4] H. E. Meyer, "Personnel Directors Are the New Corporate Heroes," *Fortune*, February 1976, p. 88.

[5]T. L. Wood, "The Personnel Staff: What Is a Reasonable Size?" *Personnel Journal,* 46 (1967), 163–167.

[6]J. A. Tirrel and T. H. Cowell, "Human Resource Development—A Mushroom?" *Training and Development Journal,* 35 (1981), 18–26.

[7]J. W. Peters and E. A. Mabry, "The Personnel Officer as Internal Consultant," *Personnel Administrator,* 26 (1981), 29–32, 49.

[8]T. C. Coffey, "Resolving a Conflict of Staff vs. Staff," *Personnel,* 46 (1969), 58–65.

[9]S. H. Applebaum, "The Personnel Professional and Organization Development: Conflict and Synthesis," *Personnel Administrator,* 25 (1980), 44–49.

[10]"Personnel Activities, Budgets and Staffs: 1977 and 1978," ASPA-BNA Survey #35, *Bulletin to Management,* 1477, II (Washington, D.C.: Bureau of National Affairs, June 15, 1978).

[11]*Occupational Outlook Handbook, 1980–81 ed.* (Washington, D.C.: U.S. Department of Labor, Bureau of Labor Statistics, March 1980), pp. 127–129.

[12]Ibid., p. 129.

[13]Ibid., p. 128.

[14]S. Langer, "Personnel Salaries: A Survey, Part I," *Personnel Journal,* 59 (1980), 983–987.

[15]*Business Week,* "Personnel Widens Its Franchise," (February 26, 1979), 116–121.

[16]Langer, "Personnel Salaries: A Survey, Part I."

[17]Langer, "Personnel Salaries: A Survey, Part I."

JOB DESIGN AND THE NATURE OF PEOPLE

LEARNING OBJECTIVES

After reading this chapter, you should be able to

1. Describe job design activities and the benefits and problems created by specialization.
2. Discuss how job design affects the organization-job and job-people relationships.
3. Discuss the relationship between job design and productivity.
4. Describe six innovative approaches to job design.
5. Explain five task characteristics and their importance to job design.
6. Discuss how individual and situational factors may affect employee reactions to job design.
7. Explain how job design is related to both monetary and psychological rewards.
8. Explain the importance of job design to effective personnel management.

Carolyn England is a punch-press operator for Macklanburg-Duncan. She has worked for the company for three years. She has been in her current job for about a year and a half. Previously she worked in the molding department for about eighteen months.

Ms. England was interviewed to gain her perspective of her job, what she does, and what she likes and dislikes.

Interviewer: Describe briefly what kinds of activities are involved in your job.

Ms. England: Basically, I run seven different dies through my machine. There are dies for a caulking gun handle, a level, etc. I have to set up the die and the machine to stamp out these pieces from a sheet of metal. The metal comes on 1,500-pound rolls. I have to get the roll and, using a crane, get it unrolled and put it on a straightening machine before feeding it into the punch press. I have to load one or two rolls a day on the average. I have to perform minor maintenance on my machine and keep it oiled. Also, I have to check for defective parts coming out of my machine. I usually check every ten to fifteen parts I turn out to see if there are any problems. If I find defective items, they go in the scrap pile and I look for machine problems causing the defects.

Interviewer: What reactions do you have to your job?

Ms. England: I like the challenge of my job. My machine can be run on automatic or manual, but I get more satisfaction out of running it on manual. I feel like I have more input that way. Also, I like to set goals for myself for motivation. I put time limits on myself to see how fast I can turn out parts or how many I can do in a day. My job is not easy. Setting up a die is difficult. There are three separate features that have to be set up and adjusted and microprocessor switches to set. Each die costs about $10,000 so I have to be careful. It takes time, but the faster you are in setting up the die, the more productive you are. Being productive is important to me.

Interviewer: What do you like least about your job?

Ms. England: I don't really like to clean up. I like to work in a clean area, but I don't like to clean it. I prefer working with the machine to cleaning. The machine is oily, and cleaning up is a monotonous procedure.

Interviewer: What is the most exciting part of your job?

Ms. England: I like being able to do everything myself without anyone else's help. I'm more satisfied that way, and it's more challenging.

Interviewer: What is the most boring part of the jobs you've held?

Ms. England: The most boring thing to do is to do the same thing over and over again. My job in the molding department was that way. When you have a job like that, there's nothing new to learn. My present job isn't like that, unless I use the automatic switch on my machine.

Interviewer: Do you do anything different on the job from the way in which you were trained?

Ms. England: Generally on most jobs, there are several ways to do the same thing. My supervisor lets me do things differently if I can come up with an easier, better, or safer way to do something. I do several things differently from the way I was trained. My primary decision criterion is time. I like to save time so I can get more done.

One example is when we work on wire screen. It comes in 700-foot rolls. When one roll runs out, I would have to stop, set up, and feed a new roll into my machine. However, I had an idea to burn the ends of two rolls together so it can be fed continuously into my machine.

Interviewer: If you could redesign any part of this job, what would you do?

Ms. England: I would do something to make the job cleaner. When I run my machine, oil splatters out. I tried putting a shield on it and it worked, but I felt cut off from my machine and I didn't like that. So, I took the shield off.

INTRODUCTION

In Chapter 1, we learned that jobs, people, and organizations are interrelated logically. Thus each of these three elements affects each of the others. Personnel managers must be aware of these interrelationships and manage them to benefit the organization and employees.

Our focus in this chapter is on jobs, how they are designed, and how they affect people. In recent years, the job has come under increasing scrutiny with emphasis on productivity and individual job satisfaction. Relative to many other developed countries, business in the United States has become less productive[1] and is experiencing growing rates of dissatisfaction among its workers.[2] Some researchers have suggested that poor design of workers' jobs is a major cause of these two outcomes.

The interview with Carolyn England illustrates how the job may affect people. Ms. England likes her job and even seems excited about it. She likes it because she can control what she does and because she can develop challenges for herself. However, she found a previous job in the molding department to be boring, having to do the same thing over and over. This is not true in her present job because she can use manual control rather than switch her machine to automatic. She can even change procedures if she develops a better way of doing things, such as fusing the rolls of screen wire together so she does not have to stop her machine and set up again when the end of one roll is reached. It seems that Carolyn England had a less than optimally designed job previously but that the present job is well designed and satisfies her needs.

The personnel manager's responsibility for the design of employees' jobs is changing. In the past, personnel managers simply analyzed the content of the job to help select the person with the appropriate skills to fill it and to set the rates of pay. However, today they must be concerned with designing the content of the job to meet the needs and expectations of the employee.

Job design: the arrangement of task contents so as to satisfy both organizational and human requirements.[3]

Personnel managers as well as all other types of managers must be concerned with the triangular relationship of the organization, jobs, and people described in Chapter 1. They must try to ensure that the relationships are established so that both the organization and its employees reach their goals through job performance. In this chapter, we discuss one element in this relationship: the job and its design. We examine the nature of job design and the effects it has. The relationship of job design, productivity, and job rewards is examined. Innovations in job design and effective means of implementing job redesign are explored. Finally, the relationship between job design and other personnel management activities is discussed.

THE NATURE OF JOB DESIGN

As noted in Chapter 1, jobs provide an important link between the organization and its employees. Jobs must be performed for the organization to meet its goals, and employees are the ones who perform the jobs. Therefore, job design affects both the organization-job relationships and the job-people relationships. The logic of job design, then, should be to accomplish organizational goals and satisfy individual needs.

Job Specialization

The design of jobs became an important issue during the Industrial Revolution in the United States. When organizations were small and tasks were few, one or a few people could perform all the necessary tasks. However, as organizations began to grow and the size and number of their tasks grew, one individual could no longer perform all the tasks effectively. Industrial growth necessitated changes in job design. The work was broken into a series of smaller, more specialized tasks. Thus large organizations have accountants, personnel managers, sales representatives, purchasing agents, machine operators, inventory clerks, assembly workers, and so on. This process of breaking work down into smaller sets of related tasks is called job specialization.

Effects of Job Design

In recent years, however, some jobs have been so specialized that they have become highly routine and repetitive. Many of these jobs occur on manufacturing assembly lines and in some white-collar departments (e.g., typing pools, file maintenance). Assembly lines have been designed to produce the maximum number of products in the most efficient manner. These assembly lines, along with the specialized jobs they perform, then, are intended to help organizations achieve their productivity goals.

However, the design of overspecialized jobs does not necessarily work well for the job-people relationship. People on these jobs have little or no responsibility, and many of these employees become bored and dissatisfied. The design of the job does not match their skills or satisfy their needs. High job specialization has frequently been cited as one of the reasons for the decline in productivity and job satisfaction in the United States.[4]

People in some professions are more satisfied with their jobs than are others. In one survey, people were asked what type of work they would choose if they started their careers again. Forty-three percent of a cross section of white-collar workers said that they would choose similar work again, whereas only 24 percent of a cross section of blue-collar workers said that they would choose the same work again. Interestingly, neither percentage is very high. However, it seems that the white-collar workers were more satisfied with their work than were blue-collar workers, whose jobs were probably more specialized.[5]

Carolyn England's previous job in the molding department was boring for her; the job was highly specialized (maybe overspecialized). Her present job, however, offers more challenge and uses a range of her skills.

We must point out that low productivity and dissatisfaction do not always result from job specialization. In some jobs, although specialized, the tasks involved are not necessarily repetitive and routine. They may be complex and challenging. Still, individuals on these jobs may become dissatisfied. Of the many reasons for this dissatisfaction, two predominate. First, the job tasks may not utilize many of the individual's skills. Thus he or she is overqualified for the job. Second, the job may not satisfy all the incumbent's needs (e.g., need for achievement and need for power). Thus we can conclude that the job must be designed to *match* an employee's *skills* and *needs* for an effective job-people relationship.

Job design must serve multiple purposes. It must help to meet organizational goals, and it must utilize employee skills and satisfy employee needs. This relationship is depicted in Figure 3-1.

Job Design and Productivity

From the organization's viewpoint, jobs should be designed to achieve maximum productivity. Much of the early work on job design focused on productivity increase, the emphasis being on the organization-job relationship.

The emphasis on productivity through increases in efficiency began with Frederick W. Taylor and the scientific management movement.[6] Taylor used time and motion studies to break the jobs into their smallest units, thereby increasing efficiency. Jobs were standardized, wage incentives were provided, and workers were trained in the most efficient (least time-consuming) ways to perform their tasks. Our knowledge of management advanced during this time with development in the organization-job relationships. However, the job-people relationship was largely ignored.

The mass-production assembly line, which allowed products to be manufactured efficiently and at a low cost per unit, was another development that focused on the

Figure 3-1

Organization-Job Design-People Interrelationship

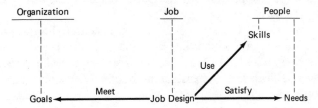

organization-job relationship. The jobs along the assembly line became highly specialized so that each worker had little or no discretion. Work was machine paced and well engineered to reduce the impact of human errors. However, it also ignored the job-people relationship. Some of the problems with repetitive, boring assembly-line work have already been noted.

Job changes in the assembly line were brought about primarily because of changes in technology.[7] Technological changes, then, affect the organization-job relationship. Much of the increased productivity in the past resulted from technological development as opposed to increased employee motivation or skill. Reportedly, employees have been dissatisfied with boring and repetitive jobs. Although no direct relationship has been found between job satisfaction and productivity, several studies have shown that dissatisfaction can lead to employee turnover, absenteeism, sabotage, theft, and other actions that weaken the organization. These actions affect long-run productivity.[8] If workers are absent from their jobs, temporary replacements must be found or other workers must take up the slack, thereby reducing output. If experienced employees quit their jobs, new employees must be recruited, hired, and trained. During the recruitment and training periods, output suffers. Obviously, sabotage and theft have a negative effect on output as well.

Carolyn England is self-motivated and likes to be productive, and her supervisor wisely allows her flexibility on the job. She may even change some of her procedures if she can develop a more productive way. Focus on the job-people relationship may allow increases in productivity. It has, at least, in Ms. England's case.

Although technology has been the prime contributor to productivity increases in the past, gains in the United States due to technology have been less than those in Europe and Japan in recent years.[9] From 1967 to 1974, for example, Japan's productivity level increased by almost 100 percent whereas productivity in the United States rose less than 30 percent.[10] Thus we cannot always expect technology to help us increase productivity. It is likely that this has led to a renewed emphasis on the job-people relationships that increase productivity. This emphasis, in turn, has produced innovations in job design activities and work scheduling discussed later in this chapter.

Two other developments that have affected the organization-job relationship are worth noting for their potential effects on productivity: the technological developments of minicomputers and the use of mechanical robots to perform routine assembly-line work. In some cases, these automated systems have replaced employees. These developments have also led to sophisticated word processing systems that replace or reduce the size of common secretarial pools. These examples of computerization are only the tip of the iceberg.

As shown in Figure 3-2, we may conclude that productivity results from both organization-job relationships (technology) and job-people (employee satisfaction and performance) relationships. Technology does not affect all jobs to the same degree, however. Therefore, increases in productivity on some jobs result largely from the job-people relationship.

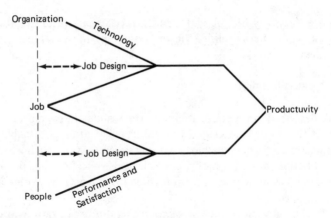

Figure 3-2

Relationship of Job Design and Productivity

INNOVATIONS IN JOB DESIGN

Several special approaches to job design have been utilized by organizations. Among them are work simplification, job specialization, job rotation, job enlargement, job enrichment, and autonomous work groups.

Work Simplification

Work simplification grew out of the scientific management work. Taylor and Gilbreth used time and motion studies to develop the best way in which to perform the job, frequently requiring work simplification and standardization. The concept of work simplification has changed since Taylor's work.

Work simplification: the process of deleting those elements of a job that are least demanding of human skills and those that are unnecessary to task accomplishment.[11]

The objective of work simplification is to improve satisfaction and productivity by allowing employees to spend more of their time performing the more challenging, complex, and important tasks in their job. Work simplification requires careful analysis of all task elements of the job. It is frequently implemented in conjunction with another job design strategy such as job enrichment.

For example, the part of Ms. England's job that is least demanding of her skills and the least critical to task accomplishment is cleaning up. If she did not have to clean up, she could continue turning out parts. It might be possible to eliminate that task as a part of her job and turn it over to a janitor or maintenance person. Thus her work would be simplified (fewer tasks), permitting greater concentration on more challenging tasks.

Job Specialization

We described job specialization and the results of "overspecialization" earlier. However, it should be understood that job specialization is a viable job design strategy. In some areas of work, we have extreme specialization, such as those noted along the assembly lines and in some types of clerical work. More of our work in organizations is becoming white-collar and professional. As new jobs evolve and grow, the work becomes specialized.

The growth in the use of computers in organizations provides evidence. At one time, most organizations using computers had a job titled "programmer/analyst," which combined the programming and systems analysis tasks. Individuals in these jobs would analyze major information systems, design improved systems, and write the necessary computer programs. As computer tasks have grown in number and complexity, many organizations have developed two specialized jobs: "programmer" and "systems analyst." The same change has occurred in television news, with a distinction emerging between the tasks of reporting and photographing news events. The original job of "reporter/photographer" has been divided into two jobs: "reporter" and "photographer." In addition, they may be specialized further in the type of reporting (Capitol beat reporter, local news) and photography (sports photographer, family features). Thus, although we do not want to overspecialize, job specialization is still an important and useful job design strategy.

Job Rotation

Job rotation is a relatively simple concept.

 Job rotation: having an employee perform several different jobs, moving from one to the other in some prearranged logical sequence over some period of time.

With job rotation, the contents of the specific jobs remain unchanged. The purposes of job rotation may be several. Rotating through different jobs may provide new job skills, change work and social relationships on the job, and provide relief from boring work. It is especially useful where some of the jobs are more challenging than others. In this way, it allows sharing of the repetitive tasks instead of assigning them to specific persons. However, job rotation may be useful only in the short run unless some of the jobs through which a person rotates are meaningful and challenging. Job rotation is most effective when combined with other job design changes where some jobs may be simplified and others enriched.

When Carolyn England was in the molding department, she was bored. Job rotation might have been a useful strategy to have employed at that time. It would have given Ms. England exposure to other jobs and helped her to develop other skills, possibly increasing her motivation.

Job Enlargement

Job enlargement was one of the first approaches used to combat too much specialization. However, it has other purposes as well.

Job enlargement: increasing the number of tasks in a job by adding tasks related to those currently performed, some of which may require a greater variety of skills.

Job enlargement adds tasks that are similar in complexity to those performed. Job enlargement may include

Increasing the number of tasks
Expanding the variety of tasks
Providing an entire unit of work to be accomplished[12]

Job enlargement is a broad concept and may serve many different types of purposes. It can help employees to develop new skills or to use a wider variety of existing skills. It may provide employees with more independence by allowing them to determine methods and pace of work. It may increase their feeling of accomplishment by providing more responsibility and having a larger part of the operation.

Job enlargement for Ms. England's punch-press operator's job might entail assigning her new tasks on her machine or having her operate other similar machines. Her job may have been enlarged already because she, to some extent, currently determines the methods and pace of her work.

Job Enrichment

Job enrichment is a more complex job design strategy than those discussed previously.

Job enrichment: the process of changing the job to allow more employee discretion over work and increased involvement in planning, decision-making, and controlling activities related to the job's tasks.

There are similarities between job enlargement and job enrichment. However, important differences exist as well. Job enlargement involves adding tasks to jobs that are similar in level and complexity to those currently required. Job enrichment involves changing the job to include more complex and challenging tasks that are required to "manage" the job. Thus when jobs are enriched, employees become managers of their own jobs. Job enrichment is sometimes referred to as *vertical job loading* as contrasted to job enlargement, which is referred to as *horizontal job loading*.

Job enrichment serves the primary purpose of providing more challenge as well as personal freedom and responsibility on the job. The intent is to increase a person's motivation by offering more challenging tasks and personal discretion. Increased job satisfaction and individual productivity often result from job enrichment.

Job enrichment on Ms. England's job might entail more decision-making responsibility regarding the timing and amount of parts she will produce in a given period of time. Carolyn England already has some of that flexibility on her job. However, job enrichment would provide her much more independence than she now has.

Autonomous Work Teams

Autonomous work teams represent an attempt to consider both the social and technical aspects of a job.

> **Autonomous work teams:** groups of employees assigned to perform a natural unit of work who are given the responsibility to manage their own work, acquire required materials, set the timing of tasks, assign tasks, and control employee efforts.

The primary concern of management in this case is with output (both quantity and quality). Therefore, both social (relationships among employees) and technical aspects (methods used to accomplish tasks) of jobs may be affected. This approach goes beyond allowing a democratic workplace. Employees do not simply *participate* in decisions; they, as a group, *make* the decisions. As long as the output meets the organization's requirements, managers allow group discretion.

Autonomous work teams were developed primarily as a response to growing dissatisfaction with lower-level jobs and changing values in U.S. and European societies. Although not as common as job enrichment, the approach has been used in such companies as General Foods, Syntex, and Volvo of Sweden. For example, at Volvo a group of workers is assigned the responsibility of assembling a complete automobile.

We should also note that there have been innovative approaches to work scheduling developed as a response to some of the problems mentioned in this chapter. Since they do not relate to the job but to quality of life, they are discussed in Chapter 22.

Carolyn England's current job probably does not need to be redesigned. She seems to have plenty of discretion and flexibility. However, her previous job in the molding department should be examined for possible redesign. She described it as monotonous.

Application of Job Redesign Strategies

There have been many published accounts of job redesign efforts. We have already discussed examples of job specialization. Work simplification and job rotation have been used in such organizations as Cummins Engine Company and Shell U.K.[13] However, most successful efforts applied multiple design strategies, and it is, therefore, difficult to sort them out. We focus, then, on the more complex and innovative job design strategies.

Job enlargement efforts at Maytag have produced several conclusions regarding fifteen separate job enlargement projects over a period of three years. Maytag found that where job enlargement was implemented quality of production increased, labor costs decreased, and the majority of participants preferred their new enlarged jobs to their old ones. In addition, workers reported higher levels of personal satisfaction, greater overall efficiency from reduced materials handling, more stable production standards, and more flexible production rates.[14]

Job enrichment has been used successfully at American Telephone & Telegraph, Texas Instruments, IBM, Corning Glass Works, and Procter & Gamble. A good example is provided by the job enrichment project at Bankers Trust Co. of New York. There, a job enrichment strategy was used that stressed the combination of tasks into "whole" jobs that make up a natural unit of work. They emphasized worker identification with bank clients, provision for performance feedback to employees, and the inclusion of vertical loading (planning, decision making, and control responsibilities). Bankers Trust chose to implement job enrichment in the deposit accounting department where productivity was low, error rates were high, turnover was high, and overall morale was low. Job enrichment was implemented in each of the three separate work units in the deposit accounting department.

The results can be evaluated by work unit. In the regular and special accounts unit, forgeries paid fell by 56 percent, misfiled items decreased 19 percent, complaints decreased 20–30 percent, staff was reduced 16 percent, and the productivity index was 110.1 compared with the target 98.5. Supervisors were able to increase the percentage of time spent developing subordinates from 17 percent to 68 percent. Turnover reduced from 38 to 14 per year, for an annual saving of $38,400.

In the business accounts unit, the productivity index increased from 88.3 to 108.6, and staff levels were reduced from 63 to 50. Turnover was reduced by over 50 percent, for a savings of $20,800. In the accounting control unit, setup clerical capacity was increased by 34.7 percent, effectively adding 30 productive hours each month. The bank calculated that the decrease in the cost of a standard business hour for the three units yielded an annual savings of approximately $305,000. William Cox, the officer in charge of deposit accounting, called the job enrichment program an "unqualified success."[15]

We noted that autonomous work groups have been used in several organizations, but probably the best-known example of their use is at Volvo of Sweden. Volvo management began job redesign efforts in the 1960s, which are still in operation, to increase job satisfaction among workers in lower-level jobs. As a result of these efforts, the traditional assembly-line process, used by most automobile manufacturers, was eliminated at its Kalmar assembly plant. The assembly line was replaced by autonomous work teams, each of which was responsible for the complete assembly of an automobile. The teams managed their own work and job assignments, acquired materials, timed their task activities, and exercised their own methods of control. In other words, the workers' jobs were expanded considerably in scope. Workers had more opportunities to make decisions, and they received more feedback on their performance.

The results are somewhat different from those of other design strategies, however. The Kalmar plant cost 10 percent more to build than did a conventional facility and produces only one-third the number of automobiles as a typical U.S. plant. But absenteeism and turnover are lower than at other plants in the area, and output quality is higher. Volvo is pleased with the results. It has implemented many of these job design changes in its other facilities, including its new U.S. plant in Virginia.[16]

IMPLEMENTING JOB REDESIGN

We have noted some examples in which job redesign strategies have been used successfully. However, not all attempts have been successful. For the most part, we do not have the opportunity to read published accounts of those that fail. Job redesign is also not appropriate in all situations. Task characteristics should be considered along with individual and situational characteristics. The sequence of activities required in job redesign is shown in Figure 3-3.

Task Characteristics

Five important task characteristics in job design have been identified. They are skill variety, task identity, task significance, autonomy, and feedback.[17] Research has found

Figure 3-3

Implementing Job Redesign Strategies

Recognition of Need for New Job Design	Analyze Task Characteristics	Analyze	Analyze Constraints	Select and Implement Appropriate Job Design Strategy
	Skill variety Task identity Task significance Autonomy Feedback	Individual Factors (e.g., growth need strength) Situational factors (e.g., satisfaction with work environment elements)	Employee ability Technology Union	Work simplification Job specialization Job rotation Job enlargement Job enrichment Autonomous work teams

that these task characteristics affect an individual's motivation. These characteristics also affect an individual's feeling of meaningfulness of work, sense of responsibility for work done, and knowledge of the results of job performance. Therefore, the more a job contains of each of these five characteristics, the more motivation it provides to workers.

SKILL VARIETY.   We noted earlier that some jobs are highly routine and repetitive. The tasks on these jobs not only require simple skills, but they also provide little opportunity for the individual to develop new or more complex skills. Individuals on these jobs frequently must perform the same task over and over again. The task is so simple that it can be done many times within a day. For example, a packer in a furniture factory may pack hundreds of folding chairs in boxes each day. It is easy to see how performing this same task day after day, week after week, for several years would become extremely monotonous and boring to the average person.

Skill variety: the provision of a number of different tasks requiring diverse skills.

Job rotation, job enlargement, and job enrichment provide opportunities for individuals to use a greater variety of their skills. Monotony may be relieved by rotating to different jobs or even adding tasks of similar difficulty. More challenging tasks would likely also decrease monotony. More variety in the tasks may provide more opportunity for the individual to develop new skills.

TASK IDENTITY.   It is important to be able to identify a task that has been completed successfully. In addition, we should be able to identify with the end product and know how we have contributed to it.

Task identity: the degree to which successfully completed tasks can be determined and the degree to which one performing those tasks can associate with the end product.

On many jobs, however, it is not only difficult to identify with the end product, it is also difficult to identify successful completion of tasks. On jobs that are highly routinized, successful completion of a task means little. Because it is so simple, it has little significance. Employees whose jobs are highly specialized may have problems identifying with the completed product. Additionally, many staff jobs in organizations make it difficult to identify with the end product. The manager of the corporate file department, a junior programmer, and even a benefits specialist may have problems identifying with the end product (e.g., card tables and chairs for a furniture manufacturer). For example, a benefits specialist may experience frustration because he or she lacks discretion to complete the task. Other managers control the decision to adopt or reject the changes and/or new benefit programs.

Task identity can be increased by increasing the number of tasks and their complexity and by adding more discretion. In addition, developing a larger, more natural unit of work may help employees to identify with the end product.

TASK SIGNIFICANCE.   Task significance along with skill variety and task identity affects the feeling of the meaningfulness of the work.

Task significance: the degree to which the job tasks have an impact on others both inside and outside the organization.

Task significance can be affected by the complexity and challenge in the work, by how closely individual job performance relates to department and company performance, and by the status accorded the job. A company president has a high degree of task significance in his or her job. The work is complex and challenging, individual performance relates closely to company performance, and the job carries high status. There is much less task significance in a mail clerk's job. Additionally, those in highly skilled production jobs are accorded more status than are those in assembly-line jobs, as can be seen in union contracts. Thus skilled production jobs generally have high task significance.

Jobs can be redesigned to increase task significance by adding more complex and challenging tasks as well as tasks that would normally afford more status. Frequently, more complex tasks will also add more status, but such is not always the case. Higher task significance increases the meaningfulness of the work.

AUTONOMY.   Autonomy on the job relates to the degree of worker discretion. The degree of autonomy affects employee feelings of responsibility on the job.

Autonomy: the amount of discretion allowed the employee on the job.

Discretion is one of the more easily manipulated aspects of a job. Discretion may be increased by allowing employees to choose the work methods to be used, decide the sequencing and timing of work to be done, obtain needed raw materials, and coordinate with other jobs and units as necessary. Frequently, the supervisor may increase worker autonomy by delegating some of the managerial responsibility over the job. However, this is not always easy, because supervisors are sometimes reluctant to delegate authority. Job enrichment and autonomous work teams are designed to increase autonomy on the job.

FEEDBACK.   Feedback affects the knowledge of personal performance on the job.

Feedback: information provided to employees regarding their performance on job tasks.

Knowledge of performance affects a person's motivation and performance on the job. If a person is performing well and knows it, he or she is likely to continue performing well. However, if a person is performing poorly but receives no feedback, he or she is unlikely to improve performance. In addition, a person who is performing well but is receiving no feedback may reduce performance because he or she becomes less motivated. Feedback, then, is an important task characteristic.

Some jobs have built-in feedback, others do not. However, higher-level jobs do not necessarily have more feedback than lower-level jobs. Recently, a vice-president of a major insurance company complained to one of the authors about the lack of feedback she received on her job. In fact, she felt that not knowing the results of her efforts was one of the most frustrating aspects of her job. Most individuals desire and need feedback on their job performance. Knowledge of the results of one's efforts are important. This aspect relates task identity and autonomy. Greater task identity allows greater opportunity for general feedback on results because one can relate to the success of the final product. Additionally, greater autonomy may bring with it less feedback from one's supervisor. Thus specific efforts must be made in job redesign efforts to provide feedback. In autonomous work teams, feedback would be provided by peers; in job enrichment programs, the supervisor must spend more time providing feedback.

We have noted that assembly-line workers seem to have low job satisfaction. This may be explained by the task characteristics of their jobs. Generally, these jobs have low skill variety, task identity, task significance, and autonomy. In contrast, professional jobs are often much higher in these dimensions. As a result, professionals generally have higher levels of job satisfaction than do assembly-line workers.

The makeup of the characteristics of tasks and jobs must be considered carefully before job redesign strategies are implemented. Jobs must be analyzed and strategies such as job enrichment must be designed to change the task characteristics that are required for highest job motivation.

Carolyn England provided information that allows us to examine her job on several of the task characteristics. First, her job seems to require at least a reasonable amount of skill variety in setting up the dies, loading the machine, and trying to spot and solve problems. She seems to identify strongly with her job and the products she turns out. Her supervisor allows her a reasonable amount of autonomy: she can run the machine manually, change work procedures, and so on. She receives feedback in two ways. She checks her output for defects. Also, she sets goals for herself and measures her performance against those. Thus there is flexibility in her job in order for her to do this. Task significance in her job is hard to analyze. However, Carolyn England stated that she feels challenged, so there may be a reasonable level of task significance as well.

Individual and Situational Factors

Individual and situational factors must be considered in addition to task characteristics prior to implementing job redesign strategies. This relationship is shown in Figure

3-3. It is likely that some job redesign efforts have failed because these factors were not analyzed carefully.

INDIVIDUAL FACTORS.   Differences have been found in the way in which urban and rural workers respond to changes in their jobs. Research indicates that rural workers are more satisfied with complex jobs whereas workers from urban areas were more satisfied with less complex jobs.[18] Perhaps more important, individual factors such as one's need for achievement, one's need for affiliation, and one's growth need strength (need for accomplishment, learning, and challenge) have been found to affect the outcomes of job redesign efforts.[19] Employees who have a high need for achievement and/or high growth need strength respond more favorably to enriched jobs than do those with low needs in these areas. Thus job enrichment should be more effective with individuals having a high need for achievement. Research, then, indicates that we should not apply job redesign strategies indiscriminately to all individuals and expect the same results. Different individuals will likely respond differently to the design efforts.

SITUATIONAL FACTORS.   In addition to individual factors, other situational factors may affect workers' responses to changes in the design of their jobs. For example, employees who are satisfied with their work environment (e.g., co-workers, supervision, pay, job security) are more likely to respond favorably to job enrichment efforts.[20] Therefore, Carolyn England would likely respond favorably to enriching job changes. Even the type of function in which one works may affect one's satisfaction with an enriched job. Therefore, consideration must be given to employees' work environment and their satisfaction with it prior to implementing job redesign. If employees were found to be dissatisfied with elements of their present work environment, job redesign efforts might be delayed until changes could be made to increase employee satisfaction. In this way, job redesign efforts would have a higher probability of producing positive results.

Constraints on Job Redesign

At least three constraints to job redesign efforts may be noted in Figure 3-3. The first is again related to the individual. Employees must have the skills to perform the job for which they are selected. If changes are made in the job (particularly enriching changes), employees must be able to perform them. If employees do not have the ability to perform the tasks added to the job, productivity will probably decrease. Therefore, employee ability places constraints on the nature and extent of job redesign.

Second, the primary technology (techniques and processes required to change raw materials into finished products) area in which job design changes are desired may act as a constraint on these changes.[21]

The benefits of these changes must outweigh the costs in order to justify them. It is difficult for some organizations to eliminate their assembly-line processes to redesign assembly workers' jobs. Volvo management did so and is pleased with its results. However, the production in the newly designed plants is considerably less than is that of comparable American automobile manufacturing plants.

The third potential constraint on job redesign efforts is acceptance by employee unions. We discuss union and management relations in Chapter 18. It is useful to note that unions may be skeptical of organizational activities to increase productivity and satisfaction. If employees are represented by a union, the organization cannot make unilateral decisions regarding jobs or conditions of work. Union acceptance and approval is necessary in these cases. Since many unions view these activities suspiciously, gaining their approval may not be easy.

Job Design and Rewards

Employees' rewards and their jobs are highly interrelated. Two basic types of rewards are tied to the job design: monetary compensation rewards and intrinsic psychological rewards. We discuss employee compensation and its relationship to jobs in Chapter 14, in which it is noted that effective pay systems are related strongly to the design of jobs. Jobs that are more complex and more valuable to the organization receive greater amounts of pay.

Additionally, job designs affect employees' psychological rewards. One of the biggest problems with overspecialized, routine jobs is that they do not provide adequate psychological rewards. They do not provide challenge or allow for personal growth and development. Many of the redesign strategies described in this chapter provide more psychological rewards.

We should note that, if employee pay and job design are well coordinated, changes in job design may require changes in pay. Many employees will, in fact, expect pay increases if they are given more demanding responsibilities.

The complexity of the job design concept has been noted in the preceding discussion on implementation. The issue of job design is more important and more complex than might be expected by the ordinary employee. Figure 3-3 summarizes the nature of implementing job redesign.

JOB DESIGN AND PERSONNEL MANAGEMENT

The job is a basic element in personnel management. A majority of personnel management activities are related to employee jobs and their design. Much of the focus in this chapter has been on redesigning the job. However, it is important that a job be designed properly from its inception. Other important personnel activities cannot be accomplished effectively if it is not.

The design of the job is the basis for human resource planning, selection, training, motivation, and compensation. It plays an important role in career development, equal employment opportunity, labor relations, organization development, and quality of work life. Thus its importance to personnel management should not be overlooked.

It is important to know the number and type of employees that will be necessary to fulfill the organization's future requirements. The numbers and types of employees needed are related to the *jobs* and their *designs* required for the organization to accomplish its goals. Human resource plans, then, are based on the numbers and types of job designs (covered in Section II).

The selection process is designed to obtain the most qualified person available to meet job requirements. Once jobs have been designed and analyzed thoroughly, the skills needed to perform the job are determined. Individuals with the appropriate background and skills are then recruited and interviewed to select the one that can best fulfill the requirements of the job (covered in Section II).

The purpose of training programs is to help personnel develop the appropriate skills to perform current and/or future jobs. Training programs are geared to the skills needed based upon the job design. Management development programs, for example, help current and future managers develop skills that are necessary for them to be effective in managerial roles (covered in Section III).

Throughout this chapter, we have discussed jobs and motivation. Individuals must be motivated to perform the job. Two forms of reward for performing the job discussed were monetary and psychological. Both are important to motivation, but some feel that, given some reasonable level of monetary rewards, psychological rewards become prominent. We also noted that the range of monetary compensation paid an individual is based appropriately on the complexity of the job and its value to the organization (covered in Section IV).

Career paths to develop individuals and to help them accomplish career goals are designed around jobs. Equal employment opportunity involves the selection process and job design. Union-management negotiations and grievances frequently focus on job activities as well as on the conditions of work. Some organization development techniques are based on the job. Most of the job design strategies discussed in this chapter (e.g., job enrichment, autonomous work teams) can be considered organization development techniques. An important part of the quality-of-life issue revolves around the job design and the quality of work life (covered in Sections IV and V).

Thus we can see that jobs and their design form the basis of many important personnel management activities. We stated in Chapter 1 and earlier in this chapter that job design affects both the organization-job relationship and the job-people relationship. The underlying logic of job design, then, becomes part of the underlying logic of each of these other personnel management activities. However, we also noted in Figure 3-3 that task characteristics, individual factors, situational factors, and potential constraints must be analyzed prior to implementation of job design strategies. Therefore, the first major step in proper job design is job analysis. We discuss the process of job analysis in Chapter 4.

SUMMARY

The focus of this chapter is on jobs, their design, and their effects on people. Job design concerns the arrangement of task contents necessary to satisfy both organizational and human requirements.

The emphasis on job specialization and on technical efficiency often leads to overspecialization, in some cases negatively affecting the job-people relationship. Many people in boring, repetitive jobs are not satisfied with their work, whereas those in more complex and challenging jobs (e.g., professionals) have been found to be more satisfied. For most effective results, job designs should be matched to employee skills and needs.

Jobs should be designed to achieve maximum productivity. This requires designs that fulfill goals (organization-job relationship) and individual needs (job-people relationship). The development of scientific management and mass-production techniques increased technical efficiency and productivity but did not account for the job-people relationship. Newer technological developments affecting productivity include the increasing use of minicomputers and the use of robots on the assembly line.

Work simplification, job specialization, job rotation, job enlargement, job enrichment, and autonomous work teams represent approaches to job design. Work simplification and job specialization narrow the number of tasks performed. Job rotation and job enlargement increase the number of tasks performed. Job enrichment and autonomous work teams focus on increasing the complexity and challenge of the jobs.

Many examples of successful application of these design strategies have been described. However, implementation of job redesign strategies is not simple. The task characteristics of skill variety, task identification, task significance, autonomy, and feedback must be identified for each job under redesign consideration. Individual factors (e.g., need for achievement) and situational factors (e.g., satisfaction with work environment) must be analyzed thoroughly. Finally, potential constraints (e.g., employee ability, union) must be considered. The results of these analyses must then be considered together and the most appropriate strategy or combination of strategies chosen and implemented.

Job design is the basis for both monetary and psychological rewards. Job design is also the basis of many personnel management activities. In fact, jobs are at the very heart of the personnel function.

INTERVIEW WRAP-UP

What I like about my job is the challenge that it presents and the autonomy to do the job by myself, with no one else's help. My previous job was monotonous because I had to perform the same tasks over and over again.

The only thing I dislike now is having to clean up, but I certainly understand the necessity of doing so. Still, I would like to find a way to change it. —Carolyn England, punch-press operator, Macklanburg-Duncan.

WHAT MANAGERS SHOULD DO REGARDING PERSONNEL MANAGEMENT ACTIVITIES

1. Personnel managers should be involved in the initial phases of job design throughout the organization. Their concern is not the technical aspects of the job but the people aspects. The purpose is to see that the organization-job and job-people relationships based on the job design are compatible.

2. They should work with and train managers in the important factors of the job design that relate to effective job-people relationships.

3. Managers should continually monitor turnover rates, absenteeism rates, and morale to spot problem areas requiring job redesign strategies. Once these areas are identified, they must work with functional managers to analyze task characteristics, individual factors, situational factors, and potential constraints. Finally, working with the functional managers, they should select, implement, and monitor the results of job redesign strategies.

Managers must be involved in each of these activities if selection, training, and compensation programs are to be successful.

REVIEW QUESTIONS

1. What are reasons for dissatisfaction and low productivity in some U.S. organizations?

2. How does job design affect the organization-job and job-people relationships?

3. In what ways do you think new developments such as sophisticated minicomputers and robots on the assembly line affect productivity? Be specific.

4. What are the similarities and the differences between the innovative approaches to job design?

5. How would you implement a job redesign strategy? Be sure to describe the complete process.

6. Why is the concept of job design so important for personnel management?

KEY CONCEPTS

Autonomous work teams   Job specialization
Autonomy   Productivity
Feedback   Skill variety
Job design   Task identity
Job enlargement   Task significance
Job enrichment   Work simplification
Job rotation

CASE

THE DILEMMA OF THE WAYWARD SECRETARY

Beverly Jackson had graduated magna cum laude with a B.S. degree in foreign languages. As the child of a military family, she had visited many parts of the world and had traveled extensively in Europe. Despite these broadening experiences, she had never given much thought to a career until her recent divorce from John Bateman.

Needing to provide her own income, Beverly began to look for work. After a fairly intense but unsuccessful search for a job related to her foreign language degree, she began to evaluate her other skills. She had become a proficient typist in college and decided to look into secretarial work. Although she still wanted a career utilizing her foreign language skills, she felt that the immediate financial pressures would be eased in a temporary secretarial position.

Within a short period of time, she was hired as a clerk/typist in a typing pool at National Washington Life Insurance Company. Six months later, she became the top typist in the pool and was assigned as secretary to Betty Anderson, manager of marketing research. Beverly was pleased to get out of the pool and to get a job that had more variety in the tasks to perform. Besides, she also got a nice raise in pay.

Everything seemed to proceed well for the next nine months. Betty was pleased with Beverly's work, and Beverly seemed happy with her work. Beverly applied for a few other more-professional jobs in the Cleveland area during this time. However, each time her application was rejected for lack of related education and/or experience in the area.

Over the next few months, Betty noticed changes in Beverly. She did not always dress as neatly as she had in the past, she was occasionally late for work, some of her lunches extended to two hours, and most of her productive work was done in the morning hours. Betty did not wish to say anything because Beverly had been doing an excellent job and her job tasks still were being accomplished on time. However, Beverly's job behavior continued to worsen. She began to be absent frequently on Mondays or Fridays. The two-hour lunch periods became standard, and her work performance began to deteriorate. In addition, Betty began to suspect that Beverly was drinking heavily, due to her appearance some mornings and behavior after her two-hour lunches.

Betty decided that she must confront Beverly with the problem. However, she wanted to find a way to help her without losing a valuable employee. Before she could set up a meeting, Beverly burst through her door after lunch one day and said:

"I want to talk to you, Betty."

"That's fine," Betty replied. "Shall we set a convenient time?"

"No! I want to talk now."

"OK, why don't you sit down and let's talk?"

Betty noticed that Beverly was slurring her words slightly and she was not too steady.

"Betty, I need some vacation time."

"I'm sure we can work that out. You've been with the company for over a year and have two weeks' vacation coming."

"No, you don't understand. I want to start it tomorrow."

"But, Beverly, we need to plan to get a temporary replacement. We can't just let your job go for two weeks."

"Why not? Anyway anyone with an IQ above 50 can do my job. Besides, I need the time off."

"Beverly, are you sure you are all right?"

"Yes, I just need some time away from the job."

Betty decided to let Beverly have the vacation, which would allow her some time to decide what to do about the situation.

Betty thought about the situation the next couple of days. It was possible that Beverly was an alcoholic. However, she also seemed to have a negative reaction to her job. Maybe Beverly was bored with her job. Beverly did not have the experience or job skills to move to a different type of job at present. Betty decided to meet with the personnel manager and get some help developing her options to deal with Beverly's problem.

CASE QUESTIONS

1. What is the problem in your opinion?

2. Assume that you are the personnel manager. What are Betty's alternatives? Be sure to describe them thoroughly.

3. What do you consider the best alternative? Why?

NOTES

[1] W. F. Christopher, *Management for the 1980s* (Englewood Cliffs, N.J.: Prentice-Hall, 1980), pp. 230–231.

[2] R. P. Quinn and G. Staines, *1977 Quality of Employment Survey* (Ann Arbor: Institute of Social Research, University of Michigan, 1978).

[3] Adapted from R. W. Woodman and J. J. Sherwood, "A Comprehensive Look at Job Design," *Personnel Journal,* 56 (1977), 384–390.

[4] *Work in America,* report of a Special Task Force to the Secretary of Health, Education and Welfare (Cambridge, Mass: MIT Press, 1973).

[5] Ibid., pp. 15–16.

[6] For more information, see J. W. Taylor, *Shop Management* (New York: Harper, 1919).

[7] R.A. Sutermeister, *People and Productivity* (New York: McGraw-Hill, 1976), pp. 7–9.

[8]Ibid., p. 51.

[9]H. Brooks, "What's Happening to the U.S. Lead in Technology?" *Harvard Business Review,* 50 (1972), 110–117.

[10]M. Fein, "Improving Productivity by Improved Productivity Sharing," *The Conference Board Record,* 13, (1976), 44–49.

[11]Woodman and Sherwood, "A Comprehensive Look at Job Design," 384–390.

[12]R. J. Aldag and A. P. Brief, *Task Design and Employee Motivation* (Dallas: Scott, Foresman, 1979), pp. 42–43.

[13]Woodman and Sherwood, "A Comprehensive Look at Job Design," 384–390.

[14]Ibid.

[15]W. P. Kraft and K. L. Williams, "Job Redesign Improves Productivity," *Personnel Journal,* 54 (1975), 393–397.

[16]R. D. Middlemist and M. A. Hitt, *Organizational Behavior: Concepts and Their Application* (Chicago: Science Research Associates, 1981).

[17]J. R. Hackman and G. R. Oldham, "Motivation Througb the Design of Work: Test of a Theory," *Organizational Behavior and Human Performance,* 16 (1976), 250–279.

[18]A. N. Turner and P. R. Lawrence, *Industrial Jobs and the Worker* (Cambridge, Mass.: Harvard University Press, 1965).

[19]J. E. Stinson and T. W. Johnson, "Tasks, Individual Differences and Job Satisfaction," *Industrial Relations,* 16 (1977), 315–322.

[20]R. M. Steers and R. T. Mowday, "The Motivational Properties of Tasks," *Academy of Management Review,* 2 (1977), 645–658.

[21]D. M. Rousseau, "Technological Differences in Job Characteristics, Employee Satisfaction, and Motivation: A Synthesis of Job Design Research and Sociotechnical Systems Theory," *Organizational Behavior and Human Performance,* 19 (1977), 18–42.

JOB ANALYSIS AND ITS USES

LEARNING OBJECTIVES

After reading this chapter, you should be able to

1. Define job analysis and explain its importance for organizations.
2. Describe seven commonly used job analysis techniques.
3. Discuss situations in which each of the job analysis techniques would be most effective.
4. Define job description and job specifications.
5. Describe how job descriptions and job specifications can be used by personnel managers.
6. Discuss the uses of job analysis.

Dennis R. Cash is the wage and salary administrator for Texas-New Mexico Power Company in Fort Worth, Texas. He has been with the company for about three years and holds an M.B.A. degree.

Texas-New Mexico Power Company provides electricity to some eighty-nine municipalities and adjacent rural areas in the southwest United States. Additionally, it provides energy to selected industrial customers who operate large plants and other facilities.

Dennis Cash was interviewed to understand why job analysis is important and how it is used in an organization.

Interviewer: The term "job analysis" may be vague in meaning. In your own words, what is job analysis?

Dennis Cash: To me, job analysis is the investigation of a job to determine (1) the principal duties and responsibilities involved, (2) the mental and physical requirements of the job, (3) the special skills needed to perform the job, and (4) the conditions under which the work is performed.

Job analysis includes writing a job description that defines the job adequately and specifies the minimum requirements of skill, ability, responsibility, and knowledge that an incumbent must possess to perform the job satisfactorily.

Interviewer: How do you analyze a job?

Dennis Cash: The first step of job analysis is gathering information concerning the job. Questionnaires, interviews, and observation are methods used for gathering this information. However, questionnaires are the primary source.

Questionnaires are completed by persons presently holding the job being analyzed. The questionnaire asks questions concerning job duties, mental requirements, skill requirements, experience requirements, working conditions, and responsibilities. After this form is completed by the employee, it will be reviewed and signed by the supervisor. Should I have any questions on the completed questionnaire, I will interview the employee, supervisor, or both.

From this information, a job description and requirement sheet can be written. These two items will be reviewed by the employee and the supervisor. After any changes, the job description and requirement sheet are ready for the department head's approval. Following this approval, the job is ready for evaluation.

Interviewer: Why is it important that the job be analyzed correctly, and what are the uses of the results of job analysis?

Dennis Cash: The results of job analysis are used in developing job requirements, in work force planning and job recruiting, in developing job performance standards on our appraisal program, and in helping to orient new employees toward responsibilities and duties. If results from job analysis are to be successful in these important areas of personnel, it is imperative that it be done correctly. However, the major use of job analysis for us is to gather information and present it in such a way that it can be used for job evaluation and salary administration purposes. Job evaluations are based on the information in the job descriptions and requirements. The job descriptions and requirement sheets written from the job analysis information are vital components for a successful job evaluation and wage administration program. It is very important that jobs be analyzed properly so that job descriptions and requirements can be written that describe the jobs accurately. Job descriptions and requirements are bases upon which to measure relative worth of jobs in the company and compensate them accordingly.

INTRODUCTION

In Chapter 3, we discussed the importance of job design. We also noted that to design jobs properly, they must be analyzed thoroughly.

 Job Analysis: a systematic process for gathering information about a job.[1]

The results of job analysis are job descriptions and job specifications. These describe the specific tasks, duties, and responsibilities, along with the personal skills, abilities, and qualifications, that are needed to perform the job.

IMPORTANCE OF JOB ANALYSIS

Dennis Cash described the importance of job analyses. He noted that job analyses were used for many purposes. Among those were the developing of job requirements, work force planning, recruiting, setting job performance standards for performance appraisal, job evaluation and salary administration. Therefore, job analyses are related directly to many of the responsibilities of personnel managers. Job analyses are useful not only to the organization but also to the employee. The results of job analyses spell out the requirements and responsibilities of the job. Thus they help employees to know what is expected from them on the job. Dennis Cash noted that they are especially useful in orienting new employees in their jobs.

A good working knowledge of the contents of jobs is necessary for effective personnel management activities. In Chapter 1, we noted that job analysis affected the organization-job and the job-people relationships. Job analysis, in part, affects these relationships through its link with job design, but it also has separate effects on these relationships. For example, people cannot perform their duties if the job has not been analyzed and they do not know what their responsibilities are. This affects both the organization (organization-job) and the employee (job-people). Most personnel management activities, in some way, relate to the job (e.g., human resource planning, selection, training, compensation).

Job analysis is important for sound management practices. The basic elements of the organization structure are jobs. Thus, to construct a logical structure, managers must have a good understanding of job contents. Knowledge of job tasks, duties, and responsibilities is necessary if managers wish to place similar jobs together in a work unit (developing a structure).

Those at the top of organizations must understand the work that their employees do. It is not enough to know that the organization has 157 secretaries, 63 cost accountants, 72 sales representatives, and 336 machinists. There must be an understanding of what employees do in these jobs. For example, if executives are considering the purchase of word processing equipment at a cost of approximately

$100,000, they must know how it will affect secretarial and clerical jobs throughout the organization and how it will influence productivity and cost saving. An effective job analysis can provide this understanding.

Job analysis is also necessary for two other important reasons: legal requirements and salary computation. It is legally necessary for all personnel activities to be related to the job rather than to the characteristics of the person to eliminate discrimination. Thus a person must be selected on the basis of his or her skills to fulfill the job duties and responsibilities rather than on some other basis (e.g., one's religion, race, sex, or age). If someone were to bring charges of discrimination, it would be necessary for the organization to show that the basis for action was job related. To do so, a thorough job analysis is necessary, along with complete job descriptions and job specifications.

In the previous chapter, we discussed job rewards, both psychological and monetary, and their relationships to job design. Analysis of job content is necessary to understand better the nature of the psychological rewards provided by the job. Also, the wages and salaries provided to an employee are largely determined by the job contents and their value to the organization. Job analysis, then, is necessary to determine the appropriate basis for rewarding an employee's performance.

Dennis Cash emphasized the importance of job analysis for both purposes just stated. For example, use of job analysis in developing job requirements, in recruiting, and in developing performance standards for appraisal purposes ensures that hiring and appraisal actions are job related. Additionally, he emphasized the importance of job analysis for wage and salary administration purposes. Job analyses are necessary to evaluate the worth of a job accurately. Wages and salaries should be based on the worth of jobs to the organization. We may conclude that job analysis is a basic activity for an effective personnel department or any managerial activity.

JOB ANALYSIS TECHNIQUES

Several techniques may be used to analyze jobs. Often, a person called a job analyst is responsible for seeing that jobs are analyzed properly and described accurately. Some of the more common analysis methods used by job analysts include observation, employee self-recording of activities, supervisory analysis, interviewing, use of questionnaires, use of critical incidents, and examination of previous job analyses and descriptions.

Observation

Direct observation of job activities, one method used for job analysis, requires a trained job analyst who observes and records the tasks performed on a specific job over some period of time. The observation method is not simple and requires close attention by the job analyst. The job analyst must ensure that all important components of the job are observed and recorded. To ensure accuracy, the analyst should observe several employees performing on the job at various times. The observation of several employees helps avoid bias due to the unique manner in which one employee may perform the job tasks. Observation at several and various times helps to ensure that all tasks are recorded (since different tasks *may* be performed, for example, at different times in the day).

Although observation is a useful analysis technique, it is not appropriate for all jobs. Observation is most useful for jobs with tasks that take a short time to complete and are primarily of a physical nature (e.g., assembly-line jobs, clerical jobs). Jobs in which the tasks take long periods to complete or are primarily of a mental nature (e.g., highly skilled jobs, planners) do not lend themselves to observation for job analysis. It is easy to observe physical activities but difficult to observe mental activity. In addition, activities that require a few minutes or a few hours to complete are much easier to observe than are those that require several weeks or months.

From this discussion, we can see that unskilled and semiskilled jobs are the most appropriate ones on which to use observation. This method is used frequently by industrial engineers for time and motion and work measurement studies. Observations can be useful in the analysis of more complex jobs if used in conjunction with one or more of the other analysis methods. It can help the analyst to become familiar with the work conditions, equipment used, and certain personal skills involved in performing tasks.

Employee Self-recording of Activities

In some cases it may be appropriate to ask the employee(s) in the job to record the various job activities. The employees in these cases are asked to provide detailed descriptions of each task performed on their jobs. The premise underlying this approach is that the person performing the job should have the best knowledge of the job tasks.

It is necessary to analyze carefully the employees' descriptions because they may provide a distorted view. But this potential bias may be controlled by having the employee's supervisor review it for accuracy. This approach is efficient and economical and is particularly useful for higher-level and more complex jobs. It also is useful when combined with other sources of job information such as supervisory analysis and interviews with employees conducted by job analysts.

In Chapter 3 we described an interview with Carolyn England, a punch-press operator for Macklanburg-Duncan. Both observation and employee self-recording of activities might be useful in analyzing Ms. England's job. Her job is simple enough so that most activities could be identified by observation. Also, she seems to be conscientious and understands her job well. Thus she probably could record her own task activities accurately if she were asked to do so.

Supervisory Analysis

Supervisors may be asked to record the activities, tasks, duties, and responsibilities of the jobs over which they have authority. Again these people should, in most cases, have a good understanding of the jobs they supervise. Many of the supervisors have performed the jobs they supervise and therefore have had the opportunity to view them from two vantage points (supervisor and job incumbent).

Supervisors can provide particular help in identifying the personal skills necessary to perform the job. However, supervisors can also be biased. They may over- or underestimate the job responsibilities and skill requirements. Bias occurs more often when the supervisor has worked in some of the jobs but not others. This supervisor generally "favors" those jobs in which he or she has worked. Therefore it is important to ensure that no bias is present in the supervisor's analysis.

Job analysts frequently use a combination of supervisor analysis and employee self-recording of activities. This combination approach allows two viewpoints of the job. In addition, it controls, at least partially, for personal bias and allows supervisors and employees to become aware of and, it is hoped, resolve differences in viewpoints.[2]

Interviews

One of the most common job analysis techniques is the interview. The job analyst serves as the interviewer. The employee(s) and/or the supervisor serve as the interviewee(s).

Interviews, as well as employee self-recording and supervisory analyses, are more applicable to a wider variety of jobs than is the observation method. Interviews are useful for jobs with both short- and long-cycle tasks and physical and mental requirements. However, job analysts should plan their interviews carefully. Structured interviews including a few open-ended questions are the most appropriate for job analysis. Job analysts must be skilled interviewers for best results. The job analysts must be adept at obtaining the required information and be excellent listeners to ensure accurate interpretation of the interviewee's remarks. Different interviewees may require different styles (e.g., machinist and director of marketing research).

As with the methods discussed previously, the respondent may provide inaccurate information. Thus it is necessary that information from other sources be used in conjunction with interview data to complete the analysis and to write job descriptions and specifications. Individual interviews are expensive, requiring the job analyst's time and the interviewee's time away from work. At times, job analysts may interview a sample of job incumbents or hold group interviews to reduce the time and expense.

Most of the methods discussed thus far must be used in conjunction with other methods or sources of information to ensure accurate analyses. Research has shown that structured observation and interviews do not necessarily yield the same information.[3] Therefore, the use of only one method may provide incomplete or inaccurate information.

Questionnaires and Checklists

A currently popular method of job analysis is through administration of questionnaires to obtain job information. Questionnaires are a popular method of job analysis because they are less costly and less time consuming than are many of the other methods.

Often questionnaires are distributed to employees who are asked to complete them on company time. Once completed, the questionnaires are reviewed by the employee's supervisor. After agreement between the employee and supervisor, the questionnaires are returned to the job analyst. The job analyst would then use this and any other relevant information (e.g., previous job descriptions) to write a job description. The job analyst often requires more information in addition to the questionnaire responses to describe the job completely and accurately. At times follow-up is necessary to clarify ambiguous or missing responses to the questionnaire. A sample job analysis questionnaire is shown in Figure 4-1.

Standard questionnaires that are used by many organizations include the Position Analysis Questionnaire (PAQ),[4] the Task Abilities Scale (TAS),[5] and the Management Position Description Questionnaire (MPDQ).[6] Each of these instruments has been constructed carefully based on research. Both the PAQ and TAS have been found to be reliable (they measure the same elements the same way consistently) and valid (they measure what they are supposed to measure, namely, task contents).[7] Reliability and validity are important characteristics for a number of reasons, not the least of which is meeting legal requirements. When we use such a questionnaire and employee responses on it to develop job descriptions and job specifications, we want to be sure that they reflect the job accurately. Job standards upon which employee performance will be evaluated, as well as selection tests are based on these descriptions and specifications. Since selection criteria must be job related, the job analysis questionnaire plays a key role.

Use of a reliable and valid questionnaire then helps ensure that people are selected to perform jobs based on job-related reasons. This helps avoid selecting employees on some other basis, say, personal characteristics (e.g., race, sex, age), that could be discriminatory.

Probably the PAQ is the most thoroughly researched of any job analysis questionnaire. The PAQ contains 194 job elements. Managers are asked to respond to a five-point response mode (ranging from "does not apply" to "very substantial"), rating the degree to which each job element appears in the job. The job elements cover six major areas including information input, mediation processes, work output, interpersonal activities, work situation and job context, and miscellaneous aspects. The intent of the PAQ is to identify the behaviors involved in performing the required job tasks, duties, and responsibilities. The PAQ may be used to develop or validate selection tests and in job evaluation systems designed to assign jobs equitably to appropriate salary ranges based on job contents.

Other Job Analysis Methods

Other job analysis methods are available for use by the job analyst as the situation dictates. These include the critical incident technique (CIT) and examination of previous job analyses and descriptions.

The CIT involves obtaining records of behaviors that have led to effective or ineffective job performance. These are called critical incidents. The critical incidents

Figure 4-1

Sample Job Analysis Questionnaire

Position Title: _____

Name: _____ Department: _____

Name of Immediate Supervisor: _____
Responsibility:
　　Please provide a short summary of the responsibilities of your job. Describe its basic purpose(s). _____

_____

_____

Job Duties
　　Please describe all the duties you perform in your job. At the end of the description of each duty, please note how often you perform each duty (e.g., daily, semiweekly, weekly, monthly, yearly). If you do not have enough space, please attach extra sheets. Number each duty and place them in order of importance with the most important duty first.

Supervision of Others
1. Please list the job titles and numbers of employees that are directly under your supervision: _____

_____

_____

2. Please describe the type of authority you have with your subordinates (e.g., assign work, discipline, instruct, coordinate activities, recommend pay increases, decide to hire and discharge, answer grievances). _____

_____

_____

Supervision Received
1. Please describe the type and amount of supervision you receive in doing your job. (Type: detailed instructions—all elements checked with supervisor; general instructions—nonstandard situations checked with supervisor; plan and arrange own work—supervisor reviews results; accountable for own results—little supervision). Amount: frequent (hourly) contact, periodic checks on performance, irregular performance checks, occasional meetings.)

_____

_____

2. Please describe the decisions you make on the job without consulting your supervisor. _____

_____

_____

Machines, Equipment, and Tools
　　Please list the type of machines, equipment, and/or tools used in your job and the percentage of time spent using them.

Figure 4-1 (*Continued*)

<u>Type</u>   %

_____

_____

_____

Work Conditions
     Please check the following conditions that best describe those of your workplace.

General Environment

☐ Good working conditions—clean, adequate light, heat, air and space
☐ Occasional exposure to some disagreeable elements (e.g., dirt, poor light, heat, air)
☐ Frequent exposure to several disagreeable elements
☐ Continuous exposure to multiple disagreeable elements

Job Hazards

☐ Occasional possibility of minor cut or abrasion; no other hazards
☐ Some exposure to minor hazards

☐ Periodic exposure to elements that might cause injury or illness
☐ Frequent exposure to elements that might cause injury or illness

Contacts with Others
     Please provide the job titles, frequency and nature of contact with persons outside of your department required in your job.

<u>Position Title</u>   <u>Frequency</u>   <u>Nature of Contact</u>

_____

_____

_____

To Be Filled out by Supervisor
1. What is the minimum level of education required to perform this job satisfactorily? _____

_____

2. What is the minimum *type* and *amount* of experience required to perform this job satisfactorily?
3. Please describe any *special* training, in addition to the education and experience noted above, required to perform the job satisfactorily. _____

_____

4. Please describe the responsibility and/or impact this job may have on the assets of the organization. _____

_____

_____

_____   _____
        Supervisor's Signature   Date

Source: Constructed on the basis of several sources: *Wage and Salary Administration: A Guide to Current Policies and Practices* (Chicago: Dartnell Corporation, 1969); U.S. Training and Employment Service, *Handbook for Analyzing Jobs* (Washington, D.C.: Government Printing Office, 1972); D. S. Beach, *Personnel: The Management of People at Work* (New York: Macmillan, 1980); and personal sources.

may be collected from supervisors, from employees on the job, or from both groups. This method is useful in complex jobs or jobs in which it takes a long time to complete some tasks. Thus the CIT may be useful in analyzing a staff planning specialist job (long task cycle). It has also been found useful in analyzing jobs with considerably varied dimensions like police officers (complex).[8]

Examination of previous job analyses and descriptions can be particularly useful if little change has occurred in the job since they were done. If change in the job has occurred, previous job analyses and descriptions may still be useful (for parts of the job that are unchanged and for a reference point) when used in conjunction with one or more of the other analysis techniques. There are several other techniques that may be useful but only in specialized cases such as the functional job analysis using the *Dictionary of Occupational Titles* provided by the U.S. Department of Labor.[9]

Most of the techniques have their disadvantages as well as their advantages. We have noted several of those in the discussion. However, even in the more quantitative approaches (e.g., PAQ, TAS), errors can be made in sampling. Therefore, it is generally advisable to use more than one job analysis method, when possible, to eliminate some of the potential error. A useful description of the components of job analysis may be obtained from the *Handbook for Analyzing Jobs,* provided by the Training and Employment Service of the U.S. Department of Labor.[10]

Dennis Cash noted that questionnaires, interviews, and observation are methods used to analyze jobs. He relies primarily on the questionnaire method. The questionnaire he uses was developed by him and was designed specifically to meet the needs of the Texas-New Mexico Power Company. He uses an interview with the employee, supervisor, or both if he needs further information.

JOB DESCRIPTIONS AND SPECIFICATIONS

Once jobs have been fully analyzed, they may be described, specifications developed, and standards set.[11] The relationship among job analysis, descriptions, specifications, and standards is depicted in Figure 4-2.

Figure 4-2

Job Analysis, Descriptions, Specifications, and Standards

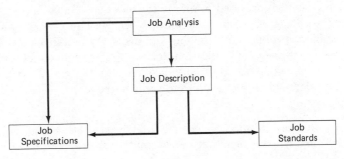

Job Descriptions

As shown in Figure 4-2, job descriptions are based on job analyses, and job specifications are based on both job analyses and job descriptions.

Job descriptions: written summaries of the basic tasks, duties, and responsibilities of jobs.

Normally, a job description contains three basic sections: identification, job summary, and specific duties and responsibilities.[12] The identification section generally contains the job title, department, and supervisor's title. Other identification elements such as job number and pay grade for the job may be included. The job summary provides a brief overview of the general nature of the job tasks. The third section provides a detailed listing of the specific duties and responsibilities contained in the job. Typical job descriptions are shown in Figure 4-3.

It is important that job descriptions be as accurate as possible. Job descriptions should contain all the major tasks assigned to the job. Accurate and complete job descriptions are necessary because they have several important uses:

> Clarifying vague responsibilities and eliminating overlapping responsibilities between jobs
>
> Developing job specifications
>
> Human resource planning and recruiting
>
> Orienting new employees to job duties and responsibilities
>
> Developing performance standards
>
> Job evaluation[13]

The importance of job descriptions then must not be overlooked.

Job Specifications

Job specifications are an important outgrowth of job analysis and job descriptions. Job specifications are used primarily for selection of qualified employees. Thus specifications should be precise as well as job related. However, they are also useful in human resource planning and training and necessary in affirmative action programs. Figure 4-4 shows the job specifications for the director and news photographer jobs described in Figure 4-3. Most job specifications list the education, experience, and general knowledge skills and abilities to perform the job.

Job specifications: summaries of the skills, background, and qualifications necessary for an employee to perform the job in a satisfactory manner.

Figure 4-3

Typical Job Descriptions from a Television Station

Job Title: <u>News Photographer</u>   Supervisor Title: <u>Chief Photographer</u>

Department: <u>News</u>   Salary Grade: _____

Number of Employees Supervised: <u>0</u>

Type of Employees Supervised: _____ (exempt vs. nonexempt)

Date: _____

Job Summary
Operates portable video camera and videotape recorder on live and recorded stories. Operates and understands microwave gear, both mechanical and electrical, in live vehicle. In coordination with assignment editor or reporter, shoots and edits assigned film/VTR within prescribed deadlines, meeting the quality criteria set by superior.

Specific Duties and Responsibilities
1. Operates portable video camera and videotape recorder on live and recorded stories.
2. Edits ¾" videotape in proper manner.
3. Operates and understands microwave gear, both mechanical and electrical, in live vehicle.
4. Shoots and edits assigned film/VTR within prescribed quality criteria and deadlines.
5. Maintains working area, vehicle, gear and editing equipment. Maintains adequate supply of film/VTR and editing supplies, as directed by superior.
6. Runs minicam pieces during newscasts, files minicam stories in permanent log, puts minicam/film reels together or files film on the cores after 10:00 P.M. newscast.
7. Accessible to assignments editor throughout work shift through personal contact, radio, or telephone. When available, accessible off shift on emergency, overtime basis.
8. Maintains and monitors news car police scanner and checks out traffic on police scanner to determine if newsworthy.

_____
Department Head's Signature

Job Title: <u>Director</u>   Supervisor: <u>Operations Manager</u>

Department: <u>Operations</u>   Salary Grade: _____

Number of Employees Supervised: <u>1–10</u>

Type of Employees Supervised: _____ (exempt vs. nonexempt)

Date: _____

Job Summary
Directs live broadcasts, assigned studio tape sessions, remotes. Directs and/or works as film photographer/editor on assigned film production work units.

Specific Duties and Responsibilities
1. Directs live broadcasts.
2. Directs assigned studio tape sessions and remotes. Coordinates time and production techniques with agency; directs clients and/or station producers.
3. Functions as film photographer/editor.
4. Assists production director and/or air control director in training and critique of production personnel.

Figure 4-3 (*Continued*)

5. Operates necessary equipment related to each assignment.
6. Schedules and coordinates studio time and crew requirements on assigned work unit.
7. Coordinates necessary information and material with other station personnel and departments on assigned units.
8. Works with agency and station producers in preplanning sessions to determine most effective approach to accomplish desired end result.

_____
Department Head's Signature

Care must be taken in the construction of job specifications, as they are used for several important purposes. It is also necessary to be able to show that the education, experience, and other qualifications required for employees are necessary to perform the job satisfactorily. If these specifications are necessary to perform the job, they are considered valid. However, if they are not specifically necessary to perform the job and individuals with minority status are eliminated from consideration as employees because of them, discrimination may be claimed. More of this relationship will be discussed in Chapter 17.

A second element based on job descriptions is job standards. Job standards represent the expected performance for each job duty described on the job description. Job standards provide the employee with performance goals to accomplish and with knowledge of performance expectations on the job. Job standards are often linked to performance appraisals. This relationship was noted by Dennis Cash. We discuss standards and performance appraisals in Chapter 15.

USES OF JOB ANALYSIS

Previously we noted some uses for job analysis. However, job analysis has multiple uses. In Chapter 1, we noted that job analysis affects both the organization-job and job-people relationships. Job analysis then affects many personnel management activities. The relationship of job analysis to these activities is shown in Figure 4-5.

We have also discussed the relationship of job analysis to job descriptions, specifications, and standards. Job analysis underlies many personnel management activities through the development of job specifications. We have already noted how job specifications are used in several personnel management activities but not in depth. The selection process is designed to find the most qualified person for the position. The job specifications, then, describe the minimum qualifications acceptable from applicants and are often used in advertisements of job openings. Thus job analyses provide the guidelines to be used in recruitment and selection of qualified employees.

Figure 4-4

Job Specifications for Director and News Photographer

Job Title: Director_____   Supervisor: Operations Manager

Department: Operations_____   Date: _____

Education
Requires a high school diploma plus two years of college.

Experience
Requires four years' prior related experience in live or taped broadcasts plus six months' learning time on the job, for a total of four years and six months.

Complexity of Decisions
Makes decisions on a variety of complex problems, some of which can be anticipated or are of a recurring nature. Must exercise sound judgment and creative thinking to plan the work and deal with factors not easily evaluated. Only a few of these decisions are subject to check. Solutions to problems often require coordination with other departments or organizations.

Physical and Visual Effort
Employee will have to stand or walk to perform most of duties. Handling of some lightweight equipment may be necessary at times. Visual concentration and manual dexterity are required approximately 50 percent of the time.

Supervision
Must be able to direct and supervise the activities of from one to a group of people engaged in director's assigned productions or work periods. Supervisory authority is confined to such periods exclusively, and no further supervisory or personnel functions are performed.

Contact with Others
Performance of duties requires appreciable contacts with persons outside the department and outside the station as a regular part of the job. Employee must exercise discretion, tact, and courtesy in these contacts.

Job Title: News Photographer   Supervisor: Chief Photographer

Department: News_____   Date: _____

Education
High school diploma plus up to two years of formal training in photography or comparable education.

Experience
One year prior related photographic experience plus three months' learning time on the job, for a total of one year, three months.

Complexity of Decisions
A variety of problems to be solved using general guides, some of which are complex and most of which are subject to check. Involves some discretion, independent action, and judgment to decide what to do.

Figure 4-4 (*Continued*)

Physical and Visual Effort
Manipulates medium- to heavyweight equipment and materials most of the shift. Regularly works in strained positions or with reaching, unrestrained movements most of the shift. Monitoring and/or operating equipment requires sustained concentration and use of visual concentration more than 50 percent of the time.

Contact with Others
Requires large number of contacts with limited categories of people both inside and outside the station. Must have a working knowledge of departmental policies and procedures and exercise tact, discretion, and persuasiveness to obtain cooperation.

Planning for future employee needs is important so that adequate recruitment and internal training and development programs may be designed. This planning is, of course, related to the job and the skills required to perform the job. Often, these plans describe the type of needed personnel by skill, education, and general qualifications. Thus job specifications are important in human resource planning.

Training and management development programs are designed to help employees acquire skills necessary to perform their current or future jobs well. Job specifications are also useful in career planning and development. To plan one's career path requires knowledge of the employee qualifications for each job in the projected career. Designing how an employee will obtain the necessary skills to make the next move along the career path is an important part of the planning.

Job analyses and equal employment opportunity are related by the way in which skills required to perform jobs affect minority hiring. Although we discuss this relationship later in Chapter 17, it is important to note that any activity that has an "adverse impact" on the employment of minorities may be considered discriminatory.[14] Thus, if job skills required are of such a type and/or level that a disproportionate number of applicants of minority status are excluded from consideration, questions of discrimination may arise. Effective job analysis, then, is critical to ensure that the job specifications are correct and are job related. In addition, job analysis may be used to develop and validate selection tests.[15] Given the most recent Equal Employment Opportunity Commission's (EEOC) guidelines on the validation of all selection procedures, effective job analyses have become even more important.[16]

Job analysis plays an important role in the development and administration of fair and equitable compensation systems. Job analyses are used in formal evaluations of the job's worth to the organization. Salary levels are often based on these formal evaluations. Thus job analysis may form the basis for the wages and salaries paid employees.

Finally, job analysis plays a role in performance and appraisal. We noted earlier that job standards were developed from the description of job duties and responsibil-

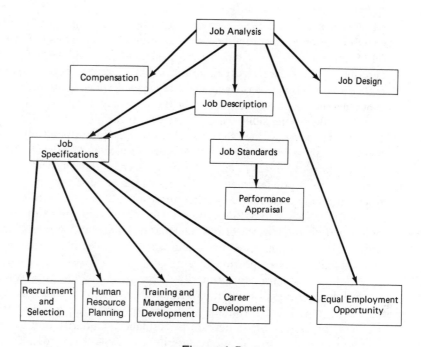

Figure 4-5

Relationship of Job Analysis to Personnel Management Activities

ities. These standards are then used in evaluating an employee's performance at the end of some predesignated period.

Dennis Cash noted that job analysis was used for many purposes in his company. In fact, he listed most of the uses described in this chapter. In addition, he strongly emphasized the importance of correct job analysis and accurate results. Without complete and accurate job analyses, many other personnel management activities could not be accomplished effectively.

SUMMARY

Job analysis is an important personnel management activity. Job analysis is a systematic process for gathering information about a job. A good working knowledge of job contents is necessary to fulfill many personnel management responsibilities.

Several techniques may be used to analyze jobs. Job analysts may select from observation, employee recording of activities, supervisory analysis, interviewing, use of questionnaires, use of critical incidents, examination of previous job analyses and descriptions, or some combination of these techniques. Observation of job activities requires alertness and concentration to ensure that all important activities are recorded. Observation is most useful on more routine jobs where tasks take only a short period of time to perform. It may be more efficient for employees to provide a detailed description of all the tasks they perform. This approach is most useful for complex, higher-level jobs. Supervisory analysis of jobs is frequently useful because supervisors should have a good understanding of the jobs they supervise. They are particularly useful for identifying skills required to perform the job.

Interviews conducted by job analysts with employees and supervisors are a common job analysis technique. Interviews are applicable to a wide variety of jobs with long- or short-cycle tasks and with varying mental and physical requirements. Questionnaires are a popular method of job analysis because they are less costly and less time consuming than are many other approaches. Some standard questionnaires, such as the PAQ, TAS, and MPDQ, are available for organizations to use. Other methods of job analysis, such as the critical incident technique and examination of previous analyses and descriptions, are most useful when used in combination with one or more of the methods discussed previously.

Job analyses are used primarily to construct job descriptions and job specifications. Job descriptions are written summaries of the basic tasks, duties, and responsibilities of jobs. Job descriptions may help to clarify vague responsibilities, to orient new employees to jobs, to develop performance standards, and to determine proper compensation. Job specifications describe the skills, background, and qualifications necessary for an employee to perform the job in a satisfactory manner. Job specifications are interrelated with recruitment and selection, training, human resource planning, and career development.

Job analyses underlie many basic personnel management functions to include job design, compensation, human resource planning, recruitment and selection, training and management development, performance appraisal, career development, and equal employment opportunity. Job analyses play particularly important roles in compensation systems (job evaluation), in selection processes, and in equal employment opportunity (development and validation of selection tests and employment procedures).

INTERVIEW WRAP-UP

Job analysis is a process to help determine the principal duties and responsibilities of the job, the mental and physical requirements of the job, the special skills needed to perform the job, and the conditions under which work is performed.

I use questionnaires, interviews, and observations to conduct job analyses, with primary emphasis on interviews. I use multiple methods to ensure that the analysis is correct. At Texas-New Mexico Power Company, job analyses are used for many purposes, including development of job requirements, work force planning, job recruiting, setting performance standards, and job evaluation to set wage and salary ranges for jobs. I am involved most heavily in the last function as the company's wage and salary administrator. —Dennis Cash, wage and salary administrator, Texas-New Mexico Power Company.

WHAT MANAGERS SHOULD DO REGARDING PERSONNEL MANAGEMENT ACTIVITIES

1. Managers should make sure that all jobs are analyzed on a periodic basis to ensure that the selection process, compensation systems, training programs, and other important personnel activities provide the most effective results.
2. Managers should attempt to ensure that the most effective means of job analysis are used. The methods used should be the most efficient and capable of obtaining maximum information for the job(s) being analyzed.
3. Personnel managers should utilize only well-trained job analysts. If they are unable to hire experienced job analysts, they should develop their own in-house training program. It may include both on-the-job and classroom training segments.
4. Managers should be responsible for ensuring that accurate up-to-date job descriptions and specifications exist for all jobs under their direction.

REVIEW QUESTIONS

1. Why do you believe that most organizations should use job analysis? Be specific.
2. For what type of jobs are the observation and interview job analysis techniques most appropriate? Why?
3. Why are questionnaires (e.g., PAQ) used frequently for job analysis?
4. What are the several uses of job descriptions and specifications?
5. Assume that you are a manager. In what ways will you use job analysis?

KEY CONCEPTS

Critical incident technique (CIT)
Employee self-recording
Interviewing
Job analysis
Job description
Job specifications
Job standards

Management Position Description Questionnaire (MPDQ)
Observation
Position Analysis Questionnaire (PAQ)
Questionnaires
Supervisory analysis
Task Abilities Scale (TAS)

CASE

THE ROUTINE DETECTIVE

Mary Peters and Sean Wilson were sitting at their desks doing routine paperwork when the phone rang. As Mary answered the phone, their supervisor, Lieutenant Taylor, burst into the office.

"A disturbance has been reported at 1716 West Rogers. The officers at the scene think that drugs may be involved, and they've requested detectives. You two are the ones. Get moving!"

Mary hung up the phone without ever knowing who was at the other end. She and Sean headed for their car. Once in the car, Mary drove, heading for West Rogers.

Sean broke the silence. "Boy, it's good to be getting some action. Things have been quiet for a while. We've been stuck in the office doing paperwork and going on routine calls the last week."

Mary responded, "Yes, I know what you mean. I was getting bored. I hate doing that paperwork. It reminds me of when I was a personnel specialist in the army. It seemed as if we had to fill out a form just to get a form to fill out."

When they arrived at the scene, no police officers were in sight. Two patrol cars were parked outside the large old three-story house. Mary and Sean got out of their car. After they carefully surveyed the scene, Mary spoke. "Something seems wrong. It's too quiet here. I'll take the front and you go around to the back."

"OK, but be careful, Mary. If you spy anything, call me."

Mary proceeded carefully to the door, which was partially open. She pushed open the door slowly. The room was extremely dark. She flipped the light switch right inside the door, but nothing happened. Mary thought to herself, "That paperwork and those routine calls don't sound so bad right now."

She took several steps into the room when she heard running footsteps. It sounded as if they were on stairs, but she could not see any stairs. She ran to the door of another room and looked in but saw nothing. Mary decided it was time to draw her weapon. Again, she heard the footsteps, moving faster this time. Just as Mary began to run toward the sound of the footsteps, she heard, "Mary, help!" and then there was silence.

Mary ran immediately out the front door to the back of the house where Sean was supposed to be. She found Sean lying unconscious just inside the back door. She pulled Sean outside the house, laid him on the ground, and tried to revive him, but she had no luck. Mary had to make a quick decision. Should she go back into that house alone and pursue Sean's assailant? The assailant may have gone out the back door and be gone by now. Was the assailant armed? Police procedures required that she call in extra help.

She decided she would follow police procedures. Mary proceeded to the car where she quickly called backup teams for help. Then Mary went back into the house. She proceeded quickly to the room where she had heard footsteps. No sounds were heard this time. She found the stairs and slowly began climbing them.

As she reached the top, the lights suddenly came on, taking Mary by surprise. A gnarled old man fell against Mary, knocking her against the wall. A young man then tried to run past her. However, Mary's reactions were fast. She tripped the young man, and he went tumbling down the stairs. Mary followed quickly and had him by the collar just after he reached the bottom. He struggled, but Mary twisted his arms behind his back and handcuffed him. Just at this time, two police officers burst through the door. Mary was pleased to see them.

The next day Mary was back at her desk in the station, filling out her report on the incidents of the night before. Sean was also at his desk but with a patch above his right eye, covering the seven stitches required to close the gash opened when he was struck by the assailant.

Sean said to Mary, "Boy, filling out these reports is boring. I wish we could get some action."

Mary looked at Sean, but before she could say anything, they both began to laugh.

CASE QUESTIONS

1. Assume that you are a job analyst called in to analyze Mary and Sean's detective jobs. Describe the methods of analysis you would use and the reasons why.

2. Based on the information provided in the case, write a job description and specifications that you feel reflect Mary and Sean's job.

3. What problems can you see in analyzing the job, describing it, and developing specifications for it?

NOTES

[1]T. A. De Cotiis and R. A. Morano, "Applying Job Analysis to Training," *Training and Development Journal,* 31 (1977), 20–24.

[2]Ernest McCormick, "Job and Task Analysis," in *Handbook of Industrial and Organizational Psychology,* ed. M. Dunnette (Chicago: Rand McNally, 1976), pp. 651–696.

[3]G. D. Jenkins, D. A. Nadler, E. E. Lawler, and C. Cammann, "Standardized Observations: An Approach to Measuring the Nature of Jobs," *Journal of Applied Psychology,* 60 (1975), 171–181.

[4]E. J. McCormick, P. R. Jeanneret, and R. C. Mecham, "A Study of Job Characteristics and Job Dimensions as Based on the Position Analysis Questionnaire (PAQ)," *Journal of Applied Psychology,* 56 (1972), 347–368.

[5]E. A. Fleishman, "On the Relation Between Abilities, Learning and Human Performance," *American Psychologist,* 27 (1972), 1017–1032.

[6]W. W. Tornow and P. R. Pinto, "The Development of a Managerial Job Taxonomy: A System for Describing, Classifying and Evaluating Executive Positions," *Journal of Applied Psychology,* 61 (1976) 410–418.

[7]E. P. Prien, "Function of Job Analysis in Content Validation," *Personnel Psychology,* 30 (1977), 167–174.

[8]W. W. Ronan, T. L. Talbert, and G. M. Mullet, "Prediction of Job Performance Dimensions: Police Officers," *Public Personnel Management,* 6 (1977), 173–179.

[9]U.S. Department of Labor, *Dictionary of Occupational Titles* (Washington, D.C.: Government Printing Office, 1977).

[10]U.S. Training and Employment Service, *Handbook for Analyzing Jobs.*

[11]W. French, *The Personnel Management Process* (Boston: Houghton Mifflin, 1970), p. 176.

[12]D. W. Belcher, *Compensation Administration* (Englewood Cliffs, N.J.: Prentice-Hall, 1974), p. 134.

[13]French, *The Personnel Management Process,* pp. 176–177.

[14]M. G. Miner and J. B. Miner, *Employee Selection Within the Law* (Washington, D.C.: Bureau of National Affairs, 1978), pp. 7–8, 15.

[15]G. A. Kesselman and F. E. Lopez, "The Impact of Job Analysis on Employment Test Validation for Minority and Nonminority Accounting Personnel," *Personnel Psychology,* 32 (1979), 91–108.

[16]T. P. Dhanens, "Implications of the New EEOC Guidelines," *Personnel,* 56 (1979), 32–39.

HIRING FOR PERFORMANCE

Once the organization has gathered needed information, designed jobs, and determined an appropriate organizational structure, the process of finding employees to perform those jobs can begin in earnest. Information that was gathered during job analysis is extremely useful at this juncture because it determines the skills and talents that the employees will need. This section, then, examines determination of the numbers and types of employees needed and which of the many job applicants have the necessary job skills.

The underlying rationale or logic of selection, presented in Chapter 5, provides a basis for examining the various personnel management activities of selecting employees who are likely to be high performers. Subsequently, in Chapter 6, we present various techniques that managers can use to plan or determine the organization's human resource needs (numbers and types of skills) and to recruit excellent employees. Specific selection tools and issues associated with choosing a particular employee are examined in Chapter 7. These tools and issues are extremely important in selecting the best employees and also in avoiding charges of discrimination. Finally, we conclude the section by examining, in Chapter 8, the unique difficulties associated with selecting managers and professional employees. The difficulty of measuring job requirements and identifying "true" levels of conceptual reasoning skills makes this activity challenging. Knowledge of how to select employees for these two groups is necessary in building your abilities to select employees effectively.

THE LOGIC OF SELECTION

LEARNING OBJECTIVES

After reading this chapter, you should be able to

1. Describe the logical purpose of selection.
2. Identify the relationships of job analysis, job description, and job specification as used for selection.
3. Describe the relationships among selection tools, job-related skills, and job performance and satisfaction.
4. Identify four major problems associated with selection of new employees.
5. Explain the need for validation of selection tools.

Xerox Corporation is an international corporation that employs over 120,000 people in the United States and abroad. It is one of the leading manufacturers of business equipment and is especially noted for its copiers and duplicators. Xerox also has divisions that are involved in electronic typewriters, information processing systems, electronic terminals, printers and plotters, educational publishing, and other related areas. Finding and hiring qualified employees to staff such a large organization is an important activity.

Douglas W. Pelino is the manager of corporate employment and college relations for Xerox. Mr. Pelino responded to our request for information regarding the general process of recruiting and selection of employees for organization tasks.

Interviewer: What is the general selection process used at Xerox?

Mr. Pelino: Xerox has a relatively consistent approach to the selection process. The process is one of deciding the kind of people we need, developing a recruiting strategy that exposes us to those people, interviewing them, and finally deciding which ones to offer the job, or jobs. We are concentrating on entry level hiring, to enable us to pursue a promotion-from-within strategy of career development. We know that, if we hire good people to begin with, then we will have good people who will grow and develop with the company.

Interviewer: What kind of information do you need about the organization, the specific job, and the job applicant before you can make a good selection decision?

Mr. Pelino: As a recruiter, I think it's important to understand the company and departmental objectives, the kind of person they are looking for and why. In practice, this means that I sit down with the line manager who needs the employee and who has final responsibility for hiring the person. Through discussion I can get a feel for the manager's needs, why there is an opening, and what the duties and responsibilities are. I can also get a feeling for the type of people that work in the department and the type of person and skills they are looking for. Occasionally I offer advice and counsel to help the manager clarify those needs if he or she is uncertain about them.

Interviewer: When you need information about the person you are considering for employment, how or where do you get the information?

Mr. Pelino: That varies a great deal. For instance, it is more difficult to get some information on a new college graduate than for someone who has worked several years. In the latter instance, we rely more on references, past accomplishments and work record. For the new college graduate, we rely more heavily on judgments based on a balance of activities, grades, evidence of leadership, interpersonal skills, and so on. In either case, the interviewer must have keen judgment to assess such things as 'can this person interact well, get along with others on a team' or 'what kind of thought process does the person have' or 'what is the person's long-range potential'. These attributes are not measured easily by such things as academic grades. Sometimes we ask several managers to interview the person in order to help us make the best decision.

Interviewer: Do you use selection tests, such as a psychological test, in the selection decision process?

Mr. Pelino: Selection tests have been criticized somewhat, perhaps because they aren't always used correctly. Although they are one indicator, they are not the "end all." We all know people who have passed tests but have failed miserably on the job, or people who failed tests but excelled at work. We use tests sparingly at Xerox, and only where they have been developed and validated over a long period of time. In these instances, the test serves as one of several aids to the manager. The manager may find the person to be ideal in almost all respects, but weak on the test, and decide to hire the person on the basis of the other strengths. Then the test helps the manager to know what the person's weakness is, and he or she can work with the person to overcome that problem.

Interviewer: If you were managing a small business, could you still make the kinds of good selection decisions that you do here at Xerox?

Mr. Pelino: Yes, but the process might be different, and in some cases more difficult. If I were the manager of a smaller business, I'd lack the resources to send recruiters all over the country to interview graduates at all the top colleges. I might have to concentrate my efforts more on the local area and universities. But, while the approach would be different, the objective would be exactly the same—that is, get the very best people who can do the job for which they are needed and who have the capability to grow.

INTRODUCTION

To the casual observer, the personnel management process of finding and hiring people for organizational jobs may seem deceptively simple. That is, it may seem that organizations "just" decide they need someone and "just" hire the person that most impresses them. However, as seen in our interview with Mr. Pelino of Xerox Corporation, the employee selection process is not at all simple. A great deal of careful thought must be given to recruitment strategies, understanding company and departmental objectives, and determining the kind of person the organization is seeking. Only by careful consideration of these, and related, issues can an organization maximize the likelihood of having a successful match between the new employee and the requirements of the job.

Many of us have experienced the frustrations of poorly conceived employee selection processes. In some cases, we were rejected from challenging jobs for which we believed that we were qualified. In other cases, we received monotonous, routine jobs that failed to utilize our skills and potential. These are typical frustrations that result from the organization's failure to design a logical selection process.

The excitement and satisfaction of finding and getting that special job that matches our needs, aspirations, and skills very closely is inevitably the result of careful consideration by organizational managers. In this chapter, we present one logic that underlies carefully conceived employee selection processes.

The basic purpose of the selection process is to ensure that the person whose skills, needs, and aspirations are best suited for a particular job is, in fact, the person most likely to be hired for that job. In reality, for most organizational jobs, there are probably many prospective employees who lack the precise job skills but who have some of the skills or can be trained in the job skills. One needs to recognize that the selection process, however, is basically intended to find individuals whose skills are closest to those required in the job.

If the objective of selection is achieved (the best suited person is hired for the job), it is more likely that the person will also be satisfied with the organization, and vice versa. That is, our total concern for the proper integration of jobs, people, and organizations can be met in part by concentrating our selection efforts on the job-to-person relationship.

FORMULATING THE LOGIC

The logic of selection is fairly straightforward. We can anticipate it by asking two questions. First, what is the likelihood that any given candidate for the job will be successful in performing the job duties? This question is fundamental to the job-to-person relationship, since unsuccessful performers negatively affect the organization's goals and must ultimately be terminated or assigned to other jobs for which they are better suited. Since we wish to avoid such actions, we should try to predict each candidate's likely success in performing the job. Except for "training" positions, we are trying to identify those candidates who have greater task abilities along the skill dimensions of the job.

Second, what is the likelihood that any given candidate for the job will be satisfied with it and want to continue in it for some reasonable period of time? When we think about job performance, we must think both in the short term and the long term. We might hire a highly qualified person but know that person would soon be unhappy in the position and resign. In this case, we would continually be repeating the expensive selection process. This question, then, causes us to consider the problems of both underqualified and overqualified job applicants. Those who lack skills are more likely to be dissatisfied because they cannot meet the demands of the task. Those who are overqualified are more likely to be dissatisfied because the job lacks challenge and is routine.

FORMALIZING THE LOGIC

The basic objective of selection activities, then, is to find and hire people who are most likely to be successful and satisfied in performing the tasks in that particular job.[1] This means that we must be able to *anticipate* or *predict* what each applicant's task performance is likely to be. Just how to make that prediction is a matter of logical thinking.

That logic begins by considering the fact that we are concerned with the match between a person and his or her job. That is, we want to assess a person's capabilities for performing a job *before* we decide to hire that person. The job consists of certain tasks, duties, and responsibilities, and if we know the exact nature of these, we will be better able to assess the possibilities that one or another person can perform them. We can then determine the skills, needs, and aspirations of people that are related to performing the tasks, duties, and responsibilities of the job and have a basis from which to predict performance. Thus selection activities will first involve the development of reliable knowledge regarding

1. the exact nature of the job's tasks, duties, and responsibilities and
2. the exact nature of the job applicant's skills, needs, and aspirations that relate to performing the job.

Figure 5-1 illustrates the ways in which this information is acquired and how it may ultimately aid in selecting new employees having a high likelihood of job success and satisfaction.

Job Design and Human Resource Planning

As illustrated by Figure 5-1, the correct design of organizational jobs results in a well-integrated structure. Each job is given a particular shape by the nature of its tasks,

Figure 5-1

Logic of Selection

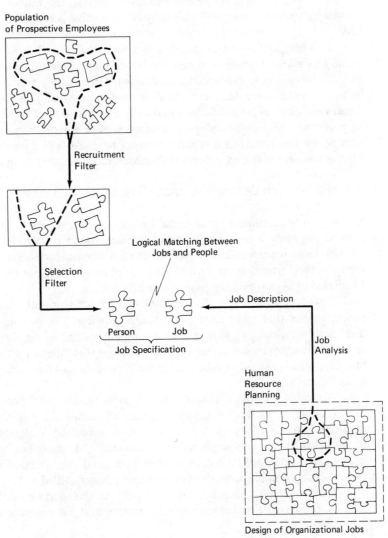

duties, and responsibilities. When each job is designed, the designer must keep in mind how it will relate to other jobs around it. For example, when deciding the exact nature of a waiter's job, the restaurant manager must be sure that there are no overlapping or conflicting responsibilities with the cook's job. He or she must also be sure that there are no duties that are overlooked; that is, at least one of the jobs must perform the necessary duties. In this way, the organization begins to resemble a jigsaw puzzle in which each job "fits" perfectly with each other job around it.

Although job design was discussed previously in Chapter 3, it is important to note here that poorly designed jobs may result in the selection of employees who lack skills for performing certain necessary tasks. If a necessary task were left out of the job design, the personnel manager would be unaware of it and would not look for employees who could perform it. Yet, in the final analysis, the missing task must be performed by someone, and the result may be ineffective performance on that particular task.

It is also useful to recognize, at this time, that a well-designed set of organizational jobs allows managers to plan for future human resource needs of the organization. By compiling sales forecasts, economic indicators, and production schedules and by analyzing turnover data, managers can determine which jobs are likely to need new employees. Since good job designs make the identification of employee skills possible, managers can locate and recruit new employees in anticipation of the need and prevent production problems that arise from not having a skilled employee available. The human resource planning process is discussed more completely in Chapter 6.

Job Analysis, Job Description, and Job Specification Links

It is logical to examine a job in detail before choosing a person to perform it. As explained, job analysis provides the detailed information from which job descriptions are written. Once managers have described the job's tasks, duties, and responsibilities accurately, their attention can turn to the issue of locating the person having the greatest likelihood of performing the job with satisfaction.

This process involves the translation of job activities into the human skills and characteristics that make their performance possible. For instance, if one of a job's tasks involves sorting various electrical components and fitting them into appropriate receptors on an electrical assembly, it would seem that "dexterity" might be an important task-related skill. The relationship between skills and job performance is illustrated in Figure 5-2.

Although we would expect that the most skilled people would always be the most productive, such is not always the case. The relationship between skills and productivity is modified by such factors as motivation and leadership. Sometimes the most skilled employee is surpassed in production by a less skilled but more motivated individual. This suggests that, no matter how good our selection process is, we can expect some job applicants who are apparently lesser skilled to be good employees.

We should also note a second difficulty in this portion of the selection logic. That is, the translation between job description and job specification involves much

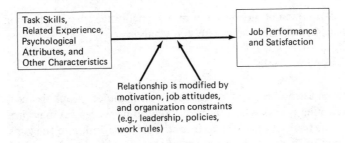

Figure 5-2

Relationship Between Task-Related Skills and Task Performance

guesswork. Although such translation is usually made by trained specialists, it is still an educated guess. We cannot be *absolutely certain* that dexterity is a basic, underlying skill for electrical sorting and assembly. It is even more risky when we determine that psychological attributes, such as intelligence or aggressiveness, are underlying skills for jobs such as selling or auditing. This difficulty demonstrates the need to verify, in a scientific manner, that the translation is accurate. We return to this point later in Chapter 7.

A third difficulty is that many of the underlying skills or attributes cannot be observed or measured physically. These types of characteristics are called hypothetical constructs. We are fairly certain that there is such a thing as intelligence and that some people have more of it than others. However, we cannot see or measure it physically. We can see intelligent behaviors (not crossing the street on a red light) and can measure intelligent answers to tests, but we cannot see or directly measure intelligence itself. Thus, when we say that characteristics, such as intelligence, underlie the performing of a certain job, we are faced with the difficulty of measuring it in the people we consider for the job. Thus, we must examine the people who might apply for organizational jobs as illustrated earlier in Figure 5-1.

Labor Markets and Recruitment

In addition to the job specifications and the skill to performance relationship, it is apparent that in any population there are likely to be many people who possess the skills required to perform any particular job. Most people have multiple skills, such as being both dexterous and intelligent. However, exact combinations of these skills vary widely among individuals. Since we generally specify several skills for task performance, we must locate the person whose skill is closest to our requirements. In other words, in job skill terms, a large population of people resembles an unassembled jigsaw puzzle, and while many are close to our specified requirements, only one or a few may be exactly what we are looking for. The first task, on the people side, is to narrow this larger population down to a manageable size consisting of those few people who may be close to our requirements. This is also a human resource planning function, consisting of a labor force analysis to identify likely sources and a recruitment activity to inform them of our openings and to encourage their application for these. This process is described more completely in Chapter 6.

Selection Tools

Once a small pool of reasonably well-qualified people is recruited, the major task of selecting that one person most likely to be successful may proceed. If we were correct in the translation of skills (from the job description to the job specification), we simply need to measure the presence of the skills the applicants hold. A theoretically ideal case of the total process of relating skill measurements to actual skills and actual skills to job performance is illustrated in Figure 5-3.

Since many skills cannot be measured directly (e.g., intelligence, assertiveness), organizations must often resort to secondary measurement tools. Such tools as intelligence tests, personality tests, achievement tests, and aptitude tests are examples of secondary tests. If these tests were direct measures, their results would be ideal or exact measures of skills. However, they are not direct measures and are therefore imperfect measures of underlying skills. That is, the person who is truly most intelligent may not have the highest score on an intelligence test. This person might not take tests well or may have been ill on test day, or the wording on the test may have affected his or her responses. Thus, we can identify another practical problem in selection, namely, measurement errors that result from having to use secondary measures of skills that cannot be verified directly.

We might conclude that the whole selection process is so contaminated with

Figure 5-3

Relationships Among Skill Measurements, Task-Related Skills, and Task Performance

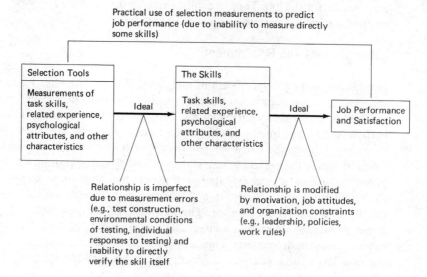

practical problems as to be useless. However, even given the problems we have identified (by thinking logically), we are usually better off using such a process than simply to flip coins to make selection decisions. What can be done, and should be done, is to discover the degree to which selection measurements (secondary and primary) accurately predict performance and satisfaction.[2] Because we are aware of the imperfections or problems (e.g., effect of motivation and leadership, inability to directly measure some skills, guesswork involved in translating from job descriptions to job specifications, and measurement errors), we should expect

1. That the predictive relationship between selection measurements and actual job performance will be imperfect.
2. That the predictive relationship between any job selection measurement and job performance *must* be validated scientifically to be sure that the guesswork was correct.

EXTENSION OF SELECTION LOGIC

We can now understand that job performance and satisfaction result from actual skills, psychological attributes, and other characteristics rather than from test scores. Test scores are merely indicators of the presence of the desired characteristics, and there are, thus, some practical problems associated with the use of test scores to predict performance. With these ideas in mind, we can begin to extend the selection logic to achieve practical desirable results in choosing new employees.

For example, there are many selection measures that are more direct measurements of underlying skills. Past job-related experiences and assessments of employee performances in those related experiences are very good predictors of future performance. Also, interviews may be good assessments of certain interpersonal skills. These skills surface in face-to-face interactions but may be hard to measure on paper-and-pencil tests. Organizations that are too small to afford the development of complex, costly psychological testing programs may be able to use these other approaches in selection.

Furthermore, validation of selection measures is not limited to paper-and-pencil tests. Nearly any predictor of job performance (e.g., interviews, past experience, education) can, and ideally should, be validated.

We can also see that selection logic is not limited in application to basic skill-oriented jobs such as typists, lathe operators, and plumbers. The prediction of managerial success follows the same logic. The difference between predicting success for skilled employees and managers lies in the types and varieties of skills associated with their jobs. It may also be more difficult to identify and measure underlying managerial skills (job specifications). However, by cautiously noting the logical problems associated with any selection decision, our accuracy in choosing successful managers can also be improved.

SUMMARY

Selecting new employees for organizational jobs is a process that can be a major head-ache for organizations. Unless one is aware of the problems associated with predicting the likely success of a job applicant, the choice of a new employee may be incorrect. However, the selection process can be a logical process, and good results can be achieved when one is aware of that logic.

The basic goal of selection is to ensure that the person whose skills, needs, and aspirations are best suited to the requirements of a job is, in fact, the person hired for the job. Predicting each applicant's likely success in the job depends on our knowledge of both the exact nature of the job's tasks, duties, and responsibilities and the exact nature of the applicant's skills, needs, and aspirations that relate to performing the job.

Data are gathered about the job (job analysis), and a translation is made from job requirements (job description) to human skills or characteristics underlying the performance of those requirements (job specification). Logic tells us that this transla-tion involves some assumptions or educated "guesswork," best made by trained ex-perts.

Once we have specified the human requirements, it is logical to work in the labor market to identify groups of people who are apt to have those abilities (recruitment). We can then set about measuring those abilities in the people who apply for job open-ings and identify the person whose abilities match our specifications most closely.

The use of logic points out several important problems in this process, including

1. The relationship between actual skills and resulting job performance is imper-fect due to the modifying effects of motivation, attitudes, leadership, and sim-ilar constraints.
2. The translation from job requirements to related human skills may be imper-fect.
3. Many human skills are not directly observable, causing us to rely on second-ary measurements.
4. The relationship between secondary measurements of skills and the true level of the skill itself may be imperfect, due to various measurement errors.

These problems lead to the conclusion that we must validate (test the truthful-ness) the predictive relationship between selection measurements and subsequent job performance. The practical results of using unvalidated selection measures may be in-effective employees and even social discrimination against certain groups of potential employees.

The remaining chapters in this section examine, in greater detail, the practical applications of selection logic. Chapter 6 examines the process of planning for human resource needs and recruiting potential employees. The practical uses of selection tools such as interviews, tests, application forms, references, and the methods of validating them are considered in Chapter 7. Finally, the more complex issues surrounding the selection of managers and other professional employees are discussed in Chapter 8.

INTERVIEW WRAP-UP

If we hire good people to start with, then we will have good people who will continue to move and grow with the company. —Douglas Pelino, manager of corporate employment and college relations, General Services Division of Xerox Corporation.

REVIEW QUESTIONS

1. How do organizations benefit from the use of a logically derived selection process?
2. How do job applicants benefit from the use of a logically derived selection process?
3. What four weaknesses are present in any selection process?
4. In what ways can managers improve their ability to choose new employees?
5. What are the differences between primary and secondary measurements of skills, psychological attributes, and similar characteristics?

KEY CONCEPTS

Human resource planning	Labor market
Job analysis	Recruitment
Job description	Satisfaction
Job design	Selection measurements
Job performance	Selection process
Job specification	Validation

CASE

SHIPPING DELAY

Jan was tired, hungry, and more than a little angry when she arrived at work. She had been with Aviation Supplies for over fifteen years and had held a responsible position for the past three years as the head of customer relations. Her biggest headache had always been the meeting of customer delivery deadlines and the regular failure of Aviation Suppliers to meet them. Jan had researched this problem carefully and had located a number of bottlenecks where delays occurred. Most of these had been dealt with and resolved more or less satisfactorily. For instance, it used to take five working days simply to log a sales order and transmit it to the inventory people. Due to Jan's efforts and an improved recording process, this was now accomplished in two days.

However, one bottleneck was still causing Jan a lot of grief. This involved the shipping department, which was responsible for crating, loading, and shipping the equipment to customers. Many pieces of equipment were specially made to customer specifications and were often bulky and heavy. Crating these orders and moving them around was a physically demanding and tiring job. Also, because the work was not particularly interesting, many of the shipping employees were hard to motivate, and it often took several days to get a shipment processed. Jan was convinced that this was longer than necessary and that the time could be shortened with an improved work process.

She had conferred with the head of shipping, Ben Gibson, explaining her need to decrease the shipping delay. Ben took her out to the floor and showed her what he considered to be the biggest problem. All the crating, lifting, carrying, and loading was done manually. He had six strong men working for him, but the work was simply too strenuous. In addition, the work was perceived as boring, and turnover among the men was high. The turnover was a major problem for the crating task, since it took a long time to train a new employee in how to build crates properly for the equipment.

Jan agreed to use her influence with management to help Ben gain approval for the purchase of forklifts, an automated conveyor setup, and some pneumatic hammers that would make the shipping job easier and more interesting. Ben assured her that this would eliminate shipping delays.

That was a year ago. Jan went to management and after a lot of serious discussion was able to help Ben get his equipment. But in the six months since the new equipment was received, shipping delays had not improved. Yesterday Jan had an angry confrontation with Ben. She noted that there were several new men in the department but each looked as strong and capable as their predecessors. Ben explained that turnover had not decreased as expected and that, furthermore, there had been a number of accidents in the department since getting the new equipment. The forklifts were apparently too complex to be driven safely, and a couple of times large crates had slipped off the conveyor, resulting in a dislocated shoulder for one worker and a fractured wrist for another. The pneumatic hammers seemed to be even more dangerous since the men insisted on using them as weapons, shooting nails at one another. Therefore, Ben explained, he had ordered the men to stop using the forklift and conveyor system and had taken their "toy hammers" from them.

After thinking about this overnight, Jan was sure that what was happening in the shipping department would be bad for her relationship with management. After all, she had stuck her neck out and customer delivery dates were still being missed with regularity.

CASE QUESTIONS

1. What factors do you think are contributing to some of the problems in the shipping department?
2. How did the change in the shipping jobs affect the types of skills that employees would need?
3. If you were Jan, what recommendations would you make to management? Why?

NOTES

[1]M. D. Dunnette, *Personnel Selection and Placement* (Belmont, Calif.: Brooks/Cole, 1966).

[2]L. E. Tyler, *Tests and Measurements,* 2nd ed. (Englewood Cliffs, N.J.: Prentice-Hall, 1971).

HUMAN RESOURCE PLANNING AND RECRUITING

LEARNING OBJECTIVES

After reading this chapter, you should be able to

1. Understand the processes involved in human resource planning.
2. Discuss the rationales for human resource planning.
3. Describe the process of inventorying an organization's human resources.
4. Describe the techniques used in forecasting the supply of personnel.
5. Describe the techniques used in forecasting the demand for personnel.
6. Discuss how realistic job expectations can be achieved in recruiting.
7. Discuss how recruiting sources can be evaluated.

Joe Shepela is the personnel manager at the Stanford Park Division of the Hewlett-Packard Company in Palo Alto, California. The division currently has approximately 1,800 employees. This division manufactures electronic communication transmitters and receivers for commercial, military, government, and research applications. The Stanford Park Division has been in existence since 1962 and has been a separate division since 1973.

Interviewer: How is human resource planning conducted in the division?

Joe Shepela: In one of the division's two methods of forecasting the demand for human resources, the personnel department works closely with the sales and marketing departments. The forecasting process begins with the new fiscal year on October 1. The sales department provides sales quotas while the marketing department provides an order forecast. These two departments then take their quotas and order forecasts to the manager of production planning in the manufacturing department. On the basis of an analysis of the quotas and forecasts, these departments then determine the types of skills and number of employees needed in the future. The second method of human resource planning is based on the personnel department's analysis of monthly turnover rates. Separate indices are calculated for those leaving the company and those transferring to other divisions within the company. Because of the company's rapid growth, there has been a high rate of transfers out of the unit to other divisions while the separation rate (for those leaving the company) has been low.

Interviewer: How is the division's recruiting handled?

Joe Shepela: For the Stanford Park Division, most job candidates are walk-in applicants who are processed by the employment office at the Palo Alto complex. In addition to walk-in applicants, Hewlett-Packard has approximately 800 managers who do some recruiting for the company. This recruiting is conducted primarily at universities and military separation centers. The company very seldom uses the services of employment agencies, and when it does use such agencies, it is usually looking for highly skilled individuals.

Interviewer: Who makes the hiring decision on those job applicants who have been recruited?

Joe Shepela: The line supervisor always makes the final decision for anyone hired for his unit. The personnel manager makes recommendations, but the line supervisor makes the final decision.

INTRODUCTION

The interview with Joe Shepela indicated that, in his division, human resource planning consisted mostly of forecasting the demand for personnel and analyzing the supply of personnel that would be with the organization in the future. In other companies, these aspects of human resource planning may receive more or less emphasis.

We have used the term human resource planning in this chapter instead of the somewhat older term of manpower planning for two reasons. The first is that some confusion has arisen over the usage of the latter term. Although the term manpower planning has been applied to human resource planning activities, as we describe them in this chapter, it has also been used to describe activities that comprise macro-planning or planning from a governmental perspective. In such contexts, manpower planners might be concerned with forecasting the demand for certain occupational specialities in the entire U.S. labor force, a state, an industry, or some other aggregate unit in the economy.[1] Our usage of the term human resource planning refers to micro-applications, that is, to those planning activities performed in an organization or an organizational subunit.

Although we do not treat macro-applications of planning in this book, such planning obviously has an effect on the organization. As an example, government macro-planning may identify an anticipated shortage of students expected to graduate with degrees in geology during the next few years. The human resource planner will want to take these macro forecasts into consideration; however, such forecasting is beyond the scope of discussion.

The second reason for using the term human resource planning is that it implies viewing an organization's personnel as resources. Organizations have financial investments in its personnel that arise from such expenditures as hiring costs, training, development, and so on.[2] In the past, organizations were acutely aware of the value of their investments in physical capital but did not always act as if they realized the value of their investments in personnel. Use of the term human resources implies a recognition of the organization's investment in its personnel and a need to preserve and enhance the value of that investment. We direct our attention in this chapter to human resource planning before our treatment of recruitment, because planning must be conducted so that an organization will know its recruiting needs.

HUMAN RESOURCE PLANNING

Human resource planning consists of several activities that must be performed sequentially. In Chapter 4, we described the process of job analysis in which job descriptions and job specifications are prepared. After jobs have been described and the requirements for jobholders have been specified, human resource planning can take place. Human resource planning is described in several ways, but typical definitions include most of the same general sequential processes with some variations.[3]

> **Human resource planning:** a sequential process that includes (1) inventorying present human resources, (2) forecasting the internal supply (within the organization) of human resources, (3) forecasting the demand for human resources, (4) determining the discrepancy between projected demand and supply, and (5) planning the actions that will be needed to correct the mismatch in demand and supply.

An exception to the described sequence is that supply and demand forecasting may be conducted in a reverse order or simultaneously. Another definition of human resource planning is the following: "Put simply, it is the process by which a firm insures that it has the right number of people, and the right kind of people, in the right places, at the right time, doing things for which they are economically most useful."[4]

We devote our attention now to the concepts and processes contained in these definitions.

The previous, more detailed, definition points out two important concerns: First, human resource planning should be thought of in terms of supply and demand;[5] Second, human resource planning involves two major processes, namely (1) forecasting the supply and demand of human resources and (2) planning the actions that will secure and develop the number and type of individuals necessary to match the projected manning requirements. The second definition emphasizes the efficient utilization of human resources or the economic justification of the process. The reasons for conducting human resource planning need to be considered first in more specific terms. Thus we discuss initially the rationales for human resource planning. Then we discuss the activities involved in inventorying present personnel, followed by considerations of techniques for forecasting supply and demand and the planning activities that are required to bring shortages and surpluses in alignment. Finally, we consider the special problems encountered in implementing human resource planning and in utilizing its information output.

Reasons for Conducting Human Resource Planning

As with any activity, human resource planning is conducted to facilitate the organization's accomplishments of its goals and to help its employees achieve their goals when such goals are consistent with the organization's objectives. An obvious rationale for such planning is to avoid shortages of qualified personnel. Nonetheless, even such an obvious rationale may not justify an expensive planning program if the personnel shortage involves low-level skills that unskilled recruits can acquire in a short period of on-the-job training. Thus human resource planning activities must first be logically justified in economic terms relative to alternative uses of limited capital and staff resources.[6] The other rationales will build on this underlying economic justification. As costing techniques have become more sophisticated and are applied more to personnel functions, it has become easier to attach a dollar value to the additional cost involved in recruiting and hiring personnel from the external market when such shortages were not anticipated.

Although the economic rationale for human resource planning has been stressed, we hasten to point out that there are other sound reasons for conducting such planning that are less related to economic considerations or are related only indirectly to economic considerations. One of these reasons may be to enable the organization to meet affirmative action objectives by providing equal employment opportunities. Specifically, the organization may utilize human resource forecasting techniques to establish minority and female hiring goals or to identify what activities should be incorporated in its affirmative action efforts.[7] Of course, even this application might have some positive economic consequence if it helps the firm to avoid litigation or federal contract cancellations that might result from a failure to implement and administer a feasible affirmative action program.

Another rationale for human resource planning involves development of the organization's current personnel.[8] If forecasts identify a future need for a specific skill, present personnel may need experience in a series of jobs that will enable them to acquire the skills needed for the higher-skill job. This is the case for managerial personnel. A firm wishing to expand in a particular product area may find that it cannot do so because of a shortage of managerial personnel who have had experience with the product line. Human resource planning efforts would identify the assignments needed for the development of a pool of managers qualified to handle such positions in the future.

Further, such planning is a prerequisite for a program of career development. A survey of private sector firms found that employees' desires for career development were cited by 41 percent of the firms as reasons for engaging in human resource planning. In fact, the same survey revealed that career development needs were one of the three major reasons for conducting human resource planning. The survey also revealed that 70 percent of the responding firms indicated that they conducted human resource planning to avoid shortages of qualified personnel and that 43 percent indicated affirmative action as another rationale for human resource planning.[9]

A final planning rationale identified by 24 percent of the responding firms was to avoid layoffs.[10] Layoffs might be avoided if an organization has forecasted with accuracy an excess supply of personnel in a skill category. Through the utilization of a variety of other actions such as transfers and retraining or reduced hiring and reliance on normal attrition, excess supply may be reduced without resorting to layoffs. Next we consider human resource inventories and methods of forecasting the supply and demand for human resources. As our interview with Joe Shepela revealed, his division made forecasts of both the supply and demand for personnel.

Inventorying Current Human Resources and Using Information Systems

As indicated in Chapter 5, the underlying rationale of selection rests on matching the right person with the right job. Human resource inventories facilitate this matching process by providing the organization with information on its current employees and serving as internal personnel search tools.[11]

Human resource inventory: a system that allows matching of an individual's experience, education, and preference with a task or function to be performed.[12]

Aside from use as an internal search tool, human resource inventories are used for a variety of purposes, one of which is human resource planning. Other uses of inventories may be for determining eligibility for promotion; for ascertaining training needs, work preferences, and location preferences; for obtaining quick access to work force characteristics needed to respond to affirmative action and other government reporting requirements; and for developing personnel research.[13] The sophistication of the inventory system varies with the size and other characteristics of the organizations. Likewise, relatively simple systems may be sufficient for organizations with a stable work force. Conversely, in larger organizations that have a less stable work force, computerized inventories are appropriate.[14]

There are several components to the typical human resource inventory. These components have been defined as "key words, work history, foreign languages, formal education, special courses, special projects, and vocational licenses."[15] Key words are used to describe the occupation or job. One crude analogy to key words would be the categories of jobs in newspaper employment advertisements. Key words may be structured in different levels of specificity to facilitate different personnel search needs. For example, the most general category might contain job key words such as business administration, whereas the next more specific category might break down business administration into accounting, personnel, management, and so on. An even more specific level of key words might break down the general occupation of accounting into cost accounting, tax, and so on.[16] The other components are essentially self-descriptive.

Human resource inventories require initial information inputs into the system on all employees. To be useful, these inventories require periodic updates on the information stored for each employee. One way in which information is updated is through the use of a turnaround form. The turnaround form contains current information on the employee and provides space for corrections and updates on items. Employees are sent such turnaround forms and are asked to verify the information and return the corrections and update portions.[17] The design of human resource inventory systems including computer software and input and output forms is an expanding business. Many vendors offer specialized services in this area. An excellent source of basic information on human resource inventory systems is *Planning and Using Skills Inventory Systems.*[18] A sample turnaround form is presented in Figure 6-1.

If the organization's human resource inventory system is to be used for planning purposes, it would probably contain "information on age, sex, race, tenure, skills, rated potential, rate of compensation, job and organizational assignment, and any other information found useful in predicting turnover, performance, and job moves in the organization."[19] A requirement for many human resource quantitative forecasting techniques is archival or historical data on manning levels. Thus inventory records for past years are needed as well as current data.

One final point on human resource inventories is that such systems need to comply with privacy legislation. Since the area of information privacy is one in which there has been a great deal of recent activity, an extensive review of the system's compliance with such legislation is warranted.[20]

Forecasting the Supply of Human Resources

Forecasting the supply of personnel from within the organization (the internal supply) requires consideration of all the possible movements of personnel into and out of the organization as well as movements within the organization. Since forecasts are typical-

Figure 6-1

Example of Human Resource Information System Turnaround Form for Professional Personnel

PERSONNEL PROFILE SHEET

SOC' SEC. NO.	EMPLOYEE NAME			BIRTHDATE	DATE OF LAST UPDATE	DATE OF THIS REPORT
	LAST	FIRST	MIDDLE			

SEX	CITIZEN?	CURRENT RANK		PERSONNEL POSITION NO.	DATE PRESENT TITLE ACHIEVED	DATE OF LAST PAY INCREASE
		CODE	TITLE			

WORK MAIL ADDRESS	EMPLOYMENT STATUS	PAYROLL TYPE	CURRENT RATE OF PAY	PERCENT EMPLOYED

CONTINUOUS EMPLOYMENT DATE	PROBATION DATE	PAY GRADE	RETIREMENT DATE	MONTHS APPOINTED	RACE	MARITAL STATUS

CAMPUS ADDRESS			HOME PHONE	PROFESSIONAL LICENSES
ROOM	BUILDING	PHONE		
				(117)
				(118)
				(119)

ADDRESSES

	STREET	CITY	STATE	ZIP CODE
HOME ▶				
PERM ▶				

EDUCATIONAL BACKGROUND

	DEGREE OR HOURS CREDIT	DATE	INSTITUTION	FIELD OF STUDY
(123)				
(124)				
(125)				
(126)				
(127)				
(128)				

SOC. SEC. NO. OF SPOUSE

SPOUSE AND DEPENDENT CHILDREN

	LAST NAME	FIRST NAME	REL	BIRTHDATE
(129)				
(130)				
(131)				
(132)				
(133)				
(134)				
(135)				
(136)				
(137)				
(138)				

PROFESSIONAL AFFILIATIONS

(120)	
(121)	
(122)	

RECORD OF LEAVES

TYPE OF LEAVE	DATE LEAVE STARTED	DATE LEAVE ENDED	REASON

PREVIOUS POSITIONS

POSITION CODE AND TITLE	FROM	TO	ENTRY REASON

PREVIOUS EMPLOYERS

	NAME	CITY AND STATE	ZIP CODE	START DATE	END DATE
(139)					
(140)					
(141)					

KEEP THIS PAGE FOR YOUR FILES

Figure 6-1 (*Continued*)

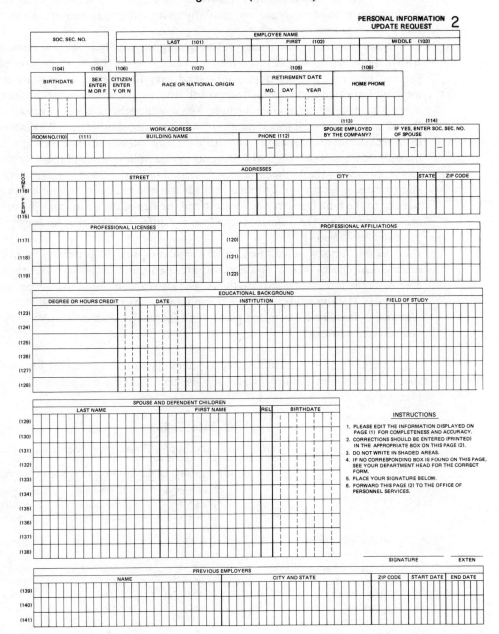

ly needed for the various skill specialties as well as by hierarchical level, lateral and vertical moves must be considered similarly to movements in and out of the organization.[21]

Several techniques are used in forecasting the supply of human resources from within the organization. Some, such as replacement charts or succession plans and personnel inventories, are quite simple and easy to develop. Others are somewhat more sophisticated and are based on probabilistic or operations research concepts. The more sophisticated techniques include Markov models, operations research models (based on linear or goal programming), and computer simulations. We discuss each of these techniques more specifically, with the exception of personnel inventories, which have already been covered, in the paragraphs that follow. Some of these techniques are less sophisticated than others; however, their simplicity does not make them any less appropriate. A recent survey found that the use of forecasting techniques differed according to the time frame of the forecast and the size of the company. The percentages of companies using the different techniques for different lengths of forecast periods are presented in Table 6-1.

As might be expected, the simpler techniques, such as personnel inventories and replacement charts or succession plans, are used quite frequently, but their use decreases as the forecast period lengthens. The survey also found that larger companies tend to use Markov models, computer simulations, operations research techniques, replacement charts and succession plans more frequently than do smaller firms for several forecasting ranges.[22]

REPLACEMENT CHARTS.   Replacement charts can be used for forecasting both supply and demand. An abbreviated replacement chart for one position is provided in Figure 6-2.

Table 6-1

Utilization of Human Resource Supply Forecasting Techniques

	Percentage of Sample Reporting Use of Technique		
	Short Range (less than 2 years)	Intermediate Range (2–5 years)	Long Range (more than 5 years)
Personnel inventories	54%	33%	22%
Succession plans or replacement charts	55	39	22
Markov or network flow models	12	13	10
Operations research techniques	11	12	10
Computer simulation	10	15	5
Other techniques	6	6	2

Source: Adapted from C. R. Greer and D. Armstrong, "Human Resource Forecasting and Planning: A State-of-the-Art Investigation," *Human Resource Planning,* 3 (1980), p. 71.

Replacement charts: may take a variety of forms but typically contain such information as position identification,[23] names of position incumbents, potential replacements, ages, performance ratings, and the number of years before an incumbent or replacement will be ready for promotion.

By examining the data in the replacement chart on probable retirement dates and years required for promotion, one can readily tell whether the supply of potential replacements will be inadequate for expected vacancies or whether there is an oversupply of qualified replacements with no likely vacancies in the near future. Knowledge of either of these two conditions will alert the human resource forecaster to the necessity of making plans to provide developmental assignments for replacements where shortages exist or reassignment where surpluses of qualified personnel exist.

MARKOV MODELS. Our interview with Joe Shepela revealed that his division made forecasts on the basis of rates of transfers within the company.

Markov models: probabilistic techniques that use historical data on personnel movements to derive probabilities for similar moves in the future.

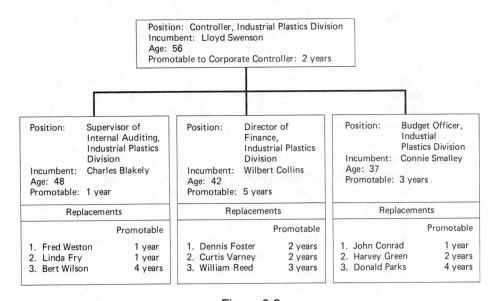

Figure 6-2

Replacement Chart

Source: Adapted from G. L. Mikovich and T. A. Mahoney, "Human Resources Planning and PAIR Policy" in *Planning and Auditing PAIR*, eds. D. Yoder and H. G. Heneman, Jr. (Washington D.C.: Bureau of National Affairs, 1976), pp. 2–15; V. R. Ceriello and L. Linden, "Management and Resource Program," *Journal of Systems Management*, 23 (1973), pp. 8–10.

Markov techniques begin with a distribution of manning levels in various positions from one time period, such as the current year. Then, through a multiplicative process utilizing the probabilities of all possible moves into and out from these positions, they develop a distribution of manning levels for these positions for a future time period, such as for the next year. The probabilities of the various moves are derived simply by determining the proportion of individuals in a position at the start of a time period who remain in that position at the end of the period as well as the proportion who moved to other positions or out of the organization. In practice, one may want to obtain an average of several time period probabilities. These transition probabilities are arranged in a rectangular configuration or array, which is called a transition probability matrix.[24] An example of such a transition matrix, including current and predicted manning levels, is presented in Table 6-2.

In using the Markov process, one needs to beware of two limitations of the technique. The first is that the probabilities are based on historical movement patterns, and it is therefore presumed that the same patterns will occur in the future. The second limitation is that small numbers of individuals in each position lead to the computation of unreliable transition probabilities.[25] Nonetheless, if these limitations are kept in mind, the Markov process provides a very systematic means of forecasting internal supply.

LINEAR PROGRAMMING AND GOAL PROGRAMMING.   One forecasting technique that has proven to be a useful diagnostic tool for analyzing personnel flows within organizations is linear programming. With this technique, the organization can have as goals a specified number of individuals at each rank or level. Manning at each level is affected by various personnel policies such as the timing of promotions, the proportion of persons promoted, the assignment of persons not promoted, retirements, and turnover rates. Through the application of linear programming, the forecaster can determine the promotion policies, turnover rates, and so on that will enable the organization to achieve its manning goals at the various ranks or levels. For example, given current personnel policies the forecaster can determine what needs to be done to avoid a surplus of midlevel managers at a future date. He can determine the promotion rates, turnover rates, and the like, that will provide personnel flows into and out from midlevel management positions and result in the desired manning levels. Although the technique is not utilized widely, it is utilized extensively in some organizations.

As with other techniques, there are limitations to applications of linear programming. The first is that the technique assumes that the goals will not change for some time; the second is that the model may assume that personnel enter the organization only at the lowest level.[26] A variation of linear programming, called goal programming, allows the human resource forecaster to specify a series of goals. Goal programming works on the principle that certain goals must be achieved before others can be considered. Through the utilization of goal programming, the forecaster can determine the personnel policies that will result in the achievement of the critical goals as well as other less important goals.[27]

Table 6-2

Markov Forecast of Internal Supply of Human Resources

Manning Levels	Job Titles	Drill Press Operator	Turret Lathe Operator	Heliarc Welder	Maintenance Technician	Multiple Spindle Screw Machine Operator	Section Foreman	Exit
1983 Distribution								
98	Drill Press Operator	.56	.14	.05	.05	.03	.00	.17
137	Turret Lathe Operator	.02	.71	.00	.02	.10	.02	.13
68	Heliarc Welder	.03	.03	.69	.02	.02	.02	.19
30	Maintenance Technician	.03	.05	.01	.65	.02	.02	.22
67	Multiple Spindle Screw Machine Operator	.02	.08	.02	.04	.65	.01	.18
24	Section Foreman	.00	.01	.00	.02	.01	.76	.20
Total 424		62	120	53	32	62	24	71

Forecasted Distribution for 1984

COMPUTER SIMULATION. Supply forecasting models based on computer simulation are designed to allow the forecaster to predict the effects of changes in personnel policies and the effects of other factors.[28] One sophisticated model has been developed that predicts the effects on the supply of human resources that result from (1) personnel policies such as salary changes, rates of promotion, and recruiting; (2) labor market influences such as job offers; and (3) individual attributes such as searches for another job, levels of work effort, aptitudes, and resignations.[29] With such a model, the forecaster can vary a personnel policy to determine the impact of such a change on the future supply of human resources or to determine how much various personnel policies must be changed to obtain a desired level of supply. Furthermore, the impact of various combinations of changes in personnel policies may also be determined through the use of computer simulations. Constraints on the utilization of computer simulations in such applications include the high costs of development and the ability of the modeler to simulate realistically the factors that affect human resource supply. In the next section, we turn our attention to the techniques of forecasting the demand for human resources.

Forecasting the Demand for Human Resources

Forecasts of the demand for human resources may be based on either top-down or bottom-up approaches. Forecasts from the top-down perspective take levels of future activities, such as an index incorporating barrels of oil refined per day in the case of a refinery,[30] and convert such activity levels into personnel requirements. Obviously, predicting an organization's activity levels at some future time would seem to be an overwhelming task. Fortunately, the human resource planner is not generally required to perform this forecast. The human resource forecaster's task is to predict the demand for personnel on the basis of activity levels that other planners and top management have provided in the form of sales levels, production levels, and so on. These activity levels are set by top executives as goals or objectives for the firm to reach in the future. As we learned in our interview with Joe Shepela the Hewlett-Packard division in which he works begins its human resource demand forecasts with activity levels forecasted by the sales and marketing departments. This is not to suggest that top management and other planners are the only members of the organization concerned with the impact of the economy and other influences on the firm. The explanation for the planner's consideration of goals or activity levels as given is that such goals or predicted activity levels are an outcome of the strategic planning process, a major responsibility of top executives. In making strategy decisions and setting goals, these executives draw on numerous sources of expertise within the organization, including that of the personnel department. We should note, however, that not all methods of forecasting involve a top-down or policy approach. Some methods of forecasting involve a bottom-up approach, in which demand (or supply estimates) are summed across units and subunits.[31] A top-down approach was described by Joe Shepela of Hewlett-Packard, using forecasts from the sales and marketing departments.

SUPERVISORY ESTIMATES. These judgmental estimates rely on the experience and intuition of the organization's supervisors to project the personnel that their units will require in the future.[32] Because these forecasts originate at the lowest levels in the organization and are then summed across organization units and subunits, they are an example of a bottom-up approach. Supervisory estimates of the demand for human resources are widely used for short-range forecasts (less than two years in length). As Table 6-3 indicates, 75 percent of the firms surveyed use such estimates for short-range forecasts. The usefulness of supervisory estimates declines for longer-range fore-

Table 6-3

Utilization of Human Resource
Demand Forecasting Techniques

	Percentage of Sample Reporting Use of Techniques		
	Short Range (less than 2 years)	Intermediate Range (2–5 years)	Long Range (more than 5 years)
Supervisor estimates	75%	31%	12%
Rules of thumb	28	15	7
Replacement charts	36	34	18
Delphi procedure	2	6	1
Time series regression analysis	13	19	13
Computer simulation	7	11	7
Other techniques	8	6	0

Source: Adapted from C. R. Greer and D. Armstrong, "Human Resource Forecasting and Planning: A State-of-the-Art Investigation," in *Human Resources Planning,* 3 (1980), p. 73.

casts, as evidenced by the fact that only 12 percent of the sample firms used them for forecasts longer than five years.

RULES OF THUMB AND HEURISTICS. Such forecasting techniques are based on past operating policies that rely on simple rules or decision processes to convert activity levels into human resource requirements. An example is to hire another machinist for every increase in estimated production of 10,000 units.[33] As indicated in Table 6-3, these rules are used much more frequently for short-range than for long-range forecasts.

REPLACEMENT CHARTS. The use of replacement charts in human resource forecasting has been described earlier in the discussion on supply forecasting techniques. Although replacement charts indicate the number of individuals available to fill future position vacancies, they also indicate through age and promotability evaluations of job incumbents the likelihood that a position will become vacant through the retirement or promotion of the incumbent. Thus the number of expected vacancies provides an indication of the future demand for human resources.

DELPHI PROCEDURE. The Delphi technique is essentially a judgment refinement process.

Delphi procedure: draws on the judgment of experts to estimate future demand and refines judgments through a series of estimates or an iterative approach.

A typical application of the Delphi procedure would involve the following: (1) The forecaster distributes a questionnaire to experts requesting an estimate of future human resource demand and the information that the forecaster needs to make such an estimate. (2) A second questionnaire is then sent to each of the experts along with the information that the expert has requested. The expert is asked to make an estimate of demand and to describe how he arrived at the forecast. (3) The estimates made by the experts are then distributed to other members of the panel along with another questionnaire requesting a refined estimate. (4) Further rounds are conducted, and the estimates tend to converge as the process continues. After a point, little value may be obtained from further iterations of the process, and the experts may not wish to spend additional time on the procedure.[34]

Advantages of the procedure relative to other group decision-making processes include less opportunity for personal factors, such as status, to bias or affect each expert's estimate, because they are not confronting one another in a common meeting. Further the process results in a forecast that is expressed in numerical values, the estimate is reached through a gradual refinement process, and, unlike quantitative techniques, there is no necessity for an extensive data base. Finally, there is evidence that the technique may provide forecasts as accurate as those possible through some quantitative techniques such as regression analysis.[35] In spite of such promising results, the survey findings reported in Table 6-3 indicate that very few organizations are using the Delphi process for human resource forecasting at this time.

REGRESSION ANALYSIS.   Regression analysis provides a very useful method for forecasting the demand for human resources. With this technique, personnel levels (a dependent variable) are regressed on one or more predictor variables (independent variables). Predictor variables are factors that vary closely with personnel levels.[36] A good data base extending over several time periods is required for accurate forecasting with this statistical procedure. When only one independent variable is used, the procedure is called simple regression analysis; when two or more independent variables are used, the procedure is called multiple regression analysis. If more than one predictor factor can be identified and if an adequate data base exists, more predictive accuracy should be forthcoming from a multiple regression analysis forecasting model. As with many other forecasting techniques, regression analysis assumes that in the future a similar relationship between personnel levels and predictor factors will continue to exist. Different models are typically developed for jobs that are fundamentally dissimilar, as an increase in activity does not have the same impact on all jobs. For example, increased production activity would likely require more production workers but no increase in clerical workers.

APPLICATION: REGRESSION ANALYSIS

While regression analysis is a sophisticated technique, simple regression analysis can be performed manually or very easily on a programmable calculator as well as on a computer. The basic principle underlying regression analysis may be understood by noting that the statistical procedure estimates the equation of a line that is used for forecasting. Thus the equation of the line $y = a + bx$, where y is the dependent variable, a is the intercept, b is the slope, and x is the independent variable, is expressed in a statistically derived regression equation as $y = \alpha + \beta x + \epsilon$, where y is the dependent variable, α is the intercept, β is the slope, x is the independent variable, and ϵ is an error term. The error term tells us that the equation cannot account perfectly for all the variation in y. The basic task in forecasting future values of y is to begin with a value for x, which reflects a future activity level such as sales or production. Next we use an equation in which values for α and β have been derived in regressions of y on x from historical data to obtain a future value for y.

Regression analysis derives the parameters for an equation "which minimizes the sum of the squared deviations of the points of the graph from the points of the straight line."[37] For this reason, the simple regression procedure described here is called least squares regression. Figure 6-3 provides a hypothetical example of a regression equation and a scatter diagram or graph.

An example of a regression analysis application in human resource forecasting is provided in Table 6-4. In this example, the number of lathe operators is forecasted on the basis of units of production. The parameters of the equation are derived from data for the years 1972 to 1983. The example is designed to forecast the number of lathe operators needed in 1984. Top management has informed us that it plans to produce 35,000 units in 1984.

In the example provided in Table 6-4, the forecasted demand for lathe operators in 1984 is forty-one operators. However, since regression analysis is a statistical procedure, a great deal must be known about the equation derived before we can use the results with any confidence. The derivation of these statistics is beyond the scope of

Figure 6-3

Scatter Diagram

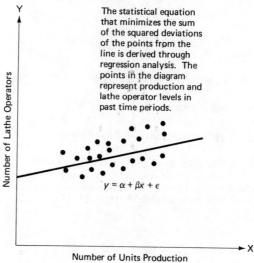

The statistical equation that minimizes the sum of the squared deviations of the points from the line is derived through regression analysis. The points in the diagram represent production and lathe operator levels in past time periods.

$y = \alpha + \beta x + \epsilon$

Number of Lathe Operators

Number of Units Production

Table 6-4

Regression Analysis Demand Forecast

Year (i)	Units of Production (000) (x)	Number of Lathe Operators (y)	$(x_i - \bar{x})$	$(x_i - \bar{x})^2$	$(y_i - \bar{y})$	$(x_i - \bar{x})(y_i - \bar{y})$
1972	11	21	-8	64	-8	64
1973	13	22	-6	36	-7	42
1974	14	23	-5	25	-6	30
1975	14	25	-5	25	-4	20
1976	17	28	-2	4	-1	2
1977	16	30	-3	9	1	-3
1978	19	32	0	0	3	0
1979	21	31	2	4	2	4
1980	20	32	1	1	3	3
1981	24	34	5	25	5	25
1982	28	34	9	81	5	45
1983	31	36	12	144	7	84

$\Sigma x_i = 228$

$\Sigma y_i = 348$

$\Sigma(x_i - \bar{x})^2 = 418$

$\Sigma(x_i - \bar{x})(y_i - \bar{y}) = 316$

$$N = 12 \quad \bar{x} = \frac{\Sigma x_i}{N} = 19 \quad \bar{y} = \frac{\Sigma y_i}{N} = 29$$

Simple regression formula:

$$y = \alpha + \beta x + \epsilon$$

where

$$\beta = \frac{\Sigma[(x - \bar{x})(y - \bar{y})]}{\Sigma(x - \bar{x})^2} = \frac{316}{418} = .76$$

$$\alpha = \bar{y} - \beta\bar{x} = 29 - (.76)(19) = 14.56$$

ϵ is assumed equal to zero.

Forecast for the 1984 production goal of 35,000 units is:

$$Y = 14.56 + (.76)(35) = 41.16 = 41 \text{ lathe operators}$$

Source: Formula adapted from R. S. Pindyck and D. L. Rubenfeld, *Econometric Models and Economic Forecasts* (New York: McGraw-Hill, 1976), p. 11–16.

this book; therefore we just present the results of these additional derivations. (A good introductory econometrics text will provide a helpful discussion of these interpretive statistics.[38])

The first interpretive statistic of concern is the coefficient of determination, R^2. In the example, $R^2 = .81$, which means that the model accounted for a good amount of variation (81 percent) in employment of lathe operators. The next statistic is the t value for the β parameter. The t statistic tells us whether there is a statistically significant relationship between the production level and the employment of lathe operators. In this case $t = 6.67$, which means that we can say with a confidence level of 99 percent that a significant relationship exists between the two variables. The final statistical procedure involves the construction of a confidence interval for our forecast. Since we are using a statistical procedure, we would like to know how much our forecasted level of lathe operators varies by chance. In the example, our confidence interval indicates that we can say with a confidence level of 95 percent that the number of lathe operators should be between thirty-six and forty-seven (rounded off) if the underlying relationship does not change.

In this example of time series regression analysis, one should be aware that serial correlation sometimes makes such results unreliable; however, there are methods for handling problems of serial correlation. As the data in Table 6-3 indicate, the utilization of regression analysis is relatively constant across time ranges of forecasts.

EXPONENTIAL SMOOTHING. This technique of forecasting is a very straightforward method that has the advantage of requiring data on only one variable. It is essentially a variation of a weighted average approach. Another advantage of the approach is its simplicity. This is an important point because, if the people who are expected to make decisions on the data supplied by a forecasting technique do not understand the procedure, its results are unlikely to be utilized. In more sophisticated applications, the technique has been used in conjunction with regression analysis, although such complicated approaches are beyond the scope of our discussion.[39]

APPLICATION: EXPONENTIAL SMOOTHING

Exponential smoothing can be understood by working through an example. The basic exponential smoothing formula is

$$\hat{Y}_{t+1} = (\alpha)Y_t + (1 - \alpha)\hat{Y}_t$$

where $\hat{Y}_{t+1}$ is the forecast being derived for the next time period, t is the current time period, Y_t is the actual observation during the current time period, $\hat{Y}_t$ is the forecast that was derived previously for the current period, and α is the weighting constant that is developed from experience or a trial and error process.[40] Table 6-5 presents an example of forecasting the same demand for lathe operators as used in the regression example. In this case, we are simply forecasting the future demand for personnel on the basis of past demand without consideration of a factor reflecting the activity level. In cases where the human resource forecaster can obtain little guidance from policy-

Table 6-5

Exponential Smoothing Demand Forecast

Year	Actual Observed Number of Lathe Operators	Forecasted Number of Lathe Operators (with different α values)		
		$\alpha = .1$	$\alpha = .5$	$\alpha = .9$
1972	21	—	—	—
1973	22	21.0	21.0	21.0
1974	23	21.1	21.5	21.9
1975	25	21.3	22.3	22.9
1976	28	21.7	23.7	24.8
1977	30	22.3	25.9	27.7
1978	32	23.1	28.0	29.8
1979	31	24.0	30.0	31.8
1980	32	24.7	30.5	31.1
1981	34	25.4	31.3	31.9
1982	34	26.3	32.7	33.8
1983	36	27.1	33.4	34.0
	Forecast for 1984 =	28.0	34.7	35.8

Example of computations for $\alpha = .1$[a]

$\hat{Y}_{1973} = (.1)(21) + (.9)(21) = 21.0$
$\hat{Y}_{1974} = (.1)(22) + (.9)(21) = 21.1$
$\hat{Y}_{1975} = (.1)(23) + (.9)(21.1) = 21.3$
$\hat{Y}_{1976} = (.1)(25) + (.9)(21.3) = 21.7$
$\hat{Y}_{1977} = (.1)(28) + (.9)(21.7) = 22.3$

Source: Formula adapted from B. M. Thornton, *CPA Review: Quantitative Methods and Statistical Samples* (Worthington, Ohio: McHugh, 1918), p. 119.

[a]Using $\hat{Y}_{t+1} = (\alpha)Y_t + (1 - \alpha)\hat{Y}_t$

makers about such goals or future targets, such an approach may be the only one available to the forecaster.

When the exponential smoothing formula is expanded to include several time periods, the terms have exponents, and the formula becomes cumbersome.[41] Fortunately, one can simply apply the basic two-period formula sequentially to a data series to derive a forecast. This approach is shown in the example in which three different values of α are tried out on historical data to determine which α level gives us the best forecasts in our particular situation. It should be noted that during the start-up of the process, where there is no previous forecast for the second period, we have simply used the actual observed number of lathe operators in the previous period as the forecasted number for the second period.

As the data in Table 6-5 indicate, the particular α value employed has a substantial impact on the forecast. The α value selected would be the value that caused the forecast to approximate most closely the observed employment level according to historical data. Thus, since the α value of .9 caused the forecast to approximate most closely the actual employment of lathe operators up through 1983, we would use $\alpha =$ .9 in our forecasts. It should be noted that higher order models may be more accurate for trend data.

Concluding Remarks on Human Resource Forecasting

Major problems encountered in human resource forecasting include (1) forecasts that sometimes have less than desired levels of accuracy, (2) data bases for planning that are sometimes inadequate, and (3) a lack of acceptance of human resource forecasting. With respect to the accuracy of forecasts, accuracy tends to vary between industries. In some industries, such as high-fashion women's clothing, only low-accuracy forecasts are possible. Conversely, high-accuracy forecasts are possible in other industries, such as public utilities. Forecasts in some public utilities have been reported to be within a 5 percent margin of accuracy with twenty-year forecasts. The explanation for such differences is that the predictability of the activity level varies greatly across industries.[42]

One final comment is that the forecaster must take care to analyze the conditions that are likely to affect the organization's future demand for human resources as well as its future supply. An examination of demand factors might include an evaluation of the staff required for a new technology. It probably cannot be assumed that the same proportions of human resources, according to skill and occupational mix, presently utilized will be appropriate in the future if there is a substantial change in technology. Likewise, factors that are likely to affect the organization's supply might be changes in retirement age options or the relocation of a large, high-wage employer into the same local labor market.[43]

The Role of Planning

As indicated earlier, the function of human resource planning is to identify and prepare qualified individuals to fill position vacancies identified by human resource forecasts. Much of planning focuses on structuring the developmental actvities that are needed to prepare an individual to perform an important job adequately in the future. Many jobs, particularly those in higher levels of management, require years of experience in various activities for development of required skills. It cannot be assumed that a large organization will have an adequate supply of individuals ready to be plant managers unless the developmental assignments of such individuals have been planned. The development process often involves a process of planned job rotation that is aimed at providing needed job experiences. As part of the developmental process, career counseling may be undertaken to provide the employee with information on the options available and to enable the employee to provide personal inputs, such as desires and interests, into developmental plans.[44]

Planning may be viewed as meeting four needs: (1) staffing, (2) employee growth, (3) prevention of motivational decline and obsolescence, and (4) replacement of individuals who retire. Planning may be more effective when stages in individuals' lives or career cycles are considered. This is because people differ in their needs and interests as they progress through life. When human resource planning takes these differences into consideration, the needs of the individual and organization can be better matched.[45]

Next, we consider recruiting the necessary personnel to meet gaps between the forecasted supply and demand of personnel. Recruiting is obviously necessary for entry-level jobs and whenever developmental activities cannot supply personnel for higher-level positions.

RECRUITING

This discussion does not consider the legal constraints on recruiting that result from equal employment opportunity regulations; we cover such legal requirements in Chapter 17. Here we simply note that, if the organization has an underrepresentation of minorities or females, it will want to expand its recruiting to sources that it may not have used previously. Furthermore, if it has relied on word-of-mouth or walk-in applications in the past, it will want to supplement these sources with others, as such sources may not have supplied very many minorities or females.

Sources of Recruits

The sources for recruits vary according to the types of jobs to be filled and the size of the organization. Applicants for jobs requiring a college education are recruited from sources that are quite different from those utilized for jobs that do not require such education.

A large survey of recruiting practices found that, for college personnel, 82 percent of the companies recruited on college campuses, 67 percent used referrals by present employees, 66 percent used employment agencies, 63 percent used newspaper advertisements, 60 percent advertised in professional journals, and 57 percent used summer interns as a source of recruits. For these employees, larger organizations tended to differ from smaller organizations in their utilization of the various sources. In the sample, 88 percent of the larger companies (1,000 or more employees) utilized campus interviews whereas only 58 percent of the smaller companies conducted campus recruiting. Other differences were that larger companies were more likely to use present employee referrals and summer interns. Conversely, smaller companies were more likely to use employment agencies and newspaper advertisements. The survey also revealed differences in the effectiveness of recruiting through such sources. For the larger companies, 55 percent found on-campus interviews to be a successful source of recruits, whereas only 16 percent of the smaller companies indicated campus interviews as a successful source. Conversely, 47 percent of the smaller companies reported employment agencies as a successful source, whereas only 20 percent of larger companies reported such agencies as successful sources.[46] Thus the recruiting sources for college graduates tend to vary for organizations of different sizes, and the success of such sources tends to be related to organization size.

For noncollege job applicants, other recruiting sources are used. The same survey indicated that 99 percent of companies recruit from walk-in applicants, 89 percent use newspaper advertisements, 86 percent hire applicants referred by present employees, 74 percent use employment agencies, and 63 percent recruit through contacts with high schools. Larger companies (at least 1,000 employees) differed from smaller companies to the extent that they recruited through employment agencies. Only 63 percent of the larger companies used employment agencies, whereas 100 percent of the smaller companies used them. Finally, another recruiting source, especially for larger companies, is separation centers for the armed forces.[47]

Evaluation of Recruiting Sources

The different recruiting sources vary in the number of applicants they attract as well as in cost per job applicant. For example, referrals from present employees are an inexpensive source of recruits. Nonetheless, if many job applicants are desired, word-of-mouth recruiting may not bring in sufficient numbers. Conversely, newspaper advertisements, although more expensive, may result in a larger number of applicants at a relatively low cost per applicant. In addition to the number of recruits that can be obtained through various sources and the costs associated with each source, there is another important consideration, one that is related to the philosophy or objective of the organization's recruiting program.

Traditional philosophies toward recruitment sometimes emphasize attracting large numbers of applicants. In this manner, organizations can be more selective in hiring. As a result, lower selection ratios (ratios of hires to applicants) are maintained.[48] A more sophisticated recruiting philosophy would evaluate sources in terms of the "favorableness" of their ratios relative to the selection ratios of other recruiting sources. A source that provides a high proportion of good applicants (applicants that are hired) relative to the number of applicants would be considered a good source. A sophisticated method of evaluating recruiting sources considers differences in the "quit rates" associated with each source. One study of quit rates found that four recruiting sources had significantly lower quit rates that did three other sources. The recruiting sources with low quit rates were rehired former employees, high school referrals, referrals by employees, and walk-in applicants. Those recruiting sources associated with high quit rates were referrals from the organization's major employment agency, newspaper advertisements, and referrals from other employment agencies.[49] A more recent study of quit rates of white-collar workers (professional, managerial, sales, and clerical personnel) in a bank, an insurance company, and an abstracting service enterprise found that employees referred by other employees typically had lower quit rates than did those referred by employment agencies or responding to newspaper advertisements.[50]

Research on Recruiting and Suggestions for Improvement

Research indicates that college students prefer middle-aged recruiters and that they often dislike the practice of sending recent graduates to recruit because recent graduates often cannot answer questions about jobs. College students have also reported that recruiters are most influential when they are knowledgeable, enthusiastic, friendly, convincing, interested, and truthful. Conversely, college students dislike recruiters who lack interest and enthusiasm. Some negative recruiting practices include attempts by recruiters to establish a status differential through sarcasm or insults, uses of pseudopsychiatric approaches based on questions that are subject to misinterpretation, and stress interview techniques.[51]

A recent review of the recruiting literature emphasizes the importance and multiplicity of influencing factors on the job choice decision and attitudes of job applicants. Negative influencing factors in addition to those just cited are inadequate recruiter knowledge and preparation, lack of recruiter credibility, interviews conducted with an extreme concern or lack of concern for structure, and excessive talking by the interviewer. Conversely, positive influences were found to be recruiting by the incumbents of jobs under consideration, verbally fluent recruiters, recruiter personality characteristics, such as those noted and warmth, timely follow-up after the interview, and high interview face validity. Finally, the review hypothesized that students just completing their schooling will be more susceptible to such recruiting factors than will experienced individuals.[52]

Managers would do well to remember that the recruiter conveys the image of the company to potential job applicants. Thus benefits can be obtained from concentrating on recruiter assignments and training. An additional suggestion is that recruiting brochures should provide information about the jobs that applicants are likely to perform, training programs, and career progressions.[53]

Realistic Job Expectations

Another point to consider in recruiting is its purpose. Although it seems abundantly obvious that the purpose is to attract job applicants to the organization, a more precise statement of purpose is to attract qualified candidates who will not only accept jobs but will remain with the organization. Thus the organization cannot simply concentrate on attracting candidates; it must not violate the expectations of those who accept jobs, because employees with unmet expectations will tend to leave.

Although it is necessary to present a positive view of the advantages of employment with the organization, exaggerating its merits typically has undesirable consequences. Employees who have accepted jobs on the basis of such exaggerations or on the basis of unrealistically optimistic expectations, will eventually leave. The organization then incurs turnover costs and must once again go to the expense of recruiting and hiring replacements. To eliminate this problem, some organizations have been using "realistic" interviews and job previews. In realistic job previews, the applicant may observe the performance of the job or actually perform the work. Some job previews may simply show "realistic" films of performing the job. Southern New England Telephone Company has used this approach with potential telephone operators, who view films that show fast-paced work, obnoxious customers, and so on. Prior to the use of previews, the company had turnover rates as high as 100 percent during the operators' first six months on the job. After the use of realistic job previews, turnover rates were in the range of 30 to 40 percent for the first nine months of employment.[54]

Other examples of realistic job previews have had applicants perform the actual work. For example, in one instance applicants actually operated sewing machines to which they would be assigned. Following the preview, several job candidates refused the job.[55] Having applicants withdraw at this stage because the work does not meet their expectations is far preferable to having them quit after they have been hired.

SUMMARY

In this chapter we have distinguished between the concepts of manpower planning and human resource planning, noting that human resource planning is a micro concept that refers to organization-specific activities. Human resource planning is based on a recognition that an organization's personnel should be viewed as valuable assets. Such planning helps the organization to develop and maintain its personnel assets. The process of human resource planning involves (1) inventorying present personnel, (2) forecasting the internal supply of personnel, (3) forecasting the demand for personnel, (4) determining the discrepancy between supply and demand, and (5) developing plans for dealing with forecasted shortages or surpluses of personnel.

Forecasting obviously plays a major role in human resource planning. An understanding of human resource forecasting may be facilitated by considering such forecasting techniques in supply and demand contexts. Techniques used to forecast supply include replacement charts, Markov models, linear programming, goal programming, and computer simulation. Demand forecasting techniques include supervisory estimates, rules of thumb, heuristics, replacement charts, the Delphi procedure, and regression analysis.

Recruiting takes place to fill current vacancies or in anticipation of vacancies that have been forecasted. In recruiting, the objective is not only to attract job applicants but to attract those who are qualified, will accept jobs if offered, and will remain with the organization. Realistic job previews are one technique that tends to lower employee turnover rates because employees develop realistic expectations about what their jobs will be like. Survey results indicate that differentials in recruiting source utilization rates are associated with the type of employees desired (college or noncollege graduates) and the size of organizations. Finally, research results reveal that there are differences in quit rates for the various sources through which employees are recruited.

INTERVIEW WRAP-UP

Even relatively low-skilled jobs require that a certain amount of human resource forecasting be conducted. Forecasts for human resources are determined through two approaches. One involves an extrapolation from sales quotas and order forecasts; the other is based on an analysis of turnover rates. Although the firm does not recruit for low-skilled positions at the Palo Alto complex, it does have a decentralized recruiting program that is conducted at universities and military separation centers as an occasional duty of some 800 managers. —Joe Shepela, personnel manager, Hewlett-Packard Company.

WHAT MANAGERS SHOULD DO REGARDING PERSONNEL MANAGEMENT ACTIVITIES

1. Managers should realize that some very important short-run and long-run benefits can accrue from human resource planning.

2. Managers need to be aware that human resource forecasts cannot be accurate if the data that they supply to the human resource forecasters are inaccurate. Thus, they must take the time to provide good data for such forecasts if any benefit is to be obtained.

3. When called upon to provide recruiters, managers should be prepared to send individuals who have a thorough knowledge of the jobs to be filled. It has been shown that candidates tend to form negative opinions of employers when their recruiters are unable to tell candidates any details about the job or their probable career progression.

REVIEW QUESTIONS

1. What are the steps involved in human resource planning?
2. Describe four methods of forecasting the supply of human resources.
3. Describe four methods of forecasting the demand of human resources.
4. What are some of the problems encountered in human resource planning?
5. In exponential smoothing, how is the α value derived?
6. How are the transition probabilities derived in Markov models?
7. Describe how to evaluate various recruiting sources.

KEY CONCEPTS

Computer simulation
Delphi procedure

Realistic job preview
Regression analysis

Exponential smoothing	Replacement chart
Goal programming	Rules of thumb and heuristics
Human resource inventory	Selection ratio
Linear programming	Supervisory estimates
Markov models	Transition probability

CASE

AN EXPONENTIAL SMOOTHING FORECASTING PROBLEM

The following are the actual manning levels for tool and die makers in the compressor manufacturing section of the Feltner Tool Company. As indicated, the data are for the years 1970 through 1983. Find the α value from those of .2, .6, and .95 that leads to the forecasted value that most closely approximates the observed or actual manning levels. Use this α value to forecast the number of tool and die makers that will be needed for 1984. Be prepared to discuss the limitations of forecasts that are based on exponential smoothing.

Year	Actual Observed Number of Tool and Die Makers	Year	Actual Observed Number of Tool and Die Makers
1970	42	1977	45
1971	42	1978	50
1972	43	1979	49
1973	43	1980	47
1974	45	1981	50
1975	40	1982	53
1976	48	1983	55

NOTES

[1] For an example of macro manpower planning as applied to local labor markets, see G. Mangum and D. Snedeker, *Manpower Planning for Local Labor Markets* (Salt Lake City, Utah: Olympus, 1974).

[2] W. Y. Oi, "Labor as a Quasi-Fixed Factor," *Journal of Political Economy,* 70 (1962), pp. 538–555.

[3] See J. W. Walker, *Human Resource Planning* (New York: McGraw-Hill, 1980); G. L. Milkovich and T. A. Mahoney, "Human Resources Planning and PAIR Policy," in *Planning and Auditing PAIR,* eds. D. Yoder and H. G. Heneman, Jr. (Washington, D.C.: Bureau of National Affairs, 1976), pp. 2–1 to 2–29.

[4] T. H. Patten, Jr., *Manpower Planning and the Development of Human Resources* (New York: John Wiley, 1971), p. 14.

[5] W. S. Wikstrom, *Manpower Planning: Evolving Systems* (New York: Conference Board, 1971).

[6] J. Fiorito, "The Rationale for Human Resource Planning," *Human Resource Planning* (in press).

[7]J. Ledvinka, "Technical Implications of Equal Employment Law for Manpower Planning," *Personnel Psychology,* 28 (1975), 299–323.

[8]E. H. Burack and T. G. Gutteridge, "Institutional Manpower Planning: Rhetoric versus Reality," *California Management Review,* 20 (1978), 13–22.

[9]C. R. Greer and D. Armstrong, "Human Resource Forecasting and Planning: A State-of-the-Art Investigation," *Human Resource Planning,* 3 (1980), 67–78.

[10]Ibid.

[11]R. A. Kaumeyer, Jr., *Planning and Using Skills Inventory Systems* (New York: Van Nostrand, 1979).

[12]Ibid., p. 1.

[13]Walker, *Human Resources Planning;* Milkovich and Mahoney, "Human Resources Planning and PAIR Policy"; Kaumeyer, *Planning and Using Skills Inventory Systems.*

[14]Walker, *Human Resources Planning;* Milkovich and Mahoney, "Human Resources Planning."

[15]Kaumeyer, *Planning and Using Skills Inventory Systems,* p. 19.

[16]Ibid.

[17]Ibid.

[18]Ibid.

[19]Milkovich and Mahoney, "Human Resources Planning," pp. 2–18

[20]Kaumeyer, *Planning and Using Inventory Systems.*

[21]M. Haire, "Managing Management Manpower: A Model for Human Resource Development," *Business Horizons,* 10 (1967), 23–28.

[22]Greer and Armstrong, "Human Resource Forecasting and Planning."

[23]Milkovich and Mahoney, "Human Resources Planning;" V. R. Ceriello and L. Linden, "Management Resource Program," *Journal of Systems Management,* 23 (1973), 8–10.

[24]K. M. Rowland and M. G. Sovereign, "Markov-Chain Analysis of Internal Manpower Supply," *Industrial Relations,* 9 (1969), 88–99; H. G. Heneman, III, and M. G. Sandver, "Markov Analysis in Human Resources Administration: Applications and Limitations," *Academy of Management Review,* 2 (1977), 535–542.

[25]Ibid.

[26]A. L. Patz, "Linear Programming Applied to Manpower Management," *Industrial Management Review,* 11 (1970), 31–38.

[27]B. M. Thornton and P. Preston, *Introduction to Management Science: Quantitative Approaches to Managerial Decisions* (Columbus, Ohio: Charles E. Merrill, 1977).

[28]D. R. Bryant, M. J. Maggard, and R. P. Taylor, "Manpower Planning Models and Techniques: A Descriptive Survey," *Business Horizons,* 16 (1973), 69–78.

[29]W. L. Weber, "Manpower Planning in Hierarchical Organizations: A Computer Simulation Approach," *Management Science,* 18 (1971), 118–143.

[30]Wikstrom, *Manpower Planning.*

[31]Milkovich and Mahoney, "Human Resources Planning."

[32]Bryant et al., "Manpower Planning Models and Techniques."

[33]G. L. Milkovich and T. A. Mahoney, "Human Resource Planning Models: A Perspective," *Human Resource Planning,* 1 (1978), 19–30; Bryant et al., "Manpower Planning Models and Techniques."

[34]G. L. Milkovich, A. J. Annoni, and T. A. Mahoney, "The Use of the Delphi Procedures in Manpower Forecasting," *Management Science,* 19 (1972), 381–388.

[35]Ibid.

[36]Wikstrom, *Manpower Planning.*

[37]R. S. Pindyck and D. L. Rubinfeld, *Econometric Models and Economic Forecasts* (New York: McGraw-Hill, 1976), p. 6.

[38]Pindyck and Rubinfeld, *Econometric Models and Economic Forecasts.*

[39]M. Drandell, "A composite Forecasting Methodology for Manpower Planning Utilizing Objective and Subjective Criteria," *Academy of Management Journal,* 18 (1975) 510–519.

[40]B. M. Thornton, *CPA Review: Quantitative Methods and Statistical Sampling* (Worthington, Ohio: McHugh, 1978).

[41]B. L. Bowerman and R. T. O'Connell, *Time Series and Forecasting: An Applied Approach* (North Scituate, Mass.: Duxbury Press, 1979).

[42]Wikstrom, *Manpower Planning.*

[43]Walker, *Human Resources Planning.*

[44]E. H. Schein, "Increasing Organizational Effectiveness Through Better Human Resource Planning and Development," *Sloan Management Review,* 18 (1977), 1–20; E. H. Schein, *Career Dynamics: Matching Individual and Organizational Needs* (Reading, Mass.: Addison-Wesley, 1978).

[45]Ibid.

[46]Bureau of National Affairs, "Recruiting Practices," *Personnel Policies Forum,* 86 (1969), 1–15.

[47]Ibid.

[48]J. P. Wanous, *Organizational Entry: Recruitment, Selection, and Socialization of Newcomers* (Reading, Mass.: Addison-Wesley, 1980).

[49]M. J. Gannon, "Sources of Referral and Employee Turnover," *Journal of Applied Psychology,* 55 (1971), 226–228.

[50]P. J. Decker and E. L. Cornelius, III, "A Note on Recruiting Sources and Job Survival Rates," *Journal of Applied Psychology,* 64 (1979), 463–464.

[51]W. F. Glueck, "How Recruiters Influence Job Choices on Campus," *Personnel,* 48 (1971), 46–52.

[52]S. L. Rynes, H. G. Heneman, III, and D. P. Schwab, "Individual Reactions to Organizational Recruiting: A Review," *Personnel Psychology,* 33 (1980), 529–542.

[53]P. Schofield, "Recruiting Graduates—Some Fresh Answers," *Accountancy,* 89 (1978), 93–94.

[54]J. P. Wanous, "Tell It Like It Is at Realistic Job Previews," *Personnel,* 52 (1975), 50–60.

[55]J. L. Farr, B. S. O'Leary, and C. J. Bartlett, "Effects of a Work Sample Test upon Self-Selection and Turnover of Job Applicants," *Journal of Applied Psychology,* 58 (1973), 283–285.

7

SELECTION TOOLS

LEARNING OBJECTIVES

After reading this chapter, you should be able to

1. Understand the psychometric properties (validity and reliability) of selection tools.

2. Be able to describe the predictive and concurrent models of test validation.

3. Describe the general legal requirements that control personnel selection.

4. Describe the various types of personnel selection tests.

5. Be aware of the errors and biases that commonly occur in interviews.

6. Have some knowledge of how to improve an employer's interviewing methods.

7. Discuss the usefulness of other selection tools.

Mike Hornbuckle is the director of human resources for American Tourister in Warren, Rhode Island. Mike has been with American Tourister for five years and has eight years of experience. He has a bachelor's degree in psychology.

Interviewer: Tell us about the difficulties involved in deciding which of several applicants is the right person to hire for a job.

Mike Hornbuckle: Well, I guess the problem is that you are able to spend such a short period of time with applicants when you are in a peak hiring period, or, if you're interviewing regularly, it's difficult to take the time out to do the hiring process unless you're totally committed to that. Even in those conditions, you're probably doing a tremendous amount of hiring, and as a result can't spend a whole lot of time and you have to do a very quick analysis of somebody while they are in here.

Interviewer: Is American Tourister seasonal in its hiring pattern?

Mike Hornbuckle: Quite often it is. But I probably should tell you about three different phases of hiring. One is exempt. Exempt personnel are those who are considered to be exempt from overtime. That's the real classification. They are your management people primarily, the ones who would normally have a college degree and be in a supervisory or management function. The next classification would be the nonexempt and those people are in the clerical area primarily, those people who provide support for the management group or they might be keeping data for you or something of that nature. Then, when you get into your manufacturing operation, you're talking primarily about hourly. So you would have those three classifications: hourly, nonexempt, and exempt. Now each of those has problem areas with the recruiting function. They all have uniqueness to them. For example, in the hourly area, you're dealing with a situation where the people are in here very quickly. It takes about fifteen minutes to interview somebody. That's all you have time for, and the interviews are very difficult because interviewees can't talk to you. If you were to come in and interview for a job, I would probably make a very simple request: "Tell me about yourself." And you could go on and on about it. If I were to ask that of an hourly employee, quite often you get a blank stare. And you normally will find a yes and no situation.

Interviewer: To follow up, are these individuals high school graduates?

Mike Hornbuckle: Exactly. Most do not even have a high school education. I guess I'm alarmed at the number of people who do come into our operation applying for jobs who have not finished school. And when you are asking them questions, you'll say, "Where do you want to go in your life?" which is an important question in trying to determine if they are going to be a stable individual. They'll say, "I don't know" or "Huh?" So the real mechanism for determining a hire situation so often with hourly employees is to review their applications to see their work experience and you want to try to look at some stability there. Have they spent a long time on particular jobs? Have they worked one place for five or six years or have they job-hopped, which means they are probably going to be very insecure in your situation. You look at the kind of companies a person has worked for. We know the general area. We know the kind of companies where a person might be. Then, of course, the tool that we like to use but can't too often because of legal requirements is the reference check. If I were to say, for example, that you had an absentee problem and I could not have justified that and shown it to you, then I really can't say that you had an absentee problem. There has to be a specific reason. Also, companies are very, very careful today about being hauled into court. More and more that becomes a legal situation. I can be taken in tomorrow for answering questions you may have. You may have asked what was your general impression of the employee and I might tell you poor. But unless I have some very strong background for that, I'd better not make that opinion. Our policy, for example, is that we do not give reference checks. If you were to call in and ask what can you tell me about an employee, I would tell you a couple of things. What they were doing here, their job classification, their date of hire, and their date of exit. That's it. That keeps me in a good situation because I can support that legally. I can tell you what the person was doing, and I can tell you the date they were hired and the date that they left.

Realistically, that really ties our hands. That makes it very difficult for me to check up on an employee. Often because of that we don't really check that much. We should do more of it, but we find ourselves having to base 90 percent of our decision on the personal interview and what the individual does.

Now there is also another phase of this that is important and that is the testing area. We don't do testing at American Tourister, because we don't require a lot of skill and experience. If I were working in a high-technology industry, I would then do testing. I'd want to make sure that there were basic skills there. I'd want to bring in some manual dexterity tests and have some vision tests done, things of that nature."

Interviewer: Is testing used in the selection of exempt employees?

Mike Hornbuckle: Not here. In other businesses that I have been in we have. You need to be in a very defensible situation with testing. You find if you are going to do testing that it comes under modern EEO laws and you must be able to show that your testing will not have a disparate effect on any minority group. And you have to go through a qualifying testing program to make sure that your testing will not disqualify people because of race. For example, I have to show that, if I gave the test to ten whites and ten blacks, they basically would have the same result. If I were to show that they had an unequal effect on any minority group, I would not be able to use that test.

Interviewer: Is there any way to tell if a particular test is appropriate in those situations where it is feasible to test?

Mike Hornbuckle: There are many tests that can apply to your situation. The psychological testing that we can do today is very sophisticated; there are many branches of it. Again, I can do a manual dexterity test. I can give you a general intelligence test. I can actually have you go out and try to use different tools. Of if you think back, you may have gone through the military process. A lot of our testing in some cases is similar, in that you have people look at different tools and tell you what they are and that would give you a basic mechanical understanding. But then it can become more sophisticated. For example, if you have a quality control area, and you are using micrometers or very technical instrumentation, then you can be very specific about your testing. And those are the ideal situations because normally you can say this relates directly to the job I have. They must have that knowledge to perform the job. By the way, that's another important criterion here. You must be able to show that any testing you do has to be a part of that job. If, for example, I said that I wanted to improve my work force and was therefore going to give a hard test, that really doesn't apply because if it can be shown that people can do the job without those skills, then I have the legal responsibility to give them opportunity to work on the job.

Interviewer (after following up on Mike's response with an example of an analytical ability test): Would you concur that the test would be inappropriate in your situation.

Mike Hornbuckle: For American Tourister in particular because ours is a very easy assembly process. If you think about it, putting together a suitcase is very easy to do. As a matter of fact, in one facility we are trying to live up to our handicapped responsibility, and we've hired some mentally handicapped individuals. But because of the simplicity of the operations we have, we are able to do very well.

INTRODUCTION

This chapter concerns the use of selection tools that enable us to maximize the job-to-person relationship. The term selection tool is defined in this chapter in a rather broad sense. Selection procedures such as interviews and evaluations of references will be considered as selection tools along with the more traditionally defined tools or instruments, such as tests and application blanks. This definition is useful because we need to think of all these tools from a common viewpoint. All these activities or instruments have a potential impact on the selection decision and consequently need to have predictive ability. Aside from the good economic sense of using only selection tools that have the ability to predict job performance, the current equal employment opportunity laws prohibit the use of invalid selection tools that have an unfair discriminatory impact.

Before proceeding with an examination of the various selection tools, we first consider their psychometric properties. Our interview with Mike Hornbuckle revealed that, before we would use tests for selection, they would have to be shown to be valid predictors of job performance. Validity is an important psychometric property.

VALIDITY AND RELIABILITY

Validity

When a selection tool is said to be valid it measures what it is expected to measure. In the selection setting, it obtains measures of whether the applicant will perform the job successfully or complete a training program. A valid tool then enables the employer to obtain an indication or prediction of the likelihood of success. Thus, in selection, a concern is with the predictive validity of selection tools. This type of validity is a criterion-based validity in that the selection tool's prediction is tested against criteria of job performance or training performance. Because criterion-based predictive validity is fundamental to legitimate selection tools, we describe how the existence of such validity is determined.

> **Validity:** the property of a selection tool indicating the extent to which the tool measures what it is supposed to measure.

PREDICTIVE VALIDITY. The predictive validity of selection tools is determined in a stepwise manner, as shown in Table 7-1. For example, a test would be validated by first administering several tests or a battery of tests to job applicants. It is advisable to administer more tests than are needed so that there is a better chance of obtaining at least one valid test. After administration of the tests, the results are kept confidential and hiring decisions are made without knowledge of test scores. After a suitable time period for the hired applicants to become proficient at their jobs, performance

Table 7-1

Steps in the Predictive Validation Process

1. Administer battery of tests to a group of job applicants.
2. Hire applicants on the basis of factors other than test scores and keep test scores confidential.
3. Wait a suitable time period for recently hired employees to develop job proficiency.
4. Collect performance criteria on employees who were tested.
5. Correlate test scores with performance criteria (such as performance appraisal data).
6. Use tests that are correlated significantly and substantially with performance criteria in the selection of future employees.

criteria are collected. The test scores are then correlated with performance measures (performance criteria). Those tests that are correlated significantly (a measure of association) with the performance criteria and explain sufficient variation in performance are chosen for use in selection. These valid tests are then administered to new job applicants, and the test scores are used in making hiring decisions.

Test scores are kept secret during the validation process because knowledge of test scores could bias the evaluations of performance.[1] Such bias might result in a self-fulfilling prophecy if raters rate the performance of individuals higher (or lower) in part because they expect them to perform better (or worse) as a result of their high (or low) test scores. In the classic validation study of all time (conducted at AT&T for assessment centers and discussed in the next chapter on managerial selection), the test results were kept secret for eight years.[2] Although predictive validation is the preferred method, it does have a major disadvantage—namely, the waiting period during which the test scores cannot be used in the hiring decisions.[3] If a test can help to maximize the job-to-person fit, the organization should benefit from a better qualified work force and reduced turnover. Since the costs of an ineffective work force and turnover are substantial, there may be pressure on the personnel department to adopt a promising test before the waiting period has ended. Thus, other means of validation may be desired. The next method of validating selection tools overcomes the waiting period limitation of predictive validation.

CONCURRENT VALIDITY. A second criterion-based form of validity is called concurrent validity (described in Table 7-2). The concurrent validity of a selection tool is determined on the basis of data obtained from current employees. The procedure is described here in the setting of validating a test. In concurrent validation, the first step is to administer tests to present employees doing the job for which the test is being developed. Next measures of such employees' job performance are collected. The test scores are then correlated with the measures of performance (performance criteria). Those tests that are significantly related to performance and explain sufficient variation in performance are then used in the selection process.[4]

Although the concurrent validation process overcomes the time delay of the predictive validation process, it has disadvantages as well. The first drawback is that the test scores of *experienced* employees are correlated with their performance ratings. To

Table 7-2

Steps in the Concurrent Validation Process

1. Administer battery of tests to current employees.
2. Correlate test scores with measures of current employees' performance (such as performance appraisal data).
3. Use tests that are correlated significantly and substantially with performance criteria in the selection of future employees.

the extent that job experience affects the way in which the individual will perform on such tests, the procedure is biased. Thus, although good, experienced employees may perform well on the tests, inexperienced job applicants may not do well on such tests, although if hired, they may be good employees after an initial learning period.[5]

Another disadvantage of the concurrent validation process is that, if there is an underrepresentation in the validation sample of a group traditionally discriminated against, there is no assurance that the statistical relationship established between test scores and performance measures for nondisadvantaged persons will hold for disadvantaged persons. It is possible that such disadvantaged persons might not do well on the tests but might perform well on the job.

A final disadvantage exists in the potential restriction in the range of test scores (and in performance ratings as well). This restriction of range occurs because, when current employees are used to validate the selection tool, it is likely that few incompetent employees will be current employees and also likely that excellent performers may have moved on to more challenging jobs. Thus, if test scores are related to job performance, it is likely that neither very low nor very high test scores will be obtained on the basis of a validation study conducted on current employees. Restriction of the test score range causes the correlation between test scores and performance to be understated.[6] Of course, there will be a restriction of the range of performance measures (with predictive evaluation as well) if incompetent performers are eliminated prior to the collection of the performance indicators used in the validation study.

Restriction in the range of performance levels because of the elimination of incompetent performers prevents the calculation of correlation coefficients on data that include combinations of low performance and expected low test scores. Thus, the correlation coefficients that are calculated may not be as large as they should be. So, although typically there is only moderate correlation between test scores and performance measures, such restrictions of range provide some indication that the true relationship between test scores and performance measures may be somewhat higher. Next we consider a type of validity that is helpful where only small numbers of employees are in the jobs of concern.

SYNTHETIC VALIDITY. The previous criterion-based forms of validity require sufficient numbers of job incumbents (at least thirty or forty according to various rules of thumb) to obtain sufficient performance measures for statistical correlation with test scores.[7] For the smaller firm and for jobs that do not require very many employees, problems of inadequate samples prevent these methods of validation. Although the preferable procedure is to validate every selection tool in each organization where it is utilized, that may be impossible. Thus synthetic validity or job component validity provides an alternate validation method. Such a procedure for validation can be used where selection tools exist that measure common subdimensions of jobs. Tests may exist that have been shown to predict performance validly on similar components in other jobs, even in other organizations. By selecting validated tests (from other jobs) that measure the likelihood of future performance on the various common subdimensions of a job, one can develop a battery of such tests that enables the prediction of performance on the whole job. This procedure is also a viable strategy for developing selection tests for a new job. The procedure is illustrated in Figure 7-1.

Later on, predictive or concurrent validation could be performed on the job if sufficient employees were available to constitute a suitable sample. It should be noted that with this method of validation (as well as with others) a good job analysis is required for the identification of the job duties to be performed and skills or abilities that are required.[8]

OTHER TYPES OF VALIDITY.   So far we have defined two types of criterion-based validity: predictive and concurrent. We have also defined a third type of validity, synthetic validity, that is also based on performance criteria although from other jobs or other organizations. These types of validity are the most important for personnel selection; however, two other types of validity, although not used in selection, may be used in constructing selection tests. These two types are content validity and construct validity.

✸ **Content validity:** asks whether the subject matter of the job is sampled adequately by the test.

Figure 7-1

The Synthetic Validation Process

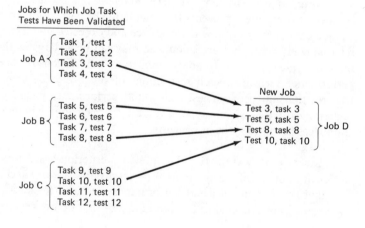

Typically, the content validity of a test is simply assessed logically.[9]

★ **Construct validity:** a concept used in the construction of psychological tests.

For instance, if a paper-and-pencil, group-administered test purports to measure anxiety, the test would be described as having construct validity if the test results were correlated significantly with a recognized, individually administered test of anxiety for the same subjects.[10] As noted earlier, in personnel selection, we are concerned only indirectly with construct validity.

Another form of validity is called face validity.

★ **Face validity:** exists simply when a test looks as if it would measure the potential to perform a job.[11]

Face validity has no value in assessing the predictive validity of a test or selection tool. Face validity, however, may have an indirect use in selection to narrow the set of possible tests to those that might be suitable candidates for criterion-based validation. Furthermore, face validity may be of use in selecting placement tools. A placement tool or test may be accepted more readily by employees if it looks as if it is valid. Where employees are unionized and can file grievances over the appropriateness of tests, the extent to which such tests look reasonable or possess face validity is important. Thus, although content validity, construct validity, and face validity have some indirect benefit in selection, they are not substitutes for criterion-based forms of validity.[12]

★ **Differential validation:** involves separate validation of selection tools for various demographic groups of job applicants.

For example, a demographic characteristic such as race may affect the relationship between test scores and job performance. When such a characteristic has this effect, it is said to moderate the relationship. Thus race may be acting as a moderating variable between test scores and performance measures. In such a case, the test should be validated separately (differential validation) for the groups in which race is acting as a moderator variable. If differential validation is not conducted, a test that is statistically valid for the group as a whole may be inappropriate for members of a demographic group because it may lack predictive validity for those individuals. Mike Hornbuckle of American Tourister noted the need to validate selection tests to ensure that they were not discriminatory. He also noted that it was not easy.

The other psychometric property that is of great importance in personnel selection is that of reliability. Before a selection test or technique is used, it must not only be valid but also reliable.

Reliability

The reliability of a selection instrument or procedure refers to its consistency—whether it obtains consistent results with repeated administrations. If a job applicant is interviewed by an employment interviewer more than one time and the rating that he or she receives is relatively constant, then we would say that the interview was reliable. Likewise, if a job applicant is interviewed by several interviewers and the ratings given in each of the separate interviews tend to be similar, the interview procedure is said to have high interrater reliability.

✱   **Reliability:** refers to the consistency of a selection instrument or procedure.

Reliability is a necessary, but not a sufficient, condition for validity. For example, Mike Hornbuckle mentioned situations where dexterity tests might be used. A manual dexterity test could be designed that measures a job candidate's ability to assemble electronic components. Applicants are found to perform at the same level (after allowing for learning effects) on repeated administrations of the test. In such case, the dexterity test is said to be reliable. If very dissimilar scores are obtained on repeated administrations of the test to the same applicants, then intuitively we know that the test is probably not a good predictor of a job applicant's ability to assemble electronic components. In such a situation the test is not valid. It cannot predict what it is supposed to predict because it lacks reliability—a necessary condition for validity.

The dexterity test may produce very reliable responses, but validity may not be established. If the test is used to predict performance on other jobs such as those involving supervisory duties, no predictive power may be found. Obviously, the ability to assemble electronic components may not be related to the supervisory ability that a foreman's job requires. Although the test may be found to be reliable, it will probably lack validity. Thus, although reliability is a necessary condition for validity, it is not a sufficient condition for validity. Next we discuss the methods of determining reliability.

METHODS FOR DETERMINING RELIABILITY.   The test-retest technique for determining reliability simply correlates individuals' scores on two administrations of a test. A problem with this method of determining reliability is that any learning effects that occur as a result of the first administration of the test will affect performance on a second administration of the text. Thus recall of responses on the first administration of the test may make responses on the second administration uncharacteristically similar to the first responses. If the interval between administrations is too short, recall effects may be more pronounced. The result is that the correlation of test scores will then be artificially high, and the reliability of the test will be overestimated. Conversely, if the interval between test and retest is too long, other factors that affect test performance may change. Consequently, changed conditions may cause the correlation between test scores to be lower than it should be. In this case, the reliability will be underestimated.

A second method of determining reliability considers a test essentially as two separate tests that are administered simultaneously. This technique is called the split-halves technique. Half the test items are considered as one test and the other half are considered as a second test. The association of the responses on these halves is then calculated using an adjusted correlation measure.[13] This measure of reliability assesses internal reliability or internal consistency.

Another measure of internal reliability is called the coefficient alpha. The coefficient alpha essentially measures the correlation among test items after making an adjustment for the length of the test (number of items).[14]

A final means of assessing reliability is the parallel forms or equivalent forms technique. In this technique, two versions of a test are constructed that theoretically ask the same questions in differently worded or differently constructed items. Now that we have described the desired psychometric properties of selection tools and the methods of evaluating such tools' validity and reliability, we turn our attention to the legal environment of personnel selection.

THE LEGAL ENVIRONMENT OF SELECTION

In our interview with Mike Hornbuckle we were made aware of the legal constraints on personnel selection. Few areas of personnel and even business and management in general have experienced such profound changes over the last two decades as the legal environment of personnel selection. Beginning with the Civil Rights Act of 1964, the selection process has come under extensive regulation. Title VII of the Civil Rights Act of 1964 (which became effective in 1965 and was amended by the Equal Employment Opportunity Act of 1972) specifies the following:

> It shall be an unlawful employment practice for an employer (1) to fail or refuse to hire or to discharge any individual, or otherwise to discriminate against any individual with respect to his compensation, terms, conditions, or privileges of employment, because of such individual's race, color, religion, sex, or national origin; or (2) to limit, segregate, or classify his employees in any way which would deprive or tend to deprive any individual of employment opportunities or otherwise adversely affect his status as an employee, because of such individual's race, color, religion, sex, or national origin.[15]

The law is enforced by the Equal Employment Opportunity Commission (EEOC) and (with the 1972 amendment) now covers the following employers:

> All private employers of 15 or more persons; all educational institutions, public and private, state and local government, public and private employment agencies; labor unions with fifteen or more members; and joint labor-management committees for apprenticeship and training.[16]

The requirement that an employer have at least fifteen employees to be covered by Title VII is tempered by the provision that coverage requires that such a level of employment must be maintained "for each working day in each of 20 or more calendar weeks in the current or preceding calendar year."[17]

Another important selection regulation is Executive Order 11246 (implemented in 1965 and amended by Executive Order 11375 in 1967), which requires nondiscrimination in employment on the part of contractors and subcontractors doing business with the federal government. The executive order is enforced by the Office of Federal Contract Compliance Programs (OFCCP) in the Department of Labor. It applies as follows:

> Generally, the executive orders cover all government contractors—both construction and nonconstruction—as well as subcontractors with the federal government. More significantly, however, all contractors with fifty or more employees and contracts of $50,000 or more are required to develop written affirmative action plans.[18]

Chapter 17, which deals with equal employment opportunity, considers this regulation in more detail.

Another federal law governing personnel selection and employment is the Age Discrimination in Employment Act of 1967 (amended in 1978). This law provides the following:

> Sec. 4(a)   It shall be unlawful for an employer (1) to fail or refuse to hire or to discharge any individual or otherwise discriminate against any individual with respect to his compensation, terms, conditions, or privileges of employment, because of such an individual's age.[19]
>
> Sec. 12(a)   The prohibitions in this Act shall be limited to individuals who are at least 40 years of age but less than 70 years of age.[20]

Finally, the law defines employers as follows:

> Sec. 11   For the purposes of this Act . . . (b) The term "employer" means a person engaged in an industry affecting commerce who has twenty or more employees for each working day in each of twenty or more calendar weeks in the current or preceding year.[21]

Other federal legislation affecting employment includes the Vocational Rehabilitation Act of 1973 and the Vietnam Era Veterans' Readjustment Act of 1974, which are considered in Chapter 17 in the discussion of affirmative action.

Thus far, our discussion has concerned only federal legislation and regulation; however, other laws and regulations of a similar nature exist at the state and local government level. These laws and ordinances are too numerous for discussion in this text; however, several excellent reference sources are available.[22]

To administer Title VII of the Civil Rights Act and Executive Order 11246 (as amended), the regulatory agencies have adopted regulations to be followed in selection practices. Two U.S. Supreme Court decisions in this area are critical to a basic understanding of the legislative environment of personnel selection. The first decision is the 1971 landmark *Griggs* v. *Duke Power Company* case. At Duke Power, there had been a history of discrimination in that blacks had been restricted to the lowest-skilled, low-est-paying jobs. After the Civil Rights Act became effective, the company stopped this practice and implemented high school education and test requirements for initial as-signment and transfer out of these low-skilled jobs. However, neither the educational requirement nor the test could be shown to be related to job performance (no predic-tive validity). Furthermore, these two requirements disqualified a disproportionate number of blacks (no differential validation). In the Court's decision on this case, a great deal of guidance on the requirements for selection was provided, as evidenced by the following two excerpts:

> The Act proscribes not only overt discrimination but also practices that are fair in form, but discriminatory in operation. The touchstone is business necessity. If an employment practice which operates to exclude Negroes cannot be shown to be related to job perfor-mance, the practice is prohibited.

> Nothing in the Act precludes the use of testing or measuring procedures; obviously they are useful. What Congress has forbidden is giving these devices and mechanisms control-ling force unless they are demonstrably a reasonable measure of job performance. Con-gress has not commanded that the less qualified be preferred over the better qualified simply because of minority origins. Far from disparaging job qualifications as such, Con-gress has made such qualifications the controlling factor, so that race, religion, nationali-ty and sex become irrelevant. What Congress has commanded is that any tests used must measure the person for the job and not the person in the abstract.[23]

Thus, the *Griggs* v. *Duke Power Company* decision tells us that tests, as well as *other* selection procedures, must provide an indication of job performance—they must be valid. (Of course, this is precisely the message that the selection literature had con-veyed for years prior to the decision.) A consequence of the decision was that many employers abandoned or de-emphasized testing. Furthermore, there was a predictable shift to tests that are less subject to cultural bias, such as work sampling.[24] The aban-donment of tests was probably due to the fact that many employers had not validated their tests or had a real concern over the costs of litigation if the validity of their tests had to be established in court. As a result, more reliance in selection may have been placed on other procedures. Some of these selection procedures, such as interviews, may be subject particularly to undesirable biases. Nonetheless, the *Griggs* v. *Duke Power Company* decision applied to other selection procedures and requirements as well as tests.

Consideration of the requirement for valid selection tools may cause one to in-quire about the situation where the selection test or procedure is valid but dispropor-tionately rejects members of a class of job applicants. In such a case, the factors that cause those applicants not to perform well on the selection test or procedure may also be expected to inhibit a good job performance. In such an instance, use of the valid test or procedure would still be appropriate. Nonetheless, it may be that remedial training or some other program can correct deficiencies in a disadvantaged person's background, so that both test performance and the likelihood of satisfactory perfor-mance may be increased. In many instances such training may be appropriate.

The other major decision of interest is the 1975 Supreme Court case of *Albemarle Paper Company* v. *Moody*,[25] which dealt with the requirements of selection test validation. To enforce Title VII, the EEOC has adopted guidelines for nondiscriminatory selection that provide direction for validation. In *Albemarle*, the company's validation efforts were found deficient. The Court's decision established that "the EEOC guidelines are 'entitled to great deference' and as measured against these guidelines, found the company's validation study deficient."[26]

Implications of the Court's decision are that tests for entry-level jobs cannot be based on a relationship with higher-level jobs (1) that are not reached automatically, (2) that are not stable in their job content, and (3) for which employees change in their ability to perform the job.[27] Since there has been substantial disagreement on the validation guidelines or principles that are to be applied by federal enforcement agencies and there is much litigation,[28] the personnel practitioner must be diligent in seeking out the latest guidelines or principles to apply and must monitor court decisions closely.[29] A summary of the federal government's Uniform Guidelines on Employee Selection Procedures is presented in Chapter 17, which deals with equal employment opportunity. One feature of the guidelines is that a selection procedure does not have to be validated as long as it does not have any adverse impact on minorities and females.[30]

A final area to be discussed concerns exceptions to the prohibitions against consideration of job applicants on the basis of religion, sex, national origin, or age. Title VII of the Civil Rights Acts states the following:

> it shall not be an unlawful employment practice for an employer to hire and employ employees . . . in those certain instances where religion, sex, or national origin is a bona fide occupational qualification reasonably necessary to the normal operation of that particular business or enterprise.[31]

Furthermore, there can be bona fide occupational qualifications (BFOQs) that permit consideration of age in selection under the Age Discrimination in Employment Act.[32] Some examples of valid BFOQs are (1) for religion—hiring only Orthodox Jews to perform rituals necessary in the preparation of kosher meats; (2) for sex—hiring only males to be male washroom attendants; (3) for national origin—hiring only Chinese cooks and staff for a Chinese restaurant; and (4) for age—hiring only a young actor for the role of a youthful character.[33] It should be noted that, although there are certainly situations in which other BFOQs to the prohibitions against using religion, sex, national origin, and age as selection criteria exist, they apply in very restrictive situations. In the next section, the procedures and tools that are used in selection are considered.

SELECTION PROCEDURES AND TOOLS

In this section, the various selection procedures and instruments are considered. Even though it is commonly recognized that selection tests should be valid for both legal and economic reasons, it is less commonly acknowledged that the validity requirement also pertains to all selection activities and procedures such as interviews. A simple rule of thumb to bear in mind when considering selection procedures and tools is that, if the information to be obtained cannot be related to the prediction of job performance or basic reporting or record-keeping requirements, it probably should not be collected. The first selection tool to be considered is the application blank.

Application Blanks

The interview with Mike Hornbuckle revealed that an applicant's work history is an important factor in the selection of hourly employees at American Tourister. Application blanks obviously provide a relatively efficient means of collecting such information from job applicants in an orderly and consistent manner.

Such information may be used for both basic screening purposes in determining whether the applicant meets the minimum requirements of the job specification and record-keeping requirements. Application blanks provide a much more cost-efficient means of collecting basic information than the practice of collecting such information in personal interviews (although this seems to be a somewhat all too common practice). Nonetheless, there are limitations to the use of application blanks. The disadvantages are that (1) application blanks require careful preparation, (2) when completed they may contain sensitive information that must be safeguarded, (3) there is no universal form that is appropriate for all jobs (especially higher-level jobs), and (4) the information collected may be inaccurate.

One study of low-skilled job applicants found considerable inaccuracies in reasons for leaving the previous job, time spent on the previous job, and salary in the previous job.[34] Conversely, another study of employed police officers found a high degree of agreement between verified information and that obtained by use of an experimental application blank. However, in this study, the subjects were already employed and were not under pressure to obtain a job.[35]

Thus, it would appear to be a good practice to verify application blank information, perhaps on a sampling basis. The *Washington Post*'s recent experience, in which one of its reporters received a Pulitzer prize for a fabricated story, revealed the importance of verifying self-reported information obtained on application forms or resumés. In the *Washington Post* case, it was found that the reporter was hired on the basis of educational credentials that were nonexistent. The obvious implication of this incident is that, had the paper followed the sound personnel practice of verifying job applicant information, the reporter would probably not have been hired in the first place and the paper could have been spared the substantial embarrassment of having to repudiate the story and award. However Mike Hornbuckle noted that American Tourister does not provide much information to other companies to avoid potential litigation.

The information sought on application forms should conform with equal employment opportunity requirements. Application forms or pre-employment inquiries can be illegal or be viewed as evidence of discrimination or an intent to discriminate if they ask information on certain applicant characteristics. A good rule to use in eliminating questions that are a potential source of difficulty is the following: "any question that tends to identify an applicant as a member of a protected group, or any question that tends on the average to disfavor members of a protected group, is a problem question."[36] Although the particular circumstances determine whether a question is permissable, blanks or questions seeking information on the following may cause potential problems: color of hair and eyes, height (with exceptions), weight (with exceptions), marital status, child care arrangements (when asked for women only), Saturday or Sunday work availability, national origin, and arrests. Furthermore, questions on military discharge conditions may be inappropriate. Even questions on criminal convictions may be inappropriate as automatic rejection criteria for job applicants. Finally, even questions on age and education can present problems. Because of the obvious link between age and age discrimination, it has been recommended that the date of birth should be requested instead of age. Questions on education should include provisions for nontraditional or less formal means of education such as on-the-job training and educational equivalence examinations.[37]

A recommended procedure for obtaining potentially troublesome information that is needed legitimately involves a two-stage information collection process. Potentially troublesome information, such as age or number of dependents, can be collected after hiring the applicant. In this manner, the hiring decision is not affected by information that could be viewed as the basis for discrimination.[38]

Weighted Application Blanks

Weighted application blanks (WAB) go a step beyond application blanks by providing a numerical score that reflects the job applicant's likelihood of succeeding on the job. Responses to the various items on the blank are given numerical values that reflect both the importance of the factor, such as years of experience in a similar job, and the degree to which the particular applicant possesses a characteristic, such as six years of experience.

The process of developing a weighted application blank essentially involves dividing present employees doing a particular job into two groups of good and poor performers on the basis of criteria, such as performance criteria, and then comparing their responses on the various application blank items. A coding scheme is developed for the various items, and after comparison of the responses on the items, those items that discriminate between the good and poor performers are retained for the weighted form. A trial and error approach may be utilized to develop weights for the various items that result in overall application blank scores that provide maximum separation of the two groups. As a final step, the items and weighting scheme are employed to predict whether employees in a separate holdout group are good or poor employees. If the weighted application blank is able to predict accurately the good and poor employees in the holdout group, then there is evidence that the instrument is a valid selection device for the particular job for which it was developed. One limitation, however, is that as a rule of thumb, each of the two groups used to develop the blank should contain at least fifty employees, whereas each of the two holdout groups require at least twenty-five employees. Nonetheless, the WAB provides a quick means of assessing the job applicants, and it can be used readily in conjunction with other selection tools.[39]

Tests

Several different types of tests are used in personnel selection. Furthermore, there are a number of ways in which these tests can be classified. Table 7-3 presents a synthesis of some of the more common classifications.[40] By examining each category of tests in Table 7-3, we should be able to gain a basic understanding of selection tests.

CONTENT OF TESTS. We will begin our discussion according to the content of tests. There are several different ways that tests may be described according to content. We can categorize according to content as follows: aptitude tests, achievement or trade tests, and motivation tests.

Aptitude Tests. Aptitude tests are designed to measure a job applicant's potential to complete a training program, perform a job that he or she has not performed before, or to grow and develop in the future.[41] There are two general types of aptitude tests: (1) cognitive, which measures mental or intellectual aptitudes, and (2) motor, which measures physical dimensions such as manual dexterity or hand-eye coordination.[42] Examples of cognitive aptitude tests are the Differential Aptitude Tests (DAT) and the Flanagan Aptitude Classification Tests (FACT), which measure such facets of

Table 7-3

Classification of Selection Tests[1]

I. Content
   A. Aptitude tests
      1. Cognitive
      2. Motor
   B. Achievement or trade tests
   C. Motivation tests
      1. Interest
      2. Personality
      3. Job preference
II. Method of administration
   A. Number of subjects
      1. Individual
      2. Group
   B. Means of testing
      1. Individual
      2. Paper and pencil or group
      3. Performance
         a. Recognition
         b. Simulation
         c. Work sample
   C. Time allocated
      1. Speed
      2. Power

[1]There is some overlap in these categories, such as between aptitude and achievement tests and between aptitude and personality tests.

intellectual aptitude as numerical ability, abstract reasoning, and coding.[43] Examples of motor aptitude tests are the Purdue Pegboard, which measures dexterity skills that might be useful in packing operations, and the Bennett Hand-Tool Dexterity Test.[44]

Achievement or Trade Tests. Achievement or trade tests measure abilities, skills, or knowledge that have been acquired through training or job experience. Examples of such tests are the Purdue Test for Electricians, which measures knowledge of electrical devices, circuits, wiring, and so on, and the Purdue Test for Machinists and Machine Operators, which measures knowledge of milling machines, lathes and the like.[45] Examples of the items that might be found on a trade test for welders are presented by Figure 7-2.

Motivation Tests. The final content category consists of tests that are designed to measure the motivation of the applicant. As Figure 7-3 indicates, three types of tests fall under this heading: interest inventories, personality tests, and job preference measures. It has been found that motivation tests do not generally provide a good indication of job performance, although such measures may be predictive of job tenure and satisfaction. However, there are some situations in which personality tests have been used successfully in predicting job success, particularly for managerial personnel.[46] Examples of questions that might be found on a test that measures motivation are presented in Figure 7-3. Interest tests may be useful in placement decisions, and there have been some successful applications of interest inventories in blue-collar jobs.[47] Because interest inventories have been subject to faking, some interest inventories now have controls for this.

Examples of personality tests are the Thurstone Temperament Survey (TTS) and the California Psychological Inventory (CPI). The Strong Vocational Interest Blank (SVIB) and Kuder Preference Records are two well-known interest inventories.[48] Finally, the Job Diagnostic Survey (JDS) is an example of a measure of job preference in that it determines the aspects of jobs that are preferred by employees.[49]

METHOD OF ADMINISTRATION. The next category in Table 7-3 is the method of administration. Tests may be classified broadly as either individually or group administered.

Individual. Individually administered tests require the tester actually to give the test through such actions as reading questions and interpreting the answers, recording responses to puzzles, and timing the applicant in various exercises. Examples of individually administered tests are the Wechsler Adult Intelligence Scale (WAIS) and the Rorschach Ink Blot Test, which is a projective (indirect measure of personality) test. Both tests require examiners to have extensive training in their administration. Because such tests require highly trained administrators and they usually take a long time to administer, they are too expensive to be of much use in most personnel selection decisions. Nonetheless, they may provide a higher degree of accuracy (as in the case of an intelligence test such as the WAIS) than can be obtained ordinarily with group tests.

Paper and Pencil or Group. Paper and pencil or group tests obviously are less expensive to administer. Contrary to their designation as "group" tests, such tests may be given to job applicants on an individual basis. Typically, such tests are of the paper-

Figure 7-2

Examples of Types of Questions That Might Be Used in a Trade Test for Welders

_____ 1. What should be done first in shutting off an exyacetylene torch?
a. Shut off the oxygen at the torch.
b. Shut off the oxygen at the tank.
c. Shut off the acetylene at the torch.
d. Shut off the acetylene at the tank.
e. Shut off both the oxygen and acetylene simultaneously at the torch.

_____ 2. Which of the following materials produces toxic fumes when welded?
a. Heat-treated steel.
b. Galvanized steel.
c. Cast iron.
d. Stainless steel.
e. None of the above.

_____ 3. What is the proper amp setting for arc welding butt welds on one-quarter inch steel plate?
a. 70 amps.
b. 90 amps.
c. 110 amps.
d. 130 amps.
e. 150 amps.

_____ 4. Which of the following is an unsafe practice when arc welding?
a. Chipping slag off beads immediately after the completion of welding.
b. Changing electrodes before shutting off the power.
c. Remove the ground connector before shutting off the power.
d. All of the above are unsafe practices.
e. None of the above is an unsafe practice.

_____ 5. What is the amp range for 1/8 inch electrodes when used on mild steel?
a. 20–75.
b. 50–90
c. 90–125
d. 100–170.
e. 120–145.

_____ 6. Which of the following is a recommended method for checking regulator connection leaks on acytylene tanks?
a. Put your ear close to the tank and listen for leaks.
b. Brush soapy water on the connections and look for bubbies.
c. Observe the movement in pressure guage settings over a five minute interval.
d. All of the above are correct.
e. None of the above is correct.

Figure 7-3

Examples of Types of Questions That Might Be Used to Assess Dimensions of Motivation

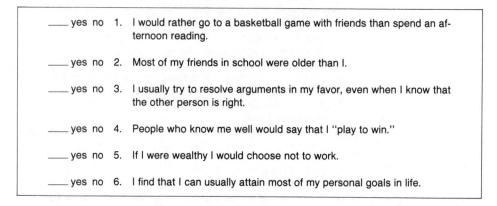

_____ yes no   1. I would rather go to a basketball game with friends than spend an afternoon reading.

_____ yes no   2. Most of my friends in school were older than I.

_____ yes no   3. I usually try to resolve arguments in my favor, even when I know that the other person is right.

_____ yes no   4. People who know me well would say that I "play to win."

_____ yes no   5. If I were wealthy I would choose not to work.

_____ yes no   6. I find that I can usually attain most of my personal goals in life.

and-pencil variety and may be scored by comparing the applicant's responses with the responses of a large number of subjects that serve as the test's norms.

Performance Tests. Another means of testing job applicants is through performance testing. In performance tests, the applicants do the work or a sample (real or simulated) of the work required in the job. Recognition tests are performance tests in which the result of the applicant's work is evaluated.[50] An example might be a collection of drawings that a job applicant would submit for evaluation. A simulation performance test would have the applicant perform a task that would ordinarily be a part of the job. An example of a simulation performance test for a labor relations specialist might involve having the applicant handle a simulated grievance. The last type of performance test, the work sample, simply requires the job applicant to do a job task for a brief period, such as having an applicant for a machinist's job operate a turret lathe for two hours.

Time Allocated. The final means of classifying tests pertains to the time allocated for the test. In speed tests, the applicant has only a limited amount of time in which to complete the items. A typing test where the score is based on the number of words typed in a time period is an example. Conversely, in power tests, the applicant is given so much time to complete the test that he or she is not hurried in his or her responses. In power tests, the items to be completed may be arranged in increasing order of difficulty. Since it has been found that older applicants may not perform on speed tests at a level that indicates their ability to perform on the job, they may be penalized unfairly. Therefore, in some cases power tests may be more appropriate.[51]

TESTING ETHICS AND OTHER CONSIDERATIONS.   Before leaving the subject of testing, we should bear in mind that testing is still a controversial issue. Tests have received a great deal of adverse publicity as a result of some abuses. Much of the criticism is probably unwarranted, but some of it has a legitimate basis. One common criticism is that carefully designed tests are often administered and interpreted by unqualified individuals. Such persons are frequently ignorant of the fact that tests are only samples of behavior, ability, knowledge, or attitudes. Consequently, small differences in scores are incorrectly afforded great meaning. Untrained testers have also been frequently guilty of failing to inform job applicants of the true purpose or real nature of selection tests. In the case of personality tests, where very sensitive information is involved, the failure to inform job applicants about the nature of such tests indicates a serious breach of ethics. Finally, the results of selection tests that are of a sensitive nature should be kept confidential. Only those persons who have a legitimate need for such information should be allowed access.

Interviews

The importance of interviews in selection was demonstrated in the interview with Mike Hornbuckle. Mike noted that American Tourister relies heavily on interviews for employee selection. Although selection decisions almost invariably involve personal interviews of the job applicants in one form or another, the overwhelming use of interviews provides no reason to assume that they are conducted properly or that the process is an effective means of personnel selection. In fact, a vast literature has evolved that details the limitations of the interview as a valid selection procedure. However, in spite of its weaknesses, the interview is likely to remain a central element in the personnel selection process, and we need to focus our attention on making good use of interviews and improving their validity.

To understand how to conduct valid interviews or to use the procedure as a valid part of the selection process, we can benefit from a discussion of what not to do in interviewing and the biases that typically occur. By first understanding the limitations of the process, we can better understand how to improve it.

Interviewing Biases and Errors

HALO EFFECT.   When a job applicant is interviewed, the underlying selection logic is that the applicant should be assessed on several dimensions that are critical for job performance. Unfortunately, this is frequently not the case, since the interviewers often allow their evaluation of the applicant on one dimension to affect their evaluation on other dimensions. In other words, the halo effect occurs when the interviewer's evaluation on one dimension carries over in the evaluations on other dimensions. If the candidate is exceptionally strong or weak on one dimension, it is falsely concluded that the candidate is similarly strong or weak on other dimensions.[52]

EFFECT OF NEGATIVE INFORMATION.   Frequently, negative information is afforded more weight than positive information. Likewise, interviews are often conducted as a search for negative information.[53] As soon as any negative information is uncovered, the job candidate may be "selected out." This practice points out the need to consider the reward system that is in effect for the interviewer. We need to consider what behaviors are actually rewarded or negatively sanctioned.

It may be that the interviewer will be adversely affected if he or she recommends a candidate who subsequently turns out to be an unsatisfactory performer. On the other hand, the interviewer may not receive a positive reward for recommending a candidate who turns out to be a strong performer because others take credit for the applicant's success. It may be quite likely that the interviewer will face some negative consequences for recommending the hiring of a candidate who turns out to be a poor performer. There is certainly less risk (under most circumstances) that the failure to recommend a strong candidate will be followed by a negative consequence because the interviewer's error will typically go undetected. An exception might occur in a small, very specialized labor market, such as in professional athletics or other sectors of the entertainment industry. Thus, under typical circumstances, there may be a strong incentive for the interviewer to avoid making a detectable error by rejecting flawed applicants who might have a good chance of succeeding. He or she may also try to minimize the likelihood of recommending an applicant who could turn out to be unsatisfactory—a high-potential, high-risk candidate.

STEREOTYPES OF THE IDEAL CANDIDATE. Many interviewers have a mental image or stereotype of the ideal job applicant.[54] Furthermore, this image may not bear a close resemblance to the realistic requirements for the job. It may vary greatly between interviewers from the same organization, and it may not take into consideration the fact that the job may be performed quite successfully by individuals who possess widely differing characteristics. Thus, if stereotypes are relied on extensively, the interviewer proceeds by determining whether each applicant fits the "mold" and then recommends only those who fit the stereotype. Even if interviewers are successful in pursuing common stereotyped candidates and eventually hire such candidates, negative long-run consequences for the organization might result from a work force that is too homogeneous.

EXPECTATIONS. A recent study has attempted to explain how interviewers' preinterview expectations about job applicants can affect applicant evaluations and hiring decisions. Expectations based on prior knowledge of applicants' success or failure in work or educational experiences were found to affect evaluations of interview transcripts and simulated hiring decisions. Specifically, the study found that

> different expectancies can indeed result in the same information being perceived and interpreted in a different manner . . . an interviewer who begins an interview with an unfavorable expectancy may tend to give an applicant less credit for past accomplishments, may blame the applicant more for past failures, and may ultimately be more likely to decide that the applicant is unacceptable.[55]

Thus, the interview may be biased by perceptual processes at work even prior to the interview.

CONTRAST EFFECTS. Another error that affects interviewers' evaluations of job applicants is the impact of the evaluation of preceding applicants.[56] Thus, if an applicant of only average ability is preceded by extremely weak applicants, his or her evaluation may be much higher than it would have been had the preceding applicants been quite promising.

EARLY DECISIONS.   When interviews are conducted in an unstructured format—that is, without regard to asking the same questions, soliciting the same information from all applicants, or assessing each of the applicants' strengths on all dimensions—the interviewer is prone to make a decision about the applicant very early in the interview.[57]

"SIMILAR TO ME" EFFECT.   It has been found that, when the job applicant and interviewer have similar biographical characteristics, the applicant tends to be evaluated more favorably.[58] Racial prejudice can easily influence an applicant's evaluation through this effect.

PRIMACY AND RECENCY EFFECTS.   The order in which positive and negative information is received in an interview may have an effect on the evaluation of job applicants. When the first information is weighted more heavily, a primacy effect is operating; when the most recently received information is weighted more heavily, a recency effect is at work. There is some evidence that, when favorable information is received before unfavorable, the applicant is rated more favorably (a primacy effect);[59] however, these order effects may be moderated or influenced by other factors such as the type of information being received.[60] It is difficult to reach strong conclusions on these effects, but we should at least be aware that the order in which information is received can affect applicant evaluations.

APPLICANT CHARACTERISTICS.   Interviewers sometimes assume incorrectly that they can assess several applicant traits validly through the selection interview. A good idea of an applicant's intelligence or mental ability probably can be obtained through interviews, but interviews are not good means for assessing such characteristics as creativity, loyalty, dependability, honesty, and other traits that are not manifested during the interview.[61]

Means of Improving Interviews

Many of the mistakes in interviewing are made by untrained interviewers. For many managers, interviewing is only an occasional duty, and the time required to develop good interviewing skills must come at the expense of other more closely evaluated duties. Nevertheless, if interviewing is to serve as a valid phase of the selection process, training is necessary so that interviewing skills may be improved. Simple instructions and practice sessions with mock interviews can help the interviewer to avoid asking questions that may be answered with a "yes" or "no," to avoid communicating desired responses through leading questions, and to enable the interviewer to probe the applicant's responses more thoroughly. Simple probing techniques such as the two-stage method are quite useful. For example, with the two-stage method, the interviewer may ask the applicant to identify the least desirable duty in his or her previous job. After the applicant identifies the duty, the interviewer might ask the applicant to explain why the particular duty was undesirable. In this manner, the interviewer is better able to determine whether certain aspects of the new job may be undesirable to the applicant as well. Furthermore, it is probably not safe to assume that even experienced interviewers are performing the task correctly, as there is some evidence that the data obtained by experienced interviewers are no more reliable than that obtained by inexperienced interviewers.[62]

There are several other means of improving interviewing validity so that many of the errors cited may be avoided or their adverse effects reduced. One of the most effective means of avoiding many of these errors is through the use of structured interviews, particularly with inexperienced interviewers. In the structured interview, the interviewer asks all applicants the same questions or similar questions. In this manner, the applicants' responses can be compared on the same dimensions. This practice also tends to improve interrater reliability (agreement among interviewers) because all interviewers have obtained information on the same dimensions.[63] The use of structured interviews also tends to reduce the early-decision error because the interviewer is forced to assess the applicant on several dimensions, not just an overall or global impression. This is particularly true if the interviewer is required to pass along written comments on each dimension.[64] Unstructured interviews should probably be used only by skilled interviewers, because such an approach, when used by an unskilled interviewer, may deteriorate into a rambling discussion of irrelevant issues.

To improve control of the impact of negative information, interviewers should be required to consider the applicant's strengths on all necessary dimensions before making the decision to recommend acceptance or rejection.[65] Stereotyping errors may be reduced by developing an accurate profile of acceptable job applicants and then communicating this profile or outline of acceptable attributes to all interviewers.[66] Early-decision errors may also be reduced by requiring interviewers to conduct longer interviews. However, more study is needed before we can reach a definitive conclusion on this suggestion.[67]

Relatively simple training sessions in which the halo error is explained followed by instructions to minimize such an evaluation of behaviors have been shown to be capable of reducing halo errors.[68] Workshops in which interviewer trainees have rated videotapes of job applicants and then have been critiqued on their evaluations have been shown to be capable of reducing halo errors, contrast effect errors, "similar to me" errors, and first-impression or early-decision errors.[69]

Another means of improving the validity of selection interviews is to utilize multiple interviewers. The use of multiple interviewers, although time consuming, is an approach commonly employed for selecting management and professional personnel today. The proper role for the interview should also be better understood. It is only one of many selection tools; however, it seems particularly well suited for use in "filling in gaps" in information about applicants and in determining how the applicant will "fit in" with the employee group when interpersonal relationships are critical.

Recent research has identified some potential areas through which interviewing may be better understood and improved. One study based on simulated employment interviews analyzed the process through which perceptions of personality characteristics are formed and inferences are drawn regarding applicants' suitability for different occupations. It was found that inferences drawn from brief occupationally related be-havioral descriptions of individuals could predict to some extent (particularly with group consensus) personality-related behavior. A question for future research concerns the role that such inferences may play in interviewer decision making.[70] Another study has found that interviewers can make better decisions on an applicant's suitability for a job when the interviewer is required to assess the job applicant on specific behavioral dimensions. Requirements for rating on such dimensions, which are relevant to job performance, enable better interviewer performance than having the interviewer rate applicants on more general dimensions.[71]

Finally, we must also remember that, not only does the interviewer obtain information about the job applicant, but during the interview, information about the employer is conveyed to the applicant. Even if the applicant is not hired, a well-conducted interview and courteous treatment may cause the applicant to apply again in future years or to become a customer or client of the organization. Conversely, a poorly conceived interview that is conducted discourteously by an unprofessional interviewer can create a future opponent for the employer. Likewise, the use of a special type of interview, the stress interview, can damage the employer's image.

> **Stress interview:** stresses the job applicant under the rationale that the employer needs to know how the applicant will react under pressure.

Pressure or stress may be induced by such methods as having the interviewer disagree or argue with whatever the applicant says. Although this is probably an exaggeration, unless the employer is hiring spies who need to withstand the stress of interrogation and torture, the adverse impression formed by job applicants probably outweighs the questionable benefits of this technique, which also may be lacking in validity.

References

Although for many jobs, especially higher-level management or professional positions, reference letters are required as a part of the selection process, their value is quite questionable. Unless the writer of the reference letter is known personally or by reputation, little weight can be placed on references. One reason for their lack of utility is that, if the information about the applicant is negative (as indicated by Mike Hornbuckle), many former employers or associates are reluctant to report such information, particularly in a letter. One may have a better chance of obtaining more accurate information through telephone contacts with former employers or associates. Because there has been litigation over negative information provided in references by former employers, some employers now require a form that authorizes the release of such information.[72]

As indicated earlier, however, there are some situations in which the references are known and play a valuable part in the selection process. An example is in the labor market for management professors. There are not very many management professors throughout the entire United States. Whenever reference letters are received for an applicant for a faculty position, the chances are usually quite good that one of the faculty members will know the reference personally. Some other professions and occupations are similar insofar as extensive knowledge of members of the profession or occupation is available.

Assessment Centers

A selection process has evolved that combines many other selection tools such as interviews, various testing procedures, and specially developed situational exercises that simulate certain aspects of jobs. This combined assessment process is called an assessment center. It is called a center because the assessment procedure has been conducted frequently over a period of one day to a week at locations that are remote from the workplace. Since assessment centers are used primarily in the selection and development of managerial and sales personnel, we discuss the subject in more depth in the next chapter.

Physical Examinations

Some jobs require certain physical capabilities. Airline pilots must have excellent vision, depth perception, and be in otherwise good physical condition. Likewise, deep-sea divers must be able to withstand the rigors of severe pressure and effects of deep water. We can probably think of other jobs that require extraordinary physical abilities. In these jobs, the physical examination is a critical part of the selection process. However, most jobs do not require such physical abilities, and for these jobs, the physical examination is not really a selection tool. If a physical examination is required, it is usually reserved as a last step in the process and is conducted only if a tentative decision has been made to hire the applicant. One reason for conducting the physical examination is to avoid placing an individual in a job where a physical problem might be aggravated by the job.[73] The physical examination may also be used to establish a baseline of the applicant's health at the time of hiring. Such information may be useful for evaluating claims of job-related injuries or illnesses and may be required by the employer's insurance carrier. Thus the physical examination can serve as a means of protecting the employer from hiring an individual who could become a substantial financial liability.

Polygraph Examinations

Polygraph examinations are utilized occasionally when the employer feels that the honesty of employees is critical. Polygraph examinations (lie detector examinations) are purported to establish whether an applicant is being truthful about his or her background. For example, has the applicant ever stolen anything from an employer? Unfortunately, two aspects about polygraph examinations make their use in personnel selection questionable. The first is that the polygraph examination has questionable validity,[74] and the second is that it can be perceived by prospective employees as an invasion of their privacy. One prominent western brewery has been charged by the union representing its employees of invading the privacy of its employees through the use of polygraph examinations. Because of the problems with polygraph examinations, its use is sometimes regulated: "The use of polygraphs as a condition of employment in private industry is restricted in 15 states."[75]

SELECTION STRATEGY

We have discussed several selection tools in this chapter, but we have not yet addressed how the information obtained from them is combined in making a decision as to whether or not to hire an applicant. We should note that hiring decisions depend on the number of applicants relative to the number of position vacancies. A low selection ratio (proportion of individuals hired relative to number of applicants) means that the firm is able to impose relatively high standards.[76] Low selection ratios may result from favorable (to the employer) labor market conditions or from intensive recruiting activities that increase the pool of job applicants.

Selection is commonly conducted in a multiple-hurdle approach, in which not every job applicant is subjected to all selection tools and procedures. Because of economic considerations, it is more efficieint to arrange the selection tools sequentially in a number of steps or hurdles so that, if the applicant fails to meet the standards on one of these steps, he or she is rejected at that point and does not proceed through all steps. A typical sequence of steps might be (1) initial screening, (2) filling out an application blank, (3) testing, (4) in-depth interviewing, and (5) physical examination. After successfully proceeding through all the steps (excluding the physical examination), the candidate is then considered along with all other applicants who have likewise made it through all the hurdles. The decision of who to hire from this pool may be made in a mechanical or systematic manner, in which scores or evaluations that are expressed in quantitative terms are combined and evaluated on the basis of their validity and reliability.

The other approach may be termed a clinical approach, in which each input from the selection tools is combined more or less subjectively. Although the systematic approach of combining these inputs is capable of producing somewhat better decisions, the clinical approach is the only one possible when only a few employees are hired for each job and the systematic approach cannot be validated.[77]

SUMMARY

In this chapter, we emphasized the importance of using selection tools that are both valid and reliable. The predictive and concurrent methods of validation were described in detail, and the means of determining their reliabilities were discussed. After the discussion of these psychometric properties, we discussed the legal environment of selection. We found that two U.S. Supreme Court decisions have had a great impact on personnel selection. The *Griggs* v. *Duke Power Company* case established that selection procedures must be valid. The *Albemarle Paper Company* v. *Moody* case established that the guidelines adopted by the EEOC to enforce the nondiscrimination provisions of the Civil Rights Act must be followed in selection tool validation.

Next we examined the various selection tools: application blanks, weighted application blanks, tests, interviews, references, assessment centers, physical examinations, and polygraph examinations. We found that interviews are subject to several errors and biases that can be controlled to some degree through interviewer training. Finally, we considered the systematic and clinical methods of combining information on job applicants for use in making the hiring decision.

INTERVIEW WRAP-UP

Because of the relatively low skill requirements for most of the hourly jobs at American Tourister, testing is not used and, instead, selection decisions are based largely on evaluations of the applicants' work histories and personal interviews. The necessity of processing large numbers of applicants can require the personnel specialist to make a rapid assessment of the applicant's capabilities and likelihood of fitting in with the work force. —Mike Hornbuckle, director of human resources, American Tourister.

WHAT MANAGERS SHOULD DO REGARDING PERSONNEL MANAGEMENT ACTIVITIES

1. Managers should be aware of the strengths and weaknesses of the various selection tools.

2. Managers need to be aware of the legal environment of personnel selection so that they do not ask applicants illegal questions or discriminate in some other way in violation of the law. Likewise, they should know the law well enough so that they will not be afraid to conduct a good interview and will be able to employ other selection practices in such a manner that will allow them to hire good employees.

3. Managers need to know the errors and biases that occur frequently in interviewing. They should realize that their interviewing skills may need improvement and that they can benefit from being better interviewers.

REVIEW QUESTIONS

1. Explain how you would determine the predictive validity of a test. How would you establish the predictive validity for an interview?

2. Describe the different methods of determining the reliability of a selection tool.

3. What are the different laws that must be considered in personnel selection?

4. Explain how a weighted application blank is developed.

5. Describe the different types of tests that are used in personnel selection.

6. What are some biases or errors that frequently affect interviewers' evaluations of job applicants?

7. How can interviewing be improved?

KEY CONCEPTS

Achievement test	Parallel forms reliability
Aptitude test	Predictive validity
BFOQ	Primacy and recency effects
Coefficient alpha	Psychometric properties
Concurrent validity	Reliability
Construct validity	Selection strategy
Content validity	"Similar to me" effect
Contrast effect	Split-halves reliability
Criterion-based validity	Synthetic validity
Differential validity	Test-retest reliability
Face validity	Validity
Halo effect	Weighted application blank
Motivation test	Work sample

CASE

THE "RECENT GRADUATE" INTERVIEW

Southwest Casualty and Diversified Risk, Inc., is a large insurance company based in Dallas, Texas. To help manage its investment portfolio, the Investments Department has decided to hire several recent college graduates with majors in finance. This year during the campus recruiting season, the Personnel Department's experienced employment specialists and the Investment Department's managers have been working day and night in helping the Legal Department prepare a defense for a lawsuit that claims that the Investments Department has discriminated against women. Since the former employees who have filed the suit are asking for $1.7 million in damages, preparations for the lawsuit have been given top priority.

As a result of the lawsuit, the task of recruiting from universities in the Southwest, from which the company typically hires, has been given to Jeff Rinehart, a recent graduate from a major university in the region. Although Jeff does not work in the Personnel Department, he has had great success as a financial analyst during his two years in the Investments Department. The vice-president for investments, Mr. Wolfson, has insisted that Jeff is the right person to do the job. He feels that, as a bright, recent graduate, Jeff can do a good job in screening candidates to bring in for intensive interviews at the home office in Dallas. The following is an account of how Jeff has been conducting the interviews.

Jeff is greatly impressed by the fact that he has been assigned to do the recruiting and initial interviews for the Investments Department. He has no formal training in interviewing or selection; however, he feels that he is a good judge of people and that because he is intelligent and has good analytical skills he can "size up" people very quickly. Jeff has been busy with his regular job and has not taken the time to read any of the resumés that the university placement offices have sent him prior to the interviews. He prefers to take five minutes during each interview to read the resumé while the job candidate sits across the table from him. Aside from obtaining some basic information about the candidate through this quick review of the resumé, Jeff is also interested in what the candidate does while he is reading the resumé. Jeff read an article on body language recently and feels that it makes a great deal of intuitive sense. Thus, if the candidate appears to move about in the chair while Jeff reads the resumé, he mentally subtracts points because the candidate lacks self-confidence.

After reading the resumé, Jeff leans back in his chair, puts his feet on the table, and asks the following question to determine how assertive the candidate is: "So what makes you think you are good enough to work in the Investments Department?" If the candidate mentions his good grades, Jeff then says that good grades do not mean anything after one goes to work and advises the candidate to join some campus organizations. Other responses are listened to only briefly before Jeff mentally tunes out in preparation for his next question. He views this question as serving a secondary purpose of communicating a warning that the company is looking for the very best candidates like himself.

Typically, Jeff has asked questions about the candidates' family background to determine whether they come from a family sufficiently affluent to know something about investments. All the female candidates have been asked whether they are engaged and whether they eventually want to get married and have children. Although Jeff has been with the firm for only two years, he has heard some of the managers complain about women who quit to have children. He has asked a few of the most attractive women to go to lunch with him so that he can tell them more about the company. Most of the remainder of the time in each interview has been filled with Jeff telling the candidate all about the company, its fringe benefits, and what the candidates need to do to improve their marketability.

As a result of Jeff's interviews, he has recommended twenty-two candidates for home office interviews. Most of the recommended candidates "look" like businessmen in that they are handsome, tall, and usually have belonged to a fraternity. Because Jeff has been aware of the firm's affirmative action goals, he also recommended one black candidate and three female candidates, even though one of the women has taken only the basic finance course. Despite her lack of a strong finance background, Jeff feels that the firm will hire her because she has a very pleasant personality, is quite attractive, and has good verbal skills.

CASE QUESTIONS

1. Comment on Jeff's interviewing practices.

2. Have you experienced an interview in which any similar behavior occurred? What were your experiences?

3. What do you think the result of Jeff's interviewing will be in the short run? What about the long run?

4. What can you conclude about the firm's initial screening and recruiting practices?

NOTES

[1] M. D. Dunnette, *Personnel Selection and Placement* (Belmont, Calif.: Brooks/Cole, 1966).

[2] A. Howard, "An Assessment of Assessment Centers," *Academy of Management Journal,* 17 (1974), 115–134.

[3] Dunnette, *Personnel Selection and Placement.*

[4] Ibid.

[5] B. Schneider, *Staffing Organizations* (Santa Monica, Calif.: Goodyear, 1976).

[6] Dunnette, *Personnel Selection and Placement.*

[7] K. W. Wexley and G. A. Yukl, *Organizational Behavior and Personnel Psychology* (Homewood, Ill.: Irwin, 1977); Schneider, *Staffing Organizations.*

[8] Schneider, *Staffing Organizations;* Dunnette, *Personnel Selection and Placement.*

[9] C. H. Lawshe and M. J. Balma, *Principles of Personnel Testing,* 2nd ed. (New York: McGraw-Hill, 1966).

[10] Lawshe and Balma, *Principles of Personnel Selection;* W. F. Cascio, *Applied Psychology in Personnel Management* (Reston, Va.: Reston, 1978).

[11] Lawshe and Balma, *Principles of Personnel Selection.*

[12] Ibid.

[13] Several sources provide excellent treatments of the split-halves and other techniques of determining reliability: Cascio, *Applied Psychology in Personnel Management;* Dunnette, *Personnel Selection and Placement;* Lawshe and Balma, *Principles of Personnel Selection;* J. C. Nunnally, *Psychometric Theory,* 2nd ed. (New York: McGraw-Hill, 1978).

[14] Nunnally, *Psychometric Theory.*

[15] Section 703(a), Civil Rights Act of 1964.

[16] E. M. Idelson, U.S. Equal Opportunity Commission, *Affirmative Action and Equal Employment: A Guidebook for Employers,* Vol. 1 (Washington, D.C.: Government Printing Office, 1974), pp. 12–13.

[17] Bureau of National Affairs, *Fair Employment Practices Manual* (Washington, D.C.: Bureau of National Affairs, 1981), p. 411:51.

[18] Ibid., p. 411:251.

[19] Section 4(a) (1), Age Discrimination in Employment Act of 1967, P.L. 90–202 (as amended in 1978).

[20]Section 12(a), Age Discrimination in Employment Act of 1967, P.L. 90–202 (as amended in 1978).

[21]Section 11(b), Age Discrimination in Employment Act of 1967, P.L. 90–202 (as amended in 1978).

[22]One such reference is the Bureau of National Affairs, *Fair Employment Practices Manual.*

[23]*Griggs v. Duke Power Co.,* 401 U.S. 424 (1971).

[24]Prentice-Hall, *Personnel Management—Policies and Practices, Report Bulletin 15,* Vol. 24 (Englewood Cliffs, N.J.: Prentice-Hall, January 11, 1977). 3–4.

[25]*Albemarle Paper Co. v. Moody,* 422 U.S. 405 (1975).

[26]M. G. Miner and J. B. Miner, *Employee Selection Within the Law* (Washington, D.C.: Bureau of National Affairs, 1979), p. 49.

[27]B. S. Feldacker, *Labor Guide to Labor Law* (Reston, Va.: Reston, 1980).

[28]Miner and Miner, *Employee Selection Within the Law;* R. H. Greenman and E. J. Schmertz, *Personnel Administration and the Law,* 2nd ed. (Washington, D.C.: Bureau of National Affairs, 1979).

[29]A comprehensive source on the legal environment of selection is provided by Miner and Miner, *Employee Selection Within the Law.*

[30]Equal Employment Opportunity Commission, Title 29—Labor, Chapter XIV, Part 1607—Uniform Guidelines on Employee Selection Procedures (1978), in the *Federal Register,* August 25, 1978, pp. 38290–38315.

[31]Section 703(3), Civil Rights Act of 1964.

[32]Greenman and Schmertz, *Personnel Administration and the Law.*

[33]Ibid.

[34]I. L. Goldstein, "The Application Blank: How Honest Are the Responses?" *Journal of Applied Psychology,* 55 (1971), 491–492.

[35]W. F. Cascio, "Accuracy of Verifiable Biographical Information Blank Responses," *Journal of Applied Psychology,* 60 (1975), 767–769.

[36]J. Ledvinka and R. D. Gatewood, "EEO Issues with Pre-Employment Inquiries," *The Personnel Administrator,* 22 (1977), 22–26.

[37]Ibid.

[38]Ibid.

[39]G. W. England, *Development and Use of Weighted Application Blanks,* rev. ed., Bulletin 55 (Minneapolis: Industrial Relations Center, University of Minnesota, 1971).

[40]The classification scheme presented in Table 7-3 is a synthesis of the classifications of Lawshe and Balma, *Principles of Personnel Selection;* Schneider, *Staffing Organizations;* J. P. Wanous, *Organizational Entry: Recruitment, Selection, and Socialization of Newcomers* (Reading, Mass.: Addison-Wesley, 1980); E. J. McCormick and J. Tiffin, *Industrial Psychology,* 6th ed. (Englewood Cliffs, N.J.: Prentice-Hall, 1974); E. E. Ghiselli and C. W. Brown, *Personnel and Industrial Psychology,* 2nd ed. (New York: McGraw-Hill, 1955).

[41]Wanous, *Organizational Entry.*

[42]Dunnette, *Personnel Selection and Placement.*

[43]Schneider, *Staffing Organizations.*

[44]McCormick and Tiffin, *Industrial Psychology.*

[45]Lawshe and Balma, *Principles of Personnel Selection.*

[46]Schneider, *Staffing Organization;* Wanous, *Organizational Entry.*

[47]Schneider, *Staffing Organizations*

[48]Ibid.

[49]Wanous, *Organizational Entry.*

[50]Ibid.

[51]Ghiselli and Brown, *Personnel and Industrial Psychology.*

[52]M. Hakel, "Similarity of Post-Interview Trait Rating Intercorrelations as a Contributor to Interrater Agreement in a Structured Employment Interview," *Journal of Applied Psychology,* 55 (1971), 443–448.

[53]E. C. Mayfield, "The Selection Interview—A Re-evaluation of Published Research," *Personnel Psychology,* 17 (1964), 239–260.

[54]O. R. Wright, Jr., "Summary of Research on the Selection Interview Since 1964," *Personnel Psychology,* 22 (1969), 391–413.

[55]D. H. Tucker and P. M. Rowe, "Relationship Between Expectancy, Casual Attributions, and Final Hiring Decisions in the Employment Interview," *Journal of Applied Psychology,* 64 (1979), 32–33.

[56]N. Schmitt, "Social and Situational Determinants of Interview Decisions: Implications for the Employment Interview," *Personnel Psychology,* 29 (1976), 79–101; K. N. Wexley, R. E. Sanders, and G. A. Yukl, "Training Interviewers to Eliminate Contrast Effects in Employment Interviews," *Journal of Applied Psychology,* 57 (1973), 233–236.

[57]Mayfield, "The Selection Interview"; Wright, "Summary of Research."

[58]L. M. Rand and K. N. Wexley, "Demonstration of the Effect 'Similar to Me' in Simulated Employment Interviews," *Psychological Reports,* 36 (1975), 535–544.

[59]Schmitt, "Social and Situational Determinants."

[60]M. London and M. D. Hakel, "Effects of Applicant Stereotypes, Order, and Information on Interview Impressions," *Journal of Applied Psychology,* 59 (1974), 157–162.

[61]Mayfield, "The Selection Interview"; McCormick and Tiffin, *Industrial Psychology.*

[62]Schmitt, "Social and Situational Determinants."

[63]Mayfield, "The Selection Interview."

[64]Schneider, *Staffing Organizations.*

[65]Ibid.

[66]Ibid.

[67]W. L. Tullar, T. W. Mullins, and S. A. Caldwell, "Effects of Interview Length and Applicant Quality on Interview Decision Time," *Journal of Applied Psychology,* 64 (1979), 669–674.

[68]W. C. Borman, "Effects of Instructions to Avoid Halo Error on Reliability and Validity of Performance Evaluation Ratings," *Journal of Applied Psychology,* 60 (1975), 556–560.

[69]G. P. Latham, K. N. Wexley, and E. D. Pursell, "Training Managers to Minimize Rating Errors in the Observation of Behavior," *Journal of Applied Psychology,* 60 (1975), 550–555.

[70]M. Rothstein and D. N. Jackson, "Decision Making in the Employment Interview: An Experimental Approach," *Journal of Applied Psychology,* 65 (1980), 271–283.

[71]H. G. Osburn, C. Timmreck, and D. Bigby, "Effect of Dimensional Relevance on Accuracy of Simulated Hiring Decisions by Employment Interviewers," *Journal of Applied Psychology,* 66 (1981), 159–165.

[72]Miner and Miner, *Employee Selection Within the Law.*

[73]P. S. Greenlaw and W. D. Biggs, *Modern Personnel Management* (Philadelphia: W. B. Saunders, 1979).

[74]F. Elkouri and E. A. Elkouri, *How Arbitration Works,* 3rd ed. (Washington, D.C.: Bureau of National Affairs, 1974).

[75]P. R. Sackett and P. J. Decker, "Detection of Deception in the Employment Context: A Review and Critical Analysis," *Personnel Psychology,* 32 (1979), 488.

[76]Dunnette, *Personnel Selection and Placement.*

[77]Ibid.

SELECTING MANAGERS AND PROFESSIONALS

LEARNING OBJECTIVES

After reading this chapter, you should be able to

1. Understand the special problems involved in the selection of managers.
2. Be able to discuss the various selection tools used in managerial selection.
3. Be able to describe a typical assessment center.
4. Understand the logic and validity of assessment centers.
5. Understand how such assessment center components as in-basket exercises and leaderless group discussions operate.

Jim Rogers is manager of personnel resources for NCR-Microelectronics, Fort Collins, Colorado. NCR is a multinational corporation involved in the sale of computer systems, point-of-sale terminals, financial terminals, and assorted equipment and services. NCR employs over 60,000 people, with about 230 at the Fort Collins plant. Mr. Rogers is responsible for personnel functions such as staffing and personnel relations. He has a degree in economics and a masters degree in Industrial Relations from North Texas State University. He has been with NCR for four and a half years, three of those years in his current position. He provided the following insights regarding the selection of managers and professional employees.

Interviewer: Can you describe, in general, the procedure NCR follows in selecting managerial and professional employees?

Jim Rogers: Basically, we first make contact with potential candidates over the telephone. This contact allows us to discuss the position and clarify any issues that help us and the candidate to assess our mutual interest. Once we have determined that we are mutually interested we establish an on-site interview with five or six of the people with whom this candidate will actually interact on the job. During this interview we try to assess both the technical and behavioral skills of the candidate.

Interviewer: What approaches, such as selection tests and interviews, are most useful in evaluating the managerial and professional candidates for employment?

Jim Rogers: We rely very heavily on the interview process in our initial selection of managerial employees. We do not use selection tests, per se, in this process. However, in evaluating our employees for promotion to higher levels of management, we may utilize various assessment techniques such as in-basket exercises. In these exercises we give the employee an opportunity to show how he or she would handle actual problems that will be faced at that level of management. In some cases we may use external consultants to help us make the promotion decision at these higher levels.

Interviewer: In general, what types of skills or characteristics are important in managerial or professional positions?

Jim Rogers: In these types of positions, perhaps the most important characteristics are the individual's previous work experiences and education. Beyond that, we need to separate managerial from technical professionals. With technical professionals we also look for technical competence in that area, the ability to look at data, evaluate it, and make good decisions regarding technical problems. We also look for communication and interpersonal skills since these people do not work in a vacuum. With managerial positions we look for people with positive work experiences in performing managerial duties such as leadership, planning, and organizing skills.

Interviewer: You mention "positive work experience." In terms of a new college graduate, what would be a positive work experience?

Jim Rogers: Especially for new graduates, we don't expect to find them with significant "managerial" experience. But summer work experiences, such as working on a production line, being a waiter, and so on, are positive work experiences, because they do learn how to work with others and build confidence. When they come to NCR, they will receive training and assistance in learning managerial duties.

Interviewer: How would a lower level manager prepare himself or herself to rise to a higher level position?

Jim Rogers: To rise to a higher position, people need to broaden the skills they already have. They should look at the types of responsibilities at the higher level and take additional coursework or training that provides skills to handle those responsibilities. For example, the higher position may require more understanding of complex financial matters, and they would want to take some cost accounting or financial strategy courses. They may need to develop skills in production scheduling or information systems. Basically, then, continuing education to broaden one's skills is one of the more useful ways to prepare for managerial advancement.

INTRODUCTION

Much of the material in the previous chapter on selection applies to the selection of managers and professionals; however, there are enough special considerations in managerial and professional selection to warrant separate treatment. Most of the research on managerial and professional selection has focused on the former. Thus, our discussion will devote primary attention to the selection of managers but will, from time to time, point out particular practices that are applicable to specific groups of professionals.

One area of difficulty in the selection of managers is the requirement for situation-specific abilities or characteristics. The following quotation from a comprehensive review of managerial selection studies describes this problem quite clearly:

> Throughout, we have emphasized the importance of situational effects on managerial behavior. Managerial behavior, more than most other behavior, is likely to be strongly affected by situational, as opposed to strictly individual difference, variables.[1]

Although this finding of situation specificity may initially seem contrary to intuition (i.e., the same basic principles of management should apply to many different types of organizations), we know after further reflection that various styles of management seem more appropriate in different situations. In fact, the development of contingency models of leadership rested on the premises that no one style of leadership works well in all situations and that the motivational makeup of the leader and the extent to which the leader can exercise control and influence in a situation determine the effectiveness of leadership.[2] Although leadership and management are not identical phenomena, we know that managerial effectiveness will be affected to the extent that leadership is important for the performance of managerial duties. Further, managerial effectiveness may thus be dependent on the situational requirements for particular leadership styles, as the following quotation illustrates:

> no single personality trait, trait pattern, or particular style of leader behavior assures good organizational performance in all leadership situations. A person may be a very effective leader in one situation but very ineffective in another.[3]

One study has examined the self-perceived areas of competence held by managerially oriented individuals and technically oriented specialists. The technically oriented specialist designation referred to those preferring work related more directly to the subject matter or work content of the functional areas of business such as marketing, finance, and research and development. Those subjects perceiving their areas of competence to be in the technical or functional specialties expressed a dislike of the "politics" of management and placed great value on reward systems that recognize them for their "expertise" and the assignment of more challenging work.[4]

In contrast to the technically oriented specialists, the managerially oriented subjects viewed themselves as having a combination of competencies or abilities in three areas: (1) analytical, (2) interpersonal, and (3) emotional. Analytical ability was defined as "the ability to identify, analyze, and solve problems under conditions of incomplete information and uncertainty."[5] Interpersonal skill was viewed as being effective in exercising influence over others (to include those outside the manager's control and the organization as well as the boss), leading, supervising, motivating, communicating, resolving conflict, monitoring work performance, and presiding over meetings.[6] Emotional competence was defined as "the capacity to bear high levels of responsibility without becoming paralyzed, and the ability to exercise power without guilt or shame."[7]

Obviously, the skills required for specialists or professionals, managers, and other types of workers are not the same. As indicated by the perceived competencies of the managerially oriented subjects of the study just considered, complex sets of abilities are associated with managerial jobs.

MANAGEMENT SELECTION TOOLS

With these caveats in mind regarding the limitations of situational factors and complex abilities required for successful managerial performance, we consider some of the managerial selection tools (Table 8-1) and their predictive ability. Although we face a difficult task in selecting managers, we should still have as a goal the maximization of the fit between the job and the person. Given the contingency view of leadership, obtaining a good "fit" is critical.

Tests and Inventories

The many studies that have evaluated the ability of tests to predict managerial effectiveness have reached mixed conclusions. In one major review of such studies, intelligence tests, personality tests, and interest inventories were found to be good predictors of the effectiveness of executives. Another review of the ability of tests to predict managerial performance was less optimistic. It found intelligence to be a useful predictor of the performance of first-line supervisors but not predictive of the performance of higher management. Of the personality and leadership tests, only the Miner Sentence Completion Scale, which measures managerial motivation, was found to have predictive ability. Finally, a third review of personality tests and interest inventories found them to be of little value in predicting managerial effectiveness. But the study found that, because of the situational specificity of managerial effectiveness, when the scoring keys for such instruments were modified to fit the situation, improved prediction could be obtained.[8]

Table 8-1

Managerial and Professional Personnel Selection Tools

Tests and inventories
Interviews
Industry and company-specific games
References
Assessment centers

Some other instruments have received attention as potential managerial selection tools. The Leadership Opinion Questionnaire (LOQ), which is an instrument that is completed by a manager or potential manager, is designed to measure one's inclination toward employing initiating structure and consideration behaviors. Initiating structure encompasses such behaviors as planning, scheduling work, and directing subordinate efforts toward goals. Consideration behaviors include those involved in maintenance of trusting relationships, showing respect for subordinates, and establishing good communications. A review of studies on the predictiveness of the LOQ found that it had little ability to predict managerial effectiveness. The Leader Behavior Description Questionnaire (LBDQ) is administered to a manager's subordinates or other persons in a position to observe his or her behavior. Although the LBDQ may have some predictive ability, its usefulness as a selection device is limited because of the fact that it is filled out by current subordinates or observers.[9]

Finally, as noted earlier, the Miner Sentence Completion Scale has been employed successfully as a predictor of performance (although there has been some debate on its validity). Essentially, the instrument has been designed to measure an individual's motivation to manage.[10]

As a final caveat on the use of tests and inventories, we should note Mr. Rogers' comments. The conventional wisdom of competent personnel managers and selection experts is that test results provide only one piece of evidence on the job applicant. Such results should never be used as the sole factor in selection decisions.

Interviews

The use of interviews as selection tools was discussed thoroughly in the previous chapter. Although, as noted, there are many potential biases in the interviewing process, it is an almost universally employed selection procedure for managerial and professional personnel. Our interview with Jim Rogers revealed that the interview was NCR's most important selection tool.

Although we know that interviews frequently are not conducted in a manner that will enable a valid prediction of managerial performance, in the previous discussion of interviewing, some suggestions were offered for improving their predictive validity. When used properly, there is potential for successful selection through interviews. One study found that, when a skilled interviewer conducted interviews of applicants for stockbrokers' positions, very good predictions of their success could be obtained when the interview covered only a narrow range of topics. These topics included the applicant's educational and work experiences, why such education and work was undertaken, the success that had been achieved, and the reasons why the applicant aspired to be a stockbroker. These interviews did not attempt to make convoluted inferences about the applicants' personalities; rather they concentrated on the candidates' previous records of achievement.[11] Thus there is potential for effective managerial and professional personnel selection if interviews are conducted properly. Furthermore, the interview provides the unique opportunity for the organization to obtain some indication for whether the applicant will "fit in." Managerial selection interviews are covered in greater detail in this chapter in the discussion of assessment centers.

Industry or Company-Specific Games

Games that may be used to evaluate managerial applicants have been proposed. Such games may be utilized separately from assessment center procedures to evaluate applicants who have never been managers. Applicants' decision-making and analytical skills may be evaluated through such games. Furthermore, although unrelated to selection, these games may have the potential to serve as valuable management development aids.[12]

References

Although references, either written or oral, are typically of only limited use in most selection circumstances, they have much more potential for managerial and professional personnel. In the case of managerial talent, references are of more value when they are used for higher-level personnel. This is because the references may have more credibility as a result of the greater opportunity for the hiring employer to know the reference source. As mentioned in the previous chapter in the case of some professionals where there is a very small job market, there is considerable personal contact through professional organizations and other professional activities. Jim Rogers told us that an important factor in NCR's selection of managers was their previous work experience. References are an important source of information on managerial applicants' work experience.

Other Management Selection Considerations

There is a trend toward increasing usage of executive search firms to recruit and help in the screening of managers. Whereas in the past such firms were used mainly to identify senior-management candidates, they are now being used to identify middle-management candidates. Explanations for this trend may be the efficiency of such search firms and limited in-house internal recruiting abilities or systems. Along with this trend, there has been an increasing centralization of management selection activities.[13]

The reasons for this centralization may be related to the identifiable and considerable costs of external searches by executive search firms. Because of these costs, some employers are centralizing these selection functions to avoid overlooking qualified internal candidates. In the absence of such centralization, there may be a greater likelihood of not identifying internal candidates across organizational units if each unit does its own managerial selection independently from the others. The opportunities for unit managers to hoard good people are also reduced by centralized search and selection activities. Another potential advantage of such centralization is that more selection expertise may be applied as a result of the greater experience of the centralized staff in making such selections.[14] In any event, the inputs of the key personnel should not receive less attention.

ASSESSMENT CENTERS

There has been an increase in the use of assessment centers. One recent report noted that nearly 1,000 organizations are using assessment centers.[15] Although assessment centers have been used in the past for managerial and sales force development, they are also used extensively in the selection of managerial and sales personnel. Furthermore, in recent years they have also been used to select professionals such as auditors, revenue agents, and engineers.[16] Unfortunately, as in several other areas of personnel, the adoption of assessment centers in some instances has been more of a fad than a deliberate, well-thought-out approach to selection. Undoubtedly, many of these adoptions have stemmed from the fact that some assessment centers have been very successful.

The assessment center approach to managerial selection is a complex process that does not lend itself to casual implementation. Thus we approach this selection procedure with care and devote substantial attention to it.

Description of Assessment Centers

As indicated earlier in Chapter 7, the assessment center is a process, not a place. The term center implies that the assessment process may sometimes be conducted at isolated locations or at sites that are separated from the normal work environment. The assessment process involves the use of multiple selection tools and evaluation of assessees by multiple assessors. Typically, these processes take one and one-half to three and one-half days to complete.[17]

> **Assessment center:** a process by which individuals participate in skill-based exercises and have their skills to perform certain activities assessed.

One interesting feature of the assessment center process is that it combines a number of selection tools, which by themselves have only limited validity, into a combined process that seems to have substantial predictive validity in many applications.[18] Later we discuss why such apparently illogical predictive success is possible.

The selection techniques or tools employed typically in assessment centers (as indicated in Table 8-2) include situational exercises such as the in-basket exercise, leaderless group discussions (LGD), various types of management simulation games, oral presentations, intelligence and personality tests, interviews, and other techniques such as creative writing assignments.[19] Each of these tools is examined later in some detail.

Applicants' performances on the various exercises and interviews are evaluated typically by several assessors. These assessors often include higher-level management personnel who have actually performed the jobs under consideration.

The purpose of the assessment center is selection; however, the job applicant is often being selected for a job that he or she has not performed previously, such as selecting first-line supervisors from rank-and-file employees. In other words, "candidates are evaluated not on what they have done in present or past jobs but on how they are likely to cope with a new type of position."[20] Of course, the process may also be used to select higher-level managers from a pool of lower-level managers who are performing the same type of job.

Finally, the dimensions on which managerial job applicants are assessed are somewhat different from those of other jobs. A review of the managerial dimensions assessed by several companies identified the following:

(a) leadership, (b) organizing and planning, (c) decision making, (d) oral and written communications skills, (e) initiative, (f) energy, (g) analytical ability, (h) resistance to stress, (i) use of delegation, (j) behavior flexibility, (k) human relations competence, (l) originality, (m) controlling, (n), self-direction, and (o) overall potential.[21]

We consider next the selection tools that are utilized typically in assessment centers for measurement of these dimensions.

Table 8-2

Typical Assessment Center Activities

Leaderless group discussions
In-basket exercises
Management games
Interviews
Individual presentations
Tests
Other procedures
  Self-evaluations
  Case discussions
  Autobiographical essays
  Personal histories
  Creative writing exercises

Leaderless Group Discussions

In the leaderless group discussion, a group of applicants is given a topic to discuss and may be asked to reach a decision of some sort on the topic. Variations in the exercises may assign different positions for each of the participants to defend. As the title implies, no leader is appointed, and the discussion is essentially unstructured. The leaderless group discussion enables the assessors, who do not participate in the discussion, to observe the applicants' skills in communicating and their abilities to channel a discussion toward an objective, to facilitate the arrival at a group consensus, to meet deadlines, and to observe interpersonal interaction skills. The exercise has the clear advantage of allowing the assessors to observe these actual skills instead of being forced to rely on indirect reports. Managerial dimensions measured through the leaderless group discussion include leadership, group acceptance, individual influence, and interpersonal skills. High interrater and test-retest reliabilities have been reported for the process.[22] Jim Rogers told us that the communication skills of managerial job applicants were important factors considered by NCR in its hiring decisions.

> **Leaderless group discussion:** a process in which a group of leaderless applicants discuss a topic while being observed by assessors.

In-Basket Exercises

As the name implies, the in-basket exercise consists of presenting applicants with a series of memos, letters, reports, messages of phone calls, and the like that would normally be received by the position incumbent. The applicant is typically given background information about the organization and then is required to play the role of a manager in the organization. Applicants are then given a limited amount of time in which they must indicate how they would respond to each of the items and to explain their reasoning. Typically, the respondents would be asked to provide some indication of the priority they would assign to each item. Evaluations of their responses may then be based upon the content of their responses as well as the style that they employed. The items could be a sample of actual in-basket items. Because of the authenticity of the items and the ease of perceiving a relationship between the exercise and the activities of the job, the procedure has high face validity.[23]

> **In-basket exercise:** an experiential selection process in which assessees respond to realistic memos, reports, records of telephone calls, and so on.

The in-basket exercise is designed essentially to measure administrative and planning skills that are required in managerial jobs, but it probably does not measure supervisory skills well. Some administrative and planning skills that seem to be measured by in-basket exercises are decision preparation, taking final action, systematic organization, and subordinate need orientation. Finally, subjects' responses on the in-basket are probably not dependent on managerial experience, although there seem to be positive relationships with intelligence and with education.[24]

Readers might note for personal reasons that the in-basket exercise will likely be encountered if they participate in an assessment center upon leaving school. The in-basket exercise has become so popular that its use in assessment centers is virtually universal.[25] Good concurrent validity has been found for the in-basket exercise between measures of managerial effectiveness and the following assessed dimensions: personally rewarding and punishing subordinates, goal setting, and enriching subordinates' jobs.[26] The in-basket technique is one of the tools used by NCR for selecting managers to be promoted. It is not used in all instances of managerial selection.

Management Games

Various kinds of management problem-solving games have been used in assessment centers. One game is a manufacturing game, in which the participants play the role of partners in a firm that produces toys. In this game the participants purchase parts, produce the toys, market the products in a simulated changing economy, and manage inventory levels.[27] Other management games have involved stock market problems, mergers, and a conglomerate game in which the participants are to gain control of other companies by trading stocks. Such games may place the participants in competition with one another or may require cooperation. The dimensions that may be assessed with such games include the ability to organize, leadership, and adeptness in interpersonal relations.[28]

Interviews

Interviews are typically used to tap such dimensions as the participants' social values, interests, objectives, feelings about the organization, and the degree to which the applicant is likely to relate well to members of the organization.[29] Although, as discussed in the previous chapter, we know that the interview is subject to several sources of bias that often detract from its validity, many assessment centers have benefitted from use of the interview. In assessment centers, interviews are frequently conducted by multiple assessors who have received training in interviewing techniques. As was pointed out in Chapter 7, such training has great potential to increase the validity of the interview. The importance of interviews in the selection of managerial personnel was emphasized in Jim Rogers' description of NCR's practices.

Individual Presentations

The abilities to communicate positions, make presentations, and otherwise communicate effectively are universally critical in managerial positions. These abilities are measured in assessment centers by requiring participants to make brief oral presentations on such topics as a new product. Sometimes these presentations are videotaped, which would be of use in management development. Such exercises are designed to allow the assessors to measure the applicants' communications skills, persuasiveness, and composure in the somewhat stressful setting of making an individual presentation to a group.[30] These communication abilities of managers are so important that some business schools are helping their M.B.A. students develop such skills by requiring them to make oral presentations and briefings to boards comprised of executives and faculty members in simulated business situations.

Tests

Various types of tests are frequently employed in assessment centers. Personality may be assessed through the use of (1) projective tests, such as the Thematic Apperception Test (TAT); (2) sentence completion tests, such as th Rotter Incomplete Sentence Blank and the Miner Sentence Completion Scale (MSCS); and (3) various personality inventories. Other tests are used to measure ability, critical thinking, interests, various types of attitudes, and other personal attributes. Such tests are administered in assessment centers as part of a battery of tests.[31]

Other Procedures

Other procedures that have been used in assessment centers include applicant self-evaluations, discussions of cases presented in films, autobiographical essays, completion of questionnaires covering personal histories, and creative writing exercises. One interesting exercise is J C Penney's "irate customer phone call," in which the applicant must deal diplomatically with an unreasonable customer.[32]

Assessors

A unique aspect of assessment centers is that, typically, many of the exercises will be evaluated by managers from the organization. Some of the procedures, however, such as the projective psychological tests, require qualified psychologists for administration, although managers who receive training in how to assess the participants conduct much of the assessment. Having performed the jobs for which the participants are being evaluated, these assessors provide the advantage of an intimate knowledge of the requirements. These assessors are usually managers at two or three levels higher in the organization than the position for which the applicants are being evaluated. Usually, there is a high ratio of assessors to participants from a range of one assessor to each four participants to one assessor for each participant. When the applicants are employees from within the organization, the assessors are generally not their supervisors.[33] Not only does the use of actual managers benefit the assessment process, but these managers may be better interviewers, observers, and evaluators of behavior as a result of their assessor training.

Validity and Reliability of Assessment Centers

Evaluations of the validity and reliability of assessment centers have been generally favorable in a number of studies.[34] One reason for the rapid, widespread adoption of assessment centers has been their apparent validity. Unfortunately, not all organizations utilizing assessment centers have validated their programs, and it is apparent that they may be accepting the process as universally valid.[35] Statements such as the following one are all too common: "A.T.&T. did such a good one [validation study] that we didn't feel that it was necessary. . . . We're too small a company to do that kind of research."[36] Such an assumption of validity is dangerous. One study of assessment centers commented on the rapid growth in their utilization:

> Assessment center growth should not necessarily be regarded favorably, because first-hand experience has shown us that many so-called assessment center programs up and running today aren't worth the paper on which their exercises are written.[37]

In general, the studies that have evaluated the validity of assessment centers—as implemented in specific organizations—have found that the centers were predictive of job performance.[38] Certainly, the classic studies of the predictive abilities of the AT&T assessment centers provided strong evidence of the procedure's ability to forecast accurately managers' potential. In the comprehensive AT&T studies, for subjects who were assessed five to eight years previously, 80 percent of those predicted to move on to middle management did so. Conversely 95 percent of those managers predicted not to move above the first managerial tier did not do so.[39] These results are even more impressive when it is considered that AT&T did not allow the managers' performance evaluations and advancement decisions to be affected by their performance in the assessment center because the performance data were kept secret during the intervening years.[40] However, these studies have evaluated only a small fraction of operating assessment centers.

The validity of the process as a selection tool is affected by a number of factors, but it is quite dependent on two concepts that serve as the rationale for its functioning. These two concepts are a behavioral philosophy and job simulation. The behavioral philosophy maintains that, when certain individual traits are inferred without direct observation (for example, assessing an applicant's loyalty through an interview), such inferences are no better than guesses. Thus the philosophy is that selection is better if based on observable, relevant, and quantifiable behaviors for evaluation.[41]

An analogy involving the selection of professional basketball players makes the advantages of a behavioral philosophy and job simulation more apparent. One might attempt to determine the best players by giving them intelligence tests and personality tests, evaluating their performance as college players, evaluating their physical attributes, or observing them in a professional basketball game. Evaluating the players' performance in a game is obviously the preferred method, since it is clearly an observation of relevant job behavior. Such a procedure may be too costly in terms of games won, but a realistic scrimmage may provide almost as good an observation at a far lower cost and, thus, be a better selection method. Assessment centers operate in the same manner as an observation of a realistic scrimmage.[42]

As noted in Chapter 7, one factor that can detract from the validity of a selection tool is its lack of reliability. Assessment centers have low reliability when the various exercises are not conducted in the same way for all candidates (unstandarized administration). The reliability of assessment centers may be improved through the implementation of the following suggestions: (1) presenting the exercises in the same order for all assessees, (2) giving the same instructions in the same manner to all assessees, (3) using the same exercise time limits for all assessees, (4) minimizing unfair advantages in role playing, such as the assignment of a role to an assessee who has a great deal of experience in the role while the other assessees have no similar experience, (5) maintaining consistent role performances by nonassessees, (6) training all assessors in a similar manner, and (7) minimizing the likelihood that the assessees and assessors have had previous experiences with one another.[43]

The validity of assessment centers for different demographic groups has been the subject of several studies. One study of the assessment center results and promotional records of 4,846 women at AT&T found that assessment centers are equally and highly predictive for women as well as men. The study also found that approximately the same proportions of women and men (about one-third) received ratings in the two highest evaluation categories.[44] Another study involving AT&T found assessment center ratings equally effective in predicting managerial job performance and the potential for further advancement for black and white women.[45] Nonetheless, there may be some differences in the ratings received that are associated with the assessee's race and sex.[46]

Although, as noted earlier, several studies have reached favorable conclusions on the validity of assessment centers, there have been some criticisms of the performance criteria employed in the studies. These criteria are typically number of promotions or salary progression. The studies typically compare assessment evaluations with the individual's number of promotions or salary progression. The problem with this procedure is that one cannot tell whether the assessment really provides any information (at considerable expense) that the organization did not have previously.

Assessment center assessors are typically astute individuals who have much experience with the subtleties of the organization. In assessing candidates, they may simply evaluate the individuals in accordance with how they think the other managers in the organization will react to individuals with such characteristics. In other words, the assessors may give a candidate a good evaluation, because individuals with similar characteristics have been viewed positively in promotion decisions by other managers in the past. Whether such an individual has truly "good" managerial skills or potential really has not been established. Thus the process may be very organization specific. Furthermore, the same information could have been obtained potentially at a much lower cost through such sources as biographical data, supervisory rankings, or peer nominations.[47] This brings us to the next subject—the utility of assessment centers in managerial and professional personnel selection.

Utility of Assessment Centers

In accordance with the underlying theme of logic in this book, we need to consider the utility of the assessment center in the selection of managers and professionals. Even if we are able to establish that an assessment center has superior predictive validity in our organization, we need to consider its cost effectiveness in relation to other selection methods. In assessing the utility of a selection tool, we need to consider its impact on training costs, recruiting costs, and other related organizational costs. The feasibility of assessing the utility of assessment centers has been demonstrated in one study, although some of the cost data are admittedly subjective. By varying such selection factors as the validity of the assessment center, cost of an assessment center, the validity of alternative selection procedures, selection ratios, and other factors, the utility of assessment centers can be assessed.[48] This approach at least points out the number of factors that should be considered in evaluating the cost effectiveness of assessment centers.

SUMMARY

In this chapter we have described some of the special requirements for the selection of managerial and professional personnel. One factor that makes managerial selection difficult is the impact of situation-specific factors that ultimately determine a manager's success. Another factor is that, for many positions involving supervisory duties, managers must be selected from among many candidates who have never had any previous managerial experience. Thus, although such applicants may have been good performers in their previous jobs, such performance is not necessarily a good indicator of good performance as a manager. Fortunately, considerable progress has been made during recent years in managerial and professional personnel selection.

Interviews that have been conducted properly have been demonstrated to have potential predictive ability. Likewise, because of the greater likelihood of source credibility, references can also be useful for managerial and professional personnel selection. Although tests and inventories have not generally proven to be strong predictors of managerial success, certain of these instruments seem to have some predictive ability. However, the greatest breakthrough in managerial selection has been the assessment center. Because of careful assessment program development, assessor training, and use of situational exercises such as leaderless group discussions and in-basket exercises, assessment centers have the potential for good predictive ability. But it is important to note that some organizations have adopted assessment centers without critical evaluation and have not attempted to validate their procedures.

INTERVIEW WRAP-UP

Managerial jobs involve a great deal of responsibility and often require substantial integration of knowledge about technical matters and company policies and practices. It is difficult for younger applicants to possess all of these abilities, but we have many different ways for aspiring young managers to enter the field. Perhaps a good entry position is first into a professional field, such as purchasing, cost accounting, engineering, or production control, and so on. The aspiring graduate who gets the professional or technical experience first can grow from there. The field is open. —Jim Rogers, manager of personnel resources, NCR Microelectronics.

WHAT MANAGERS SHOULD DO REGARDING PERSONNEL MANAGEMENT ACTIVITIES

1. Managers need to recognize the existence of situation-specific factors that must be considered in selecting managers.
2. Managers should be familiar with the logic that underlies assessment centers and the requirements for successful conduct of assessment centers.
3. Managers should not be complacent with their current methods of selecting managerial and professional personnel or forget that such selection is critical to organizational effectiveness.

REVIEW QUESTIONS

1. Describe how a leaderless group discussion is used in managerial selection.
2. What is an in-basket exercise, and what is it supposed to do?
3. Describe a typical assessment center.
4. How can an assessment center have good potential for predictive ability, when some of its typical components have not been very predictive in the past?
5. Explain how the selection of managerial personnel differs from the selection of other personnel.
6. On what grounds should an organization decide to adopt an assessment center for selection purposes?
7. What are some criticisms of assessment centers?

KEY CONCEPTS

Assessment centers	Management games
Creative writing exercises	Miner Sentence Completion Scale
In-basket exercises	References
Individual presentations	Reliability
Industry- or company-specific games	Situationally specific requirements
Interviews	Tests
LBDQ	Utility
Leaderless group discussions	Validity
LOQ	

CASE

LATIMER CONSOLIDATED OIL FIELD SERVICES

Latimer Consolidated Oil Field Services (LCOS) is a rapidly growing company that provides services for the mushrooming oil drilling industry. The energy crisis and the consequent rapid growth in oil drilling activity has created a great demand for oil rig maintenance services.

LCOS was established in 1957, when Tom Latimer graduated from Texas A & M University with a B.S. degree in petroleum engineering. Tom's family had always been involved in the oil business, and while Tom was a student, he worked in the oil fields during the summers. It was during these summer jobs that he observed a need for oil field maintenance services. He began the firm with used equipment and only one employee, but his prompt service and willingness to provide service at any time of day assured a steady demand for his company.

During the 1960s, the firm incorporated and grew steadily. It had 208 employees in 1973, just before the Arab oil embargo signaled the beginning of the energy crisis. By 1981, the firm had 892 employees and was operating in five states: Texas, Louisiana, Oklahoma, Kansas, and Arkansas. Because of the nature of the industry and the necessity of providing maintenance services where the oil rigs are located, the firm operates in a decentralized manner at twenty-seven service locations throughout the five-state region. The manning levels at these various locations range from an approximate low of fifteen employees to a high of fifty-five to sixty employees in a few areas in Texas and Oklahoma.

A continuing problem for the firm, especially during the last two years when more service locations have been added, is a shortage of location managers. Typically, these managers have come from current employees who have had a few years of experience in the oil industry. However, the great demand for such location managers, which has resulted from the firm's expansion and raiding by competitors, has caused the firm to draw location managers from young employees who have not had managerial experience. Furthermore, it has not been able to recruit any experienced managers from other similar companies. As a result of these constraints, a high proportion of new location managers have not performed well, though a few have been quite successful.

In the past, the selection of these managers has been rather informal. The company's personnel director, headquartered in the executive offices in Dallas, has typically polled other executives and location managers for the names of employees who might be promising candidates for the positions. The candidates have been brought to Dallas for interviews with the president, the vice-president of operations, and the personnel director. These interviews have been discussed by the three executives at a meeting in which all the qualifications of the job candidates are evaluated (including their last five years' performance evaluations). It is at this meeting that the hiring decision is made.

The job of local manager entails the complete supervision of the maintenance centers. Each maintenance location has drivers of oil well service trucks, mechanics, welders, and supply deliverymen. Each location office also has some accounting, budget, and billing activities. Although it has never been established that a petroleum engineering background is necessary for holding the job, preference has usually been given to those applicants with degrees in petroleum or chemical engineering because of a general feeling that such people have a better feel for oil field operations.

CASE QUESTIONS

1. How can LCOS improve its success in selecting location managers?
2. Is the firm's rapid expansion the cause of its managerial selection problems?
3. How typical is the company's approach to managerial or professional personnel selection?

NOTES

[1] J. P. Campbell, M. D. Dunnette, E. E. Lawler, III, and K. E. Weick, Jr., *Managerial Behavior, Performance and Effectiveness* (New York: McGraw-Hill, 1970), p. 139.

[2] F. E. Fiedler and M. M. Chemers, *Leadership and Effective Management* (Glenview, Ill.: Scott, Foresman, 1974).

[3] Ibid., p. 73.

[4] E. H. Schein, *Career Dynamics: Matching Individual and Organizational Needs* (Reading, Mass.: Addison-Wesley, 1978).

[5] Ibid., p. 135.

[6] Ibid.

[7] Ibid., p. 136.

[8] Campbell et al., *Managerial Behavior.*

[9] Ibid.

[10] J. B. Miner, "Levels of Motivation to Manage Among Personnel and Industrial Relations Managers," *Journal of Applied Psychology,* 61 (1976), 419–427. For information on the controversy over the psychometric properties of the instrument, see A. P. Brief, R. J. Aldag, and T. I. Chacko, "The Miner Sentence Completion Scale: An Appraisal," *Academy of Management Journal,* 20 (1977), 635–643; J. B. Miner, "The Miner Sentence Completion Scale: A Reappraisal," *Academy of Management Journal,* 21 (1978), 283–294.

[11] Campbell et al., *Managerial Behavior.*

[12] C. Gooding and T. W. Zimmerer, "The Use of Specific Industry Gaming in the Selection, Orientation and Training of Managers," *Human Resource Management,* 19 (1980), 19–21.

[13] A. R. Sells, "Viewing Advancement on a Corporate-wide Plane," *Personnel Administrator,* 25 (1980), 25–27.

[14] Ibid.

[15] S. L. Cohen, "Validity and Assessment Center Technology: One and the Same?" *Human Resource Management,* 19 (1980), 2–11.

[16] A. Howard, "An Assessment of Assessment Centers," *Academy of Management Journal,* 17 (1974), 115–133.

[17] B. Schneider, *Staffing Organizations* (Santa Monica, Calif.: Goodyear, 1976).

[18] Ibid.

[19] Ibid.

[20]Ibid., p. 116.

[21]Ibid., p. 117.

[22]Campbell et al., *Managerial Behavior.*

[23]S. L. Cohen and L. Sands, "The Effects of Order of Exercise Presentation on Assessment Center Performance: One Standardization Concern," *Personnel Psychology,* 31 (1978), 35–46; H. H. Meyer, "The Validity of the In-basket Test as a Measure of Managerial Performance," *Personnel Psychology,* 23 (1970), 297–307; D. J. Bass and G. R. Oldham, "Validating an In-basket Test Using an Alternative Set of Leadership Scoring Dimensions," *Journal of Applied Psychology,* 16 (1976), 652–657; Howard, "An Assessment of Assessment Centers,"; Campbell et al., *Managerial Behavior.*

[24]Meyer, "The Validity of the In-basket Test."

[25]S. D. Norton, "The Empirical and Content Validity of Assessment Centers vs. Traditional Methods for Predicting Managerial Success," *Academy of Management Review,* 2 (1977), 442–453.

[26]Bass and Oldham, "Validating an In-basket Test."

[27]D. W. Bray and D. L. Grant, "The Assessment Center in the Measurement of Potential for Business Management," *Journal of Applied Psychology,* 80 (1966), 1–27.

[28]Howard, "An Assessment of Assessment Centers"; K. Anundsen, "An Assessment Center at Work," *Personnel,* 52 (1975), 29–36.

[29]Bray and Grant, "The Assessment Center"; Howard, "An Assessment of Assessment Centers."

[30]Howard, "An Assessment of Assessment Centers"; Cohen, "Validity and Assessment Center Technology"; Anundsen, "An Assessment Center at Work."

[31]Bray and Grant, "The Assessment Center"; Howard, "An Assessment of Assessment Centers"; Schneider, *Staffing Organizations;* Miner, "Levels of Motivation."

[32]G. M. Worbois, "Validation of Externally Developed Assessment Procedures for Identification of Supervisory Potential," *Personnel Psychology,* 28 (1975), 77–91; Howard, "An Assessment of Assessment Centers"; Bray and Grant, "The Assessment Center"; Anundsen, "An Assessment Center at Work."

[33]Howard, "An Assessment of Assessment Centers."

[34]Cohen, "Validity and Assessment Center Technology."

[35]Ibid.

[36]Anundsen, "An Assessment Center at work," p. 35.

[37]Cohen, "Validity and Assessment Center Technology," pp. 2–3.

[38]Ibid.; J. R. Huck and D. W. Bray, "Management Assessment Center Evaluations and Subsequent Job Performance of White and Black Females," *Personnel Psychology,* 29 (1976), 13–30.

[39]Bray and Grant, "The Assessment Center."

[40]Howard, "An Assessment of Assessment Centers."

[41]Cohen, "Validity and Assessment Center Technology."

[42]Ibid.

[43]Ibid.

[44]J. L. Moses and V. R. Boehm, "Relationship of Assessment-Center Performance to Management Progress of Women," *Journal of Applied Psychology,* 60 (1975), 527–529.

[45]Huck and Bray, "Management Assessment Center Evaluations."

[46]Ibid.; N. Schmitt and T. E. Hill, "Sex and Race Composition of Assessment Center Groups as a Determinant of Peer and Assessor Ratings," *Journal of Applied Psychology,* 62 (1977), 261–264.

[47]R. J. Klimoski and W. J. Strickland, "Assessment Centers—Valid or Merely Prescient," *Personnel Psychology,* 30 (1977), 353–361.

[48]W. F. Cascio and V. Silbey, "Utility of the Assessment Center as a Selection Device," *Journal of Applied Psychology,* 64 (1979), 107–118.

THREE

TRAINING FOR PERFORMANCE

After employees have been selected for jobs in an organization, training them for the specific tasks to which they have been assigned becomes important. Again, we find that the information on job tasks gathered during job analysis is necessary in designing training programs. Further, information regarding employee skills gathered during selection testing and performance appraisals provides for individualized training approaches. Training is necessary because of selection errors that inevitably occur, because organizations prefer to develop their employees' skills regularly in preparation for advancement to more challenging jobs and opportunities, and because the nature of the organizations' jobs changes over time. This section, then, examines the training phase of personnel management.

An underlying logic presented in Chapter 9 is intended to prepare the student for dealing with more complex issues of training. The rationale is developed from the viewpoint that training is a process of learning and, therefore, effective training programs must "teach" job-relevant skills and attitudes. Specific training approaches, presented in Chapter 10, are examined from a learning as well as from an effectiveness perspective. We find that different approaches accomplish different learning objectives and that attitude, as well as skill training, is important. The section ends with specific attention to the needs for continuing development of employees for career and/or managerial growth (Chapter 11). We believe that training is an economic investment in the organization's human resource that compares favorably with alternative investments in capital equipment and other resources. Training expenditures can be investments that offer returns to the firm as favorable as other investments.

THE LOGIC OF TRAINING

LEARNING OBJECTIVES

After reading this chapter, you should be able to:

1. Explain the similarities and differences between training and education.
2. List the six fundamental elements in training.
3. Explain how assessments are made of skills and abilities required by the job.
4. Discuss the assessment of employee skills and abilities.
5. Describe how training needs are specified.
6. Discuss the impact of training on job performance and satisfaction.

Jane Kurtiss is the training center director for Massachusetts Mutual Life Insurance Company in Springfield, Massachusetts. She has been in this position for four and a half years. Her primary responsibilities include the design of companywide training programs for both managerial and nonmanagerial personnel. Massachusetts Mutual Life Insurance Company has over 3,000 employees who perform a variety of jobs such as actuarian, salesperson, computer programmer, and financial analyst. Comprehensive training is available for all 3,000 employees, so Jane Kurtiss's responsibilities are quite demanding. She took time from her busy schedule to respond to several general questions regarding important issues in training.

Interviewer: To some people, it may seem strange that, with all the attention given to the selection of the most qualified applicants, training is necessary. Can you tell me why training is still necessary even if the company has a good selection process?

Jane Kurtiss: This question depends on a rather basic assumption, which is that the "most" qualified applicant is fully skilled in all aspects of the job. This is rarely the case, since for most people a "new" job will require them to perform activities that they have never experienced. They may possess rudimentary skills, but they must be trained to sharpen these into the refined skills needed for the job.

We might also see that jobs rarely stay the same over time. That is, an employee will find that tasks required in a job change as new techniques, new products, and other forces cause the job to grow. Training is necessary to keep employees abreast of these changes and to keep their skills developing with those changes.

Finally, people don't stay at the same entry-level job for which they are first selected. As they are promoted and transferred to more responsible jobs, the skills required of them will change. Training allows employees to acquire these skills in anticipation of being promoted or transferred. So an employee may be a good salesperson, but might be receiving managerial training with the expectation that he or she will one day be promoted and need managerial skills at that time.

Interviewer: How do you know what skills to train or teach?

Jane Kurtiss: At MMLIC we are constantly performing "needs analyses" for the development of our training programs. Basically, this is done by surveying various people to find out what they feel their needs are. For example, we try to get departmental managers to sit down on a regular basis and, as a group, identify critical areas in which employees will need training. We also ask training participants to list areas in which additional training would be useful, and we regularly interview other employees for the same purpose.

Interviewer: If two people had different experiences or backgrounds, would their training for an identical job be identical or different? Why?

Jane Kurtiss: This is a difficult question to answer, because it assumes that we have a specific training program for each specific job, which we don't. The training we provide out of my office is in terms of companywide programs, programs that might be attended by sales people, actuarians, medical technicians, and almost any other person. However, each employee will receive different training according to his or her needs because both will receive on-the-job training that is adjusted by the supervisor according to the unique needs of each trainee. Second, each trainee will examine the array of companywide programs and identify the ones most appropriate to his or her own needs. Thus, two employees on the same job will receive different training because their on-the-job training and selection of companywide programs will vary according to their needs. It is important to state here that each employee can take advantage of any training that we offer that will improve either his or her job performance or career development. Supervisors constantly work with their employees to identify useful training experiences and encourage employee growth and development.

INTRODUCTION

Training in industrial organizations is a major activity. One needs only to look at the popular magazines (*Reader's Digest, Psychology Today,* etc.,) to see discussions of sensitivity or T-group training, executive encounter seminars, or other human relations programs. The importance of training can also be seen in the growth of a technical training industry (e.g., "vo-tech" schools, business schools, programming schools). Or one can talk to a training specialist employed by any one of thousands of organizations that provide in-house training for their employees. Jane Kurtiss, the training center director for Massachusetts Mutual Life Insurance Company, is one of those specialists whose career centers on the ability to train others and improve their skills at work.

One gets the impression from talking to Jane Kurtiss, and other training specialists, that employees' abilities to function effectively in the organization requires almost constant exposure to new training programs. That is, the patterns of our society, socially, technologically, and economically, are changing at such a rapid rate that today's skills quickly become obsolete. The plumber who fails to develop the skills required to handle plastic tubing and the tool and die maker who has not learned to handle exotic new alloys will become obsolete and of little value to an organization. While we may tend to think of training as an expensive cost with little benefit to organizations, examples such as these demonstrate its importance.

In this chapter, we examine some of the basic issues that underly the design of effective training programs. As is true of most major personnel activities, designing effective training programs requires the use of a certain logic or rationale.

TRAINING AND EDUCATION

Before we examine the logic of training, it is necessary to understand the meaning of the term training. Casual observation of training processes in organizations reveals that the major outcome of training is that the trainees "learn." That is, trainees acquire or learn new habits, refined skills, or useful knowledge that helps them to improve their performance of required tasks. Thus training involves the process of learning.

However, learning can occur in the absence of a formalized training program. For example, development of speech and behaviors in children normally occurs without much formalized training. Similarly, employees can learn to operate machines without training, but such learning will be haphazard and often dangerous. A formalized process for learning is more likely to achieve the desired new skills and behaviors.

In reality, most individuals have been exposed to formalized training programs, such as those found in institutions of education. It is useful to examine the similarities and differences between training and education. Both share the common purpose of helping people to learn and acquire new behaviors and knowledge that are useful for effective functioning in society.

> **Education:** the systematic acquisition of skills, rules, knowledge, and attitudes that have broad or general applicability in one's total social environment.[1]

It is important to note that education is intended to relate to one's total social environment. Because modern society is so complex, the skills necessary to function in it effectively are quite diverse. That is, we may find a use for algebra (determining gas mileage, calculating grocery costs), history (conversations, comparison of world events), economics (budgeting, investment planning), and so on. In this case, educators cannot be sure about the specific situations one may face later that require such knowledge. Therefore, education tends to be more theoretical or conceptual in approach, which enables one to extract the applications according to the various situations confronted. If education provided only specific (rather than broad or general) applications, one would be unprepared for the many unique and unanticipated situations that one would face later.

> **Training:** the systematic acquisition of skills, rules, knowledge, and attitudes that have specific or narrow applicability to a limited set of situations in a specific job environment.[2]

As opposed to education, training deals only with a relatively narrow aspect of one's total social environment—the job in which one works. Although some jobs may be quite complex and require several skills, we can be much more certain as to the situations that one is likely to face in the job. The unexpected job situation will require the application of broad conceptual skills (such as those acquired by education), but the more routine and expected job situations and required skills can be specified. Therefore, training tends to focus on the *specific applications* of a relatively narrow set of skills, rules, knowledge, and attitudes. These will compose the basic and predominant activities allowing one to function effectively in the job environment. As indicated by Jane Kurtiss, even broad skills learned in education must be refined to specific skills needed for the job.

TRAINING LOGIC

Given our understanding of the purpose of training, we can examine the logic that is likely to underlie the development of effective training programs. Our discussion of training and education has implied that there are six fundamental elements in training:

1. The specific job environment (situations to be faced and the skills, rules, knowledge, and attitudes corresponding to those situations).
2. The individual (the skills, rules, knowledge, and attitudes held that may or may not correspond to the job situation).

3. Assessments of the job and individuals (measuring the types of skills, etc., and the degree to which they are required by the job *and* possessed by the employee).

4. Application of a sound learning strategy (the actual process of teaching job-required skills, etc., in which the individual is deficient).

5. Changes in employee skills, rules, knowledge, and attitudes (acquired through the training experience).

6. Improved performance on the job (the result of newly acquired skills, rules, knowledge, and attitudes).

As illustrated in Figure 9-1, these six elements are interrelated in a logical arrangement with the intended final result being improved job performance and employee satisfaction. An effective training process achieves these results since employees become more prepared to perform the tasks, duties, and activities in the job as their abilities become matched to job requirements.

Job Environments and Employees

As explained in previous chapters, personnel management activities are, in part, concerned with matching people and jobs. Since we have already examined one major personnel management activity, selection, which is intended to accomplish that match, it

Figure 9-1

The Training Process

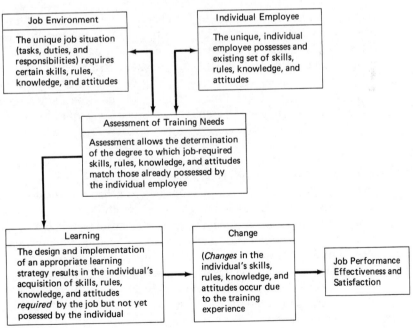

may be necessary to explain why a second activity with the same general purpose is required. That is, if we do a good job of selecting people who are likely to possess job-related talents, why should they need to be trained? As Jane Kurtiss of Massachusetts Mutual Life Insurance Company explained, this question depends on a simplistic assumption that "most" qualified means "fully" qualified. For most new employees, their new job will require them to perform some activities with which they have little experience and to learn new methods of performing jobs that are unique to their employer.

Furthermore, the need for training is not limited to new employees. Jobs are frequently redesigned by organizations to take advantage of new technologies and developments. Product changes often necessitate changes in work methods. Thus, even if an individual never changed jobs during his or her work career, training may be a necessary activity for maintaining the match between job requirements and individual characteristics and abilities.

Finally, our work society is very mobile. Few people work at the same job for their entire careers. It is common for our interests to change and for us to seek challenges associated with these changes. Thus employees may seek lateral transfers (no promotion involved) or vertical transfers (involving promotion or demotion). Each job transfer will necessitate training either prior or subsequent to the transfer.

Assessment of Training Needs

Because we recognize the inevitable need to conduct training in organizations, it is logical to ask next, "How can we determine exactly what skills, rules, knowledge, or attitudes need to be developed or learned?" We might have a "nice-looking" training program that teaches new abilities effectively, but if these abilities are not needed on the job, the training will prompt neither job performance nor satisfaction. Conversely, if these are needed job abilities but individuals already have them, the organization will have absorbed unnecessary costs that contributed little to performance or satisfaction. Therefore, the design of an effective program depends first on our ability to assess or measure the type and amounts of various skills, rules, knowledge, and attitudes required by the job and possessed by the employee.

ASSESSING JOB REQUIREMENTS.   The importance of job analyses, job descriptions, and job specifications is once again apparent. Job analyses yield information regarding work procedures and methods that are then described in terms of employee tasks, duties, and responsibilities. The job description is then translated into specifications of the human skills, knowledge, and attitudes that relate to job performance. We can see at this point that personnel activities are interlocked inextricably, since the validation of these translations (as described in the section on selection) will yield better assessments for training purposes. The assessment of job requirements for training purposes, then, is not a costly process, since such assessments already exist, given that job analyses, job descriptions, and job specifications have been conducted.

This conclusion holds only for training on an employee's current job. If the job is redesigned, new assessments must be made. Also, we may anticipate that the individual will be transferred to a different job or promoted in the future. In these cases, we will train for skills, rules, knowledge, and attitudes not necessarily contained in the employee's current job but in a future job. We must then look at assessments of jobs that the employee is likely to hold in the future. This is especially important in managerial employees who may receive frequent promotions to higher levels and who must acquire the needed abilities for those jobs prior to promotion.

ASSESSING EMPLOYEE ABILITIES. The assessment of employee abilities requires that we recognize two groups of employees: new employees and incumbent employees. This is because our concern is with measuring the types and levels of abilities held by employees *at the time* training is to occur.

For new employees, types and levels of abilities are measured primarily during the selection process. Various skill measurements (e.g., dexterity, visual acuity), knowledge measurements (e.g., education, experience), and attitude measurements (e.g., assertiveness, sociability) may have been made. These measurements are contained in application forms, in references, and in the specific skill and psychological instruments that were administered. Some organizations may prefer to develop additional measurements that are used only for training need assessments; however, it remains that the selection measurements are a logical source of such information.

For incumbent employees, selection measures are less likely to prove useful for training purposes. This is because job experiences produce changes in the types and levels of employee abilities. Even in the absence of formal training, individual abilities change and develop. What was true of abilities at the time of selection is unlikely to be true later on. Further, we may be considering an incumbent employee for possible transfer or promotion to a different job. In this case, the types of abilities we assessed at selection may not be appropriate. Abilities that were not considered at that time may now have to be assessed.

The primary means of assessing incumbent employees' abilities is through performance appraisals by supervisors and other managers and by surveying the incumbents as to their perceived needs as they consider their own career plans. These methods of assessment were of great importance to Jane Kurtiss in developing training programs at Massachusetts Mutual Life Insurance Company.

SPECIFYING TRAINING NEEDS. As Figure 9-2 illustrates, the specification of an individual's training needs requires that the assessment of job requirements be compared with the assessment of individual abilities. This is true whether one is considering new or incumbent employees, whether it is an existing job, a job being redesigned for technology, or work method purposes, and whether it is simply to prevent employee obsolescence or to prepare the individual for a transfer or promotion. However, we must be sure that the job assessment corresponds to the job situation for which the training will be conducted.

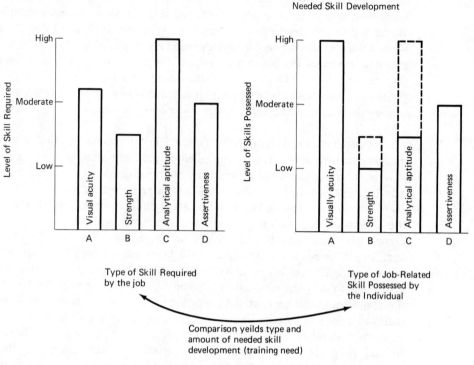

Figure 9-2

Specifying Training Needs for Individuals

As seen in Figure 9-2, such a comparison might easily reveal training needs for one individual. In this hypothetical case, the job requires four basic skills, in varying amounts. The comparison reveals that the individual

Possesses a greater level of visual acuity than is required by the job.

Has less strength than required.

Has less analytical aptitude than required.

Possesses an adequate level of assertiveness.

In this case, then, an ideal and logically derived training program for the individual would focus only upon strength and analytical skills. Further, the starting point would be at the level of these skills already possessed by the candidate. For example, since the employee already possesses some analytical skills, the training might begin, say, with advanced computer languages (e.g., PL1) rather than Basic.

However, we can see that the ideal case will also be expensive, as an organization will have to conduct a unique training program for every individual in the company. From a cost perspective, it may be better to design one or two rather standardized training programs for a job that can accommodate such differences in individual skills. This can be accomplished by establishing a basic level at which new skills are introduced (say, multiplication in the example) and then allowing more skilled individuals to either skip or progress more rapidly through the basic level. Less skilled individuals would progress more slowly. This same principle is seen at Massachusetts Mutual Life where employees are permitted to choose from standardized companywide programs according to their perceptions of their own skill deficiencies. This would seem to avoid costly and redundant training.

Learning Theory

As shown by the model in Figure 9-1, once we have specified training needs, it is necessary to apply a learning theory that will promote the development of skills, rules, knowledge, and attitudes in the training program. That is, there are many means by which we could attempt to have employees learn the new skills, but some methods are better than others. Effective training programs are designed around logical and sound learning theories. Since this is a critical element in training, we examine it more closely in Chapter 10.

Job Performance and Satisfaction

Finally, the obvious goal of any training program is to achieve more effective employee job performance and satisfaction. The exact relationship between job satisfaction and performance has been somewhat controversial.[3] Some argue that satisfaction causes one to be productive; others argue that being productive causes one to be satisfied. While we do not wish to debate this issue, it is important to note that both are desirable goals and that they are interrelated.

Training is a direct cause of job performance levels. Since performance derives from job-related skills, rules, knowledge, and attitudes, any training program that enhances these characteristics will be likely to achieve an increase in productivity.

Job satisfaction is influenced by training in a complex manner. That is, job satisfaction is first an attitude that is learned.[4] Thus, one aspect of most training programs is simply to teach appropriate attitudes that will enhance satisfaction directly. Second, self-esteem and ego are affected by one's perception of one's own skills and abilities. If skills are enhanced by training, pride and ego are enhanced, which then may result in increased satisfaction with one's job. And, finally, increased productivity may cause one to be more satisfied. Pride and ego may be affected by *both* enhanced skills *and* the result of those skills—productivity.

SPECIAL TRAINING CONSIDERATIONS

A good understanding of the logic underlying training programs allows us to examine several special aspects of job and people relationships. Two of these are training for professional and managerial employees.

The Professional Employee

While we have assumed primarily that most organizational jobs lend themselves easily to job analysis, job description, and job specification techniques, in some cases the range and variety of tasks, duties, and responsibilities may be so large as to be nearly impossible to identify completely. It may also be because the types of activities in these jobs change frequently as new technologies develop. One such category is that group of jobs commonly referred to as professional. Examples are accountant, chemist, engineer, lawyer, and doctor.

In these jobs, employees cannot simply follow a narrow list of job duties. The employees must rely upon their own skills, expertise, and knowledge and make work-related decisions alone. Thus a major training problem will be the assessment of job requirements. In the case of professional employees, the primary purpose of training may be to prevent obsolescence of skills. That is, these employees must be kept abreast of developing technologies in their areas of expertise.[5] By staying current, employees will be able to change their jobs (a type of self-directed job redesign) to take advantage of new developments.

Thus we see that training for professionals is less concerned with learning the specifics of a job as it is designed currently. Rather, it is concerned with learning new concepts that go well beyond current job requirements and that may not be applied to the job until some future time. Such training may not be conducted by the organization itself, but may be acquired from outside agencies such as universities or professional organizations (e.g., professional engineers' society). The importance of "staying abreast of these changes" was cited by Jane Kurtiss as a training goal.

The Managerial Employee

A second group of jobs that poses unique training problems is that of managers. Again, managerial jobs are not analyzed or described easily. Underlying skills are rarely technical, tending instead to emphasize problem-solving abilities and human relations skills. As with professionals, managers cannot simply follow a list of job duties; rather, they must be able to analyze each unique problem they face and to apply knowledge in solving the problems.

Thus managerial training rarely focuses on specific job duties. Managers must learn broad skills and knowledge that allow them to solve problems or to guide subordinates toward the achievement of organizational goals. This training is, in part, conducted within the organization and, in part, by outside agencies. Because of the importance of managerial training we examine it in some detail in Chapters 10 and 11.

THE ECONOMICS OF TRAINING

We have been, thus far, concerned primarily with the logic of training as a process of learning and the relationship between learning of job-related skills and job performance or satisfaction. That is, if we train an employee, we want it to be an effective learning process that leads to improved job performance and satisfaction. This type of logic allows us to design learning programs that accomplish training purposes.

However, we would be remiss if we failed to recognize that training expenditures are investments. One recent survey estimates that $100 billion is invested in training programs by industrial and governmental organizations each year.[6] As with other investments (e.g., new product development, new production plant or equipment), the costs of developing the organization's human resource skills must be justified by the returns or benefits of those investments. The process of justifying the economic benefits of organizational investments is called cost-benefit analysis. Economically, the investment in training is justified only if benefits exceed the costs of training, and some would add that these training benefits should be greater than benefits that would accrue from alternate investments (say, in equipment).

Such economic logic does not deter our learning logic, since effective learning programs based on accurate needs assessment will be more cost/benefit effective than will poorly designed training programs. However, even effective training programs should be justified by cost-benefit analysis.

For training to be an integral part of management's investment plan, it must be evaluated just as other investments are. We can then see that, ideally, any training program should contain both learning objectives (skill, performance, satisfaction) and financial objectives (return on investment).

However, many companies find that it is very difficult to perform cost-benefit analyses on their training expenditures. Partially this is so because many of the costs are indirect and hard to monitor. For instance, employee salaries received while attending a training program are, in fact, training costs. Yet training budgets rarely include these as direct training expenses. Similarly, many of the benefits are hard to assess, especially in economic terms. What, for instance, is the dollar value of increased satisfaction? Furthermore, the financial impact of improved employee skills may not be felt for several years and in that time period become interwoven inextricably with other financial revenues. In some cases, the financial benefits are related indirectly to training (lower turnover), and estimates of such revenues are difficult to make.

Still, organizations should attempt to justify training expenditures by cost-benefit analyses. As shown in Figure 9-3, many of the direct and indirect costs of training

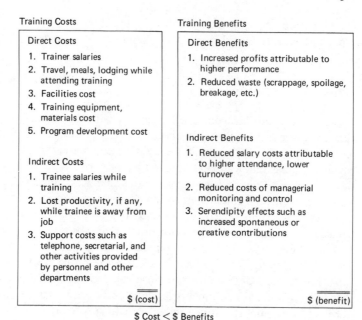

Figure 9-3

Cost-Benefit Analysis of Training

can be estimated, if not measured directly. The ability to assess these costs accurately improves when accounting systems are designed to monitor such costs. Similarly, when accounting systems develop better means for measuring benefits, cost-benefit analysis becomes a useful tool for evaluating training programs.[7] This type of evaluation truly expresses the philosophy that training is a legitimate *investment* in valuable human resources.

SUMMARY

In this chapter, we have outlined a basic logic that underlies the training function of personnel management. We have seen that training and education are similar in that they both involve the systematic learning of skills, rules, knowledge, and attitudes. They are dissimilar in that training involves skills, rules, knowledge, and attitudes that relate to the narrower job environment.

The logic of training involves assessment and measurement. To determine what skills, rules, knowledge, and abilities need to be learned, we must measure or assess the specific requirements of a job. Then, logically, we must measure the corresponding ability levels of the employee. Comparison of these two sets of measurements allows us to design a "learning" or training program.

The logic of training also involves the application of a learning theory. The effectiveness of training depends upon the ability to design training activities that "teach" new or different skills required by the job. Programs that are weak in learning theory are unlikely to accomplish the intended goals of improved job performance and satisfaction.

Finally, we have seen that some types of jobs pose greater difficulties than do others in training. Jobs for professionals and managers are more difficult to assess, and the variety of required abilities may be great. In these cases, training focuses upon learning new techniques that may not be present in the current job or upon improving one's problem-solving and human relations abilities. A solid understanding of the logic of training prepares us to deal with these special training considerations.

INTERVIEW WRAP-UP

We have seen a rapid change in the state of the art in training in the last three to five years. Partially this is caused by the equal opportunity legislation requiring us to deal with employees who are seriously deficient in job skills and to provide them with the ability to perform complex tasks and progress upward in their careers. Our training programs today are better, more logical, than ever before. —Jane Kurtiss, training center director, Massachusetts Mutual Life Insurance Company.

REVIEW QUESTIONS

1. In what ways are training and education similar? Dissimilar?
2. Why is it important to assess the job requirements before developing a training program for it?
3. In what ways might employee abilities be assessed?
4. How are job performance and satisfaction affected by training?
5. Why do professional and managerial jobs pose special training problems?

KEY CONCEPTS

Assessment	Job satisfaction
Assessment of employee abilities	Job specification
Assessment of job requirements	Performance appraisal
Education	Professional employee
Job analysis	Selection measures

Job description

Job environment

Job performance

Specification of training needs

Training

CASE

MANAGEMENT TRAINEE

Sandy Moore sat dejectedly at her desk. She had just had her first official performance appraisal on her new job, and she was very disappointed in the ratings she had received.

Sandy was a management trainee for a large eastern bank that had extensive holdings overseas as well as within the United States. One of the primary reasons she had accepted the position was because of the opportunity to one day work in a foreign location. The bank, also, had hired her with the same expectations, that one day she might be assigned as a manager in one of the European locations. Sandy had majored in international business at college and was fluent in three languages. These qualifications led to her selection.

However, before assignment overseas, it was customary for new managerial trainees to learn domestic operations. All trainees went through a three-year training program designed to acquaint them with the various bank services, such as commercial loans, trusts, savings, and related operations. Sandy's first assignment, for six months, was to the commercial loan department.

Bud McDonald, her new supervisor, had told her that the best way for her to get acquainted with the procedures was to start analyzing customer applications and to actually make some of the loans. He told her to get with Jayne Adams, an experienced loan officer, and have Jayne "show her the ropes." Then Bud left for a meeting.

Although Jayne was kind and patient, Sandy found it very difficult to learn everything that she was supposed to. There were very tricky procedures for evaluating financial statements, an array of bank policies covering interest rates (of which there were several "standard" and numerous "special" rates), and a constant influx of customers with unique requests. Sandy was afraid to make any loan decisions on her own since she was unable to grasp all the finer points of analysis and policies. Mostly, she helped Jayne, gathered credit reports, investigated credit references, and whatever else Jayne needed. During all this time, Bud McDonald had spoken to her only a few times.

However, during the performance appraisal session today, he emphasized that Sandy was far behind in her training and that he would have to recommend that she be retained for an additional six months in commercial loans. Until she actually became adept in analyzing customer loan requests, he could not approve her rotation into the next bank operation.

CASE QUESTIONS

1. What do you see as the major problems in this case?

2. Is Bud correct in insisting on complete learning of consumer loan activities? Why or why not?

3. If you were to design a management training program for this bank, where would you start? Why?

NOTES

[1] I. L. Goldstein, *Training: Program Development and Evaluation* (Monterey, Calif.: Brooks/Cole, 1974), p. 3.

[2] Ibid., p. 4

[3] C. N. Greene, "The Satisfaction Performance Controversy: New Developments and Their Implications," *Business Horizons,* 15 (1972), 31–41.

[4] A. D. Szilagyi, Jr., and M. J. Wallace, Jr., *Organizational Behavior and Performance,* 2nd ed. (Santa Monica, Calif.: Goodyear, 1980), pp. 88–90.

[5] R. D. Middlemist and M. A. Hitt, *Organizational Behavior: Applied Concepts* (Chicago: Science Research Associates, 1981), pp. 167–169.

[6] L. Lien, "Reviewing Your Training and Development Activities," *Personnel Journal,* 58 (1979), 791–807.

[7] J. S. Jenness, "Budgeting and Controlling Costs," in *Training and Development Handbook: A Guide to Human Resource Development,* ed. R. L. Craig (New York: McGraw-Hill, 1976), pp. 4–1 to 4–12.

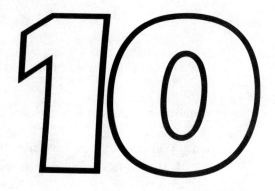

ORIENTATION AND TRAINING

LEARNING OBJECTIVES

After reading this chapter, you should be able to:

1. Explain the four basic concepts of learning theory and describe their relationships.
2. Discuss the similarities and differences between classical and instrumental learning.
3. Explain the importance of orientation in the training process.
4. Describe several on-the-job and off-the-job training approaches.
5. Discuss the differences between managerial or professional training and training for lower-level employees.
6. Explain one method of evaluating training programs and why evaluation is necessary.

Xerox Corporation is a major, international organization familiar to most people. It is the dominant firm in an industry that supplies office equipment, and its office copying equipment has become a generic name. When a duplicate copy needs to be made, one "makes a Xerox."

Judy Mason-Mertz is a marketing support specialist for Xerox Corporation in the Office Products Division. She has been employed by Xerox for nine years. Her job involves supporting the marketing effort of information processing softloaded systems. In this she makes demonstrations; performs applications analyses, concept presentations, and ministudies; exercises cancellation control; and must have comprehensive knowledge of competitive equipment. She also deals with customers to support their needs through preinstallation calls, in-depth training, and ongoing follow-up. She also trains other Xerox employees at various branch locations.

This is a demanding set of job responsibilities. It would be normal for a new employee to experience considerable anxiety when coming into such a job. A great number of new skills and much knowledge must be learned. We asked Judy to describe the manner in which Xerox helped her as a new employee to reduce these anxieties and learn her job effectively.

Interviewer: Can you describe your emotions about the job and the company during your first two or three months here? Did the company do anything to help make you "feel at home" during that time?

Judy Mason-Mertz: My first two or three months as a marketing support representative should, in retrospect, have been difficult. Xerox moved me from Jacksonville, Florida, to Tallahassee, Florida, where I knew no one. Along with the headaches that accompany any move, new job responsibilities, new business contacts, traveling three weeks a month, and trying to settle my affairs in Jacksonville, I only remember the fun and excitement of it all.

My immediate supervisor was located in Miami. Even though the distance could have caused me to feel "left out or forgotten," he seemed always to be just a phone call away.

Interviewer: Was it necessary for you to receive some initial training by the company before you could perform the job? If so, what was the training like?

Judy Mason-Mertz: Because of the technical/sales skills required, the training was extremely extensive and thorough. I spent three weeks in Dallas, Texas, learning how to operate the equipment. Two weeks were spent in Miami, Florida, with my manager and other experienced marketing support representatives, observing them in all possible functions and responsibilities. Then I spent three more weeks in Leesburg, Virginia, at the Xerox International Center for Training and Management Development. During these weeks, concentrated time was spent on such items as demonstration skills, sales skills, PSS (professional selling skills), teaching techniques, behavior modification, competitive training, and application analysis.

Interviewer: Do you ever get more training now that you are a skilled employee? If so, what is it like?

Judy Mason-Mertz: I am in a constant state of training. For example, since the beginning of the year, I have been to our training facility in Virginia for one week; to Dallas, Texas, for a week on three separate occasions. Additional in-branch training occurs approximately one or two days a month and is given by region support training specialists on various aspects of our fast-changing business.

INTRODUCTION

Jobs, in an advanced industrial society, can be enormously complex—because of the types of technical skills required, the breadth of knowledge demanded, and the myriad of organizational relationships that must be mastered. This complexity places special emphasis on the importance of training.

We can see this importance in jobs such as that described by Judy Mason-Mertz. Xerox is a complex, modern organization. Her job involves the use of many technical skills as well as skills in human relations. The length of her initial training program, and the complex array of skills being taught, suggests that Xerox invested a considerable sum in her training. This investment has paid off because Ms. Mason-Mertz is an effective employee.

In this chapter, we examine various training approaches that can be used to teach employees the skills and knowledge needed for performing their jobs. The effectiveness of these approaches requires logically that we design them according to the process by which people learn and that we deal with trainees' anxieties and uncertainties before exposing them to the learning process.

LEARNING PROCESS

The scientific study of learning began in 1885 with the work of Ebbinghaus on learning and memory.[1] But this area of study continues to be surrounded by considerable controversy, primarily between those who strongly believe that learning is the result of internalized mental or motivational processes and those who believe that learning is a result of external or environmental contingencies. While we do not wish to belabor the various merits of these viewpoints, it is useful to note that learning can be either a largely mental process or an environmental product. That is, learning of knowledge, such as memorizing the alphabet or reading and digesting a textbook, requires mainly mental processes.

However, when the focus of attention is on acquiring new behaviors, environmental contingencies play the more important role. Industrial training of employees involves the acquisition of new behaviors, behaviors that must be practiced and improved for performance purposes. Although such learning is often accompanied by mental processes (reading instruction manuals), the desired behaviors must be practiced, their results observed, and corrections made to acquire effective performance behaviors. The external or environmental theory of learning, then, is one that has the greater applicability to industrial training.[2]

Four Basic Concepts of Learning

Although the environmental theories of learning refer to a great many concepts, there are four basic concepts to which frequent reference is made. These concepts are drive, stimulus, response, and reinforcer.[3]

DRIVE. *Drive refers to a state of arousal.* A state of arousal can result from deprivation (e.g., having been deprived of food), in which case we are "driven" to seek food. A state of arousal can also result from external stimulation (e.g., an "opportunity" to gain recognition), in which case we are "driven" to seek recognition. Some drives are innate, such as the need for food or sleep; others are learned in society, such as the need for recognition, status, power, or satisfaction.

STIMULUS. *A stimulus is an event or object that serves as the occasion for a particular response or behavior.* Many events act as stimuli for responses. For example, a red light at a crosswalk is a stimulus that causes us not to step into the street. The sound of a doorbell is a stimulus to answer the door. A disapproving look from our supervisor is a signal for us to change our behavior to something more acceptable, perhaps to return to work.

RESPONSE OR BEHAVIOR. *Response refers to what we do in reacting to a stimulus.* Responses are behaviors in which we engage because we feel that they will be correct for the situation or stimulus. Not stepping into the street, answering the door, or getting back to work are correct responses to the described stimuli and will obtain favorable results.

REINFORCER. *A reinforcer is any result or event following a response that acts to maintain the strength of the response to similar, future stimuli.* For example, not being struck by a speeding car, seeing a friendly face at the door, or being given a look of approval from the supervisor are all results (events) that would strengthen the given responses. This reinforcement makes it likely that we will continue the responses the next time we face a red light, hear the doorbell, or see our supervisor's disapproving look.

Statement of Learning Principle

The basic principle of learning theory can be described as

> Any response or behavior occasioned by a stimulus and followed closely by a reinforcer that satisfies a drive or need will be strengthened and the likelihood of the same response to the same or similar stimulus in the future will be increased.[4]

This statement is related easily to organizational situations of training. When employees learn new tasks or duties, they will observe stimuli that occur and repeat behaviors that are reinforced. If managers provide reinforcers for correct behaviors, employees will learn operations. Learning is less effective when stimuli are not present or are hard to identify, when reinforcers are not provided, or when incorrect behaviors are reinforced inadvertently.

The Case of Classical Conditioning

The advancement of a theory of environmental learning began with Pavlov's work in the late 1800s. To describe this well-known research briefly, Pavlov observed that his laboratory dog salivated when food was placed in its mouth. The salivation response is an innate or unlearned response that is a reflexive aid to digestion. Food, in this case, is called an *unconditioned stimulus* and salivation an *unconditioned response.*

In a series of revealing studies, Pavlov rang a bell at the same time the dog was fed. After doing this several times, Pavlov found that the dog would salivate when the bell was rung, even though the dog was given no food. Apparently, the dog had learned that a ringing bell was a stimulus signaling that food would soon follow. In this case, the bell is called a *conditioned stimulus* and the associated salivation is called a *conditioned response,* because the pattern of stimulus-response has been learned.[5]

The Case of Instrumental Conditioning

People are not much like animals. Most of our behaviors are not reflexive, although we have many reflexive and unconditioned behaviors. Rather, most of our behaviors result from our attempts to accomplish specific and desired goals or purposes. These behaviors are said to be *instrumental* in achieving such goals.

We can contrast these behaviors to the one that Pavlov conditioned in the dog. We can see that "salivation" as a conditioned response is not different from the behavior "salivation" as an unconditioned response. Only the precipitating stimulus had changed. Further, in either case the salivation behavior did not help get food for the dog. Such behavior was not, then, instrumental in gaining the dog's goal of eating.

In contrast, stopping for a red light is the result of a higher-order reasoning process in which, by previous experience, we have learned such behavior is instrumental in not being hit by a car. Thus, in the case of human functioning, the instrumental theory of learning accounts for

> External stimulus events
>
> Internal information processing systems and regulatory codes
>
> Reinforcing responses and feedback processes

The instrumental conditioning process is illustrated in Figure 10-1. We can see that responses can have positive or negative consequences and, therefore, that the response is reinforced with positive consequences but not with negative consequences. As individuals experience the lifelong cycle of responding to various situations (stimuli), they observe the consequences of their behaviors and usually learn appropriate responses that are instrumental in achieving their purposes.

Finally, we must recognize that people can learn, instrumentally, by observing others. That is, we can see another's response to a stimulus, observe the consequences to the other person, and thereby learn vicariously what is an effective or ineffective behavior in that situation.

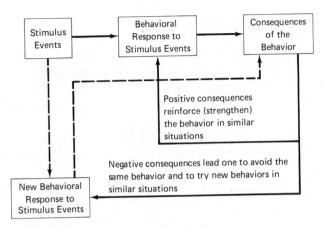

Figure 10-1

Environmental Learning Theory: Instrumental Learning

Source: Adapted from R. D. Middlemist and M. A. Hitt, *Organizational Behavior: Applied Concepts* (Chicago: Science Research Associates, 1981), p. 64.

Important Rules of Instrumental Conditioning

Research in instrumental conditioning theory has shown that the learning of new behaviors is most effective when the following rules or principles are observed:

1. The timing of reinforcers—the reinforcing quality of any consequence (event) of a behavior being greatest when that consequence immediately follows the behavior. Large lapses of time obscure the stimulus-response-reinforcement relationship.

2. The size of the reinforcer—the intended reinforcer being neither too large nor too small. Excessively large reinforcers make people dependent on them and unlikely to repeat the behaviors for more reasonable consequences. Small reinforcers may not be valued enough so as to occasion a desired response.[6]

3. Generalization or transfer—the extent to which learned responses to a specific stimuli in one specific setting will carry over to similar stimuli in other, but similar, settings. In other words, will behaviors learned in a classroom, say, be applied to a real world situation?

4. Goal gradient—the time span between the individual's behavior and the reinforcer. When this time span is short, the behavior is stronger. Thus we might see employee performances improve substantially in the last month prior to an annual bonus payment.

5. Knowledge of results—the process of feeding back information on the effectiveness of responses. Without this information a person might learn to do things that merely seem to be correct but that in fact lead to poor results later.[7]

Latency

6. Successive approximation—the schedule or sequence in which complex behaviors are learned. It has been found that complex behaviors are learned best beginning with the simplest basic behavior, then adding the next most simple and so on, until the entire complex sequence has been learned. This is similar to the manner in which math abilities are learned, beginning with simple counting and moving on to addition, multiplication, and so on, until complex math such as calculus is learned.

7. Modeling—the process of vicarious learning achieved by observing another person (the model) demonstrating the behavior and seeing the stimuli and reinforcers that apply.[8]

8. Extinction—the withholding of reinforcement, which decreases the strength of a response. Extinction has been found to be more effective than punishment in eliminating incorrect or ineffective behaviors.[9]

ORIENTATION PROCESS

Before we examine actual training approaches used by organizations, it is useful to discuss what might be considered a pretraining process referred to as orientation. Even though many organizations have training programs that are based on sound learning theory, some experience difficulty because of fears and anxieties held by new employees. In fact, if we examine learning curves, such as those illustrated in Figure 10-2, we see that the rate of learning is very low during the initial stages of a training

Figure 10-2

The Relationship Among Learning, Anxiety, and Turnover

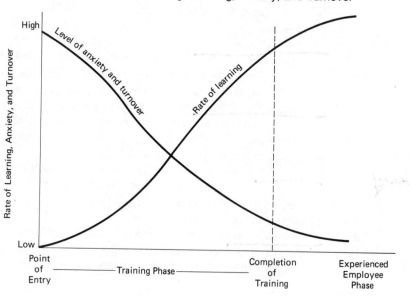

program. Furthermore, researchers have found that employee turnover is highest during the initial stages of the employee-employer relationship.[10] Judy Mason-Mertz described her initial contact as "fun and exciting" but recognized that it could have been difficult. Although different employees react differently, organizational training is less successful when employers neglect the possibilities that many new employees experience fear or uncertainty in their new jobs.

Orientation Perspectives

The early experiences of new employees in an organization are illustrated in Figure 10-3. In this view, employees bring certain expectations with them when they join the organization. During the first few days (weeks), employees discover that some of their expectations were either unrealistic or not provided for by the organization. As they compare their expectations with what is discovered as reality, large deviations may lead to turnover. If the employees find that the deviations are small they may decide to stay with their new jobs and therefore, experience a socialization process in which they become integrated with the rules, values, and personalities of the organization.

Orientation: a systematic organization strategy for helping new employees form their expectations and for becoming socialized to the organization.

Figure 10-3

Orientation, Turnover, and Employee Effectiveness

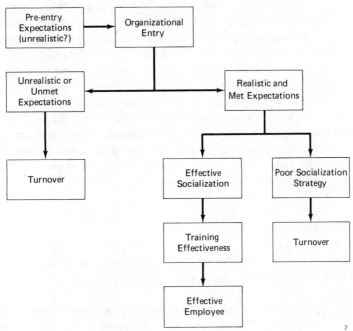

UNREALISTIC AND UNMET EXPECTATIONS.   New employees' expectations are often inflated unrealistically as a result of the organization's recruiting efforts. These inflated expectations are called "unrealistic expectations." Alternatively, even though some expectations are indeed realistic, it may be that the organization (for whatever reason) simply does not meet those expectations. These are referred to as "unmet expectations."[11] It is important that managers design a strategy to reduce early turnover by ensuring that employee expectations are both realistic and met.

One strategy is to help recruits form more realistic expectations during the recruiting process. It has been found that greater realism results when recruits receive orientation information through booklets, films, or other media that describe factual rather than idealistic conditions of organizational employment.[12]

A second strategy is for managers to meet with new employees when they are first hired. At this time, the manager can solicit the new employee's expectations, clarify them, and exchange viewpoints on what the employee may face or expect. The purpose is to reach an understanding by which neither the employee nor the manager will be disappointed before training is completed. Research has found that both strategies reduce early turnover.[13]

SOCIALIZATION.   Assuming that the individual does not leave the organization before training has begun, socialization occurs. Socialization is the process of integrating the individual's values, abilities, behaviors, and social knowledge with those of the organization. Thus part of the orientation strategy must be to socialize the new employee. This strategy must include imparting of an understanding of the organization's broader mission, what the work culture is like ("how things are done around here"), and the norms of employee groups. Training is generally aimed at acquiring technical performance skills and does not account for this needed socialization.

It must be recognized that employee training is likely to be ineffective unless the organization takes steps to reduce employee anxieties and fears. Further, new employees must be socialized into the organization by relating their expectations to organizational realities. At a practical level, the "sink or swim" approach is not effective. Uncertainty and fears may develop as new employees seek the needed understanding. Again, socialization is the manager's responsibility. Successful strategies may include the fostering of links to reliable, experienced co-workers (such as buddy systems) and frequent managerial appraisal of new employees to provide feedback and information exchange. Orientation strategies such as these must precede the training experience, thereby enhancing training effectiveness.

TRAINING APPROACHES

Broadly conceived, there are four basic steps that managers must take to train their employees effectively. These are

1. Identify the target group for training—are these new employees or older employees who need additional training?

2. Identify the training goals and needs—this is done by referring to the job analysis, description, and specification and contrasting these to measures of existing abilities and skills of the trainee(s).
3. Design the training programs in terms of appropriate principles of learning—learning theory and orientation concepts that we have examined suggest that the training program will be more effective to the degree that
   a. Dysfunctional uncertainties and unrealistic (unmet) expectations of the trainee are reduced.
   b. New behaviors to be learned do not conflict with old behaviors or means are provided to extinguish old, dysfunctional behaviors.
   c. The trainee is an active participant (asks questions, etc.).
   d. Training is broken into basic units arranged in a meaningful sequence.
   e. Provisions are made for demonstrating (modeling) the new behaviors.
   f. The program provides opportunities for practice and repetition of the behaviors.
   g. New, correct behaviors are reinforced by some means.
   h. The trainee is motivated to improve his or her own performance.
   i. The trainee is provided with knowledge of the results from attempts to improve.
   j. The learning situation allows for individual differences in the speed of learning.
   k. Provisions are made for generalizing or transfer of the new behaviors from the training setting to the actual job setting.
4. Evaluate the outcomes of the training experience with a scientifically designed evaluation scheme—the manager must determine whether the training accomplished what it was supposed to.[14]

There are a number of ways in which we could look at common training programs or approaches. However, we have chosen to examine them in terms of on-the-job and off-the-job approaches. We consider learning theory issues associated with step 3 as each is discussed and then discuss evaluation as a separate issue.

On-the-Job Training Approaches

The most common general method of training employees is to have the training carried out on the job. That is, the employee reports to his or her work station and, with some form of guidance, begins to perform the task, learning while doing so. Most of us have been trained, at one job or another, in this manner. But if we discussed our experiences, we would find great differences in how on-the-job training was actually conducted and in our feelings about it. This is because some managers and organizations give careful consideration to specific methods used, whereas others allow such training to be haphazard and unplanned. Four methods can be employed to make on-the-job training more effective.

COACHING. *Coaching refers to the assignment of a specific person to act as either an instructor or resource person for the trainee.* Usually, the training is done by an experienced employee or by the manager. Occasionally, a trained instructor is assigned to the trainee's job setting, but this is more costly and also more rare. The coach's task is usually to demonstrate (model) the task operations, to answer questions, and to provide guidance in developing understanding.

Coaching, without support from other methods, is not particularly effective. That is, coaching is better than not coaching, but it should be used in conjunction with other methods. This is so primarily because observational learning (watching a coach) effectiveness is highly dependent on trainees' internal capacities. The rate and level of learning by observation are limited by the extent to which

1. Trainees possess necessary sensory capacities for accurately detecting the modeled stimuli.
2. Trainees possess motor capacities for precisely repeating the modeled behavior.
3. Trainees possess the capacity for mentally visualizing and rehearsing the modeled sequence of behaviors.[15]

With these thoughts in mind, we can see that some trainees may learn from coaching alone but that others will not possess each required capacity. Therefore, on-the-job training must employ other methods to support coaching.

APPRENTICESHIP. *Apprenticeship refers to a combined on-the-job, off-the-job training approach in which the trainee agrees to work for a salary below that of fully qualified employees in exchange for a specified number of hours of formal training by the organization.* This is a common approach used in certain occupations, such as electrician, plumber, and welder, and is often coordinated with a particular union or certifying agency. Examples of apprenticeship programs, registered with the U.S. Department of Labor, are shown in Table 10-1.

Table 10-1

Occupational Apprenticeships

Occupation	Usual Length of Apprenticeship Training
Cosmetician	Two years
Butcher	Two to three years
Bricklayer	Three years
Sheet metalworker	Three to four years
Carpenter	Four years
Machinist	Four years
Boilermaker	Four years
Electrician	Four to five years
Patternmaker	Five years

Source: U.S. Department of Labor, *The National Apprenticeship Program* (Washington, D.C.: Government Printing Office, 1972), pp. 9–27.

Apprenticeship programs often combine on-the-job coaching by a skilled journeyman with classroom training in applied math, materials, and technical knowledge. Because apprenticeship programs employ many of the principles of learning, such as modeling, feedback, and appropriate learning sequence, they are often quite effective. Drawbacks include the length of training at which trainees are paid at the lower rate and an overreliance on the coach who may not be trained in applying reinforcement.

JOB ROTATION.   *Job rotation is the process of training employees by rotating them through a series of related tasks.* In this method, trainees are exposed to various coaches, points of views, and task operations. It is not generally useful for training technical skills, such as programming or welding, since it does not focus on these. However, it is very common for training managers. The wide exposure to different operations provides them with a general knowledge of company procedures and how coordination is achieved. In most cases of managerial training, the new trainee is assigned to each of the various operations for a three- to six-month period and receives a final, managerial assignment in about two years. This is the type of training described by Judy Mason-Mertz as a central aspect of her training at Xerox. We should note that such training is often combined with coaching and classroom activities.

Primary weaknesses of the approach relate to the difficulty of coordinating the various assignments, the fact that some of the coaching managers may not be motivated to spend time with a trainee assigned for only a short period, the fact that different coaches may espouse conflicting viewpoints of company policies and procedures, and the fact that the socialization of new employees into more or less "permanent" work groups is delayed.

JOB INSTRUCTION TRAINING.   *Job instruction training (JIT) is a set of coordinated procedures for conducting on-the-job training, developed by the War Manpower Commission during World War II.* This comprehensive set of procedures incorporates many of the principles laid out earlier in this chapter, including modeling, practice, feedback, active participation, generalization, and orientation. JIT procedures specify the need to have coaches (trainers) who are trained in giving instruction, an analysis of the job, a measure of what the trainee knows prior to instruction, and a schedule for training activities. An abbreviated list of steps for JIT is shown in Table 10-2.

CONCLUSIONS.   On-the-job training methods are useful to organizations for a number of reasons. They often require little additional effort and no special equipment except that used in the job, and the organization obtains some production while the employee is learning. In addition, on-the-job training methods can apply several principles of learning and generalization is maximized.

However, on-the-job training methods also invoke risks. Production equipment is more likely to be damaged, instruction may be haphazard (especially in job rotation), and pressures of the work setting may increase trainees' anxiety. Managers must evaluate these advantages and risks, consider the nature of behaviors and attitudes to

Table 10-2

Job Instruction Technique

Pretraining
1. Develop timetable in terms of each skill to be learned and speed at which proficiency will be attained.
2. Break job into simple, component parts.
3. Assemble all needed materials, machines, and supplies.
4. Arrange training location in the same manner as the employee will be expected to keep it.

Training
1. Begin with introductory statement of the purposes of the job.
2. Follow up with step by step review and demonstration of the job operations.
3. Have trainee perform the operations and repeat explanations for the trainer.
4. Have trainer ask questions and correct errors as trainee progresses through step 3.
5. Have trainee practice until satisfactory proficiency is attained.
6. Remove close supervision but have trainer check back on a periodic basis.

Trainer's Duties in Summary
1. Focus trainee's attention to relevant and critical tasks.
2. Estimate difficulty of each task and adjust
   a. trainee's rate of practice.
   b. the number of operations required at specific times.
   c. the range of permissible errors at specific stages.
3. Detect incorrect behaviors and correct them before they become habits.
4. Detect individual trainee weaknesses and provide extra practice and guidance accordingly.
5. Provide immediate knowledge of results.

See: War Manpower Commission, *The Training Within Industry Report,* (Washington, D.C.: U.S. Government Printing Office, 1945).

be learned, and determine whether on-the-job methods are likely to be superior to off-the-job methods.

Off-the-Job Training Approaches

Many organizations either supplement on-the-job training with off-the-job methods or in some jobs use off-the-job methods as the primary means of training. Off-the-job training refers to training conducted away from the actual work setting, be this at a special site in the organization or in a nonorganization location, such as at a vocational school or university.

Off-the-job training is particularly appropriate for certain managerial skills (such as interpersonal abilities), for certain production jobs where machinery controls the pace of work (an assembly line operation), and for some technical jobs (programmer) where teaching expertise is found elsewhere. Four common off-the-job approaches are vestibule training, programmed instruction, classroom training, and sensitivity training.

VESTIBULE TRAINING.   *Vestibule training refers to training that occurs in a special site, usually on the organization's premises, away from the actual work setting, but using equipment and procedures similar to those used at the work setting.* Vestibule training offers a number of advantages. First, on-the-job pressures are avoided and the rate of learning can be slower. Second, a trained trainer is more feasible because several trainees can be taught at once. Third, it tends to reduce training time and maximize skill acquisition.[16] Fourth, there are no problems with breakage of equipment needed for actual production.

However, equipment is often that which has been replaced by newer equipment. This is because duplicating exact equipment may be prohibitively expensive. Thus generalization is sometimes problematic. Also, vestibule training is expensive in other ways. Costs include training space, loss of production from trainees, and the trainer's salary. Still, this method is valuable for training in assembly-line type jobs.

An example of vestibule training was observed by one of the authors at an aircraft parts manufacturer. The company had recently acquired a new, automated lathe used in the manufacturing process. The old lathe was semiautomatic involving a more manual-based setup process, but the actual machine operation was quite similar. The old machine was moved to a remote area of the plant, and new employees trained on this machine, learning the operation procedures, but not the setup process. Good parts produced by trainees were added to the plant's production. Minimal time was required, then, to learn the setup procedure on the new lathe, a distinct advantage considering manufacturing requirements on the main production line.

PROGRAMMED INSTRUCTION.   *Programmed instruction refers to learning materials that are organized in a sequential fashion so that correct understanding of one set of materials must be indicated before the trainee can progress to the next set.* This method often uses books or manuals, but it may be supported by electronic teaching machines and computer systems. In practice, the trainee reads a set of materials and then responds to questions (usually multiple choice, or true or false). If the answer is correct, the trainee goes to the next section. However, if the answer is incorrect, the trainee reads additional information and again responds to questions on that material. This procedure is repeated until the trainee answers correctly, at which time he or she goes forward.

This method utilizes several learning principles, including movement from simple to complex material and provision of feedback. It is limited in that reinforcement is difficult and interaction with a coach is minimal. However, research has shown it to be one of the more effective methods for building knowledge and retention of that knowledge.[17]

CLASSROOM INSTRUCTION.   Perhaps the most common method of off-the-job training is that referred to as classroom instruction. Instruction of this type is familiar to nearly every individual in our society since it is the process used in education. Only the contents of training, not the methods used, are different from those used in educational classrooms, and in some cases the content is similar or identical. This method is particularly useful for imparting cognitive, as opposed to physical, skills. Classroom instruction content runs a wide gamut from technical knowledge (e.g., accounting concepts, engineering concepts) to broader social issues (e.g., human relations concepts, social responsibility concepts).

Classroom instruction may be appropriate for lower-level employees wanting to build skills for advancement purposes, for professionals needing to stay current with technological developments, and for managers needing to build broader perspectives of societal relationships. Classroom instruction is available from many institutions such as high schools, vocational training centers, colleges, and universities. Also, a number of specialized organizations cater to the training needs of industry and offer a wide range of classroom courses.

The specific methods that may be used in a classroom setting also vary widely. For example, a course may use the lecture as its primary method or it may draw on demonstrations, audiovisual aids, case studies, role playing, or in-basket techniques. The technique to be used depends on both the content and the type of trainees. The effectiveness of classroom training varies widely because of the difference in techniques used and the type of skill being developed, as shown in Table 10-3.

SENSITIVITY TRAINING.   *Sensitivity training is a process in which several individuals work together for several days for the purpose of building self-awareness, understanding of group processes, and greater understanding of interpersonal relationships.* Under the guidance of a qualified trainer, the trainees are encouraged to probe their feelings, abilities, and needs in building interpersonal relationships. The process involves a penetration of their psychological defenses, and some emotional reactions are experienced.

Sensitivity training has been criticized because of the emotional responses it can evoke and because it cannot be established firmly that the trainees actually change

Table 10-3
Effectiveness of Off-the-Job Training Methods

Training Goal	Training Methods	
	Most Effective ────────▶	Least Effective
1. Knowledge acquisition	Programmed instruction, case study	Sensitivity training, lecture
2. Problem-solving ability	Case study, simulations	Audiovisual, lecture
3. Interpersonal skills	Sensitivity training, role play	Programmed instruction, lecture
4. Attitude change	Sensitivity training, role play	Programmed instruction, lecture

Source: Adapted from S. Carroll, Jr., F. Paine, and J. Ivancevich, "The Relative Effectiveness of Training Methods," *Personnel Psychology*, 25 (1972), 495–499.

their interpersonal behaviors when they return to their jobs.[18] Still, many organizations firmly believe that such training is an essential aid in the development of their managers. As reflected in Table 10-3, some research indicates this type of training is very effective in changing managers' attitudes and in developing intended interpersonal skills.

CONCLUSIONS.   Off-the-job training methods are useful because they are cost effective (e.g., many trainees can be trained at the same time by one instructor). They are invaluable in developing cognitive and interpersonal skills but may be weaker in building physical skills. In terms of learning principles, it can be seen that anxiety may be lower in the classroom, that modeling may be used, and that allowances may be made in the speed of learning. However, classroom methods are generally weaker than on-the-job methods in providing reinforcement, practice, generalization, and knowledge of results (as applied to the job).

MANAGERIAL AND PROFESSIONAL TRAINING

Our discussion of orientation and training, thus far, has tended to ignore important issues surrounding differences between various types of employees. Although all the methods have applications to most employee groups, the training approach that is most effective will differ considerably. This is because the goals of training and the needs of the employees are widely different. This difference is great, especially between technicians and unskilled employees and between nonmanagerial and managerial and other professional employees.

The Goals of Training

For lower-level employees, the goals of training deal most often with hands-on skills that relate to current performance. Hands-on skills are those that require physical activity or contact with some object, such as a wiring assembly. It should be noted that hands-on skills may also require high levels of knowledge; for example, a machinist must know various metal strengths, cutting speeds, and other complex information.

However, the goals of managerial and professional training relate more often to decision-making skills and leadership skills that are likely to affect future performance or promotion opportunities. Many firms are experiencing high turnover rates among their young professional and managerial employees. Some researchers feel that this problem is the result of the employees perceiving a "dead end" job from which promotion is unlikely.[19]

Thus the goals of managerial and professional training are developmental. Many of the methods described earlier (i.e., in-basket simulations, case study, role playing, laboratory or sensitivity training) are appropriate means for developing the potential of these employees. We should also recognize that current performances are generally improved as a result of the training, since the employees are likely to put the new knowledge to work in their immediate jobs.

The Needs of Managerial and Professional Employees

The effectiveness of managerial and professional training depends on a number of factors, including

> Intellectual skills and education level of the trainees
> Self-concept of the trainees
> Job assignment(s)
> The trainees' immediate supervisors

New managerial and professional employees, today, are highly educated (advanced degrees), above average in intelligence, interpersonally competent, and motivated. They also tend to have positive self-concepts.[20] These factors indicate that training must be geared to the high level of trainee skills. That is, basic training may be redundant with trainee skills and negatively affect the trainees' responsiveness to the organization. Job assignments and supervisory coaching must be matched to the needs of these employees. Poor work assignments (e.g., unchallenging, dead end) coupled with poor supervisory coaching may reduce trainees' self-concepts and lead to turnover. Thus managerial and professional training must be designed around proper job assignments and supervisory coaching.

JOB ASSIGNMENTS.   We have already seen that job rotation is one training method that is used in managerial and professional training. However, the nature of the jobs to which these employees are assigned is of critical importance. Repetitive job operations are less useful than are jobs that incorporate responsibility and challenge. Jobs that are particularly useful in this training tend to

1. be nonroutine *projects.*
2. have observable results.
3. require integration of inputs and knowledge from different areas.
4. expose the trainee to a comprehensive view of the organization's operations.
5. involve important policy or financial matters, rather than repetitive decisions.
6. require full use of decision skills.[21]

For example, asking a managerial trainee to help develop the departmental budget will be nonroutine, have observable results, and so on. However, having that trainee responsible for entering supply vouchers on a daily basis is routine, repetitive and requires few decision skills. From a training perspective, the first assignment is more developmental.

PERFORMANCE COACHING.   Many organizations rely on supervisory coaching as a major means of training new managerial and professional employees. This method is of such importance that supervisors may be trained to act as coaches. The method, when formalized, requires the supervisor regularly to observe the trainee's performance and then to hold frequent discussions with the trainee, focusing on performance improvements. Because of its focus, this process is often referred to as performance coaching and consists of

Development of learning and performance objectives

Establishing time frames for achieving goals

Measurement of achievements

Regular task-related and personal feedback by the supervisor to the trainee that is both positive and negative

Reinforcement of desired behaviors

Supervisors who are effective performance coaches provide good role models and are not necessarily "nice persons." It is through constructive feedback and criticism that new managers and professionals develop their potential. An example of the impact of effective performance coaching is seen in Judy Mason-Mertz's case. Performance feedback, provided by her supervisor, was felt to be a major contribution to her development.

EVALUATION OF TRAINING

It might seem, given all the guidelines and principles for learning and training, that any logically designed training program must, by definition, accomplish its purposes. However, closer inspection of the complexities of training reveals that even the most logically designed program might not benefit either the trainee or the organization. We must evaluate the results of a training effort, after its completion, to be sure of its benefits.[22] Although a wide variety of evaluation procedures can be applied to training programs, it is nearly always true that the evaluation procedure should

1. Be planned at the same time that the learning objectives for the training are outlined.
2. Be based on objective information gathered as trainees progress through training.
3. Follow rigorous scientific principles.

Following this rationale, evaluation of training will attempt to answer several important questions.

1. Did the behavior of trainees change?
2. If it did change, was this due to the training program or to some other cause?
3. If it did change, is the change consistent with the learning objectives?
4. Has the change improved trainees' performances on the job?

Criteria

To answer the four questions above, the evaluator must be able to measure the specific results of training. Criteria refers to the measurements of those outcomes. A number of criteria are of possible use in the evaluation of training, some of which are shown in Table 10-4. As illustrated, there are four major types: reaction criteria, learning criteria, behavioral criteria, and results criteria. These are often referred to as "levels" of criteria because each one is successively more rigorous, requiring more effort to obtain but yielding a better and more relevant evaluation.[23]

REACTION CRITERIA.   These are the least rigorous of the evaluation criteria. They are simply measures of the trainer's or trainees' reactions or impressions about the program. They are usually obtained by questionnaires given at the end of the training program. While it may be useful to know how trainees "feel" about the training, such information cannot substitute for other criteria.

Table 10-4

Examples of Evaluation Criteria for Training Programs

Reaction Criteria
    Trainee ratings of usefulness of program
    Trainer rating of usefulness of program
    Trainee ratings of satisfaction with program

Learning Criteria
    Trainee scores on test items
    Trainee scores on skill demonstration tests

Behavioral Criteria
    Ratings of acceptable behaviors by supervisor
    Number of safety rules broken
    Grievance reports
    Length and frequency of unauthorized breaks from work station
    Number of complaints against trainee by co-workers

Results Criteria
    Number of units produced, items sold, etc.
    Dollar volume of sales
    Number of letters typed
    Rate of turnover
    Rate of scrappage or errors
    Length of time taken to reach minimum performance standard
    Supervisor rating of performance

LEARNING CRITERIA.   These measurements are usually related to tests that cover the training material and are taken at the completion of training. They answer the question, "Did the trainees understand the information provided by training?" In some cases, these may be skill exams (e.g., wiring a toaster), but more often they pertain to facts, information, and other conceptual understanding.

BEHAVIORAL CRITERIA.   These are measures of trainee behaviors on the job. They are an attempt to determine if the things learned in training are being applied on the job. For example, if the manager attended sensitivity training, a behavioral criterion might be the amount to which he or she allows subordinates to participate in making decisions. It should be understood that these criteria relate only to behaviors, not to the results of those behaviors. The measures might be obtained by observing the trainees' on-the-job behaviors or by asking co-workers, supervisors, and subordinates for their observations.

RESULTS CRITERIA.   These are the most rigorous criteria and pertain to the actual achievement of organizationally desired objectives or results. Such measures might be cost or productivity figures. They might also be employee morale figures, absenteeism rates, profits, and so on. We must recognize that these criteria are not interchangeable with reaction, learning, or behavioral criteria. For example, it might be that trainees *liked* the training, *learned* what was taught, and *have changed* their behaviors on the job, but achieve poor results because we designed the *wrong* content. To conclude that nothing was *learned* in training would be wrong. The trainee, indeed, learned what we taught, but *we* taught the wrong things. This example points out one of the important reasons for evaluating training programs—that is to be sure we train the right skills.

Evaluation Design

There are a great many ways in which to evaluate training. It is not our intention to discuss them all. We suggest that proper evaluation designs are a function of many factors and that rigorous evaluation procedures are best designed by trained specialists. However, the basic design that has general application is similar to the design used for validating selection instruments (see Chapter 7). This basic design consists of the following steps:

1. Determine the objectives to be achieved by the training program.
2. Establish the criteria measurements that relate to those objectives. It may be that we wish to use only one set of criteria (say, results criteria) or all four sets of criteria. It is generally better to look at all four sets, since we probably want to know how trainees react, whether learning occurs, whether learned behaviors transfer to on-the-job, and if training results in desired objectives.
3. Establish the content of training that seems appropriate to the objectives.
4. Randomly select one group of employees (from the target group to be

trained) to actually receive the training experience. The group of employees not selected is used as a control group to ensure that other factors do not account for changes in behavior or results.

5. Train the selected employees.
6. Obtain the criteria measures. It should be noted that behavioral measures and results measures cannot be obtained until trainees actually have been placed on the job and have performed in that job for some time. Reaction measures and learning measures are taken earlier, at the completion of training. Finally, all criteria measures are taken from *both the trained and the untrained employees.*
7. Compare the criteria measures from the trained group with the criteria measures from the untrained group. Differences in the measures will indicate the effect of training.
8. If the training program results in the desired effects, the untrained employees should then be trained. Otherwise, modifications must be made to the training program and a second evaluation then be undertaken.

This evaluation procedure is not always possible, especially in smaller organizations. However, managers should strive to evaluate their training programs in some similar manner because it is only from evaluation that we can know whether the investment made in training is beneficial. An example of the usefulness of evaluation is provided by two researcher-consultants who wished to know if a particular human relations training program made managers more effective. One-half of the target management group was selected randomly for training and the other half was not trained. Several criteria of effectiveness were measured for both groups, and a comparison revealed that the trained managers were more considerate of their subordinates (a training objective) and were rated by their superiors as more effective (a training objective). This evaluation demonstrated the beneficial effects of the training program, and the organization then confidently sent the remaining managers to the human relations training program.[24]

SUMMARY

In this chapter, we have examined the learning process and its application to the design of effective training programs. Four basic concepts of learning—drive, stimulus, response or behavior, and reinforcement—were described. The basic principle of learning is that any behavior occasioned by a stimulus and followed closely by a reinforcer that satisfies a drive will be strengthened and that the likelihood of the same response to the same or similar stimulus in the future will be increased. This principle is applied to employee training when we can determine behaviors that lead to organizational effectiveness and identify the situations or stimuli in which employees should so behave. By reinforcing these behaviors in the correct situations, employees learn how to be productive. This theory of training is called instrumental conditioning.

Orientation is a pretraining process that reduces anxiety by correcting unrealistic expectations and socializing employees to their new work environments. Orientation facilitates the training process.

Broadly conceived, the four basic steps of the training process are the identification of the target group needing training, the identification of training goals and needs, the application of appropriate principles of learning so as to design the training program, and the evaluation of the outcomes of training. Several training approaches were examined, including on-the-job and off-the-job designs. These approaches are used for varying groups of employees (e.g., unskilled, skilled, managerial, professional), but each approach has certain limitations and advantages. The choice of a particular approach depends on the nature of the trainees, the type of material or skills being learned, and the nature of the job to which the trainee is assigned.

Since the choice of a training approach is always a somewhat tenuous decision, it is best to evaluate the results of training. It is necessary to determine if trainees change their behaviors, if the changes are in fact the result of training, and if the changes are consistent with the training objectives. Further, we must determine if the changes benefit the organization in terms of improved performance. The training activities, approaches, and evaluations were derived from the training logic set forth in Chapter 9. This logic invariably leads to a superior training program, but we should not forget that training is not a one-time experience for employees. The best training program, if limited to new employees only, will not yield an effective organization. Training, designed and evaluated logically, must be provided to employees throughout their organizational careers.

INTERVIEW WRAP-UP

Occasionally, training is late in getting to me (a need-to-know arrives and I must train myself), which can make it a bit repetitive. But, overall, training is necessary, timely, and extremely effective. —Judy Mason-Mertz, marketing support specialist, Xerox Corporation.

WHAT MANAGERS SHOULD DO REGARDING PERSONNEL MANAGEMENT ACTIVITIES

1. Managers should study, understand, and apply a sound learning theory in the design of employee training programs. We suggest that instrumental conditioning is especially useful in training that involves acquisition of new behaviors.

2. Managers should spend time with new employees or otherwise provide for their orientation in the organization. Orientation should be designed to reduce uncertainties and fears as well as to develop reasonable expectations and socialization.

3. Managers should analyze the job and determine whether on-the-job or off-the-job

training is most appropriate. Guidelines suggested in this chapter can assist managers in this decision.

4. All training programs should be evaluated to assess their usefulness. Such evaluations may be used on the best combination of reaction, learning, behavioral, and results criteria, according to the organization's needs.

REVIEW QUESTIONS

1. What are the four basic concepts of learning theory? Describe their relationships.
2. In what ways are classical conditioning and instrumental conditioning dissimilar?
3. Why does orientation play an important role in the training process?
4. In what ways does managerial or professional training differ from training for lower-level employees?
5. If, in question 4, these differences exist, why can it be that a particular training approach (say, coaching) might be appropriate for managers and also lower-level employees?
6. Why is evaluation a necessary function in the training process?

KEY CONCEPTS

Apprenticeship
Behavioral criteria
Classical conditioning
Classroom instruction
Coaching
Drive
Evaluation
Evaluation design
Extinction
Generalization/transfer
Goal gradient
Instrumental conditioning
Job instruction training
Job rotation
Knowledge of results
Learning criteria
Learning theory
Managerial training

Modeling
Off-the-job training
On-the-job training
Orientation
Performance coaching
Professional training
Programmed instruction
Reaction criteria
Reinforcer
Response
Results criteria
Sensitivity training
Socialization
Stimulus
Successive approximation
Unrealistic expectations
Vestibule training

CASE

A LEARNING EXPERIENCE

Bernie Bloom was a little older than the average doctoral student. He had worked in business for several years in a variety of managerial positions before deciding that he would like to become a professor. He was thirty-three when he accepted an offer to pursue doctoral studies in the business school at Urban State University. He accepted this offer because of the high reputation of the Urban State program and because they offered him a part-time position as a teaching assistant that would help support his financial needs.

Bernie sold his house and moved to the city where Urban State was located. He reported to the dean two weeks before classes started to arrange his own studies and to get his teaching assistantship assignment. Although Bernie had been successful in business, he was concerned about the possibility of failing at Urban State. His concern related only partially to his own studies. He was much more concerned about his teaching assistantship, especially when Dean Warner told him that he had sole responsibility for teaching the introduction to management class. Bernie had thought he would be assisting a professor and was shocked to discover he would be alone in the classroom.

Bernie expressed some of his fears to Dean Warner, including the facts that he'd never taught before, that he'd never taken a class in education or teaching methods, and that he didn't have any idea of what to include as material for the class. Dean Warner smiled and said, "Bernie, you want to become a professor so you've got to start teaching in the classroom sometime. Now is as good a time as any. You'll do just fine. Remember that most professors were just like you when they started. They had never taught before. But, like you, they had good, solid business experience, were studying advanced management, and were bright. These are more important than a course in teaching methods."

Bernie smiled weakly, realizing that Dean Warner was right, but still he was a little apprehensive. Dean Warner then sent him to see Professor Wilson to get a copy of a previous course outline used for the class.

The semester seemed to go on forever. Bernie noticed that class attendance was poor, that several students seemed bored, and that it was nearly impossible to get meaningful discussion from the students. When he passed out the student class evaluation questionnaire on the last day, he knew the results would be disastrous. He wasn't sure he would ever be a good professor.

CASE QUESTIONS

1. What factors are important in this situation?
2. What should Dean Warner have done when Bernie first visited him?
3. What alternative solutions would prevent this problem in the future?

NOTES

[1]B. M. Bass and J. A. Vaughan, *Training in Industry: The Management of Learning* (Belmont, Calif.: Brooks/Cole, 1966), pp. 9–10.

[2]F. Luthans and R. Kreitner, *Organizational Behavior Modification* (Glenview, Ill.: Scott, Foresman, 1975), pp. 11–12.

[3]Bass and Vaughan, *Training in Industry,* p. 10.

[4]E. L. Thorndike, *Animal Intelligence* (New York: Macmillan, 1911), pp. 244–45.

[5]C. B. Fester and M. C. Perrott, *Behavior Principles* (New York: Appleton-Century-Crofts, 1968).

[6]Y. Yinon, A. Bizman, and M. Goldberg, "Effect of Relative Magnitude of Reward and Type of Need on Satisfaction," *Journal of Applied Psychology,* 61 (1976), 325–328.

[7]L. Becker, "Joint Effect of Feedback and Goal Setting on Performance, A Field Study of Residential Energy Conservation," *Journal of Applied Psychology,* 63 (1978), 428–433.

[8]H. Weiss, "Subordinate Imitation of Supervisor Behavior: The Role of Modeling in Organizational Socialization," *Organizational Behavior and Human Performance,* 19 (1977), 89–105.

[9]Fester and Perrott, *Behavioral Principles,* pp. 6–7.

[10]P. M. Muchinsky and M. L. Tuttle, "Employee Turnover: An Empirical and Methodological Assessment," *Journal of Vocational Behavior,* 14 (1979), 43–77.

[11]M. R. Louis, "Surprise and Sense Making: What Newcomers Experience in Entering Unfamiliar Organizational Settings," *Administrative Science Quarterly,* 25 (1980), 226–250.

[12]J. P. Wanous, "Organizational Entry: From Naive Expectations to Realistic Benefits," *Journal of Applied Psychology,* 61 (1976), 22–29.

[13]M. D. Dunnette, R. D. Arvey, and P. A. Banas, "Why Do They Leave?" *Personnel,* 50 (1973), 25–39.

[14]Bass and Vaughan, *Training in Industry: The Management of Learning*

[15]A. Bandura, *Principles of Behavior Modification* (New York: Holt, Rinehart and Winston, 1969), pp. 147–150.

[16]W. McGehee and D. H. Livingston, "Persistence of the Effects of Training Employees to Reduce Waste," *Personnel Psychology,* 7 (1954), 33–39.

[17]S. Carroll, Jr., F. Paine, and J. Ivancevich, "The Relative Effectiveness of Training Methods," *Personnel Psychology,* 25 (1972), 495–499.

[18]A. Szilagyi, Jr., and M. Wallace, Jr., *Organizational Behavior and Performance* (Santa Monica, Calif: Goodyear, 1980), 562–564.

[19]J. Aplin, "Issues and Problems in Developing Managerial Careers and Potential," *Business Quarterly,* 43 (1978), 22–29.

[20]Ibid.

[21]Ibid

[22]L. L. Cummings and D. P. Schwab, *Performance in Organizations: Determinants and Appraisal* (Glenview, Ill.: Scott, Foresman, 1973), p. 19.

[23]D. L. Kirkpatrick, "Techniques for Evaluating Training Programs," *Journal of the American Society of Training Directors,* 13 (1959), 3–9, 21–26.

[24]H. Hand and J. Slocum, "A Longitudinal Study of the Effects of a Human Relations Training Program on Managerial Effectiveness," *Journal of Applied Psychology,* 56 (1972), 412–417.

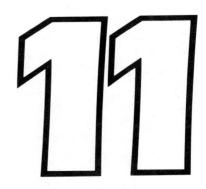

CAREER AND MANAGEMENT DEVELOPMENT

LEARNING OBJECTIVES

After reading this chapter, you should be able to:

1. Define the terms career and career development.
2. Describe the major reasons for both career development and management development.
3. Discuss the four career planning processes.
4. Explain the general management development process.
5. Describe three methods to assess needs for management development.
6. Discuss the best climate in which to implement management development programs.
7. Explain the four areas in which management development programs can be evaluated.
8. Discuss the importance of integrating personal and professional development.

Mr. Lewis Lash is manager of management development and training for Eastern Airlines. He has been with Eastern Airlines for twelve years. He has an M.B.A. degree from the University of Michigan and is currently working on a Ph.D. near his current location in Florida. He has a total of seventeen years of experience, and ten of those in managerial positions. In his current capacity, Mr. Lash reports directly to the senior vice president of personnel and corporate administrator.

Interviewer: What are your career aspirations?

Lewis Lash: My own career goals entail playing a key role in human resource development for a major organization. Human resource development includes traditional training efforts along with development programs to ensure appropriate strategies for meeting long-range needs.

Interviewer: How is your current organization helping you to realize these goals?

Lewis Lash: Eastern Airlines assists me in meeting my personal career goals by encouraging self-development. Self-development opportunities include job rotation, enrollment in external education programs, and coaching and counseling efforts by my superiors.

Interviewer: What is the major focus of management training programs?

Lewis Lash: Management training programs focus on skills that managers need to function effectively in their work environment. The programs tend to be pragmatic and focus, for the most part, on short-term payoffs. This is particularly true when contrasted to management education provided by universities. Large companies provide more specialized training than smaller companies.

Interviewer: Can you and others expect to continue receiving training as you go higher up the management ladder?

Lewis Lash: In general, formal company training diminishes as a manager's responsibility broadens. However, when the company goes into a new endeavor, higher-level managers may receive exposure through training or use of consultants, for example, implementation of Japanese productivity strategies and the quality circle concept. As one gets higher in the managerial hierarchy, there is only a limited amount of new material available. Also, there are few developmental opportunities. And those selected programs are offered only to high-potential candidates.

Interviewer: What makes the difference between a successful young manager and an unsuccessful one?

Lewis Lash: Management's role is becoming more complex. The successful manager is one who can manage an environment that is complex and continuously changing. A successful young manager should have the following traits:

Is able to focus clearly on his or her own career needs.

Is capable of assessing needs and values and is willing to commit to achieving goals. Goal achievement may involve long work hours, social business commitments, and integration of personal and organizational definitions of success.

Is continually in the process of learning.

Takes personal inventories regularly.

Gains the skills needed for career development through self-directed learning.

Has the ability to integrate a variety of disciplines.

Maintains a social and political awareness of his or her internal work environment and the environment external to the organization.

Is aware of the changes in the external environment and ways of relating the changes to the organization.

In other words, successful managers stay "tuned in" to the changes going on around them. In the current decade, the major factors influencing corporate strategy are government involvement in corporate management, interest group pressures, energy issues, and escalating costs of energy and human resources.

INTRODUCTION

Lewis Lash is an experienced manager who recognizes the importance of career and management development. These are essential for the development of the organization's key human resources. Mr. Lash noted that successful young managers were concerned about career development and that management training is designed to provide managers with the skills needed to be effective in their personal work environments. He also noted the increasing complexity of managerial jobs making development and training more important for managerial effectiveness.

Career development and management development are interlinked. For management development to be effective, both the skill needs of the organization and of the individual must be met. Career development involves career planning in which one may identify the skills needed at each stage of his or her career. In addition, needs assessment (e.g., assessment center) techniques used to identify necessary management development programs may be used for career planning purposes.

In Chapter 9 we described six fundamental elements in training, which are equally important to both career and management development: job environment (requirements); individuals (skills, knowledge); assessments of job and individual; sound learning strategy; changes in employees (skills, knowledge, attitudes, etc.); and improved or constantly effective performance. We will learn how these interact in career and management development to produce effective performance.

The focus in this chapter is career development and management development. We examine the reasons for career development, career planning, and career counseling. Within the discussion of management development, we describe means of identifying needs, management development strategies, and the ways in which to make management development effective.

CAREER DEVELOPMENT

A person's career is one of the most important elements in his or her life. A career may be seen in several ways. It may be seen as vertical mobility (advancement), an occupation (profession), a lifelong sequence of jobs, and a lifelong sequence of role-related experiences.[1] For our purposes, career is defined as follows:

Career: sequence of attitudes and behaviors associated with the series of job- and work-related activities over a person's lifetime.[2]

The focus of career development within an organization is the series of jobs that one holds in that organization. Career development is a fairly recent phenomenon. Twenty or thirty years ago, for example, it was rare for someone to help an employee map out a career within the company and then develop the necessary strategies to ensure that the employee would be able to meet the job requirements at the appropriate time. Many professional employees now expect organizations to provide such information and assistance in support of their careers. Most such efforts are limited currently to managerial and professional employees.

Career development: process of planning the series of possible jobs one may hold in the organization over time and development strategies designed to provide necessary job skills as the opportunities arise.

One's career development is greatly affected by job mobility in the organization. Job mobility is affected by the organization's size, technology, and structure; for example, career development may imply transferring an employee across departmental lines to develop new job skills. However, research has shown that, when the technology used is complex, the ability to transfer personnel across departmental lines is limited.[3]

It can be seen then that the matching of skills, attitudes, and knowledge required by the job and those of the individual is crucial in career development. Thus a sound learning strategy and changes in employee skills, attitudes, and knowledge are important for effective performance as one moves through a series of jobs.

Our discussion of career development includes the reasons for it, career planning processes, and career counseling.

Reasons for Career Development

Organizations receive benefits from career development activities as do employees. There are several reasons, then, for career development efforts.

1. A rapidly changing environment is making managerial jobs more complex, as noted by Lewis Lash of Eastern Airlines. Thus employees need to be better prepared for higher-level executive positions. Career development also allows the organization to identify future managers with more accuracy.
2. Career development programs help to assure that the organization receives maximum contribution from employees. It does so by ensuring that employees' skills are developed preparing these employees for their jobs. Therefore, underemployemnt is reduced.
3. Organizations need increasing adaptability and technical updating on the part of their employees because of rapidly changing technology. A career development program helps to satisfy these needs.
4. Career development offers a sensible approach to moving women and minor-

ities more rapidly into higher-level managerial positions, fulfilling affirmative action programs, and meeting equal employment opportunity requirements.
5. The benefits to individual employees are multiple. Employees generally acquire more skills; obtain better jobs, have increased responsibility, increased job mobility, and increased work satisfaction; and develop a career orientation.[4,5]

It may be hard to understand why organizations have not used career development more often until recently, given the number of potential benefits described. However, it should be noted that employees now expect such activities. In addition, because of new federal laws and employee demands, personnel activities have received increasing emphasis in recent years.

Career Planning Processes

The focus of this discussion is on organizational career planning as differentiated from individual career planning. *An organizational career plan is a map of a sequence of jobs for an employee within that organization;* individual career planning, on the other hand, involves a map of job sequence without regard to the organization.

Among various career planning activities are career pathing, personnel skills inventories, career information systems, and career counseling.[6] To conduct career planning effectively, several things are required. Detailed information of jobs is required so that skills needed for success on the job are known. Therefore, an effective system of job analysis and job descriptions (Chapters 3 and 4) is required. A useful performance appraisal system is necessary to monitor performance and identify not only current skill levels but also the skills that need to be developed. The individual employee must have clear career goals if planning and development are to take place. These goals must be realistic and must not only assess potential but also interests. The organization must have an effective human resource planning system (Chapter 6) to identify human resource needs in advance, a necessary function if development is to occur in time to have personnel prepared as the need arises. Organizations must have clearly designated career paths and job families so that career planning may proceed logically and the paths be understood by employees. Finally, an effective information system is necessary to make these data available to the appropriate parties at the appropriate time.[7]

CAREER PATHS. *Career paths are a series of jobs representing potential progression tracks that employees may follow.* In some organizations, these paths are clearer and easier to understand than in others. Career paths should represent logical job progressions that develop employees for preselected key jobs. This becomes particularly important because job experiences apparently contribute more to managerial success than a person's ability.[8]

Major parts of career paths are career ladders and job families. Figure 11-1 shows a simple job ladder in a sales department. Figure 11-2 shows a complex career

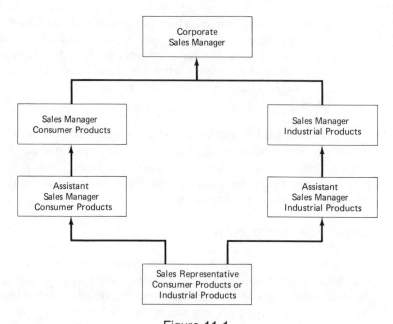

Figure 11-1

Career Ladder in a Sales Department

ladder network in a manufacturing unit. In each figure a logical progression of jobs is shown. The career ladder network shown in Figure 11-2 provides much more information than does the one presented in Figure 11-1. However, the career path in the manufacturing unit is much more complex than is the one in the sales unit. The information contained in the career ladder should be appropriate for the complexity of the path.

Job families are groups of jobs with similar characteristics and requirements. The jobs in Figure 11-1 represent a job family. Once job families are identified and career ladeers are developed for all units in the organization, career paths may be laid out. They may be shown on the career ladder, or they may be mapped out extending across ladders from separate units. This is useful when higher-level management positions represent the focal jobs.

Once career paths are developed, we can identify the requisite skills for any position along those paths. The knowledge of these skill levels then aids in developing employees to fill the position and in selecting the person with appropriate skills for the position.

PERSONNEL SKILLS INVENTORIES. Identification of employees with the appropriate skills to fill a position may be a cumbersome process, particularly for large organizations. A manager has a position opening in New York City, for example, and the organization (20,000 employees) may have employees qualified to fill the position

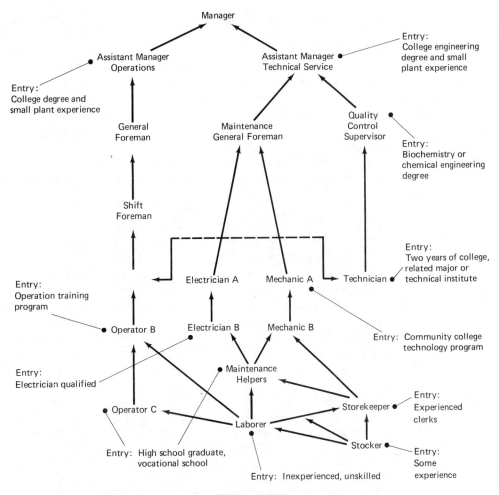

Figure 11-2

Career Ladder Network for a Manufacturing Unit

Source: E. H. Burack and N. Mathys, "Career Ladders, Pathing and Planning: Some Neglected Aspects," *Human Resource Management,* 18 (1979), 6. Used with permission.

in Houston, Los Angeles, and Detroit. That manager probably is not aware of all employees in the organization qualified to fill the vacant position. Therefore, organizations need an information system that provides up-to-date information on its employees' skills. The systems were introduced earlier in Chapter 6.

 Skills inventory: an information system containing data on employees' important skills and career goals.

Skills inventories, then, are data banks usually containing information on employees' education, training, experience, and career goals. Frequently, these inventories contain information on the employee's past performance ratings, ratings of the individual's potential by the immediate supervisor, and even the employee's location desires and constraints. These systems are usually computerized. This allows the manager in New York to request a listing of all employees in the organization with certain skills, whose career goals are appropriate for the position, and who are willing to locate in New York. In this manner, he or she will be able to consider qualified employees regardless of current location.

These systems, then, are vital to providing equal career opportunities to all in the organization and in assuring that the organization selects the best person for the job.

CAREER INFORMATION SYSTEMS. Career information systems supplement skill inventories. These systems usually contain two programs: succession planning or replacement charts, which show personnel who are being developed to take over higher-level positions as they become vacant, and a job-posting system, in which all nonofficer position vacancies are posted so that employees are aware of them. Employees may then submit a bid to be considered for the position. The files of those submitting bids are reviewed, and those meeting the minimum job requirements are considered for the position. This system is particularly effective for lower-level jobs (e.g., hourly nonexempt positions). The final part of most career information systems is career counseling.

CAREER COUNSELING.   An increasingly important part of career development is career counseling. Employees may need career counseling at different stages throughout their careers, especially early in their careers, at the midpoint, and prior to retirement. Preretirement counseling is discussed in Chapter 22.

Career counseling is a complex process that is difficult to conduct effectively. It must include examination of personal resources, life goals, work opportunities, and attitudes toward work environments.[9] Examination of personal resources includes surveying skills, special talents, interests, and even personality attributes. Discussion of life goals really involves examination of how work fits into a person's value system. Particular emphasis is placed on a person's life-style and the targets that he or she has set. An attempt is made to interrelate work and life-style goals.

Next the individual's attitudes toward work and particular work environments are assessed. Emphasis is placed on the role that the individual sees for himself or herself in the work environment. Attention is given to the individual's need for status, power, security, and autonomy, among others. Thus the counselor and individual try to identify the most positive type of work environment for the individual.

The final area that should be covered in career counseling is an examination of career opportunities. Here the counselor and individual examine specific careers. Both current job prospects and the long-run outlook for advancement should be examined. Personal skills, education, training, experience, and interests may be matched with job and career opportunities. The career counseling process must be comprehensive, as described, to be effective.[10]

Comprehensive counseling is particularly important in the early stages of one's career and again at midcareer. In the early stages, it helps to provide a plan to guide the person along his or her tailor-made career path. It also points to developmental needs for which a person may plan and develop new skills as required for career advancement. At midcareer, the plan should be reassessed. Individual life-styles and life goals often change. Attitudes toward work and work environment may change. Finally, advancement in one's career may have differed from the original plan. Thus the reassessment should be made to develop a new plan that will lead the individual through to the end of his or her career. Of course, each individual is unique and has different needs. Career counseling is an important part of a complete career development program.

Career development and career planning are important to organizations and to individuals alike. Lewis Lash pointed this out in describing the traits he believed a successful young manager should have. Among these traits Mr. Lash included one's ability to focus on one's career needs, regularly assess one's personal inventory, gain skills needed for career development, and integrate goal achievement with both personal and organizational definitions of success. As noted by Mr. Lash, once career needs are assessed, the appropriate skills must be developed. Organizations often help their employees to develop these skills through development and training programs.

Research tends to support the importance of career development activities; for example, career experiences (sequence of jobs held) have been found to be related to both interest in and effort put forth to further one's career. The better the experience, the greater the amount of interest and effort put forth. In addition, positive experiences with job mobility lead to improved job satisfaction. Clearly, organizations need to provide both vertical and horizontal job mobility.[11] Organizations that practice effective career development try to plan the development of employees, thereby improving opportunities for job mobility.

Lewis Lash noted that his own career goals entailed playing a key role in human resource development in a major organization. To an extent, he does so already as manager of management development and training for Eastern Airlines. His next position might be one of similar responsibility in the personnel area such as compensation director (horizontal). Or he could develop his skills to undertake a vice president of personnel position (vertical). He noted that his superiors encourage self-development and provide him with career counseling.

MANAGEMENT DEVELOPMENT

Once career paths are identified and career goals are established, individuals must develop the basic skills necessary to proceed along the ladder. Part of those skills can be obtained through experience from the jobs they hold. In many cases, the present job does not prepare employees fully to hold the next highest position. These employees, then, must develop the "extra" skills necessary to advance. Management and professional development programs are designed for this purpose.

For example, General Electric has introduced a variety of programs to ensure that its professional employees maintain and increase competence in their respective fields. Its management believes that these programs are essential for the company to meet its technical skill needs for technology growth. In addition, the programs are seen as aiding in the recruiting, retaining, and retraining of personnel.[12]

Reasons for Management Development

With the strong link between it and career development, at least some of the reasons for management development become obvious. The reasons are as follows:

> To prepare employees for current and future jobs.
> To increase productivity and overall effectiveness of employees.
> To prevent employee obsolescence on the job.

EMPLOYEE JOB PREPARATION.   The purposes served by professional and management development programs are multiple and varied. However most, in some way relate to the three major reasons just presented. The preparation of employees for current and future jobs serves both the employee and the organization. It serves employees by helping them to gain the skills necessary for moving along their career paths and attaining higher-level positions. Thus the opportunity to participate in development programs may increase employee satisfaction and general morale.

The organization is benefited because it is assured of a ready supply of employees with appropriate skills to assume higher-level positions. Second, it may help to satisfy equal employment opportunities and affirmative action programs by providing minorities (e.g., women, blacks) with the skills necessary to assume higher-level positions.

PRODUCTIVITY AND EFFECTIVENESS.   Developmental programs also help to increase employee productivity and enhance overall organizational effectiveness.[13] They do so by providing new skills and updating others. Often, application of these new skills allows employees to improve their performance. In addition, those in managerial positions may increase the productivity of subordinates by applying new managerial skills. In this manner productivity and organizational effectiveness may be increased.

Phillips Petroleum Company, for example, has recently increased its management development program offerings, one of which focuses on development of middle- and first-line managers' performance counseling skills. The expectation is that managers can enhance employee productivity through improved performance coaching and counseling. In the long run, organizational effectiveness should also increase.

EMPLOYEE OBSOLESCENCE.   With rapid changes occurring in technology and knowledge, the possibility increases of employee skills becoming obsolete for their jobs; in fact, it has been estimated that technological and other changes make a professional's skills obsolete ten years after graduation from college.[14] Professional and management development programs, then, are necessary to ensure that employees continue to have the skills necessary for adequate performance of current jobs. It is certainly better to prevent obsolescence than to attempt to retrain individuals with obsolete skills.

Age is not a major factor in employee obsolescence. Low motivation, low self-esteem, and limited intellectual capabilities explain why employees let themselves become obsolete.[15] Development programs may be used to overcome the first two factors. Little can be done with the third. When employees become obsolete, organizations must change job responsibilities, ensure that employees develop new skills through development programs, or terminate the obsolete employees. The most positive approach is use of a development program.

Mr. Lash noted that managerial jobs were becoming more complicated because of the complex and changing environment with which managers must deal. We may speculate that it is now easier for managers to become obsolete. Management development programs, then, are critical for preventing managerial obsolescence.

Management Development Process

Effective management development programs follow a consistent pattern reflected in Figure 11-3. As shown, the first step in management development is identification of needs. Next the appropriate management development programs should be designed and implemented. Implementation requires that an effective climate be established. Finally, the program should be evaluated to ensure that its goals have been achieved.

Figure 11-3

Management Development Process

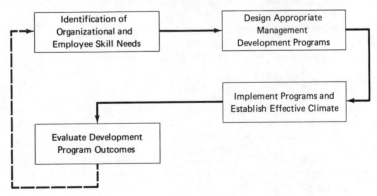

Identification of Needs

Need for development activities can be identified in several ways. Chief among these is the performance appraisal (discussed in Chapter 15). Other need assessment devices include a training needs survey and assessment center techniques.

ASSESSMENT OF NEEDS. Performance appraisals should be used to evaluate performance but, in addition, should be used to assess developmental needs.[16] Therefore, it becomes the responsibility of the supervisor to identify the skills that employees need to develop. Of course, these skills may be related to the current or to a future job. They may then relate to current deficiencies or to skills necessary for advancement. The supervisor should be in the best position possible to make an assessment of an employee's skill needs. However, the process is purely subjective.

A somewhat more objective process is the training needs survey. The first step in developing such a survey is analyzing the tasks of those to be covered, the purpose being to identify the range of skills necessary for these employees (e.g., managers) to perform their jobs in the particular organization. Next a questionnaire can be constructed listing each skill and asking several questions about it. The questions generally relate to a perceived *need for training* in each skill and the perceived *importance* of the skill in the employees' jobs. Thus the objective is to determine the training needs and to be able to order those needs on the basis of importance. Figure 11-4 is an example of possible questionnaire items.

Usually, then, these questionnaires are administered to the employee group targeted for management development and their supervisors. In one use of a training needs survey for the U.S. Forest Service, thirty-seven major skills were identified from

Figure 11-4

Possible Items in a Training Needs Survey

1. Measuring performance of subordinates
   a. Need for training

Almost no need	Some need	Average need	Strong need	Very strong need
1	2	3	4	5

   b. Importance of the skill to your job

Unimportant	Relatively unimportant	Average importance	Important	Very important
1	2	3	4	5

2. Developing plans
   a. Need for training

Almost no need	Some need	Average need	Strong need	Very strong need
1	2	3	4	5

   b. Importance of the skill to your job

Unimportant	Relatively unimportant	Average importance	Important	Very important
1	2	3	4	5

job analysis. Based on responses to the survey, several training needs were identified for first-level supervisors in the organization. Skills in which training was needed and was considered important included developing plans and objectives, using time effectively, motivating employees, appraising or measuring employee performance, and training subordinates on the job.[17]

ASSESSMENT CENTERS. Another needs assessment device is the assessment center. Assessment centers were discussed in Chapter 8 as a managerial selection tool. Prior to use of the assessment center, it is necessary to develop a clear set of behavioral objectives and a set of skills that should be assessed. Assessment centers were defined in Chapter 8.

Next the individuals must be selected who are to have their skills assessed. Since assessment centers are complex, only ten to twelve participants are assessed at any one time. Therefore, this method is not used generally for large numbers of personnel.

Assessment centers were used originally for promotional decisions, particularly for selecting potential managerial talent (see Chapter 8). However, because they assess employee strengths and weaknesses, they are now being used frequently for determining management development needs and for career planning. Currently, many assessment centers are conducted to provide two types of outcomes: to report on participants' strengths and weaknesses and to detail developmental activities for strengthening the limitations noted.[18]

A recent study on assessment centers found that assessors tend to focus on only a few major managerial skills, regardless of the number they are supposed to assess. In this study, the assessors consistently focused on leadership, organizing, planning, and decision-making skills.[19]

Assessment centers require a great deal of planning, time, and effort to conduct and to utilize their results effectively. A recent study showed that assessment centers seem to be valid predictors of subsequent managerial performance.[20]

Management Development Strategies

Once the development needs have been identified, the appropriate program must be designed fo fulfill those needs. These programs must be designed on the basis of the organization and the skill needs of the individuals. Thus a contingency approach should be taken.[21] Highly structured continuing management development programs may not fully meet both organizational and employee needs. These needs, then, determine the shape of the program and the methods used to develop the skills in those programs. For example, standard repetitive courses may be useful when the task variability is not high and the skill needs are relatively simple. Case studies may be useful when task variability of managers' jobs is high but the organization exists in a relatively stable climate. Examination of others in similar situations is useful. However, when skill needs are complex and many, and the organizational environment changes frequently, more complex group and problem-solving exercises may be necessary.[22]

PROGRAM CONTENTS AND METHODS.   Although use of a contingency approach provides varying program contents and methods, some common threads do exist throughout most management development programs. Typical programs may use programmed instruction, case studies, group and individual experiential exercises, and lectures as described in Chapter 10. Frequent topics include planning, leadership, motivation, and measuring employee performance. The key is to design a program in which the content thoroughly covers the needed skill areas and through which participants really learn these skills. Often, it is necessary to maintain participant enthusiasm and desire to ensure that learning occurs. Frequently, effective programs accommodate a diverse set of participants varying in age, sex, tenure with the organization, and job experience.[23]

Lewis Lash of Eastern Airlines noted that most management training programs focus on skills managers' need to function effectively in their current work environment. He also stated that the number of management training programs available decreases as one moves up the managerial hierarchy. This is because higher-level managers have broader responsibilities and because there is a limited amount of new material available that can be of use to them.

PROBLEMS IN MANAGEMENT DEVELOPMENT.   Many organizations have ongoing management development efforts. However, some do not achieve the desired objectives because of:

- failure to link management development to long-run strategic plans.
- failure to ensure that employees need the training.
- failure to use effective training methods.
- failure to differentiate individual and group skill development.
- failure to provide support after the training.
- failure to evaluate training results.[24]

If management development efforts are not coordinated with long-run strategies of the organization, managers may not be developing the skills needed to meet new challenges and opportunities. In addition, it is important to be sure that those attending development programs need the skill. If participants already possess the skill or if the skill is of little use to them in current or future jobs, the participants will show little enthusiasm. Even if training needs have been assessed properly and participants have been chosen carefully, the training methods must be appropriate to teach the skills. Often, the most effective programs use a variety of teaching methods as discussed earlier in the chapter.

Differentiating between skills that can be used individually and those that must be used by a group is important. If a development program is teaching a skill that must be used by a group of people, *all* who might use it must participate in the development program. If some participate and others do not, those who participate may never be able to use the skill with those who do not understand the technique. When group skills are being taught, individual participants are less important. The transfer of skills from training to the job may not occur without posttraining support. Supervisors can provide assistance and encouragement in applying the newly developed skills on the job. If they are not used, the value of the training is low. Finally, all developmental programs should be evaluated to ensure that desired objectives were achieved. Evaluation is discussed in more depth later in the chapter.

Effective Management Development Climate

If the proper psychological climate does not exist within the organization, management development programs have little chance of success. Employees must feel, for example, that there is adequate support and reward, not only to develop new skills, but to use them. Without the proper support and reward, there would be little incentive to participate in developmental programs. One recent study found three climate dimensions to be of particular interest for developmental activities:

Stimulation—degree of achievement and high standards.
Support—degree of opportunities provided and fairness in rewards.
Teamwork—degree of team spirit and social responsibility.[25]

A developmental climate should be high in each of these dimensions. When this type of climate exists, the transfer of learning in developmental activities is greatest. An effective developmental climate will greatly aid the implementation of a management development program.

Evaluation of Management Development Programs

Many organizations have invested thousands of dollars in management development programs. Thus, it seems certain that these organizations want to know what return they are receiving for their investment. To do so, they must in some way evaluate the results of management development efforts. It is difficult to evaluate these results accurately, however.

Because of the multiple factors that may affect individual and organizational effectiveness, most programs can be measured only in subjective ways. However, there are some means of evaluating the effectiveness of development programs. Successful evaluation requires assessment in four areas.[26] The first is the participants' emotional acceptance of the material presented in the program. Usually, this information is obtained by having the participants evaluate the program's content, method, and instructor(s) at the end of the program. The second assessment area is the degree to which the participants learn the material presented. This can be assessed by a pre- and posttraining examination. The third area is the degree to which the learning results in actual behavioral changes on the job—a factor that is more difficult to measure. One method is to have each of the participants set behavioral job-related objectives to implement learned material. A follow-up six months later with participants can deter-mine if objectives have been met. The fourth and final area is the impact of these changes on departmental or organizational effectiveness. This is most difficult. Even if improvements are noted, they could be caused by other factors. Thus this fourth as-sessment may have to be subjective. However, the assessment should be made.[27]

It should be emphasized that, no matter how subjective the evaluation must be, management development programs should be evaluated. If not, many ineffective pro-grams will be allowed to continue without needed changes. As with all other realms of organizational activity, effectiveness of management development programs must be evaluated.

Management Development Issues

Several issues are important to note in a discussion of management development. Two of these are the impacts of management development on attitude formation and change and the integration of personal and professional development.

IMPACT ON ATTITUDES.   Many management development programs are aimed at the acquisition of new attitudes or the change of existing ones. This is particularly evident in leadership development and human relations development programs. In leadership development programs, the objective is to change participants' attitudes and have them acquire new ones to exhibit effective leadership styles. In one study of an intensive ten-week management development workshop, measures of attitudes were taken before and after the program. Participants ranged in age from the early twenties to the late fifties, but most were in their thirties and forties. These individuals were middle-level managers from a variety of national companies. Industry classifications included aerospace, banking, construction, electronics, food products, insurance, pub-lic utilities, and transportation. Thus there was a good cross section of industries, companies, and ages in the program.

The results of the attitude assessment suggested that attitudes were changed by the program. Those attitudes showing the most change were related to the organiza-tion's social responsibility, willingness to accept the expanding role of the manager, and faith in their employees. In addition, the participants showed strong agreement on the attitudes at the end of the program.[28] These results are from only one study. How-ever, they do point to the purpose of many development programs—new attitude for-mation or attitude change. Some argue that attitudes cannot be changed or that attitude change is not lasting. Therefore, the issue of attitude change is an important one for management development.

Mr. Lash noted that successful managers must stay "tuned in" to the changes around them. This implies that they must also be flexible and willing to change as the need dictates.

INTEGRATING PERSONAL AND PROFESSIONAL DEVELOPMENT.   Personal de-velopment is as important an issue today as is professional development. Organizations are becoming increasingly sensitive to a person's need to balance personal and work lives. Thus personal and professional development must be integrated. As stated by Gordon Lippitt, a person's work identity plus social identity equals self-integration or that person's quality of life.[29] The workaholic does not have his or her life in balance. Neither does the self-indulgent who strongly emphasizes social life over work. Organizations must help individuals to achieve this balance if they are to be fully productive employees. Employees then must experience a high quality of work life and a high overall quality of life. Achievement of this balance should be integrated into developmental programs.

Individuals who have achieved this balance have, at least, some of the following characteristics:

Mobility readiness

Life/career plans

Flexibility

Esteem and security (psychologically and economically)

Clarified set of values

Good interpersonal relationships

Job satisfaction

Opportunity to influence work situation

Support of one's organization to grow and develop

Support of peers and supervisor

Career opportunities[30]

Lewis Lash noted many of these same characteristics in his description of a successful manager.

EFFECTIVE MANAGEMENT DEVELOPMENT.   Management development can succeed only if the organization and top management sanction it. Top management should fully support the concept of management development. Rewards must be available (e.g., in the form of career opportunities) when employees develop appropriate skills through development programs. For management development programs to be successful, managerial responsibilities must be well defined and clearly delineated. Without this, objectives of developmental programs cannot be met, and learned skills will not be fully implemented. The organization must be flexible and open to change if attitude change from development programs is to persist. Lasting attitude change will not occur in closed, inflexible organizations. Finally, management development does not come from training programs alone. An objective of developing personnel to utilize their skills fully should persist throughout the organization. In summary, the general organizational philosophy and climate must be conducive to management development, if it is to be effective.[31]

SUMMARY

Career development and management development are highly interrelated. For example, career planning may help to identify skills necessary to further one's career. These skills may be obtained through management development programs.

Career development is the process of planning for the series of possible jobs that one may hold in an organization over time and the developmental strategies to provide the needed skills as job opportunities arise. Career development is important for several reasons. Managerial jobs are becoming more complicated, requiring a more complex set of skills. Career development ensures that the organization has the skilled personnel necessary. Career development helps to keep employee skills up to date, in turn helping the organization adapt to technical changes. Career development helps organizations to meet equal employment opportunity goals and provides personal benefits to the employees as well.

Career planning includes career pathing, personnel skills inventories, career information systems, and career counseling. Career paths are series of jobs representing potential progression tracks for employees to follow. These should be delineated clearly. Personnel skills inventories are information systems containing data on employee skills and career goals. These are necessary particularly in large organizations to ensure that the best employee for any one job is chosen. It allows managers to consider employees at various geographic locations for a position vacancy. Career information systems supplement skills inventories. These systems usually include replacement charts (showing potential successors to key positions) and a job-posting system (announcing vacancies so that employees may bid for consideration). Career counseling is especially important early in an employee's career (to examine skills and priorities and set goals); in midcareer (to re-examine goals and career; make changes, if necessary); and prior to retirement (to prepare for retirement).

Once career paths are identified and career goals are established, the requisite skills for jobs must be developed. Management development programs serve at least three major purposes: they prepare employees for current and future jobs, they aid in increasing employee productivity and effectiveness, and they aid in preventing employee obsolescence on the job.

The management development process has several steps. First, organizational and employee skill needs must be identified. This may be done through performance appraisal activities, specially designed surveys, and/or assessment centers. Second, appropriate management programs must be designed. These programs must contain not only the appropriate contents for the needed skill development but also the most effective methods to achieve skill development. Some of the biggest problems with management development programs include the failure to relate them to long-run strategies, failure to see that the appropriate employees are trained, failure to use the most effective training methods, failure to differentiate between individual and group development, failure to provide support after training, and failure to evaluate the effectiveness of training efforts.

Third, the appropriate climate must be established to ensure effective implementation. The best climate is one that emphasizes high standards, achievement, fairness in rewards, and provides employees with opportunities, team spirit, and a sense of social responsibility. Finally, management development programs should be evaluated in terms of the participants' emotional acceptance, degree of learning, and degree of behavioral change on the job, and the impact on individual and organizational effectiveness.

Two management development issues that should be recognized are the emphasis on attitude acquisition and change and integration of personal and professional development. Many developmental programs focus on attitude change. Thus this change must be monitored over the long run to assess program effectiveness. Organizations are now recognizing the need to emphasize both personal and professional development to ensure well-balanced employees. Those whose lives are in balance will be more productive in the long run. Management development programs will be effective only to the extent that they are well supported by the organization's philosophy and climate.

INTERVIEW WRAP-UP

I am pleased that Eastern has provided me the support to develop my own specialized skills. Most management development programs are designed to provide pragmatic skills with short-term payoffs; fewer development programs are available for higher-level managers than those in lower levels in the hierarchy.

Additionally, management is becoming more complex and thus it takes more skill to be a successful manager. Successful managers stay "tuned in" to the changes around them. —Lewis Lash, manager of management development and training, Eastern Airlines.

WHAT MANAGERS SHOULD DO REGARDING PERSONNEL MANAGEMENT ACTIVITIES

1. Managers must be aware of the importance of career development for their employees. They must provide career guidance where appropriate (e.g., explaining potential career paths) and encourage them to seek career counseling from specialists in the organization when necessary.

2. Managers should participate in and use skills inventories and career information systems to their own maximum advantage. It will benefit their own employees (provide opportunities) and themselves by helping them to select highly qualified personnel for their position vacancies.

3. Managers should use management development programs wisely. They should select those employees to attend development programs and time these events carefully. Employees would then develop skills as they need them to perform current tasks or future tasks.

4. Managers should be flexible and open to new ideas provided in development programs. In addition, they should attempt to implement these new ideas on their own jobs.

5. Managers should evaluate the results of development programs. They should be willing to make constructive suggestions for improvements.

REVIEW QUESTIONS

1. Why has career development become such an important issue in recent years?

2. What are the four elements in career planning? Describe each of them briefly.

3. What is management development and what is its purpose?

4. What are some of the problems with management development and how can they be overcome?

5. How would you evaluate a management development program? Describe the methods you would use.

6. Why is it important to integrate personal and professional development? How would you recommend doing so?

KEY CONCEPTS

Assessment center	Career paths
Career	Career planning
Career counseling	Employee obsolescence
Career development	Management development

CASE

THE THREE CAREERS

Michael Alders is a young and independent "junior executive." He received his M.B.A. degree from the University of Chicago, one of the top U.S. universities, in economics and finance. Upon graduation he went to work for a large bank in Atlanta. After a year during which he was unhappy, he went to Union Oil Company in San Francisco in the insurance department.

Angela Nichols is forty-five years old and is a middle manager in Union's corporate accounting department. She has spent her career in accounting positions since graduation from college. She worked for two companies prior to her association with Union. She has been employed by Union in the corporate accounting department for almost ten years.

Bill Donaldson is sixty-four years old and has spent his entire career with Union. He is currently manager of vendor and quality control. Bill started with Union in the maintenance department and worked his way up through the organization. He has always worked hard and has been a loyal employee. He went to school at night and earned his college degree when he was forty-nine years old. He was promoted into the managerial ranks shortly after that.

What do these people have in common? They are not satisfied; in fact, they are unhappy. The following represents current feelings:

Michael: I've been in the insurance department for almost nine months now and I don't see any future in the department for me. I have my job mastered and my boss is only thirty-nine and not about to leave any time soon. There are only two other professional job classifications in my department. I want a management job. I want some responsibility and challenge. Also, I want to use some of the skills I developed while in college. No job I've had so far has allowed me to use many of my skills.

Angela: I've been in accounting my whole career and I feel that I'm getting stale. I can see many opportunities in accounting with growth of the profession and its importance. But I'm not sure I want to stay in accounting for the rest of my working career. I also feel that I've just been putting in too many hours the last few years. I'm still young and want to do other things in life besides just work.

Bill: I've worked for Union for forty-six years now. I've enjoyed every minute of it. Sure there have been rough spots here and there but the company has always treated me right. Now I'm sixty-four and I can retire with full retirement in less than a year; in fact, my boss has hinted that I might enjoy retirement. My wife wants me to retire and have us travel around the country. However, I've worked all my life and I wouldn't know what to do with myself if I weren't coming to the office every day. I believe I would be really unhappy. Besides, the law now allows me to work until I'm seventy.

CASE QUESTIONS

1. What are the problems of Michael, Angela, and Bill?

2. What are the similarities and differences in each of their situations?

3. What would you recommend in each of their cases?

NOTES

[1]D. T. Hall, *Careers in Organizations* (Santa Monica, Calif.: Goodyear, 1976), pp. 2–3.

[2]Ibid., p. 4

[3]Y. Vardi and T. H. Hammer, "Intraorganizational Mobility and Career Perceptions Among Rank and File Employees in Different Technologies," *Academy of Management Journal,* 20 (1977), 622–634.

[4]M. A. Morgan, D. T. Hall, and A. Martier, "Career Development Strategies in Industry—Where Are We and Where Should We Be?" *Personnel,* 56 (1979), 13–30.

[5]S. Gould, "Career Planning in the Organization," *Human Resource Management,* 17 (1978), 8–11.

[6]Morgan et al., "Career Development Strategies."

[7]E. H. Burack and N. Mathys, "Career Ladders, Pathing and Planning: Some Neglected Basics," *Human Resource Management,* 18 (1979), 2–8.

[8]Morgan et al., "Career Development Strategies."

[9]I. R. Swartz, "The Quadrant Construct: A Conceptual Framework for Midlife Career Counseling," *Training and Development Journal,* 32 (1978), 50–52.

[10]Ibid.

[11]Vardi and Hammer, "Intraorganizational Mobility and Career Perceptions."

[12]"Increasing Technical Skills: How GE Upgrades Professional Staff," *Management Review,* 69 (1980), 29–31.

[13]C. P. McNamara, "Management Productivity: How to Uncover a Hidden Corporate Asset," *Management Review,* 68 (1979), 20–23.

[14]D. F. Harvey and C. R. Brown, *An Experiential Approach to Organization Development* (Englewood Cliffs, N.J.: Prentice-Hall, 1976), p. 22.

[15]H. Kaufman, *Obsolescence and Professional Career Development* (New York: AMACON, 1974).

[16]N. B. Winstanley, "Performance Appraisals and Management Development: A Systems Approach," *The Conference Board Record,* 13 (1976), 55–59.

[17]A. Braun, "Assessing Supervisory Training Needs and Evaluating Effectiveness," *Training and Development Journal,* 33 (1979), 3–10.

[18]J. C. Quick, W. A. Fisher, L. L. Schkade, and G. W. Ayers, "Developing Administrative Personnel Through the Assessment Center Technique," *The Personnel Administrator,* 25 (1980), 44–46.

[19]P. R. Sackett and M. D. Hakel, "Temporal Stability and Individual Differences in Using Assessment Information to Form Overall Ratings," *Organizational Behavior and Human Performance,* 23 (1979), 120–137.

[20]L. D. Alexander, "An Exploratory Study of the Utilization of Assessment Center Results," *Academy of Management Journal,* 22 (1979), 152–157.

[21]J. Brian, "A Contingency Approach to Management Development: Some Perspectives and a Diagnostic Model," *Management International Review,* 19 (1979), 123–128.

[22]Ibid.

[23]J. E. Dittrich, "Management Development in Nonbusiness Organization: A Design and Its Evaluation," *Journal of Management Studies,* 15 (1978), 340–346.

[24]W. G. Miles and W. G. Biggs, "Common, Recurring and Avoidable Errors in Management Development," *Training and Development Journal,* 33 (1979), 32–35.

[25]D. C. Pheysey, "Managers' Occupational Histories, Organizational Environments, and Climates for Management Development," *Journal of Management Studies,* 14 (1977), 58–79.

[26]D. L. Kirkpatrick, "Techniques for Evaluating Training Programs," *Training and Development Journal,* 33 (1978), 78–92.

[27]Braun, "Assessing Supervisory Training Needs."

[28]J. K. Leidecker and J. L. Hall, "The Impact of Management Development Programs on Attitude Formation," *Personnel Journal,* 53 (1974), 507–512.

[29]G. L. Lippitt, "Integrating Personal and Professional Development," *Training and Development Journal,* 34 (1980), 34–41.

[30]Ibid.

[31].A. W. Hill, "How Organizational Philosophy Influences Management Development," *Personnel Journal,* 59 (1980), 118–120, 148.

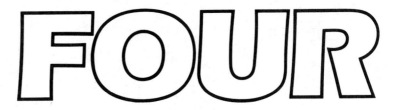

FOUR

MOTIVATING AND COMPENSATING FOR PERFORMANCE

To this point, we have followed the employee-organization relationship from the design and preparation of jobs to the selection of employees and the training or development of their job-related skills. It is now appropriate to consider a fourth phase of personnel management, that of determining employees' salaries and motivating them to perform. Although we would certainly consider these issues even while designing jobs, they are especially important after employees have been trained. Managers sometimes feel that a trained, skilled employee will naturally be productive, and if not, the responsibility for failure lies with the employee. That is, management has met its obligations by providing training and from then on employees are on their own.

However, progressive organizations recognize that even skilled employees may not be productive if the organization fails to establish an effective compensation and motivational program. The design of compensation and motivation programs depends on information gathered during job analysis, selection, testing, and performance appraisals. A simple rationale for understanding essential elements of these programs is presented in Chapter 12. The rationale emphasizes that motivation is not necessarily equivalent to compensation; that is, employee productivity is not guaranteed simply because employees are compensated. Thus we examine in Chapter 13 several important concepts of motivation and some more recent motivational applications within organizations.

Compensation is viewed as a two-part process: the compensation of jobs (Chapter 14) and performance appraisal and compensation of people for performance (Chapter 15). As discussed in the logic of compensation, employee salaries depend on both *what employees do* (jobs) and *how well they do it* (performance). Finally, we conclude the section by examining employee benefit programs and the special case of incentive compensation in Chapter 16. These chapters should prepare managers to consider carefully and design motivation and compensation programs that encourage high levels of performance.

THE LOGIC OF MOTIVATION AND COMPENSATION

LEARNING OBJECTIVES

After reading this chapter, you should be able to:

1. Define direct and supplemental compensation.
2. Describe the basic concept of equity.
3. Discuss the relationship of equity in the determination of time-based compensation.
4. Describe the nature of qualification and effort factors in a salary system.
5. Discuss the difference between time-based and productivity-based compensation.
6. Describe the relationship between compensation and motivation.

Texas Instruments is a well-known organization with an established reputation in the electronics field, manufacturing such products as pocket calculators and home computers. Texas Instruments also has been widely recognized for its innovative approaches in personnel activities and has achieved excellent relationships with its employees. Wayne Wright is the director of industrial relations for Texas Instruments and has been with the organization for fourteen years. His lengthy experience with Texas Instruments, and other organizations, has given him a valuable insight into issues involved with compensating (paying) and motivating employees. Mr. Wright shared these insights with our interviewer.

Interviewer: Two important terms in personnel management are "motivation" and "compensation." Can you tell me how motivation is different from, or similar to, compensation?

Mr. Wright: In motivating employees, it's "different strokes for different folks." Although some people cannot truly be motivated, we find the things that can best motivate are related to the job itself—the amount of freedom and the ability to use one's brain on the job. There have been attempts to tie motivation to compensation through the use of piece-rate systems and profit sharing. In these, companies try to reward employees for their contributions or according to the market value of their jobs. Generally, however, happiness with one's work is the biggest motivator. Merit pay is more like recognition; it can alleviate some negative aspects of the job, but it is seldom the biggest motivator.

Interviewer: What are the most important things your company does to motivate its employees? How does your compensation system fit into this?

Mr. Wright: Texas Instruments motivates its employees with participative management. We do not "hire hands," but rather "people." People, employees, are our best experts about what's happening on the production floor. A large percentage of our hourly employees participate in a broad range of problem solving, that is, using their brains to solve problems they see in their jobs. This participation enriches their jobs and removes tediousness from it.

Our compensation system simply encourages employees to stick around long enough to be motivated by job enrichment and other factors. We know that almost anyone can find some other job that pays more; thus it is the day-to-day job atmosphere that is more important. Still, administration of the compensation plan is critical. The employee must have a good understanding of the plan and accept it as fair and just. We know our plan must be generally competitive in the job market, uncomplicated, and not operated on whims.

Interviewer: What do you have to do to decide how much money to pay an employee?

Mr. Wright: Many factors contribute to our decisions about salaries. First we assess the job market. We look at union-negotiated contracts with other companies, perform wage surveys, and look at the U.S. Bureau of Labor Statistics and consumer price indexes. We also assess our own abilities to pay as a company. We have 80,000 employees nationwide, and labor costs run about 42 percent of our total sales dollars. With labor costs that high or higher, companies cannot afford to make poor compensation decisions.

Interviewer: What are your biggest headaches in designing a wage and salary structure?

Mr. Wright: There are three major problems. First, and very important, is the internal administration of the salary structure. The compensation structure must be internally equitable. This is extremely difficult because there are so many types and levels of job. Second, a merit system takes care and feeding. We must look after it daily and be sure that salary increases are "earned," not simply automatic. Third, we must educate employees to understand the salary system. They must believe in the plan and in the managers who will carry it out.

INTRODUCTION

> Where do you work?
> What kind of work do you do?
> How do you like your work?

These three questions have something in common. They are all questions we ask of others or have had asked of us about our job. These questions are ways of learning about others and sharing our excitement, or frustration, regarding the occupation at which we earn our living. However, there is one question that we never ask, even though our curiosity may be extreme. That question is

> How much money do you make?

Although we may be curious, we are usually reluctant to ask how much other people earn from their jobs. Perhaps we feel that is none of our business. Or perhaps it is because we are afraid of the answer. That is, if we find out that the other person makes more than we do, we will be unhappy about our own salary—we will feel underpaid.

As we discover in interviews with personnel managers, the issues surrounding compensation (paying salaries to employees) are complex and sometimes misunderstood. One common misunderstanding pertains to the relationship between compensation and motivation. Somehow it seems that, if we pay people more money, they should be more motivated. This is often not the case, as Mr. Wright has explained. Organizations are becoming aware of the fact that, while it is difficult to motivate underpaid employees, simply increasing (or promising to increase) their salaries may not increase their motivation to perform the job better.

The purpose of this chapter is to explore some basic factors that underlie compensation and motivation of employees. We intend to demonstrate the basic thought that must go into the development of any salary structure for an organization and how managers can improve employee motivation within that structure. We should note that the logic we use is based on one theory of motivation, equity theory. However, our intent here is *not* to examine theories of motivation; rather, it is to set a logical framework from which to examine compensation issues. A more comprehensive review of motivation theories appears in Chapter 13.

THE LOGIC OF COMPENSATION

There are many methods by which employees are compensated for their contributions to organizations. The basic methods are direct compensation and supplemental compensation.[1]

Direct compensation: payment for employee performance in terms of productivity or amount of time worked.

Supplemental compensation: some additional amount received for which the employee is not required to exert additional time or productivity.

In terms of direct compensation, most employees receive a salary or a wage based on time, that is, an hourly, weekly, or monthly salary. However, many employees receive payment based on some measure of their productivity. These latter compensation programs are generally referred to as incentive systems. Although incentive systems are felt by many to have a direct effect on employee motivation, many managers, including Wayne Wright, recognize that salary alone has little to do with motivation. Primarily, salary systems are best designed to maintain an equitable or fair distribution of organizational rewards among employees. The notion of equity, then, is the basic premise from which organizational salary structures can be designed.

Equity Concept

Most people develop a sense of equity, or fair play, quite early in life. As children, we are bothered if a sibling receives more attention from our parents. If this happens, we feel treated unfairly and seek to re-establish a more equal distribution of parental attention. As we grow older, we become concerned about "fair play" between playmates or unfair grading in classrooms. Most of us prefer situations in which fairness exists, as compared with situations in which someone receives unjustified preferential treatment.

Perhaps the most widely researched theory of equity is that offered by Stacy Adams.[2] According to Adams, equity between two people exists when the ratio of rewards to investments for one person is equal to the ratio of rewards to investments for the other person. These ratios can be expressed in a simple equation:

$$\frac{Op}{Ip} = \frac{Oa}{Ia}$$

where
    Op = person's outcomes (such as salary, promotion, recognition, etc.)
    Ip = person's inputs or investments (such as education, training,
        effort exerted, etc.)
    Oa = the other person's outcomes
    Ia = the other person's inputs or investments

In terms of an organization's salary structure, then, one employee's ratio of outcomes over inputs should be equal to another's ratio if equity is to be maintained. For example, if the first person received $500 for five units of inputs, a second person who had three units of inputs should receive only $300.

Logically, then, the determination of any employee's salary should be based on that individual's inputs or investments and maintain a constant ratio $\frac{O}{I}$ with other employees. To determine an employee's salary, therefore, it is necessary to understand more completely the term "investments" or inputs. This understanding is not simple and requires two related lines of thought: first, a consideration of the values of certain qualification factors versus values of certain effort factors and, second, a consideration of job value versus employee value.

QUALIFICATION AND EFFORT FACTORS. Research has found that workers consider two basic types of factors when reacting to payment situations.[3] First, most people feel that certain types of backgrounds or qualifying factors should be compensated. That is, individuals who have more seniority, experience, education, and so on should be paid more than co-workers who have less seniority, experience, or education. Regardless of how hard one actually works, superior qualifications should be compensated. These qualifications are one type of input or investment.

Second, most people feel that actual performance or effort should be compensated separately. That is, if one works harder, or produces more parts, that person should be paid more than one who works less or is less efficient. Thus an individual's pay should be based, in part, on qualification factors and, in part, on performance or effort factors. These performance or effort factors are a second, distinct type of input or investment. A more complete equity expression would be

$$\frac{Op}{Qp + Ep} = \frac{OA}{Qa + Ea}$$

where O = outcomes
Q = qualification factors
and E = effort or performance factors

JOB AND INDIVIDUAL VALUES. We can turn our attention now to an equally important consideration: the values that occur because of the *kind of work* one does and other values that occur because of *how well the person* does that work. Consider for a moment the case of four employees, John, Mary, Mike, and Roberta. John and Mary are both accountants employed by a department store, and Mike and Roberta work in the night cleanup crew (janitors) for the same company. John is a better accountant than Mary, and Roberta is the best janitor in the cleanup crew. What are the relative values associated with each?

First, we would probably feel that accountants perform more demanding or responsible tasks and are worth more than janitors; that is, there are different values that arise because of the work itself that one performs, and most accountants (regardless of their actual efforts) will be paid more than most janitors. These are job value inputs.

Also, we know that John's achievements as an accountant entitle him to more pay than Mary and that Roberta's janitorial performance entitles her to more pay than Mike. Thus John will probably be paid the most, Mary the second most, Roberta the third most, and Mike the least. Their pay, then, depends on both job-related value and employee-related value. Therefore, an alternative equity expression would be

$$\frac{Op}{JV_p + IV_p} = \frac{Oa}{JV_a + IV_a}$$

where JV = job-related value inputs and IV = individual-related value inputs.

Arriving at Total Compensation

As we turn to the simultaneous consideration of qualification, effort, and job-related and individual-related values, we can see their relationship as illustrated in Figure 12-1. Job-related value is composed of minimum qualification factors required by the job and minimum effort factors demanded by the job. Individual-related value is composed of the actual qualifications held by the employee and the actual level of performance achieved by the employee.

The normal, and logical, processes for determining an employee's salary will then be to place a value on the job (the qualifications and efforts it requires) and also a value on the employee's contributions (the actual qualifications and efforts—whether greater or lesser than the minimum job requirements). This establishes equity among employees. However, the resulting equitable relationship must be anchored to the external labor market for the organization to attract and hire employees for these jobs. Thus final compensation for employees is derived by adding some *market value* to the equitable structure, as shown in Figure 12-1.

As will be shown in the following chapters of this section, several different pro-

Figure 12-1

Relationship Among Qualification, Effort, Job, and Employee Factors

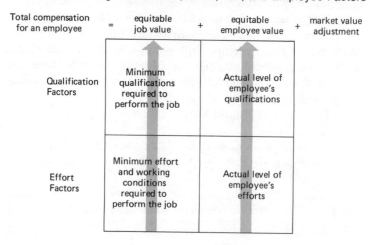

cedures may be applied in the determination of salary, but all of them are intended to result in an equitable structure that is competitive with the labor market. Those procedures that establish the value of job-related factors are referred to as job evaluation. Procedures that establish the value of individual-related factors are called performance evaluation and performance appraisal. The market value factor is obtained by conducting wage surveys on selected jobs.

THE LOGIC OF MOTIVATION

It is difficult to argue that salary does not motivate employees. In fact, few employees would continue to work for their employers if they were not paid for doing so. However, it does not take much investigation to discover that salary, as administered typically in organizations, is severely restricted in its usefulness as a motivator. As Mr. Wright of Texas Instruments stated, "Merit pay is more like recognition; it can alleviate some negative aspects of the job, but it is seldom the biggest motivator."

Motivational Consequences of Inequities

We can begin to understand the weakness of salary as a motivator by looking again at the equity expression

$$\frac{Op}{Ip} = \frac{Oa}{Ia} \tag{1}$$

Motiviation, defined as the "willful desire to direct one's effort (behavior) toward achieving given goals,"[4] is a major aspect of one's inputs. As effort increases (motivation), one's inputs are higher. Hence we can see that it should be possible to cause an increase in one's motivation by the simple act of first increasing one's outcomes, that is, by intentionally creating inequitable overpayment for that person.

For example, consider a person who is paid equitably given some current level of effort, so that he or she receives five units of outcome (pay) for five units of input (effort) while co-workers are also receiving five units of outcome for five units of input. The numerical equity relationship would be

$$\frac{5p}{5p} = \frac{5a}{5a} \tag{2}$$

To increase this person's effort, we would overpay him or her; for example,

$$\frac{7p}{5p} = \frac{5a}{5a} \quad \text{(inequitable relationship)} \tag{3}$$

To resolve this inequity, the person should increase his or her efforts to 7, resulting in a new expression:

$$\frac{7p}{7p} = \frac{5a}{5a} \quad \text{(equitable relationship)} \tag{4}$$

However, if we return to expression (3), we can see that not only was the person overpaid but that each and every co-worker had been underpaid. It was also possible, and highly likely, that the co-workers would also attempt to resolve the inequity *by reducing their efforts,* as

$$\frac{7p}{5p} = \frac{5a}{3.57a} \quad \text{(equitable relationship)} \tag{5}$$

Thus, the attempt to use salary increases as a means to *cause* motivation may not achieve increases in effort at all. Rather, it may result in a large net loss in employee efforts due to the dissatisfaction of all other co-workers with their inequitable underpayment. We can conclude that the use of money or salary will not often result in organizational improvements.

Stacy Adams proposed initially that employees facing inequities would be motivated to do one, or more, of the following:

1. Increase or reduce their outcomes (according to whether they were underpaid or overpaid, respectively).
2. Reduce or increase their inputs (according to whether they were underpaid or overpaid, respectively).
3. Reduce or increase their co-workers' outcomes.
4. Increase or reduce their co-workers' inputs.
5. Cognitively distort or misperceive the inequity (that is, mentally "rearrange" the facts) so that it is seen to be equitable.
6. Leave the field (e.g., quit their jobs) or otherwise change their comparison group.

Since overpayment of one employee results in underpayment of all others, managers should be mostly concerned about the underpayment. *None* of the six motivational effects of underpayment is desirable organizationally. Furthermore, researchers have largely verified these predicted effects to be widespread consequences of inequitable underpayments. For example, Leventhal and Michaels found that individuals divide rewards among themselves according to perceived inputs.[5] This has been confirmed by at least three other studies.[6] Also, Lawler and O'Gara found that underpaid subjects subsequently distorted their own qualifications and efforts to be less so as to perceive equity.[7]

Organizational research has also shown that employees who perceive that high performance inputs are rewarded by higher salary or promotion outcomes are more satisfied with their pay.[8] Finally, an interesting study of a large aircraft manufacturer found that work groups that perceived higher inequities in salary also experienced substantially greater employee turnover (leaving the field).[9] These results are representative of the findings in a large area of research on inequitable compensation and the likelihood of negative consequences to organizations that permit inequities to exist.

Although increases in salary may not be likely to cause widespread improvements in effort throughout the organization, this does not mean that salary and motivation are not related. Any of the five equity expressions we examined contain both monetary and effort (motivation) factors. Thus salary increases should not be used to precipitate increases in motivation. However, it can be seen readily that increases in effort *should* precipitate increases in salary.

For example, if one worker increases his or her efforts (motivation), expression (2) might become

$$\frac{5p}{7p} = \frac{5a}{5a} \quad \text{(inequitable relationship)} \quad (6)$$

This act may cause other co-workers to increase their efforts as

$$\frac{5p}{7p} = \frac{5a}{7p} \quad \text{(equitable relationship)} \quad (7)$$

Further, the organization should increase the person's outcomes through salary increases as

$$\frac{7p}{7p} = \frac{5a}{5a} \quad (8)$$

and ultimately any co-workers who had also increased their efforts as

$$\frac{7p}{7p} = \frac{7a}{7a} \quad (9)$$

Unless such increases in salary followed increased efforts, employees would soon reduce their efforts to the original levels. Thus, while salary cannot be used to elicit motivation from an employee, motivation should inevitably elicit salary from the organization.[10] Salary, then, supports and maintains employee motivation, even if it is used infrequently to elicit increased motivation.

Prompting Motivation

If organizations cannot use salary safely as a means of eliciting employee motivation, how then can motivation be encouraged? A great many organizations feel that motivation is aroused by the nature of the job itself and from internal needs and drives of the employee that relate to that job. This view was espoused by Wayne Wright, who stated, "Happiness with one's work is the biggest motivator." As we see in Chapter 13, the relationship between an employee's goals and the manner in which job performance helps to achieve those goals is perhaps the most important factor in motivation. Motivation may be induced by creating a job situation that permits employees to control the achievement of their goals and needs.

Incentive Systems and Motivation

There is some evidence that employee effort or motivation is higher when the employee's salary is based on some measure of his or her productivity, instead of time.[11] Productivity-based compensation plans are commonly referred to as incentive payment systems. In these systems, we might expect an assembly-line worker to be paid so much (say, 15¢) for each part assembled. At the end of the day, after having assembled 200 parts, the worker would have earned $30. Incentive systems are also common in sales positions where a salesperson might receive 10 percent of his or her total sales. If, for example, the salesperson sold $400 worth of goods, the commission would be $40. Typically, the earnings are accumulated for a one- or two-week period and are then given to the employee in the form of a paycheck rather than immediately as each part is assembled or each product is sold.

The psychological process by which such incentives arouse employee motivation is debated by some, but it appears to be related to reinforcement processes; that is, immediately following the employee's behavior (a completed assembly or closed sale), the employee can determine the impact that such behavior will have on his or her earnings. If the impact is positive (more earnings), it will reinforce the behavior, making it more likely that the employee will repeat the behavior.

In the case of incentive compensation, money does appear to be related to motivation. However, even in this case it can be seen that effort precedes payment; that is, the employee must first assemble the part, or close the sale, *before* the payment is received. It can also be seen that equity is an important issue in such systems. If one employee receives 15¢ a part while another receives only 10¢ a part, inequity will be perceived and will negatively affect the lower-paid employee. Furthermore, when employees receive the same piece rate, any employee who exerts greater effort (more inputs) receives greater payment (more outcomes), which maintains equity.

The essential differences between time-based and productivity-based payment, in terms of motivation and equity, are:

1. With incentive systems, the inequity that occurs when one employee exerts more effort than another is resolved more quickly (e.g., immediately), whereas inequity in time-based systems is not resolved until some performance review period (which may be annual).
2. With incentives, the relationship between one's productivity effort and compensation received is direct and clear, whereas the relationship between one's productivity effort and compensation received is obscure with time-based payment, because salary is calculated on the basis of hours worked rather than on parts produced.

We can conclude that higher levels of productivity associated with incentive payments are probably due to the rapid resolution of inequities and the reinforcement properties of a clear relationship between productivity and earnings. It is difficult to imagine that money, under either a time-based or an incentive system, is the primary means by which motivation is aroused. Again, the nature of the work itself, regardless of compensation system features, may be a more significant source of motivation arousal.

SUMMARY

In this chapter, we have tried to formulate some of the basic logic and thought processes underlying the issues of compensating and motivating employees. Individuals who work in the personnel management field, such as Wayne Wright of Texas Instruments, tend to see compensation and motivation as distinct and different issues; that is, employee motivation is not simply a matter of how much employees are paid. Attempts to arouse motivation through the use of money often create inequities that may cause widespread dissatisfaction among employees. However, equitable compensation may support and reinforce motivation that is aroused by the nature of employees and the jobs they perform.

Most employees are paid under time-based compensation systems. In these systems, the underlying concept is that of equity. An employee's salary (outcome) is based on qualification and effort factors (inputs) and must be in the same ratio as other employees' salaries, qualifications, and efforts. These compensation systems include both job and individual inputs and are adjusted to keep the wage level competitive with the general labor market.

Productivity-based compensation systems are less common but occur frequently in certain occupations, such as individuals employed as salespeople. These incentive structures reinforce efforts aroused by the nature of employees and their jobs. The maintenance of equity, and the clarity of relationships between earnings and productivity, probably explains the high productivity that can occur under such systems.

Since any compensation system tends to pay people after, rather than before, effort is exerted, the arousal of motivation by means other than salary is important. We believe that motivation may be induced by creating a job situation that permits employees to control the achievement of their goals and needs. In this case, the nature of the job itself and the internal needs and drives of employees become paramount in personnel management activities.

INTERVIEW WRAP-UP

I would like to emphasize two points that I've made before. First, different people are motivated by different things, but most are motivated by the job itself. This puts enormous responsibility on the line manager to be sure that employees find their jobs interesting, challenging, and with at least some personal freedoms. Second, organizations must educate employees to understand and believe in the compensation plan. Even the best planned salary system can be poor if employees reject it. —Wayne Wright, director of industrial relations, Texas Instruments.

REVIEW QUESTIONS

1. Why is the design of a salary system related more closely to the concept of equity than to some concept of motivation?

2. What are the major sources of inputs from which salary (outcome) can be determined?

3. If an employee is overpaid in an attempt to induce motivation, what are the likely results?

4. Describe two situations in which employees may feel equitably paid, even though they earn different salaries.

5. How are the reinforcement properties of incentive payments different from the "arousal" of motivation?

KEY CONCEPTS

Direct compensation	Market value
Effort	Motivation
Employee value	Productivity-based compensation
Equity	Qualifications
Incentive payment	Supplemental compensation
Job value	Time-based compensation

CASE

A DISGRUNTLED TRAINEE

Mary leaned back to proofread the letter. She wanted to be sure that the letter said what she wanted to say. She didn't really want to quit her job, but unless the salary issue was resolved, she felt that she had no other choice. She wanted to be sure that Dave Reardon, her boss, knew this. She wanted to give him every chance to resolve the salary dispute, not to force his back to the wall where he had no choice but to accept her resignation. As she read the letter, her mind reviewed the events of the past year.

A year ago, Mary had graduated from City College, receiving her B.S. degree in management. She had interviewed with several companies during the on-campus interviewing period, but it seemed as if all these companies wanted her to move to another state. Since she wanted to continue to live in Manhattan, she declined a couple of attractive offers, choosing to take her chances in the local job market.

She visited some employment agencies, answered many newspaper ads, and asked for help from several friends and relatives who were employed at different firms around the city. After several weeks of interviewing, she finally accepted an offer from Union Bank as a loan officer trainee. Although the starting salary of $1500 per month was somewhat lower than others that had been offered, she felt that Union Bank had more job opportunities. First, it had a definite training program for new employees, which others did not. Second, she liked the chance to combine quantitative and analytical skills with interpersonal skills. Most other jobs were either technical or interpersonal, but not both. As a loan officer she would have to evaluate credit risks, interest rates, labor market factors, and so on, while dealing on a personal level with bank customers. Finally, the bank promised a definite career plan, which included both promotional and salary increase factors. Mary thought she could see a promising future for herself upon completing the training program.

The bank employed twenty-seven loan officers, including commercial and consumer specialists. Mary was one of three new, inexperienced loan officer trainees hired during the summer. For each of them, the training program was identical, and they pursued their training together, becoming good friends in the process. The first phase of their training consisted of a six-week assignment to the clerical and posting section. Their activities consisted of making credit investigations of prospective customers, filling in for account payment posters, and occasionally backing up the teller windows. Subsequently, Mary and the other trainees were rotated through the collections department, insurance group, interest assessment group, and consumer and commercial loan departments.

During this fourteen-month period, Mary's performance had been evaluated by her training supervisor on a quarterly basis. Dave Reardon was very positive in his evaluation, offering good guidance, and Mary's salary had risen to its current level of $1750. She was pleased with her progress and found the work to be extremely interesting. She anticipated completion of the training program in the next four months and hoped to be assigned to the commercial loan unit.

However, last week one of her fellow trainees, Ralph Snowden, approached her with some information that upset her greatly. Her conversation with Ralph, as she recalled it, went something like this:

"Hey, Mary, do you know that new loan officer, Pete Williams, that they hired a few days ago over in commercial?"

"Yes, I met him yesterday. Why?"

"Well," Ralph said, "I was talking to him and he tells me he had only a year's experience with People's Savings and Loan. It really upsets me that he's already been made a loan officer, while we have been here longer than that and are still in training."

Mary had started to say something but Ralph interrupted her.

"What's even more disgusting is that he's getting loan officer salary. He says he's getting $2000. What do you think about that?"

Mary finished proofreading her letter. She really didn't like doing this. Damn Union Bank! Damn Pete Williams! She folded the letter, sealed the envelope, and addressed it to Dave Reardon. Now she would go to bed and sleep on it, but she knew she would give him the letter in the morning.

CASE QUESTIONS

1. What seem to be motivational forces for Mary?
2. Describe the role that her salary plays throughout the case.
3. What factors might have caused the bank to hire Pete Williams as a higher-paid loan officer?
4. If you were Dave Reardon, what steps would you take when you receive Mary's letter in the morning?

NOTES

[1] A. N. Nash and S. J. Carroll, Jr., *The Management of Compensation* (Monterey, Calif.: Brooks/ Cole, 1975), p. 193.

[2] J. S. Adams, "Inequity in Social Exchange," in *Advances in Experimental Social Psychology*, ed. L. Berkowitz (New York: Academic Press, 1965), pp. 267–300.

[3] R. D. Middlemist and R. B. Peterson, "Test of Equity Theory by Controlling for Comparison Co-workers' Efforts," *Organizational Behavior and Human Performance*, 15 (1976), 335–354.

[4] R. D. Middlemist and M. A. Hitt, *Organizational Behavior: Applied Concepts* (Chicago: Science Research Associates, 1981), p. 136.

[5] G. S. Leventhal and J. W. Michaels, "Extending the Equity Model: Perception of Inputs and Allocation of Reward as a Function of Duration and Quantity of Performance," *Journal of Personality and Social Psychology*, 4 (1969), 303–309.

[6] See I. M. Lane and L. A. Messé, "Distribution of Insufficient, Sufficient, and Oversufficient Rewards: A Clarification of Equity Theory," *Journal of Personality and Social Psychology*, 21 (1972), 228–233; G. S. Leventhal and J. T. Bergman, "Self-depriving Behavior as a Response to Unprofitable Inequity," *Journal of Experimental Social Psychology*, 5 (1969), 153–171; D. R. Schmitt and G. Marwell, "Withdrawal and Reward Reallocation as Responses to Inequity," *Journal of Experimental Social Psychology*, 8 (1972), 207–221.

[7] E. E. Lawler, III, and P. W. O'Gara, "Effects of Inequity Produced by Underpayment on Work Output, Work Quality, and Attitudes Toward the Work," *Journal of Applied Psychology*, 51 (1967), 403–410.

[8] S. J. Carroll, Jr., and H. L. Tosi, Jr., *Management by Objectives: Applications and Research* (New York: Macmillan, 1973).

[9] C. S. Telly, W. L. French, and W. G. Scott, "The Relationship of Inequity to Turnover Among Hourly Workers," *Administrative Science Quarterly*, 16 (1971), 164–172.

[10] Middlemist and Peterson, "Test of Equity Theory," p. 354.

[11] D. P. Schwab and L. D. Dyer, "The Motivational Impact of a Compensation System on Employee Performance," *Organizational Behavior and Human Performance*, 9 (1973), 215–225.

MOTIVATION

LEARNING OBJECTIVES

After reading this chapter, you should be able to:

1. Define the term motivation and discuss several issues raised by motivational researchers.
2. Briefly describe Maslow's need hierarchy, McClelland's achievement needs theory, and Herzberg's two-factor concept of motivation.
3. Demonstrate how various notions from other motivation theories are related to the expectancy theory of motivation.
4. Define and describe the terms expectancy and valence.
5. Explain job enrichment as a motivation activity.
6. Discuss goal setting and management by objectives as personnel management activities and show how principles of expectancy theory are applied in these activities.
7. Describe the motivational impacts of performance appraisal and counseling.
8. Discuss motivational properties of incentive systems.

GTE Sylvania is among the twenty largest companies in the United States. As one of the largest companies, it has a well-developed personnel management program that is staffed by individuals with a high degree of experience and qualifications. The problem of motivating employees is especially important to large companies.

Fred Brown is a personnel manager at one GTE Sylvania location. He has been with GTE Sylvania for twenty-three years and has developed keen insight into many personnel activities. He shared some of these insights with us.

Interviewer: What is the most important factor in employee motivation?

Fred Brown: Enjoyment of the job. Employees' enjoyment of the job accomplishes two things: it leads to a higher level of performance and also helps to keep employees with the company for a longer period of time. That secretary across the room, for example, is one of our better employees and has been here for ten years.

Interviewer: Tell us about the differences among employees.

Fred Brown: Certainly, different employees and groups of employees are motivated by different things. For example, there is a difference between union and nonunion employees, and between salaried and hourly employees. While it is very difficult to establish comprehensive programs to deal with these differences at a corporate level, supervisors often recognize them at the department level.

Interviewer: How does GTE Sylvania, at the department level, actually motivate employees?

Fred Brown: One of the most critical elements, personnel policy, has to do with the annual appraisal session that each employee has with his or her supervisor. In addition to simply discussing the nature of past performance and reviewing salary issues, the employee and manager discuss employee performance and improvement goals for the upcoming year.

These goals are arrived at by mutual discussion and are agreed upon by both the employee and the manager. The communication between the two is critical, and therefore about 30 to 45 minutes is set aside for this discussion. The goals are written down on the appraisal form and signed by both the manager and the employee. For example, a secretary could set a goal to improve her shorthand. The improvement plan of action might include her taking a class and practicing at home. It would be understood that, if the secretary reaches the goal, her salary at the next appraisal would reflect her achievement.

Employees' motivation is affected positively by the participative discussion session, by having specific goals and plans to achieve the goals, and by supervisory support throughout the year. Also, since the employees help set the goals, you can be sure they are ones that are important to them and that they will be committed to achieve. The salary increase they will subsequently receive is after the fact and merely recognizes the employees' motivated achievements.

INTRODUCTION

The motivation of employees is admittedly one of the more important aspects of managing an organization successfully. When employees work harder, the organization usually prospers; when employees work less hard, the organization is likely to suffer. However, as Fred Brown of GTE Sylvania explained, the issues of motivation are not easily understood. Different employees are motivated by different forces. This often makes it difficult to design systematic approaches for motivating employees on a companywide basis.

Our recognition that different people are motivated by different forces generally leads us to study motivation as it applies to individuals. That is, we focus on understanding individual need and motive structures and examine various organizational factors that affect these individual structures. However, when we view motivation as a personnel management activity, it is important to recognize that we must evolve strategies that can be applied more widely to larger numbers of employees. Motivational systems must be designed so that consistent and fair procedures are used from manager to manager and from employee to employee. Otherwise, motivational efforts may be offset by inconsistencies and inequities that occur as a result of widely divergent, individualized approaches.

What is needed, then, is a motivational process that has wide applicability across an organization but that allows individual factors to play an important role. Such a system is seen in the job-oriented appraisal approach described by Fred Brown.

The purpose of this chapter is to review briefly several theories of motivation that are commonly encountered by students in basic psychology and management courses and then to develop an understanding of how these theories can be translated into a more systematic personnel activity.

THE NATURE OF MOTIVATION

Several definitions of the term motivation have been written by interested researchers. Despite certain differences, most agree that the primary organizational purpose of motivation is to encourage employees to direct their efforts toward the organization's goals. Thus we can define motivation as, simply, *the willful desire to direct one's behavior and skills toward the accomplishment of certain goals.*[1]

This definition raises several issues that have been the focus of considerable research in motivation. For example, what factors would activate a willful desire? What is the role of skill in motivated behavior? Does accomplishment, in itself, enhance future motivation? Is the choice of type of goal, or level of goal difficulty, an important issue in motivation? These questions, while not exhaustive, are indicative of the kinds of issues that have been investigated systematically and have led to several important theories of motivation. An understanding of these theories will help us to develop personnel activities that encourage higher levels of employee motivation. These theories are reviewed here briefly.

Maslow's Need Hierarchy

Perhaps one of the more popular motivation theories was proposed by Abraham Maslow in the 1940s.[2] Basically, this concept addresses issues related to the activation of willful desire and the choice of types of goals.

According to Maslow, individual behavior is activated by the desire to fulfill unsatisfied needs. That is, if a person has an unsatisfied need for clothing, he or she will take actions that will lead to obtaining clothes. From this rather simple example, we can see that the unsatisfied need provides some basis for choice of goal and also activates the desire. The five needs that Maslow specified, and the types of personal goals that satisfy them, are shown in Table 13-1.

It was proposed that these needs are arranged in a hierarchical order, from physiological (lowest) to self-actualization (highest), although the exact order may vary somewhat among individuals. Also, each lower need is prepotent over higher-order needs or must be largely satisfied before the unsatisfied higher need will activate behavior. Once satisfied, any need tends to lose its capacity for activating behavior, since the higher, unsatisfied need becomes the focus of the individual's activity.

Maslow's need concept has not been well supported by empirical research.[3] This may be due to the difficulty of identifying the exact order of an individual's needs or weaknesses in measuring prepotencies or other problems. However, the idea that unsatisfied needs activate seeking behavior and clarify personal goals is widely accepted.

McClelland's Achievement Needs Theory

A second motivation concept that relates to job performance was developed by David McClelland in the late 1950s. This concept is also based on individual needs: the needs for achievement, power, and affiliation.[4] While all three needs affect one's behavior, the need for achievement is generally thought to exert a greater effect on one's motivation to perform elements of a task.[5] Individuals who have a high need for achievement

1. Prefer to take personal responsibility for solving task-related problems.
2. Work their hardest when assigned to tasks of moderate difficulty, neither too easy nor impossible to achieve.
3. Prefer tasks in which they receive regular concrete feedback on their performance and achievements.[6]

Table 13-1

Maslow's Need Hierarchy

Needs	Personal Goals/Satisfiers
Self-actualization	Development of full potential; goals that can be obtained through less rigid organizational structure and encouragement of independence and creativity.
Esteem or recognition	Recognition of achievements; factors that derive from supervisory and peer praise and various organizational status symbols.
Social or belongingness	Acceptance by peers and friends; satisfiers that are developed through team and group relationships.
Safety or security	Shelter and stability; satisfiers that may be purchased by salary or assured by employment contracts.
Physiological	Food, water, and so on; factors that for the most part are purchased by money or salary.

These findings suggest that accomplishments, in themselves, have motivational properties for some people. Further, the level of difficulty in a task or goal does influence an individual's motivation.

Herzberg's Two-Factor Concept

Frederick Herzberg was also examining employee motivation in the late 1950s. As a result of his research with engineers and accountants, he concluded that employee attitudes toward their jobs were influenced by two groups of factors: motivators and hygienes. Motivators are factors that are contained within a person's job and include the chance for achievement and recognition, opportunity for responsibility and advancement, the nature of the work itself, and the potential for personal growth in the job. The more a job has these characteristics, the more likely an employee is to be satisfied and, hence, to exert greater effort. Hygienic factors are not within the job but involve the conditions under which the job is performed, such as the level of pay, type of supervision, job security, working conditions, organizational rules and policies, and type of interpersonal relationships in the work environment. These factors, when inappropriate, tend to be associated with employee dissatisfaction.[7]

According to this concept, managers may prevent dissatisfaction by providing good pay and working conditions and by reducing restrictive work rules, for example. However, these alone would not cause motivation. To enhance motivation, managers should also design jobs in which employees can be recognized for their achievements and that lead to personal growth and development of the employees.

Expectancy Theory

The most popular current theory of motivation is called expectancy theory. Two frequently cited models of expectancy theory, developed originally by Vroom[8] and by Porter and Lawler,[9] have since been modified according to various research findings. One reason for the importance of this theory is that it integrates most concepts from other motivation theories and therefore offers a more powerful understanding of employee motivation.

The theory is based on two central ideas: expectancy and valence.

Expectancy: a person's assessment of the subjective probability of attaining a particular outcome.

Valence: the anticipated value of an expected outcome—if such outcome did, in fact, occur.

According to the theory, an employee chooses the behaviors in which he or she engages on the basis of the valences of outcomes from such behaviors and the subjective estimate of the probability that his or her behavior will indeed result in the outcomes.[10]

As illustrated in Figure 13-1, employee motivation is viewed as a complex behavior in which a variety of factors play important roles. These factors include needs, achievement, and work context. They also include several other factors, such as goal difficulty, perceived probabilities, organizational support, employee skills, and the values placed by employees on the various rewards they may receive for task performance. Since this model underlies many personnel activities that affect employee motivation, it is important to understand its complexities.

VALENCES.   Three types of valences affect employee motivation. While earlier research had identified various rewards associated with task performance, subtle differences between them were overlooked. First, most employees experience psychic or intrinsic rewards simply in performing the task (IV_1). If they enjoy the task and feel that it is important, or if it involves doing things related to the employees' central skills, they are likely to feel a sense of satisfaction (an intrinsic reward) or a sense of contribution (also an intrinsic reward). If they do not enjoy the task and feel that it is unimportant or that it involves unimportant skills, they are likely to experience dissatisfaction and a sense of noncontribution (intrinsic negative rewards). When these intrinsic rewards are more valued by employees, they will be more motivated to perform the task.

Figure 13-1

Expectancy Theory Model

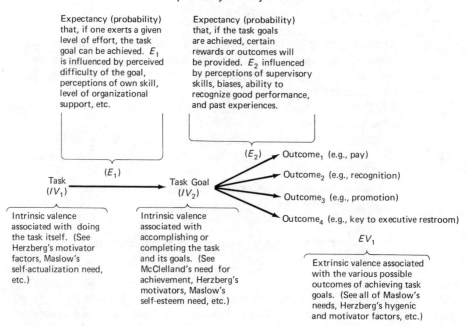

Also, performance goals are assigned to most tasks. For example, a goal may be to produce fifty wiring assemblies per work day or to increase sales of oxford shoes by 10 percent. Regardless of the valence associated with the job itself, most employees perceive intrinsic rewards (satisfaction, personal growth, contributions, and achievement) when performance goals are reached. If one has a high need for achievement, the achievement of performance goals should have more intrinsic valence (IV_2) than for employees with a lower need for achievement. Also, we might expect that the achievement of task goals is more valued for jobs we like (IV_1) and for goals that are at least somewhat difficult to achieve. The achievement of goals that are too easy may have little intrinsic valence.

Finally, employees are given rewards such as salary and promotion that are based on their achieved level of performance. The degree to which these rewards are desired or valued by the receiving employees is referred to as extrinsic valence (EV). Rewards having greater extrinsic valence are more likely to lead to higher levels of motivation.

EXPECTANCIES.   While there are three types of rewards in the model, there are only two sets of expectancies. Expectancies refer to subjective probabilities that a particular outcome (reward) will actually be attained. For rewards associated with doing the task itself, the probability is always 100 percent. That is, the employee either does enjoy or does not enjoy the task; thus there is no expectancy associated with intrinsic rewards for simply performing the task.

However, the intrinsic rewards that derive from achieving task goals are never certain. Regardless of the employee's enjoyment and satisfaction with the task, reaching performance goals involves uncertainties. The employee may feel that the goals are too difficult or that he or she lacks a crucial skill or that necessary resources (a new tool, information, for instance) will not be provided by the organization. In this case, the employee would perceive a low probability (E_1) that the task goal will be achieved. Thus, even if the employee highly values intrinsic goal achievement rewards, he or she may be poorly motivated to perform. A certain sense of futility may be experienced, for example, "Why waste my efforts if I can't get it done?" This is an especially important element in motivation that the earlier researchers overlooked.

Finally, organizations may not be consistent in rewarding employees for achievement of goals. Because of their perceptions of supervisory biases, the absence of supervisory skill in appraising performance, or other reasons, subordinates may perceive a low probability that organizational rewards will be received (E_2) regardless of the quality of their own achievements. Employees who perceive a low probability of extrinsic rewards may be less motivated to achieve task goals than may employees who perceive a higher probability.

This complex theory of motivation incorporates many features of earlier motivation research. It also fits nicely with the way in which personnel managers, such as Fred Brown, feel employees are motivated. Motivation begins with the task itself and the pleasures and satisfactions that employees derive from it. Improvement goals and the possibilities of achieving them also influence employee motivation. Compensation, in terms of pay and promotion, support the motivation system, but they cannot be thought of as the primary cause.

PERSONNEL ACTIVITIES FOR MOTIVATION

With a solid understanding of motivation theory, it is possible to examine several specific personnel activities that affect employee motivation. Most of these activities have been researched extensively as to their organizational usefulness. These activities tend to be focused on the task itself (job enrichment), task goals (goal setting and management by objectives), and expectancies (performance feedback). There is some interaction of these activities, as between goal setting and feedback, which we examine as well. We also see that selection and training activities, although not designed specifically for employee motivation, have significant effects on motivation. Finally, we examine the nature of compensation effects that interact with some of these motivation programs.

Job Enrichment

Job enrichment (discussed in the sections on job design) is the process of adding tasks to jobs that allow employees to have more discretion in performing their jobs.[11] This involves permitting employees to become managers of their own jobs by allowing them to plan, organize, and evaluate task activities. Employees tend to view the planning, organizing, and evaluating elements as more interesting and challenging, thus enhancing the intrinsic valence associated with performing the task itself.

AT&T, Corning Glass Works, IBM, and Procter & Gamble are among numerous companies that have implemented job enrichment programs. Although many researchers have questioned the results of such programs,[12] the literature has many examples of astounding results. For example, employees of General Foods at the Topeka, Kansas, plant were assigned to work teams that handled customer complaints, made decisions on performance evaluation and compensation of team members, and performed basic task elements. In addition to lower turnover and absenteeism, this plant produced at a rate 40 percent higher than did other General Foods plants.[13]

The primary difficulty in implementing job enrichment is that neither researchers nor practicing managers have been able to identify a precise set of procedures for accomplishing enriched jobs. In fact, the procedure should be expected to vary from job to job. Some jobs may already be rich in planning, organizing, and evaluating activities. Others may be poor in those ingredients, but difficult to enrich due to technological or resource constraints. Still, it is obvious that the underlying objective is the task itself and, therefore, that the task design procedures, identified earlier in this text, may be appropriate. As such, cooperation among personnel management specialists, employees who perform the tasks, and their supervisors may lead to specific steps for enriching job contents.

Goal Setting

The setting of goals to be achieved in task performance is an extremely important personnel management activity. Fred Brown of GTE Sylvania is typical of personnel specialists who recognize the motivational properties of setting task performance goals. An examination of the motivation model (Figure 13-1) suggests this importance, as *achievement* of goals provides intrinsic rewards and may also lead to organizational rewards.

The research on goal setting is fairly convincing insofar as the act of setting clear goals for employee tasks generally results in better performance than not setting such goals. This has been found in organizations as well as in research laboratories.[14] Based on this research, it is possible to conclude that motivating employees through goal setting depends on the manager's attention to several issues.

CLARITY OF GOALS. Managers who attempt to motivate employee task performance by establishing task goals must be sure that the goals, or performance targets, are clear and specific. It is well established that specific goals such as "reduce customer complaints by 20 percent" or "increase sales calls on retail firms by 15 percent" are much more likely to lead to employee performance improvements than are vaguely stated goals such as "do your best."[15]

DIFFICULTY OF GOALS. One of the questions that managers must answer is, "How difficult should the tasks' goals be?" Goals can be set low so that all employees can achieve them, or so difficult that hardly any employees can achieve them, or someplace in between. The research on this is more ambiguous, but early research suggested that difficult goals that are achieved by only a small portion of employees are better motivators.[16] However, more recent research has found that difficult goals may not motivate employees under two conditions.

First, unless information is provided frequently, employees may be unable to assess their progress toward the goal. The lack of such information seems to deter performance. Therefore, when employees are assigned task goals, they must also be given frequent feedback relative to their progress toward those goals. Unless this is done, the employees may not be motivated.[17]

Second, it has been found that the effects of difficult goals differ between piece-rate and bonus payment systems. If individuals are paid by piece (e.g., 5 cents per widget), performance is highest when goals are set very high. In this case, the goal acts as a target, but even if unreached, the employee still receives full compensation for all pieces produced. However, if individuals receive part of their compensation in terms of a bonus that is given only when the goal is achieved, performance is highest when goals are only moderately difficult. This may be due to the fact that part of the employee's efforts are not rewarded in the event that a goal is not reached.[18] Therefore, managers must examine the payment system when deciding how difficult employee task goals should be.

PARTICIPATION IN GOAL SETTING.   When managers think of employee motivation, they often think first of the effects of employee participation in decisions. An abundance of early research in organizations suggested that employee participation in decisions causes increased productivity. It was believed that the increased productivity was due to simple increases in employee commitment to the goals. That is, since the *decision* about how high the performance goal should be set *was basically the employees',* they were more committed to achieve them.

However, recent research suggests that it is more likely that participation in seting goals leads employees to set higher goals (than would their managers) and yet not perceive the goals to be extremely difficult to attain.[19] Since higher goals tend to lead to higher performance (except in bonus incentive systems), it may be that the impact of participation on performance is due to the setting of higher goals.

Regardless of the reason, it is clear that participation will often lead to improved performance, especially if higher goals result from the participation. Furthermore, such participation usually results in greater employee satisfaction.[20] Many managers, as Fred Brown of GTE Sylvania explained, believe that employee motivation is affected positively by participative discussions in setting performance goals.

NEED FOR ACHIEVEMENT AND GOAL SETTING.   The effect of setting task goals is not always the same from individual to individual. Some people welcome the chance to set and work toward fairly difficult goals. Others prefer to set lower goals and thus assure themselves that they will be able to achieve the performance targets. Although we do not understand all the characteristics of people that cause them to react differently to goal setting, it seems that one characteristic—the need for achievement—is particularly important.

To examine the relationship between one's need for achievement and the effect of goal setting, one researcher studied supervisors in a large West Coast public utility. Goal setting was used as a motivational program throughout the organization. The researchers gathered information relative to supervisors' needs for achievement, difficulty of goals they set, the degree to which they participated in goal setting, the clarity of their task goals, and the measures of their actual levels of performance.

Interestingly, it was found that the relationship among need for achievement, goal difficulty, and performance was more complex than originally thought. It was found that goal difficulty had very little to do with level of performance, regardless of one's need for achievement. However, individuals with a high need for achievement were motivated to higher performance when *goals were clear* and when feedback on their performance was received regularly. Individuals with a low need for achievement were motivated to perform when allowed to *participate* in setting their goals.[21]

Clearly, the motivation of employee performance by setting task goals is complex. Line managers must be assisted by personnel managers in designing goals that are compatible with individual characteristics of the employees.

Management by Objectives

Many organizations have formalized some of the principles of goal setting into a structured process—management by objectives (MBO)—in which managers work with their subordinates to establish objectives for employee tasks. These objectives are taken from departmental objectives that derive from plantwide objectives, and so on, until all objectives have been integrated into the highest-level corporate objectives. By using this procedure, the organization accomplishes coordination between various parts of the organization as well as motivational benefits of involving employees in the setting of task performance objectives.

Although there are differences in the specific steps taken by various organizations, several general steps are involved in most MBO programs. First, managers at all levels collect information that relates to setting realistic goals and diagnosing various problems on which to focus MBO efforts. Second, workshops are conducted to help instruct managers in the correct use of MBO techniques. Then major organizational objectives are defined in team meetings among top executives. These objectives are then coordinated throughout the organization into work unit objectives. At this point, managers and individual employees mutually discuss and agree on each employee's performance goals. The agreed-upon goals are then used in evaluating each employee's performance during the coming evaluation period (generally one year).[22]

While this process often results in higher levels of employee performance, it is time consuming and often requires a great deal of paperwork. Each manager may be required to complete records of employee discussions and to report on these to the next higher manager. The next higher manager also makes records and reports to an even higher manager, and so on. This has discouraged many managers, and they may fail to give the MBO effort the attention it needs. Lack of attention may result in poor goal setting or in an attitude of indifference. In these cases, the MBO effort fails to achieve the expected levels of employee motivation. Thus MBO requires a great deal of managerial effort and commitment if it is to be of motivational value.

Performance Appraisal and Counseling

One major personnel activity that affects motivation is the process of appraising employees' performance and counseling them in methods of improving. Although we think of performance appraisal as a personnel management tool for determining salary adjustments, it is also a useful process in motivation.

Two important elements in motivation (see Figure 13-1) are the expectancies between performing a task and task-goal achievement and between task-goal achievement and valued outcomes such as pay, recognition, and promotion. Motivation is affected positively when these expectancies are high. Performance appraisal and counseling are personnel management activities that can influence these expectancies.

Most employees need some structure within their work assignments and feedback regarding their standing within the organization. Without structure and feedback, the relationship among employee, job, and organization is ambiguous and perhaps stressful. High performers need to know how their performance is linked to organizational rewards. Low performers need to know how their performance can be improved. The feedback provided by performance appraisal and counseling should be designed for these purposes.[23]

Goal setting is also accomplished at this time. In the case of low performers, managers should establish personal development goals (training programs) as well as moderately challenging task goals that can be accomplished. For high performers, career development goals (training for the next promotion) and more challenging task goals will lead to greater motivation.

This personnel management activity is one of the major motivational efforts explained by Fred Brown. Performance appraisal is performed annually at GTE Sylvania. In addition to discussing past performance and salary increases, GTE Sylvania managers discuss both personal improvement goals and task performance goals in a lengthy meeting with each subordinate. The goals become the focus of the employee's efforts during the next year, which serves to motivate the employee.

MONETARY INCENTIVES IN MOTIVATION

While many researchers have questioned the role of salary in employee motivation, most would not deny that properly administered salary systems can be important. We have reviewed some research that suggests certain kinds of incentive payments affect the motivational effects of goal setting. In addition, incentive systems based on employee productivity have been associated with high levels of productivity in many organizations.[24] Although incentive payment systems are described more fully in Chapter 16, it is important to discuss their motivational properties at this point.

Incentives can take many forms, but generally they are financial rewards that prompt employees to behave so as to achieve some specified job performance or other goal desired by an organization. Thus an organization could provide incentives for a number of desired goals such as improvements in work processes, increases in productivity, decreases in waste, increases in sales, and so on. In some cases (improving some work process), the incentive may be earned as a result of "working harder." The point is that the impacts of incentives on employee behaviors can be varied, depending on the goal to be achieved.

By re-examining Figure 13-1, we can see that an incentive system that specifies that an employee can earn $1.50 for each wiring bank assembled will affect the expectancy between task goal and reward. The incentive agreement removes most uncertainty that may have existed about whether task achievement would, in fact, be rewarded.

However, incentives may not have the desired motivational effects in a number of circumstances. For instance, the assembly may require extreme effort and the $1.50

may not be deemed by employees as worth the effort. Also, it may be that the employee lacks the skills to complete wiring bank assemblies, in which case the first expectancy (E_1) is low, and subsequently motivation is also low. These are only two of the great many problems that can reduce the motivational properties of incentive plans.

Motivational properties of incentive plans can generally be enhanced by designing them in a manner consistent with the expectancy model of motivation. This suggests that several issues be explored during their design. Specifically, the following guidelines seem logical:

1. Be sure that the performances to be paid by incentives are consistent with the task goals of the particular job. In some cases, incentive arrangements may discourage some desired performances that are not included in the incentive system.
2. Specify clearly the exact levels of task performance that are required of employees to earn the incentive(s). General or ambiguous formulas for payment do not clarify the task goal-reward expectancy.
3. Be sure that task goals are set at levels that most employees can obtain, but not at lowest levels. If a goal is reached by everyone, even poorly skilled employees, it will offer very little challenge or intrinsic satisfaction for most employees.
4. Be sure that the incentive is large enough to have valence, but not so large as to create inequities for employees performing other jobs.
5. All payment systems, especially incentive systems, require a supporting structure of training and supervision. Therefore, design the incentive system with training needs in mind. In some cases this may mean that a second incentive structure is devised for new employees who have not completed their training.

SUMMARY

In this chapter, we have explored some basic concepts of motivation as they are applied to personnel management activities. Motivation is described as the willful desire to direct one's behavior and skills toward the accomplishment of certain goals. These goals can include both those of the organization and those of individual employees.

Much of the early research in motivation concerned theories of individual behavior. Such work led to the development of Maslow's popular need hierarchy, McClelland's need for achievement concept, and Herzberg's two-factor theory. While knowledge of individual motivation is important, these concepts were hard to apply in organizations composed of hundreds or thousands of individuals. Because each individual is likely to have slightly different needs from every other individual, applying these concepts might necessitate the development of several different motivational programs in an organization.

However, the expectancy theory of motivation that grew out of the early research efforts is applied more easily in organizations. This theory emphasizes task performance, task goals, reward valences, and the relationships among them—expectancy. Important factors that can be structured by the organization play an important role in determining the level of effort employees exert in performing their tasks. These include task-goal difficulty, organizational support programs, employee skills, perceived probabilities of task success, and the values of various rewards to employees. The expectancy model also accounts for individual differences in intrinsic rewards such as satisfaction and self-esteem.

The expectancy theory of motivation leads to several systematic motivational programs that are viewed as important personnel management activities. Job enrichment is a program that enhances the intrinsic rewards that employees receive for performing the task. This activity focuses on the task itself. Goal setting is an activity that focuses on task goals and the expectancy relationships. Task goals that are perceived as challenging but that employees perceive as achievable have been found to lead to higher performance than have goals that are either too easy or too difficult. Employee participation in setting performance goals also enhances efforts.

Management by objectives is a third, widely applied approach to employee motivation. This activity is a goal-setting approach that utilizes participation and encourages manager-subordinate cooperation. Performance appraisal and counseling is a common personnel management activity that also affects motivation. The feedback and goal setting that occur during appraisal, and focus on training or development needs, affect expectancies that lead to improved employee performance.

Finally, incentive payment systems are useful motivational tools, but only if careful attention is given to expectancies and valences. Incentive structures generally affect the expectancy between task goal and extrinsic rewards. They remove doubts that the employees might have about whether supervisors will recognize task achievements and reward them for it. However, goals must be clear, and the levels of achievement that will be rewarded must be explicit. Caution must be exercised to ensure that other desired behaviors are not threatened by narrowly defined task goals and that equity with other employees is not lost.

The concepts of motivation and personnel management activities described in this chapter are approaches that are used by many organizations. Fred Brown, commenting on employee motivation, summarized his views for us.

INTERVIEW WRAP-UP

The most important factor in motivation has to do with the employee's enjoyment of the job. Basically, this means whether the tasks and duties the employee performs are meaningful and important to the employee. If they are not, then we will have a difficult time motivating the employee. We can pay more money, but unless we can design challenge and excitement into the job, the employee may just put in time until something else comes along. —Fred Brown, personnel manager, GTE Sylvania.

WHAT MANAGERS SHOULD DO REGARDING PERSONNEL ACTIVITIES

1. Managers should acquaint themselves thoroughly with the major theories of motivation. The correct implementation of a plan for motivating employees often depends on the manager's understanding of basic, underlying principles found in these theories.

2. Managers can increase employee motivation by increasing the intrinsic valence of the employee's job through job enrichment. Adding challenge and skill variety increases employee interest in the job.

3. Employee motivation can be increased by attending to characteristics of task performance goals. Clear, challenging goals generally lead to higher motivation, whether or not the employee has participated in setting them. However, managers should, as a rule, involve employees in goal setting since it often results in setting more challenging goals. A well-designed MBO program should lead to these results.

4. Managers must develop their skills in appraising employee performance and counseling employees in methods for overcoming performance weaknesses. This activity is one that many managers avoid because it can be uncomfortable to provide such feedback. However, the benefits derived from effective performance appraisal and counseling are well worth the time invested in developing the skill.

5. If monetary incentives are used as a motivational tool, they should be designed with the guidelines presented in this chapter. This includes consideration of consistency, clarity, goal difficulty, size of incentive, and the need to train managers in the supervision of the incentive-employee relationship.

REVIEW QUESTIONS

1. Why is it often difficult to apply concepts of motivation in organization settings?

2. What are some of the ways in which the expectancy theory of motivation makes use of earlier efforts such as Maslow's, Herzberg's, or McClelland's?

3. Would it be possible for an employee to have a high valence for some organizational reward, such as promotion, and yet have a low level of motivation? Why or why not?

4. Goal setting is a personnel management application of expectancy theory. Explain three issues that affect the motivational impact of organizationwide applications of goal setting.

5. Explain two outcomes of performance appraisal and counseling that might enhance the motivation of either high or low performers.

6. What might be an unexpected consequence of incentive payment systems? How can this be avoided?

KEY CONCEPTS

Expectancy	Need for achievement
Feedback	Need hierarchy
Goal clarity	Participation
Goal difficulty	Performance appraisal
Goal setting	Performance counseling
Incentives	Task goal
Intrinsic reward	Task performance
Job enrichment	Two-factor concept
Management by objectives	Valence
Motivation	

CASE

THE RELUCTANT PROFESSORS

Dr. John Grayson was perplexed. He had been department head for nearly twelve years and was proud of the group of faculty members he had enticed to join Milton College. When he first took over the department, the faculty consisted of a few professors nearing retirement and one instructor. With a great deal of personal effort, however, Dr. Grayson had managed to hire several young, promising scholars from some of the most prestigious universities in the country. Dr. Grayson had enticed them by promising financial support for research projects and reduced teaching loads for doing research. He had fulfilled his promises, with the help and encouragement of the dean, Dr. Ralph White.

At first, Dean White had been skeptical of Dr. Grayson's suggestion regarding the annual appraisal and promotion policy. Milton College had always rewarded its faculty for excellence in the classroom, in terms of both annual salary increases and promotion decisions. Milton's conservative promotion policy had a long-standing tradition and, in Dean White's opinion, was the primary reason for the low turnover among its faculty. But it was this very point that Dr. Grayson used to his advantage in persuading the dean to adopt a new appraisal and promotion policy.

"Look, Dean White," he had said, "our appraisal and promotion policy was excellent at one point in time. It used to be that most professors chose this career because of the opportunity to teach and mold young minds. Being good in the classroom was their primary satisfaction and was the basic means of being recognized as a scholar in the academic community. But times have changed."

Dr. Grayson paused for effect, and then continued, "Where are the young faces in the faculty? There aren't any. Do you realize that we haven't been able to hire one, not even one, new Ph.D. in over five years? Oh, sure, we've found some older faculty who've been willing to join us, but we haven't hired any faculty members under the age of thirty-five since we got Greg Morrison in 1975.

Dean White had nodded. "I realize that, John, but I'm not sure it's the result of our appraisal and promotion policy. I rather think it's because there are so many schools out there, competing for these young graduates, that we are just at a disadvantage with our limited financial resources."

"That's a problem all right," Dr. Grayson had agreed, "but every school has limited finances. We're not that far off on our starting salaries. That's not what we're fighting. But, when I tell these young people, during the interview, that we emphasize teaching in the salary and promotion decisions, I lose them. They are all into research these days. If we can't promise them recognition and support for research, we've lost them. They're getting offers for a six-hour teaching load, release for research, research assistants, and three-year promotion with half-a-dozen publications. Then I offer a twelve-hour teaching load, few research facilities, and a five-year promotion if they please their students. I can see them get all tense, and I've lost them. We just have to change our priorities."

Eventually, Dean White was persuaded. The criteria for salary and promotion decisions was altered to reflect a new emphasis on research and publication. The new policy dictated that promotion eligibility would be based on research and publication activity. To be promoted from the assistant to an associate level required five published research articles, and from associate to full professor required an additional seven publications. Performance appraisal for salary purposes was to be based on "research, teaching, and overall contribution to the college." Although it was not formalized explicitly into a written policy, the new guideline was made clear to the older professors as well as to all new prospects.

At first, Dr. Grayson and Dean White were very pleased with the results of the new policy. It seemed to help their recruiting efforts as they were able to hire two young men with a great deal of promise and two more outstanding graduates the following year. These individuals seemed to be living up to their promise, and several publications had resulted.

However, during this, the third year, some problems seemed to be surfacing. First, several of the older faculty had complained to Dean White about the underemphasis on teaching. They maintained that the purpose of the college was to educate students and that some of the bright newcomers were neglecting this responsibility. They also complained about their small salary increases, which didn't reflect their value to Milton College. Loyalty and teaching ability were being downgraded, they had claimed.

Then, this morning, Dr. Grayson received the student evaluations for all courses offered during the fall semester. He was dismayed as he scanned through them, noting that the department's ratings were much lower than they had ever been. Even more troublesome was the fact that lower ratings were being received by both the newer faculty members and the older group. He had expected that

some of the young scholars might have slightly lower ratings, but he had not anticipated the large decline in the older faculty group. But, in fact, the ratings for both
groups were "horrible."

CASE QUESTIONS

1. From your point of view, which theories of motivation seem to be involved in this
   case?
2. Why would the change in the salary-promotion policy affect the classroom performance of the older faculty?
3. Is there an alternative personnel approach that could have been used in this case?
   What is it and why might it have been better?
4. If you were Dr. Grayson, what would you do now?

NOTES

[1] R. D. Middlemist and M. A. Hitt, *Organizatonal Behavior: Applied Concepts* (Chicago: Science Research Associates, 1981), p. 136.

[2] A. H. Maslow, "A Theory of Human Motivation," *Psychological Review,* 50 (1943), 370–396.

[3] M. A. Wahba and L. G. Bridwell, "Maslow Reconsidered: A Review of the Research on the Need
Hierarchy Theory," *Organizational Behavior and Human Performance,* 15 (1976), 212–240.

[4] D. C. McClelland, "That Urge to Achieve," *Think,* 32 (1966), 19–23.

[5] Ibid.

[6] Ibid.

[7] F. Herzberg, B. Mausner, and B. Snyderman, *The Motivation to Work* (New York: John Wiley,
1959).

[8] V. H. Vroom, *Work and Motivation* (New York: John Wiley, 1964).

[9] L. W. Porter and E. E. Lawler, *Managerial Attitudes and Performance* (Homewood, Ill.: Irwin-
Dorsey, 1968).

[10] M. A. Wahba and R. J. House, "Expectancy Theory in Work and Motivation: Some Logical and
Methodological Issues," *Human Relations,* 27 (1972), 121–147.

[11] Middlemist and Hitt, *Organizational Behavior,* p. 465.

[12] R. J. Aldag and A. P. Brief, *Task Design and Employee Motivation* (Glenview, Ill.: Scott, Foresman, 1979).

[13] R. E. Walton, "How to Counter Alienation in the Plant," *Harvard Business Review,* 50 (1972), 70–
81.

[14] R. M. Steers, "Task-Goal Attributes, *n* Achievement, and Supervisory Performance," *Organizational Behavior and Human Performance,* 13 (1975), 392–403.

[15] J. M. Ivancevich, "Different Goal Setting Treatments and Their Effects on Performance and Job
Satisfaction," *Academy of Management Journal,* 20 (1977), 406–419; also, see G. P. Latham and G. A.
Yukl, "Assigned Versus Participative Goal Setting with Educated and Uneducated Wood Workers," *Jour-
nal of Applied Psychology,* 60 (1975), 299–302.

[16] Latham and Yukl, "Assigned Versus Participative Goal Setting," pp. 299–302; also, see E. A.
Locke, "Toward a Theory of Task Motivation and Incentives," *Organizational Behavior and Human
Performance,* 3 (1968), 157–189.

[17]H. R. Strange, E. C. Lawrence, and P. C. Fowler, "Effects of Assigned Goal Level and Knowledge of Results on Arithmetic Computation: A Laboratory Study," *Journal of Applied Psychology,* 63 (1978), 446–450.

[18]J. C. Mowen and R. D. Middlemist, "Joint Effects of Goal Level and Incentive Structure on Task Performance: A Laboratory Study," *Journal of Applied Psychology,* 66 (1981), 598–603.

[19]G. P. Latham and L. M. Saari, "The Effects of Holding Goal Difficulty Constant on Assigned and Participatively Set Goals," *Academy of Management Journal,* 22 (1979), 163–168.

[20]Ivancevich, "Different Goal Setting Treatments," pp. 406–419.

[21]Steers, "Task-Goal Attributes, *n* Achievement, and Supervisory Performance," pp. 392–403.

[22]J. R. Hackman and G. R. Oldham, "Motivation Through the Design of Work: Test of a Theory," *Organizational Behavior and Human Performance,* 16 (1976), 250–279.

[23]L. L. Cummings and D. P. Schwab, *Performance in Organizations: Determinants and Appraisal* (Glenview, Ill.: Scott, Foresman, 1973), p. 55.

[24]H. G. Zollitsch and A. Langsner, *Wage and Salary Administration* (Chicago: South-Western, 1970), p. 487.

COMPENSATING JOBS

LEARNING OBJECTIVES

After reading this chapter, you should be able to:

1. Define the terms compensation, salary, and wages.
2. List and describe briefly six major pieces of legislation affecting compensation policies and practices.
3. Describe the major factors affecting the level at which organizations set their pay.
4. Define job evaluation and describe the general process for determining pay for jobs.
5. Explain four methods of evaluating jobs.
6. Describe the purpose of wage and salary surveys and how they are conducted.
7. Discuss how wage ranges and career curves are developed.

Norman L. "Tex" Holton is secretary-treasurer of the Food Process Workers, Warehouse-men and Helpers Union Local Number 228. This union is affiliated with the International Brotherhood of Teamsters. Norman's local represents workers at Campbell Soup's Sacramento, California, plant. Norman has ten years of experience and has been with the union for that period of time.

Norman has an important job. He is the principal officer in the local and was elected for a three-year period. As the principal officer, he has the final decision regarding whether a grievance case should be sent to arbitration or not. Also, he tries to maintain up-to-date knowledge in his field. For example, he took a labor course at California State University at Sacramento. To his credit Norman was asked to speak recently at the Center for Labor Research and Education at the University of California at Berkeley.

Interviewer: What is the union viewpoint on the importance of compensation? Should compensation be related to the job? How can employees be compensated fairly?

Norman Holton: Currently, wages are the number one concern of employees, and hourly wages have been the most important issue in the last two contract negotiations. The reasons for this are severalfold. The increasing inflation rate and high cost of living have contributed to the importance of compensation to the workers. In addition, the work force, at least at the Sacramento plant, is younger than in the past. Younger workers seem to care more about the fringe benefits. Fringe benefits (e.g., insurance programs, retirement benefits) seem to be running a close second to hourly wages in importance.

Definitely, the amount of compensation paid to the employee should be related to the type of job performed. Too, the employer has to make a reasonable profit. Otherwise, none of them will have a job. It seems to me that the fairest way to compensate most employees is through an hourly wage rate tied to the type of job performed. An accurate job description should be developed and a fair job classification or evaluation should be used to establish the proper wage rate. As the job changes (i.e., becomes more involved), the job description can be changed along with the classification as necessary. Job descriptions should be explicit so that employees know what must be done to accomplish the whole job.

Performance is an important element in pay, but incentive or piece-rate systems, whereby pay rates are based on the amount of items produced, do not seem to be effective. They produce too much competition among employees and even may lead to "cheating." The incentive pay system may lead to a higher quantity of output but also leads to lower quality. Although performance is important, it must be measured in broader terms than simply "quantity of output." Take the case of a nineteen-year-old employee and a fifty-five-year-old employee, both in the same job and same pay rate. The younger worker may be able to turn out more products but the older worker is steadier, more dependable, and generally has lower levels of absenteeism. Therefore, their work is generally equal in the long run.

INTRODUCTION

An officer in a local union affiliated with one of the most powerful unions (the Teamsters) in the United States, Norman is in a unique position to view the mood of American workers. He noted that the amount of hourly wages paid has been the most important issue to employees in the last two contract negotiations at his plant. Given the reasons for the importance of this issue, particularly high inflation rates, it is likely these workers reflect the mood of most workers in the United States, unionized or not.

Money is an important issue to most employees regardless of level, type of position, or type of skills they have. Few would perform the tasks they now perform if they were not paid for it. In Chapters 12 and 13, we learned that money was not the only source of reward, and in some cases may not be a motivator. However, it is important. Employees need certain levels of compensation to maintain their standard of living or to attain their desired standard of living. In addition, and perhaps more important, employees are concerned about equity. Most employees like to feel that they are compensated fairly (equitably) in comparison with other employees in the organization; that is, they want to receive levels of pay similar to those performing jobs similar in complexity and similar in productivity or performance. Research has shown that the most important ingredient in employees' pay satisfaction is a feeling of equity.[1] The relationship of pay and feelings of equity was discussed fully in Chapter 12.

Other work suggests that more emphasis should be given to equity of pay or fairness than to employee satisfaction with pay. This is because high performers and those with satisfactory levels of performance should be satisfied, but those who are performing poorly *should be* dissatisfied with their pay. In other words, those who are performing below acceptable standards should be paid accordingly.[2] Therefore, a marketing research analyst may not be concerned with what a personnel manager makes in another company, but he or she may be concerned if a marketing research analyst in the same company with fewer years' experience makes twice as many errors and receives a higher salary.

The second reason for the emphasis on pay as described by Norman was a younger work force. Although this is not a universal occurrence for all employee groups, demographic analyses have shown that, from the late 1960s through the 1970s, the number of younger people in the work force has increased rapidly.[3] However, this trend is expected to reverse because of the declining birth rate and changes in retirement laws. Over the next twenty years, the average age of the work force is expected to increase.

From the previous discussion, we know that amount of pay and equitable pay are both important to employees. Actually organizations have the potential to influence many types of behavior and attitudes with pay. Pay may affect the choice of job by a person and his or her behavior, such as job performance and attendance, satisfaction (or dissatisfaction), and the desire to leave the organization or termination.[4] Thus a compensation program can serve several purposes. First, it aids in producing an effective employee recruitment program. It serves as a means to promote higher-quality performance on the job. An effective compensation program ensures equitable treatment (pay) of all employees, thereby minimizing employee complaints and reducing unwanted turnover. Finally, it allows the organization to administer and control employee pay (ensuring equity) and therefore helps the organization to control labor costs.[5] We may then conclude that an effective compensation program is important to the effective operation of organizations.

Thus far we have used the term compensation. However, the term compensation has a broad meaning.

Compensation: the total of all direct and indirect pay received by an employee.

Compensation covers all pay received by employees. As such, it is composed of at least three factors: direct salary and wages, benefits, and special pay incentives or bonuses. Direct salary and wages are the focus of this chapter. Incentives and benefits are the focus of Chapter 16.

Some employees are paid on a salary basis; others are paid hourly wages. Some differentiation is required by law (Fair Labor Standards Act discussed later in this chapter); other distinctions may be based on the needs of the organization, type of employees, and/or type of jobs performed.

Salary: direct pay for performing a certain job that is not tied to the amount of time worked.

Wages: direct pay for performing a certain job that is tied directly to the amount of time worked (e.g., hourly).[6]

In this chapter we discuss legal wage and salary issues, the development of organizational pay levels and pay systems, the development and use of job evaluation systems and wage surveys, the development of wage and salary structures, and the effects of cost of living. Thus the focus of this chapter is on the establishment of an equitable job value and a market value adjustment as parts of a total employee compensation package (Chapter 12).

LEGAL WAGE AND SALARY ISSUES

A number of laws either directly or indirectly affect organizational compensation practices. Our purpose is not to review each one but, rather, to discuss the most important pieces of federal legislation directly affecting compensation policies and practices.

Davis–Bacon Act of 1931

This act requires all firms involved in construction of federal projects over $2,000 in value to pay prevailing wage rates. The Labor Department must determine the prevailing wage rates in the local area (usually accomplished through the use of a wage survey) for construction workers on federal projects. The prevailing wage rate is frequently close to the average union rates in the area. Therefore, if the prevailing wage rate for metalworkers in an area is $10 per hour, a firm involved in constructing a federal office building must pay its metalworkers at least $10 per hour.

Walsh–Healy Act of 1936

This piece of legislation extended the use of the local area prevailing wage rate as the minimum wage paid to employees of firms that have contracts with the federal government in excess of $10,000. The Davis–Bacon and the Walsh–Healy acts were the first minimum wage laws. In addition, the Walsh–Healy Act requires that time and one-half be paid for all work in excess of eight hours in one day or over forty hours in one week.[7]

Fair Labor Standards Act of 1938

The Fair Labor Standards Act is one of the most significant pieces of federal legislation affecting organizations. It deals with both minimum wage and overtime pay provisions for employees. In addition, it outlawed oppressive child labor.[8] The Fair Labor Standards Act has been amended several times, primarily for the purpose of extending the coverage to more types of organizations and to raise the minimum wage. Currently, almost all organizations are covered by this law. The minimum wage as of January 1, 1981 is $3.35 per hour (based on 1977 amendments).

The overtime provisions are similar to those of the Walsh–Healy Act. Time and one-half must be paid for all hours in excess of forty worked within one week (any seven-day period). The only exception is for hospitals, due to the nature of their work. They must pay overtime for any hours worked in excess of eighty in any fourteen-day period. There is no requirement that the organization pay overtime for time worked on a daily basis. This is helpful to organizations that have adopted a four-day forty-hour workweek, since employees must work ten-hour days.

Based on the provisions of the Fair Labor Standards Act, most organizations set up three employee classifications: salaried exempt, salaried nonexempt, and hourly. By law, all employees paid on a salary basis (e.g., $1,500 per month) must be separated into exempt and nonexempt classifications. Salaried exempt personnel are exempt from the overtime provisions of this law. Salaried nonexempt personnel may also be paid on a salary, but they must also receive time and one-half for all hours worked in excess of forty in the workweek (or in excess of eighty in two weeks for hospitals). The law has specific definitions of what personnel can be considered exempt. Usually, the exempt classification includes managers and professionals. Hourly personnel are those who receive pay on the basis of the number of hours worked.[9] It should be noted that there are some variations in the provisions by industry.

Equal Pay Act of 1963

The Equal Pay Act is an important amendment to the Fair Labor Standards Act. The primary purpose of this act is to prohibit sex discrimination in the rates of pay. Thus males and females performing equal jobs under equal conditions within the same organization must be paid equal rates of pay. Differences in pay may occur for legitimate reasons such as seniority, merit level of performance, and productivity differences.[10]

In the past, females sometimes received lower rates of pay than males performing equal jobs. However, this law prohibits such practices. Any differences in pay must be for legitimate, job-related reasons. Pay is interpreted to include all forms of compensation including benefits. For employee benefits, the law allows a choice between providing equal benefits or benefits with equal costs.[11] The law has been pressed in the courts. In fiscal 1974, almost 33,000 employees were found to have been underpaid by an amount totaling over $20 million. Two of the most important court cases involved American Telephone & Telegraph Company (AT&T) and Corning Glass Works. As a result, AT&T paid out approximately $7 million to some 7,000 employees. The Corning Glass Works case is important because it was the first equal-pay-law case to be reviewed by the U.S. Supreme Court. As a result of the Supreme Court's decision, Corning had to pay almost $1 million in back wages.[12]

Civil Rights Act of 1964

Because of its far-reaching effects in United States society, most of us are familiar with the basic provisions of this law. Title VII prohibits compensation differences related to race, color, religion, sex, or national origin. It is administered by the Equal Employment Opportunity Commission (EEOC). The notion of equal costs allowed under the Equal Pay Act is rejected.[13] This law has many important impacts that are still being felt. The enforcement of this law and court interpretations continue. For example, changes in job evaluation systems (discussed later in this chapter) are anticipated to delimit any discriminatory actions. This and other antidiscrimination laws along with their implications are discussed in more detail in Chapter 17.

Age Discrimination Act of 1967

This act applies to all employers with twenty or more regular employees. It extended the prohibition of discrimination to those in age groups over forty and less than seventy. The provisions of this law apply to pay, job security, advancement, status, and benefits. This act affects, in particular, the manner in which job content is defined, measurement of job worth, methods used to relate pay to performance, and the motivation of people to retire.[14] Any differences must be based on bona fide occupational qualifications to perform the job. This law was amended in 1978. Effective in 1979, the permissible retirement age was raised from sixty-five to seventy. Only those individuals in an "executive or high policymaking position" for two years prior to reaching the age of sixty-five and who may receive a nonforfeitable pension of at least $27,000 per year may be *forced* to retire at age sixty-five.[15]

As we can see, there are many legislative constraints on the development of compensation policies and their implementation. In addition, continuing court interpretation of these laws presents changing requirements for personnel departments.

ORGANIZATIONAL PAY LEVELS

Organizations must decide at what general level they wish to compensate their employees. They may decide to pay employees at high, average, or below-average levels as compared with market rates. The decision at which level to pay is not an easy one.

Figure 14-1

Factors Influencing an Organization's Pay Level

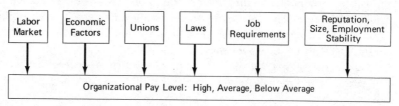

A number of factors should be considered in determining the organization's pay level, including nature of the labor market, economic factors, unions, federal and state laws, and job requirements as illustrated in Figure 14-1.

The extent to which the labor market is tight or loose (amount of unemployment) may affect the wage level. Low unemployment may mean that an organization must pay more to obtain needed employees. Also, what other organizations are paying for similarly skilled employees affects an organization's pay level. Organizations must consider the quality of the applicants they desire. The higher the wages, the higher the probability for obtaining more qualified applicants. Thus recruitment is easier.

Economic Factors

A number of economic factors may impact on the level of pay an organization provides. The organization's ability to pay, for example, greatly affects its general level of compensation. A highly profitable company can usually afford to pay more than an unprofitable one. The state of the U.S. and world economies also affects pay level. Generally, in times of recession, organizations have less ability to pay and unemployment is higher. These have a deflationary effect on general pay levels. The high inflation rates in recent years have produced strong pressures to increase general levels of pay. Norman Holton emphasized that, because of high inflation rates, members in his union had pushed for higher pay scales as their first priority in their last two contracts. Also because of differences in cost of living among different parts of the country, organizations have been forced to pay area cost-of-living differences to their professional personnel.[16] Other factors affecting an organization's level of pay are related to industry characteristics such as the competitiveness of the product market and the level of capital intensiveness.

Unions

Existing unions and/or the threat of unionization generally impact an organization's pay levels. As a rule, pay levels tend to be higher in organizations that are unionized. Unions tend to have both direct and indirect effects on the pay levels. The direct effects come from bargaining for higher pay for all employee classifications represented. Indirect effects are found in union pressures to substitute skilled labor for unskilled labor, raising hiring standards and pay levels[17] and in the tendency of nonunion firms to pay more than they might otherwise in order to discourage unionization. In addition, nonunionized organizations' pay levels are generally more responsive to individual worker levels of education and experience and to area pay differentials than are unionized organizations' pay levels. However, unionized organizations still generally have higher pay levels.[18] Recall Norman Holton's comments. He noted that his local union had emphasized direct wages in the last two contract bargaining sessions. He felt that benefits were a close second in importance.

Federal and State Laws

Federal and state laws affect the general pay levels of organizations, specifically in minimum wage and overtime pay requirements. Most of the important pieces of federal legislation were reviewed in the previous section. Several states also have minimum wage laws, the effects of which are important for state and local government employees. Of course, the tax structure imposed by government also influences general pay levels.

Job Requirements

Organizations should consider the job requirements and average skill level of employees when setting their general pay level. If the average skill level is low, organizations can set their pay levels lower and still obtain qualified employees. However, if their average skill level is high, organizations may have to set higher levels of pay to recruit qualified employees.

Other Factors

There are, at least, several other factors that may affect the determination of an organization's general pay levels. These include company reputation in the community, stability of employment in the organization, and organization size. An organization that wants to maintain a strong positive image in the community may wish to establish higher pay levels. Higher pay levels generally aid the reputation of the organization in the community. Some organizations offer greater employment stability than do others. This occurs because they have consistent demand for their product or services and/or they are managed more efficiently than others. Regardless of the reason, these organizations may be able to offer lower pay levels and still attract qualified employees because they offer more employment security. Finally, organization size generally affects the organization's ability to pay. In general, small organizations cannot afford to pay at the high end of the scale. They have fewer resources and less flexibility than do larger organizations.

When looking specifically at the determination of general pay levels for managerial personnel, fewer factors may be important. Research has shown that the general pay levels are based on the average number of employees supervised, number of reporting levels below the chief executive officer, the company's annual return on equity, after-tax profits and annual sales volume, and the average number of managers in each of the various functions. Location and type of product sold has little effect on managerial pay levels.[19]

JOB EVALUATION

Once an organization has decided how to position its general level of employee pay, it must then develop some means for setting basic rates of pay for jobs in the organization. The pay levels should, in some way, reflect the importance of the job to the organization and allow comparative equity in pay between jobs of varying levels of difficulty and importance to the organization (discussed in Chapter 12). Job evaluation is a means for doing this. Norman Holton, the representative of the union local affiliated with the Teamsters, emphasized the importance of evaluating a job's worth.

> **Job evaluation:** the process by which the worth of jobs to the organization is assessed relative to all other jobs in the organization.

The first step in job evaluation requires a thorough job analysis. Based on the job analyses, job descriptions are written. Job analyses and job descriptions were discussed in Chapter 3. Norman noted the importance of job descriptions for several reasons. The information contained in the job descriptions is then used to evaluate jobs. This process is shown in Figure 14-2.

There are several methods from which an organization may choose to evaluate its jobs. These include ranking, classification, factor comparison, and point. The rank-

Figure 14-2

Process of Determining Pay for Jobs

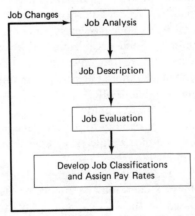

ing and classification systems are nonquantitative methods; the factor comparison and point systems are quantitative systems. The point system is the most frequently used job evaluation method and the ranking system is the least used of the four.[20] We describe each of these four systems briefly, but due to its importance, more emphasis will be placed on the point system. More detailed descriptions can be found in books on wage and salary administration.[21]

Ranking Method

The ranking method is the simplest of the job evaluation methods. Essentially, use of this method requires that jobs be arranged in order of their value or merit to the organization from highest to lowest. As such, the jobs are examined as a whole rather than on the basis of important factors in the job.

Rankings may be made by simply ordering all jobs or by a paired comparison (comparing two jobs at a time and then combining the comparisons to obtain a final ranking). Regardless of the method used, the jobs will usually be ranked in each department, and then the department rankings are combined to develop an organizational ranking.

The ranking method is suited best for a small organization. In large, complex organizations, its simplicity works to its disadvantage. The rankings are highly subjective and become more difficult to develop as the number of jobs becomes larger. The rationale for ranking certain jobs may be difficult to defend to employees and the validity of a ranking system may be difficult to determine. Therefore, it is not used frequently.

Classification Method

The classification method of job evaluation places groups of jobs into job grades or classes. The grades and grade descriptions are established first. Then jobs are fitted into the grade with the appropriate description. Thus jobs in the same grade receive the same relative pay rates within some range. Frequently separate classes are established for different types of jobs (e.g., office/clerical, manufacturing, managerial/professional). The U.S. Civil Service System uses a series of classes called GS (general schedule) and WS (wage schedule) grades. Generally, a committee of individuals is used to develop the grade descriptions and place specific jobs in grades. The committee usually selects representative jobs and rank orders them. It then separates them into grades and uses these jobs to develop grade descriptions. Once the grade descriptions are complete, the other jobs are evaluated and placed into the appropriate grade based on the committee's judgment.

This system is only slightly less subjective than the ranking system. Again, the whole job is examined instead of its various factors. The system is easier for employees to understand and can be used with a variety of jobs. However, when individual job descriptions and grade descriptions do not match well, the evaluators must simply classify the job using judgment. The validity of this method may also be questioned but less so than the ranking method. Most government agencies are now shifting to other methods.

Factor-Comparison System

The factor-comparison system is a complex ranking method. Rather than ranking complete jobs, each job is ranked according to a series of factors such as mental effort, physical effort, skill, responsibility, and working conditions. In general, key jobs in the organization are selected and are rank ordered on each of these five factors. The key jobs are those that are differentiated easily from others and are judged to have the correct pay assigned relative to the other key jobs. Once the key jobs are selected and are ranked according to the factors, other jobs can then be ranked on each of the factors in comparison to key jobs.

There are two methods by which pay may be assigned. First, the present wages paid for the key jobs may be divided among the factors weighted by importance (the most important factor, for example, mental effort, receives the highest proportion of the money). Next wages are assigned to the job in comparison to its ranking on each factor. Another method is a combination of factor-comparison and point systems. Rather than assigning money by factors, points are assigned by factors. The total of a job's points determines the pay range for the job. The ranking using either method should be done by a committee to obtain a pool of judgments. The federal government adopted such a system in the mid-1970s. The Hay system developed by Hay and Associates, a consulting firm, uses a variation of this system. The Hay system is used widely and involves three factors: know-how, problem solving, and accountability.[22]

This system is undoubtedly complex and difficult to explain to employees. In addition, use of key jobs and current pay can create problems. Jobs change over time, and thus so do key jobs. If these key jobs change, they should be ranked again; and if rankings change, all jobs should be re-examined. Use of present wages also does not allow flexibility for future changes. This system also presents several advantages. With the use of key jobs, the system is oriented specifically to each organization. In addition, there is no upper limit on the rating a job may receive on each factor.

Point System

The point system is the most widely used method of job evaluation as noted earlier. Reasons for its wide use include its quantitative approach, use of important components of a job, and the weighting of each component. These components are frequently referred to as compensable job factors. Several "universal" point systems are used by many organizations (adapted for their specific organization). The National Electrical Manufacturers Association (NEMA) and the National Metal Trades Association (NMTA) have widely used point evaluation systems. An organizaton may use a universal system or develop one of its own.

First, general job factor categories are chosen such as skill, effort, responsibility, and work environment. Next compensable job factors are developed for each category. For example, the compensable job factors for skill may be education, experience, judgment, and manual dexterity. Once the compensable job factors are developed for each job factor category, each of these factors must be "weighted" by assigning a number of points to it. The number of points assigned should be based on the importance of the job factor. Next the job factors are broken down into degrees and point values are assigned to each degree. An example of job factor categories, compensable job factors, degrees, and points appears in Table 14-1. Table 14-2 shows an example of degree definitions for one factor.

With the degrees defined and points assigned, jobs may then be evaluated. Usually, the evaluation is conducted by a committee to ensure that all important information is considered and that multiple inputs are available when judgments are required. Furthermore, input from several organizational members helps to facilitate acceptance of the job evaluation results. However, simple jobs can be evaluated by one individual. The points are added up to determine the rating of the job. Generally jobs with similar point totals are grouped into classes or grades. Pay ranges are then assigned to each classification.

Point systems, once developed, are, for the most part, the most sophisticated yet simple job evaluation systems available. They are flexible in that they can be used with most types of jobs. Since no pay rates are considered at the time of evaluation, no bias from previous evaluations is involved. However, point evaluation systems are complex and time consuming to develop. In addition, they still entail some subjective judgment (but less than other evaluation systems). However, the point system is probably the best general job evaluation method.

Table 14-1

Point Job Evaluation System: Factors, Degrees, and Points

Factor Categories	Compensable Factors	Degrees							
		I	II	III	IV	V	VI	VII	VIII
Skill	Education	20	40	60	80	100			
	Experience	15	35	55	75	95	115	135	
	Judgment	20	40	60	80	100	120		
	Manual dexterity	10	20	30	40	50			
Effort	Physical effort	5	15	25	35	45			
	Visual effort	5	15	25	35	45			
	Mental effort	5	15	25	35	45			
Responsibilities	Directing others	20	40	60	80	100			
	Assets	25	50	75	100				
	Interpersonal relations	10	30	50	70	90	110		
	Policy development	15	35	55	75	95	115	135	155
Work environment	Working conditions	5	10	15	20	25			
	Job hazards	5	10	15	20	25			

Table 14-2

Example of Degree Definitions for One Compensable Factor

Education: This factor is designed to measure the general education development through formal schooling or its equivalent required to perform the job in a satisfactory manner.

Degree	Definition	Points
1	Less than a high school education (simple knowledge of arithmetic and basic communication skills	20
2	High school education or its equivalent (knowledge of normal arithmetic functions and acceptable writing skills).	40
3	High school plus two years of college, trade or technical school, or its equivalent (complex mathematical/technical skills and good communication skills).	60
4	College education or its equivalent (complex skills in specialized professional field and good communication skills).	80
5	Graduate education or its equivalent (complex skills in professional field, complex mathematical/technical skills, and complex communication skills).	100

Avoiding Discrimination in Job Evaluation

Job evaluation systems are designed to provide equity in pay among the various jobs in the organization. However, some job evaluation systems have only perpetuated past bias in pay in favor of traditionally white male jobs. In fact this is the basic question in the *comparable worth* controversy involving the argument that traditional female jobs are evaluated lower than comparable male-dominated jobs. Thus the Equal Employment Opportunity Commission has begun auditing organizations' job evaluation systems.

The following represent some recommendations that can help organizations to develop nondiscriminatory practices:

1. Use a formal, well-documented point job evaluation system that ties directly to job descriptions.
2. Use evaluation factors such as responsibility and interpersonal skills that can be validated as important to achieve job and organizational goals.
3. Do not use factors such as education, experience, or skill (defined by education and/or experience) unless they can be validated in the same way as in the selection process.
4. Do not use factors that can discriminate against an occupational minority group such as females or the physically handicapped.
5. Assign points to factors using regression analysis that best predict current pay levels for white male jobs.
6. Allow changes in job descriptions as necessary.

7. Audit your system continually to ensure that no group is discriminated against in pay.
8. Validate the system periodically.[23]

If these criteria were applied today, few organizations' job evaluation systems would pass the test. Many organizations, for example, use different evaluation systems for salaried exempt, salaried nonexempt, and hourly employees. In addition, many use factors such as education and experience without validating them. However, changes are coming with the new EEOC audits and emphasis on job evaluation programs. Research has shown that married women with children tend to earn less than married men with families.[24] Thus changes are inevitable.

Some feel that it is difficult, if not impossible, to develop and implement one system for all jobs in an organization. However, H. F. and Ph. F. Reemtsma in West Germany has done so successfully. It has integrated three thousand employees from four diverse locations and in two hundred different job categories into one wage structure. All employees in the same job class receive the same level of pay. All differences in pay because of age, sex, length of service, experience, or family responsibilities have been abolished.[25]

In Chapter 12, we noted the importance of equity in compensation systems. Inequity in pay, no matter what the reason, will create problems for the organization (e.g., lowered productivity, turnover). Therefore, it makes good business sense to correct *any* and *all* inequities that exist in an organization's compensation system.

ADMINISTRATION OF A COMPENSATION SYSTEM

As noted, a job evaluation system is designed to develop internal equity among jobs in the organization. However, it is necessary also to develop external equity. In Chapter 12 we referred to this as a market value adjustment. In other words, jobs must be paid competitively with rates paid similar jobs in the marketplace. To do so, organizations must determine what other organizations are paying for similar jobs. They do so by means of wage and salary surveys as reflected in Figure 14-3.

Norman Holten noted the importance of evaluating the job and thus of establishing internal equity. Unions are also concerned with external equity. In fact, a frequent bargaining tactic is to use wage rates of employees from other companies in the area, from other companies represented by the union, and/or from those covered by other contracts with locals of the same national union. Therefore, unions are generally concerned with both internal and external equity, as are most employees.

Wage and Salary Surveys

Wage surveys help organizations to establish and maintain competitive compensation structures.

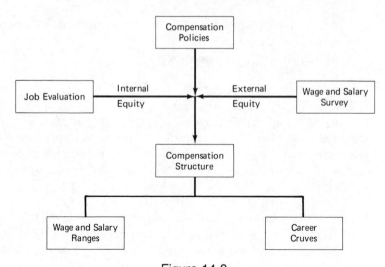

Figure 14-3

Internal and External Pay Equity

Wage and salary survey: a questionnaire designed to obtain data on compensation practices and actual compensation paid to jobs similar to those in the focal organization.

Organizations may purchase available wage and salary survey data from such organizations as American Management Association, Dartnell Corporation, and other consulting firms along with trade associations, local chambers of commerce, and even federal government agencies such as U.S. Department of Labor and Bureau of Labor Statistics. However, many organizations need to conduct their own surveys because of the uniqueness of the jobs in their industry.

To conduct a wage survey, the organization must first select *key* jobs to be surveyed. These key jobs must represent important benchmark jobs in the organization and be common to the other organizations surveyed. Second, organizations to be surveyed should represent the organizations with which the focal organization must compete for employees (e.g., local community, industry). Finally, the types of compensation information desired must be decided. The organization may desire information related to pay increase policies, extent of unionization, and benefit programs in addition to pay rates for specific jobs. Organizations must be assured of anonymity so that they can receive the general results necessary for cooperation.

The results of wage surveys are used primarily to establish or update wage and salary ranges. However, if other data such as pay increase policies and benefit programs are included on the survey, the results may be used to update or change compensation policies (if needed to remain competitive).

Compensation Structure

WAGE RANGES. The data from the survey may be used to construct wage and salary ranges. These ranges are generally tied to wage or salary grades. A typical example of wage ranges is shown in Table 14-3. The key jobs have already been classified into different grades through a job evaluation system. Thus, the salary ranges may be established by making the *average* wage or salary from the survey the midpoint (or close to it) of the particular grade or classification in which the key job(s) exists. In the example shown, the ranges have a 50 percent spread between the minimum and maximum. This is typical but by no means required. The spread should be suited to the organization's purpose. As can be seen, the ranges generally overlap purposely. Thus, it is possible for a person in a lower grade but with more time and experience on the job to make more than another in a higher grade. However, the minimum rate paid in a higher grade is higher, and the potential to receive a higher rate of pay (maximum) exists.

Figure 14-4 shows how job evaluation points, salary grades, and salary ranges may be linked together. The circled jobs above the salary range are called *red-circle rates*. Theoretically, persons receiving those rates cannot receive pay increases because their pay now exceeds the maximum of their range. The circled jobs below the minimum of their range are called *blue-circle rates*. The pay for persons receiving these rates should be raised to the minimum in a short period of time.

The salary range is important because it affects recruitment and hiring, pay increases, promotions, and so on. Frequently, for example, pay increases are adjusted by the position of the person's current rate in the range. Those lower in the range can receive higher percentage increases than do those higher in the range. This is discussed in more detail in Chapter 15.

Table 14-3

Wage Ranges

Wage Grade	Wage Ranges (per hour)		
	Minimum	Midpoint	Maximum
1	$3.60	$4.50	$5.40
2	3.95	4.95	5.95
3	4.35	5.45	6.55
4	4.80	6.00	7.20
5	5.30	6.65	7.95
6	5.85	7.30	8.80
7	6.45	8.05	9.70
8	7.10	8.90	10.65
9	7.80	9.75	11.70
10	8.60	10.75	12.90

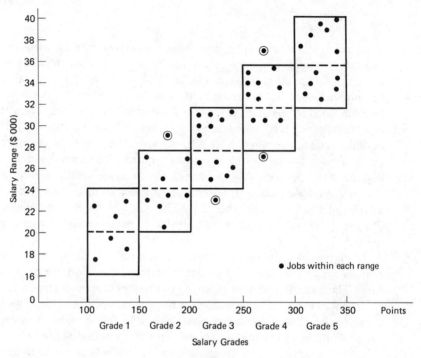

Figure 14-4

Salary Structure

CAREER CURVES. On occasion, rates for individual jobs become noncompetitive where a system such as the one just described is used and rapid changes occur in the marketplace. Thus the rates for these jobs are usually adjusted to put them in line with the market. However, this puts them out of line internally. Some argue that more future-oriented organizations that design career or maturity curves using comp-ratios to determine salary increases and movement through the ranges avoid some of the problems such as the one described above.[26]

Career curves are generally applied to professional positions, particularly those in engineering and science. However, they are applicable to any large groups of individuals filling similar professional positions. Usually, the career curves are constructed from external salary survey data and internal job data. Generally, these curves are used in place of job evaluation systems and apply to all employees in the jobs under question. They are generally linked to a merit pay increase system as well. An example of curves for one job is shown in Figure 14-5.

Examination of the figure shows that a person on this job for five years performing at a level 3 should be making approximately $22,000. However, a person performing at a level 1 with five years on the job should be making approximately $26,000 annually. The main disadvantage of career curves is that they do not distinguish be-

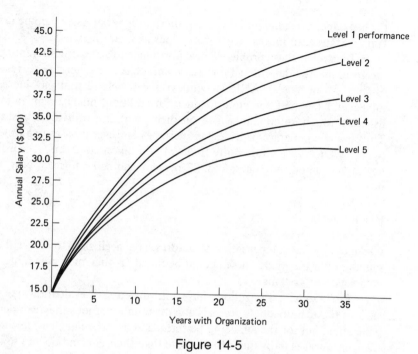

Figure 14-5

Career Salary Curve for a Professional Position Linked to Performance Appraisal System

tween jobs based on job content. Thus, if these jobs are not relatively constant and/or similar at different years, this system may not be useful or defensible.

Pay Increases

Initial wage or salary rates for individuals are set generally based on a person's background and experience. However, many organizations do not like to hire individuals at rates of pay above the midpoint of their range unless they expect them to be promoted quickly. It leaves them little room for salary increases. Once these initial rates are set, policies must be established to guide increases in pay as a person performs the job, gains more experience, and becomes more valuable to the organization. The most frequent pay increases are based on merit or seniority. Merit versus seniority is discussed in Chapter 15. But note that it is rare for an organization to pay exclusively on performance.[27]

Another problem is how to account for rapid increases in the cost of living. Norman Holton noted that cost-of-living increases had made direct wage increases a top priority in his union in recent years. The viability of pay increases is affected by the cost of living. A high inflation rate creates many problems. Regardless of the base for pay increases—merit or seniority—employees feel that they have received little if increases do not exceed the increases in the cost of living, usually reflected in changes in the consumer price index (CPI). In addition, the progressive income tax system in the United States also means larger deductions as salary increases.

To combat these problems, organizations have chosen different approaches. Pay increases may be determined on visible and objective criteria (e.g., reaching mutually established job goals). At least employees can believe that pay increases are determined in a fair and equitable manner. In addition, many organizations have established (through union contract or on their own) cost-of-living adjustments (COLA). Thus many companies provide pay increases on several bases (e.g., merit and cost of living). COLAs are found quite frequently in union contracts. According to one survey of 248 unionized companies, 97 percent had some form of cost-of-living adjustment.[28]

Pay Innovations

Changes in basic compensation structures have been slow to evolve, but some are beginning to be adopted. These should be noted, as they may play major roles in future compensation systems.

First, some organizations have introduced skill-evaluation pay plans. In plans such as these, individuals are paid for the number of jobs they can perform in the organization, not for the job being performed at a particular point in time. This system, then, encourages individuals to do more than their current job and to learn new skills. This type of system has been found to be particularly effective in organizations that make frequent use of job rotation.[29] However, this system requires that the organization be committed to substantial investments in training.

Another change from the traditional approach tried by some organizations has been to allow employees to participate in pay decisions. The results of this approach have been quite positive. Employees who participated in pay decisions had a more accurate picture of how their pay compares with others'. Additionally, they were involved in the decision and felt that the system was fair. In one such instance, employees designed their own pay plan resulting in an 8 percent increase in the firm's salary costs. After six months they showed significant improvements in turnover, job satisfaction, and satisfaction with pay.[30]

One final area in which important changes seem to be occurring is in the secrecy of the pay systems. Traditionally, compensation systems have been shrouded in secrecy. Some organizations are now starting to make pay information public (e.g., Corning Glass Works and Bell Laboratories). Secrecy tends to cause people to be suspicious and overestimate the pay of their peers. In addition people tend to underestimate the pay of their supervisor. They become dissatisfied when this occurs. Therefore, secrecy of pay may create more dissatisfaction than it resolves.[31] Most compensation experts believe that pay secrecy should be removed.[32]

Job and Individual Pay

The emphasis in this chapter has been on the manner in which organizations establish the value and thus the compensation rates for jobs. In most organizations, compensa-

Figure 14-6

Compensation Based on Job and Employee

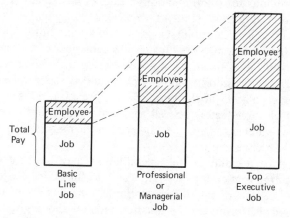

Source: Adapted from H. G. Zollitsch and A. Langsner, *Wage and Salary Administration* (Cincinnati, Ohio: South-Western, 1970), p. 143.

tion of employees is based on both the job and the employee. This split is shown in Figure 14-6.

Figure 14-6 shows that, as the job becomes more important, total pay increases. Also, notice that the percentage of total pay related to the employee increases as the job becomes more complex and more valuable to the organization. Some of the pay related to the individual may be related to seniority or merit increases and/or incentive programs. Compensating employees is the topic of the next chapter.

SUMMARY

Money is an important issue to most employees, and therefore the manner in which an employee's compensation is determined is important. Compensation may be defined as the total of all direct and indirect pay received by an employee. Salary is the direct pay for performing a job and is not tied to the amount of time worked, whereas wages are the direct pay for performing a certain job and are tied directly to the amount of time worked.

A number of laws affect compensation policies and practices in some manner, among the most important being the Davis–Bacon Act, Walsh–Healy Act, Fair Labor Standards Act, Equal Pay Act, Civil Rights Act, and Age Discrimination Act. The Davis–Bacon Act requires all firms involved in federal construction projects over $2,000 in value to pay prevailing wage rates. The Walsh–Healy Act requires all firms with federal government contracts in excess of $10,000 to pay local area prevailing rates. It also requires time and one-half to be paid for all hours worked in excess of eight hours in one day or forty hours in one week. The Fair Labor Standards Act established a minimum wage and required time and one-half pay for all hours worked in excess of forty in one week. Most private organizations are covered by the law, and amendments have continued to raise the minimum wage over time. The Equal Pay Act prohibits sex discrimination in rates of pay. The Civil Rights Act prohibits compensation differences related to race, color, religion, sex, or national origin. The Age Discrimination Act prohibits age discrimination in rates of pay.

Organizations generally consider a number of factors in determining the level of the organization's pay to employees. These include nature of the labor market, economic factors, unions, industry characteristics, federal and state laws, job requirements, reputation of the organization, organization size, and employment stability. Based on these factors as well as on internal organizational policy, the organization decides whether to pay rates higher than the market, average for the market, or below average for the market.

After deciding on the general level of pay, basic rates of pay for each of the jobs in the organization must be set. Many organizations use job evaluation to help in setting these rates of pay. Job evaluation is a means by which the relative worth of jobs is assessed. Performing job evaluation requires thorough job analyses and well-written job descriptions. Based on job evaluations, jobs are slotted into job classifications, and pay rates are assigned. Several job evaluation methods may be used, including ranking, classification, factor-comparison, and point systems.

The ranking method, the simplest, requires that jobs be arranged in order of their value to the organization. The classification method places jobs of similar assessed value (based on job description fitted to grade description) into a job grade or class. The factor-comparison system is a complex ranking method insofar as jobs are ranked in comparison with key jobs (already ranked) on the basis of important factors (weighted by importance). The factors often include mental effort, physical effort, skill, responsibility, and working conditions. The point system is the most widely used method in job evaluation. Jobs are evaluated usually by a committee of people on the basis of a series of compensable factors. Each compensable factor (e.g., experience) is broken down into degrees, and points are assigned to each degree. A job is judged on each factor, is assigned to a certain degree, and receives the points for that degree. The worth of the job is determined by the total number of points received.

It is important to note that the Equal Employment Opportunity Commission has been examining job evaluation systems recently. Changes may have to be made in traditional systems to avoid being discriminatory.

While a job evaluation system provides internal equity (with other jobs in the organization), a wage and salary survey helps to provide external equity (pay in the labor market). Thus wage and salary surveys are important to maintain a competitive compensation system. A wage and salary survey usually contains questions regarding compensation practices and compensation paid to jobs similar to those in the focal organization. Once data are collected on wages and salaries from organizations that are competitive in the labor market, wage ranges can be established. The wage ranges are matched to job grades or classifications obtained from job evaluation. Therefore, wage ranges provide the minimum and maximum that should be paid to employees on specific jobs. Of course, in unusual circumstances, some employees may be receiving red-circle rates (pay rates above the range maximum) and blue-circle rates (pay rates below the range minimum).

Pay increases may be across-the-board to handle cost-of-living increases or they may be based on merit or seniority. The across-the-board pay increase is frequently referred to as a cost-of-living adjustment.

A number of innovations in pay are currently being tested. These may become the compensation systems of the future. These include skill-based evaluation plans, employee participation in pay decisions, and the provision of more public information on employee pay.

Total pay generally increases as the job becomes more important. Also, pay based on the employee versus pay based on the job often increases as a percentage of total pay as the importance of the job increases.

INTERVIEW WRAP-UP

The importance of direct wages to employees today is the result of high inflation rates. This importance places more emphasis on compensation procedures. The high cost of living has led to an increased number of COLAs, particularly where unions represent employees.

The amount of compensation paid to an employee should be highly related to the job being performed. In addition, accurate job descriptions and a fair method of classifying jobs into wage grades are important. The emphasis placed on various forms of pay by unions plays a large role in the way many employees are paid, even nonunion employees. Therefore, effective job evaluation systems and total compensation procedures play a major role in an organization's dealings with its employees. —Norman "Tex" Holton, secretary-treasurer, Food Process Workers, Warehousemen and Helpers Union, Local 228.

WHAT MANAGERS SHOULD DO REGARDING PERSONNEL MANAGEMENT ACTIVITIES

1. Managers should have an operating knowledge of the relevant laws regarding employee compensation. In particular, they should be aware of the laws to ensure that their actions are not illegal. If in fact they are unsure about the legality of some action, they should contact those in the organization who are knowledgeable of the laws before they act.

2. Managers must have a reasonable understanding of the factors that underlie the general level of pay in the organization. Top managers are the ones who set the general pay levels and must consider each of the relevant factors. However, other managers in the organization must administer the pay system, and they should understand the factors on which it is based.

3. Managers should be intimately familiar with the organization's method of job evaluation. They want to ensure that it is fair and equitable and that it establishes the

proper rate of pay for the jobs under their direction. In addition, they should be able to explain to employees how their job was classified and thus the basis of their pay.

4. Managers ultimately make and implement pay decisions. As such they must understand the organization's compensation system and how it should be implemented. They are the ones who make the decisions on pay increases for their subordinates.

REVIEW QUESTIONS

1. Why does money (direct wages and salary) seem to be such an important issue to employees?

2. How do the Davis–Bacon and Walsh–Healy acts affect employee compensation?

3. How do the Civil Rights and Fair Labor Standards acts affect employee compensation?

4. What do you believe are the most important factors affecting the level at which organizations set their pay? Why?

5. If you were asked to develop a job evaluation system, what type would you design and why?

6. What is the purpose of wage and salary surveys and how are they used?

KEY CONCEPTS

Age Discrimination Act	Job classifications or grades
Blue-circle rate	Job evaluation
Civil Rights Act	Organizational pay level
Classification method	Point system
Compensation	Ranking method
Compensation structure	Red-circle rate
Cost-of-living adjustment	Salary
Davis–Bacon Act	Wage ranges
Equal Pay Act	Wages
Factor comparison system	Walsh–Healy Act
Fair Labor Standards Act	

CASE

THE HOT POTATO

Marsha Winters is compensation director for Lake Enterprises, a large manufacturer of recreational products. Marsha has held her present position for almost two years. Prior to her current job, she had experience in a variety of personnel positions, including employee and union relations, training and development, and benefits administration. She has a good working knowledge of personnel activities and employee needs.

Currently, Marsha and her staff have been studying the total compensation structure in the company to ensure equity in pay. Specifically, they have been examining the job evaluation system and the manner in which pay increases are determined. She has scheduled interviews with key executives in the company to obtain their feelings on the compensation structure and current compensation policies. So far she has had two interviews, one with the vice-president of marketing and one with the vice-president of finance. Both went relatively well. The vice-president of marketing seemed uninterested and the vice-president of finance was pleased with current policies and practices.

Marsha's third meeting was with Sam Roman, director of management information services. Her meeting with Sam went as follows:

"Hello, Sam. How are you today?"

"Oh, OK, I guess. I'm keeping my head above water. Marsha, I understand our meeting is to discuss our salary program."

"Yes, that along with other compensation programs."

"Well, I've got a number of comments on our compensation programs. Overall, I think they are quite poor. I've got people on my staff who are grossly underpaid, but I can't do anything about it because the system is so rigid."

Marsha was surprised by Sam's statement and decided to probe further. "In what way is the system inflexible and why do you think you have employees who are underpaid?"

"Well, I can answer both questions at the same time. The job evaluation system does not take into account factors important in some of my jobs such as time pressures and highly technical work. Also, my employees are not being paid what they are worth in the labor market. We should have our own salary ranges and not be grouped with all other jobs in the company. We are different."

Well, Marsha had heard this before and was tired of hearing it.

"Sam, we've bent over backward trying to accommodate you. We have to be equitable to everybody in the company. Besides we cannot have different ranges for your group only. Eventually, every group would want the same, and then there would be no standardized compensation policies. In addition, the job evaluation system was developed and implemented by one of the top consulting firms in the United States."

"Well, it just does not fit the kind of jobs in my department. I can see you are about as inflexible as the compensation program you administer. I am frustrated by the whole system and see no reason to continue our discussion. Good day, Marsha."

With that Marsha left Sam's office. Her next appointment was with Berle Martin, the vice president and general manager of the Sports Equipment Division. Her meeting with Berle went something like this:

"Hello, Marsha. It's good to see you again."

"Hello, Berle. I guess you know the reason for our meeting today."

"Yes, as I understand it, we are to discuss the compensation system here at Lake."

"Yes, that is correct."

"Well, Marsha, I have an important issue on my mind with regard to pay, and we should discuss it. In our preliminary session with the union preparing for our upcoming contract negotiation sessions, it looks as if two factors are going to be hot issues. They are going to ask for large increases in direct wages, and they want a cost-of-living adjustment built into the contract. As you and I have discussed, a cost-of-living adjustment would be very costly."

"Yes, Berle, not only costly for you but for the total company, because other employees will desire the same. What do you think our strategy should be?"

"I've been thinking about that, and frankly I think we may have to give in on the cost-of-living adjustment to avoid a strike. If we give that we may be able to hold down the increase in direct wages some."

"Berle, this will really put pressure on our total compensation program. Our wage and salary ranges were not developed with the intent of having cost-of-living adjustments per se. Besides, it will mess up the equity of our pay internally. Some of your plant employees may make as much as our professional employees. I don't know what all of this will do to our job evaluation program and our present slotting of jobs into job grades."

"Well, Marsha, I am afraid I can see it at some time in the future, if not now. However, realistically, we cannot afford a strike, and, therefore, I think that you can expect large pay increases for the employees in the bargaining unit. Inflation has been terrible."

"I know it has created problems for every company's compensation programs."

They continued to discuss strategies. However, when Marsha left she could not help thinking about her two problem areas she discovered today. In addition, the projected union contract would only create more pressure from Sam Roman to increase the pay of his employees.

CASE QUESTIONS

1. What are Marsha's two problems?

2. How does each of these problems affect the compensation program?

3. What recommendations do you have for Marsha to deal with these problems?

NOTES

[1]H. J. Shapiro and M. A. Wahba, "Pay Satisfaction: An Empirical Test of a Discrepancy Model," *Management Science,* 24 (1978), 612–622.

[2]D. W. Belcher, "Pay Equity or Pay Fairness?" *Compensation Review,* 11 (1979), 31–37.

[3]R. B. Freeman, "The Effect of Demographic Factors on Age-Earnings Profiles," *The Journal of Human Resources,* 14 (1979), 289–318.

[4]L. Dyer, D. P. Schwab, and J. A. Fossum, "Impacts of Pay on Employee Behaviors and Attitudes: An Update," *The Personnel Administrator,* 23 (1978), 51–58.

[5]D. S. Beach, *Personnel: The Management of People at Work* (New York: Macmillan, 1980), pp. 559.

[6]B. R. Ellig, "Compensation Management: Its Past and Its Future," *Personnel,* 54 (1977), 30–40.

[7]D. W. Belcher, *Compensation Administration* (Englewood Cliffs, N.J.: Prentice-Hall, 1974).

[8]Ellig, "Compensation Management."

[9]Belcher, *Compensation Administration.*

[10]R. L. Greenman and E. J. Schmertz, *Personnel Administration and the Law* (Washington, D.C.: Bureau of National Affairs, 1979), pp. 44–51.

[11]Ellig, "Compensation Management."

[12]Greenman and Schmertz, *Personnel Administration and the Law.*

[13]Ibid., pp. 65–66.

[14]S. T. Beachum, "Managing Compensation and Performance Appraisal Under the Age Act," *Management Review,* 68 (1979), 51–54.

[15]Greenman and Schmertz, *Personnel Administration and the Law,* pp. 82–85.

[16]E. C. Miller, "Consensus," *Personnel,* 56 (1979), 4–11.

[17]L. M. Kahn, "Unionism and Relative Wages: Direct and Indirect Effects," *Industrial and Labor Relations Review,* 32 (1979), 520–532.

[18]F. E. Block and M. S. Kuskin, "Wage Determination in the Union and Nonunion Sectors," *Industrial and Labor Relations Review,* 31 (1978), 183–192.

[19]K. E. Foster and J. Kanin-Lovers, "Determinants of Organizational Pay Policy," *Compensation Review,* 9 (1977), 35–41.

[20]"Personnel Policies Forum," *Job Evaluation Policies and Procedures,* PPF Survey, #113 (Washington, D.C.: Bureau of National Affairs, June 1976).

[21]For example, see Belcher, *Compensation Administration;* A. Nash and S. J. Carroll, Jr., *The Management of Compensation* (Monterey, Calif.: Brooks/Cole, 1975); H. G. Zollitsch and A. Langsner, *Wage and Salary Administration* (Cincinnati, Ohio: South-Western, 1970).

[22]H. Suskin, ed., *Job Evaluation and Pay Administration in the Public Sector* (Chicago: International Personnel Management Association, 1977).

[23]D. J. Thomsen, "Eliminating Pay Discrimination Caused by Job Evaluation," *Personnel,* 55 (1978), 11–22.

[24]M. S. Hill, "The Wage Effects of Marital Status and Children," *Journal of Human Resources,* 14 (1979), 579–594.

[25]"Paying Workers What Their Jobs Are Worth," *International Management,* 34 (1979), 31–34.

[26]E. J. Brennan, "The Problem with Salary Ranges (and a Realistic Solution)," *Personnel Journal,* 59 (1980), 187–191.

[27]W. J. Kearney, "Pay for Performance? Not Always," *MSU Business Topics,* 27 (1979), 5–15.

[28]D. A. Weeks, *Compensating Employees: Lessons of the 1970's* (New York: Conference Board, 1976), p. 21.

[29]E. E. Lawler, III, "New Approaches to Pay: Innovations that Work," *Personnel,* 53 (1976), pp. 11–23.

[30]Ibid.

[31]Ibid.

[32]J. G. Frank, "Compensation and Industrial Relations—In the 1980's," *Compensation Review,* 12 (1980), 64–73.

PERFORMANCE APPRAISAL: COMPENSATING PEOPLE

LEARNING OBJECTIVES

After reading this chapter, you should be able to:

1. Distinguish between seniority and merit-based compensation systems.
2. Define performance appraisal and describe its uses.
3. Describe at least five methods of appraising employee performance.
4. Discuss the legal requirements for performance appraisals.
5. Explain five potential problems with performance appraisals.
6. Describe how to conduct an effective performance appraisal interview.
7. Explain how performance appraisals and employee compensation can be linked together.
8. Describe how to use four different styles in performance coaching and counseling to be most effective.

Betty Myers is a benefits specialist for Texize Chemicals, Inc. In her job she processes workers' compensation and insurance claims and explains the company's different benefit programs to employees having trouble understanding them. Ms. Myers has been a part of the labor force for twenty-three years, the last ten of which she has worked for Texize. Texize is the manufacturer of Fantastic spray cleaner and other household products.

Interviewer: What is the importance of compensation and how do you, as an employee, feel that pay and performance on the job should be related?

Betty Myers: The amount of pay I receive is very important. I am self-supporting and thus must pay for rent, food, clothes, and so on from one income. However, I'm not so sure if I would go to work for another company doing the same job if they offered more money. Other things, such as the "people orientation" of the company, are also important to me. And my personal associations at work have rewards.

My job performance is not affected by the amount of money I receive. When I am given a job I do it right. If I can't do it right, I won't accept the work.

It seems to me that there are three different bases on which anyone should be paid. These are (1) the value and importance of the job to the company, (2) the employee's ability to do the job, and (3) the amount and quality of the employee's work on the job. However, the amount and quality of an employee's work should determine that employee's pay level. In other words, employees should be paid on the basis of their performance.

Equity of the pay between individuals is important. There may be some inequity in my organization, but it is not so severe that I want to find another job. For example, suppose that three people were doing the same job but that two of them work hard trying to do a good job and the third one "goofs off" most of the day. I don't think that it would be equitable to pay these three people the same amount.

Interviewer: Would you prefer to be paid by the hour or on the basis of the amount you produce?

Betty Myers: If I had incentive pay and was paid by the amount of paperwork I handle, I would get rich. However, an hourly wage would be better. Of course, there is probably no definitive answer to the question; it would depend on the characteristics of the job and the company.

INTRODUCTION

In the previous chapter, we learned of the processes by which organizations compensate jobs. Betty Myers noted that one of the bases of compensating employees is the value of their job to the organization. However, she also noted that employee compensation should be based on the employee's ability to do the job and performance on the job. One can see from the interview that Betty Myers clearly believes that there should be some link between employee pay and performance.

In Chapter 12 we noted the importance of including an equitable employee value as a part of the total compensation package. To determine employees' equitable employee value requires evaluation of their qualifications and efforts or performance on the job. In this chapter, we emphasize compensating employees on the basis of their performance.

Our discussion includes seniority and merit systems, performance appraisal, problems in appraising performance, legal considerations, making performance appraisals effective, and linking appraisals and compensation.

In Chapter 14 we discussed how organizations set up salary or wage ranges. However, we did not discuss how pay levels were set within these ranges for new employees nor did we discuss how employees' pay levels progress through the range. These are the topics of discussion within this chapter.

ESTABLISHING PAY LEVELS

Once salary and wage ranges for jobs are established, the procedures by which new employee pay is set and the means for progressing through the range must be developed.

New Employee Compensation

Betty Myers felt that one of the bases of employee pay should be employee qualifications. We usually determine employee ability by education, experience, training, and, in some cases, pre-employment skill tests (e.g., typing, key punching). Examination, then, of a person's education, experience, and/or training is used to determine his or her ability to perform the job. One's skills are matched with the job requirements.

Compensation of new employees is generally based on two factors: ability to perform the job and the demand in the labor market for personnel with the desired skill levels. When the demand is average, ability is the dominant factor in determining pay. If the new employee's skills and abilities match minimum qualifications for the job, then his or her pay should be set at the minimum of the range. If the new employee's abilities exceed the minimum qualifications, pay should generally exceed the minimum of the range. The amount by which new employee pay exceeds the range minimum should be based upon procedures established by the organization and on managerial judgment. Frequently, however, organizations have policies limiting new employee pay to the midpoint of their jobs's salary/wage range.

When the labor market is such that a strong demand (demand for skills exceeds supply of personnel with them) exists for certain types of employee skills, it becomes the dominant factor in new employee compensation. When the demand for skills exceeds the supply of personnel with those skills, new employee pay becomes dependent on the strength of general demand, the strength of the organization's needs for personnel with those skills, and the organization's ability and/or desire to pay. The results, then, are simply a matter of supply and demand. In these cases, organizations must pay what is necessary to obtain the needed personnel or forgo the opportunity of having their skills. Organizations must balance their need for the employee skills with the potential pay inequities that may develop with existing employees. Because of rapid changes in the labor market, some organizations may have to pay the same rate of salary or wages to a new employee that they do to one or more employees in similar jobs with several years of experience. This creates an inequitable situation and may hurt employee morale.

Finally, when the demand in the labor market is low (supply of personnel exceeds the demand for their skills), it is sometimes possible to pay new employees at a level below that required normally for their abilities. However, this approach has potential hazards. When a person is paid less than required normally for his or her abilities, morale problems can develop and performance could suffer. If the labor market changes, these people generally have less loyalty to the organization than do others paid more equitably. Thus it is always advisable to pay for a person's abilities, with reasonable constraints.

Seniority Versus Merit

Once an employee's initial pay level is established, the way in which the employee's pay will progress through the established range must be determined. In other words, the basis on which an employee receives pay increases must be developed. The two primary bases for employee pay increases are seniority and merit.

When pay increases are based on seniority, employees progress through the salary/wage ranges based on their length of service. Seniority systems are easy to administer and are usually favored by unions. In seniority systems, employees working in the same job and who have been in the job for the same length of time receive the same pay raise. Seniority systems are found more often in jobs that offer little latitude in individual performance (e.g., along a mass-production assembly line) and in jobs where performance is difficult to measure (e.g., police officer). However, managers generally do not like seniority pay systems. Rather, they prefer pay based on performance.[1]

With merit systems pay increases are based on employee performance on the job. Thus pay increases are individualized, whereas with seniority systems, pay increases are depersonalized. Merit systems are designed to improve job performance by increasing motivation with pay increases. There are several complicating factors with merit systems. First and foremost, accurate measurement of employee performance is required. Measurement of employee performance is usually accomplished through the use of performance appraisals. Performance appraisals are discussed thoroughly later in this chapter. Suffice it to say at this point, that accurate measurement of performance is difficult to obtain.

Second, the problem of increases in cost of living are interrelated with employee expectations of fair treatment in pay. Should firms, for example, provide cost-of-living increases in addition to merit increases? Firms differ in philosophy on this point. Some build cost of living into their ranges by adjusting them upward over time and into their pay increases by providing some monies for cost of living and some for merit. Other organizations have developed programs that call for automatic cost-of-living adjustments.[2] However, managers frequently provide at least minimal increases for all employees because of cost-of-living increases even when using a merit system. This practice has the tendency to lessen the amount of money perceived by the employee for merit purposes. Figure 15-1 compares pay increases based on seniority and based on merit.

Using the seniority system chart shown in Figure 15-1, all machinists who have been in their jobs for thirty-six months will receive $12 per hour in wages. Those who have been on the job for only twelve months will receive $8 per hour. In contrast, the merit system chart shown in Figure 15-1 is not tied to total wages paid but to increases in pay. For example, if a cost accountant received a performance rating of excellent by her supervisor, she could receive a pay increase totaling as much as 15 percent of her current base pay ($20,000 × .15 = $3,000). Another accountant who received a performance rating of good could obtain a pay increase up to 6 percent of his or her current base pay ($19,000 × .06 = $1,140).

Although it is likely that employee preferences for either a seniority system or a merit system would vary by individual, Betty Myers made her views clear. Betty prefers pay based on performance rather than on other factors. From her discussion, it

Figure 15-1

Comparison of Seniority and Merit Systems

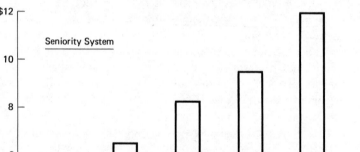

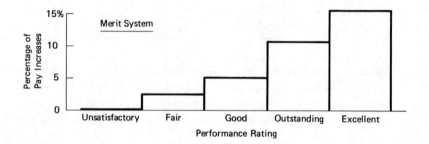

seems that she feels a merit-based pay system to be the most equitable for all employees.

PERFORMANCE APPRAISAL

Merit-based pay systems require that employee performance be evaluated in some manner. This evaluation is usually accomplished through the use of some form of a performance appraisal.

> **Performance appraisal:** assessment of employee work behavior with the general purpose of determining the degree of employee effectiveness on the job.

Performance appraisals are used extensively in all types of organizations. Studies have shown that performance appraisals are used with approximately 84 percent of office workers and 54 percent of production workers.[3] Performance appraisal systems are generally designed by personnel specialists and are then used by managers throughout the organization.

Uses of Performance Appraisal

Performance appraisals may serve several purposes, including salary administration and employee development.

SALARY ADMINISTRATION. As noted in our discussion of merit systems, the overall evaluation of employee performance is usually linked to pay increases allowed for employees. Recall Figure 15-1, in which employees who were given an overall evaluation of outstanding were allowed to receive up to a 12.5 percent pay increase, whereas those employees with an overall evaluation of good could receive up to a 6 percent pay increase. Although merit pay systems are generally more complex than this simple illustration, it does show the manner in which performance appraisals may be used for salary administration.

Therefore, performance appraisals are the primary method by which an employee's effort is evaluated to establish the equitable employee value portion of that employee's total compensation package.

EMPLOYEE DEVELOPMENT. Performance appraisals are also used for employee development. If deficiences found in employee performance stem from a lack of the necessary skills, these deficiencies can be noted. Plans can then be made during performance appraisal sessions to develop these skills to overcome the deficiencies. A second important area of employee development is the preparation for new jobs (career planning discussed in Chapter 11). Thus, the evaluator can aid the employee by discussing what skills will be needed for the next logical job in his or her career plan and make plans to develop those skills. Usually, most performance appraisal forms have space for the evaluator to comment on employee development.

OTHER PURPOSES.   Performance appraisals may serve other purposes such as for placement or guides to job changes, for evaluation of selection procedures, and for development of rapport between supervisor and subordinate. Information from appraisals is useful for placing individuals in jobs appropriate for their skills. Individuals may have more, less, or the appropriate level of skills for their present jobs. Thus, the job changes may include promotion, demotion, or lateral transfer. In addition, performance could be so poor that termination is necessary. Performance appraisals may be used to evaluate selection procedures in that, if individuals have been well matched to the job requirement during the selection process, they should generally perform satisfactorily on those jobs. If most perform well, the selection process can be assumed to be operating well. However, if a number of new employees do not perform well in some job class, personnel managers should examine the selection procedures used for that job. The appraisal process can help to build rapport between supervisors and subordinates if they are conducted properly. The supervisor can develop a better knowledge of subordinates, and subordinates can develop more trust toward the supervisor.

Raters of Performance

Often, the person who conducts the performance appraisal is the supervisor. Supervisors are in a position to observe employee behavior and are charged with the responsibility of meeting work unit goals. Supervisors are supposed to help motivate employees to perform their jobs well and can link rewards with performance. Thus they are the likely persons to rate employee performance. Appraisals may be made by peers, subordinates, outsiders, or employees may rate their own performance. However, these approaches are employed infrequently and are probably useful only when utilized in conjunction with supervisory appraisals.

Performance appraisals are generally conducted on an annual basis (e.g., on the employee's anniversary date) for ease of administration. Preparation for each employee's performance appraisal usually requires approximately two hours.[4] Thus an effective performance appraisal may require approximately three hours per employee for a supervisor to prepare and to conduct the appraisal discussion with the subordinate. Research has shown that feedback on performance can affect future performance.[5] As a result, performance feedback should be given frequently to have more impact on employee behavior. If organizations continue to use only annual formal reviews because of the time required and for ease of administration, supervisors must provide informal feedback on performance more frequently.

Appraisal Methods

Several methods of performance appraisal may be used. A recent study of major corporations showed that 78 percent of the companies used some combination of rating scales and essays or narratives, 17 percent used narratives alone, and only 6 percent used ratings alone.[6] Possible methods include rating scales (e.g., traits, job dimension scales), essays, critical incident method, behaviorally anchored rating scales (special case of rating scales and critical incident methods), management by objectives (MBO), and others (e.g., checklist, ranking, forced distribution).

RATING SCALES.   Of the several forms of rating scales, one of the most common lists personal and/or behavioral traits, and the employee is rated on these traits. An example of this form of rating scale appears in Figure 15-2. A variety of traits may be used in these types of rating devices, the most common ones being quantity and quality of work. These rating scales can be adapted by including traits that the organization considers important for effectiveness on the job. The most important part of the rating is the overall evaluation. Some rating scales may be more precise than that shown in Figure 15-2. They are made so by adding benchmark statements describing each of the separate levels of performance for each trait.

Figure 15-2

Traditional Rating Scale

Employee Name: _____   Job Title: _____

Department: _____   Rate: _____

Date: _____

	Unsatis-factory 1	Fair 2	Satis-factory 3	Good 4	Excellent 5
Judgment: Analyzes facts and uses sound judgment in job-related decisions.	☐	☐	☐	☐	☐
Quantity of Work: Produces an acceptable amount of work under normal conditions.	☐	☐	☐	☐	☐
Dependability: Carries out assigned duties as expected (is reliable).	☐	☐	☐	☐	☐
Knowledge of Job: Has the understanding and technical knowledge necessary to perform all phases of job requirements.	☐	☐	☐	☐	☐
Attitude: Exhibits enthusiasm and cooperativeness on the job.	☐	☐	☐	☐	☐
Quality of Work: Exhibits accuracy and thoroughness of work in producing desired output.	☐	☐	☐	☐	☐
Overall Rating	☐	☐	☐	☐	☐

Several criticisms of this type of rating scale exist. It assumes that each factor or trait is of equal importance in developing the overall rating. However, different job situations may require emphases on different traits. Along the same line, because these traits are generalized to all jobs, special characteristics or conditions of each job are not considered.

To overcome this last criticism, some organizations use a rating system focusing on separate dimensions of the job. The dimensions relate to separate factors or job duties described in the job description (discussed in Chapter 4). The job factors or duties may be presented in the form of performance standards. Performance standards are specific to each job. For a sales representative, a performance standard could be expressed in terms of units of sale (e.g., 1,000 units per year) or expected number of new customer contacts (e.g., 100 per year). The performance standards then may be used by the supervisor to compare with actual employee performance in determining his or her performance rating. Clearly, these performance standards may be helpful to the supervisor in rating performance. For maximum value, they should be communicated to the employee at the beginning of the rating period. A performance appraisal form using performance standards is shown in Figure 15-3.

ESSAYS.   Examination of Figure 15-3 shows that this performance appraisal system is a combination of rating scales and an essay. The essay is required in three parts of the form: areas needing improvement, recommendations, and description of the reasons for the overall rating. As noted earlier, the trend is to combine both rating scales and essays or narratives describing or assessing employee performance for some period of time. Some organizations use a total essay format to describe employee performance, which allows the supervisor or rater to describe more completely how an employee performed for some period of time. The supervisor or rater has more freedom and flexibility in attempting to describe performance. The rater is not limited by the confines of rating performance on general traits. In addition, the rater designs the evaluation for the specific job and employee on that job. The major disadvantage of this approach is that it provides no specific structure to employee performance appraisals. Thus it is hard to compare the performance of two separate employees. There also may be legal liabilities regarding this approach as we discuss in a later section of this chapter. Therefore, fewer organizations are using an essay-only approach to performance appraisals, and more are moving to a combined approach (ratings plus essay), capitalizing on the advantages of each.

CRITICAL INCIDENTS.   The critical incident method was popularized by its use in the Minnesota Mining and Manufacturing Company a number of years ago.[7] There are three stages of appraisal when using the critical incident method. First, personnel specialists must develop critical incidents of behavior that represent outstanding and poor work behavior on the job. They do so for each job category or family of jobs (e.g., sales representatives). Second, supervisors maintain logs on each employee whereby they periodically record critical incidents of an employee's behavior. Third, at the end

Figure 15–3

Performance Appraisal Form Using Performance Standards

Job Title: _____   Employee: _____

Date: _____

	1	2	3	4	5
	Poor	Fair	Satisfactory	Good	Excellent

Performance standards:*

_____

_____

Areas needing improvement: _____

_____

_____

Recommendations (e.g., training, steps for improvement): _____

_____

Overall rating:

_____ Excellent   Performance is exceptional.
_____ Good   Performance exceeds normal requirements.
_____ Satisfactory   Performance meets normal requirements.
_____ Fair   Performance shows need for further improvement.
_____ Poor   Performance shows need for immediate and considerable improvement.

Concisely describe the reasons for the overall rating given: _____

_____

_____

_____

_____   Date: _____
Supervisor's Signature

_____   Date: _____
Employee's Signature

*Performance standards specific to each job. For a sales representative, a standard may be expressed in terms of the expected units of sales, expected number of new contacts, and so on.

© Michael A. Hitt, R. Dennis Middlemist, and Charles R. Greer.

of the rating period, these recorded critical incidents are used in the evaluation of the employee's performance. The advantage of this method is that it provides a record of extremely good and/or extremely bad employee work behavior over the rating period. The major disadvantage is that employees begin to fear the "black book" used by the supervisor. Also, supervisors may oversee employee activities too closely to record these behaviors thereby creating negative reactions from subordinates.

BEHAVIORALLY ANCHORED RATING SCALES.   Behaviorally anchored rating scales (BARS) is a relatively new approach to performance appraisal. It represents a combination of both the rating scale and critical incident methods. The BARS system identifies specific employee behaviors for each performance by job category.[8] For example, Figure 15-4 shows a behaviorally anchored rating scale for a stocker/sacker in a supermarket. These rating scales are then anchored with behavior that can be expected or is typical of an employee performing at a given level. For example, stocker/sackers performing at a below-average level will likely have to be told to help unload trucks with new stock rather than initiate the work on their own. These anchored behavioral expectations for each job family in the organization are difficult and time consuming to develop. Managers must work together to develop critical incidents for each group of jobs. Next the managers must tie these behaviors to a rating scale. The behaviors are developed for each important job dimension. This method may help supervisors in rating performance by giving them examples of behaviors relating to specific levels. This system should lead to more consistency in ratings among supervisors because they have the same behavioral anchor points. Also, the BARS method makes ratings more job related, which is now a legal necessity, and leads to more objective appraisals. These behavioral anchors, then, relate to the important dimensions of a job, and thus the important job behaviors are those being evaluated. The development of BARS requires several steps and the time of several managers.

MANAGEMENT BY OBJECTIVES.   Management by objectives (MBO) has been a popular performance appraisal method for several years, particularly in appraising the performance of managers and professionals. MBO involves the development of performance objectives for each employee for the next rating period (e.g., twelve months). These objectives are supposed to be mutually agreed on by the supervisor and employee. The objectives should relate to important dimensions of the job. At the end of the rating period, the employee evaluates his or her own performance, and the supervisor

Figure 15-4

Behaviorally Anchored Rating Scale for One Component of a Stocker/Sacker's Job

Performance		
Extremely good	7	Can expect S/S to make suggestions for higher stock sales and to have positive relationship with customers.
Good	6	Can expect S/S to initiate creative displays of stock to increase sales.
Above average	5	Can expect S/S to keep shelves well stocked, stock rotated and fronted.
Average	4	Can expect S/S to keep aisle clean and neat (free of trash, clean floor).
Below average	3	Can expect S/S to help unload trucks with incoming stock after being asked by supervisor.
Poor	2	Can expect S/S to leave shelves only partially stocked.
Extremely poor	1	Can expect S/S to take extended coffee breaks.

evaluates the performance against the established objectives. The employee and supervisor then discuss their appraisals and develop a mutually agreed-upon performance appraisal. If a disagreement cannot be resolved, it is so noted; but the supervisor's appraisal usually is used for compensation and other purposes. However, with explicit measurable objectives, and each party comparing actual performance against the objectives, most disagreement is resolved. In fact, this system of appraising performance usually produces less conflict than do most other methods. MBO is useful both in rewarding employees on performance and in developing employees' skills preparing them for future jobs.[9]

OTHER APPRAISAL METHODS. Other appraisal methods that may be used include checklist, ranking, and forced distribution. The *checklist* usually involves a list of adjectives and/or descriptive statements. Raters check those that seem to describe the employee. A rating score is developed based on the number of checks. Also, a weighted checklist may be used whereby each item on the list contains a predetermined weight or value. A rating score is developed by adding up the values of the items checked in this case.

Ranking is a relatively simple technique whereby the supervisor places his or her employees from highest to lowest on several predetermined criteria or characteristics. While simple, this method may become cumbersome when large numbers of employees are involved. Also, the differences among employees are not necessarily identified.

The *forced-choice method* was developed to help eliminate bias and the preponderance of high ratings that occur in some organizations. The use of this technique requires managers to judge employee characteristics by choosing from two seemingly favorable statements for each characteristic. Personnel specialists have predetermined which of these statements is related to effective job performance (based on research). Thus they take the supervisors' ratings and develop an overall score. Although it eliminates potential bias, supervisors do not know whether they are evaluating the employees favorably or not. This method is not used much because of managerial resistance to it.

IMPORTANCE OF APPRAISING PERFORMANCE. Several methods of appraising performance have been discussed. Each has advantages and disadvantages. However, managers must become proficient at appraising performance whenever merit-based compensation systems are used. Betty Myers favors a merit-based system and suggests that is the approach used in her firm. She related an instance whereby two employees outperformed another on the same job, in which case she believed that they should not receive the same pay. If an effective performance appraisal system is used at Texize, the employee performing at higher levels is likely to receive higher rates of pay than is the one who has poor performance.

Recall in Chapter 13 Fred Brown of GTE Sylvania, who noted that he believed his firm's system of annual performance appraisal, similar to MBO whereby employees and managers agree on goals, served as a motivational tool. Employee performance is compared with the goals, and if the goals are reached, the employee is rewarded. Fred believes that the appraisal program offers an important avenue for communication between manager and employees. Thus, performance appraisals are important for compensation, employee development, motivation, and communication purposes.

Performance Appraisal Problems

Performance appraisals are not easy to conduct. There are many potential pitfalls or problems that managers may encounter. These problems, if not avoided, may reduce the value of performance appraisals measurably. These problems include halo effect, varying standards, recency effects, rater bias, and rater patterns.

HALO EFFECT. The halo effect is a common problem with performance appraisals. It occurs when the supervisors rate an employee high or low on all appraisal criteria based on one characteristic of that employee. For example, an employee may do quite well in one aspect of the job such as quantity of work, and the supervisor rates the employee high on all aspects of the job such as quality of work, dependability, and so on, on the basis of it. Also, it may occur because a person's personal traits are perceived favorably by the supervisor. The employee may be physically attractive or may hold political beliefs similar to those of the supervisor. If an employee receives a high performance rating because of these factors, it is because of the halo effect. The halo effect is more common in rating scales than in other forms of performance appraisal.[10]

VARYING STANDARDS. A frequent problem with performance appraisals is that different supervisors apply different standards. Some tend to be more lenient than others, which creates problems particularly when pay increases are linked to performance ratings and when ratings are used to determine employee potential for promotion. Thus, if two supervisors perceive a "good" rating differently, comparing the performance ratings of their employees could provide a distorted picture of which employees are truly the best performers. In addition, a supervisor may apply different standards to different employees. This may be because the supervisor has different expectations from these employees based on perceived differences in ability. However, this creates an inequitable situation and should not occur. When varying standards are applied by separate supervisors, behaviorally anchored rating scales may help to reduce differences in the performance ratings.

RECENCY EFFECTS. It is common for all of us to make judgments weighing factors that have occurred recently most heavily. Supervisors have this problem with performance appraisals. An employee's actions and performance in the few months preceding the appraisal are often weighted most heavily in a supervisor's overall rating of the employee's performance. This is generally done subconsciously. Thus an employee may perform extremely well or poorly in the short period before the performance appraisal and have it unduly affect the overall performance rating received. Supervisors must try to consider employee performance over the complete rating period. The critical incident method is helpful in this regard because employee behaviors are recorded throughout the period.

RATER BIAS.   Some supervisors allow their values, beliefs, and/or prejudices to affect the manner in which they appraise employee performance. This, of course, is likely to result in a distorted rating of employee performance. These prejudices may show themselves in many ways, but only employee activities and factors relating to performance should be evaluated in performance appraisal sessions. Bias is not easy to overcome. However, an effective personnel program with documentation requirements to support performance ratings given employees helps to reduce bias in performance appraisal.

RATER PATTERNS.   Earlier, we noted that some supervisors tend to give more lenient ratings than others. Another problem is that of raters using only a narrow range of that allowed in the system. For example, the overall performance rating allowed may range along a five-point scale from poor to superior. However, some supervisors may employ only the two- to four-point range, using neither the poor nor the superior ratings. Therefore, the supervisor's ratings tend to group around the central point and are all similar. Frequently, this is referred to as the central tendency error. Many raters are more reluctant to give low ratings as well. Personnel specialists can observe performance ratings and provide feedback to supervisors when they are found to follow certain patterns. Also, the central tendency problem can be reduced by providing wider ranges for potential ratings.

OTHER APPRAISAL PROBLEMS.   Other appraisal problems may also exist in an organization. For example, it is common practice for managers to give those in higher-level jobs higher ratings simply because of their position. In a company with which the authors recently consulted, the personnel department had, in fact, just identified such a trend. Top management was concerned and wanted to try to overcome the problem. We should point out that managerial personnel are the most difficult to evaluate because their individual performance and the performance of their unit must be evaluated and combined into one rating.[11] Also, on occasion, supervisors, have insufficient evidence on which to rate an employee's performance accurately. This occurs where job results are difficult to measure (e.g., research scientist) and when the job does not require much contact between supervisor and employee. This problem can be overcome by setting *measurable* objectives at the beginning of the rating period and using those to rate performance at the end of the period.

To have effective performance appraisals, these problems must be prevented or overcome. The problems become compounded when performance appraisals are used for determination of merit pay increases and employee development. Betty Myers noted that three secretaries of whom she was aware did not perform at equal levels and thus should receive different pay. Problems such as those we have just described could create situations in which all might receive equal pay increases. It might even be possible, if the problems were severe, for the lowest (actual) performer to receive a higher rating (say, because of a lenient supervisor) than the others and therefore receive a higher pay increase.

Therefore the inaccurate performance appraisal leads to an inequitable situation as described in Chapter 12. The employee value portion of the total employee compensation then is inequitable. The inequity is likely to cause lower motivation and performance. This is not in the best interests of the organization.

These performance appraisal problems can have serious negative effects on employee morale and satisfaction. Eventually, they could lead to lower performance or even to turnover. Let us assume that two employees are performing similar jobs and, at least in their opinion, are performing at similar levels. However, the supervisor agrees with the political viewpoints of one of the employees and allows this to influence his appraisal of the employee's performance (halo effect). Thus he rates one employee's performance higher than the other, but they have, in fact, performed equally. If the employee receiving the lower rating were you, what would you do? There is little doubt that you would not be happy. Each person will react differently, but most reactions to this situation will be negative.

Legal Considerations

Although we have devoted a complete chapter to equal employment opportunity (Chapter 17), it is necessary to note the legal implications of performance appraisals at this point. The civil rights legislation and subsequent court cases have put emphases on how organizations promote and reward employees, particularly those in minority classifications. Many times, performance appraisals are used in making promotion and reward decisions. Thus performance appraisals have received considerable scrutiny from government agencies and the courts.

Some decisions (e.g., *Brito* v. *Zia Company,* 1973) have found that performance appraisals are tests and must be validated against job duties. Thus they must be based on job analyses. In addition, as tests, they must be administered and scored under controlled and standardized conditions.[12] Therefore rating scales using generalized traits are open to question because they may not relate to specific job duties. Also, systems that allow varying standards (easiest to occur with essays and rating scales) could not meet the requirement for controlled and standardized conditions.

Other decisions (e.g., *Albemarle Paper* v. *Moody,* 1975) have ruled against performance appraisals based on subjective supervisory ratings that are not based on job analyses. Thus generalized rating scales and essay forms of performance appraisal are subject to legal questions.[13] Probably the best methods of performance appraisal from the legal standpoint are the behaviorally anchored rating scales (BARS) and management by objectives (MBO).[14]

In one company with which the authors consulted, an employee who had been fired because of poor performance filed suit claiming that the loss of job was based on age discrimination. The employee had been a news announcer for a number of years with the company. Most employees were aware of this employee's "on-the-air performance" and agreed that it had been poor. However, the firm used a rather loose essay evaluation system and did not require supervisors to discuss ratings with subordinates. Most of the poor ratings were stated in general terms and were not specifically job related. In addition, the employee was not informed of these ratings until he was fired. The court ruled in favor of the employee, that he had, in fact, been discriminated against on the basis of age and even if the performance ratings had been valid, the individual had not been given a fair chance to improve performance. The company immediately began work to improve its performance appraisal system. Later, after the new system had been in effect for a few years, a female reporter filed suit claiming that a male reporter was making more money than she was and that the difference was because of sex discrimination. The courts ruled in favor of the company in this case because the pay increases had been based legitimately on job-related performance differences.

The results of these court cases suggest that organizations must take care with the development of performance appraisal systems. They must have a performance appraisal system to ensure that promotions are made on the basis of job-related performance and not some other basis such as race, sex, religion, color, nation origin, or age. These systems must be validated (shown to be job related) and administered under controlled and standardized conditions. Thus, organizations must relate performance appraisal systems to effective job analyses (Chapter 4), must develop standards of performance, and must train supervisors to become effective evaluators of performance. In addition, organizations must observe ratings closely to see if rater patterns suggest bias. If some patterns are found suggesting bias, immediate action should be taken to alleviate the problem.

Making Performance Appraisals Effective

The appraisal interviews between supervisors and employees are important for achieving the desired results from performance appraisals. With appraisals, organizations desire to reinforce effective employee behavior and guide employees to improve their performance where needed. To do so, the appraisal interviews must be conducted properly under the appropriate conditions by a supervisor motivated to do so.

According to Samuel Beacham, a vice president of Towers, Perrin, Forster and Crosby and specialist in compensation programs, "No management tool has been given more lip service and used less effectively than employee performance appraisals."[15] He believes that the problems center on the vagueness of performance standards, subjectivity, and inconsistency between raters and inconsistent use of results. Further, he believes that performance appraisals must be based on job-related criteria, must be reliable and valid, must be standardized in their application across the organization, and must be nondiscriminatory. To do so, organizations must set goals for their appraisal programs and train their supervisors to appraise performance and feed back performance in an effective manner.[16]

Several systems have been designed to help organizations implement performance appraisal systems more effectively. Corning Glass Works uses the Performance Management System (PMS) to appraise the performance of all managerial and professional employees. The PMS represents the result of several years of research conducted at Corning, and emphasizes psychometric accuracy (reliability and validity) and practical use. The PMS is a complex system composed of employee development and management by objectives systems and innovative measurement techniques.[17] Another system, the Performance Evaluation Monitoring System (PEMS), is designed to standardize supervisory ratings statistically while allowing supervisors flexibility to establish their own norms. It provides a means to overcome the problem of inconsistency between supervisors and the problems whereby supervisors develop specific rating patterns (e.g., consistently high ratings).[18]

However, the systems are not enough. They also must be implemented effectively. Thus we come back to the process of conducting the performance appraisal. Several studies have emphasized the importance of a number of factors in conducting effective performance appraisals. One such study found that the degree of subordinate participation, degree of supervisor helpfulness, extent to which job problems were solved, extent to which performance standards were set, amount of preparation for the appraisal interview (by both supervisor and employee), and degree to which appraisal results were tied to organizational rewards all affected the effectiveness of performance appraisal interviews.[19]

EMPLOYEE PARTICIPATION. Employees should be allowed to participate in the appraisal process. They can help to develop the performance standards on which they will be measured, and they can help to appraise their performance against results. This participation helps to increase employee satisfaction and performance in several ways. Most notably, employees will feel more committed to standards and goals that they help to set. Also, it provides employees' input into the appraisal process by helping to develop perceptions of fairness and equity in the system used.

Interview Preparation

Earlier in this chapter, we noted that each appraisal interview required approximately two hours of preparation to be conducted properly. If supervisors are not well prepared for appraisal interviews, they may miss certain key points, they may overlook important employee responses (both verbal and nonverbal) because they are having to focus on the form, and/or they may simply conduct the interview too mechanically. As we stated, it is also important for the employee to prepare for the interview. When an employee is prepared, he or she can ask pertinent questions and delve into more specific job-related material. Employees who analyze their job duties and problems on the job, and give thought to their performance, tend to be more active in the interviews. Therefore, both supervisors and employees should prepare for appraisal interviews.

SUPERVISOR HELPFULNESS.   Supervisors should attempt to be helpful, taking a positive approach to the interview. They should criticize employees in a constructive manner.[20] The approach they take will have a big impact on the way in which an employee reacts to the interview. A negative approach may cause an employee to react defensively, thus reducing the developmental value of the interview.

SOLVING JOB PROBLEMS.   The appraisal interview must focus not only on an employee's rating for past performance and future development but also on any job-related problems that may hamper performance. Specifically, the interview should focus on ways in which to solve these problems. Some of these problems may be related to the employee (e.g., attitude toward peers); others may be related to the supervisor (e.g., need for more supervisory support); still others may be related to organizational conditions (e.g., cooperation from other units). The supervisor and employee should jointly consider ways in which to solve these problems.

PERFORMANCE STANDARDS.   Performance standards relating to specific job requirements should be set. Since the performance rating should be based on performance standards, the appraisal interview is the appropriate time at which to discuss performance standards for the next rating period. These standards should be agreed upon mutually. In fact, it is preferable to have the employee first try to develop standards and discuss them with the supervisor. If the job does not change, performance standards may not change. However, they should be reviewed to ensure that they continue to be appropriate. Performance standards provide a set of expectations for the employee.

TYING REWARDS TO RATING RESULTS.   In the next section, we discuss how appraisals and compensation can be related. It is important to note that tying rewards to appraisal results is important, particularly if a merit pay system is used. In addition, other forms of reward such as promotions and recognition may also be related to appraisal results. Recall our discussion in Chapter 13 on motivation. Employees are more likely to be motivated to perform well if they expect to receive rewards for positive job outcomes.

APPRAISALS AND COMPENSATION

Performance appraisals and employee compensation may be highly interrelated as we noted earlier in the chapter. In the first part of this chapter, we discussed the fact that starting salaries or wages were usually determined by two factors: the worth of the job to the organization and the experience and qualifications of the employee.

However, we described in the previous chapter how organizations establish pay ranges for jobs. For example, the pay for a cost accountant may range from $16,000 to $26,000. A cost accountant hired with one year of experience may be given a beginning salary of $18,600. Some decisions have to be made on how the employee's salary will progress through the range. Earlier we discussed the approaches based on seniority and merit. If an organization chooses seniority, the progression through the range is simple. Salary would change as an employee collected the appropriate time in the job. On the other hand, if a merit system is used, the progression may be relatively more complex.

Organizations employ varying ways by which employees progress through their salary ranges based on merit. A simple approach is described in Figure 15-5.

Let us use the cost accountant for an example. If our cost accountant's beginning salary was $18,600, it would be barely into the second quartile of the previously mentioned range (second quartile: $18,500–20,999). Let us assume that our new cost accountant received a performance rating of "good" after being on the job for a year. Figure 15-5 shows that the supervisor may provide this employee a 6 to 9 percent merit salary increase. Let us also assume that his rating was good but that the supervisor felt that the performance was strong and almost outstanding. On that basis, the supervisor decides to give this employee a 9 percent salary increase, or $1,674. The employee's new annual salary is now $20,274.

The reason for the decreasing percentages as an employee's salary advances into higher-range quartiles is to keep the employee from reaching the top of the salary range so quickly. When an employee reaches the top of the salary range for the job, he or she is no longer eligible for merit salary increases, and this could have a negative effect on performance. In practice, inflation effects and changes in the market frequently require upward adjustments in the ranges, creating more room for employee salary progression.

The reason for the range of percentage salary increase in each cell is to provide the supervisor with some flexibility. Supervisors must take into account situational factors such as budget constraints. Also, a rating system that places an employee in a category may not allow enough for differences in employee performance. For example, one student may earn a "B+" and another may earn a "B−" in the same class.

Figure 15-5

Progression Through Salary Range by Merit

Performance Level	Quartile 1	Quartile 2	Midpoint Quartile 3	Quartile 4
Excellent	12-15%*	11-14%	10-13%	9-12%
Outstanding	9-12%	8-11%	7-10%	6-9%
Good	7-10%	6-9%	5-8%	4-7%
Fair	4-6%	3-5%	2-4%	1-3%
Poor	0	0	0	0

*Maximum allowable percentage salary increase when
employee performance rating and salary are at this level.

Thus, they both receive a "B" as a course grade. In practice the supervisor may feel one employee's performance was a "good+" and another's a "good−." They both receive good ratings, but the supervisor may provide differential rewards for the differences in performance. Care should be taken with such systems to disallow any discriminatory actions. Thus salary increases should be well documented and monitored closely.

If such a system combining performance appraisals and merit pay increases were used at Texize, Betty Myers's comment about the differentials in performance among three secretaries should be no problem. Of course, it may not be a problem since Texize may use such a system as described. We do know that Ms. Myers is strongly in favor of a merit-based system. Research has shown that employees are concerned about pay equity as we stated in Chapter 12.[21] Systems such as the one just described, when administered properly, can increase employee feelings of equitable treatment in pay.

PERFORMANCE COACHING AND COUNSELING

There are many times when a supervisor should interact with employees outside of the formal performance appraisal system. These interactions are related to performance appraisals, however. Many of the supervisor's interactions with subordinates entail performance coaching and counseling.[22]

Coaching: helping employees to learn and apply job-related skills and abilities.

Counseling: helping employees to deal with important career or personal issues.

The performance appraisal process, then, will likely entail both coaching and counseling. Additionally, supervisors must deal consistently with job-related employee problems and help to develop employee skills. Thus coaching and counseling are continuous processes for supervisors and are important parts of a supervisory job.

Coaching and Counseling Styles

When coaching or counseling employees, supervisors may use several styles. The styles vary to the extent to which feedback is given willingly and is constructive and to the extent to which employees are involved in solving problems. The relationship of these two dimensions of supervisory behavior to coaching and counseling styles is shown in Figure 15-6.[23]

As shown in the figure, there are four coaching and counseling styles: boss, humanist, parent, and colleague. A supervisor who uses the "boss" style is reluctant to give constructive feedback and does not involve employees in solving job-related problems. This supervisor then is emphasizing a short-run goal of reaching immediate ob-

Figure 15-6

Coaching and Counseling Styles

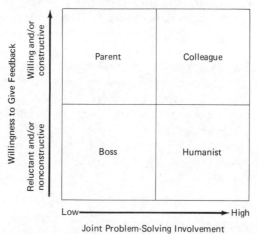

jectives. The supervisor solves the problem and/or performs the task. Quite obviously, the boss style is not developmental.

A supervisor using the "humanist" style allows employees to participate jointly in solving job-related problems but does not provide constructive feedback to them. Thus emphasis is placed on finding mutually agreeable solutions to problems but not on developing employee skills. Again, generally the short-run goals of reaching immediate objectives are emphasized. Underlying causes of problems are not explored; only short-run solutions are desired.

A supervisor using the "parent" style provides constructive feedback but solves job-related problems without employee participation. Therefore, this supervisor is being instructive, while at the same time, tries to solve job-related problems easily. The supervisor instructs the subordinate on why the problem arose and how it can best be solved, hoping that subordinates' behavior will change to avoid future similar problems.

The "colleague" style is both instructive and developmental. A supervisor using a colleague style provides constructive feedback and allows employees to participate jointly in solving problems. Generally, this approach is considered to emphasize long-run effectiveness. Employee performance improvement is sought through a blend of constructive feedback and skill development by participation in solving existing problems.

Using the Styles

Observation of the previous discussion may lead one to believe that the colleague style is the best to use. Although this may be true in many cases, there are situations in which each of the four styles would be most effective. For instance, the boss style would be most effective when

1. A quick solution is imperative.
2. Employees reject developmental efforts and/or insist on a poor solution.
3. Employees lack concern for the problem.

The humanist style would be most effective when

1. The problem is relatively unimportant to the supervisor.
2. The employee has potential but seems to rely on others for decisions.
3. The employee can solve the problem effectively and too much other input might make the solution less effective.

The parent style would be most effective when

1. It is the supervisor's responsibility to make the decision but the employee needs instructions.
2. The supervisor, alone, has the information (and skills) to solve the problem, but the employee must implement the solution.
3. The employee is inexperienced in dealing with the problem at hand.

The colleague style would be most effective when

1. Success depends on mutual input to and/or acceptance of the solution.
2. The supervisor and employee are equally skilled.
3. Employee development is at least equal in importance to the problem.[24]

Therefore we may conclude that each of these styles may be appropriate under the right conditions. Supervisors should then be able to analyze the situation and determine which coaching or counseling style to adopt. They may already have dominant styles that they use most of the time. Thus they need to analyze their own styles and attempt to be as flexible in the application of them as possible. There is an instrument that may be used to measure these styles.[25] It could be administered to supervisors to give them helpful feedback to become effective coaches and counselors.

SUMMARY

In this chapter, we focused on compensating people on the basis of performance. Once wage or salary ranges are established, organizations must set new employee wage or salary levels and decide on what basis an employee's wage or salary progresses through the range. New employee compensation is usually based on the worth of the job to the organization (at least the minimum of the salary range established) and on the employee's experience and abilities. An inexperienced employee may likely begin at the minimum salary of the range for the particular job. An experienced new employee is likely to receive a beginning salary higher in the range.

Once the beginning pay level is established, increases in pay are likely to be based either on merit or on seniority. When seniority is used, employees' pay increases are based on length of service. When a merit approach is used, pay increases are based on employees' performance. To pay employees according to their performance, a performance appraisal system is required.

A performance appraisal is an assessment of employee work behavior with the general purpose of determining the degree of employee effectiveness on the job. Performance appraisals may be used for employee development, for salary administration, for guides to job changes (promotions, transfers, demotions), for evaluation of selection procedures, and for developing rapport between supervisors and their employees. Supervisors commonly rate performance. However, an employee's performance may be rated by peers, subordinates, outsiders or by the employees themselves.

There are numerous performance appraisal methods, the most common ones being rating scales and essays. Also, the critical incident approach is used by some organizations. Probably behaviorally anchored rating scales (BARS) and management by objectives (MBO) represent the better overall approaches. Other less frequently used techniques include the checklist, ranking, and forced-choice methods. Regardless of the system used, performance appraisals are important, particularly when merit-based compensation systems are used.

Many common pitfalls or problems may be encountered with performance appraisals, among them the halo effect, varying standards, recency effects, rater bias, rater patterns, the practice of giving higher ratings to employees on higher-level jobs, and insufficient evidence. These problems must be prevented or overcome if performance appraisals are to be effective.

Performance appraisals have important legal implications, particularly with regard to providing equal opportunity to all employees. Systems must be used that are reliable and valid (shown to be related to performance on the job and administered under controlled and standardized conditions). Behaviorally anchored rating scales and management by objectives are two of the best methods for providing the appropriate conditions.

Effective performance appraisals must do more than simply meet legal requirements. Studies have shown that effective performance appraisals depend on the degree of subordinate participation, degree of supervisor helpfulness, extent to which job problems are solved, extent to which performance standards are set, amount of preparation by both supervisor and subordinate for the appraisal interview, and the degree to which appraisal results are tied to organizational rewards.

Compensation and appraisals are then interrelated in merit-based pay systems. The appraisal ratings determine the amount of merit pay increase provided to employees.

Supervisors must be good coaches and counselors to conduct performance appraisals effectively. However, they must coach and counsel employees on a continuous basis to be effective supervisors. There are four coaching or counseling styles supervisors may use: boss, humanist, parent, and colleague. Each of these styles may be applied effectively if the situation warrants it.

INTERVIEW WRAP-UP

My own job performance is not affected by the amount of money I receive because I always try to do my best on any job. There are three bases on which employees should be paid: (1) worth of the job to the company, (2) employee's ability to do the job, and (3) employee's performance on the job. Pay equity between individuals is important and pay increases should be based on employee performance (merit). A merit-based pay system would require an effective system of performance appraisal and linking it to pay increases. —Betty Myers, an employee of Texize Chemicals, Inc.

WHAT MANAGERS SHOULD DO REGARDING PERSONNEL MANAGEMENT ACTIVITIES

1. Managers should have a voice in the general pay level of the organization. They should make their feelings known to top executives and personnel staff members. The general pay level will affect the quality of the employees obtained.

2. Managers play a key role in performance appraisals. They are the ones who use the organization's appraisal system to evaluate the performance of their subordinates. Since performance appraisals are so important to the organization and to the employee (used for salary administration, employee development, etc.), managers must understand the system well and do an effective job of evaluating performance.

3. Managers should be aware of the potential problems (halo effect, varying standards, recency effects, rater bias, rater patterns) with evaluating performance and avoid them.

4. Managers can make the appraisals more effective if they are well prepared to conduct the interview.

5. Managers must understand fully how performance appraisals are related to compensation in their organization. They should be prepared to explain it to their employees.

REVIEW QUESTIONS

1. Why do you think some employees, for example, Betty Myers, prefer merit-based pay systems?

2. What are the differences between seniority and merit-based pay systems?

3. What performance appraisal methods are used most commonly? How are they implemented?

4. How are BARS and MBO effective in meeting legal requirements?

5. What are some of the more common problems with performance appraisals and how do you think they can best be overcome?

6. How can performance appraisals be made more effective?

7. How can performance appraisals and employee pay be linked together?

8. Under what conditions is each of the coaching or counseling styles most appropriate?

KEY CONCEPTS

Behaviorally anchored rating scales	Rater bias
Critical incidents	Rater Patterns
Essays	Rating scales
Halo effect	Recency effect
Management by objectives	Seniority
Merit	Varying standards
Performance appraisal	

CASE

THE ERRANT APPRAISALS

Richard Feeney was news director for KZMA television, the largest television station in the state. KZMA had a reputation of having the best news team and presenting the best news in the state. In fact, Richard had the largest news staff of any television station in the state. His department had fifty-five employees.

Richard had been news director for only six months. His predecessor had gone to Philadelphia to become general manager for a television station there. Richard had worked his way up through the ranks, starting as a general reporter. He then held a series of jobs including beat reporter, assignments editor, and chief producer prior to his current position. He's been in the television news business for over fifteen years and likes the excitement and the fast-paced atmosphere it presents.

Although Richard was pleased to be the news director of the top news department in the state, the job had many pressures. For example, he well remembers the comment of Sean McCormick, general manager of the station, when he was given the job, "Richard, we are pleased to have someone of your caliber among our staff ready to step in and take over when we need it. I believe we have the top news team in the state, and I want it to stay that way. Members of our board of directors watch our news every day and call me if they don't like something. I'll let you know when they call." Richard knew there would be a lot of pressure, but he liked the status of the job, and he was earning the best pay of his career.

There were also many pressures on his employees as well. There was constant pressure to maintain the number one standing and so they were always trying to eliminate on-the-air mistakes. In addition, there was a lot of competition among the professional staff to perform best on camera. The competition created some staff conflict and professional jealousies. Finally, the nature of the business created some time pressures. News stories had to be written and the script prepared by air time for the news. Promptly at 6:00 P.M., the news had to go on the air, ready or not. There is no slack time for live television news programs.

All these pressures combined to make Richard's job intense. Richard found his most difficult decisions did not deal with the news content or the department's operating budget, however. Certainly, they were important, but his most difficult decisions dealt with personnel. The sessions he dreaded most were the annual performance appraisals. The personnel were so competitive that they generally reacted quite defensively if they received any criticism. His predecessor filled out performance appraisal forms when he felt like it. Therefore, the personnel files were not up to date, and several of the staff, who were not high performers but were "complainers," had not received performance appraisals for two years or more.

This fact bothered Richard, and he figured that everyone should have had a performance appraisal once a year. Thus he began filling out the appraisal forms and conducting the appraisal interviews. He started with a couple that he knew would be easy. They went relatively well and Richard began to gain confidence.

As Richard was making plans to schedule appraisal interviews with all other department employees whose time was due, he received a phone call. It was Sean McCormick.

Sean boomed into the phone, "Richard, it's that Maggie Smith again. She really blew it this time. She screwed up on the air and one of our board members saw her. They've called me on her three times now. We've got to get her off the air."

Richard knew this was going to be a problem. Maggie was one of the complainers and had not had a performance appraisal interview for over two years. Richard retorted, "Sean, Maggie has not had her performance reviewed for over two years. I agree that she has not been doing a good job but no one has told her about it."

"I don't care, Richard. We can't continue making a mistake because we made one in the past. I don't want her on the air any more!" At that he hung up.

Richard thought about several "special assignments" he could give Maggie and get her off the air for a while. But he would only be postponing the inevitable. Maggie had been doing a poor job for quite some time, and everyone knew it.

Richard decided that he had no choice but to terminate Maggie. He was very nervous as the interview time approached. When the time came, he sat down with Maggie and explained that her performance had been poor for some time. Maggie seemed to take it calmly, but said she was disappointed that no one had informed her of her poor performance before. At that she left the room, cleared out her desk and then left the building.

Richard was pleased that it went so smoothly. He had expected a rough time. Everything seemed to be going well until he received a phone call two weeks later.

"This is Joan Rambo, investigative agent for the Equal Employment Opportunity Commission. Ms. Maggie Smith has filed a complaint with us charging that she was terminated because of sex discrimination. I would like to set up an appointment to discuss the complaint with you and to inspect your records."

CASE QUESTIONS

1. What seems to be the problem in this case?

2. Why were no performance appraisals conducted? Do you think Maggie has a case? Why?

3. How could this situation have been prevented?

NOTES

[1]L. Dyer, D. P. Schwab, and R. D. Theriault, "Managerial Perceptions Regarding Salary Increase Criteria," *Personnel Psychology,* 29 (1976), 233–242.

[2]H. Mustafa, "Escalator Pay Plans," *Public Personnel Management,* 3 (1974), 4–9.

[3]"Employee Performance: Evaluation and Control," *Personnel Policies Forum,* 108 (Washington DC: Bureau of National Affairs, 1975).

[4]Estimated by Development Systems International, management consultants, in a training program on performance counseling and coaching for Phillips Petroleum Company.

[5]For example, see D. A. Nadler, "The Effects of Feedback on Task Group Behavior: A Review of the Experimental Research," *Organizational Behavior and Human Performance,* 23 (1979), 309–338.

[6]K. S. Teel, "Performance Appraisal: Current Trends, Persistent Progress," *Personnel Journal,* 59 (1980), 296–301.

[7]W. K. Kirchner and M. D. Dunnette, "Identifying the Critical Factors in Successful Salesmanship," *Personnel,* 34 (1957), 54–59.

[8]D. P. Schwab, H. G. Heneman, III, and T. A. DeCotiis, "Behaviorally Anchored Rating Scales: A Review of the Literature," *Personnel Psychology,* 28 (1975), 549–562.

[9]S. J. Carroll, Jr., and H. L. Tosi, Jr., *Management by Objectives, Applications and Research* (New York: Macmillan, 1973).

[10]W. Borman, "Effects of Instruction to Avoid Halo Error on Reliability and Validity of Performance Evaluation Ratings," *Journal of Applied Psychology,* 60 (1975), 556–560.

[11]R. L. Mathis and R. H. Sutton, "Performance Appraisal," *Journal of Systems Management,* 30 (1979), 16–18.

[12]R. I. Lazer, "The Discrimination Danger in Performance Appraisal," *The Conference Board Record,* 13 (1976), 60–64.

[13]W. H. Holley and H. S. Feild, "Performance Appraisal and the Law," *Labor Law Journal,* 26 (1975), 423–430.

[14]Lazer, "The Discrimination Danger in Performance Appraisal."

[15]S. T. Beacham, "Managing Compensation and Performance Appraisal Under the Age Act," *Management Review,* 68 (1979), 51–54.

[16]Ibid.

[17]M. Beer, R. Ruh, J. A. Dawson, B. B. McCaa, and M. J. Kavanagh, "A Performance Management System: Research, Design, Introduction and Evaluation," *Personnel Psychology,* 31 (1978), 505–535.

[18]M. E. Schick, "The 'Refined' Performance Evaluation Monitoring System: Best of Both Worlds," *Personnel Journal,* 59 (1980), 47–50.

[19]R. J. Burke, W. Weitzel, and T. Weir, "Characteristics of Effective Employee Performance Review and Development Interviews: Replication and Extension," *Personnel Psychology,* 31 (1978), 903–919.

[20]G. G. Alpander, "Training First-Line Supervisors to Criticize Constructively," *Personnel Journal,* 59 (1980), 216–221.

[21]M. R. Carrell, "A Longitudinal Field Assessment of Employee Perceptions of Equitable Treatment," *Organizational Behavior and Human Performance,* 21 (1978), 108–118.

[22]M. A. Hitt, H. K. Downey, R. D. Ireland, and R. D. Middlemist, "Coaching and Counseling Styles: Effective Performance Appraisals," unpublished working paper, Oklahoma State University, Stillwater, 1981.

[23]Ibid.

[24]Ibid.

[25]H. K. Downey, M. A. Hitt, R. D. Ireland, and R. D. Middlemist, *PAS, Performance Appraisal Styles: Coaching and Counseling for Effectiveness* (Stillwater: College of Business Administration, Oklahoma State University, 1981).

INCENTIVES AND BENEFITS

LEARNING OBJECTIVES

After reading this chapter, you should be able to:

1. Discuss the development of fringe benefits and describe the legally required benefits.
2. Explain the important insurance benefits.
3. Describe the payment for time not worked and service benefits.
4. Discuss retirement programs, ERISA, and retirement patterns.
5. Explain the concept of cafeteria benefits.
6. Describe three individual incentive programs.
7. Discuss three group incentive programs.

Woodward Governor Company was founded in 1870 in Rockford, Illinois. Today it is an international organizaton with domestic manufacturing facilities in Rockford; Fort Collins, Colorado; and Stevens Point, Wisconsin. It also has manufacturing facilities in Holland, England, and Japan, with sales and service locations in Australia, Brazil, and South Africa. Woodward Governor employs over 2,500 persons. The company is one of the world's leading producers of governors, which are sophisticated fuel and speed control devices for large engines, providing precise and constant speeds over a wide range of load conditions. Woodward's governors are used in a variety of industrial applications such as hydroelectric operations, ocean-going vessels, aircraft, gas and steam turbines, and gas and diesel engines. The company enjoys an excellent reputation for high quality products, attributable in large part to the consistent efforts of its members.

Bob Kleven, manager of personnel for Woodward Governor in Fort Collins, Colorado, spoke to us regarding the importance of incentives and fringe benefits in compensation programs. Mr. Kleven holds a bachelor's degree in business administration, with a major in industrial relations. He has been associated with Woodward Governor since 1960.

Interviewer: Can you give us a general idea of how important fringe benefits are in a company's total compensation program?

Bob Kleven: I think most personnel managers would agree that fringe benefits are a very important part of compensation programs. I believe we can see this by looking at some of the basic principles of management, in particular by looking at Maslow's need hierarchy. Initially, employees need a basic salary to provide for fundamental needs such as for housing, food and transportation. However, as they mature and grow in their job they look beyond to other higher order needs. Some of the fringe benefits provided by companies help employees address these needs

Also, I think that different employees have quite different needs. As people become more involved with family and community responsibilities, their perceived needs will change. Reflecting this change will be the varied importance given one or another benefit.

Interviewer: When individuals consider a company's offer of employment, how much weight do you think the fringe benefits package carries in their decisions?

Bob Kleven: Again, I think we see a great deal of difference from person to person. Some people give fringe benefits little attention at all, while others give benefits a lot of thought. Most employees want to know their direct compensation first, and then consider the benefit package. As a guess, I would estimate that in the decision to accept or reject an offer, fringe benefits carry perhaps one-half the weight of direct compensation. As family obligations increase, however, so will the importance of benefits. Also, we know that this decision is affected by such factors as opportunity for promotion, enjoyment of the work and co-workers, and the environment in which one will be working.

Interviewer: What types of employee benefits do you consider to be important here at Woodward?

Bob Kleven: Let me first state that we maintain a progressive view of the company-employee relationship here; a view that we truly put into action. The people at Woodward are, in fact, "corporate partners," and there is a genuine mutual interest between the company and all of us. There is a commitment on both parts that is reflected in the benefits package, and also in employee, or member, efforts.

When we talk about benefits, it is important to recognize that these are not simply "freebies," they are specific types of compensation that all employees "earn" in much the same sense that they earn their cash wage. This is true no matter with what company a person works. With regards to specific benefits, I think our members place great importance on the health care and insurance coverages. We have both a medical doctor and a dentist on staff, and their services are available, without charge, to members. Beyond this, Woodward provides health, disability, and life insurance. We also have a unique vacation program that allows our members to have major control over their time-off preferences. It provides them flexibility in scheduling their time-off according to their needs. There are other benefits such as our cafeteria, barbershop, seniority recognition, and retirement program, that while certainly appreciated, are of less importance. I think an increasingly important benefit is the education reimbursement program. Woodward reimburses its members up to 100 percent of the cost for tuition, books, and related fees for any educational program related to their work if completed with a C grade or above. This includes not only university courses, but vocational and correspondence courses as well.

Interviewer: If we can switch tracks for a minute, would you tell me about any incentive programs that you feel are important to Woodward and its members?

Bob Kleven: Yes. Let me begin by saying that there are many types of incentives, some being tangible, but others being intangible. Some of the intangible incentives that encourage people to be productive are being associated with a high quality product line, opportunity for promotion, accountability for one's performance, interest in the work, and interactions with and respect from one's peers. Our major tangible incentives are our cash profit sharing program and our deferred profit sharing. These incentives are distributed to all members without distinction between job classifications. Therefore, everyone is interested in making the company profitable since they are, in fact as well as in philosophy, partners in sharing the company's success. It is also designed to place heavy emphasis on safety and product quality, unlike some incentive plans that might emphasize quantity alone—at the expense of safety and quality.

The deferred profit sharing plan is funded completely by the company through annual deposits, separate and distinct from the cash profit sharing plan. The company provides this incentive from its share of the profits, providing a fully vested trust for each member following their second year of employment. These deferred earnings belong to the member and may be withdrawn when they leave Woodward Governor Company.

Interviewer: Do you see, either in the company or the industry, any trends in fringe benefits or incentive programs?

Bob Kleven: I'd say that companies will probably begin to supplement educational reimbursement benefits with more educationally oriented in-house programs. The extremely rapid developments in technology are causing major problems for employees in terms of keeping up on skills and knowledge. I think companies may begin to provide theoretical, science, and liberal arts oriented training in-house and at no cost to employees.

Second, I think childcare facilities for working mothers and single parents will become very important. Some companies are already doing this, and it will become even more attractive as people with this need are increasingly present in the work force.

Company sponsored recreation and recreational facilities will continue to expand to meet the interests and physical needs of a workforce no longer required to exert large amounts of physical energy on higher technology jobs.

"Elective benefits" may be implemented whereby an employee is required to participate in several benefits programs, but they can exercise the option to receive additional cash in their paycheck rather than be covered by some other programs.

Finally, larger companies are becoming more attuned to employees in a holistic way. This is perhaps similar to some of the Japanese methods of caring, being concerned about the employee's needs, not only in terms of quality-of-work life, but also for quality-of-life in total. I'm not sure exactly what form this will take, in terms of specific benefit programs, but I'm sure it will become a major influence.

INTRODUCTION

Fringe benefits are a major part of employees' total compensation package today. Bob Kleven stated that fringe benefits are a very important part of compensation programs. Some of the fringe benefits provide higher order need satisfaction for employees that they could never obtain alone. Fringe benefits also provide employees with opportunities. For example, group medical coverage usually offers better benefits at much lower cost than does individual medical insurance coverage. Individuals can rarely develop reasonable retirement income based only on their own resources. Therefore, fringe benefit programs are important to the security and well-being of many employees.

Incentive programs may also be useful primarily as a motivator to achieve high levels of performance. Woodward Governor provides a profit sharing incentive that is distributed to all members. The resulting sense of partnership leads to high performance in safety, quality, and quantity of production.

Recall from Chapter 12 on the logic of compensation and motivation that fringe benefits are generally considered supplemental compensation. However, also note that we emphasized the importance of employee feelings of equity in compensation for proper motivation. Woodward Governor maintains these feelings of equity in compensation by extending the profit sharing incentive and other benefits to all members of the organization.

In this chapter, we consider incentive and benefit programs and how benefit programs have evolved into important compensation elements. The discussion includes both those programs required by law and those offered voluntarily by organizations. The major emphases are on payment for time not worked, insurance programs, and retirement packages. The cafeteria plan approach to benefits is noted. Discussion of incentives centers on individual incentives, such as piece-rate systems, and group incentives, such as executive bonus systems.

BENEFITS

Many fringe benefits are provided employees today. We discuss many of these but emphasize the important ones. First, however, we focus on how and why benefit programs have developed into an important part of the employee's total compensation package.

Growth and Development of Benefit Programs

In the early 1900s, benefits were rare; today, they are common and expensive. Within the last fifteen to twenty years, the cost of benefits has risen from 10 to 15 percent of direct wage and salary payments to as much as 30 to 50 percent.[1] Part of the increased cost is because of inflation in some costs, such as medical insurance coverage, but part is based on increased benefits.

The 1930s, the depression years, changed views regarding employee needs and stimulated interest in benefits, such as pension plans. Many benefits are designed to reduce the financial risk of employees. As economic growth occurred after the Depression, there was more desire and pressure to provide benefits protecting employees. As employees' pay has increased, there has been a desire to obtain part of their compensation in increased benefits. As noted earlier, group benefits usually provide more service at lower cost. Most benefits are not considered taxable income to the employee. Thus employees receive more value for their money than if they were paid the same amount of dollars in direct wages. Also, organizations can negotiate from a stronger position with insurance companies and investment firms than can individuals. Better employee benefits result.[2]

Strong pressure for increasing fringe benefits came from labor unions, particularly during World War II when there were strong wage controls. Fringe benefits were sometimes viewed as means of increasing total compensation by circumventing the wage regulations. Since a ruling by the courts that benefits could be a bargaining issue (1948), and are now a mandatory bargaining issue (if either party brings up the issue) unions have usually included benefits as a part of contract demands.

There are many different types of fringe benefits. Some are required by law; others are provided voluntarily to employees. An outline of some of the more common benefits appears in Table 16-1. We discuss the most important of these.

Legally Required Benefits

Legally required benefits include social security, unemployment insurance, and workers' compensation.

SOCIAL SECURITY.   Most of us are familiar with social security. It is required by federal law, and both the employer and the employee make contributions, based on a percentage of the employee's direct pay. The primary intention of social security is to provide retirement income for employees. In 1980, the maximum taxable wage was $25,900 and the percentage of tax or contribution was 6.13 percent ($1,587.67). By 1987, the maximum taxable wage will be $42,600, and the percent of the tax will be 7.15 percent ($3,045.90). The employer and the employee make matching contributions. For an employee making $25,900 in 1980, the employee and the employer each made contributions of $1,587.67.

Employees may retire at age sixty-two with reduced benefits or at age sixty-five and after with full benefits. In recent years, Congress has improved social security benefits by tying them to the cost of living, substantially increasing the cost both to employees and employers.

Recent concern has grown over the financial stability of the social security fund. Important changes proposed include raising the retirement age, eliminating minimum benefit payments, and increasing the tax on income. It is expected that some changes will be required in the next few years.

Table 16-1

Types of Fringe Benefits

Legally required benefits
  Old Age, Survivors, Disability, and Health Insurance
    (social security)
  Unemployment insurance
  Workers' compensation

Voluntary benefits
  Insurance
    Health insurance (medical/hospital)
      (surgical/major medical, catastrophic illness)
    Life insurance
    Accident and disability insurance
    Dental insurance
    Drug insurance

  Payment for time not worked
    Vacations
    Holidays
    Supplemental unemployment benefits
    Paid sick leave
    Other (personal leave, jury duty, military reserve duty, severance pay)

  Retirement
    Pension
    Profit sharing
    Thrift or savings plans
    Stock purchase plans

  Service
    Discounts on company products
    Recreation programs
    Credit unions
    Subsidizing food service
    Financial counseling[1]
    Annual physicals[1]

[1]Usually provided only to executives.

UNEMPLOYMENT INSURANCE. The Social Security Act of 1935, which created social security, also provided unemployment insurance. It provided incentives to states to pass unemployment insurance laws meeting federal guidelines. Actual state laws vary. The benefit periods range from twenty-six to fifty-two weeks. The primary purpose of these laws is to provide income to individuals while they search for a new job. Employers pay a tax to finance unemployment compensation. The amount varies by state. To be eligible for unemployment compensation, individuals generally must have lost a job through no fault of their own and be conducting a search for a suitable job.

WORKERS' COMPENSATION. Workers' compensation laws can be found in all fifty states. Their purpose is to provide cash benefits for injuries sustained on the job. These benefits apply regardless of fault of injury. In some states, the laws are compulsory; in others, they are elective.

Employers under compulsory laws must comply with the provisions and provide the appropriate compensation to work-related injuries, whereas elective employers decide voluntarily whether or not to comply with the law's provisions. However, those choosing not to comply with the law lose the normal common law defenses[3] that help to limit the employer's liability. Employers pay premiums to private insurance funds or state-operated plans. The amount of compensation received by the employee depends on the type and severity of the injury. Most workers' compensation plans cover only physical injury. However, some have been amended to include job-related mental and emotional illnesses.

Most all other benefits are voluntary. Even voluntary benefits may be subject to legal regulations and requirements.

Insurance

Most employers provide several types of insurance benefits to employees. The most common of these are medical and life insurance benefits. One study found that 99 percent of all companies provide some form of group life insurance, and 98 percent of all companies provide some form of hospitalization and surgical insurance to employees.[4]

MEDICAL INSURANCE. A number of different types of medical benefits are provided to employees. The most common include payment of hospitalization costs and doctors' surgical fees. The plans pay these costs up to some established maximum. Usually, dependents of the employee are also covered by the insurance. In addition to the basic medical insurance coverage, many organizations also provide major medical insurance coverage. Major medical insurance covers medical costs that go beyond the basic plan. This type of insurance is designed to aid in medical costs associated with prolonged and serious illness. The costs of this insurance may be paid wholly by the organization or on some shared basis between employer and employee.

Another somewhat recent benefit being adopted by some organizations is the health maintenance organization (HMO). This unique form of health coverage provides comprehensive health care for a prepaid annual fee. The HMO is composed of a group of medical professionals who provide the health care. The emphasis is on prevention as well as on overcoming medical problems.

The purpose of this program is to encourage patients to have early checkups and avoid hospitalization where possible. Growth of HMOs was spurred by the Health Maintenance Act of 1973. This act requires firms (with twenty-five or more employees) to offer membership in an HMO to employees as an alternative to any existing health plan if an HMO is available in the area.[5] Under this law, the federal government is also supposed to encourage the development of HMOs. Some large organizations are establishing their own HMOs rather than paying for coverage as a part of a larger system.[6] An example of this form of medical coverage in operation for several years is the Kaiser Foundation plans on the West Coast.

Medical insurance coverage is important to most people. Bob Klevin felt that Woodward Governor's employees placed great importance on the health care and insurance coverages. Further, Woodward Governor had both a medical doctor and a dentist on staff for prevention of health problems, a benefit similar to the HMO's just described.

LIFE INSURANCE.   Most group life insurance programs are straightforward and easily understood. These programs usually involve term life insurance carried on the employee as long as he or she remains an employee. The amount of the coverage either is fixed, such as $30,000, or is tied to the amount of salary or wages received such as two times annual salary. Therefore, if a person earned $25,000 per year in salary, he or she would have life insurance coverage in the amount of $50,000. Life insurance coverage provides benefits upon death to survivors of the deceased. Thus it is designed to help protect the financial well-being of the employee's family. In most cases, the employer pays the full premium for the coverage. In addition, many employers allow employees to continue with the coverage after retirement.

OTHER INSURANCE.   Many employers offer several other insurance programs for their employees. Among these are accident and disability, dental, drug, and vision care insurance plans. The most common among these are the accident and disability insurance plans. This type of insurance is designed to compensate employees for wage losses because of nonjob-related accidents or illnesses. These may be of the short-term (e.g., less than twenty-six weeks) or long-term variety. More common today are long-term disability plans. These plans usually compensate employees for up to 60 percent of normal wages when they become permanently disabled due to illness or injury.

The other plans such as dental, drugs, and vision care insurance operate much like medical insurance coverage. These are helpful to employees offsetting some of the major costs in each of these areas. Bob Kleven described that Woodward's members, as well as employees in general, place great importance on health care and insurance benefits.

Payment for Time Not Worked

The most common benefits that involve pay for time not worked are vacations and holidays. In addition, supplemental unemployment benefits, paid sick leave, personal leave, and severance pay fall into this category. This area has been growing in recent years with the pressure from employees for more leisure time.

VACATION AND HOLIDAYS.   In recent years, the average workweek has decreased in hours until some workers spend less than forty hours on the job. Employees are also showing a preference for three-day weekends.

Paid holidays are granted to all employees regardless of length of service or wage level. The average company today grants ten holidays a year. These usually include all major holidays such as Christmas and Thanksgiving. In addition, some employers grant time off for employees' birthdays.

All workers, be they management, professional, clerical, or hourly production-line employees generally receive paid vacations. Most vacation plans grant increasing time off as the employee attains greater seniority with the organization. Table 16-2 shows typical holiday and vacation schedules. Time away from work is important because it combats both physical and mental fatigue. Having a break from work can build an employee's enthusiasm for the job.

SUPPLEMENTAL UNEMPLOYMENT BENEFITS. Supplemental unemployment benefits (SUBs) generally occur as a result of union contract negotiations. They are designed to provide normal wages or some major percentage thereof (e.g., 90 percent) to employees who are laid off by the company for a temporary period. These benefits may continue for as long as a year. The company makes contributions to a fund that is then used to pay wages to employees who are laid off. SUBs are particularly useful in industries whose fortunes fluctuate with the economy's. However, they can be quite costly to the employer. SUBs are found in such major industries as automobile, steel, rubber, and glass.

In recent years SUBs have become increasingly important, particularly in industries hit especially hard during economic recessions. They were most helpful to workers in the automobile and steel industries during the recession in the early 1980s. In some cases, such as in the auto industry, SUBs paid up to 95 percent of a worker's wages for as much as a year's time after being laid off. SUBs then provide for income until, it is hoped, the firm can recall the workers or they can find other employment.

Table 16-2

Typical Holiday and Vacation Schedules

Holiday Schedule

All employees will be granted the following holidays with full pay:

New Year's Day	Labor Day
Washington's Birthday	Thanksgiving Day
Good Friday	Day after Thanksgiving
Memorial Day	Christmas Eve
Independence Day	Christmas Day

Any employee who works on one of these holidays will receive pay at two times the normal rate.

Vacation Schedule

Employees will receive paid vacation according to the following schedule:

Length of Service	Vacation time
After 1 year	2 weeks
After 5 years	3 weeks
After 10 years	4 weeks
After 20 years	5 weeks

PAID SICK LEAVE. Another common benefit involving pay for time not worked is paid sick leave. This benefit allows employees to stay at home when they are ill without loss of pay. Given the normal cycle of short-term illnesses such as colds and flu, employees may be expected to be ill for a few days annually. However, this benefit may be abused. For example, some employees are not ill and use the time to conduct personal business. Also, some employees view it as a right and stay at home when they are not ill simply to use their allotted time. This occurs particularly when the policy does not allow employees to accumulate sick leave time. Therefore, many companies have designed their sick leave plan to provide at least partial direct payment to employees who do not use all of their allotted sick leave. This encourages them to stay on the job and only use the sick leave when it is truly needed.

Retirement

One of the major benefit programs provided most employees is a retirement program—because of its substantial cost to the company and its importance to employees. It is also important because the federal government now plays a major role in the regulation and control of retirement programs. Organizations may use one or a variety of plans as a part of their retirement package. These include pension, profit sharing, thrift, and/or stock purchase programs. The most common of these is the pension plan.

ERISA.   The Employee Retirement Income Security Act (ERISA) was enacted by the federal government in 1974. Regardless of the type of retirement program, ERISA mandates several basic provisions, as shown in Table 16-3. These provisions have changed some retirement programs substantially. The law provides benefits to both the employer and employee yet at the same time eliminates several of the inequities that existed with the old rules.[7] However, many employers dislike the reporting requirements and amount of paperwork created by the law.[8]

Pension costs prior to the passage of ERISA were estimated to be 5 to 10 percent of payroll costs. Some have estimated that ERISA may increase the cost to as much as 20 to 30 percent of payroll costs.[9] Therefore, organizations must be efficient in managing their pension plans while maintaining maximum benefits to employees. Regardless of the issues revolving around ERISA, its effects will be felt for years to come.

PENSIONS.   Between 30 million and 35 million people are covered by private pension plans.[10] Millions more (20 million) are covered by government-administered public pensions. These plans have in excess of $160 billion in assets.[11] There are a number of different types of pension plans. For example, some are contributory (employees and employers contribute), and some are noncontributory (employer provides all contributions). The primary distinction in pension plans is defined benefit and defined contribution. A defined benefit plan specifies the benefits that a person will receive based on years of service and earnings. For example, an employee may receive a benefit equal to 2 percent times years of service times the average of the highest three consecutive years' compensation. With the defined contribution plan, the employer

Table 16-3

Major Provisions of ERISA

Eligibility	Eligibility requirements can be no more than one year of service or over 25 years of age, whichever is later. Employee then becomes a participant six months after meeting these requirements or on the first day of the new plan year, whichever occurs first.
Vesting	Employer must provide at least one of the following minimum standards: (1) 100 percent vesting after 10 years of service. (2) 25 percent vesting after five years of service increasing each year to 100 percent after 15 years of service. (3) 50 percent vesting when age and years' service equal 45 (with minimum of five years service) increasing up to 100 percent vesting five years later.
Funding	Employers must annually fund the full cost of current benefits accrued. In addition, initial past service costs must be amortized over not more than 30 years for new plans and 40 years for existing plans.
Fiduciary responsibility	Establishes the "prudent person" rule requiring the trustee to diversify investments and prohibiting several types of transactions. (Investments of more than 10 percent in employer securities real estate leased to the employer or affiliates of the employer are prohibited.)
Portability	When an employee leaves the organization, vested benefits may be transferred tax free to a qualified plan of the new employer or to an individual retirement account (with the consent of employer).
Maximum benefits	The annual retirement benefit cannot exceed the lesser of $75,000 per year or 100 percent of the three consecutive years' highest average compensation. (However, annual adjustments may be made for cost-of-living increases.)
Maximum contributions	The maximum annual addition to profit-sharing, money purchase, or thrift plans by the employer is limited to the lesser of $25,000 or 25 percent of the employee's compensation that year.

Sources: S. Becker, "An Overview of the Pension Reform Act of 1974," *CPA,* 45 (1975), 27–31; D. G. Carlson, "Responding to the Pension Reform Law," *Harvard Business Review,* 52 (1974), 133–144; D. G. Carlson, "What Management Must Do Under the New Pension Reform Law," *Administrative Management,* (1974), 27–30, 32, 36.

makes a contribution equal to a certain percentage of an employee's compensation each year to a retirement fund. These funds are invested and the employee receives the benefit of the funds plus investment earnings upon retirement.

Other Retirement Programs

Other retirement programs include profit sharing and savings or thrift plans. Usually in profit-sharing plans, the company makes a contribution to the plan based on each year's profits. Thus contributions may vary from year to year. Employees then share in these funds upon retirement, based on a formula of years of service and salary level. Thrift plans allow employees to save a portion of their pay, which is usually matched by a company contribution. Upon retirement, the employee may withdraw his or her own contributions and employer contributions, plus investment earnings. Often, these funds are invested in company stock and/or government bonds.

One other program that may be considered a part of an organization's retirement package is an employee stock purchase plan, in which employees are encouraged to buy company stock, with the purchase usually being subsidized by the company. Generally, there are certain rules governing the sale or disposition of the stock. Each of the three additional programs noted have other objectives in addition to the provision of retirement benefits. In each case, there is a desire to provide incentives to help make the organization more effective (especially with profit-sharing and stock purchase plans).

RETIREMENT PATTERNS. The Age Discrimination in Employment Act of 1967 and its more recent amendments have created the possibility for some employees to work past the "normal" retirement age of sixty-five, up to age seventy. These changes have important effects on a number of different fringe benefit programs.[12] However, their largest single impact is on retirement programs. Prior to the passage of these amendments, it was predicted that the changes would have little effect on retirement patterns. This was because early retirement seemed to be the trend. But recent high inflation rates have hurt retirees severely. Their buying power has been reduced substantially so that fewer are retiring early. Based on the new law, many are electing to remain on their jobs after age sixty-five, and others are coming out of retirement. These changing patterns will require the retirement programs to be reworked and thought be given to the effect on other benefit programs (e.g., medical and long-term disability benefits). These changes may mean increasing costs. However, there are no legal requirements for additional pension credits beyond age sixty-five if the employer has only one plan. If supplemental plans are in existence, these employees must be included.[13] A more complete discussion of changing retirement patterns and their effects appears in Chapter 22.

Service Benefits

A number of other benefits may be provided by employers that can be considered service benefits, including discounts on the organization's products or services, physical fitness facilities, recreation programs, and payment for tuition related to employee educational programs. These benefits are primarily service oriented and are designed to maintain the morale and even the health of the employees. The education reimbursement benefit described by Bob Kleven is an example of a service benefit. Service benefits such as these represent cost savings to employees and are important. They also affect employee attitudes and satisfaction with the company and, thus, may be effective investments in human resources.

Cafeteria Plans

The cafeteria approach to benefits allows employees to choose the type and amount of benefits, within constraints, that best fit their own needs and life-styles. For example, a divorced person of fifty-five with grown children may have needs significantly different from those of a younger (age thirty-five) married person with two small children. The younger person may desire higher amounts of term life insurance than the older person who has fewer responsibilities for others.

Cafeteria benefit programs may be administered in a number of different ways. In most cases, organizations offer a core of benefits to all employees. Then, past the core up to some maximum, employees are given a choice in the type and amount of benefits they receive. Generally, the constraints imposed are in the form of a specified dollar cost or value up to a certain percentage of salary (e.g., 10 percent).

The cafeteria plan is not yet common practice in industry. It does offer advantages to employees, but it has not been used widely for several reasons. First, the costs of administering a variable benefit program are much larger than normal because of its complexity. Second, some benefits may cost more if only a few employees select them (fixed costs would then not be spread over a large number of people). A third problem is the Internal Revenue Service. If it concludes that employees effectively control fringe benefit monies, it may decide that they are taxable to the employee. This would severely restrict the value of the benefits.[14]

Some major organizations have adopted the cafeteria plan approach. Among these are TRW, Inc., and American Can Company. American Can first implemented what it called a flexible benefit program as a pilot study for seven hundred salaried employees in its Consumer Towel and Tissue business unit. The purpose was to make the benefit program more responsive to employee needs. In this program, the company provided a core of common basic benefits to all these employees. The difference in value between core benefits and existing plans was broken down into an average per individual and was converted into flexible credit dollars. Employees used these dollars to purchase additional benefits from a wide range of options. The two additional benefits chosen most often were a vision/hearing preventive health care plan (86 percent) and additional long-term disability protection (88 percent). To administer the flexible benefits program, the company developed a computer system that can handle over 10,000 individual benefit programs.[15]

Benefits Overview

The costs of benefits have risen dramatically in the last several years. The sharply rising medical costs have led to major escalation in the cost of medical insurance. ERISA and increasing social security payments have led to higher costs for retirement programs. In addition, organizations have added many new benefits to their benefit packages.

Because of these increasing costs, it is likely that profit-sharing plans may be implemented instead of pension plans when new retirement programs are initiated. These permit varying contributions based on the firm's profits. More organizations are likely to self-insure to reduce benefit costs. Thus more pressure will be placed on personnel administrators to become familiar with insurance administration and tax laws dealing with insurance. In addition, some firms may offer a package of additional benefits that are not subsidized by the company. In these cases, the costs would be borne by the employees if they desire to participate. Also, more organizations are likely to implement the cafeteria benefits approach to obtain maximum appreciation by employees.[16]

If benefits are to be valuable in the future, they must meet several criteria:

1. Benefits must be maintained up to date with the current environment.
2. Benefits must meet employees' needs and be well received by them.
3. The benefit programs must be communicated to employees and they should have a good understanding of those benefits.
4. The benefit programs should provide for an easy transition from employment into retirement without a serious threat to income security.[17]

INCENTIVES

Organizations frequently provide incentives for their employees. These incentives often are monetary and are tied to performance. Thus the purpose is to encourage high levels of performance. Employees can then earn more by increasing performance. Incentives may provide the basic compensation or may provide supplementary compensation. Incentives may be designed for individuals or groups.

You may recall from Chapter 12 that equity in compensation was emphasized as important for employee motivation and performance. Incentive programs, when designed properly, generally provide greater feelings of equity than do other forms of compensation because they are tied directly to individual performance.

Individual Incentives

Individual incentives are rewards based on the performance of each person. There are several different types of individual incentives that may be offered, the most popular being the piece-rate system and bonus.

PIECE RATE.   Many variations of the piece-rate system exist. The basic notion of piece-rate systems remains consistent, however. Piece-rate compensation systems pay individuals a certain amount for each unit produced. For example, a production worker may be paid 25 cents for each buckle stamped out. In addition, some systems allow for a graduated scale of pay per item produced as certain levels of performance are reached. The following is an example:

Buckles per Day	Pay per Unit
1–200	15¢
201–400	20¢
401 and up	30¢

With the schedule shown, a worker who produced 450 buckles in a day would earn 200 × 15¢ + 200 × 20¢ + 50 × 30¢ = $85.00 When a worker is paid a set amount for each piece produced and the amount does not change (e.g., 25 cents per unit), it is called a *straight piece-rate plan*. *A differential piece-rate plan* provides for graduated pay per unit as performance reaches certain levels as shown in the example. Generally, the latter system establishes a standard of performance that the average worker can easily reach. In the case given, the standard may be two hundred units. The higher rates paid for units produced above standard then are to provide incentive for higher production levels.

In general, piece-rate systems are easy to understand. However, complex systems with a variety of rates for a large number of jobs and in which workers are transferred from one job to another regularly may become overly burdensome. Most important, the systems must be designed to be equitable and fair.

Piece-rate systems are not without problems. Administration of these systems often is difficult, and establishment of standards is frequently a problem area. The authors encountered one situation in which a company had such a complex system that mistakes were made in the calculation of employee pay. These mistakes occurred regularly and led to the feeling that the company was trying to cheat employees. In addition, many employees did not fully understand the basis of their pay. The result was high employee turnover (over 100 percent per year). In this case, the piece-rate system was not simple or well understood, and it failed. Also, when pay rates increase (e.g., a general increase mandated by a collective bargaining agreement), implementation becomes difficult. It is also necessary that minimum wages be paid, regardless of the employee's performance level, and this must be provided for in the incentive system. Piece-rate systems are also problematic where there is informal group pressure to restrict output.

BONUS. A bonus is also based on performance but not in the same manner as in the piece-rate system. In these instances, a base wage or salary is paid, but when performance exceeds certain predetermined levels, a bonus is earned. Usually, bonuses are earned only if performance is quite high. These types of individual bonuses are found quite often in sales poisitions and, in some cases, in executive management positions. However, most executive bonus plans are based on group performance and are thus discussed in the group incentives section. An example of a bonus is a trip to Hawaii awarded to sales representatives who sell a large number of their company's products. The reward also may be provided in extra dollars rather than in prizes (e.g., $1,000 bonus for selling fifty new automobiles in one month).

CONTINUOUS VERSUS VARIABLE PAY SCHEDULES. With the desire to design a monetary incentive plan that will increase employee productivity, much research has been undertaken. Currently, research is focusing on continuous and variable incentive pay systems. The continuous system is similar to the straight piece-rate system in which the employee receives a fixed amount per unit produced. The variable system allows the amount per unit produced to be higher than the continuous schedule but the timing of the payment varies.

For example, workers planting trees on a continuous incentive pay schedule may receive a $2 bonus for every 1,000 trees planted. Workers on a variable schedule would receive an $8 bonus when 1,000 trees are planted some times and other times would receive no bonus. The basis for the variable incentive pay model is the work of B. F. Skinner on operant conditioning.[18] This work suggests that the desired behavior will occur more often when reinforced on a variable schedule.

The research results are not conclusive. The results show that in some cases the continuous schedule produced the highest productivity, whereas in others the highest productivity was found with the variable schedule. The research does suggest that individual differences should be taken into account in developing pay systems. For example, employees with more education and those in a higher economic class seemed to prefer the variable schedule; employees with less education and those in a lower economic class preferred the continuous schedule.[19] In addition, inexperienced workers were found to perform better under a continuous schedule while experienced workers performed better under a variable schedule.[20]

IMPLEMENTING INDIVIDUAL INCENTIVES. Several problems with individual incentive programs should be recognized. First, individual productivity must be identified clearly and measured precisely. If this cannot be done, individual incentives will be of little use. Second, the pay system must be kept current with rates of inflation and competition. This is necessary for all pay systems, but it may be overlooked more easily with incentive systems. Third, employees must trust management and the organization. Without trust, incentive systems may produce more negative results as in the example discussed earlier where annual turnover exceeded 100 percent. In some cases employees have become dissatisfied with incentive systems because they perceived that management may have lowered the set rate for each piece produced. Incentive standards must take into account the fact that a certain amount of learning will take place and that if the standard is too "easy" it will be difficult to lower the rate for each piece produced.

Group Incentives

Group incentives have some of the same advantages and disadvantages as individual systems, but they are designed to achieve larger productivity goals. Their major advantage over individual incentive plans is promotion of cooperation among group members to achieve the performance goals. Among group incentive plans are the Scanlon Plan, executive incentive compensation, and stock options. In some manner, each of these may be considered a profit-sharing plan.

SCANLON PLAN. Under the Scanlon Plan, the group incentive is provided on a plantwide basis. The Scanlon Plan consists of two parts: a plantwide wage incentive and a unique form of suggestion system. The wage incentive is based on a calculation of a labor cost norm. As efficiency increases and/or productivity increases so that the cost per unit is reduced, the increased profit is shared by the company and the employees by mutual agreement on a predetermined basis.

The second part of the program consists of suggestion committees established to evaluate employee suggestions for improvements. There are two levels of committees: departmental and plant. The departmental committees review all proposals for changes within the department. Generally, the departmental committee consists of one employee and the department supervisor. The plant committee usually consists of several management personnel and several employees or union representatives. The departmental committee can approve and implement suggestions for departmental improvement. The plant screening committee considers those suggestions involving larger areas or large expenditures of funds. The savings from these suggestions are passed on to employees in some manner such as a plantwide bonus. Individual employees who make suggestions that are adopted usually receive an award based on a percentage of the calculated cost savings.[21]

EXECUTIVE INCENTIVE COMPENSATION.   Incentive compensation has become a popular form of compensation for executives in recent years. Frequently, top executives receive a reasonable and competitive base salary, but a majority of their compensation comes from incentive compensation. This incentive compensation is tied to the results of the company or the major unit (profit center) they are managing. These plans vary from quite sophisticated and complex to simple. Results may be measured by a complex or simple financial formula. For example, results measurement may vary from being based on residual return on assets to being based on simple net profit figures. The incentives or awards may be cash, stock, or a combination of cash and stock. In addition, the award may be paid in full each year that it is earned, or part of it may be deferred and spread over a few years. In some cases, the awards are deferred until retirement for tax purposes. Often, the awards are based on percentages of base salary, that vary from 10 percent to 80 or 90 percent. Some firms provide no more than 50 percent of base salary in incentive compensation.

These plans are usually reserved for top executives only, though some plans include middle-level managers, such as the one in use by Samsonite Corporation. Woodward Governor's plan is even more progressive, including all subordinates as well as managers and executives. This plan supports the company's "corporate partnership" philosophy and is a major factor in the high quality of Woodward's products.

When lower-level managers are included, the amount of award is generally constrained by level in the company. For example, let us say that a 50 percent award performance level were attained. Top executives in this case would receive a bonus of 50 percent of their salary. However, those in middle management may receive lesser amounts, because they have a lesser impact on results. These may be calculated on some sliding scale based on salary grade level as follows:

Salary Grade	Participation in Awards
15	10%
16	25
17	40
18	55
19	70
20	85
20 plus	100

A person in salary grade 17 making $35,000 salary per year would receive a (40% × 50% × $35,000) $7,000 bonus. A top executive (above salary grade 20) making $100,000 salary per year would receive a (100% × 50% × $100,000) $50,000 bonus.

It should be noted that executive incentive compensation is visible and frequently noted in special reports to stockholders; it comes under the close scrutiny of the Internal Revenue Service.

STOCK OPTIONS. As noted, executive incentive awards may be paid in the form of stock. The purpose is to have managers own part of the company, providing further incentive to perform well. Stock options have a similar purpose. Stock options are issued to executives based on company performance with a set price. The executive may exercise that option at a later date, for example, when the price of the stock in the stock market is above the option price. However, the option will likely not be exercised when the option price is above the price of the stock on the open market.

Stock options were designed to provide increased income without increasing taxable income. However, the tax advantages of stock options have been virtually eliminated, thus substantially decreasing their use in recent years.

Incentives Overview

Monetary incentives are not the only incentives that managers can use, and some feel that they are less effective than others. This is particularly true for the professional employee. Research on two separate groups of professional employees found financial incentives to be one of the weakest motivators.[22] In addition, incentive plans must be fair and be perceived as equitable by those who are participating. If the plan is perceived as inequitable, it may have a negative impact on performance.[23] To serve a motivational purpose, incentive programs for managers should be considered as additional compensation for exceeding what is recognized as good performance. In addition, at least some part of the incentive should be tied to overall corporate performance to encourage cooperation between the various units to achieve overall organizational goals.

Thus we may conclude that an effective incentive compensation plan should have the following characteristics:

1. Incentives should be tied directly to distinct and measurable performance.
2. The program should be fair and equitable.
3. The program should be well understood by all participants.
4. Individual differences should be taken into account to maximize the motivational properties of the incentives.
5. A climate of trust should exist between management and employees.
6. The incentive plan should have part of the incentive rewards tied to overall organizational performance to encourage cooperation among the several organizational units.

SUMMARY

Fringe benefits are a major part of an employee's total compensation package. However, fringe benefits have not always been as important as they are now. Benefit programs were extremely rare until after the Depression and World War II years. People became concerned about personal and financial security, and pressure was placed on organizations to reduce employees' financial risk. Much of this pressure came from labor unions. Organizations could provide tax-free services, could negotiate from a stronger position than could individuals, and could provide group plans that could lower the overall cost per individual.

There are several legally required benefits. Among these are social security, unemployment insurance, and workers' compensation. The social security system was set up to provide basic retirement income and looms as a large cost to both employers and employees today. All states have some form of unemployment insurance. It is designed to provide income while individuals search for a new job. Workers' compensation laws are designed to provide cash benefits for injuries sustained on the job.

Most other benefits are voluntary. There are several types of insurance benefits. These include medical, life, accident and disability, vision care, dental, and drug insurance programs. The most important of these are medical and life insurance. Medical insurance usually includes hospital, doctor's surgical fees, and major medical coverage. Some organizations have implemented a health maintenance organization that provides comprehensive health care for a basic fee each year. It emphasizes preventative as well as corrective health care. Most life insurance programs provide term life insurance coverage based on some multiple of annual salary (e.g., two times).

Payment for time not worked is another important group of benefits. The most common of these are vacations and holidays. Generally, the length of vacation time provided varies with the length of employee service. Holidays are provided to all employees regardless of length of service. Other payments for time not worked include supplemental unemployment benefits (SUBs) and paid sick leave.

Retirement programs represent a major employee benefit. Retirement programs may be composed of one or a combination of pension, profit sharing, thrift, and stock purchase plans. Retirement programs are regulated closely. The Employee Retirement

Income Security Act (ERISA) places a number of constraints on the provisions of retirement programs. Pension plans are the most common form of retirement benefits. Pension plans may be contributory and noncontributory. Some are defined benefit plans (person receives a specified benefit), and some are defined contribution plans (employer makes specified contributions for each employee each year).

Based on current retirement patterns, employees are working longer. The early retirement trend of the past several years is reversing. This is due to high inflation rates and a change in the law making mandatory retirement illegal before age seventy.

Service benefits such as discounts on company products and services, recreational programs, and physical fitness facilities are valued by employees.

Some organizations have adopted a cafeteria plan benefits approach, in which a core of basic benefits is provided to employees who are then allowed to choose from among various benefits that meet their needs, up to some dollar cost maximum per employee. Although employees like this approach, it can be costly and difficult to administer.

Organizations frequently provide some form of individual and/or group incentives to employees. Among the individual incentive programs are piece-rate systems and bonuses. Piece-rate systems pay a specified amount for each unit produced. These systems may be simple or complex. However, they must be well understood by employees if they are to be effective. Bonuses may also be based on individual performance and are usually provided for high levels of performance. Bonuses are frequently found in sales representative jobs.

Research has been conducted to determine if a continuous (fixed amount of pay per unit produced) or a variable (generally higher amounts of pay but vary in the number of units produced in order to receive the incentive) pay schedule is better. The findings are that those with lower income and who are inexperienced desire continuous schedules. Those with higher levels of income and more experience prefer variable schedules.

Group incentive plans include the Scanlon Plan, executive incentive compensation plans, and stock option plans. The Scanlon Plan generally includes a plantwide incentive and suggestion system. Plantwide savings through increased productivity are shared between employer and employees. Executive incentive compensation programs are often limited to top executives. These programs provide for incentive awards, frequently a percentage of salary, based on attainment of predetermined profit-related goals. Sometimes these plans include middle-management personnel as well. Stock options had been a popular incentive but are used less often now because Congress removed the tax advantages.

INTERVIEW WRAP-UP

Something that made a lasting impression on me was a sign on my first sergeant's desk which read, "take care of your people and your people will take care of you." I think this means caring, responding, being involved, and assuring that employee needs are met in all areas. Fringe benefits and incentives are two ingredients that help meet those needs. —Bob Kleven, personnel manager, Woodward Governor Company, Engine & Turbine Controls Division, Fort Collins, Colorado.

WHAT MANAGERS SHOULD DO REGARDING PERSONNEL MANAGEMENT ACTIVITIES

1. Managers should have a good understanding of the organization's complete benefit program and ensure that employees do as well.

2. Managers should try to develop employee appreciation for the benefit program as a part of the total compensation package.

3. Managers play a key role in the implementation phase of any program. Thus the success or failure of an incentive program may hinge on effective implementation. Managers should work to ensure proper implementation of these programs.

REVIEW QUESTIONS

1. Why are benefits important to such employees as those at Woodward Governor?

2. What are the legally required benefits and why are they required?

3. What are some of the most common insurance and payment for time-not-worked benefits?

4. Why is a retirement program considered a major employee benefit?

5. What are the basic provisions of ERISA?

6. What is the basic concept behind cafeteria plan benefits and how does it operate?

7. How are piece-rate and individual bonus systems used?

8. What are two common group incentive programs and how do they operate?

KEY CONCEPTS

Accident and disability insurance	Profit sharing
Benefits	Scanlon Plan
Bonus	Social security
Continuous pay schedules	Stock options
Executive incentive compensation	Stock purchase plans
Holidays	Supplemental unemployment benefits
Life insurance	Thrift plans
Medical insurance	Unemployment insurance

Paid sick leave
Pensions
Piece-rate plans

Vacations
Variable pay schedules
Workers' compensation

CASE

THE THREE EXECUTIVES

Benjamin Carter: Age sixty-four, vice-president of marketing, married, three grown children.

Kathryn Waters: Age forty-two, director of cost accounting, married, two children in college.

Randall Lowe: Age thirty-two, manager of quality control, single.

Ben, Kathy, and Randy are all managers for X-Ray Equipment, Inc. The company is large, and thus they barely know each other. However, they occasionally run into each other at lunch and at social events. This evening they happened to be at a party given by a mutual friend, Sue Keating, the corporate personnel director.

Ben, Kathy, and Randy were all gathered near the fireplace, discussing business and personal philosophies.

Ben stated, "Boy, I'm not looking forward to retirement. I just don't know what I will do with myself. I've put most of my efforts into my job instead of outside interests."

"Well, why retire? The law eliminated forced retirement until age seventy. You have several years left," Kathy responded.

"I know, but I'm tired of putting in so many hours at work. I would like to slow down some."

Randy half jokingly said, "Well, maybe you should step down. If more of you old geezers would do it, it would give more room for Kathy and me to move up.

Everyone quieted down with that remark. Finally, Ben broke the ice, "There's another problem with retirement. I'm afraid my life-style will suffer if I'm forced to live off income from our pension plan. With inflation so high these days, our pension income may be worthless just a few years after retirement."

Kathy suggested, "Ben, you are exaggerating some, but I understand. Perhaps we need to upgrade our retirement benefits and build cost-of-living increases into the program."

"Well, I think we would be wasting the company's money, frankly," Randy interjected. He continued, "I plan to build my own nest egg; plus, I plan to be a top executive and have a very comfortable income."

Ben noted, "That's all easier said than done. You can't always just build that nest egg. Your desires tend to increase as your income increases, and it's hard to put money away in savings."

"Well, I think that the company should take care of employees while they are working but not after they quit," Randy continued. "I'm more interested in time off. I'd like more three-day weekends so I can work on my tennis game and spend more time with Jane and Sheila and . . .".

Kathy interrupted, "You're being awfully self-centered. I'd like more time off, too, but not at the expense of our retirees. I'm more concerned with why the company doesn't allow anyone but top executives to participate in their incentive compensation program. I know I would be more motivated if I thought I might get a nice bonus at the end of the year."

About this time Sue came in. Everyone converged on her asking why the company didn't have better benefit programs.

Poor Sue. She wasn't sure what hit her.

CASE QUESTIONS

1. Why do each of these people seem concerned with different benefit or incentive programs?

2. Do you agree with Randy's philosophy on benefits? Why or why not?

3. Would a cafeteria plan benefit program be helpful here? Why or why not? Do you see any potential hazards with a cafeteria plan approach if implemented here? Describe.

NOTES

[1] R. Schulz, "Benefit Trends," *The Personnel Administrator,* 22 (1977), 18–20, 35.

[2] W. B. Werther, Jr., "Implementing Flexible Fringe Benefits Through Variable Incentive Plans," *CLU Journal,* 33 (1979), 37–43.

[3] R. L. Greenman and E. J. Schmertz, *Personnel Administration and the Law* (Washington, D.C.: Bureau of National Affairs, 1979), p. 188.

[4] *Employee Health and Welfare Benefits,* Personnel Policies Forum Survey #107 (Washington, D.C.: Bureau of National Affairs, 1974).

[5] G. E. Rejda, *Social Insurance and Economic Security* (Englewood Cliffs, N.J.: Prentice-Hall, 1976).

[6] P. Snider, "Health Maintenance Organizations—A Can of Worms?" *Personnel,* 51 (1974), 36–44.

[7] S. Becker, "An Overview of the Pension Reform Act of 1974," *CPA,* 45 (1975), 27–31.

[8] "What Management Must Do Under the New Pension Reform Law," *Administrative Management,* 35 (1974), 27–30, 32, 36.

[9] D. G. Carlson, "Responding to the Pension Reform Law," *Harvard Business Review,* 52 (1974), 133–144.

[10] *Employee Health and Welfare Benefits.*

[11] H. A. Williams, Jr., "Development of the New Pension Reform Laws," *Labor Law Journal,* 26 (1975), 135–138.

[12]D. H. Gravits and H. Von Wodtke, "Benefits for Employees over 65: What Are the New Rules?" *Risk Management,* 26 (1979), 41–58.

[13]R. M. Yaffe, "Changing Retirement Patterns: Their Effect on Employee Benefits," *The Personnel Administrator,* 24 (1979), 29–33.

[14]Werther, "Implementing Flexible Fringe Benefits."

[15]D. Rhodes, "What Employees Choose When Benefits Are Flexible" *Management Review,* 67 (1978), 41–42.

[16]R. Schulz, "Benefit Trends," *The Personnel Administrator,* 22 (1977), 18–20, 35.

[17]C. E. Beadle, "Revitalizing Employee Benefits Programs," *Risk Management,* 26 (1979), 63–64, 66, 68.

[18]B. F. Skinner, "Operant Behavior," in *Operant Behavior: Areas of Research and Application,* ed. W. K. Honig (New York: Appleton-Century-Crofts, 1966), pp. 12–32.

[19]G. A. Yukl, G. P. Latham, and E. D. Pursell, "The Effectiveness of Performance Incentives Under Continuous and Variable Ratio Schedules of Reinforcement," *Personnel Psychology,* 29 (1976), 221–231.

[20]G. P. Latham and D. L. Dossett, "Designing Incentive Plans for Unionized Employees: A Comparison of Continuous and Variable Ratio Reinforcement Schedules," *Personnel Psychology,* 31 (1978), 47–61.

[21]F. G. Lesieur and E. Pluckett, "The Scanlon Plan Has Proved Itself," *Harvard Business Review,* 47 (1969), 110–118.

[22]D. S. Pathak, G. E. Burton, and R. M. Zigli, "A Comparative Study of Work Incentives for Professional Employees," *University of Michigan Business Review,* 29 (1977), 27–32.

[23]H. F. Floyd, "Profit Center Incentives: Stimulants or Depressants," *Management Review,* 68 (1979), 50–52.

MAINTAINING AN EFFECTIVE WORK FORCE

A work force must be maintained beyond the time that employees are hired and trained. Many issues emerge during this period and require the attention of managers and organizations. We have chosen to present these issues at this point because of their impact on the long-term relationships among organizations, jobs, and people. However, we must recognize that these issues are important during initial job design activities and may continue to affect employees into their retirement. The four broad issues concern some of the most emotional that arise in modern organizations: equal employment opportunity, labor relations, occupational safety and health, and employee discipline.

In Chapter 17, we examine the complex legal and emotional issues of equal employment opportunities. These issues arise first during job design activities and have important impacts on selection processes. They also affect career development and employee growth. Another group of emotional issues involves labor relations and collective bargaining. The emphasis in Chapter 18 is that managers and union members must, and can, work together to achieve effective relationships. Chapter 19 presents an overview of occupational safety and health. Historical and legal bases of occupational safety and health are reviewed; then fundamental techniques for implementing safe and healthy work environments are suggested.

Finally, Chapter 20 reviews the use of discipline in organizations. Our view is that disciplinary actions may be minimized by the correct application of personnel management practices (presented throughout the text). However, when discipline becomes necessary, the establishment of fair work rules will lead to a positive approach consistent with both the organization's and the employee's needs. Effective managerial applications of the concepts presented in this section will help to maintain employee satisfaction and productivity throughout the long-term relationship between organizations and employees and will have many implications.

EQUAL EMPLOYMENT OPPORTUNITY

LEARNING OBJECTIVES

After reading this chapter, you should be able to:

1. Describe the provisions of the various laws that provide for equal employment opportunity.
2. Discuss the steps that are recommended by the EEOC for implementation of affirmative action programs.
3. Explain how to facilitate the assimilation of minorities in an organization where they have been previously underutilized.
4. Understand how personnel selection should be conducted according to the Uniform Guidelines on Employee Selection Procedures.
5. Discuss strategies for affirmative action compliance.
6. Explain how to minimize the potential for a backlash response to the implementation of an affirmative action program.
7. Describe the enforcement powers of the Equal Employment Opportunity Commission and the Office of Federal Contract Compliance Programs.

R. J. Christensen is the Corporate Manager—Human Resource Information for the Thomas and Betts Corporation. Rick has been with Thomas and Betts for about five years. The first four years he was the Employee Relations Manager at one of their newest facilities located in Tulsa, Oklahoma. He recently assumed his current position as Manager—Human Resource Information which includes responsibility for Affirmative Action on a Corporate-wide basis. He spent one-and-one half years as a manufacturing supervisor prior to moving to personnel/labor relations work. He has a total of eight years experience in personnel and holds a Bachelor of Science degree in business administration. The company has been highly successful with both U.S. and international operations. Thomas and Betts manufactures products for such markets as electronics and communications, electro-mechanical, industrial, and commercial construction and maintenance. The products include electrical and electronic terminals and connectors, flat cable and connectors, and related products.

Thomas and Betts is an equal employment opportunity employer. It has a corporate-wide affirmative action philosophy in which it strives to recruit, hire, train, and promote persons at all job levels without regard to race, color, religion, age, sex, or national origin. As such, Rick answered questions regarding more specifics of how organizations can provide equal employment opportunities.

Interviewer: What kinds of programs does your company have to insure equal employment opportunity?

Richard Christensen: My company has a significant corporate-wide affirmative action philosophy with each separate organizational unit having an Affirmative Action Program. There are a number of programs which help insure equal opportunity for all. My company presently has a tuition reimbursement program for job-related educational programs at most of its facilities. This program is available to those employees regardless of job level.

Thomas and Betts is in the process of developing a comprehensive Human Resources Development and Career Counseling Program for all employees. For example, a machine operator would receive formal counseling on the type of training needed to progress to toolmaker. Each facility has a job posting procedure whereby all employees may apply to be considered for any job vacancy occurring in the facility. Finally, recruiters work closely with the State Employment Service in each state and with minority agencies and groups to obtain qualified minorities for employees. These are only a part of the process used to insure equal opportunity at Thomas and Betts.

Interviewer: What do you feel are characteristics of effective affirmative action programs?

Richard Christensen: There are two key characteristics of effective affirmative action programs—good communication and availability of personnel information. Communications are important both within and outside the company. Managers must be aware of the affirmative action program and what it means. The company must communicate to the community that it is an equal employment opportunity employer to be successful.

Secondly, the company must have a good personnel information system for monitoring and to have appropriate information (i.e., job history, career goals) for considering all qualified employees for position vacancies. Special emphasis must be given to identification of qualified minority and female candidates.

Interviewer: Does equal employment opportunity require a lot of effort and time?

Richard Christensen: I spend a significant amount of time on EEO activities. My time is spent predominantly in proactive rather than reactive activities, however. My ability to spend time this way is due to the company's emphasis on its employee relations and a good affirmative action program. If a company is well managed, it will have good employee relations, which should lead to high productivity, low turnover, and equal opportunity for all potential and current employees.

Interviewer: Where do you look for hiring most of your personnel, the local or national market?

Richard Christensen: For plant and clerical personnel, hiring is accomplished in the local market. Professional and management personnel are usually hired from the national market.

INTRODUCTION

Equal employment opportunity (EEO) has emerged since the passage of the Civil Rights Act of 1964 as the law of the land as well as a policy that is perceived widely as a standard of social responsibility. Although there are sometimes disagreements over the means of providing EEO, there is little controversy over its underlying objectives.

The legislation and regulations that have been adopted to provide for EEO were discussed first in Chapter 7, on the selection of employees. EEO is required by several federal laws and executive orders as well as by similar state and local laws and regulations.[1] Because of space limitations, only the federal laws and regulations are discussed in this chapter.

Legal Requirements for Equal Employment Opportunity

As indicated in Chapter 7, EEO was adopted as public policy when the Civil Rights Act of 1964 went into effect in 1965. Other federal laws have some provisions related to EEO. These include the Equal Employment Opportunity Act of 1972 (which amended the Civil Rights Act of 1964), the Age Discrimination in Employment Act of 1967 (as amended in 1978), the Equal Pay Act of 1963, the Rehabilitation Act of 1973, and the Vietnam Era Veterans' Readjustment Assistance Act of 1974.[2]

In addition, there are executive orders having EEO provisions that apply to federal government contractors and subcontractors. These are E.O. 11246, which was issued in 1965 and amended by E.O. 11375 in 1967 and E.O. 12086 in 1978. Affirmative action programs (AAPs) are required of contractors and subcontractors coming under the jurisdiction of these executive orders.[3] Table 17-1 lists these executive orders along

Table 17-1

Federal Laws and Regulations Pertaining to Equal Employment
Opportunity and Affirmative Action

Civil Rights Act of 1964, as amended by the Equal Employment Act of 1972
Equal Employment Opportunity Act of 1972
Age Discrimination in Employment Act of 1967, as amended in 1978
Equal Pay Act of 1963
Rehabilitation Act of 1973
Vietnam Era Veterans' Readjustment Assistance Act of 1974
Executive Order 11246 (1965) as amended by Executive Order 11375 (1967)
    and Executive Order 12086 (1978)

with the federal laws that pertain to equal employment opportunity and affirmative action.

Title VII of the Civil Rights Act of 1964 (as amended by the Equal Employment Opportunity Act of 1972), which prevents discrimination in employment, applies to private sector employers having at least fifteen employees. That level of employment must be maintained for each day of work for at least twenty weeks in the year. Unions, employment agencies, educational institutions, and state and local governments are also covered by the act. Employers covered by the Age Discrimination in Employment Act of 1967 (as amended in 1978) include private sector employers having at least twenty employees (for each day of work for at least twenty weeks), employment agencies, and unions. The coverage for the Equal Pay Act of 1963 is the same as that for the Fair Labor Standards Act. Those employees engaged in interstate commerce or those producing goods for interstate commerce come under the act under "individual" coverage. "Enterprise" coverage by the act is obtained when an employer has at least two employees involved in interstate commerce or is producing goods for interstate commerce and has $250,000 in annual gross volume, although there are several exceptions. Federal contractors whose contracts are in excess of $2,500 are covered by the Rehabilitation Act of 1973, whereas federal contractors whose contracts are in excess of $1,000 are covered by the Vietnam Era Veterans' Readjustment Assistance Act of 1974. Finally, Executive Order 11246 (as amended) applies to contractors having contracts in excess of $10,000. [4] The major provisions of these laws and regulations appear in Table 17-2.

These laws and regulations prevent employment discrimination of a variety of types, namely, those based on race, color, religion, sex, national origin, and age (forty to seventy), as well as discrimination against qualified handicapped individuals, qualified disabled veterans, and Vietnam era veterans. Despite these prohibitions, as noted in Chapter 7, there are exceptions. These exceptions are called bona fide occupational qualifications (BFOQs). No BFOQ exceptions apply to race or color; however, BFOQs do apply to age, sex, religion, and national origin. [5] These BFOQs are very specific and apply to only a few very narrowly defined situations. Thus managers should be acutely aware that BFOQs do not allow one to hire on the basis of sex, age, and so on except in rare instances.

Enforcement of Equal Employment Opportunity

As with some other forms of social legislation, such as the Occupational Safety and Health Act and the National Labor Relations Act, which have administrative agencies, the Civil Rights Act of 1964 is administered by the Equal Employment Opportunity Commission (EEOC). In enforcing the act after discrimination charges have been filed, the EEOC can attempt to settle the issue on an informal basis in preliminary meetings or through conciliation, after the EEOC finds cause to believe that the charge of discrimination is valid. [6] Consent decrees have also been used by the EEOC to enforce the act. They are more powerful enforcement tools in that they are enforced by the federal courts. Conciliation agreements are not court action, they are simply agreements between the government and employers.[7] A consent decree that mandated many sweeping selection and promotion practices was utilized in the American Telephone & Telegraph case that is discussed later.

One of the early difficulties faced by the EEOC during the initial period after passage of the Civil Rights Act of 1964 was that it had to rely on voluntary measures to secure compliance. The lack of EEOC power was remedied when the Equal Employment Opportunity Act of 1972 gave it the ability to take its cases to the court system through direct procedures.[8] The remedies for EEO violations that the courts have imposed on employers have included requirements for back pay and adoption of affirmative action programs.[9] Some of the detailed requirements have included the following:

> Courts have required fundamental changes in all aspects of employment systems and they have specified numbers or percentages of minorities and females to be hired, trained, or promoted in specific job categories, until certain goals are reached. They usually require an employer to undertake such action quickly, with follow-up monitoring by the court.[10]

In contrast to the EEOC, the Office of Federal Contract Compliance Programs (OFCCP), the organization charged with the enforcement of federal contracts, has always had a great deal of power to enforce the EEO requirements. The OFCCP has the power to bar employers who discriminate in employment from further contacts with the government and to terminate contracts.[11] Furthermore, employees coming under OFCCP coverage are also required to adopt affirmative action programs, the subject of the next section.

AFFIRMATIVE ACTION

Most of us know a little about affirmative action.

> **Affirmative action:** specific personnel steps—in recruiting, hiring, upgrading, and other areas—which are taken for the purpose of eliminating the present effects of past discrimination.[12]

Not all employers are required to implement affirmative action programs or to file written affirmative action plans. Those employers who are found to have violated EEO laws and regulations may be required to implement affirmative action programs. As indicated earlier, federal contractors (and subcontractors) having contracts of a specified dollar amount (see Table 17-2) must implement affirmative action programs. Those having contracts of at least $50,000 and at least fifty employees must put their affirmative action programs in writing. Thus most large employers are required to have affirmative action programs. As Richard Christensen explained, the Thomas and Betts Corporation has an affirmative action program that enables it to carry out the requirements of the laws and to implement its social responsiveness objectives.

Table 17-2

Partial Texts of Major Equal Employment Opportunity and Affirmative Action Laws and Regulations

---

Civil Rights Act of 1964, as amended by the Equal Employment Opportunity Act of 1972

Sec. 703(a)   It shall be an unlawful employment practice for an employer (1) to fail or refuse to hire or to discharge any individual, or otherwise to discriminate against any individual with respect to his compensation, terms, conditions, or privileges of employment, because of such individual's race, color, religion, sex, or national origin; or (2) to limit, segregate, or classify his employees or applicants for employment in any way which would deprive or tend to deprive any individual of employment opportunities or otherwise adversely affect his status as an employee, because of such individual's race, color, religion, sex, or national origin.

Age Discrimination in Employment Act of 1967, as amended in 1978

Sec. 4(a)   It shall be unlawful for an employer (1) to fail or refuse to hire or to discharge any individual or otherwise discriminate against any individual with respect to his compensation, terms, conditions, or privileges of employment, because of such an individual's age.

Sec. 12(a)   The prohibitions in this Act shall be limited to individuals who are at least 40 years of age but less than 70 years of age.

Equal Pay Act of 1963

Sec. 3(d)(1)   No employer having employees subject to any provisions of this section shall discriminate, within any establishment in which such employees are employed, between employees on the basis of sex by paying wages to employees in such establishment at a rate less than the rate at which he pays wages to employees of the opposite sex in such establishment for equal work on jobs the performance of which requires equal skill, effort, and responsibility, and which are performed under similar working conditions, except where such payment is made pursuant to (i) a seniority system; (ii) a merit system; (iii) a system which measures earnings by quantity or quality of production; or (iv) a differential based on any other factor other than sex . . .

Rehabilitation Act of 1973

Sec. 503(a)   Any contract in excess of $2,500 entered into by any federal department or agency for the procurement of personal property and non-personal services (including construction) for the United States shall contain a provision requiring that, in employing persons to carry out such contract the party contracting with the United States shall take affirmative action to employ and advance in employment qualified handicapped individuals . . .

Vietnam Era Veterans' Readjustment Assistance Act of 1974

Sec. 2012(a)   Any contract in the amount of $10,000 or more entered into by any department or agency for the procurement of personal property and non-personal services (including construction) for the United States, shall contain a provision requiring that the party contracting with the United States shall take affirmative action to employ and advance in employment qualified special disabled veterans and veterans of the Vietnam era.

Table 17-2 (*Continued*)

Executive Order 11246 (1965), as amended by Executive Order 11375 (1967) and Executive Order 12086 (1978)

Sec. 202(1)   The contractor will not discriminate against any employee or applicant for employment because of race, color, religion, sex, or nation origin. The contractor will take affirmative action to ensure that applicants are employed, and that employees are treated during employment, without regard to their race, color, religion, sex, or national origin.

The Office of Federal Contract Compliance Programs has defined, in Revised Order Number 4, affirmative action programs as follows:

> An affirmative action program is a set of specific and result-oriented procedures to which a contractor commits himself to apply every good faith effort. The objective of those procedures plus such efforts is equal employment opportunity. Procedures without effort to make them work are meaningless; and effort, undirected by specific and meaningful procedures, is inadequate. An acceptable affirmative action program must include an analysis of areas within which the contractor is deficient in the utilization of minority groups and women, and further, goals and timetables to which the contractor's good faith efforts must be directed to correct the deficiencies and, thus, to increase materially the utilization of minorities and women, at all levels and in all segments of his work force where deficiencies exist.[13]

Developing an Affirmative Action Program

Several steps should be followed in implementing an affirmative action program. Our interview with Richard Christensen revealed that Thomas and Betts has many activities that are directed toward implementing its affirmative action program. Steps involved in developing an affirmative action program are presented in Table 17-3.

The EEOC has provided some practical guidance on how to carry out each of these steps in its publication *Affirmative Action and Equal Employment: A Guidebook for Employers.* We have drawn on some of the EEOC's suggestions to expand on some of the steps contained in Table 17-3.

POLICY, COMMITMENT, AND PROGRAM MANAGEMENT.   Implementation of an EEO policy and an affirmative action program should be accompanied by, among other things, a statement from the chief executive that he or she is personally supporting the program. The statement of policy should inform the organization's members that EEO will apply to all aspects of employment. Further, it should state that the program will go beyond simple neutrality and set goals to increase the representation of groups that have incurred discrimination. The level of the organization's commitment to the affirmative action program is communicated by the ability and stature of the individual placed in charge. Thus a capable executive of a relatively high position should be given responsibility for the program on a full-time basis. Such an individual should be attuned to the subtle manners in which discrimination can enter into the

Table 17-3

Steps in Affirmative Action Program Development Recommended by the Equal Employment Opportunity Commission

A. Issue written equal employment policy and affirmative action commitment.

B. Appoint a top official with responsibility and authority to direct and implement your program.
   1. Specify responsibilities of program manager.
   2. Specify responsibilities and accountability of all managers and supervisors.

C. Publicize your policy and affirmative action commitment.
   1. Internally: to managers, supervisors, all employees and unions.
   2. Externally: to sources and potential sources of recruitment, potential minority and female applicants, to those with whom you do business, and to the community at large.

D. Survey present minority and female employment by department and job classification.
   1. Identify present areas and levels of employment.
   2. Identify areas of concentration and underutilization.
   3. Determine extent of underutilization.

E. Develop goals and timetables to improve utilization of minorities, males, and females in each area where underutilization has been identified.

F. Develop and implement specific programs to achieve goals.
   This is the heart of your program. Review your entire employment system to identify barriers to equal employment opportunity; make needed changes to increase employment and advancement opportunities of minorities and females. These areas need review and action:
   1. Recruitment: all personnel procedures.
   2. Selection process: job requirements; job descriptions, standards, and procedures; pre-employment inquiries; application forms; testing; interviewing.
   3. Upward mobility system: assignments, job progressions, transfers, seniority, promotions, training.
   4. Wage and salary structure.
   5. Benefits and conditions of employment.
   6. Layoff, recall, termination, demotion, discharge, disciplinary action.
   7. Union contract provisions affecting above procedures.

G. Establish internal audit and reporting system to monitor and evaluate progress in each aspect of the program.

H. Develop supportive in-house and community programs.

Source: E. M. Idelson, U.S. Equal Employment Opportunity Commission, *Affirmative Action and Equal Employment: A Guidebook for Employers* Vol. 1 (Washington, D.C.: Government Printing Office, 1974), pp. 16–17. References to explanations of some terms are deleted.

employment situation.[14] Richard Christensen serves in such an important position at Thomas and Betts. His company's commitment to affirmative action has been emphasized by his appointment and its special support programs.

PUBLICITY.   Several means of publicizing the organization's program should be utilized. Better compliance with the program may be obtained if managers are aware that performance in this area will affect their overall performance evaluations and rewards. Employees may be informed of the program through company papers, orientation programs, posters, handbooks, and meetings. The program should be publicized outside the organization through contacts with sources of minority and female job applicants, in job advertising, through recruiting correspondence, and through correspondence with those companies that do business with the organization.[15] Our interview with Richard Christensen of Thomas and Betts reinforced the importance of both internal and external communications.

SURVEY AND ANALYSIS OF EMPLOYMENT.   There are specific requirements for the analysis of the present work force that must be followed in determining the representation of minorities and females in the different job classifications. Whenever the proportion of minorities and females in the various jobs is lower than the proportion of such individuals in the applicable labor market, there is underutilization. Conversely, such persons may be overrepresented or concentrated in lower-paying jobs. Either of these conditions may be an indication of discrimination.[16]

Although the details of a labor market analysis are beyond the scope of our discussion, the major considerations can be summarized briefly. For the applicable labor market, the percentage of females and minorities in the population and the labor force are determined along with their unemployment. The distribution of the necessary skills among such individuals is also determined. The analysis considers the trainability, transferability, and promotability of such individuals within the organization, and the ability of schools and the organization's internal resources to provide the training required for increased utilization.[17]

GOALS AND TIMETABLES.   The next step in affirmative action program implementation involves setting goals for increased utilization of minorities and females. The ultimate goal is to increase their utilization to the level indicated by the analysis of the labor market. Annual targets for achieving these goals should then be developed. These targets consider the increased utilization of minorities and females that can be obtained, given expected personnel turnover, the supply of such individuals having the necessary skills, and lead times necessary for skill development. Internal employment processes should also be evaluated at this step to eliminate organizational barriers to increased minority and female utilization.[18]

DESIGN AND OPERATIONALIZATION OF PROGRAM COMPONENTS.   Following the establishment of goals and timetables, programs must be designed and operationalized for eliminating barriers to minority and female employment. Means of increasing minority and female employment in job classifications showing underutilization must be implemented. Starting with recruiting, the organization should not rely on word-of-mouth referrals as the sole source of job applicants, as this is not likely to result in increased minority employment where few minorities are currently employed.

Applicant flow records that detail the demographics of applicants, job offers, reasons why an applicant was not offered a job, names of interviewers, and names of the individuals making the hiring decisions should be maintained.

Recruiting needs and the organization's affirmative action policy should be advertised through various minority- and female-oriented media. Likewise, such individuals should be recruited at educational institutions having high proportions of minority or female enrollments.[19] Richard Christensen told us about Thomas and Betts' recruitment contacts with minority groups and agencies and state employment agencies.

Selection should be guided by the Uniform Guidelines on Employee Selection Procedures that were adopted in 1978 by the EEOC, OFCCP, Department of Justice, and Department of Labor. Although tests are covered by the guidelines, other selection procedures that affect hiring decisions are also covered.[20] Information to be obtained on an application form or through interviews should be job related in compliance with the guidelines.[21] Obviously, an important part of these guidelines deals with test validation. It may come as something of a surprise, but not all selection procedures (including tests) must be validated. Only those selection procedures having an "adverse impact" on the selection of females or minorities must be proven to be valid.

> Although validation of selection procedures is desirable in personnel management, the Uniform Guidelines require users to produce evidence of validity only when the selection procedure adversely affects the opportunities of a race, sex, or ethnic group for hire, transfer, promotion, retention, or other employment decision. If there is no adverse impact, there is no validation requirement under the Guidelines . . .[22]

Means of determining "adverse impact" have been specified in the guidelines. As a rule "adverse impact" may be described as follows:

> Under the Guidelines adverse impact is a substantially different rate of selection in hiring, promotion, or other employment decision which works to the disadvantage of members of a race, sex, or ethnic group. . . .The agencies have adopted a rule of thumb under which they will generally consider a selection rate for any race, sex, or ethnic group which is less than four-fifths ($\frac{4}{5}$) or eighty percent (80%) of the selection rate for the group with the highest selection rate as a substantially different rate of selection.[23]

Although validation is not required unless there is "adverse impact," it makes little sense to use selection procedures that have not been validated. The types of validation that are acceptable under the guidelines are the following:

> Validation is the demonstration of the job relatedness of a selection procedure. The Uniform Guidelines recognize the same three validity strategies recognized by the American Psychological Association:

(1) Criterion-related validity—a statistical demonstration of a relationship between scores on a selection procedure and job performance of a sample of workers.

(2) Content validity—a demonstration that the content of a selection procedure is representative of important aspects of performance on the job.

(3) Construct validity—a demonstration that (a) a selection procedure measures a construct (something believed to be an underlying human trait or characteristic, such as honesty), and (b) the construct is important for successful job performance.[24]

Although affirmative action is greatly concerned with selection, the upward mobility of minorities and females into positions where they are underutilized is another major concern. The organizational processes that act to retard such upward mobility should be changed when they have an invalid and disproportionate effect on minorities and females. Training programs can enable minorities and females to move into higher positions more rapidly where inadequate skills may have limited their prior rate of advancement.[25] Richard Christensen indicated the importance of personnel information systems to equal employment opportunity and affirmative action. Such a system enables Thomas and Betts to identify qualified females and minorities for advancement into higher positions.

AUDITING AND MONITORING. A system for assessing the progress of the affirmative action program should be operationalized. Essentially, such a system would circulate quarterly reports among managerial personnel on such matters as the current distribution of minorities and females, the underutilization of minorities and females (in the various job classifications), job applicant flows, and the supply of minorities and females.[26]

INTERNAL AND EXTERNAL SUPPORT. Finally, support for the affirmative action program can be improved among the organization's managerial personnel through training designed to increase their "awareness" level of the subtleties of discrimination. Unfortunately, unless top management has made a definite commitment to the program, such awareness training accomplishes little. Supportive programs designed to facilitate minority employment may involve transportation assistance, where the job site is some distance from minority population centers, and child care facilities in the case of females. Other supportive programs may involve counseling on personal matters such as finances, housing, or education. Thomas and Betts' Human Resources Development and Career Counseling Program is an example of a counseling program that can help females and minorities (as well as others) gain knowledge about the training they need to move up in the organization. Some programs should be designed to interface with community organizations where minority and female employment may be subjects for action.[27]

A program that has been created to improve managers' awareness of their racial biases was developed for the Xerox Corporation. In this program, managers completed pre- and post-training attitude questionnaires that enabled the measurement of changes in their awareness and understanding. The training consisted of an in-basket exercise, role playing, discussion, watching a film, and writing a memorandum on the subject to the company president. Changes in awareness were found immediately after completion of the training as well as after a five-month period. As with other attempts to change attitudes and behavior, changes that occur as a result of training are not likely to persist unless there is support for such changed attitudes and behavior when the manager returns to the regular job environment.[28]

As a final point on affirmative action, the personnel practitioner should become conversant with the detailed selection guidelines and EEOC or OFCCP reporting requirements. An excellent reference on this subject is provided in the Bureau of National Affairs publication, *Fair Employment Practices Manual,* a loose-leafed supplemented source.

Affirmative Action Strategies

There are essentially two strategies that an employer can follow in attempting to satisfy affirmative action requirements. One is to make good faith efforts to identify and correct the organization's defects that have caused an underrepresentation of minorities and females. The other approach involves treating goals as quotas. In the good faith strategy, disadvantaged minorities may be trained so that they can qualify for jobs. Job opportunities are communicated to females and minorities, and accommodations are made for flexible working hours, child care for working mothers, and so on. Although it is assumed that these measures will increase the representation of females and minorities, in case goals and timetables are not satisfied, these efforts provide evidence of reasonable attempts to comply.[29]

On the other hand, some employers may not wish to rely on the likelihood that their good faith efforts will be evaluated by contract compliance officers as reasonable excuses for failure to achieve goals. As an alternate strategy, they hire sufficient minorities and females to meet goals, regardless of the availability of qualified individuals. Since the ultimate test of affirmative action is whether increased representation of females and minorities is achieved, this strategy may seem to minimize risk. Employers utilizing this strategy, however, may encounter another risk, namely, the likelihood that other employees will charge them with reverse discrimination.[30] There are two potential costs associated with reverse discrimination: (1) the damages incurred by the employees unfairly denied promotions or jobs and (2) the adverse effect on performance and morale that discriminatory hiring and promotion policies are likely to produce.

In the recent *Weber* case, which we consider in some detail in a subsequent section, a white male charged his employer with reverse discrimination. The employee had been denied admission to a training program while blacks with less seniority had been admitted because the company was trying to increase the representation of blacks in certain jobs. Even though the Supreme Court ruled in favor of the company, the decision probably should not be viewed as a general protection against charges of reverse discrimination.[31]

Thus a preferable strategy might be to adopt the good faith compliance strategy with the intent that an effective program can increase the representation of females and minorities. Employers would probably benefit from an awareness of good faith program efforts that are viewed as reasonable excuses for failure to meet goals.

A recent study asked some of the federal government's contact compliance officers to assess the importance of different compliance activities in the determination that good faith efforts have been made. In this particular study, the compliance officers were told to assume that an adequate utilization analysis had been conducted and that, because there was underutilization, goals and timetables were in effect. The study found that the relevant compliance activities can be categorized in terms of six factors.[32] These factors are the following:

1. Increasing the minority/female applicant flow.
2. Demonstrating top-management support for the equal employment policy.
3. Demonstrating equal employment commitment to the community.
4. Keeping employees informed.
5. Broadening the work skills of incumbent employees.
6. Internalizing equal employment policy.[33]

The *Bakke* Decision

The 1978 case of *Regents of the University of California v. Bakke*[34] considered the issue of reverse discrimination. Bakke, a white male who was denied admission to the medical school at the University of California at Davis, claimed discrimination because lesser qualified minorities were admitted as part of the university's affirmative action program.[35] Although the court ruled that the university had to admit Bakke to medical school,[36] it failed to strike down the university's use of race as a factor in making admission decisions as part of an affirmative action program:

> race was not for all times and all purposes forbidden to American government as the basis for some legal distinctions, even though any use of race must still be the subject of the greatest suspicion and rigorous scrutiny.[37]

Although the court found that the university's affirmative action policies, which caused the denial of admission to Bakke were not illegal, the use of this decision as a defense against reverse discrimination charges in employment situations is problematic. One difference between the *Bakke* case and employment situations is that much of it rested on interpretation of Title VI of the Civil Rights Act of 1964. Title VI deals with discrimination in institutions receiving federal funding, such as universities; Title VII deals with discrimination in employment.[38] A second difference is that education seems to receive special consideration in the Supreme Court's views on discrimination.[39]

The *Weber* Decision

Unlike the *Bakke* case, *United Steelworkers of America* v. *Weber et al.*[40] in 1979 involved a charge of reverse discrimination in an employment setting. In this case, Kaiser and the steelworkers union had agreed that Kaiser should undertake a training program to enable blacks to learn skilled crafts. This training was viewed as necessary because, as a result of past racial discrimination in the region, blacks had not been able to join craft unions and, consequently, had not been able to learn the skills of the various crafts. Thus Kaiser could not find and hire blacks who possessed the requisite craft skills. Kaiser and the union agreed that admission of unskilled employees to the training program would be in accordance with seniority, except that separate seniority lists would be utilized, with one list being for blacks and another for whites. Admission would be decided by alternate selections from the lists as training opportunities occurred. The black employees typically had less seniority than did the white employees.[41] As a result of the operation of this plan, Weber claimed that he had been denied admission to the training program on the basis of racial discrimination, because blacks and females with less seniority were admitted.[42]

In this case, the Supreme Court ruled in favor of the company in concluding that "Title VII does not prohibit the kind of affirmative action taken by Kaiser under the circumstances facing that employer."[43] Nonetheless, three specific circumstances of this case were important in the court's decision. The first was that, had there been no problem with an underrepresentation of blacks in the skilled crafts, Kaiser would not have conducted the training. The second was that past discrimination had caused the exclusion of blacks from the crafts. The third point was that, as soon as sufficient representation of blacks in skilled craft positions was obtained, the training would be stopped.[44]

Even though the court ruled in the company's favor, because of the importance of the particular circumstances of this case, the *Weber* decision probably should not be viewed as a sure defense against affirmative-action-based charges of reverse discrimination.[45]

Backlash Responses to Affirmative Action

Although the objectives of affirmative action, the correction of past wrongs, is creditable and generally accepted, the manner in which affirmative action programs are implemented often creates the perception of unfair treatment among unprotected groups. Whenever affirmative action programs cause race, sex, and age to be considered in hiring, training, or promotion decisions, perceptions of race discrimination may result among the unprotected class, usually white males. A recent survey of 884 male workers from 66 different organizations found that 50 percent of the workers felt that, in promotions, women were afforded preferential treatment. In general, the survey revealed on several issues that approximately 20 percent of the workers felt that women received preferential treatment. Frustration resulting from backlash responses may have negative impacts on satisfaction, performance, and tenure; it may also create tension among unprotected workers and cause lowered expectations of career progress.[46] An accurate statement of this dilemma is the following:

> It appears that management is caught in the middle of a struggle between protected groups, such as women and blacks, who demand restitution for past organizational ineq-

uities, and the unprotected majority of white male employees, who allege that they are victimized by reverse discrimination.[47]

Suggestions for reducing such backlash responses include identification of inequities in the implementation of affirmative action programs, correction through education of misunderstandings on program policies, and adoption of participative approaches to the development and implementation of such programs.[48]

Several reasons exist as to why equal employment opportunity and affirmative action programs have been viewed by some employees as reverse discrimination. (1) Some employers have incorrectly interpreted the goals of affirmative action as quotas. Quotas have been imposed in rare cases, and in such cases, it is the courts that have imposed them. In contrast to quotas, goals are targets for employment that are set after consideration of the supply of qualified minorities and females in the employer's labor market. (2) Following the passage of the Civil Rights Act of 1964, only voluntary measures were used to enforce the act. Because the voluntary measures were not effective, affirmative action was required for federal contractors and subcontractors. (3) During a short period of time, a great deal of legislation was passed, only one part of which was the Civil Rights Act and its amendment, the Equal Employment Opportunity Act. The extensiveness of legislation and the mass of accompanying publicity may have caused an overreaction that reverse discrimination was taking place. (4) During the 1970s, the economy did not expand as it had during the 1960s when affirmative action policies had been developed. Thus such actions as layoffs placed minorities and females in competition with white males for limited employment opportunities. The result was that some whites and males perceived reverse discrimination.[49]

As indicated, some employers have implemented affirmative action programs in a manner that creates perceptions of reverse discrimination. Simply complying with affirmative action requirements will not assure success or do anything to prevent perceptions of reverse discrimination. Some affirmative action program failures have resulted from (1) overreactions, (2) unplanned promotions, (3) inadequate performance evaluations, and (4) counterproductive supervisory responses to affirmative action programs. As noted earlier, overreactions have occurred as some employers have hired and promoted unqualified minorities and females or terminated nonminorities and males in a more perfunctory manner. Some employers have promoted minorities and females lacking the proper experience and development just to be able to report favorable personnel actions. This strategy is unfair to qualified nonminorities and males as well as to the minorities and females. Such promoted individuals, who are unqualified for their positions, are more inclined to quit. Furthermore, when performance evaluations are not carried out in a manner that accurately informs employees of their performance, marginal performers may not be aware that they are unqualified for promotion. Thus, when a minority member or female is promoted, such marginal performers may feel that they have been treated unfairly. Finally, poor management and leadership are contributors to misperceptions of affirmative action programs and equal employment opportunity.[50] Such poor management is sometimes manifested as follows:

priorities in decision making have often been out of balance. Instead of improving organizational climate and revamping human resource planning, legal staffs have been beefed up to fight discrimination cases. Instead of validating selection processes, more emphasis is placed on winning the statistical battle.[51]

The Experiences of American Telephone & Telegraph

As noted, affirmative action programs sometimes have been perceived incorrectly as promoting reverse discrimination. Unfortunately there is some evidence that this has taken place. As we have discussed, affirmative action programs require goals and timetables. Quotas have been imposed only in infrequent cases by the courts. However, the experiences of American Telephone & Telegraph have involved actual quotas. Since AT&T is the country's largest employer (980,000 employees), its experiences are too important to dismiss.[52]

In 1973, AT&T signed a consent decree with the EEOC and other agencies in which it technically admitted no wrongdoing but agreed to certain promotion and hiring practices that would increase the representation of women and minorities in certain higher-paying jobs and management (although in 1972 the Bell System was composed of 52 percent females, they constituted only 9 percent of second level and higher management). AT&T also agreed to compensate females and male minorities financially for the effects of possible discrimination and to raise the pay rates of women where they were receiving lower wages than men performing comparable work. Under the terms of the consent decree, AT&T was required to increase the representation of females and minorities in various jobs by specific percentages. It was also required to increase the representation of men in previously all-female jobs, such as telephone operators' jobs. To ensure that these changes were made, AT&T had to meet certain goals by specified times.[53]

Prior to the consent decree, AT&T promoted its unionized employees on the basis of the best qualified persons to fill the job despite pressure from the union (the Communication Workers of America) to promote on the basis of seniority. Only when employees had the same qualifications did seniority govern. The consent decree required AT&T to deviate from this policy (which was part of the contract with the union) and to promote females and minorities who were basically qualified. Because of AT&T's lack of progress during 1974 in gaining representation of females and minorities in certain jobs, the government imposed a supplementary order. At this time, AT&T found itself obligated to meet a set of quotas.[54]

> The sternness of the government's approach in the supplemental order convinced AT&T that it was dealing not with goals, as it had previously assumed, but with quotas . . .[55]

As a result of AT&T's attempts to follow the terms of the consent decree and supplement, there were charges of reverse discrimination. Approximately twenty-four cases eventually went to court. In one of these, the union claimed reverse discrimination because of the consent decree's promotion policy favoring basically qualified females and minorities. The district court and appeals court ruled against the union and essentially upheld preferential treatment and quotas on the grounds that such actions were justified to correct the abuses of past discrimination. Shortly after the U.S. Supreme Court handed down the Bakke decision, it announced that it would not hear the union's case. Most of the reverse discrimination cases were unsuccessful because of the loss of the union's case. However, one white male won a reverse discrimination decision for which AT&T made an out-of-court settlement for damages.[56]

The practices that AT&T was obligated to follow and their relevance in the future are perhaps best summed up in a statement by its chairman, John deButts:

> It was necessary for this period of time. But my personal feeling is that this is not the way promotions should be made—not a way to run a business forever.[57]

OTHER EQUAL EMPLOYMENT OPPORTUNITY ISSUES

Although it is obviously critical for most sizable organizations to implement EEO and affirmative action programs, and to deal effectively with any associated negative reactions, we should not lose sight of the goal of achieving true integration of the work force beyond the requirements of goals, timetables, legal compliance, and so on. If such a socially responsive goal had been pursued previously by organizations, the complex legal requirements of today would be unnecessary.

Assimilation of Minority Employees

Some suggestions have been offered for improved assimilation of nonwhites into the organization's work force. These suggestions are based on assumptions that nonwhites have had some negative experiences as a result of different treatment by a white society and that, consequently, they may often be apprehensive and skeptical of their reception into the work situation. Further, it is probably safe to assume that such individuals will desire acceptance, respect, trust, no "easier" work standards, and the same level of supervision that other new employees receive. Likewise, they do not want to be compelled to prove themselves continuously or to work at a higher standard for the same rewards that whites receive.[58]

With these assumptions in mind, acceptance of nonwhites may be facilitated by supervisors. Supervisors should not assume that they can minimize new minority employees' apprehension, but they should communicate their understanding and acceptance of such insecurity and be supportive by providing information necessary for survival in the organization. Likewise, supervisors should anticipate incidents involving prejudice toward new minority employees. White employees should be provided information on the organization's actions so that perceptions of preferential treatment of nonwhites are avoided. White supervisors who lack experience with minority employees sometimes tend to be hesitant in their interactions (lack spontaneity) with nonwhite employees. Such supervisors may also do the new minority employee a disservice by not criticizing inadequate performance or not enforcing rules out of concern for being charged with prejudice or discrimination. In fact, the failure to impose discipline may be perceived by the new minority worker as a sign that the supervisor does not care about him or her.[59]

The informal interaction of the work group with the new minority employee is critical. Such informal matters as including new minority employees in plans for lunch, after-work activities, and so on, communicate acceptance by co-workers.[60] It is difficult to overstate the importance of creating a climate of acceptance.

> One key problem of black Americans, according to Yale psychiatrist James Comer, is their inability to experience that automatic sense of belonging and "right to be here" that whites experience.[61]

Minority employees should not be viewed as ethnic representatives, for example, being "asked for the 'black point of view' or the 'Mexican-American point of view'."[62] Instead, they should be treated as individuals (e.g., asked for their individual views on problems). The organization should be willing to change in assimilating minorities. Too often, the socialization of minorities involves a process that emphasizes changing the employee so that a fit will be obtained with the white organization's mold. Such emphasis may convey to the new employee that minority culture has no value and that it is foolish to expect the organization to accommodate the employee to any extent.[63]

Of course, if the employee has been a member of the hard-core unemployed, changes in work attitudes and values on such issues as work attendance and punctuality may be necessary.[64] Regardless of race, the work attitudes and values of the hard-core unemployed often constitute significant obstacles to their employment. In the case of the hard-core unemployed black, managers need to consider that "adopting the white manager's work ethics means a major rejection of the behavior patterns he had learned in his society."[65]

Such observations point out the need for managers to view these workers' actions from a new perspective. When viewed from white middle-class norms, certain hard-core behavior does not seem to make sense. For example, consider why a hard-core unemployed black may not ask questions to obtain information necessary to perform a job. The explanation for such behavior may be that "for the black man to seek help is to admit ignorance and lack of power—to be subservient to the white man's technology and know-how."[66] Thus the assimilation of the hard-core poses some special problems that go beyond those for minority employees in general. Aside from concentrating on the establishment of acceptable work attitudes and values, managers need to counsel with such employees to assist them in developing goals that are acceptable to the organization. The organization needs to reward those supervisors who are conscientious and skillful in aiding the assimilation of these employees.[67]

Aside from the special issues involving the hard-core unemployed, supervisors need to expect individual cultural differences and to tolerate them. The sense of isolation of the new minority employee must be overcome. A simple policy that can eliminate potential isolation is to assign at least two minority employees with similar ethnic backgrounds to units made up of all white employees. Further, support groups made up of minority employees having longer tenure can provide helpful counseling for new minority employees. Finally, continuing top management involvement in assimilation program direction, managerial training, and appraisal is important.[68]

Special Issues in EEO

Several special EEO issues have created some controversy. One of these concerns the treatment of pregnant women. In 1976, the Supreme Court decided the *General Electric Company* v. *Gilbert*[69] case in which General Electric was accused of sex discrimination because its disability benefits plan contained no provision for disability benefits for women who were temporarily disabled as a result of pregnancy.[70]

In ruling that General Electric did not discriminate against such women, the majority of the court adopted the view that the absence of pregnancy benefits was essentially like any other policy exclusion. General Electric did not discriminate solely because its disability benefits plan did not cover all possible disabilities. Another point in the company's favor was that pregnancy was viewed by the court as a special disability as opposed to an involuntary disability. Not all the justices took the same view. In one opinion, the exclusion of pregnancy disability benefits was viewed as inherently discriminatory, since only women can become pregnant. Likewise, the voluntary nature of pregnancy disabilities was not viewed, in another dissenting opinion, as a point in the company's favor since General Electric did not deny all disability benefits that resulted from voluntary disabilities, such as venereal disease, attempted suicides, or injuries suffered in athletic contests.[71]

As a result of significant disapproval of the decision by some groups, Title VII of the Civil Rights Act of 1964 was amended in 1978 to preclude several pregnancy-related employment practices.[72] A summary of the impact of the amendment is as follows:

> Henceforth pregnancy and childbirth must be treated the same as other disabilities covered in fringe-benefit plans. The amendment prohibits refusal to hire or termination on the grounds of pregnancy, bars mandatory leaves for pregnant women arbitrarily set at a certain time in pregnancy, and protects job rights of women on pregnancy leave.[73]

Another issue concerns discrimination on the basis of religion. As explained earlier, Title VII of the Civil Rights Act of 1964 prevents employment discrimination on the basis of religion. Charges of religious discrimination sometimes arise when work schedules conflict with employees' observance of the sabbath or religious events.[74] The legal obligation of the employer may be stated as follows: "Title VII of the Civil Rights Act requires the employer to make reasonable efforts to accommodate the religious needs of its employees short of undue hardship."[75]

A U.S. Supreme Court decision clarified the requirements of Title VII in *Trans-World Airlines, Inc.,* v. *Hardison.*[76] In this case, a Trans-World Airline employee joined a church in which work on Saturdays was not permitted. On occasion, Saturday work was required at TWA. Such work assignments were made on the basis of the seniority provisions contained in the union contract. Attempts were made by TWA to accommodate the employee's request not to work on Saturdays. The various means of accommodation that TWA evaluated were a four-day work-week, work substitution by supervisors, and hiring off-duty employees at overtime rates. All these attempts to accommodate the employee were found to be unworkable, and TWA found that it could not grant the employee's request. Eventually, the employee was terminated for refusing to work on Saturdays. The court ruled in favor of TWA on the basis that TWA made reasonable efforts to accommodate the employee's interests and that TWA was not required to violate the seniority-based work assignment provisions of the union contract.[77]

Other court cases have dealt with employees' requests during pre-employment meetings to obtain guarantees that they will not have to work on the sabbath or days of religious observance. The court's decisions on these cases may be summarized as follows:

> The employer need not issue a blanket guarantee to a prospective employee that work on a certain day will *never* be required. However, if the applicant merely declares that he has certain religious needs, the employer must make some attempt to accommodate them.[78]

SUMMARY

In this chapter, we have seen that a variety of laws and executive orders protect job applicants and employees from discrimination. The enforcement of these laws and orders is a function of the EEOC and OFCCP. To ensure that personnel selection is conducted in a nondiscriminatory manner, Uniform Guidelines on Personnel Selection Procedures have been adopted by these compliance agencies. Thus employers need to conduct selection in accordance with these guidelines. In reality, these guidelines require nothing more than the good selection practices that selection experts have been advocating for years.

Those employers who have contracts with the federal government (most large companies) and employers who have been found in noncompliance with the EEO laws are required to implement affirmative action programs. Affirmative action programs are complex activities that facilitate the correction of underutilizations of minorities and females in an organization's various job classifications. Unfortunately, the goals and timetables of such programs have been viewed as quotas by some employers and employees. Quotas have been imposed in only limited instances and are not characteristic of affirmative action programs. Thus, although goals are not quotas, it is important for the employer to make good faith efforts to correct underutilizations of minorities and females. The purpose and operation of affirmative action programs must be communicated to employees and managers to avoid backlash responses and perceptions of reverse discrimination.

For an affirmative action program to have positive long-run effects, care must be taken to facilitate the assimilation of minorities and females in the workplace. Supervisors play a key role in such assimilation and thus need to relate well to new minority or female employees. A climate of acceptance is important for successful assimilation.

Finally, there are some special issues regarding pregnancy and religious discrimination that have been the subject of litigation in recent years. Employers need to be careful not to discriminate on the basis of pregnancy and to make reasonable attempts to accommodate employees' requests for work schedule exceptions for religious reasons.

INTERVIEW WRAP-UP

Thomas and Betts has several special programs that help to support its affirmative action program. The company has a tuition reimbursement program that helps employees to gain skills, a career counseling program, and job posting, and it maintains contact with the state employment service and minority groups to attract minority applicants. Communication of the program to managers and an information system capable of monitoring its performance are both necessary for program effectiveness. —Richard Christensen, corporate manager-human resource information, Thomas and Betts Corporation.

WHAT MANAGERS SHOULD DO REGARDING
PERSONNEL MANAGEMENT ACTIVITIES

1. Managers should realize that affirmative action programs may fail if they are viewed as inequitable. The operation of the programs must be communicated properly to employees.

2. Managers should be prepared to facilitate the acceptance of minorities and females by the work group. If equal employment of minorities and females is to become a long-run reality, such individuals must be socially integrated into the work group.

3. Managers should realize that the equal employment opportunity laws do not require the hiring or promotion of unqualified individuals.

REVIEW QUESTIONS

1. What is "adverse impact" in personnel selection?

2. What laws or executive orders provide for equal employment opportunity?

3. What is an employer's obligation to an employee who does not work on certain days because of religious reasons?

4. Describe how an employer should determine whether there is underutilization of minorities and females in the organization.

5. Discuss the equal employment opportunity experiences at American Telephone & Telegraph.

6. How might an organization improve the performance of its managers in affirmative action program implementation?

7. Describe the Supreme Court's decision in the *Weber* case.

8. How does the pregnancy of a woman affect her status in the employment situation?

KEY CONCEPTS

Adverse impact

Affirmative action program

Age Discrimination in Employment Act of 1976

Applicant flow

BFOQ

Civil Rights Act of 1964

Conciliation agreement

Consent decree

Construct validity

Content validity

Criterion-related validity

EEOC

Equal Employment Opportunity Act of 1972

Equal Pay Act of 1963

Executive Order 11246

General Electric v. *Gilbert*

Good faith efforts

OFCCP

Regents of the University of California v. *Bakke*

Rehabilitation Act of 1973

Underutilization

Uniform Guidelines on Employee Selection Procedures

United Steelworkers of America v. *Weber*

Vietnam Era Veterans' Readjustment Assistance Act of 1974

CASE

KELSON AND HATHAWAY, INC.

Kelson and Hathaway, Inc., is a small manufacturing firm located in Wichita, Kansas. The firm manufactures hydraulic valves, controls, lines, and cylinders for use in aircraft and industrial equipment. Approximately 60 percent of the firm's output is purchased by aircraft manufacturers. Most of the hydraulic systems components manufactured by the firm require several machining operations. Because of the extensive machining requirements, a large proportion of Kelson and Hathaway's 165 employees are skilled machine operators; the rest of the employees are engineers, manufacturer's representatives, and clerical staff.

Because the firm is a subcontractor for aircraft companies having large contracts with the federal government, for several years it has been required to maintain an affirmative action program. Although the firm has never consciously discriminated against minorities and females in either selection or promotion decisions, as is the case in so many other companies, it has an underutilization of minorities and females in the higher-paying, skilled production job classifications.

To date, the firm has had only limited success in attracting minority job applicants who have the skills required for the higher-paying production jobs. Furthermore, because of the high quality control requirements for aircraft components, the firm has been unwilling to conduct on-the-job training for the skilled jobs. The firm believes that other types of training, such as vestibule training, for the skilled jobs are too expensive for such a small firm. Although the firm has been able to hire minorities at the entry-level low-skilled production jobs, it has been unable to meet its affirmative action goals for the skilled jobs.

The case for females has been worse. Currently, there is only one female production worker who drives a delivery truck and stocks parts. In the past, females have been hired for entry-level production jobs, but none of them have remained on the job for more than six months. Although the male production workers have accepted minority workers, many of them have rejected the idea of having female co-workers. As an example of the negative attitudes toward female workers in the shop, one incident seemed to convey the attitude of many of the workers. Last year, a woman working in one of the regular low-skill production jobs made the mistake of asking one of the men to help her lift a shield on one of the machines. The man replied, ''Do it yourself, you're getting paid the same wages as me.''

No progress has been made in filling any of the ten manufacturer's representative jobs with women either. These jobs ordinarily involve travel, except for the three jobs that have Wichita as their territory, and are occupied by senior male employees. Although three women were hired in these jobs over the last five years, all the women quit after a year. The sales manager maintains that the women quit because of the extensive travel requirement.

CASE QUESTIONS

1. Suggest an alternative approach to filling more of the skilled production jobs with minorities.

2. What could explain the apparent resistance of the male production workers to female co-workers? What should the firm do to correct the underutilization of women in these jobs?

3. How can the firm do a better job of keeping female manufacturing representatives?

NOTES

[1]Commerce Clearing House, *Labor Law Course,* 24th ed. (Chicago: Commerce Clearing House, 1979).

[2]D. A. Brookmire and A. A. Burton, "A Format for Packaging Your Affirmative Action Program," *Personnel Journal,* 57 (1978), 294–304; E. M. Idelson, "U.S. Equal Employment Opportunity Commis-

sion," *Affirmative Action and Equal Employment: A Guidebook for Employers,* Vol. 1 (Washington, D.C.: Government Printing Office, 1974).

[3]Ibid.

[4]*Fair Employment Practices Manual,* (Washington, D.C.: Bureau of National Affairs, 1981).

[5]R. L. Greenman and E. J. Schmertz, *Personnel Administration and the Law* (Washington, D.C.: Bureau of National Affairs, 1979).

[6]R. H. Sheahan, "Responding to Employment Discrimination Charges," *Personnel Journal,* 60 (1981), 217–220.

[7]M. G. Miner and J. B. Miner, *Employee Selection Within the Law* (Washington, D.C.: Bureau of National Affairs, 1979).

[8]Idelson, "Equal Opportunity Employment."

[9]Miner and Miner, *Employee Selection Within the Law.*

[10]Idelson, "Equal Opportunity Employment," p. 8.

[11]Miner and Miner, *Employee Selection Within the Law.*

[12]*Fair Employment Practices Manual,* p. 443:1.

[13]Office of Federal Contract Compliance, Revised Order Number 4, §60-2.10.

[14]Idelson, "Equal Opportunity Employment"; *Fair Employment Practices Manual.*

[15]Ibid.

[16]Idelson, "Equal Opportunity Employment."

[17]Ibid.

[18]Ibid., *Fair Employment Practices Manual.*

[19]Idelson, "Equal Opportunity Employment."

[20]Equal Employment Opportunity Commission, Title 29—Labor, Chapter XIV, Part 1607—Uniform Guidelines on Employee Selection Procedures (1978), in the *Federal Register,* August 25, 1978, pp. 38290–38315.

[21]*Fair Employment Practices Manual.*

[22]Equal Employment Opportunity Commission, Title 29—Labor, Chapter XIV, Part 1607—Uniform Guidelines on Employee Selection Procedures, in the *Federal Register,* March 2, 1979, pp. 11997–11998.

[23]Ibid., p. 11998.

[24]Ibid., p. 12001.

[25]Idelson, "Equal Opportunity Employment."

[26]Ibid.

[27]Ibid.

[28]B. M. Bass, W. F. Cascio, J. W. McPherson, and H. J. Tragash, "PROSPER—Training and Research for Increasing Management Awareness of Affirmative Action in Race Relations," *Academy of Management Journal,* 19 (1976), 353–369.

[29]K. E. Marino, "Conducting an Internal Compliance Review of Affirmative Action," *Personnel,* 57 (1980), 24–34.

[30]Ibid.

[31]Ibid.

[32]Ibid.

[33]Ibid., p. 30.

[34]98 S. Ct. 2733 (1978).

[35]A. Cox, "Minority Admissions After Bakke," in *Bakke, Weber, and Affirmative Action,* working papers of the Rockefeller Foundation, New York City, December 1979.

[36]S. E. Tallent, "A Legal Perspective on the Bakke Decision," *Personnel Journal,* 58 (1979), 296–302, 325.

[37]Ibid., p. 299.

[38]Cox, "Minority Admissions After Bakke"; Tallent, "A Legal Perspective."

[39]Tallent, "A Legal Perspective."

[40]99 S.Ct. 2721 (1979).

[41]Cox, "Minority Admissions After Bakke."

[42]Marino, "Conducting an Internal Compliance Review."

[43]Cox, "Minority Admissions After Bakke." p. 98.

[44]Ibid.

[45]Marino, "Conducting an Internal Compliance Review."

[46]B. Rosen and F. H. Jerdee, "Coping with Affirmative Action Backlash," *Business Horizons,* 22 (1979), 15–20.

[47]Ibid., p. 19.

[48]Ibid.

[49]G. Pati and C. W. Reilly, "Reversing Discrimination: A Perspective," *Human Resource Management,* 16 (1977), 25–35.

[50]Ibid.

[51]Ibid., p. 30.

[52]C. J. Loomis, "A.T.&T. in the Throes of 'Equal Employment'," *Fortune,* January 15, 1979, pp. 45–57.

[53]Ibid.

[54]Ibid.

[55]Ibid., p. 50.

[56]Ibid.

[57]Ibid., p. 57.

[58]G. D. Klein, "Beyond EOE and Affirmative Action: Working on the Integration of the Work Place," *California Management Review,* 22 (1980), 74–81.

[59]Ibid.

[60]Ibid.

[61]Ibid., p. 77.

[62]Ibid., p. 77.

[63]Klein, "Beyond EOE and Affirmative Action."

[64]D. R. Domm and J. E. Stafford, "Assimilating Blacks into the Organization," *California Management Review,* 15 (1972) 46–51.

[65]Ibid., p. 47.

[66]Ibid., p. 48.

[67]Ibid.

[68]Klein, "Beyond EOE and Affirmative Action."

[69]429 U.S. 126 (1976).

[70]Greenman and Schmertz, *Personnel Administration and the Law.*

[71]Ibid.

[72]Ibid.

[73]Ibid., p. 107.

[74]J. M. Norwood, "But I Can't Work on Saturdays," *Personnel Administrator,* 25 (1980), 25–30.

[75]Ibid., p.30.

[76]97 S. Ct. 2264 (1977).

[77]Norwood, "But I Can't Work on Saturdays."

[78]Ibid., p. 30.

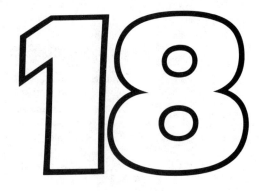

LABOR RELATIONS

LEARNING OBJECTIVES

After reading this chapter, you should be able to:

1. Discuss why employees join unions and how unions affect management.
2. Outline the legal environment of labor relations.
3. Describe the employer unfair labor practices.
4. Discuss the union unfair labor practices.
5. Explain the processes that occur in labor negotiations.
6. Describe some of the dimensions of the structure of collective bargaining.
7. Describe a typical grievance procedure.
8. Explain the process of arbitration.

Ralph Glancy is a machinist for Moon Specialties, Inc.* Moon Specialties is located in southwestern Pennsylvania. The company's primary product is hydraulic cylinders. It also manufactures gear cases, mining machines, and other types of equipment that use hydraulic cylinders. The company is still privately held.

Ralph has been with Moon Specialties for nineteen years. He has fifteen years of experience on his present job. He is also a member of the American Flint Glass Workers' Union. Another interesting point is that Ralph was recently appointed to the Board of Directors of Moon Specialties.

Ralph was interviewed to obtain his views on unions and the relationship between the union and management in his company.

Interviewer: What are the benefits an employee receives from being a member of a union?

Ralph Glancy: The union provides a bridge between employer and employee. Unionized employees can approach a company with a united front. The union negotiates with the company and provides employees with better wages, better fringe benefits, and more protection. Employees have more job security because they cannot be fired except for good reason. The national union provides the local union with good advice. Decisions regarding employees are made for the good of the group rather than just for the good of some employees and thus favoritism is minimized.

Interviewer: Should the union and company attempt to work together cooperatively?

Ralph Glancy: To have a really well-run organization, they have to work together. They have to recognize each other, the powers of each, and the benefits each can provide. Each one oversees the actions of the other. Neither one can get away with anything that way. There should be a balance between them.

Interviewer: What problems, if any, have you seen between union and company activities?

Ralph Glancy: The biggest problem is the company's apparent failure to recognize the abilities of union members. They don't seem to have a system for evaluating employee suggestions for improvement. This occurs even when employee suggestions might save them money. Employees may have suggestions for increasing production or improving working conditions, but quite often the company doesn't respond.

Interviewer: What is the job of those who work in labor relations for the company?

Ralph Glancy: We have only one person who works in what I could call labor relations. He's primarily a liaison between the company and employees, particularly on insurance and unemployment compensation matters. He doesn't make major decisions alone. He reports to the top man and together they make all of the decisions. He gathers information and serves primarily as a "man-in-the-middle."

He has helped in some ways. For example, we had a slack period last year and it resulted in a work schedule consisting of two weeks' work followed by a one-week layoff. He worked with us getting forms from the unemployment office and filling them out. This caused us a lot less trouble and the employees appreciated it.

Interviewer: Do you feel that the union can fairly represent your interests?

Ralph Glancy: The union has fairly represented me in the past. I've never been disappointed in the union's efforts, although the results sometimes leave something to be desired. I've always been satisfied with the union's efforts but less so with the company's responses.

Interviewer: Have you ever been disappointed with what the union has tried to accomplish but not succeeded?

Ralph Glancy: No, for the most part. A few grievances have been filed that seemed to work to the company's advantage. It's hard to tell if they could have been avoided.

Interviewer: Does the international union offer the local union assistance?

Ralph Glancy: Yes, they offer assistance in contract negotiations, legal advice on filing grievances, and other areas. They will send a national representative to help us.

Interviewer: You've just recently been appointed to the Board of Directors of your company. How is your participation going, getting involved on the inside?

Ralph Glancy: I don't really know how the situation will work out, being a union member on the Board of Directors. Only time will tell if it will succeed.

*The name of the person interviewed and that of the company have been changed for their protection. The facts are accurate as reported to us.

INTRODUCTION

Ralph Glancy has been a union member for several years and seems satisfied with it. As he noted, unions provide their members several benefits. Unions also make the relations between the organization and its employees complex. In many ways, these relations are unique when unions are involved. Management no longer has the unilateral right to make decisions concerning the conditions of work when unions serve as the legal bargaining agent for employees. These decisions (e.g., pay, hours of work) must be negotiated with union representatives. Therefore, the relationships between managers and employees change. For example, managers deal with a large *group* of employees instead of with individual employees. Employees have more power collectively than they do individually. Because unions create a somewhat unique relationship and because of their profound impact in American society, it is important to examine them and understand why they exist. Also, labor relations is one of the major functions of most personnel departments and thus deserves study.

In this chapter, we examine the motivation to join unions, their membership, and growth patterns. In addition, we consider the nature of collective bargaining in depth, with emphasis on the legal framework, negotiations, grievances, arbitration, and strikes. Finally, we explore the potential issues of the 1980s.

UNIONS IN THE UNITED STATES

Unions represent a prominent force in American society. Unions affect the conditions of work, wages, and fringe benefits for millions of workers. They affect the political process in the United States by supporting or not supporting various candidates for office and by lobbying for and against legislation. The growth and membership of unions provide information on their impact.

Union Membership

For several years during the 1960s, total union membership in the United States declined. However, during the period 1976–1978, total union membership rose. The increase was due primarily to some fundamental changes in the types of union members, namely, the growing number of professional and state and local government employee groups that have unionized. Additionally, the number of women in labor unions has increased steadily. Currently, women comprise 27.4 percent of total union membership.[1]

Unions have broadened their traditional emphasis on blue-collar workers to a greater focus on organizing white-collar, professional, and government employees. As the recent statistics show, women are moving into white-collar and professional positions and into the work force in general in greater numbers that at any time in the past. Therefore, these numbers are reflected in union membership totals. These trends can be expected to continue over the next several years.

However, not all is well in the union movement. Although the number of union members has increased, the percentage of the labor force that is unionized has declined in recent years. As Table 18-1 indicates, union members constituted 19.7 percent of the labor force in 1978, while two decades earlier, they constituted 24.2 percent of the labor force.[2] Moreover, the number of decertifications of unions representing groups of employees in 1976 and 1977 was approximately three times the number in 1962.

Decertification: employees voting against the union to continue to represent them in their relations with their employer.

There are several reasons for these results. One is that many of the benefits and rights for which the unions fought in earlier periods are standard practice today. Employers are more enlightened in their personnel practices. Also, the labor force is younger, better educated, and more individualistic. Unions have not been flexible enough in all cases to meet the needs of the changing work force. However, unions are beginning to adapt.[3] Even though the number of decertifications has increased, the number of members lost through decertification is not great, because it mainly occurs in smaller bargaining units.[4]

Motivation to Join Unions

Unions provide benefits to their members, otherwise their membership would not total over 20 million workers. Many of these benefits were described by Ralph Glancy. Unions provide employees with a collective voice and thus more power, protection against arbitrary actions, job security, and individual favoritism is minimized, as Mr. Glancy described. Mr. Glancy also feels that unions help workers obtain better wages and fringe benefits than they could obtain otherwise.

Interestingly, research supports these contentions. An analysis of survey data collected for the U.S. Department of Labor by the Survey Research Center at the University of Michigan found that blue-collar workers' desire to join a union was affected more strongly by dissatisfaction over wages, fringe benefits, and working conditions than by dissatisfaction over other aspects such as the nature of the work or supervision, whereas white-collar workers were motivated to join unions because of the job aspects.[5]

Table 18-1

Trends in Union Membership[1], 1958–1978
(000)

Year	Membership Excluding Canada	Total Labor Force		Employees in Nonagricultural Establishments	
		Number	% Members	Number	% Members
Unions and associations					
1968	20,721	82,272	25.2%	67,897	30.5%
1969	20,776	84,240	24.7	70,384	29.5
1970	21,248	85,903	24.7	70,880	30.0
1971	21,327	86,929	24.5	71,214	29.9
1972	21,657	88,991	24.3	73,675	29.4
1973	22,276	91,040	24.5	76,790	29.0
1974	22,809	93,240	24.5	78,265	29.1
1975	22,361	94,793	23.6	77,364	28.9
1976	22,662	96,917	23.4	80,048	28.3
1977	22,456	99,534	22.6	82,423	27.2
1978	22,880	102,537	22.3	84,446	27.1
Unions					
1958	17,029	70,275	24.2	51,324	33.2
1959	17,117	70,921	24.1	53,268	32.1
1960	17,049	72,142	23.6	54,189	31.5
1961	16,303	73,031	22.3	53,999	30.2
1962	16,586	73,442	22.6	55,549	29.9
1963	16,524	74,571	22.2	56,653	29.2
1964	16,841	75,830	22.2	58,283	28.9
1965	17,299	77,178	22.4	60,765	28.5
1966	17,940	78,893	22.7	63,901	28.1
1967	18,367	80,793	22.7	65,803	27.9
1968	18,916	82,272	23.0	67,897	27.9
1969	19,036	84,240	22.6	70,384	27.0
1970	19,381	85,903	22.6	70,880	27.3
1971	19,211	86,929	22.1	71,214	27.0
1972	19,435	88,991	21.8	73,675	26.4
1973	19,851	91,040	21.8	76,790	25.9
1974	20,199	93,240	21.7	78,265	25.8
1975	19,553	94,793	20.6	77,364	25.3
1976	19,634	96,917	20.3	80,048	24.5
1977	19,902	99,534	20.0	82,423	24.1
1978	20,246	102,537	19.7	84,446	24.0

[1]Totals include reported membership and directly affiliated local union members. Total reported Canadian membership and members of single-firm unions are excluded.

Source: U.S. Department of Labor, Bureau of Labor Statistics, *Directory of National Unions and Employee Associations, 1979,* Bulletin 2079 (Washington, D.C.: Government Printing Office, 1980), p. 59.

UNIONS' IMPACT ON MANAGEMENT AND PRODUCTION

Unions have had a substantial impact on management and personnel management, in particular. In fact, the first personnel departments were organized to avoid unionization. One of the first effects of unionization is that policies or rules that previously were informal must now be formalized and put in writing. This is not to say that all the rules of the workplace are written or that unwritten rules are invalid. The rules are so numerous that even the most comprehensive contracts cannot mention all of them.

Some of the consequences of the formalization of rules and policies are not always desirable. Frustration that results from unreasonable adherence to formal procedures and policies is an all-too frequent occurrence in our daily work lives. Nonetheless, if following the rules does not become an end in itself, formalization of them and the union's insistence on uniform application of such rules can eliminate potential sources of dissatisfaction. Dissatisfaction resulting from arbitrary application of rules may be a contributing cause of unionization in many instances. As Ralph Glancy indicated, he feels that his union protects the workers from unfair arbitrary actions.

As noted earlier, another result of unionization is that management loses some of the flexibility that it had prior to unionization. For example, management may not be able to subcontract out some types of work without bargaining with the union. Work scheduling becomes more critical in that overtime or weekend work may become too expensive to serve as a remedy for poor planning or uneven flows of work. The impact on managerial decision making is great. In many areas that were once exclusive managerial prerogatives, the union may have decision inputs. For example, in the case of layoffs, management might have had a great deal of discretion in choosing employees for layoff, whereas after unionization, layoffs are conducted in accordance with negotiated procedures that typically emphasize seniority.

Management prerogatives: rights of management to act unilaterally in directing and coordinating the conduct of work.

The job security that workers frequently seek through unionization is often a cause of managerial complaints. Such job security results from limitations on how discharges and layoffs are conducted.

Unfortunately the requirements for due process (following procedural requirements) in disciplinary actions are viewed by some managers as obstacles to effective discipline or work standards enforcement. While there is some truth to these claims, if discipline is progressively assessed and documented in accordance with the proper procedures, effective discipline can be maintained along with work standards. Of course, there have been some unfortunate abuses of these job security safeguards by unions and union members.

Due process: following standard procedural requirements in the administration of personnel actions such as discipline.

Because job security is often obtained through union security devices such as the union shop agreement, which requires workers to join the union within thirty days after employment, unions constitute unique institutions.

Union Shop Agreement: employees must join the union within 30 days after employment.

Unions are one of the few private organizations that individuals may be required to join. Furthermore, by definition, collective bargaining places the interest of collective groups above the interests of the individual worker. Thus, because of the often involuntary nature of union membership and the difficulty of protecting individual worker interests, the process of collective bargaining and the internal functioning of unions are closely regulated by an extensive body of law. We turn our attention next to the legal environment of labor relations and collective bargaining.

LEGAL ENVIRONMENT OF COLLECTIVE BARGAINING

Labor relations and collective bargaining activities are probably the most extensively regulated of all personnel management functions. In the private sector, all but the smallest employers are covered by federal law. This law consists of three major pieces of legislation: (1) the National Labor Relations Act of 1935 (NLRA), referred to as the Wagner Act; (2) the Labor-Management Relations Act of 1947 (LMRA), referred to as the Taft–Hartley Act; and (3) the Labor Management Reporting and Disclosure Act of 1959 (LMRDA), referred to as the Landrum–Griffin Act.[6] Collectively, this legislation is called "the Act" by labor practitioners.

The law is so comprehensive that, when the NLRA was passed in 1935, the National Labor Relations Board (NLRB), an independent governmental agency, was created to administer the law. We concentrate in this chapter on the act, and NLRB and federal court interpretations of the Act.

Before delving further into this body of law, we should note first that other labor laws cover various employees. Many states have labor relations laws that cover employers who are too small to come under the Act according to the NLRB's jurisdictional standards. Those firms that have no effect on interstate commerce are also excluded from the act's coverage, but these are essentially the same small employers. Public sector employers are covered by other laws. Federal government employees are covered by the Federal Service Labor-Management and Employee Relations Law,[7] while state and local government employers are subject to state laws that vary widely in their level of comprehensiveness. Finally, in some cities, municipal ordinances cover labor relations activities. Because these laws exhibit substantial diversity, space limitations preclude coverage in this text. However, since the vast majority of private sector employers are covered by the Act, we concentrate on it and other federal legislation that applies to these employers.

Coverage of the Law

Current NLRB jurisdictional rules apply minimum size standards on the basis of dollar volumes of activity, such as goods purchased by nonretail employers from out of state (either directly or indirectly) and gross volume or gross revenue in the case of other employers. In the general case of nonretail employers having either $50,000 of annual out-of-state purchases or sales (direct or indirect), the Act applies. For retail establishments, the minumum standard for coverage is $500,000 annual gross volume. Specific minimum volume standards apply to several industries and types of employers, such as public utilities, hotels, motels, and transit systems.[8]

Aside from size consideration in the Act's coverage of employers, several types of employers and employees are excluded from coverage. Excluded employees are agricultural laborers, domestic servants, employers' children and spouses, independent contractors, supervisors, and managers. Also excluded are government employees who are covered by other legislation noted earlier and railroad and airline employees. Railroad and airline employees are covered by separate federal legislation, the Railway Labor Act of 1926.[9]

Representation Proceedings

The Act provides for representation elections that allow employees to determine through a secret ballot vote whether their unit will be represented by a union. This process ordinarily begins with a union-organizing campaign in which the union attempts to obtain employees' signatures on authorization cards or some other evidence of employee interest in unionization. After obtaining authorization cards from at least 55 to 60 percent of such employees, the union will typically petition the NLRB to conduct a representation election. The union (more than one union may be on the ballot) usually tries to obtain more than a majority of authorization cards because there may be some attrition in union sentiment during the period prior to the election.

> **Representation election:** an election conducted by the NLRB in which employees vote to determine whether they will be represented by a union.

The NLRB will conduct such an election if it determines (1) that there is sufficient interest in an election as evidenced by authorization cards from at least 30 percent of the employees, (2) that there has not been a representation election in the unit during the past twelve months, and (3) that there is no current valid contract with a certified bargaining agent (union that has won an NLRB representation election).

For purposes of the election (and bargaining, if the union should win), the election unit is comprised of nonsupervisory employees who basically tend to have common working condition interests. An example of a common election unit would be all production and maintenance (P and M) workers. If the union receives a simple majority of votes cast (50 percent plus one vote), it will be certified by the NLRB as the exclusive bargaining agent (exclusive representative) for these employees. At such time, the election unit then becomes the bargaining unit, although the parties may combine such units into larger bargaining units at some future time. All employees in the bargaining unit are represented by the union regardless of whether they are members. Thus, although only one union can be the bargaining agent for the employees in the unit (exclusive representation), the union is legally obligated to represent all of them (including processing their grievances, etc.).

Exclusive representation: a group of employees is represented by only one union.

The conduct of the employers and unions are both regulated carefully by the NLRB during the period leading up to the representation election so that "laboratory conditions" will exist for the election. The rationale is that employees should be able to vote in an atmosphere free from coercive influences. Thus very detailed rules govern the conduct of employers and unions during this period.

Laboratory conditions: rules governing the conduct of employers and unions during the period leading up to the representation election.

Essentially, the employer cannot threaten retaliation or promise benefits contingent upon voting behavior. The employer and unions cannot restrain or coerce employees in exercising their right to unionize or to refrain from unionization. There has been some criticism of the amount of detailed regulation that governs organizational campaigns in the pre-election period. These criticisms maintain that employees' predisposition to vote for or against unionization are not affected materially by most pre-election activities.[10] Nonetheless, a proliferation of consulting firms, books, and seminars is directed at assisting firms to remain nonunion.[11] Furthermore, although there is currently detailed regulation of the election process, the NLRB's remedial powers may be inadequate to protect employees against unfair labor practices, such as discriminatory discharges, that are attempted as means of avoiding unionization.[12]

The number of elections conducted within thirty days after the filing of election petitions has been declining in recent years as some employers have apparently been following a strategy of attempting to win elections through the use of delay tactics.[13] In recent years, there has been a trend, in part because of such practices and increasing managerial sophistication, toward fewer union "wins" in representation elections (46.5 percent of 6,837 elections in 1978).[14] There has also been an increase in the number of decertification elections (as noted earlier) that are conducted in a similar manner as representation elections.

Although we have described only the representation election process as a means by which unions become the bargaining agent for employees, there are other means as well. First, the employer can voluntarily grant recognition to a union. The employer, however, should be careful not to do so if the union does not have the support of a majority of employees in the unit. Second, in the construction industry, an employer can sign contracts with the various trade unions such as the carpenters, plumbers, and so on. In such cases, the employer is supplied labor that is referred to the job by the union hiring halls. Third, if during the period leading up to an NLRB election, the employer violates the laboratory conditions with such a blatant threat, promise of benefit, or other act of restraint or coercion that a fair election cannot be held in the future, the NLRB will order the employer to bargain with the union. This is called a bargaining order. Even though the employer may have won an election, because of illegal actions, the employer must bargain with the union.[15]

Hiring hall: a union office that maintains lists or rosters of craftsmen (predominantly the union's members) who are available for work.

Unfair Labor Practices

In 1935, the Act contained a series of employer unfair labor practices. As a result of these protections against certain employer actions, unions gained a great deal of power relative to their pre-Wagner Act status. Partially as a result of this shift in power, in 1947 the Taft-Hartley Act added a series of union unfair labor practices. The law's basic statement of employees' rights and unfair labor practices are presented in Table 18-2.

It is readily apparent from reading excerpts of the Act presented in the Table that many of the unfair labor practices must be interpreted in terms of specific practices. For example, what constitutes restraint or coercion? The interpretation of these unfair labor practices is a continual job of the NLRB and the courts in which NLRB rulings are contested. Many of these seemingly simple provisions in the Act are quite complex and have been the subject of years of litigation. However, the basic intent of each of these unfair labor practices can be described.[16]

EMPLOYER UNFAIR LABOR PRACTICES.   The 8(a) series describes the employer unfair labor practices. The first, 8(a)(1), states that employers cannot restrain or coerce employees who are exercising their rights to join and form unions and engage in collective activities. Examples of 8(a)(1) violations are surveillance of employees who are attempting to unionize, blacklisting union activists, threatening to close down the plant solely on the basis of whether employees decide to unionize, and promising to raise wages if employees do not vote to unionize.[17] Violations of the NLRB laboratory condition rules during the prerepresentation election period constitute 8(a)(1) violations. Furthermore, 8(a)(1) is not mutually exclusive with respect to the other employer unfair labor practices, since violations of the others also constitute restraint and coercion and are consequently violations of 8(a)(1).[18]

The next unfair labor practice, 8(a)(2), essentially outlaws company unions that are employer controlled through the placement of managerial representatives as union

Table 18-2

Partial Text of The Labor Management Relations Act of 1947
(as amended in 1959 and 1974)

Rights of Employees

Sec. 7. Employees shall have the right to self-organization, to form, join, or assist labor organizations, to bargain collectively through representatives of their own choosing, and to engage in other concerted activities for the purpose of collective bargaining or other mutual aid or protection, and shall also have the right to refrain from any or all of such activities except to the extent that such right may be affected by an agreement requiring membership in a labor organization as a condition of employment as authorized in Section 8(a) (3).

Employer Unfair Labor Practices

Sec. 8(a)   It shall be an unfair labor practice for an employer

(1) to interfere with, restrain, or coerce employees in the exercise of the rights guaranteed in Section 7.

(2) to dominate or interfere with the formation or administration of any labor organization or contribute financial or other support to it . . .

(3) by discrimination in regard to hire or tenure of employment or any term or condition of employment to encourage or discourage membership in any labor organization . . .

(4) to discharge or otherwise discriminate against an employee because he has filed charges or given testimony under this Act . . .

(5) to refuse to bargain collectively with the representatives of his employees . . .

Union Unfair Labor Practices

Sec. 8(b)   It shall be an unfair labor practice for a labor organization or its agents

(1) to restrain or coerce (A) employees in the exercise of the rights guaranteed in Section 7 . . . or (B) an employer in the selection of his representatives for the purposes of collective bargaining or the adjustment of grievances;

(2) to cause or attempt to cause an employer to discriminate against an employee in violation of subsection (a)(3) or to discriminate against an employee with respect to whom membership in such an organization has been denied or terminated on some ground other than his failure to tender the periodic dues and the initiation fees uniformly required as a condition of acquiring or retaining membership;

(3) to refuse to bargain collectively with an employer, provided it is the representative of his employees . . .

(4) (i) to engage in, or to induce or encourage any individual employed by any person engaged in commerce or in an industry affecting commerce to engage in, a strike or a refusal in the course of his employment to use, manufacture, process, transport, or otherwise handle or work on any goods, articles, materials, or commodities or to perform any services; or (ii) to threaten, coerce, or restrain any person engaged in commerce or in an industry affecting commerce, where in either case an object thereof is:

(A) forcing or requiring any employer or self-employed person to join any labor or employer organization or to enter into any agreement which is prohibited by section 8(e);

(B) forcing or requiring any person to cease using, selling, handling, transporting, or otherwise dealing in the products of any other producer, processor, or manufacturer, or to cease doing business with any other person, or forcing or requiring any other employer to recognize or bargain with a labor organization as the representative of his

Table 18-2 (*Continued*)

employees unless such labor organization has been certified as the representative of such employees. . . . *Provided* that nothing contained in this clause (B) shall be construed to make unlawful, where not otherwise unlawful, any primary strike or primary picketing;

(C) forcing or requiring any employer to recognize or bargain with a particular labor organization as the representative of his employees if another labor organization has been certified as the representative of such employees . . .

(D) forcing or requiring any employer to assign particular work to employees in a particular labor organization or in a particular trade, craft, or class rather than to employees in another labor organization or in another trade, craft, or class, unless such employer is failing to conform to an order or certification of the Board determining the bargaining representative for employees performing such work . . .

(5) to require of employees covered by an agreement authorized under subsection (a)(3) the payment, as a condition precedent to becoming a member of such an organization, of a fee in an amount which the Board [NLRB] finds excessive or discriminatory under all the circumstances . . .

(6) to cause or attempt to cause an employer to pay or deliver or agree to pay or deliver any money or thing of value, in the nature of an exaction, for services which are not performed or not to be performed; and

(7) to picket or cause to be picketed or threaten to picket or cause to be picketed, any employer where an object thereof is forcing or requiring an employer to recognize or bargain with a labor organization as the representative of his employees, or forcing or requiring the employees of an employer to accept or select such labor organization as their collective bargaining representative, unless such labor organization is currently certified as the representative of such employees . . .

Employer and Union Unfair Labor Practice

Sec. 8(e)   It shall be an unfair labor practice for any labor organization and any employer to enter into any contract or agreement, express or implied, whereby such employer ceases or refrains or agrees to cease or refrain from handling, using, selling, transporting or otherwise dealing in any of the products of any other employer, or to cease doing business with any other person, and any contract or agreement entered into heretofore or hereafter containing such an agreement shall be to such extent unenforceable and void . . .

Source: Excerpted from the Labor Management Relations Act (1947), as amended by Public Laws 86-257 (1959) and 93-360 (1974).

officers, financial support, or other means. Employers must be careful in organizing employee committees because committees that deal with wages, grievances, and other conditions of work may be defined by the NLRB and courts as "labor organizations," and as such, their formation by the employer would risk 8(a)(2) violation. Thus new ideas of worker participation in committees may conflict with 8(a)(2).[19]

Company union: an employer dominated union that is illegal under the Act.

Discriminating in hiring, employee tenure, or in other working conditions on the basis of union activity or membership constitutes a violation of 8(a)(3). This unfair labor practice essentially prevents the closed shop requiring an individual to be a union member before being hired.

> **Closed shop agreement:** employees must be members of the union before being hired.

This unfair labor practice does not prevent the employer from enforcing a valid union shop agreement in which the employer would be required by the union to terminate an employee who refused to join the union within thirty days or who has not been paying required union dues. Of course, union shop agreements are not legal in right-to-work states, although the agency shop agreement may be legal. The agency shop agreement requires the employee to pay dues, but membership in the union is not required.

> **Agency shop agreement:** employees do not have to join the union but must pay union fees or dues.

Unfair labor practice 8(a)(4) simply prevents an employer from retaliating against employees who file charges or testify to the NLRB about the employer's conduct.

The final employer unfair labor practice, 8(a)(5), requires bargaining with the union if it is the certified bargaining unit for employees (has won a representation election). In 1947, the duty to bargain was broadened to include the concept of "good faith" bargaining. *Good faith bargaining* includes requirements that the parties must make counterproposals to demands, refrain (in the case of employers) from unilaterally implementing concessions during negotiations, meet within a reasonable time period to negotiate or renegotiate the contract, put the contract in writing if either party insists, send representatives to negotiate who have sufficient authority to bargain, refrain from reneging on concessions, and conduct bargaining so that the totality of their conduct indicates a genuine intent to reach agreement.[20] Essentially, these requirements mean that the parties must conduct negotiations according to an "auction model" in which counterproposals are offered. The parties cannot initiate negotiations with a firm and final offer and then adopt a "take-it-or-leave-it" stance. Nevertheless, the law does not require the parties to make real concessions.

The obligation to bargain in good faith on an issue depends on the type of issue. There are three types of issues: mandatory, voluntary, and illegal. Mandatory issues concern wages, hours, and conditions of employment. If either party (the union or management) brings up the issue in negotiations, the other party must bargain over the issue. Voluntary issues require no bargaining if either party declines. However, a party wishing to bargain over a voluntary issue cannot insist on such an issue to the point where an impasse (deadlock or stalemate) occurs. An example of a voluntary issue for management is a union demand to have an input on promotions beyond supervisory levels. For a union, a voluntary issue is a management demand that the union conduct a vote of the membership before going on strike. An illegal issue is the closed shop. If either party brings up the issue, it is illegal for the parties to bargain over it.[21]

Union Unfair Labor Practices

The 8(b) series pertains to the unfair labor practices of unions. The first one, 8(b)(1), as in the case of employers, prevents restraint and coercion of employees in exercising their rights to join a union and engage in collective bargaining activities or to refrain from such activities. Prohibited actions include acts of violence; mass picketing, which blocks entrances to the employer's premises and threatens violence; offering to obtain work for a member and paying him or her for withdrawing union unfair labor practice charges; and failing to process grievances on the basis of the grievant's race.[22]

Grievance: a charge that a provision of the labor agreement has been violated.

Unions are prevented from causing employers to operate closed shops by 8(b)(2).[23] Even where there is a valid union shop agreement, the union cannot force an employer to discharge an employee who has been expelled from the union as long as the employee pays the required union dues and fees.

Unfair labor practice, 8(b)(3), requires bargaining on the part of the union. Typically, the union does not refuse to bargain since it is the union's goal to secure more wages, benefits, or improvements in working conditions from the employer.

Secondary boycotts are prevented by 8(b)(4). The regulation of secondary pressure is very complicated because although secondary pressure on neutral third parties is felt to be undesirable, the rights of unions and employees must also be preserved at the same time. An example of a secondary boycott follows. A union has a dispute with employer A. Employer A sells a large portion of its output to employer B. To gain more leverage in its negotiations with employer A, the union asks employer B to stop purchasing materials from employer A. To enforce its request of employer B, the union sets up a picket line at employer B's premises and employer B's employees, who also belong to the same union, honor the picket line and refuse to work. Thus putting pressure on employer B, a neutral third party uninvolved in the primary dispute, constitutes a secondary boycott.

Unreasonable union dues and fees are prohibited by 8(b)(5). The reasonableness of such dues and fees depends on such factors as the typical earnings of union members and prevailing dues and fees in the industry.

Featherbedding practices were supposed to be prohibited by 8(b)(6); however, the manner in which the provision was written precludes any effective regulation of such practices. Featherbedding practices involve "make-work" requirements, the performance of unnecessary work, or overmanning for the amount of work required. The only practice actually made illegal by 8(b)(6) is requiring the employer to pay for work that is not performed. Thus, even though the work is not needed or wanted by the employer, as long as it is performed, there is no violation of the law.

Featherbedding: inefficient work practice requirements such as the performance of unnecessary work, overmanning, or make-work.

Finally, 8(b)(7) prevents *recognitional or organizational picketing* (picketing directed at causing an employer to recognize and bargain with the union) when (1) there has been a NLRB representation election within the previous twelve months, (2) there is an existing contract with a certified bargaining agent (union), or (3) the union has not filed a petition for an NLRB representation election within thirty days of commencement of picketing.

The final unfair labor practice, 8(e), applies to both employers and unions. This provision prohibits the parties from entering into *hot cargo agreements.* In a hot cargo agreement, an employer agrees not to process or handle materials made by an employer with whom the union has a dispute.

Hot cargo agreement: an agreement not to process or handle certain goods such as those made by nonunion employers or employers with whom the union has a dispute.

COLLECTIVE BARGAINING:

Collective bargaining: the process in which the union and management negotiate and administer written agreements of their understanding of the terms and conditions of employment (e.g., wages, hours, work rules).

The primary concern of collective bargaining is with rules—the rules of the workplace. Essentially, two kinds of rules are negotiated: substantive rules, that are concerned with terms such as the wage rate, and procedural rules, that are rules for rule making. An example of the latter are the procedures that define the processing of grievances. Because the rules that govern the conditions under which work is performed are so specific and numerous, labor contracts or agreements in the United States for industrial unions, that organize workers without regard to craft or skill, are often upwards of 150 to 200 pages in length. Craft unions that organize along craft or skill lines have much shorter contracts.[24]

When collective bargaining is discussed, most persons think of contract negotiations. Contract negotiations constitute only a small, but important, phase of collective bargaining. The actual administration of the final negotiated agreement constitutes the bulk of collective bargaining activity. Much of this administrative activity consists of processing grievances. In our discussion of collective bargaining, we deal first with contract negotiations; then we turn to contract administration.

Contract Negotiations

Four major processes seem to occur in most labor negotiation contexts: (1) distributive bargaining, (2) integrative bargaining, (3) attitudinal structuring, (4) intraorganizational bargaining.[25]

DISTRIBUTIVE BARGAINING.   Distributive bargaining is essentially a pure conflict process in which one party wins what the other party loses. In distributive bargaining, the opposing parties may be described as if they were maximizing subjective expected utility. Not all increases in wages and other issues would have the same utility. Thus, given this goal orientation, there is a tendency to pursue a wage settlement that takes into consideration (1) the likelihood that the opponent will resist agreement until a strike occurs, (2) strike costs, (3) the settlements that other employers and unions have reached, and (4) the difficulties in future negotiations and administration of the contract that are likely to result from that particular settlement. Thus it is probably not accurate even in the distributive process to say that a party will try to settle for all it can obtain (in the case of unions) or the least (in the case of management), because to do so would make administration of the contract very difficult. In addition, the opponent may retaliate in the next set of contract negotiations. Furthermore, it is unlikely that the negotiator would push an issue to the extent that the viability of the company (or union) is endangered. Nonetheless, distributive bargaining is a win-lose process in which information is hoarded and distorted to gain at the other party's expense.[26]

INTEGRATIVE BARGAINING.   Integrative bargaining is a problem-solving process in which there is open identification of the parties' needs and maximum information sharing. Issues that are resolved through integrative bargaining have the potential for both parties to win. An example of an integrative issue is work rules. The union may have bargained in the past for restrictive work rules that were for safety or for the preservation of union members' jobs. Changes in technology may have eliminated the need for such rules. Furthermore, the employer may be at a competitive disadvantage as a result of antiquated work rules. An integrative solution may enable both parties to win in such circumstances. Union members' jobs may be preserved through reassignment of personnel, whereas the financial viability of the employer is maintained through the elimination of inefficient work rules or manning requirements. Needless to say, the trust required for parties to enter into integrative bargaining is not obtained easily, especially when the parties' previous bargaining interactions have been distributive. When extreme levels of antagonism exist between the parties, integrative bargaining activities are not feasible. Unfortunately, in such circumstances, issues that have integrative bargaining potential may end up as distributive issues and may be handled in a win-lose contest.[27] Ralph Glancy seemed to be talking about the need for integrative bargaining when he stated that management and the union needed to cooperate more.

ATTITUDINAL STRUCTURING.   The process by which the relationship between the parties is changed so that positive outcomes, such as integrative bargaining, can take place is called attitudinal structuring. Since attitudes are quite resistant to change, attitudinal structuring activities may be directed toward improvement of relationships over long time frames, which in some cases may take years. In some situations, outside parties are brought in to improve the relationship between the parties. These parties may employ techniques based on a reinforcement theory or cognitive balance theory (which operates on the resolution of dissonance in a person's beliefs or cognitions) to try to improve the parties' attitudes toward each other.[28]

INTRAORGANIZATIONAL BARGAINING.   Intraorganizational bargaining is concerned with resolving conflict within the parties' own organizations. This is particularly important in the case of unions. A student of personnel management can benefit greatly by understanding that unions are political organizations and that union leaders can retain their positions only as long as they satisfy the wishes of their members. A union leader's actions that may seem inexplicable initially may be quite rational when it is considered that some actions are necessary to maintain continued favor with a constituency. Furthermore, it is often forgotten that unions have internal conflict. Various factions within the union have different needs and may consequently place incompatible demands on union leaders. For example, younger members may be more interested in increased wages, whereas older members may be more interested in larger pensions. Other sources of internal conflict may involve expectations of what can be obtained in negotiations. Because union leaders are more aware of the employer's financial situation, they may have lower expectations of what can be obtained realistically in negotiations than do the members. These internal conflicts must be controlled or resolved if the union leader is to retain his position. Thus the employer must realize that the union leader's actions, such as a public statement critical of the employer, may be for the "internal consumption" of the membership and not be intended to influence the employer.[29]

Collective Bargaining Structure

The structure of collective bargaining may be described in terms of four concepts: (1) size of the bargaining unit, (2) scope of the bargaining unit, (3) distribution of decision-making power, and (4) relationships between bargaining units. Size refers to number of both employees and establishments. Scope pertains to the number or type of industries, geography, and so on. The distribution of decision-making power pertains to the power balance between the parties. Finally, relationships among units pertain to coalitions of bargaining units, the locus of decision making in negotiating units, and pattern following arrangements in settlements.[30]

Because the bargaining structure in the United States is so complex, we describe it in only the most general terms for the country as a whole and then analyze in some detail, according to the concepts just outlined, two industries that illustrate extremely different bargaining structures.

THE UNITED STATES.   Compared to the bargaining structure in other countries, the U.S. system of collective bargaining is relatively decentralized. In the United
States, greater emphasis is placed on plant-level relationships and negotiations than in
other countries. Evidence of great decentralization is provided by the fact that there
are approximately 150,000 separate contracts. One reason for such decentralization is
that in the United States unions are vitally concerned with the specific "rules of the
shop" that reg ilate working conditions. Nonetheless, there is an almost overwhelming
amount of diversity in bargaining structure. For example, although there are approximately 150,000 contracts, 50 percent of the workers represented by unions are covered
by only 1,700 of these contracts. Because of the great amount of diversity in bargaining structure, we are oversimplifying the case to describe the United States structure
as decentralized. [31]

An indication of the differences in structure that occur across industries can be
obtained by reviewing the bargaining structure in two vastly different industries: the
construction industry (many small employers, several employer associations, many
unions)[32] and the steel industry (a small number of large employers, one employer
council, one union).[33]

THE CONSTRUCTION INDUSTRY.   Construction firms are dispersed throughout
the country. In contrast to many industries, production is not concentrated geographi-
cally. Although nineteen national unions represent construction workers, negotiations
are mostly conducted at the local union level where there is a great deal of autonomy,
especially among the building trade locals. Combinations of employers for bargaining
purposes in employer associations is common. These associations provide several services for the employers, many of whom are relatively small and could not afford such
services individually. These services include negotiating, lobbying, and public relations.[34]

Labor agreements with the individual construction unions are negotiated locally
by the employer or contractors' associations. The associations also administer these
agreements for their employer members. In contrast to industries characterized by
centralized bargaining (such as automobiles and steel), there are approximately 6,000
contracts in effect in the construction industry. Although local negotiations are prevalent, negotiations that are coordinated among different unions and employer associations are conducted at regional levels. Also, building trade councils, which consist of
several unions, conduct coordinated negotiations with employer associations in some
municipalities. Finally, within the construction industry there are variations in bargaining structure according to geographic region. Thus there is a rich diversity in
structure in the construction industry.[35]

THE STEEL INDUSTRY.   The bargaining structure in the steel industry provides
a striking contrast to that of the construction industry. In the steel industry, production is concentrated largely in the northern midwestern and northeastern states. As of
1976, there were eighty-nine steel producing companies. The largest twenty-five of
these produced 72 percent of domestic steel during that year. Steelworkers are repre-

sented by an industrial union, the United Steelworkers of America, which in 1976 had 1,400,000 members and was the second largest union in the country. Iron mining and basic steel employees comprise approximately 35 percent of the union's membership.[36]

Bargaining is conducted on an industrywide basis in which the national union negotiates with representatives of the steel companies on national issues. Although the companies have individual contracts with the union, the provisions on national issues, such as wages, are the same. Local issues are negotiated between the individual companies and the union. An interesting negotiating procedure has been developed in the steel industry. Because strikes have played a major role in placing the steel industry at a competitive disadvantage with imported steel, a remedy for such work disruptions was sought. An *Experimental Negotiating Agreement* (ENA) was adopted by the parties that would substitute binding interest arbitration (arbitration over the terms of a new contract) for strikes on national bargaining issues that could not be resolved during negotiations. So far, the ENA has proved successful in eliminating strikes.[37]

Interest arbitration: a procedure in which a neutral third party decides the terms of some provisions that will be included in a new labor contract.

STRUCTURE WRAP-UP.   We have purposely chosen two widely different industries to help explain the extremes and diversity in bargaining structure. One of these industries features decentralized bargaining; the other illustrates highly centralized industrywide bargaining. Neither structural form is superior to the other because each is appropriate for its industry's unique product market, employer concentration, and geographic dispersion. Most of the remaining industries can be described as fitting on a continuum between these two industries. We hasten to warn, however, that collective bargaining structures are diverse.

Strikes

On occasion, new contracts cannot be negotiated without recourse to the application of economic leverage. The cost of disagreement on a new contract for both unions and employers are the costs of a strike. The union loses wages and runs the risk of losing jobs through replacement. Employers lose potential profits, risk losing market shares, and incur overhead costs during the strike. The right to strike is the force that causes the parties to reach agreements on contracts voluntarily.

Thus, although strikes are necessary for the practice of free collective bargaining, are the costs of strikes excessive? An examination of recent strike data reveals that in 1978 there were 4,230 work stoppages or strikes. The average duration for these strikes was 33.2 days, the median was 17.0 days. Although 1,623,000 workers were involved in these strikes only .17 of one percent of total working time was lost due to strikes. In fact, total working time lost due to strikes has not exceeded 1 percent in any one year since 1946 when 1.04 percent of total working time was lost. Thus, although there is a cost to strikes in terms of days lost, it is not as excessive as one might imagine.[38]

CONTRACT ADMINISTRATION

Negotiations are critical, sometimes dramatic, and often newsworthy, but we cannot overstate the importance of the day-to-day administration of the contract. The best written contract will not produce effective labor relations if grievances are filed continually and the parties spend time and resources in the arbitration of excessive grievances.

> **Grievance arbitration:** a neutral third party decides whether a provision in the existing contract has been violated. Grievance arbitration is concerned with interpretation of an existing contract.

The U.S. collective bargaining system is unique in that there is a well-developed private system for processing disagreements over interpretation of the contract that culminates in binding arbitration. If there can be no other justification of unions than this, the unique U.S. system of "industrial jurisprudence" is a remarkable success. This is not to say that the system is without faults or that no abuses of the system have occurred. Nonetheless, the grievance system protects workers from arbitrary treatment. Furthermore, while there may be disagreements, work proceeds while the issue is resolved. This is in direct contrast to the practice in the United Kingdom where unions conduct short strikes to resolve such disagreements.

Grievances

Grievance procedures are designed by the parties and are incorporated into the contract. Although such procedures vary from contract to contract, there are some general similarities. A typical grievance procedure is outlined in Table 18-3.

In the first step, the employee who has a grievance (the grievant) must take it to his immediate supervisor. The supervisor has three days in which to respond to the grievant. If the grievant is dissatisfied with the supervisor's response, the grievant then takes the grievance to the second step. In this step, the grievance is put in writing and

Table 18-3

Typical Grievance Procedure

Step 1. The grievant discusses grievance with immediate supervisor who has three days in which to prepare a response.

Step 2. Within seven days, the grievant prepares the grievance in writing. After two other union officials sign the grievance, it is submitted to the immediate supervisor and unit manager who have seven days in which to prepare a response.

Step 3. Within ten days, the union grievance committee submits the grievance to the plant manager or his representative who has ten days in which to prepare a response.

Step 4. The grievance is taken to binding arbitration.

is signed by the grievant and two union representatives. At this step, the union has seven days in which to submit the grievance to the supervisor. The supervisor and unit manager then have seven days in which to respond to the union. If the union is dissatisfied with the employer's response, the grievance is then taken to the third step. At the third step, the union's grievance committee has ten days in which to submit the grievance to the plant manager or his representative. The plant manager or his representative then has ten days in which to respond to the grievance. If the union is dissatisfied with the response from the plant manager or his representative, the grievance is then taken to the fourth step. In step four, the union notifies the plant manager or his representative that it is going to take the grievance to arbitration. The union then has thirty-five days in which to request a list of seven arbitrators from the American Arbitration Association. After the parties receive the list, they take turns striking off names of unacceptable arbitrators until one arbitrator is left. The parties then contact the arbitrator to schedule a hearing on the grievance. The arbitrator's ruling on the grievance is binding on the parties.

As in our example, approximately 25 percent of all grievance procedures contain four steps. Some grievance procedures even have five steps; however, the most common number of steps is three. A majority of grievance procedures (63 percent) require the grievance to be in written form at the first step, although a substantial number (37 percent) permit such grievances to be oral. In general, as the grievance is processed through the steps of the procedure, the time limits on responses are more lengthy. A common problem with grievance procedures is the time delay before final disposition of the case. In 1975 there was an average delay of sixty-eight days between the filing date of a grievance (for one going all the way through the steps to arbitration) and the date of the request for a list of arbitrators.[39]

The example of a typical grievance procedure brings up several questions. The first question might be, "Are all contract disagreements subject to the grievance procedure and arbitration?" In some contracts, management prerogatives are spelled out in which some issues are identified that are not subject to the grievance procedure. This practice is somewhat more prevalent in industries in which the parties have not had much experience with collective bargaining and may not want to allow grievances on all matters.[40]

Another question may be, "Can the employer file a grievance?" Although it is unusual for an employer to file a grievance, the procedure may provide for this action. A company grievance against the union could occur when the union strikes in violation of a no-strike clause. As a result of filing such a grievance, the company's claims could be handled in arbitration.[41]

Processing Grievances

If used properly, the grievance procedure can serve management in several valuable ways. Not only does the grievance procedure enable the employer to have production uninterrupted by disagreements over contract interpretation, but it also provides a valuable channel for upward communication from employees. Further, frequent grievances on the same issue may pinpoint trouble spots. Likewise, frequent grievances involving the same supervisor may indicate poor supervisor performance or, conversely, that the supervisor could be enforcing high standards. In any event the grievance procedure provides a valuable source of communication and a potential diagnostic tool. Ralph Glancy stressed the point that the union provides a link between employees and management. One type of such a linkage is the grievance procedure.

Suggestions for management that will allow the grievance procedure to be utilized more effectively include the following: (1) The grievance procedure should be simple enough to be understood by all employees. (2) The procedure should resolve grievances quickly. (3) Grievances that do not have policy implications for other departments or units should be settled at the lower levels in the management hierarchy. (4) Grievances involving disciplinary matters should be given priority handling. (5) The goal in resolving grievances should be a fair settlement instead of "winning."[42]

The first two suggestions have the effect of promoting employee confidence in the grievance procedure. If employees do not understand the procedure or if the backlog of unresolved grievances builds up over a period of time, employees will lose patience with the procedure and work disruptions could occur. The rationale for handling grievances at the lower managerial levels when possible is that not only is there potential for rapid resolutions of grievances but the authority of first-level supervisors and foreman is emphasized. For some time, the authority of first-line supervisors has been challenged. Of course, there is good reason for centralizing grievance handling and resolving grievances at higher managerial levels. If grievances with potential policy implications are decided incorrectly by first-line supervisors, the union may attempt to use the decisions as precedents and apply them to the employer's other departments or units. Thus first-line supervisors may need training in grievance handling. Handling grievances enables supervisors to re-establish an increment of authority.

Grievances involving disciplinary measures, for example, or discharge, should be handled expeditiously because, if such a grievance is ultimately resolved in arbitration and the employer's actions are overruled, the arbitrator may require the employer to pay the grievant back pay during the period in which he was suspended or discharged. Finally, management should decide grievances on their merits instead of taking an adversarial role. Management should also resist "trading" or "bargaining" with the union over how grievances will be resolved and should, instead, resolve each individual grievance on the basis of its merits.

Arbitration

In describing the grievance procedure, the subject of grievance arbitration or "rights" arbitration was introduced. Although in the grievance example, the list of arbitrators from which one was to be chosen was supplied by the American Arbitration Association (AAA), there are other sources. The Federal Mediation and Conciliation Service (FMCS) also provides lists of arbitrators to requesting parties. Sometimes both parties may simply know an arbitrator. In such cases, they may appoint the arbitrator directly to hear the case instead of going through either the AAA or FMCS.

An arbitrator's acceptability to the parties depends not only on competence but on neutrality. It is not surprising, therefore, that the most common method of paying for arbitration services involves equal sharing of costs by both parties.[43] This method of payment also provides an incentive to the parties to settle grievances on their own without resorting to arbitration since it is quite expensive. In 1975, the AFL-CIO estimated the union's costs of going to arbitration on a relatively simple case involving a one-day hearing to be $2,220. These costs included the arbitrator's fees and expenses as well as lawyer's fees, transcript expenses, and other costs.[44] Thus there are sound economic reasons against abusing the arbitration procedure by using it to resolve grievances that lack merit. Although the union is required by law to process the grievances of all the employees it represents (either members or nonmembers), it does not have to take any grievances to arbitration that it feels lack merit.

Although at this point we know that arbitration is the final step in most grievance procedures and that it provides a final and binding resolution of grievances, little has been said about the actual procedure. *Grievance arbitration* is over the parties' rights and results from a contractual arrangement. The arbitrator's limited authority flows from the arbitration provisions in the labor agreement that the parties negotiated. The arbitrator's jurisdiction is limited to interpreting the contract with respect to the grievance at issue. It is not uncommon in an arbitration hearing for one of the parties to charge that the grievance is not arbitral under the provisions of the contract. This charge then becomes a subject of arbitration itself as the parties arbitrate questions of arbitration.[45] Likewise, it is not uncommon for the arbitrator to rule, after deliberations, that the grievance cannot be arbitrated.

Unlike court procedures, arbitration hearings are private proceedings and are not open to the public. Privacy is a distinct asset because sensitive personal or proprietary issues are often the subject of such hearings. Further, the hearing procedure is informal, and the rules of evidence are much more relaxed than in litigation. Although there are no specified procedural rules or rules of evidence that the parties are legally required to follow, such hearings usually follow a generally accepted pattern that assures a fair hearing and fair consideration of the evidence.[46] Those hearings conducted under the auspices of the AAA must follow procedural rules established by the association[47]

One result of the absence of requirements for following legal procedures is that the parties do not have to be represented by attorneys and the arbitrator does not have to be an attorney. The most important requirements are that the arbitrator must be familiar with industrial relations practices, neutral, of good character, and reasonable. Thus, although many arbitrators are attorneys, many are labor relations professors, labor economists, or members of the clergy. However, a working knowledge of the rules of evidence is quite useful for the parties presenting the union and employer's cases.[48] Another result is that arbitration hearings are conducted with minimal reliance on technical language. Likewise, arbitrators' awards are usually written in nontechnical language. The use of nontechnical language allows employees to understand the arbitrators' reasoning. Unfortunately, given some of the complex issues on which arbitrators must rule, it is doubtful that the average employee would want to read through some arbitrator's lengthy and involved awards.

After hearing the case, the arbitrator issues an award that is binding on the parties to the extent that it will be enforced by the courts under Section 301 of the Act.[49] An advantage of arbitration versus litigation is that the arbitrator has a great deal of flexibility in fashioning an award that will provide the most equity under the circumstances. For example, the arbitrator may order an unfairly discharged employee to be reinstated to his or her previous job with or without back pay, commute the discharge to a suspension of so many days, or rule in favor of the employer by denying the grievance. In other words, the arbitrator does more than decide guilt or innocence and apply a punishment as defined in statutes. In fashioning the award, the arbitrator (who is chosen because of his or her familiarity with industrial relations practices, or sometimes even on the basis of specialized knowledge of the unique practices in the particular industry) considers all the implications of the award on morale, production efficiency, future contract administration, and so on.[50] (In reality, the parties often read the arbitrators' past awards and try to select an arbitrator who is, in their opinion, more likely to rule in their favor on the particular issue in the grievance.)

Unfortunately, the process has not been particularly expeditious in recent years.[51] In fact, in 1975, the average number of days between the filing of the grievance and the arbitrator's award had risen to 223 days.[52] If grievances were handled by courts, however, even more time would probably be required. Such delays detract from the value of the process. Several factors contribute to such delays (e.g., tardiness by the parties or their representatives), but much of the delay comes from the time it takes to obtain a date on which the desired arbitrator can hear the award. Many unions and employers prefer to wait months for a seasoned arbitrator rather than to take a chance on an unproven individual.

The American Arbitration Association has offered several suggestions that inexperienced parties may find of some use. Of course, it is best to devote great effort to resolving the issue before reaching the arbitration step of the grievance procedure. Having reached arbitration, however, the parties will want to present their arguments on the grievance with some credibility. Most of these suggestions are summarized as follows: (1) The original grievance should be reviewed along with any provisions in the contract that may appear to have only limited applicability to the issue. (2) The grievance should be analyzed from the other party's viewpoint. In this manner, their arguments may be anticipated and responses can be prepared. (3) Witnesses for each side should be interviewed and notes on their testimony should be compiled. These notes can be incorporated into a checklist that can be utilized in the hearing to go back to any points that have been omitted from testimony. (4) Tentative case presentation outlines should be reviewed with other members of the organization so that deficiences can be identified. (5) A review of published arbitration awards on similar grievances may provide some guidance as to how the arbitrator will reason on the grievance.[53]

Ralph Glancy noted several issues that the union negotiated with the company (i.e., wages, job security). He noted that both parties should work together for best results. This is accomplished more in contract administration than in negotiations. He seemed fairly well satisfied at the present.

LABOR RELATIONS IN THE 1980s

Aside from the traditional "bread and butter" issues involving wages, hours, discipline, and other conditions of work, some issues are emerging that may be topics of future negotiations. One issue will undoubtedly be productivity. Productivity bargaining is not new, having received some attention during the 1960s. Productivity bargaining has typically involved attempts to eliminate restrictive work rules and practices or to obtain changes in job duties or jurisdictions that have detracted from efficiency.[54] Since such rules often have their origins in the preservation of the union members' jobs, the negotiations are often over the trade-off or quid pro quo that will make such concessions acceptable.

The preservation of union members' jobs has clearly been a major issue in the early years of the 1980s, particularly in the automobile industry where the combined pressures of competition from Japanese automobile manufacturers, high interest rates, and reduced consumer demand have placed many autoworkers' jobs in jeopardy. As the U.S. automobile manufacturers have been forced to close plants, workers have lost their jobs. These adverse conditions have caused unions and management to cooperate in attempting to negotiate novel alternatives that have previously been unacceptable. Some of the provisions have included concessions in work rules and wage increases in return for management concessions, such as job security and profit sharing.[55]

A novel approach to the issue of unions and productivity has recently been articulated. In the past unions have often been viewed as having an adverse impact on productivity through such practices as work rules and restrictions on management's flexibility. Now a few researchers are saying that unions may have a positive influence on productivity through a phenomenon known as collective voice. In the absence of unions, if employees are dissatisfied with working conditions, as individuals there is little they can do to exert influence to change such conditions other than personal persuasion. As a result, dissatisfied employees frequently "vote with their feet" by leaving or exercising an "exit voice." Thus, in the absence of collective bargaining, turnover-related disruptions in the workplace resulting from exit voice detract from productivity.[56]

Another issue may be incomes policies or wage and price controls. As a result of stagflation (a condition of high unemployment and high inflation), more pressure may be exerted on government to control negotiated wage settlements as well as prices.[57] Furthermore, in the past union membership growth has been associated positively with declines in unemployment and increases in prices.[58] Although the decade of the 1980s has begun with increases in prices, it has also begun with high unemployment. Thus a question is whether union membership will grow or decline in the 1980s. Recent research on union membership has found that, if unions are to grow in the future, they will have to reach out to sectors of the economy that traditionally have not been unionized heavily, such as the health care industry, and the public sector.[59]

Although we have not considered the unique features of public sector bargaining that distinguish it specifically from the private sector or differences in the legal environments of the two sectors (because of space limitations), the public sector will become critical in the future. It has been stated that unionization will become almost universal in the public sector. We have already seen that public sector collective bargaining has taken over many of the functions of civil service systems because of the failure of such systems to operate as effectively as they should.[60] The increasing number of public sector work stoppages in the United States, which reached 488 in the period between October 1977 and October 1978, points to a need for effective impasse resolution techniques[61] (such as mediation and interest arbitration). Likewise, the air traffic controllers' strike in 1981 in which nearly 12,000 strikers were discharged for conducting an illegal strike points to the need for the development of public sector bargaining expertise.

Another issue that is likely to assume greater importance in the future is quality of work life. So far, unions have not done much on this issue through traditional collective bargaining activities.[62] One observer has stated the following:

> But far from being an integral part of the movement to improve the quality of working life, American unionists have been almost totally divorced from it. Even more, they have been (or been portrayed as) opposed to it.[63]

The basis for such surprising resistance seems to be fundamental. Unions are sometimes apprehensive that management will implement such quality-of-work-life changes as job enrichment and work teams. They feel that hard-earned union rights to make inputs in workplace decision making will be gradually eliminated. The fact that most quality-of-work-life programs have occurred in nonunionized organizations lends credibility to this explanation.[64]

Finally, the Western European adoptions of codetermination, in which employees are represented on boards of directors and on boards concerned with the day-to-day management of companies, has raised questions about whether such a trend will carry over to the United States. In answer to this question, the conventional industrial relations wisdom is that this will not take place in the United States on any meaningful scale, as the following quotations indicate:

> American unionists strongly disavow Western European type worker participation schemes such as job control and codetermination . . .[65]

> Even as such beachheads [codetermination] are established, there is little likelihood that codetermination will become a major force furthering employee participation in U.S. management.[66]

The rationale for this view is that the origins and nature of the union movements in Western Europe and the United States are quite different. As opposed to Western European unions, which are frequently based on ideology, class consciousness, and a politically oriented power base, U.S. unions have preferred to concentrate pragmatically on job conditions and to pursue their objectives through collective bargaining rather than through socialism or employee ownership plans. As a result, U.S. unions are much more concerned with the detailed rules that govern the employer-employee relationship. The length of contracts that U.S. industrial unions typically negotiate provides evidence of the concern for the rules of the shop. Furthermore, the U.S. unions' roles as a challenger of managements' decisions would be compromised if the unions were involved in making such decisions as in codetermination systems.

However in recent years there have been some indications of changes in the United States. The president of the United Autoworkers Union is on the board of directors for Chrysler. Ralph Glancy, in our interview, was recently elected to the board of directors of Moon Specialties.

SUMMARY

In this chapter, the trends in union membership, reasons why employees join unions, and the impact of unions on management and personnel management have been described. When an organization is unionized, management loses some of the flexibility it had previously. Furthermore, policies become more formalized and many rules are reduced to writing. The conduct of disciplinary action becomes subject to the grievance procedure that dictates that management must follow rules of due process.

Relations between employers and unions are regulated extensively by federal law. With a few exceptions, all but the smallest private sector employers are covered by the Act. Union representation procedures are regulated by the NLRB, and the conduct of both employers and unions must maintain the laboratory conditions of a representation election. The labor relations activities of both employers and unions are restricted by a series of employer and union unfair labor practices that are designed to protect the rights of employees to engage in collective bargaining as well as the rights of employers and unions.

The processes involved in collective bargaining were examined. Four models of bargaining behavior were described: distributive bargaining, integrative bargaining, attitudinal structuring, and intraorganizational bargaining. Although the structure of U.S. collective bargaining may be described as decentralized because of its emphasis on local-level negotiations, the structure is complex and varies widely from one industry to another. Although negotiations occasionally result in strikes, the total working time lost in the United States as a result of strikes is typically less than a fraction of 1 percent in any one year.

Although negotiations are obviously critical in collective bargaining, the administration of the contract on a day-to-day basis comprises the bulk of collective bargaining activity. Use of multiple-step grievance procedures culminating in binding arbitration is the prevalent mode of resolving disagreements over labor contract interpretation. The grievance procedure and arbitration allow production to continue while disagreements are resolved.

Several labor relations issues of the 1980s were identified. Productivity may become a more important labor relations issue during the next decade along with incomes policies or wage and price controls. Likewise, public sector unionization seems likely to occupy a great deal of attention in the future. Whether unions will become strong proponents of the quality-of-work-life movement remains to be seen. To date, they have not been involved actively to any great extent with such issues. Finally, although there may be some experiments with workers on boards of directors, as with Ralph Glancy, U.S. unions are not likely to push for codetermination in the near future.

INTERVIEW WRAP-UP

The union is a bridge between management and employees and both must cooperate if they are to survive in the future. The union has enabled the employees to have better wages and benefits, protection, and job security. The union has also reduced the opportunity for management to exercise favoritism. One problem, however, is a perception among union members that management does not recognize their abilities or listen to their suggestions. —Ralph Glancy, machinist and company board member.

WHAT MANAGERS SHOULD DO REGARDING PERSONNEL MANAGEMENT ACTIVITIES

1. Managers should understand how their actions or failures to act sometimes cause employees to join unions.
2. Managers operating in a union environment should be familiar with the legal environment of labor relations. They should also realize that not all negotiations have to be distributive.
3. Managers should understand the role of the grievance procedure and arbitration and not try to abuse the system.

REVIEW QUESTIONS

1. How does rights arbitration (grievance arbitration) differ from courtroom procedures or litigation?
2. What is the relationship of the product market in the construction industry to the relatively great amount of local union autonomy?
3. Describe the bargaining structure in an industry of which you have some knowledge.
4. Describe the process by which a union becomes the certified bargaining agent for a group of employees.
5. What union actions are prohibited by the 8(b) series of unfair labor practices?
6. Who is excluded from coverage by federal labor relations law?

7. How does unionization affect the process of management and personnel management?

8. What employer actions are prohibited by the 8(a) series of unfair labor practices?

KEY CONCEPTS

AAA
Agency shop
Attitudinal structuring
Bargaining order
Bargaining unit
Closed shop
Codetermination
Company union
Craft union
Decertification
Distributive bargaining
Due process
Election unit
Exclusive representation
Featherbedding
FMCS
Good faith bargaining
Grievance procedure
Hot cargo agreement
Illegal bargaining issue
Incomes policies
Industrial union
Integrative bargaining

Interest arbitration
Intraorganizational bargaining
Job security
Labor agreement or contract
Labor conditions
Laboratory conditions
Labor Management Relations Act
Labor Management Reporting
  and Disclosure Act
Management prerogatives
Mandatory bargaining issue
National Labor Relations Act
NLRB
Productivity bargaining
Quality of work life
Recognitional or organizational picketing
Representation elections
Rights arbitration
Secondary boycott
Strikes
Unfair labor practices
Union shop
Voluntary bargaining issue

CASE

SIMMONS LAWN EQUIPMENT, INC.

Simmons Lawn Equipment, Inc., was founded in 1946 by George Simmons as a result of his success in designing a heavy-duty power lawn mower for industrial customers. Golf courses and industrial plants provided a strong market for the heavy-duty riding lawn mowers, which he built in his garage on a part-time basis.

The durability of his lawn mowers made them popular among groundskeepers, and after three years of manufacturing on a part-time basis, George quit his job at a local manufacturing plant and devoted his full-time efforts to his new business. Soon he hired two workers to help produce the mowers and moved into a rented building that provided more space.

The company grew steadily, and by 1960 George had thirty employees. Because of George's easygoing nature, the informality of the workplace, and wages that were about average for the area, relations with employees had always been good, and few employee relations problems were experienced. In fact, George always had a Christmas party for his employees at his own home as well as a Fourth of July picnic. Nonetheless, a few larger lawn mower companies had begun manufacturing heavy-duty lawn mowers, and George realized that he needed to keep up with these companies in product design and manufacturing quality. Fortunately, in 1969 George's oldest son, Tom, who had just graduated with a degree in mechanical engineering, returned to work in the plant with his father. Tom had some good ideas that led to better designed lawn mowers, and the company managed to keep its sales at the same level that it had maintained for several years. Nevertheless, both George and Tom felt that eventually they would have to expand into other areas of the commercial lawn care equipment business if they were to grow in the future.

In 1972 the company added a line of lawn fertilizer spreaders and a line of lawn sprinklers. Employment doubled in the next two years. By 1977, when George Simmons retired, the company had ninety-seven employees. The company by this time had lost its informality, and there had been quite a few problems with some of the older employees who were beginning to demand a pension program. Tom explained to them that the company was just too small for such benefits and that the employees were supposed to save money from their regular pay for retirement.

Low product demand caused two short layoffs in 1978 and 1979; however, in 1980 the company permanently reduced its work force to eighty-two employees because of a decline in sales in all three of its product lines. By 1982, grumblings about unionization had increased. On April 5, 1982, Tom received a letter from the NLRB informing him that it had received a petition for a representation election from his employees and that an election would be held in the near future. Tom felt betrayed and disappointed. Many of his employees who apparently wanted to unionize had been employees of the company for over twenty years.

QUESTIONS

1. Do you think that the experiences of Simmons Lawn Equipment, Inc., are typical? Why?

2. If the company is unionized, how will it be affected?

3. Why are the employees apparently willing to unionize?

NOTES

[1]"Union Membership Increases to 21.7 Million," *Labor Law Journal,* 30 (1979), 718.

[2]U.S. Department of Labor, *Directory of National Unions and Employee Associations, 1979, Bulletin 2079* (Washington, D.C.: Government Printing Office, 1980).

[3]P. J. Pestillo, "Can Unions Meet the Needs of a New Work Force?" *Monthly Labor Review,* 102, (1979), 33–34.

[4]M. H. Sandver and H. G. Heneman, III, "Union Growth Through the Election Process," *Industrial Relations,* 20 (1981), 109–116.

[5]T. A. Kochan, "How American Workers View Labor Unions," *Monthly Labor Review,* 102, (1979), 22–31.

[6]R. A. Gorman, *Basic Text on Labor Law, Unionization and Collective Bargaining* (St. Paul: West, 1976).

[7]Commerce Clearing House, *Labor Law Course,* 24th ed. (Chicago: Commerce Clearing House, 1979).

[8]Ibid.

[9]Ibid.

[10]J. G. Getman, S. B. Goldberg, and J. B. Herman, *Union Representation Elections: Law and Reality* (New York: Russell Sage Foundation, 1976).

[11]This trend has been noted by M. Roomkin and H. A. Juris, "Unions in the Traditional Sectors: The Mid-Life Passage of the Labor Movement," *Proceedings of the Industrial Relations Research Association,* (Madison, Wisconsin: Industrial Relations Research Association; 1978), 212–222.

[12]C. R. Greer and S. A. Martin, Jr., "Calculative Strategy Decisions During Organization Campaigns," *Sloan Management Review,* 19 (1978), 61–74.

[13]R. Prosten, "The Longest Season: Union Organizing in the Last Decade, a/k/a How Come One Team Has to Play with Its Shoelaces Tied Together?" *Proceedings of the Industrial Relations Research Association* (Madison, Wisconsin: Industrial Relations Research Association, 1978), 240–249.

[14]Sandver and Heneman, "Union Growth through the Election Process."

[15]Gorman, *Basic Text on Labor Law,* contains a good discussion of bargaining orders and the *Gissel* case, *NLRB* v. *Gissel Packing Company,* 395 U.S. 575 (1969).

[16]For more in-depth discussions of these unfair labor practices, the reader may wish to consult Commerce Clearing House, *Labor Law Course;* Gorman, *Basic Text on Labor Law;* C. O. Gregory and H. A. Katz, *Labor and the Law,* 3rd ed. (New York: W.W. Norton, 1979); B. J. Taylor and F. Witney, *Labor Relations Law,* 3rd ed. (Englewood Cliffs, N.J.: Prentice-Hall, 1979).

[17]Commerce Clearing House, *Labor Law Course.*

[18]Gorman, *Basic Text on Labor Law.*

[19]J. G. Getman, *Labor Relations Law, Practice and Policy* (Mineola, N.Y.: Foundation Press, 1978).

[20]Commerce Clearing House, *Labor Law Course.*

[21]Taylor and Witney, *Labor Relations Law.*

[22]Commerce Clearing House, *Labor Law Course.*

[23]Ibid.

[24]E. F. Beal, E. D. Wickersham, and P. K. Kienast, *The Practice of Collective Bargaining,* 5th ed. (Homewood, Ill.: Irwin, 1976).

[25]R. E. Walton and R. B. McKersie, *A Behavioral Theory of Labor Negotiations: An Analysis of a Social Interaction System* (New York: McGraw-Hill, 1965). Empirical support for the existence of these models is provided in R. B. Peterson and L. Tracy, "Testing a Behavioral Theory Model of Labor Negotiations," *Industrial Relations,* 16 (1977), 35–50.

[26]Walton and McKersie, *A Behavioral Theory of Labor Negotiations.*

[27]Ibid. Empirical evidence confirming much of the integrative bargaining model has been found by R. B. Peterson and L. Tracy, "A Behavioral Model of Problem-Solving in Labour Negotiations," *British Journal of Industrial Relations,* 14 (1976), 159–173.

[28]Walton and McKersie, *A Behavioral Theory of Labor Negotiations.*

[29]Ibid.

[30]A. R. Weber, *The Structure of Collective Bargaining* (New York: Free Press, 1961).

[31]F. Bairstow, "The Structure of Bargaining: International Comparisons—A Story of Diversity," *Proceedings of the Industrial Relations Research Association* (Madison, Wisconsin: Industrial Relations Research Association, 1980), 514–525.

[32]J. Barbash, "Collective Bargaining: Contemporary American Experience—A Commentary," in *Collective Bargaining: Contemporary American Experience*, G. G. Somers, ed. (Madison, Wisc.: Industrial Relations Research Association, 1980), pp. 553–588.

[33]Ibid.

[34]D. Q. Mills, "Construction," in *Collective Bargaining: Contemporary American Experience*, pp. 49–97.

[35]Ibid.

[36]J. Stieber, "Steel," *Collective Bargaining: Contemporary American Experience*, pp. 151–208.

[37]Ibid.

[38]U.S. Department of Labor, Bureau of Labor Statistics, *Analysis of Work Stoppages*, 1978, Bulletin 2066 (Washington, D.C.: Government Printing Office, 1980).

[39]J. Zalusky, "Arbitration: Updating a Vital Process," *The AFL-CIO American Federationist*, 83 (1976) 1–8.

[40]F. Elkouri and E. A. Elkouri, *How Arbitration Works*, 3rd ed. (Washington, D.C.: Bureau of National Affairs, 1974).

[41]Ibid.

[42]Ibid.

[43]Ibid.

[44]J. Zalusky, "Arbitration."

[45]A party cannot escape the obligation to arbitrate by claiming an issue to be an improper subject for arbitration. Questions of arbitration must be arbitrated according to *United Steelworkers of America* v. *Warrior and Gulf Navigation Company*, 363 U.S. 574 (1960).

[46]Elkouri and Elkouri, *How Arbitration Works:* M. Hill, Jr., and A. V. Sinicropi, *Evidence in Arbitration* (Washington, D.C.: Bureau of National Affairs, 1980).

[47]American Arbitration Association, *Labor Arbitration: Procedures and Techniques* (New York: American Arbitration Association, 1975); R. Coulson, *Labor Arbitration—What You Need to Know*, 2nd ed. (New York: American Arbitration Association, 1978).

[48]Hill and Sinicropi, *Evidence in Arbitration.*

[49]See the discussion of Section 301 and the *Textile Workers Union* v. *Lincoln Mills*, 353 U.S. 448 (1957), in Gorman, *Basic Text on Labor Law.*

[50]Elkouri and Elkouri, *How Arbitration Works.*

[51]Ibid.

[52]Zalusky, "Arbitration."

[53]Coulson, *Labor Arbitration.*

[54]J. P. Goldberg, "Bargaining and Productivity in the Private Sector," in *Collective Bargaining and Productivity*, eds. G. Somers, A. Anderson, M. Denise, and L. Sayles (Madison, Wisc.: Industrial Relations Research Association, 1975), pp. 15–43.

[55]T. Nicholson, J.C. Jones, and H. Fineman, "The UAW and GM Fail to Agree," *Newsweek*, February 8, 1982, pp. 65–66 and *UAW-GM Report*, Special Edition (March 1982).

[56]R. B. Freeman and J. L. Medoff, "The Two Faces of Unionism," *Public Interest*, 57 (1979) 69–93.

[57]E. M. Kassalow, "Collective Bargaining: In the Grip of Structural Change," *Proceedings of the Industrial Relations Research Association* (Madison, Wisc.: Industrial Relations Research Association, 1980), 118–127.

[58]F. Elsheikh and G. S. Bain, "American Trade Union Growth: An Alternative Model," *Industrial Relations*, 17 (1978), 75–79.

[59]M. Roomkin and H. A. Juris, "Unions in the Traditional Sectors: The Mid-Life Passage of the

Labor Movement," *Proceedings of the Industrial Relations Research Association,* (Madison, Wisconsin: Industrial Relations Research Association, 1978), 212–222.

[60]A. R. Weber, "Prospects for the Future," in *Labor Relations Law in the Public Sector* (Chicago: American Bar Association, 1977), pp. 3–10.

[61]U.S. Department of Commerce, Bureau of the Census and the U.S. Department of Labor, Labor-Management Services Administration, *Labor-Management Relations in State and Local Governments, 1978,* State and Local Government Special Studies No. 95 (Washington, D.C.: Government Printing Office, 1980).

[62]D. Lewin, "The Impact of Unionism on American Business: Evidence for Assessment," *Columbia Journal of World Business,* 13 (1978), 89–103.

[63]Ibid., p. 97.

[64]Ibid.

[65]Ibid., p. 98.

[66]K. A. Kovach, B. F. Sands, Jr., and W. W. Brooks, "Is Codetermination a Workable Idea for U.S. Labor-Management Relations?" *MSU Business Topics,* 28 (1980) 55.

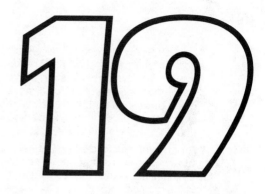

OCCUPATIONAL SAFETY AND HEALTH

LEARNING OBJECTIVES

After reading this chapter, you should be able to:

1. Describe the development of occupational safety and health programs prior to 1970.
2. Describe three federal agencies created by the Occupational Safety and Health Act and their responsibilities.
3. Discuss employers' general and specific duties (responsibilities and rights) under the Occupational Safety and Health Act.
4. Outline seven elements of an effective safety and health system organization.
5. List four primary means for reducing occupational hazards.

Hewlett-Packard Company is a well-known manufacturer of desk-top computers and peripheral equipment such as tape drive and printer units. However, Hewlett-Packard is a much more diverse international organization. It manufactures a wide variety of electronics products, especially electronic measuring devices such as stethoscopes and EKG equipment, as well as hand-held calculators, integrated circuits, and other products. It employs over 60,000 persons worldwide and has manufacturing facilities in nine states and eight countries outside the United States.

As a major employer, Hewlett-Packard feels it is important to assure that its employees work in conditions that are as safe and free from health hazards as possible. Its record as an industrial leader in providing safe, healthful working conditions is enviable; it is below industry accidental injury and illness rates. One reason for Hewlett-Packard's success in preventing employee injury and illness is attributable to professional safety experts such as H. Peter Perkins, safety and health coordinator for its 2,500-employee division in Fort Collins, Colorado.

Mr. Perkins is well qualified to deal with safety and health factors. He graduated from the University of Colorado with a degree in environmental biology, is a certified safety professional, and has eight years of safety and health experience in industry. He has been with Hewlett-Packard for two years and provided the following interview.

Interviewer: Can you describe some of the major duties of your job?

Peter Perkins: My job is basically a service position. That is, I provide safety and health services to anyone at Hewlett-Packard who requests the services. This involves *safety* consultation or advice relative to such things as storage of chemicals, building evacuation, code constructions, and employee training for accident prevention. It also involves industrial hygiene or health service to reduce health hazards such as airborne contaminants that result from some manufacturing processes.

Interviewer: It is hard for me to imagine safety and health hazards that would exist in this type of industry as opposed, say, to the mining industry where the hazards are more obvious. Can you describe some of the safety and health hazards you deal with here?

Peter Perkins: Well, the electronics industry in general is not comparable to heavy industry, such as mining, in terms of safety and health hazards. We are rated as a low to moderate hazard industry. Perhaps our major hazards at Hewlett-Packard, in terms of *potential* for injury or illness, are from chemicals used in the manufacturing process. For example, the process involves the use of small quantities of strong acids, toxic and flammable gases, and solvents. Although only small amounts are used, we must be extremely cautious and aware of the potential risks involved.

Interviewer: Do these hazards, then, account for most instances of injury or illness of your employees?

Peter Perkins: Actually not. Although they have potential for *serious* injury or illness, we have very few instances of injury or illness involving them. The most frequent problem is back injury due to lifting and is found mostly with materials handlers. Second are repetitive motion injuries, such as tendonitus in the wrist caused by repeated use of tools by assembly workers. Third comes slips and falls. Chemical and physical agents are far down the list in terms of actual injuries and health accidents.

Interviewer: Can you describe some of the things you have done to improve the safety and health conditions at Hewlett-Packard?

Peter Perkins: Actually, I'd like to talk about our comprehensive safety program in general as the major thing, but you probably want to hear about a specific activity. Right now we are involved in redesign of tools and work stations to fit employees. For so many years, the people who designed tools and work stations considered only what the product needed, not what the employee needed. Now we are trying to consider the employee first, by doing such things as rounding table edges or making chairs and benches that support the human body properly. A good example is the wrist tendonitus problem I mentioned earlier. By the simple action of purchasing pneumatic screwdrivers for assemblers, we reduced that problem substantially.

Interviewer: You mentioned a comprehensive safety program. Can you describe this?

Peter Perkins: Yes, it is the most important aspect of our safety and health success, since such things as tool and work station redesign flow out of it. It consists of several elements beginning with top management support and policy statements on safety and health. This was the key feature to our success, and top management's commitment is obvious. For example, the latest executive conference was devoted entirely to safety and health and featured speakers from OSHA and industrial safety groups. The remaining features of the program are:

> Definitions of safety responsbilities for each level of management and type of employee job.
> Assignment of accountability so that each employee's and manager's evaluation includes safety and health criteria.
> Safety training for supervisors, employees and trainees.
> Safety inspections.
> Proper engineering of the work area or work station.
> Gathering of statistics and investigation of likely problems.
> Medical and first-aid facilities in that we have two nurses and thirty-five emergency response team members (employees who are trained and certified in first-aid procedures).

Interviewer: Can you tell me how you feel about the Occupational Safety and Health Administration?

Peter Perkins: That's a tricky question, because my feelings have changed from time to time, as have those of most safety and health professionals. But I think it has been good for industry, since many companies might not have safety and health programs or might not be as far along without the pressures applied by OSHA. For many, it provided the basic foundation or motivation for getting a safety and health program going. Also, I view the current administration in OSHA as changing the relationship to a positive one where OSHA assists rather than resists business needs.

INTRODUCTION

On the morning of April 27, 1978, a group of construction workers was waiting on the arrival of a bucket of concrete rushing up to them from 170 feet below. The 1,500-pound bucket was about two-thirds of the way up when it broke loose and plunged to the ground. As it fell, it jerked the crane, poorly anchored on top of the partially completed tower wall on which 51 workers stood, from its structure. As the crane fell, it caused the wall, the workers' scaffolding, and safety nets to crumble. Fifty-one workers fell to their deaths.[1] The Willow Island cooling tower tragedy is familiar to most Americans and demonstrates the importance of providing safe, healthful working conditions.

Most organizations today are involved in activities designed to make working conditions safe and healthy for employees. In fact, tragedies like Willow Island are rare because many employers are successful in these efforts. As Peter Perkins, safety and health coordinator for Hewlett-Packard indicated, employers do care about safety and health.

This chapter concerns safety and health considerations in the employee, task, and organization relationships. We review the nature of safety and health developments including those of voluntary industry actions and those prescribed by governmental legislation. Then we acquaint the reader with the health and safety responsibilities of personnel management professionals.

SAFETY AND HEALTH IN INDUSTRY

American industry has long recognized the importance of accident prevention. Job-related accidents produce both social and economic losses, impairing not only productivity for the organization but also disrupting individual growth in society. Thus safety and health issues in organizations reflect both productivity and moral concerns.

The major reasons for preventing accidents and threats to employee health are:

1. The needless destruction of health and/or life involves moral responsibility by management.
2. Accidents and illnesses limit efficiency and productivity.
3. Injuries and illnesses produce far-reaching social harm.
4. Safety and health technology is capable of preventing most accident and health hazards.

History of the Movement

The movement toward providing safe, healthy work environments coincides with the industrialization of work, or about the mid-1800s in the United States. The evolution of large industrial organizations brought with it an increase of work-related accidents and inferior health conditions. By 1867, Massachusetts required the use of factory inspectors, and by 1877 it required the use of protective safeguards for dangerous machinery. In 1911, the first effective workmen's compensation act was passed by Wisconsin.[2]

However, the impetus for safety and health improvement was not due entirely to the enactment of mandatory laws. While many employers were negligent in their responsibilities to provide safe, healthy working conditions, many others began to improve their environments voluntarily. Progressive managers realized that a large proportion of accidents could be prevented and that health hazards were not necessarily an unavoidable by-product of industrial progress. By 1912, the first voluntary association, the First Cooperative Safety Congress, was formed. This organization later became the National Safety Council, a group still actively involved in promoting industrial safety and health objectives. Many other voluntary industrial groups also formed, and by 1970 safety and health standards had been adopted by various groups such as the National Association of Manufacturers, the American National Standards Institute, the Industrial Health Foundation, Inc., and the National Fire Protection Association.

Effect on Injury and Illness (Prior to 1970)

In assessing the voluntary safety and health efforts of industry, it is necessary to examine the accomplishments of the early movement. From 1912 to 1970, the death rate of persons ages twenty-five to sixty-four (the age range of most employed persons) declined by 67 percent. While part of this decline is due to medical advancements, a substantial amount is attributable to employment safety programs. Further, this progress relates to both job-related deaths as well as injuries. For example, in 1936 death rates in manufacturing industries reached about 26 employees per 100,000 workers and 48 per 100,000 workers in nonmanufacturing industries. By 1970, these rates had steadily decreased to about 9 and 20 per 100,000 workers, respectively.[3]

Injury and Illness Today

Although organizations have made remarkable progress in providing safe, healthy working environments for their employees, we can see that safety and health are still very serious employment problems. By 1965, the death rate for the total private sector of employment was still about 10 per 100,000 workers. In fact, this rate has remained rather static at the same level. This leads to some concern whether more progress is possible and whether safety technology has reached its limits. Over 5 million occupational injuries and illnesses occurred in 1975, and there were nearly 5,300 occupational fatalities in the same year.[4] Financial costs to employers run in the billions of dollars ($11.4 billion or higher),[5] including compensated sick leave, insurance and direct compensation costs, and medical expenses. Financial and social costs to employees are incalculable.

OCCUPATIONAL SAFETY AND HEALTH ACT OF 1970

Perhaps the biggest influence on safety and health practices today is the Occupational Safety and Health Act, which was signed into federal law on December 29, 1970. Given the reductions in occupational injuries, illnesses, and deaths that had been achieved by the voluntary efforts of organizational leaders, whether such legislation was necessary or not has been a matter of considerable debate. Regardless of this debate, passage of the act signaled recognition by U.S. congressional leaders that many employees still worked in job conditions that were unsafe and that presented serious injury or health hazards. The intent of the act was to create consistent standards of safety and health so that even the most recalcitrant employer would take steps to protect the health and well-being of its employees.

Coverage of the Act

The Occupational Safety and Health Act became effective on April 28, 1971 and immediately covered over 60 million workers in over 5 million different workplaces. The act covers *every* employee in the private sector except those covered specifically by separate federal legislation (such as employees in mining, atomic energy, and railroading). Federal employees are covered by separate provisions in Section 19 of the act and by the related Executive Order 11807.[6]

It is important for us to realize that, unlike many federal laws covering employer-employee relations, this act exempts no employers. For instance, small employers are *not* exempted. Even if an employer hires only one part-time employee, the act applies. It also applies to all agricultural employers. In essence, it is one of the most comprehensive employee relations acts ever passed. It covers *every* employer not otherwise covered by other, specific laws.

Administration of the Act

The act authorized the creation of three new federal agencies, each having distinct duties and responsibilities to fulfill in the effort to reduce job-related injuries, illnesses, and deaths. These agencies are the Occupational Safety and Health Administration (OSHA), the Occupational Safety and Health Review Commission, and the National Institute of Occupational Safety and Health (NIOSH).

OCCUPATIONAL SAFETY AND HEALTH ADMINISTRATION.   Perhaps the most controversial and influential agency is OSHA, an agency located within the U.S. Department of Labor, which has the following primary duties and responsibilities:

1. Encourage employers and employees to reduce job hazards and implement improved safety and health practices.
2. Establish "separate but dependent responsibilities and rights" for employers and employees in safety and health conditions.
3. Maintain a reporting and record-keeping system to monitor job-related accidents, injuries, and illnesses.
4. Develop mandatory job safety and health standards.
5. Enforce those job safety and health standards.
6. Provide for the development, analysis, evaluation, and approval of state occupational safety and health programs.[7]

Although its duties are fairly broad, OSHA has tended to concentrate its efforts on the development and enforcement of safety and health standards. As a regulatory agency, it has the power to create specific standards, consistent with the act, and to assess penalties and fines on employers failing to meet these standards. However, OSHA may not decide the guilt or innocence of employers accused of violating the standards.

OCCUPATIONAL SAFETY AND HEALTH REVIEW COMMISSION.   The Occupational Safety and Health Review Commission is an independent agency not affiliated with any pre-existing cabinet-level department. The commission consists of three members, appointed by the President, with the primary responsibility of carrying out adjudicatory functions under the act. That is, the commission acts as a court rendering judgments in disputed enforcement actions between OSHA and employers or employees.[8] It does not act as the court of last resort, since all cases may be appealed to the U.S. Court of Appeals. It is important to recognize the separation of powers, OSHA may determine regulatory standards, but it may not render judgments of guilt.

NATIONAL INSTITUTE OF OCCUPATIONAL SAFETY AND HEALTH.   This agency was established as a unit of the Department of Health, Education and Welfare. Following reorganization of this large department, NIOSH became a unit of the Department of Health and Human Services. NIOSH's primary duties are to conduct research into occupational hazards (safety and health) and to conduct educational and training programs on safety and health. It is responsible for identifying unknown workplace hazards and developing ways of eliminating them. Often, its findings form the basis for new or modified regulatory standards in OSHA. NIOSH's investigation of toxic substances and its development of criteria for the use of such substances in the workplace is especially important.[9] Peter Perkins mentioned the care with which Hewlett-Packard handles toxic materials. Hewlett-Packard's good record in safely handling toxic materials may be partially attributable to some of the research conducted by NIOSH.

Employer Responsibilities and Rights

Each employer covered under the act has two duties: a general duty and a specific duty. The general duty is to provide, for each employee at all work locations, a work environment that is free from recognized hazards that are causing, or that may cause, death or serious injury or illness. The specific duty is to comply with safety and health standards created by OSHA. The act provides for both civil and criminal penalties if the employer fails to meet these two duties. In addition, each employer is required to display a poster that informs employees of their rights and responsibilities regarding safety and health hazards. Furthermore, employers are required to maintain safety and health records and to report all statistics annually to OSHA. Some of these record-keeping responsibilities are shown in Table 19-1.

In addition to certain responsibilities, the act provides rights to employers that ensure due process of law. For example, employers may request variances from standards when, for certain reasons, the specific standards cannot be met. Such variance

Table 19-1

Reporting Requirements Under the Occupational Safety and Health Act of 1970

Log of occupational injuries and illnesses (OSHA Form 100). Employer must record each occupational injury or illness on the log no later than six (6) working days after receiving knowledge of such injury/illness. Log is established on a calendar year basis and must be made available to OSHA inspector on request.

Supplementary record (OSHA Form 200). This information supplements that in Form 100 and is subject to the same provisions.

Annual summary (OSHA Form 102). Employer must compile an annual summary of occupational injuries and illnesses for each establishment, based on information in the log (Form 100). This summary must be completed by February 1 of each year, certified by the employer, and submitted to OSHA. A copy must be posted in the workplace for employee purposes by February 1 and left in place for thirty consecutive calendar days.

Reporting fatal or catastrophic events (no form). Employer must report to OSHA, within forty-eight hours of occurrence, any event resulting in a fatality to one or more employees or the hospitalization of five or more employees. The report may be oral or written, for the purpose of allowing OSHA to dispatch a compliance inspector to the scene if deemed necessary.

Occupational injury and illness surveys (OSHA Form 200-S). The Bureau of Labor Statistics is responsible for assessing national, regional, and industrial trends in occupational safety and health. To do this, the Bureau of Labor Statistics surveys, on a random basis, a selected portion of employers. Those selected are notified in writing and are sent OSHA Form 200-S to complete and return within three weeks. Not all employers will receive this form.

requests are submitted to OSHA, which then decides upon the request. Employers also have the right to contest any OSHA action felt to be unjustified. The employer may contest

A citation

A proposed penalty

A notice of failure to correct a violation

The time permitted for correcting a violation

Any other action felt to be unjustified

The act also provides for financial assistance to small businesses that find the costs of meeting OSHA standards prohibitive. Such funds are available from the Small Business Administration, as that act was amended by the Occupational Safety and Health Act. Finally, as a result of a U.S. Supreme Court decision (*Barlow* v. *OSHA,* 1978), it is the employer's right to demand a search warrant before an OSHA inspector is authorized to conduct a safety or health inspection. Less than 2 percent of employers insist upon the search warrant, since many feel this would only antagonize the compliance officer and result in more citations or costlier penalties.[10]

OSHA Safety and Health Standards

Perhaps no other act of Congress has promulgated so quickly the volume of regulatory standards created by the Occupational Safety and Health Act. Although the act is only 31 pages long, the resulting OSHA regulatory standards quickly grew to a stack of volumes over seven feet high. The original rules filled 254 pages of fine print, and employers soon grew exasperated in their attempts to stay abreast of all the safety and health activities required of them.[11] As a result of employer complaints, 1,100 "nit-picking" regulations were repealed, but there are a great many more left in place.[12]

The quick issuance of these thousands of standards occurred because OSHA liberally adapted industry standards that had long been in place, such as the National Fire Protection Association Standards.[13] Up to this time, virtually all standards have been of the "specification" type. For example, one standard requires that a fire extinguisher be placed 48 inches above the floor. Another requires that stair railings be at a vertical height of not more than 34 inches or less than 30 inches from the top of the tread. Such "specification" standards are severely criticized because they prevent employers from placing fire extinguishers at an even safer location or from adjusting railings according to the physical nature of employees. There has been some pressure to change to "performance" standards that would allow the employer to decide how to make certain conditions "safe." As of this time, OSHA has firmly resisted such pressures.

In fact, OSHA has recently shown greater willingness to bring criminal charges against employers whose negligence in applying safety standards contributes to worker deaths. Conviction of criminal neglect could bring up to $10,000 in fines, or six months in jail, or both. Most commonly, these cases involve noncompliance with construction safety and health standards and involve multiple employee deaths. The most prominent case is that against Research-Cottrell, Inc., the New Jersey firm charged in the deaths of the fifty-one workers in the Willow Island cooling tower accident.[14]

BEYOND OSHA

Achieving the goal of providing safe and healthy working conditions is a difficult task that goes well beyond the regulatory standards and enforcement actions of OSHA. Companies such as Hewlett-Packard, as described by Peter Perkins, view employee safety and health as an obligation to be provided willingly regardless of legal considerations. This viewpoint is reflected in H-P's excellent records of employee safety and health. As Peter Perkins explained, OSHA serves as a motivator for some companies, prompting them to at least provide minimally safe and healthy conditions. For most employers, however, OSHA standards serve only as a floor or referent point as they seek higher goals of employee safety and health.

In point of fact, regulatory standards, alone, have not proven sufficient to further reduce worker injury, illness, and death rates. Data collected by the Bureau of Labor Statistics showed that, between the years 1972 and 1975, occupational injuries in the total private sector declined from 10.5 per 100 employees to 8.8. As indicated in Table 19-2, the rates vary from industry to industry. In that same time period, there was no change in the total incidence rates of occupational fatalities.[15] Although the statistical reporting lags, safety consultants note that current rates of occupational injury and illness are close to 9.4 per 100 employees, a rate equivalent to that at the inception of OSHA in 1970.[16]

This is not a condemnation of OSHA, since technological changes may have caused increases in injuries or illnesses without OSHA control. Also, it is possible that standards, alone, cannot make further decreases possible. Further decreases, such as those achieved by Hewlett-Packard, depend on the development of a company safety and health program reflecting a managerial and employee attitude that safety is an important organizational objective. Although this is a standard company approach for Hewlett-Packard, such an approach to safety and health management may be nontraditional for many companies.

Under the traditional method, management discovers a hazardous condition and solves it. For instance, it might be that an employee puts his or her fingers too close to the saw blade in a lumber milling operation. Management solves this directly by placing a guard over the blade to eliminate the hazard. This traditional approach is similar to following OSHA standards and is effective in the saw blade hazard but ineffective in making the total plant safer. That is, this approach is not good at locating other

Table 19-2
Injury and Death Statistics, 1972–1975

Industry Division	Incident Rates							
	1972		1973		1974		1975	
	a[1]	b[2]	a[1]	b[2]	a[1]	b[2]	a[1]	b[2]
Agriculture, forestry, fishing	—	.32	10.8	.25	9.1	.28	7.2	.35
Mining	—	.29	—	.68	10.0	.68	10.9	.61
Contract construction	18.4	.51	19.4	.33	17.9	.39	15.7	.33
Manufacturing	14.9	.08	14.7	.07	14.0	.07	12.5	.07
Transportation, public utilities	10.5	.28	10.0	.27	10.3	.26	9.2	.24
Wholesale, retail trade	8.2	.05	8.5	.07	8.3	.05	7.2	.06
Finance, insurance, real estate	2.4	.02	2.3	.03	2.3	.03	2.2	.03
Services	5.8	.05	5.9	.04	5.6	.06	5.2	.03
Total average private sector	10.5	.10	10.6	.10	10.0	.10	8.8	.10

[1]Injury rates per 100 employees.
[2]Fatality rates per 1,000 employees.
Source: U.S. Department of Labor, Bureau of Labor Statistics, *Occupational Injuries and Illnesses in the United States by Industry, 1975.* Bulletin 1981 (Washington, D.C.: Government Printing Office, 1978), 3–4.

hazards, or in making employees safety conscious, or in assuring that employee safety and health is a primary managerial objective.

The nontraditional approach emphasizes safety management as a system, similar to other managerial systems.[17] That is, safety management must be seen as a program involving a wide variety of actions. Such a program will be similar to that described by Peter Perkins.

Safety and Health System Organization

The prevention of injuries and illnesses is achieved basically through control of the working environment and control of employee behaviors. To achieve this control, it is necessary to design a systematic plan for organizing the attack against safety and health hazards. One such plan, suggested by the National Safety Council, consists of management leadership and policy, assignment of responsibilities, maintenance of safe working conditions, establishment of safety and health training, an accident record system, medical and first-aid systems, and employee acceptance of responsibilities.[18] This system is illustrated in Figure 19-1.

MANAGEMENT LEADERSHIP.   To reduce injuries and illnesses, it is necessary for top management to develop both a safety and health attitude and a policy dealing with occupational hazards. In many instances, it is necessary for personnel managers to foster such attitudes, perhaps by pointing to OSHA standards or by pointing to the costs associated with occupational hazards (poor morale, lost work time, hospitalization costs, lost productivity, etc.). This attitude is critical, since any program is less likely to succeed without top management's complete endorsement.

Once a safety and health attitude is present, it is necessary for top management, personnel specialists, and safety consultants to develop a policy that will guide the safety and health program. Basic to this policy are statements such as:

The safety and health of employees and company operations are of paramount importance.

Safety and health concerns will take precedence over expediencies or shortcuts.

Every attempt will be made to reduce or eliminate the possibility of safety and health hazards.

The company intends to comply fully with the Occupational Safety and Health Act.

ASSIGNMENT OF RESPONSIBILITY.   Once the safety and health policy has been established, it is necessary to delegate the responsibilities to lower-level managers who will actually implement the policy. Included in this delegation are various operating managers, personnel and training specialists, safety engineers, and other specialists. In some instances, it may be advisable to create safety and health committees consisting of appropriate specialists who make these assignments. The committees may deem it

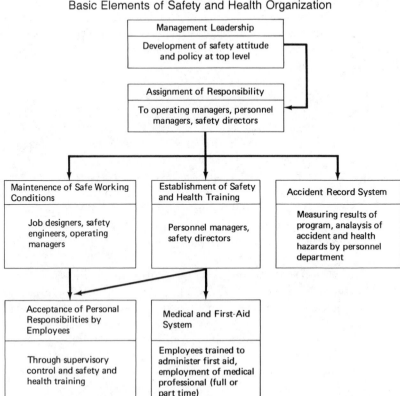

Figure 19-1

Basic Elements of Safety and Health Organization

best to analyze accident and health statistics within the organization before delegating specific responsibilities.

MAINTAINING SAFE WORKING CONDITIONS.   It is widely recognized that occupational safety and health depend first on the safety and health factors present in the job environment. That is, no matter how much we train employees, unless the job is largely free of hazards; accidents, injuries, and/or illnesses will occur. The responsibility for designing safe, healthy working conditions is usually assigned to safety engineers, job design specialists, and the operating managers. Because of its importance, we offer some useful guidelines later in this chapter.

SAFETY AND HEALTH TRAINING.   The rate of injuries and illnesses can be reduced considerably by better design of working conditions, but further reduction or elimination of injuries and illnesses then depends on the employees. A safety and health training program must consider both the types of hazards present in the work environment and the types of hazards presented by people. By this we mean that it makes little sense to train someone to watch out for a train if there are no tracks through town. But when we discover the tracks, we must be aware that some people will, by their nature, want to race the train to the crossing.

In terms of occupational safety and health training, the job must be evaluated, residual hazards and potential hazards identified, and procedures established to avoid such hazards in employee operations. The trainer must then consider human motives and behaviors that are likely to expose employees to greater risks. For example, even typing can be hazardous if the employee is tired or complacent and may result in a tipped chair, shock from an electric outlet, or a severe finger cut.

Safety and health training then is designed to

1. create an employee attitude that safety and health protection is important.
2. focus employee attention to potential hazards and how to deal with them.
3. help employees recognize potential hazards of which managers and safety experts may be unaware.
4. alter unsafe, employee behaviors in job operations.

ACCIDENT RECORD SYSTEM.   Perhaps one of the most often neglected elements of a safety program is the accident record system. This may be because of the paperwork it involves and because of the regular reports that must be filed with OSHA. If one looks at accident and health records as just so much busy work, it makes little sense to maintain them. However, many safety professionals, such as Peter Perkins of Hewlett-Packard, recognize that good safety and health record systems are a close ally in the fight against injuries and illnesses. A good record system can help the safety and health program by

1. providing for the objective evaluation of the program's effectiveness.
2. identifying jobs, departments, machines, employees, or supervisors with high rates of injuries or illnesses so that efforts may be concentrated in areas where they do the most good.
3. providing data that may point to specific circumstances associated with accidents and illnesses, such as a time of day when employees are accident prone.[19]

Many types of records and data collection forms exist. Examples are presented in Figures 19-2 and 19-3. A simple first-aid report, in Figure 19-2, provides information about a type of employee behavior that led to an injury. This knowledge will help the safety trainer and will give the supervisor information about unsafe behaviors that he or she should look for in their employees.

Figure 19-3 presents a typical supervisor summary sheet used to tabulate safety and health activities in a department. It serves as both a reminder to the supervisor to conduct certain inspection and training activities and as an analytical device for identifying high hazard conditions.

Figure 19-2

First Aid Report

```
Case No. 164                                          Date  2-12-
                        First Aid Report
   Name    S. D. Smith                        Department  Shipping
   Male [X]  Female [ ]  Occupation  Packer        Foreman  Miller
   Date of                      a.m.  Date of
   Occurrence 2-12  Time 10  p.m.  First Treatment 2-12  Time 10  a.m.
                                                              p.m.
   Nature of
   Occurrence  Splinter in index finger of left hand


   Sent:  Back to Work [X]      Doctor [ ]     Home [ ]     Hospital [ ]
   Estimated Disability  0  days
   Employee's Description of Occurrence  Handling wooden crates
     without gloves, ran splinter into finger


                                  Signed  Mr. Miller
                                                First Aid
   Issued by National Safety Council, Inc.
   Form IS-6                 Printed in U.S.A.              STOCK No. 129.26
```

Source: Reprinted by permission of National Safety Council, Inc.; 444 N. Michigan, Chicago, Ill.

Figure 19-3

A Safety Activity Report and Summary

FOREMAN'S SAFETY ACTIVITY REPORT

DEPARTMENT *Pipe Shop* FOREMAN *J. R. Kelly* NO. MEN SUPERVISED 20 WEEK OF *Aug. 9 1982*

DATES	NO OF INJUR.	CONTACTS			OBSERVATIONS		DISCIPLINE		JSA CONFERENCES		UNSAFE CONDIT.	INSPECTIONS	
		INDI-VIDUAL	GEN-ERAL	PLAN-NED	VIOLATION Rules, Proc. Instruction	UNSAFE ACTS	WRITTEN	TIME OFF	HELD	NO. EMPL. ATTENDING		HOUSE KEEPING	EQUIP.
8-10	0	5		1		1							1
8-11	0	3	1	4	2		1					1	
8-12	0	7		2							1		
8-13	1	4		2	1			1				1	
8-14	0	6	3	1					1	3			1
TOTAL	1	25	4	10	3	1	1	1	1	3	1	2	2

MEDICAL AND FIRST-AID SYSTEM. Although not all companies can afford a medical and first-aid system, it is important to make provisions for employee medical and first-aid treatment. If the company is small, it is still necessary to identify the closest source of emergency treatment. Larger companies may institute first-aid training for selected employees as a means of providing immediate attention in accident cases. Further, companies such as Hewlett-Packard provide professional nurses and medical doctors for the purpose of occupational health evaluations and monitoring.

ACCEPTANCE OF PERSONAL RESPONSIBILITY BY EMPLOYEES. Employees must recognize that even the best designed safety and health program depends largely on the personal acceptance of responsibilities. In part, this is achieved in the safety and health training program. In part, it is achieved through supervisory monitoring and control. Employees must be reminded that OSHA standards apply to employee behaviors also. They are required by law to comply with standards governing protective clothing and safe operations of safety devices (such as saw blade guards). While safety and health provisions can often be overridden by operators looking for shortcuts, it is their responsibility to keep a job safe.

Reducing Occupational Hazards

The primary means for reducing occupational hazards are

1. Eliminating the hazard from
   a. the job operations (machines and processes).
   b. the material (product).
   c. the physical setting (plant, office arrangement).
2. Controlling the hazard by enclosing or guarding it.
3. Training employees to be aware of and use proper procedures to avoid hazards.
4. Designing protective equipment for employees to shield them against the hazard, for example, asbestos clothes, respiratory masks.[20]

The reduction of occupational injuries and illnesses depends first on the ability to engineer them out of the operation in which employees are exposed. The ultimate goal is to design equipment, work processes, and work settings to eliminate employee exposure to hazards. When a high level of safety is designed into the job, employee carelessness or errors are less likely to result in injuries. Furthermore, protective equipment may fail, so a job that is designed to be safe eliminates this possibility.

JOB ANALYSIS FOR SAFETY. The basic personnel activity for eliminating job hazards is job analysis and design. The best point at which to recognize and eliminate safety and health hazards is when the job is being designed. However, the job designer must take such an analysis beyond the normal procedures for simply making an efficiently operated job. That is, the analysis must look not only for methods by which jobs can be performed faster or more accurately, but also for methods by which operations will be safer. The four basic steps for analyzing the safety of jobs are

1. Selecting the job to be analyzed.
2. Breaking the job into successive steps.
3. Identifying potential hazards and accidents in the steps (including the operations, the machines, the materials, and the work surroundings).
4. Developing ways in which to eliminate or reduce the potential hazards. (Find a new way to do the job, change the physical conditions that create the hazard, change the job procedure, reduce the necessity or frequency of doing the job.)

Effective safety analysis of jobs often requires skills beyond those of the typical personnel specialist. We recommend the use of a certified safety professional to assist in this process. When professional assistance is unavailable, we suggest that step 3 may be the critical step. To work through this step, the job analyst must ask such questions as:

Is there a danger of being struck by one or another type of object (moving equipment, doors, etc.)?
Can the worker be caught on or between objects (moving equipment, etc)?
Do some factors increase the chances of slipping or falling (slick floors, loose wires, etc.)?
Must the worker overstrain by lifting (pushing, etc.)?
Are environmental hazards present (toxic gases, acids, radiation, etc.)?

EMPLOYEE TRAINING.   In most occupational accidents, the precipitating cause is *both* an unsafe condition and an unsafe employee action. Evaluation of over 80,000 work injuries showed that an unsafe condition was present in 98.4 percent of the cases.[21] For example, in one case, an employee in a statistical library used a stool with casters to replace books on a shelf, as she had done many times without incident. However, this time she was hurrying, and the stool rolled backward and she fell to the floor, fracturing her right knee and resulting in two months of injury time off.[22]

In the case described, it is obvious that there was an unsafe condition. That condition was the presence of casters on the stool used by the employee. It is also obvious that the employee acted carelessly by hurrying to put the books away. Perhaps because she had grown so accustomed to this condition, she became complacent and careless. In any event, the accident was caused by both unsafe conditions and an unsafe act.

Even when equipment is otherwise designed to be safe, and when the job is felt to be free of recognizable hazards, operators can behave in ways to jeopardize their own safety or health. To reduce the employee's likelihood of self-inflicted accidental injury, most organizations provide safety training. Safety training is similar to other training in terms of training approaches, but the objective and content are different.

In safety training, both the supervisor and the employee are instructed in the job safety operations. The supervisor has several responsibilities that contribute to the safe or hazardous operation of a job. These include establishing work methods, assigning people to jobs, supervising and monitoring employees, and maintaining equipment and the workplace environment. Training for the supervisor includes content that places emphasis on recognizing hazards and hazardous behaviors.

Employee safety training includes both attitudinal and behavioral instruction. The attitudinal instruction often includes the beliefs that:

Management is sincerely interested in employee health and safety.

It is possible to prevent accidents.

Employee alertness to potential and actual hazards is critical to reducing injuries.

No employee should accept a job in which the level of skills required or in which the design of operations causes the job to be apparently unsafe.

Each employee must report observed hazards to his or her supervisor.

Behavioral training of employees consists primarily of procedures examined previously in Chapter 10. That is, the employee is instructed in operations and known hazards are identified. By learning correct operating procedures, it is intended that employees will not be exposed so readily to injuries.

SUMMARY

In this chapter, we have examined occupational safety and health factors that affect the relationships among employees, their jobs, and their employers. Organizational concern about employee safety and health is not a recent phenomenon. Organizations have long recognized that employee injuries, illnesses, and deaths are morally wrong and also costly in economic terms.

Although a great deal of progress in protecting employees from occupational hazards had been made through voluntary efforts of industry, Congress passed the Occupational Safety and Health Act in 1970. This act governs all organizations (except those covered by other acts) and provides for certain standards of employee safety and health. Three agencies were created by this act: the Occupational Safety and Health Administration, the Occupational Safety and Health Review Commission, and the National Institute of Safety and Health. The most influential of these is OSHA, which is responsible for developing standards and for inspecting workplaces to ensure the enforcement of the standards.

A great deal of controversy has surrounded OSHA activities, part of which involves the number of standards created by the act. These standards were adopted largely from existing voluntary industrial standards and sometimes place constraints that may prevent even further advancement in actual safety in operations. Still, employers must adhere to OSHA standards or face fines and other penalties.

Penalties for violation of safety and health standards are assessed by the review commission, which acts as a court in the event that employers dispute the findings of OSHA inspectors. Employers are promised certain rights under the act, and the Occupational Safety and Health Review Commission is responsible for adjudicating cases and protecting the rights and obligations of both employers and employees.

The third agency, the National Institute of Occupational Safety and Health, is responsible for conducting research into potential work hazards, designing procedures for eliminating work hazards, and presenting safety and training programs. NIOSH regularly publishes lists of health hazards and researches procedures for minimizing risk or exposure to these hazards.

Despite the efforts of OSHA, the review commission, and NIOSH, many safety professionals believe that further improvements in occupational safety and health depend more on voluntary than on mandated industry efforts. As suggested by Peter Perkins, a sound safety and health system organization begins with top management commitment and a statement of policies regarding the effort. Responsibilities are then passed down to the supervisors, safety specialists, and personnel employees who will set the operating procedures necessary to reduce hazards. Effective safety and health programs, such as Hewlett-Packard's, then provide safety training, accident record systems, first-aid or medical systems, and methods for analyzing and designing safe working conditions.

Because most industrial accidents involve both unsafe conditions and unsafe actions, safe operations require both a detailed job safety analysis and an effective safety training program. In most cases, it is felt that safety specialists should assist personnel managers in these activities, since they often require technical skills that safety specialists have acquired through lengthy and specialized training. By learning correct operating procedures and attitudes relevant to safety, employees are less likely to suffer occupational injuries and illnesses.

INTERVIEW WRAP-UP

A safe and healthy environment is a positive and valuable benefit to both the employee and the company. It is not separate from other managerial activities; it is built into the whole managerial system.   —Peter Perkins, safety and health coordinator, Hewlett-Packard Company.

WHAT MANAGERS SHOULD DO REGARDING PERSONNEL MANAGEMENT ACTIVITIES

1. All managers should be aware of their responsibilities and rights as provided in the Occupational Safety and Health Act (1970). They should be especially aware of both their legal and moral obligations to provide safe and healthy work environments, to display OSHA posters, and to maintain complete safety and health records.

2. Managers, personnel managers, and safety professionals should work together to establish an effective safety and health system organization. The development of a supportive attitude among top executives is paramount in this effort.

3. Managers should regularly analyze employee jobs for potential safety and health hazards as well as for task performance purposes. Safety professionals should be consulted for assistance in the reduction or elimination of hazards that are beyond the scope of managerial understanding.

4. Managers should upgrade their safety and health skills and encourage employees to do the same by attending various workshops conducted by NIOSH or other safety organizations.

REVIEW QUESTIONS

1. What was (were) the primary source(s) of development in the field of occupational safety and health prior to 1970?

2. What are the three central agencies created by the Occupational Safety and Health Act and what are their main purposes?

3. Describe the general duty and specific duty of employers under OSHA.

4. What are the seven elements of an effective safety and health system organization?

5. What are four primary means for reducing occupational hazards?

KEY CONCEPTS

Accident record system

Employer responsibilities under OSHA

Job safety analysis

National Institute of Occupational Safety and Health

Occupational injury and illness

Occupational safety and health

Occupational Safety and Health Act

Occupational Safety and Health Administration

Occupational Safety and Health Review Commission

Safety and health standards

Safety and health training

CASE

IT'S MY BUSINESS

Vincent Gomez was a successful businessman. Several years ago, he had purchased a single dump truck and, by working hard and making a couple of fortunate business arrangements, had expanded to a substantial operation. Currently, he owned ten heavy-duty dump trucks, which were kept busy most of the time hauling dirt from various construction sites. His was basically a subcontracting business, and as long as there was a lot of new construction going on, he would be busy. His largest job at present was with Jorgensen's Construction and Engineering Company, the prime contractor on a new twenty-seven-story building downtown.

Although Vincent was too busy with office work these days to do much driving, he occasionally liked to take a truck out. He felt that it gave him a chance to see operations up close, to stay on top of a job's progress, and to check out his employees. Today he was in a large Peterbuilt truck, waiting his turn at the loader.

As he looked around, he noted that good progress was being made. Jorgensen's had demolished the old structure last week, and by the end of the day Vincent guessed that his crew would have the old rubble cleared away. The loading crane made a lot of noise and created waves of dust as it steadily swung, lifted, swung, and dumped load after load into the large trucks. Vincent had seen this many times before.

Finally, it was Vincent's turn to move into position as Chuck Ferris took off with a full load. Vincent put his dump truck into gear and crept into position.

"My God, it's nasty up here," he thought to himself. Reflexively, he pulled off his hard hat, took out his handkerchief, and wiped his forehead as he leaned out the cab door to check his positioning. The loading bucket, full of rubble swung by, almost directly overhead, preparing to dump into the truck, which was in nearly perfect position.

CASE QUESTIONS

1. What types of hazards can you identify in this case? Are they hazards in the job operations, in the environment, or in the material?

2. Define one unsafe condition and one unsafe act in the case. How can these conditions be improved?

3. Do you suspect that OSHA regulations apply in this instance (Vincent's case)? Why or why not?

NOTES

[1]"Behind the Tower Tragedy," *Newsweek,* June 19, 1978, pp. 59–60.

[2]*Accident Prevention Manual for Industrial Operations.* 7th ed. (Chicago Ill: National Safety Council, 1974).

[3]U.S. Department of Labor, Bureau of Labor Statistics, *Occupational Injuries and Illnesses in the United States by Industry, 1975,* Bulletin 1981, (Washington, D.C.: Government Printing Office, 1978).

[4]Ibid.

[5]*Accident Prevention Manual for Industrial Operations,* p. 14.

[6]Occupational Safety and Health Administration, U.S. Department of Labor, *A Safe and Healthful Workplace,* OSHA 2263 (Washington, D.C.: Government Printing Office, 1976).

[7]*Public Law 91-596, 91st Congress, S. 2193, December 29, 1970,* 0-238-363 (Washington, D.C.: Government Printing Office, 1977).

[8]R. D. Moran, "Here's How the OSHA Review Commission Adjudicates Disputed Enforcement Actions," *Fuel Oil and Oil Heat,* 32 (1973), 49–50, 67.

[9]U.S. Department of Labor, Occupational Safety and Health Administration, *All About OSHA,* OSHA 2056, (Washington, D.C.: Government Printing Office, 1980).

[10]R. G. Riley, "Update on OSHA Policies and Their Impact on the Pulp, Paper Industry," *Pulp and Paper,* 53 (1979), 134–136.

[11]R.G. Riley, "Employers Face Increasing OSHA Pressure to Insure Worker Safety," *Pulp and Paper,* 51 (1977), 121–123.

[12]Riley, "Update on OSHA Policies."

[13]R. H. Davis, "Reflections on Current Safety Legislation," *Personnel Administrator,* 25 (1980), 53–54.

[14]"An OSHA Crackdown on Job-Related Deaths," *Business Week,* August 20, 1979, p. 25.

[15]U.S. Department of Labor, Bureau of Labor Statistics, *Occupational Injuries and Illnesses in the United States by Industry, 1975.*

[16]H. V. Hodnick, "Occupational Safety: Manager Approach Offers Help," *Business Insurance,* May 18, 1980, p. 37.

[17]Ibid.

[18]*Accident Prevention Manual for Industrial Operations,* pp. 51–60.

[19]Ibid., pp. 122–123.

[20]Ibid., p. 105.

[21]*Industrial Injuries in Pennsylvania* (Harrisburg,: Pennsylvania Department of Labor and Industry, 1960).

[22]*Accident Prevention Manual for Industrial Operations,* p. 350.

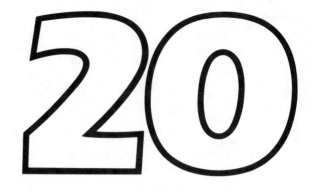

DISCIPLINE

LEARNING OBJECTIVES

After reading this chapter, you should be able to:

1. Define discipline and describe why its use is necessary in organizations.
2. Describe the positive and negative approaches to discipline.
3. Explain corrective discipline and progressive discipline.
4. List and discuss the six characteristics of effective discipline.
5. Explain the role of unions in disciplinary systems.
6. Describe the difference in discipline for professional and nonprofessional employees.
7. Discuss how to guarantee individual rights and avoid discrimination when discipline is used.

James Grimaldi is assistant vice-president, business development programs, for Equibank. Equibank is located in Pittsburgh, Pennsylvania. The following is an interview with Mr. Grimaldi on the topic of disciplinary actions.

Interviewer: Do you believe that discipline should be used by a supervisor or company?

Mr. Grimaldi: I believe that discipline should be used appropriately when justified. However, it should be used only within controlled guidelines.

Interviewer: In what situations do you believe discipline should be used by the supervisor or company?

Mr. Grimaldi: Discipline is appropriate when employee performance is unsatisfactory or when behavior deviates from established codes of conduct.

Interviewer: What types of discipline should be used and how should employees be informed of disciplinary action?

Mr. Grimaldi: Employees whose behavior or performance is unsatisfactory should be placed in a special evaluation status. At Equibank the program is called Plans for Improvement. When employees are placed in this program, their overall performance is evaluated. At this time, supervisors explain in detail (and in writing) the areas in which problems exist and outline specific courses of action designed to improve the situation. In addition, standards are established for the next performance appraisal. Supervisors also explain the company's role in assisting the employees while they are in this special status. The company wants employees to feel it, and the supervisors are sincerely committed to help eliminate the problem. Termination of employees should result only if all reasonable actions have proven unsuccessful.

Interviewer: Have you ever observed the use of discipline when it helped to solve a problem for the company?

Mr. Grimaldi: Yes, our Plans for Improvement program works quite well in most cases.

Interviewer: Have you ever observed the use of discipline when it failed to serve its purpose? Why was it not successful?

Mr. Grimaldi: Yes, in some cases problems simply cannot be solved. In these cases, termination of the employee is in the best interest of all concerned. However, termination is an avenue of last resort, and the employee is given full and complete consideration. Employees are always given the benefit of the doubt. Employees are assumed to be qualified and have a desire to do well until all corrective measures fail. In this manner, we all work together.

INTRODUCTION

Discipline is necessary in organizational life. Employees must cooperate and work together for the common good of the organization. Although an exception, a few employees may deviate from established codes of conduct to the detriment of the organization. In such cases, discipline may be required.

Where possible, discipline should be avoided. In most situations, if organizations use effective behavioral practices with employees and manage the employees with fairness and consistency, disciplinary action will be required only in exceptional circumstances. However, organizations must be prepared to apply discipline when necessary.

Mr. Grimaldi of Equibank emphasized this point. He also emphasized that discipline should be used only when necessary and under controlled guidelines.

> **Discipline:** action taken against employees when their behavior does not conform to the rules of the organization.[1]

Thus discipline is the use of some form of punishment administered when employees deviate from the rules. There are divergent views of the application of punishment and its effects on behavior. Some (e.g., B. F. Skinner) feel that punishment is not an effective means of controlling behavior and has undesirable side effects. Others (e.g., L. Berkowitz) feel that punishment can be an effective behavior control. These divergent views have led to a moderation of approaches in most current organizations.[2] Discipline is still used, but a positive approach to discipline is emphasized much like the program noted by Mr. Grimaldi at Equibank.

In this chapter, we discuss the necessity for discipline, approaches to discipline, and characteristics of effective discipline. In addition, we look at the role of unions, professional employees, and discrimination in discipline cases.

WHY DISCIPLINE IS NECESSARY

Absenteeism is a constant and costly problem for industry. A survey in the late 1970s showed that absences amounted to 3.5 percent of scheduled work time, or 82 million hours of work lost per week. This level of absenteeism costs approximately $20 billion a year.[3] The sheer cost alone shows that industry cannot sit by and allow the activity to go unchecked. Additionally, there are many other costly offenses that may require some form of disciplinary action. Some of the potential offenses are shown in Table 20-1.

Costs of certain of these activities, of course, provide reason for disciplinary actions. However, an established system of discipline is important for several reasons. Rules and policies are useless if they are broken without penalty. If this occurs regularly, employees will regard the rules as meaningless and moral problems could ensue. Rules are usually broken only by a small number of employees. The vast majority of employees abide by the rules and policies. Thus lack of disciplinary action when rules are broken is unfair to the employees who follow rules. An established disciplinary system is also necessary to ensure that all employees are treated in the same manner. Employees who commit offenses should receive the same discipline as all others who act in the same way. Another reason for the necessity of discipline relates to the employer's obligation to maintain a safe work environment. Occasional disciplinary action may be needed to ensure that safety rules are followed.

Some of the offenses noted in Table 20-1 are serious, for example, assault on peers or supervisors and refusal to accept job assignments. And, earlier, the high cost of absenteeism was emphasized. A system of discipline communicated to all employ-

Table 20-1

Potential Disciplinary Offenses

Absenteeism	Damage to machinery or materials
Tardiness	Refusal to accept job assignment
Leaving job post	Refusal to work overtime
Dishonesty	Illegal strike
Theft	Insubordination
Sleeping on the job	Misconduct during strike
Assault and fighting	Work slowdown
Falsification of records	Possession or use of drugs (on job)
Threats or assault on management representative	Possession or use of intoxicants (on job)
Profane or abusive language	Obscene or immoral conduct
Incompetence	Gambling
Violation of safety rules	Abusing customers
Moonlighting	Negligence of work responsibilities

Source: Adapted from F. Elkouri and E.A. Elkouri, *How Arbitration Works* (Washington, D.C.: Bureau of National Affairs, 1973), pp. 610–666; H.N. Wheeler, "Punishment Theory and Industrial Discipline," *Industrial Relations,* 15 (1976), 235–243.

ees and applied consistently can act as a deterrent to these offenses as well as ensure that all employees receive fair treatment. Mr. Grimaldi noted that when unsatisfactory performance is a major reason for discipline, performance must improve or termination may be required.

Also, a well-designed system of discipline fits the disciplinary action to the seriousness of the offense. Discipline, however, should not have to be applied regularly. If it is, it is a symptom of a much larger problem. In these cases, management must look beyond the offenses to determine the causes. When discipline is not likely to correct the problem (e.g., 10 percent absenteeism rates in a major plant), the cause must be eliminated.

APPROACHES TO DISCIPLINE

Discipline may be applied in a negative or positive manner. The negative approach emphasizes the punitive effects if certain undesired actions are taken. This approach then leads to management based on fear. This approach often includes frequent verbal and written warnings and even supervisory threats. The success achieved by this approach is limited. Research has shown that the negative approach will lead to only minimum desired behavior. In other words, employees will do just enough to get by. They do just enough to avoid punishment. Incentive to cooperate and reach desired goals is not provided. The negative approach to discipline then is suboptimal.

The positive approach to discipline offers a much better alternative. The positive approach attempts to obtain employees' cooperation in adhering to organizational rules and policies. The positive approach is frequently referred to as constructive discipline, its goal being to correct or change the employee's behavior.[4] Discipline is not carried out in a punitive manner but in a supportive manner. Additionally, the proper actions are rewarded and praised. Positive discipline requires that the proper work climate be established and is only one part of the supervisor's total relationship with employees. The supervisor's job then is not one of imposing discipline but rather one of creating an environment that emphasizes an employee's own responsibility and self-discipline. The supervisor's role is one of support.[5]

The program at Equibank whereby employees with unsatisfactory performance or behavior are placed in a special evaluation status called Plans for Improvement is a positive approach. Mr. Grimaldi emphasized that the company tries to assist the employee to improve performance. Termination is used only after all other reasonable actions have failed.

In line with the positive or constructive approach is the progressive discipline approach.

> **Progressive discipline:** a system of discipline whereby a sequence of penalties is administered, each one slightly more severe than the previous one. The goal is to change behavior and use maximum punishment as a last resort.

One form of progressive discipline for unexcused absences from work is presented in Table 20-2. As shown, the disciplinary action taken becomes progressively more severe as the offense continues. The purpose of this progressive approach is to correct

Table 20-2

Policy on Unexcused Absences from Work

If an employee is absent from work without an appropriate or acceptable excuse,[1] the following actions will be taken by the company:

1. The first time an employee has an unexcused absence, he or she will be given an oral warning by his or her immediate supervisor and the warning will be noted in the employee's personnel file.
2. If an employee is absent from work without an acceptable excuse for the second time, he or she will receive a written warning from his or her immediate supervisor. The written warning will also be placed in the employee's personnel file.
3. For a third unexcused absence, the employee in question will receive a three-day layoff without pay.
4. An employee who has four unexcused absences will be laid off without pay for one full workweek.
5. Five unexcused absences will be cause for immediate discharge from the company.
6. If no unexcused absences accrue over a two-year period, all previous unexcused absences will be eliminated from the employee's record.

[1]An acceptable excuse is personal illness (verified by a doctor's note), death in the immediate family, severe illness in the immediate family, jury duty, reserve military duty, approved vacation, and other absences approved by management of the company.

or change behavior. In addition, it provides employees with a fair chance, disallowing maximum punishment for one error in judgment. Arbitrators and courts look on progressive disciplinary systems with favor. In fact, arbitrators may award the decision to employees when progressive discipline has not been followed, regardless of fault.

In one case, an employee who had been absent seven times and tardy twenty-three times in a period of two and one-half months was ordered reinstated by an arbitrator because the company had not used a progressive disciplinary system.[6]

A progressive discipline system is a much fairer means of administering discipline. Would it be fair to discharge an employee who had been with the company for twenty years and had a good work record for one unexcused absence? The obvious answer is "no." In addition, it would not be in the best interests of the organization. Discharge is a severe action. Because of its severity it is often called "industrial capital punishment." Those who are discharged lose their means of livelihood; they lose pension rights and other benefits; and they may have problems finding new employment. Therefore, there are both legal and moral questions involved in disciplinary cases.

CHARACTERISTICS OF EFFECTIVE DISCIPLINE

Previous discussion has provided some characteristics of effective disciplinary systems. Effective discipline should result as a part of a formal established system, should be corrective, and should be progressive. Other characteristics include fair and reasonable rules, communication of rules and disciplinary procedures, proof of offenses, consistency in application of discipline, providing due process, and providing the right of appeal.

Fair and Reasonable Rules

The rules being applied must be considered fair and reasonable. For example, would it be reasonable to discipline an employee for an absence on a severe weather day? Arbitrators always consider the reasonableness of the rule before proceeding with further consideration of actions taken. Personnel managers have found that employees tend to obey reasonable rules while they tend not to obey unreasonable rules. In addition, it is important that employees perceive the rules as fair. Rules perceived as unfair by employees can create morale problems.

Communication of Rules and Procedures

Employees must know and understand the rules if they are to abide by them. Thus all rules and policies should be provided to employees in writing and supplemented with verbal explanation to ensure understanding. To discipline an employee for breaking unknown or misunderstood rules does little good for the organization or the employee. Also, the procedures to be used when rules are broken should be communicated. Employees then know what is expected of them and what to expect if they do not meet company expectations.

Proof of Offenses

Every disciplinary action should be supported by possession of all possible facts.[7] The system of justice in America and sense of fair play requires that individuals be considered innocent until proven guilty. Allegation of wrongdoing is then insufficient for discipline. Clear proof is required. The supervisor must investigate fully and keep complete and accurate records of employee actions.[8] Poor record keeping can be a basis for reinstatement of an employee in arbitration hearings.[9]

Consistency

Organizations must be consistent in their enforcement of rules and in their administration of discipline. To do otherwise would be both unfair and unwise. Selective rule enforcement may be grounds to order reinstatement in arbitration hearings.[10] Also selective enforcement of rules can cause employees to lose respect, not only for the rules but, more important, for the managers who enforce them.

Due Process and Right of Appeal

Many of the elements just noted could be set under the heading of due process. However, it is important to emphasize that disciplinary systems should provide due process to the employees involved. This means that proof should occur before disciplinary action is taken, employees should know and understand the rules, and employees should have the right of appeal. Timing of disciplinary action is important.[11] Disciplinary action should not occur until all avenues have been considered and facts known. Hasty decisions are inadvisable. The right of appeal assures the employee that all alternative approaches will be exhausted to ensure fair treatment.

In many cases, length of employment is considered by arbitrators in determining the reasonableness of the discipline taken. Possibly, companies could do the same during the appeal process, if not before.[12]

For example, should an employee with twenty years of faithful service and effective job performance be disciplined in the same manner as an employee with six months of service? Although equal treatment is important, it also is important to consider the quality of employees' past actions as well as their potential contributions to the organization. Judges usually make similar considerations in sentencing individuals who have committed crimes.

The design and implementation of a disciplinary system is complex and must be done with care. About 40 percent of all arbitration cases involve a review of disciplinary actions taken for some infraction of company rules. Thus discipline is a controversial issue and should not be administered without effective consideration of all issues. Disciplinary systems that contain the characteristics noted will have not only a higher probability of being supported in arbitration or in the courts but will also be perceived as fair and equitable by employees. They also have a greater likelihood of producing positive change in employee behavior.

ROLE OF UNIONS IN DISCIPLINE

Unions often play important roles in the design and implementation of disciplinary systems. Most bargaining agreements contain clauses that discuss employee discipline. As a rule, disciplinary systems in unionized organizations contain more of the effective characteristics described previously than do those in nonunion organizations. In the absence of a collective bargaining agreement, the only restrictions on management's right to discipline employees are in federal and state labor relations acts and other laws dealing with discrimination.[13] Therefore, unions have brought about the development of more effective discipline systems.

In addition, a key element in most collective bargaining agreements, the grievance procedure, provides an automatic system of right of appeal and ensures due process. Of course, union and management representatives disagree at times, which means that many discipline cases go to arbitration. Nonunion organizations would do well to follow the principles outlined in the previous section to ensure a more effective system of discipline.

PROFESSIONAL EMPLOYEES AND DISCIPLINE

The right of management to take reasonable disciplinary actions when warranted is generally accepted. However, discipline of a professional employee is a special case. Most organizations have formal rules and discipline procedures for employee groups in nonprofessional jobs. Few have the same rules or procedures for professional employees. Lack of rules and disciplinary procedures could be interpreted as providing a free hand to management to discipline as it feels necessary and equitable. In practice, however, this has not occurred often. Discipline of professionals is not prevalent.

Employees who are exempt from the requirements of the Fair Labor Standards Act (discussed in Chapter 14) are generally considered professionals. These individuals often exercise a high degree of independent judgment, have high levels of education and/or training, and work with little supervision. Professionals hold key positions in organizations. These include accountants, managers, scientists, engineers, health care specialists, and computer specialists, among others. The work of these specialists is of critical importance to organizations.[14]

More Professional Employee Discipline

A number of factors have led to changes in the manner in which professional employees have been managed. First, many of these employees want and expect a voice in decisions regarding the nature of their work. Second, some feel that employees in general have become more independent, voice more concern for individual rights, and are less willing to accept authority. Third, some organizations have instituted cost controls and more formal discipline systems for professional employees.[15] Fourth, professional employees have the right to organize under the National Labor Relations Act, and they have been organizing more frequently in recent years.[16]

Professional and Nonprofessional Employees

The use of discipline and the reasons for its use vary with professional employees as opposed to nonprofessional employees. For example, one study showed that absenteeism and tardiness was reported to be the most serious disciplinary problem with non-professional employees.[17] Yet another study found that the major disciplinary issue with professional employees was job performance.[18] Additionally, some practices may be disciplinary offenses for one class of employee but not for another. Possession or consumption of alcoholic beverages on employer premises may warrant strong disciplinary action for nonprofessional employees but is rarely regarded as an offense for professional employees. Professional employees may even be encouraged to provide alcohol when socializing with clients or visitors.[19] Moonlighting on the part of non-professionals is generally allowed if it does not interfere with the conduct of the job. However, moonlighting by professionals is often regarded with serious concern.

As an example, some blue-collar workers (e.g., construction workers, factory workers) may hold a second job, particularly when required by their personal financial situation. A construction worker may work eight hours each day in his or her regular job and then work another eight hours as a night security guard. As long as fatigue does not interfere with performance on either job, neither employer may care. However, a second job or outside work by a professional employee (e.g., manager of labor relations, financial analyst) is not condoned as easily. These individuals, if working in a second job, would likely do so in their field of expertise. As such, a second job or outside work could be perceived as a conflict of interest (e.g., manager of labor relations as an arbitrator, financial analyst as a financial consultant to other companies). Additionally, these jobs often cannot be performed at other than normal business hours.

Since job performance is the most frequent disciplinary issue with professional employees, measurement of that performance becomes critical. In nonprofessional jobs, objective standards are usually set for the measurement of performance. Setting performance standards for professional employees is difficult. More acceptable alternatives for the measurement of professional employees' performance are peer review and accomplishment of managerial goals.[20] These methods also have problems because they rely on the use of judgment rather than objective criteria.

Therefore, one may conclude that disciplining professional employees is both a complex and problematic issue. The rules governing their behavior are less clear. They exercise more freedom and flexibility on the job. Performance expectations and measurements are less precise. Yet more emphasis is now being placed on discipline of professional employees for just cause.

More established rules and procedures for discipline of professional employees are likely to develop over time, particularly with the growing amount of professional unionism. However, a positive approach to the correction of problems with professional employees is likely to be more effective than is a disciplinary one.[21] Professional employees are better educated and may be more willing to challenge discipline. However, with their education, they should have the capacity to understand a problem-solving approach. If problems can be resolved through a positive, helpful approach by management and with participation on the part of the employee, all parties will benefit.

Mr. Grimaldi did not distinguish between professional and nonprofessional employees. The Plans for Improvement program at Equibank may apply in a similar manner to all employee classes.

EMPLOYEE RIGHTS: DISCIPLINE, DISCRIMINATION, AND FREEDOM OF SPEECH

Earlier, it was noted that the only legislation outside of federal and state labor relations acts affecting organizations' rights to discipline were laws banning discrimination. Organizations must be sensitive to the potential for discrimination in discipline. In one study of hospitals, the largest number of appealed cases for disciplinary actions involved complaints of discrimination.[22] Organizations can protect themselves by developing a system with the characteristics described earlier in this chapter. Most important for avoiding discrimination are full proof of offenses and consistent application of disciplinary actions.

Also important are employee perceptions of organizational actions. Morale could suffer if employees perceive the organization's actions as discriminatory. Additionally, the organization's recruitment program could be harmed. In one study that pointed to the problems in maintaining a nondiscriminatory discipline system, it was found that those in positions traditionally considered as male jobs were considered more competent than were those in traditional female positions. Furthermore, men in traditional male jobs were less likely to be disciplined for mistakes than were either men or women in traditional female positions.[23] Organizations must guard against just this type of action. Concern must be applied to all potential forms of discrimination: race, sex, age, physical handicaps, and the like.

Employees are entitled to freedom of speech, as are all U.S. citizens. This freedom extends to employees who provide information on misdeeds of their employers.[24] Thus employers cannot automatically discharge employees for disloyalty under these conditions. The rights of employees cannot be abridged in any employer actions. Disciplinary cases represent only a minor portion of personnel actions in which discrimination and freedom of speech may be of concern.

Employees have many other rights that must be considered in discipline cases as well. For example, employees have the right to organize for the purpose of collective bargaining,[25] and they have the right to receive due process in disciplinary decisions.[26] Additionally, the burden of proof of wrongdoing and of ensuring consistent and impartial administration of discipline is on management.[27] Thus employees have the right to consistent and impartially applied discipline and to be disciplined only in cases where there is *clear* proof of wrongdoing. Other employee rights exist under federal and primarily state statutes recognizing special cases. These are too numerous to describe here. However, personnel administrators should be cognizant of all laws regarding employee rights in discipline cases, both federal and state.

SPECIAL CASES: ALCOHOLISM AND DRUG ADDICTION

Earlier we noted that possession or use of alcohol or drugs on employers' premises were considered just cause for disciplinary actions. However, many employees who use alcohol or drugs frequently use them off employer premises but come to work under their influence. Thus the effects are far more important than simple possession or use of intoxicants on the job. More important is the value of these employees. Many are highly educated, skilled, and well trained, and they perform quite well under normal conditions. In such cases, managers should be less concerned with discipline and more concerned with rehabilitation.

Many times, employees use alcohol or drugs to reduce tension or boredom or to block out stress.[28] Stress is an increasing problem in organizations and is discussed in greater detail in Chapter 22. Alcohol and drug use is a widespread organizational problem.[29] The important action for managers in these cases is to obtain help for employee rehabilitation. Most organizations have set up their own alcoholism and drug treatment programs or have developed cooperative efforts with other organizations. The desire then is to take *positive* actions to save valuable employees.

SUMMARY

Discipline is a sensitive but necessary issue in organizations. Discipline is action taken against employees when their behavior does not conform to the rules of the organization. Discipline is necessary because some employees do not adhere to important organizational policies. For example, a recent survey noted that absences amounted to a total of 82 million hours of work lost per week, costing about $20 billion a year. There are many employee actions that may be considered offenses, ranging from tardiness and unsatisfactory job performance to fighting and insubordination. In fact, discipline is necessary to ensure fair and equitable treatment of the majority of employees who abide by the rules.

Discipline may be applied in a negative or in a positive manner. The negative approach emphasizes punishment for undesired behavior. This managerial style is based on fear. The negative approach is rarely successful in the long run.

The positive approach emphasizes constructive discipline. This approach is designed to work with employees to change behavior benefiting both employee and organization. A positive supporting environment is established.

Most arbitrators and courts expect organizations to use progressive discipline. Progressive discipline provides a sequence of organizational actions, each one slightly more severe than the previous one. Its goal is to change behavior with maximum punishment used only as a last resort. A progressive discipline system provides employees with a fair chance.

Effective discipline systems possess several characteristics: they are based on fair and reasonable rules, provide for communication of rules and procedures to employees, only implement disciplinary action where offenses are proven, are applied consistently to all employees, and provide due process and right of appeal to all employees. An effective discipline system is corrective and progressive and is fair to both employees charged with offenses and the majority of employees who abide by the rules.

Unions play important roles in the design and implementation of discipline systems. Most collective bargaining agreements detail disciplinary procedures and some specify disciplinary actions to be taken for particular offenses. Formalized discipline systems are the result of union insistence.

Professional employees represent a group for which discipline becomes more difficult and complex. Professionals expect more freedom on their jobs and expect to participate in decisions affecting their careers. They are becoming increasingly unionized. Additionally, as organizations institute more cost controls and desire to improve productivity, more discipline of professionals has occurred.

There are differences between professional and nonprofessional employees with regard to discipline. The largest disciplinary offense for nonprofessional employees is absenteeism and tardiness; for professional employees, it is job performance. Some practices regarded as offenses for nonprofessional employees are accepted for professions and vice versa (e.g., consumption of alcohol on organization premises, moonlighting). A formal system of discipline should be established for professional employees as well as for nonprofessional employees.

Discipline must be administered fairly and applied consistently. Discriminatory practices cannot be allowed. In addition, all employees' individual rights must be protected including freedom of speech.

Alcoholism and drug addiction are special cases. These should be treated not as discipline but as situations requiring rehabilitation. Alcohol and drug abuse may stem from many factors, not the least of which is stress. Regardless of the cause, managers should try to obtain help to rehabilitate valuable employees.

INTERVIEW WRAP-UP

Discipline is necessary but should be used only when appropriate; it should also be closely controlled, as, for example, when employees' performance is found to be unsatisfactory. Many of Equibank's employees are professionals or skilled nonprofessionals. Thus probably the primary disciplinary offense of Equibank employees is unsatisfactory performance. Discipline does not always correct performance, and, in these cases, the organization has no choice but to terminate the employee. However, employees should be given every chance; it is hoped that, in a majority of cases, termination will be unnecessary. —James Grimaldi, assistant vice-president, Equibank.

WHAT MANAGERS SHOULD DO REGARDING
PERSONNEL MANAGEMENT ACTIVITIES

1. Managers should recognize the importance of discipline as well as the importance of using it wisely. They should not be afraid to take disciplinary actions when required to enforce organizational rules and policies, to protect the organization's integrity, and to protect the interests of all employees. They should administer discipline in a fair and consistent manner to all employees.

2. Managers must follow the procedures for discipline outlined in any collective bargaining agreement covering their employees. When in doubt, managers should seek interpretation and guidance of labor relations specialists in the personnel department of their organization.

3. A manager's goal in applying discipline should be to change employee behavior rather than to punish. In addition, a progressive discipline approach should be used to give employees a fair chance.

4. Managers should recommend that a formal system of discipline be established for the organization if one does not exist. Additionally, they should insist that it have all important characteristics described in this chapter for maximum effectiveness.

5. Managers should recognize the differences between professional and nonprofessional employees regarding discipline but use a fair and equitable discipline system for both groups.

6. Managers should ensure that all disciplinary practices are nondiscriminatory and that all individual rights including freedom of speech are ensured when disciplinary actions are taken.

REVIEW QUESTIONS

1. Why is it important for organizations to have a discipline system?
2. What is the best approach to discipline that could be used? Why?
3. What are the requirements of an effective disciplinary system?
4. What impact have unions had on discipline in organizations?
5. How is discipline for professional employees different from that used with nonprofessional employees? Why is discipline for professional employees difficult to apply?
6. How can discrimination be avoided when applying discipline?

KEY CONCEPTS

Consistency in discipline   Freedom of speech
Corrective discipline   Professional employees
Discipline   Progressive discipline

Discrimination   Punishment
Due process   Right of appeal

CASE

THE COMING OF THE MALE NURSE

Wilburton Municipal Hospital is located in Wilburton, Pennsylvania, a city of 250,000 people. It is one of several hospitals in the city. Wilburton Municipal Hospital (WMH) is large, with almost 500 beds. WMH has been in operation for nearly sixty years. Nurse Hall has been with WMH for half its existence. She is well respected by hospital administration and is felt to be one of the most capable supervisors on the staff. She was recently promoted to chief nurse in charge of all nursing operations in the hospital.

The following is an encounter between Nurse Wilma Hall, Bill Thomas, personnel director, and Michael Ireland, hospital administrator.

"Wilma, Bill thought we should meet to discuss rumors floating around the city that nurses may unionize at several of Wilburton's hospitals, including ours. Wilma, what do you think the general mood of our nursing staff is?"

"Well, Mike, I think it's generally pretty good. However, there are a few troublemakers on the staff who are consistently trying to stir up things."

"So, do you think there are sufficient numbers for the union to call a representation election?" Michael asked.

"Boy, that's hard to say because they don't naturally talk to me about such things." Wilma replied.

"Our staff in personnel thinks that there may be enough even to approve a union. As personnel director, I am very worried about the whole situation."

"How did you obtain your information?" Wilma asked.

"Oh, primarily through links to the informal channel of communication, exit interviews, and a few comments made to me by some nurses on our central staff. Can you identify them?"

"Well, I don't have proof, but I believe it's two of our new male nurses, Tom Bixby and Walter Kelley."

"Why do you think so?"

"Their attitude has always been poor. They seem to feel the world owes them a favor. They are continually complaining about rules and policies of the hospital that they think are unfair. Also, I've had several complaints from other nurses who do not like to work with them."

Bill stated, "I assume the complaints are coming from female nurses since we have only three other male nurses on the staff."

Wilma retorted, "What do you mean by that? My nurses are professionals and *only* complain when another is incompetent. Besides, we all like men when they stay in their place." With her last statement Wilma gave Bill a penetrating look.

Bill knew that no one in the hospital crossed Wilma and that it was time for him to stop talking. Mike decided that the meeting was not going much further and decided to bring it to a conclusion. "Wilma, our biggest concern is to operate WMH in an effective and efficient manner. We prefer to treat our employees fairly and equitably without a union. Also, if there are legitimate concerns and complaints from our nursing staff, I want to know about them. I hope we can correct any problems we have. I want you and Bill to go out and find out as much as you can about this potential union and the concerns of our nurses. Let's meet again at the end of the week and see what information each of you has been able to uncover."

As Nurse Hall walked down the hall to her office, she mumbled, "The damn male nurses—they can't do as good a job as my ladies; and yet, they come in here and make trouble. Why can't they just stay where they belong."

When she reached her office she called Tom Bixby and Walter Kelley and set up an appointment with them for the afternoon. She did not notify Tom and Walter's supervisors of the meeting.

When time for the meeting rolled around, Tom and Walter appeared nervously at Wilma's office. As they walked in, she gave them the same glare she had given Bill Thomas earlier in the day. Tom and Walter sat where she motioned for them to sit.

Nurse Hall began as soon as they sat down, "I wanted to talk to you boys today to let you know that I'm not pleased with your activities around here. I've had complaints about your performance."

Tom didn't like the tone of her voice and interrupted, "But I've heard nothing of this from my superior."

"Shut up, I'm not through yet. In addition, you are continually complaining about hospital rules and policies, and I hear that you are making noises about unionizing here."

Walter then interrupted. "Wait a minute, all these accusations are serious, but you are not offering any specifics. Besides, I don't agree with you. I have been doing my job and quite well, too."

"No, you haven't. I have had several nurses complain that you don't do your share on teams, take longer than others to do certain tasks, and make mistakes when you shouldn't?"

"Have you talked to my supervisor?"

"I don't have to. Obviously you two really don't know what it takes to be a *professional nurse.*"

Tom was really mad now, "Why, you old bag! How can you make that accusation? You are twenty years behind the times."

Walter chimed in, "We don't have to sit and listen to this nonsense. This is exactly why nurses need a union at WMH."

Nurse Hall responded, "I will not allow insubordination and lack of professionalism on my staff. As of now, you are officially discharged. Pick up your personal items and leave WMH at once!"

CASE QUESTIONS

1. Was Nurse Hall correct in the actions she took? Why or why not?

2. What type of disciplinary approach would you follow? Discuss.

3. If Tom and Walter appealed their case in the courts, what do you think the likely results might be?

4. Were the individual's rights protected in this case? Discuss. Were there any potential illegal actions taken? Does the movement to unionize pose any special problems for management's approach to discipline in this case? Discuss.

NOTES

[1] H. N. Wheeler, "Punishment Theory and Industrial Discipline," *Industrial Relations,* 15 (1976), 235–243.

[2] Ibid.

[3] R. Rosenthal, "Arbitral Standards for Absentee Discharges," *Labor Law Journal,* 30 (1979), 732–40.

[4] R. G. Martin, "Five Principles of Corrective Disciplinary Action," *Supervisory Management,* 23 (1978), 24–28.

[5] R. Discenza and H. L. Smith, "What's New in Discipline: A Supportive Approach," *Supervisory Management,* 23 (1978), 14–19.

[6] Arbitrator A. Allen, Jr., *Mason County Road Commission,* 78-1, ARB 8066.

[7] W. E. Lissy, "Necessity of Proof to Support Disciplinary Action," *Supervision,* 40 (1978), 13.

[8] M. J. Shershin, Jr., and W. R. Boxx, "Due Process in Discipline and Dismissal," *Supervisory Management,* 21 (1976), 2–9.

[9] For example, see Arbitrator J. Alutto, *Shepard Niles Crane & Hoist Corp.,* 71 LA 828; Arbitrator L. Smundo, Jr., *Georgia Pacific Corp.,* 71 LA 195.

[10] Rosenthal, "Arbitral Standards."

[11] R. S. Wolters, "Moral Turpitude in the Industrial Envirnoment: A Real Dilemma," *Labor Law Journal,* 27 (1976), 245–254.

[12] Rosenthal, "Arbitral Standards."

[13] F. Elkouri and E. A. Elkouri, *How Arbitration Works* (Washington, D.C.: The Bureau of National Affairs, Inc., 1973), 10.

[14] E. L. Harrison, "Discipline and the Professional Employee," *The Personnel Administrator,* 24 (1979), 35–38.

[15] Ibid.

[16] D. Chamot, "Professional Employees Turn to Unions," *Harvard Business Review,* 54 (1976), 119–127.

[17] "Employee Conduct and Discipline," *Personnel Policies Forum Survey 102* (Washington, D.C.: Bureau of National Affairs, 1973).

[18] Harrison, "Discipline and the Professional Employee."

[19] I. Unterberger and S. H. Unterberger, "Disciplining Professional Employees," *Industrial Relations,* 17 (1978), 353–359.

[20] Ibid.

[21] Harrison, "Discipline and the Professional Employee."

[22] Ibid.

[23]L. Larwood, P. Rand, and A. D. Hovanessian, "Sex Differences in Response to Simulated Employee Discipline Cases," *Personnel Psychology,* 32 (1979), 539–551.

[24]K. Walters, "Employee Freedom of Speech," *Industrial Relations,* 15 (1976), 26–43.

[25] Harrison, "Discipline and the Professional Employee."

[26]Shershin and Boxx, "Due Process in Discipline and Dismissal."

[27]Lissy, "Necessity of Proof"; E. L. Harrison, "Discipline and the Professional Employee."

[28]R. D. Middlemist and M. A. Hitt, *Organizational Behavior: Applied Concepts* (Chicago: Science Research Associates, 1981), p. 165; A. Bandura, *Principles of Behavior Modification* (New York: Holt, Rinehart and Winston, 1969), p. 529; R. Cook, D. Walizer, and D. Mace, "Illicit Drug Use in the Army: A Social-Organizational Analysis," *Journal of Applied Psychology,* 61 (1976), 262–272.

[29]*Drug Use in America: Problem in Perspective,* (second report of the National Commission on Marijuana and Drug Abuse (Washington, D.C.: Government Printing Office, 1973).

COMPLEX ISSUES

The final section in this text examines some of the more intricate issues in organization-job-employee relationships. These issues arise for a variety of reasons and may require creative solutions by managers. No one has all the answers or even knows all the questions. However, managerial and organizational research has provided many insights and suggestions for confronting these issues. Personnel management activities that correspond to this large body of research literature are presented in three chapters.

Chapter 21 introduces the problem of organizational change in our modern society. Individual and organizational development programs can confront this problem effectively and are also examined. The implementation of these programs depends on the diagnostic and human relations skills of managers, skills that will be enhanced with concepts in this chapter. Quality-of-life issues have also become a societal problem that managers must confront. Quality-of-work-life programs that deal with job design, work environment, health and safety, and stress are explored in Chapter 22. Retirement issues are also examined. Finally, in Chapter 23, we present personnel management activities that are expected to be important in the future. We feel that the future will offer many challenges and opportunities that can be surmounted through the study of personnel management concepts.

21

ORGANIZATION CHANGE; INDIVIDUAL AND ORGANIZATION DEVELOPMENT

LEARNING OBJECTIVES

After reading this chapter, you should be able to:

1. Describe the internal and external change pressures faced by an organization.
2. Provide three reasons why resistance to change occurs.
3. Explain the change process.
4. Discuss how force-field analysis may be used to overcome resistance to change and help implement change.
5. Describe individual development in the three-step process.
6. Define organization development and list the five steps in the OD process.
7. Explain eight OD techniques.

Wayne Smith is senior representative for management training and development for Phillips Petroleum Company; Wayne has a Ph.D. in psychology and has seven years of experience. He has been with Phillips for two years. His current job includes both training and organization development responsibilities. Phillips is a major company in the petroleum, chemicals, and mineral industries employing about 33,000 employees. Mr. Smith had the following answers to our questions.

Interviewer: What are the most important internal and external factors creating need for your organization to change?

Wayne Smith: Internal factors creating a need for Phillips to change include demographic factors, a strong projected growth trend, changing direction of the company, growing international operations, and increasing emphasis on productivity. Phillips has a problem in the age distribution of its professional employees, which is an industrywide problem. A large number of the company's professional employees are under thirty or over forty-eight years of age. We don't have enough employees between the ages of thirty and forty-eight, the group from which middle managers are drawn. Additionally, Phillips has projected significant growth over the next ten years with an increasing emphasis on coal, minerals, and chemicals. Also the company has moved from being largely domestic to becoming an expanding international operation.

The external factors are changing technologies, changing employee expectations, diminishing conventional petroleum resources, the general state of the U.S. economy, and dealing with various governments, those of the United States (federal and state) and other countries. With the gradual sophistication of technology, people's skills can become outmoded. Employee expectations are based on changing societal values and expectations that Phillips increasingly faces with many new, young employees. Phillips has moved to emphasize coal, new technologies, and new research areas as directions for the future. Dealing with a multitude of governments is highly problematic because of the constraints they place on the company's activities.

Interviewer: What do you believe the result would be if your organization failed to change in response to these factors?

Wayne Smith: Phillips has been continually responding to these changes. However, if it did not, it probably would not meet its growth goals, might not maintain its position in the industry, and might possibly even decline. For example, Phillips wants to maintain a positive work environment for younger and older employees alike. But, if it did not, it would probably have trouble hiring top-quality personnel. Also, the company must continue to adapt to and develop good relations with different governments and, over time, increase the role of overseas nationals in foreign operations.

Interviewer: What are some of the tools your organization uses to diagnose organizational problems?

Wayne Smith: Phillips uses several tools to diagnose problems. Among these are small, localized employee surveys, personal manager observations, diagnostic instruments in training programs (e.g., climate surveys, minineeds analysis), and outside consultants. Additionally, Phillips is considering the use of a companywide employee survey.

Let me give you three examples of how OD could be used to effect change in Phillips. First, a survey feedback technique may be used. Employee survey results help make management aware of potential or actual problems, form the basis for action, provide information on employee perceptions, and help management and employees to reach a common understanding. Other interventions using a third party such as myself or a colleague can focus on particular problems identified and help find solutions. Finally, quality circles are being utilized to emphasize productivity along with the quality of work life for employees.

Interviewer: What are the most commonly used organization development approaches or techniques in your organization?

Wayne Smith: The most commonly used OD approaches in Phillips are employee surveys (localized) and feedback, interventionist projects, quality circles, and training and professional development. Additionally, Phillips places emphasis on at least three programs that supplement other OD programs including performance appraisals (which is a modified management by objectives system), developing managers' key skills, and large-scale human resources programs.

Basically, Phillips has recognized the need for change and is responding to it positively.

INTRODUCTION

Change is something we all must face. In fact, we see changes every day. We see prices of goods we purchase go up; we see new businesses started; we see old buildings being torn down and new ones being built; we see people die and babies being born. Thus we experience much change over time. However, people must not only adapt to these changes; they must also change. When a baby is born, the parents often must change their life-style and habits. Employees must develop new skills as the technologies of their jobs change to meet the employer's standards. As do individuals, organizations also experience much change.

The importance of change was emphasized by Wayne Smith. He noted not only several major change pressures Phillips faced but also the consequences if successful change were not implemented. As he explained, Phillips is responding to the pressures with positive changes. Therefore, both individuals and organizations must cope with this change. To do so, they must develop their skills and resources. This chapter focuses on the need for change, resistance to change, and the means to overcome resistance and make effective changes. In addition, considerable space is allocated to the discussion of both individual and organization development, both being within the purview of the personnel function.

CHANGE IN ORGANIZATIONS

We have noted the amounts of change that individuals and organizations face every day. There are reasons for these changes. Not only do changes occur, but they have done so at an increasing rate in recent years.

Change Pressures

Most organizations today face a turbulent external environment. Rapidly fluctuating interest rates, uncertain energy supplies, price inflation, government regulation, an uncertain economy, and new technological advancements are but a few of the factors in the external environment with which organizations must cope. These same factors place pressures on individuals as well.

Organizations have many pressures for change. From inside the organization, employees often demand changes either collectively, through a union, or individually, based on their expectations. Personnel managers must be particularly aware of employee expectations if they desire to recruit, select, and maintain a high-quality work force. Also, with rapid technological developments, production systems, jobs, and work techniques frequently change. Organizations must adjust, retrain personnel, and hire new personnel with the necessary skills to perform the new tasks.

Possibly even more problematic are the pressures for change from outside the organization. Among these are changing societal values, shortages of natural resources, government regulation, and interdependence among countries in the world. Changing societal values may be evidenced in several ways. They affect what consumers desire to purchase; they affect employee attitudes and expectations; and they affect government legislation and action. For example, in recent years, concern has developed over increasing government regulation and debt. These concerns likely had some impact on the changes in Congress and in the White House in the 1980 elections.

Demands for natural resources have increased dramatically in the last two decades, but discoveries of new natural resources (e.g., oil, minerals) have not kept pace. Therefore, shortages of some resources have developed. These shortages have major impacts on individuals who use energy to heat their homes and run their automobiles. They affect organizations in the same way. Additionally, raw materials required in the manufacture of organizations' products may be difficult to obtain and/or very expensive.

Government involvement in the affairs of individuals and organizations alike increased greatly in the 1960s and 1970s. This involvement is seen in legislation and regulatory actions. Important examples for personnel administrators are the Civil Rights Act and the Occupational Safety and Health Act. We discussed these in Chapters 17 and 19, respectively. New jobs have been created simply to deal with specific laws and enforcement agencies (e.g., Equal Employment Opportunity Commission) as evidenced by the growing number of affirmative action coordinators and safety directors.

The increasing interdependence among countries of the world has occurred because of limited natural resources, increased communications capabilities, and growing multinational marketing of goods and services. This interdependence has both positive (new markets) and negative effects (potential loss of energy supplies) on organizations. One of the greatest impacts this factor has on the personnel function is in the training of personnel and particularly managers Managers must be trained to deal with cultures different from their own, not only in negotiation and marketing of goods, but in the management of people when facilities are located in foreign countries.[1]

Many of these change forces were predicted. In the early 1970s, a symposium of industrial psychologists forecasted expectations about the work world in the later 1970s and 1980s. Several expectations were identified for this period. They believed that more education would be required in work, that rewards would be tied more closely to performance, that computers would become increasingly important, that interpersonal skills would continue to grow in importance, and that more autonomy would be desired but less would be available. Also they felt that customer demands, international markets, and government regulation would become more important.[2]

Additionally, the industrial psychologists noted that people are living longer and will work longer. More women, highly educated workers, professionals, technicians, and managers will be in the work force over the period of the 1980s. Managers will have to contend with this changing work force. They also forecasted continuing rapid technological development and changing values and expectations of the work force.[3]

The change pressures described affect most people and most organizations. For example, Wayne Smith described multiple change pressures faced by Phillips Petroleum Company. Several of those he described for Phillips are similar to the general pressures just noted. More important is how organizations react to the change pressures. Wayne explained that he felt that Phillips might not grow, might lose its place in the industry, and might even decline if it did not respond to its change pressures.

Resistance to Change

Although it is necessary, people and organizations often resist change. It is natural for most human beings to resist change. Most organizational resistance to change comes from employees. It is important to recognize and expect resistance to change programs and to find ways of overcoming it. Personnel administrators, for example, should be prepared for resistance when they make changes in personnel programs. People will resist change even when they are dissatisfied with the current state of affairs.

People resist change for several reasons, including fear of the unknown, feelings of insecurity, redefined power relationships, and inconvenience. Any change brings with it some uncertainty. For example, an individual facing a new job has at least some, if not much, uncertainty. A new job may require the use of different personal skills, developing new interpersonal relationships, and even a change of work locations. Any of these changes may be threatening; there is uncertainty in each.

Any type of change often creates inconvenience to people. When changes occur people must change habits they have developed over time, and, as most people know, well-developed habits are difficult to break.

Let us look at an example. Bob has been working for XYZ Company, a large firm, for five years and has been in the same job for that period. Bob becomes restless and desires a promotion. He tells his supervisor of his desire and at the same time begins pursuing opportunities on the outside.

Bob and his family are now located in Denver, Colorado. He has three children ages thirteen, nine, and seven. His wife works part time in a retail outlet, and Bob has been attending school at night, working toward his M.B.A. degree. Bob and his family love to ski and go camping in the mountains.

Bob's supervisor began working on his stated desires immediately, contacting other company operations. After a few weeks, the supervisor had developed an interesting possibility. The job looked as if it was tailor made for Bob's skills. It was in Atlanta, and, although it would be a lateral move for Bob, chances for promotion would be good within two years.

The supervisor was excited, but when he approached Bob, he got an unexpected reaction. Bob listened attentively and without enthusiasm, said he would like to think it over, and discuss it with his wife.

Why didn't Bob jump at the chance to move to a jew job? There are probably several reasons. First, a new job presents uncertainty. With no promotion, Bob may not be willing to take the chance. Second, the change would require becoming a part of a new work group and separating from close friends in Denver. Third, the move would be an inconvenience to Bob and his family. They would have to sell their home, move, and buy a new one. The children would have to change school systems; his wife would have to leave her current job. Bob would have to get used to new traffic patterns. These and other reasons may have contributed to Bob's response.

However, there are ways to overcome resistance to change. The best way is to use the change process effectively.

Change Process

To implement change properly requires preparation for the change and solidifying the change in addition to the change itself. A general model of the change process was developed by Kurt Lewin.[4] The change process is illustrated in Figure 21-1.

Using the change process of unfreeze-change-refreeze can help to combat or overcome resistance to change. In fact, the model shows why change may not be effective if resistance is not overcome. If people are not unfrozen, that is, prepared to accept the change, the change may never occur.

The first step in the change process involves unfreezing the forces that prevent change. This may require an attitude change, or it may require showing the positive benefits of the change and/or changing some other factors first. After people are, at least, prepared for and willing to make the change, change must be implemented. Finally, the change must be reinforced (refrozen). If the change is not reinforced, people may fall back into their old habits. Unfreezing and refreezing then are certainly as important as the actual implementation of change for the change process to be effective.

Not only should one understand the change process, but one should know how to use it. Force-field analysis may be used to help supervisors diagnose the forces preventing change and help them to overcome these forces.

Figure 21-1

The Change Process

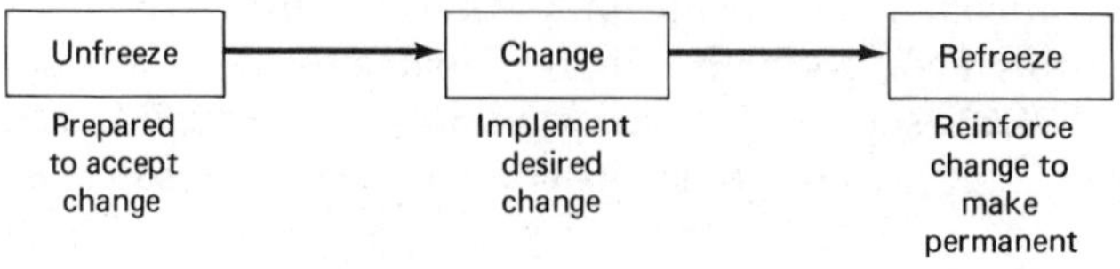

Force-Field Analysis

Force-field analysis may be used to diagnose the forces that cause a person to behave in a certain way. These forces are depicted in Figure 21-2. As shown, two types of forces act on a person to create a certain behavior: driving forces and resisting forces.[5]

Generally, there are several driving and resisting forces working on a person's behavior at any point in time. Additionally, these forces vary in strength with some being stronger and others being weaker. To make a change, a supervisor must identify the forces acting on a person at the present time. The supervisor must then attempt either to increase the driving forces or to reduce the resisting forces to change the employee's behavior. To show how force-field analysis may be used as a diagnostic tool and to help overcome resistance to change, let us consider Bob's situation and the probability of his accepting the new job. This situation is illustrated in Figure 21-3.

As the figure suggests, Bob may resist taking the new job unless the supervisor increases the driving forces or reduces the resisting forces. Of course, the supervisor must first recognize these forces. Once identified, the supervisor can then decide which forces he or she has the ability to affect. There will be some forces that the supervisor cannot affect.

Let us look at the supervisor's options:

Supervisor may talk to Bob stressing the importance of the job and his or her belief that Bob should take it (increasing driving force).

Supervisor can emphasize future promotional opportunities (increasing driving force).

Figure 21-2

Force-Field Analysis and Behavior

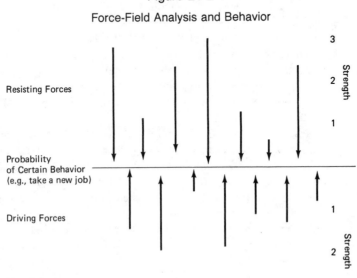

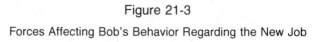

Figure 21-3

Forces Affecting Bob's Behavior Regarding the New Job

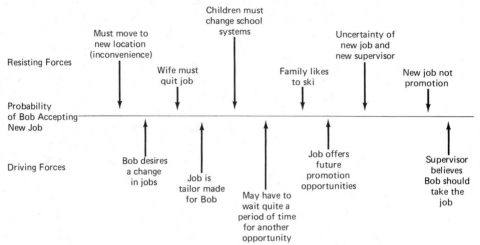

Supervisor could tell Bob that the company is responding to his stated desires and that it may be a while before another opportunity occurs (increasing driving force).

Supervisor can make Bob aware of the company's moving policy (e.g., pays moving costs, helps sell current home), reducing the inconvenience of moving (reducing resisting force).

Supervisor can get company representatives in Atlanta to search for job opportunities for Bob's wife (reducing resisting force).

Supervisor could have company pay for a trip to Atlanta for Bob and his wife. There Bob could talk to his potential supervisor about the job and learn more about it, his co-workers, the work environment, and future promotional opportunities. Also, the school system, recreational opportunities, and housing possibilities could be explored (reducing resisting forces).

The supervisor has several options. Research shows that the best way of unfreezing a person is to reduce resisting forces rather than to increase driving forces. In fact, increasing driving forces may pressure people into making the changes, but with the resisting forces continuing, they never really accept them and thus the change can never be reinforced (refrozen) effectively. Therefore, the supervisor should probably utilize the last three alternatives noted, attempting to unfreeze Bob's behavior and have him make the change. Once the resisting forces are reduced, Bob may feel less uncertainty and insecurity with the move, and his family may be more positively disposed toward the move.

The change model and force-field analysis are useful in any change process, be it individual or organizational. Next we focus on individual development. Then we examine the process of organization development.

INDIVIDUAL DEVELOPMENT

Individual development: the process by which individuals gain new skills, thereby increasing performance on the job.

Many organizations state in their public relations materials that their most valuable assets are human resources. Therefore, it makes sense to invest in developing these assets so that they perform as well as possible. The two most common and specific reasons for individual development are to improve performance and to prepare for future jobs. Desire to improve performance may occur with substandard performance or with good performance. Also, the desire may be simply to maintain good performance. As new technology is developed, new job skills are required. In these situations, individuals must develop those new skills to maintain their performance on the job. As organizations grow, new jobs are formed. Additionally, people leave the organization through retirement and for other jobs. Thus employees must be prepared to take on these jobs as the need dictates, and, organizations must continually develop employees' skills to have a pool from which to draw to fill job vacancies.

Millions of dollars are spent each year by organizations to develop their employees' skills. Some even operate their own colleges, offering a variety of courses. Earlier, we discussed training, management development, and career development processes (Chapters 10 and 11). In this chapter, it is necessary to relate these personnel management processes to individual development.

The process of individual development is presented in Figure 21-4. As shown, the first step in individual development is to determine both organizational and individual needs.

Identification of Needs

Organizational and individual needs may be identified in several ways. Organizational needs are usually identified through human resource planning described in Chapter 6 and, to some degree, through career development. Since development programs require substantial investments, it is necessary to ensure that they fulfill organizational

Figure 21-4

Individual Development Process

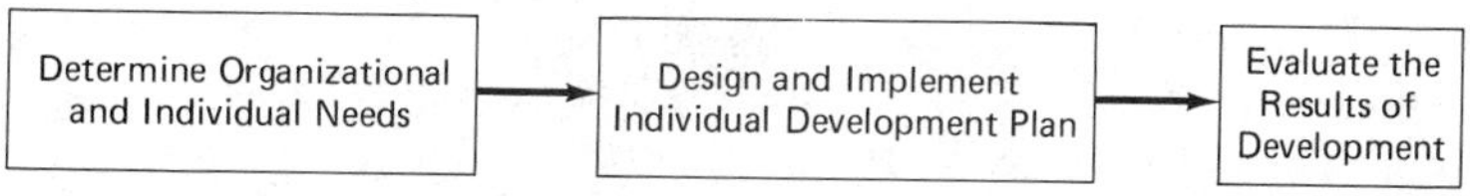

| Determine Organizational and Individual Needs | → | Design and Implement Individual Development Plan | → | Evaluate the Results of Development |

needs. Human resource planning identifies the types and numbers of jobs the organization will have in the future, along with the employee skills required to perform them. For example, many organizations in the oil and related industries project substantial growth in their work force over the next decade (e.g., Exxon, Phillips Petroleum). To meet these strong needs, they expect not only to have a large recruiting program for college graduates but also to increase their investment in development programs. Wayne Smith noted, for example, that Phillips was placing particular emphasis on professional development. One petroleum company projected a growth in employee numbers by 20,000 in a six-year period. Additionally, it expected to develop over 1,000 brand-new managers during this time. The projected investment costs were substantial.

Organizational needs and individual needs may overlap. As an example, if an employee is performing at a substandard level, the organization needs to have improved performance. For performance to improve, the employee may need new skills. Additionally, employees may need to develop skills to fill new jobs created by the organization.

The most common process for identifying employee needs is the performance appraisal process. We discussed the formal performance appraisal process and cited its role in employee development in Chapter 15. Performance appraisal sessions should detect needed improvement in individual performance. If actual performance is lower than desired performance, the supervisor and subordinate must explore the reasons. If the reason for the lower-than-desired performance is lack of employee skills, an individual development program should be designed. However, not all performance discrepancies are the result of a lack of employee skills. Other means of identifying employee needs include career counseling and training needs surveys. Both have been discussed in previous chapters (10 and 11). In career counseling, employee career goals are explored and skill needs examined to reach those goals. Then plans for skill development and career paths are designed. Training needs surveys are usually administered to supervisors. Supervisors are asked to identify employees who have or may have problems with performance. In addition, they are asked to identify the type of training or development that those individuals need.[6]

Development Plan

Once needs have been identified, the development plan may be designed to fulfill those needs. Numerous development techniques may be used, including supervisory coaching, on-the-job training, formal training programs, outside educational courses, and training videotapes. Some development plans may be relatively simple; others may be exceedingly complex.

Supervisory coaching is a common and useful developmental technique (discussed in Chapter 15). In coaching, the supervisor tries to help the employee learn the skills necessary to do the job. Coaching may take the form of showing subordinates how to do a certain job, providing instructions on how to perform a task, or simply providing advice on a task as needed. On-the-job training may require supervisory coaching. However, its approach is to help the employee learn by doing. The supervisor tries to delegate or assign tasks requiring new skills. Over time, the employee then develops new skills by performing the newly assigned tasks.

Formal training programs were discussed in Chapter 10. It is important to note, however, that employee needs be matched to training program objectives for best results. Outside educational courses and training videotapes may be useful in individual cases. For example, a personnel analyst may desire to become a wage and salary administrator. It may be useful for that person to enroll in a university-offered course on wage and salary administration. Training videotapes are becoming popular because they offer time flexibility. Employees may choose slack times in which to view the videotapes rather than to attend formal classes at a specific date and time. They also have the disadvantage of providing only one-way communication. Thus they are more useful in combination with other development strategies or as refreshers.

Regardless of the technique used, the development program should fulfill organizational and individual needs. To do so, specific objectives should be set and the development program then designed to meet those objectives. After the development program is complete, the results should be evaluated.

Evaluation

Evaluation of training program outcomes was discussed in Chapter 10. It is important to recall that all development programs should be evaluated. The objectives for the program can be stated in the form of skills, behaviors, attitudes, or organizational outcomes desired. After the program is finished, the results may be compared with the objectives. This is easier said than done, however, because some of the outcomes are hard to measure. Nevertheless, supervisors should evaluate performance to see that individuals are able to apply new skills, attitudes, and so on.

ORGANIZATION DEVELOPMENT

Development of individuals is an important part of the total process that helps organizations to change and be more effective. However, developing organizations involves more than developing individual skills and improving individual performances. Organizations are made up of multiple groups, and the effectiveness of these groups is important for organizational effectiveness. Group effectiveness is dependent not only on intragroup factors but also on intergroup development. It is important then that emphasis be placed on developing the organization as well as the individual.

Organization development: a planned, continuous process designed to increase organizational effectiveness by focusing on improving problem-solving skills, coping with environmental change, and changing organizational processes and structure.[7]

Therefore, organization development (OD) is a systematic and ongoing process designed to ensure continued survival and effectiveness of the organization.

OD Process

OD focuses on changing the organization in some manner. To be systematic, a planned process must be followed. Several steps are required in the OD process, which are shown in Figure 21-5.

DIAGNOSIS.   The first step in the OD process is to diagnose the situation, so as to know the cause of an existing problem or to predict future problems. Too often OD techniques have been used more as cure-alls rather than as fitting the solution to the cause of the problem. In fact, diagnosis and constant monitoring of both the internal organization and external environment may make a crucial difference in whether the organization simply *reacts* to events that have already occurred or *proacts* before problem events occur (thus preventing them).[8]

A number of different approaches may be used for diagnostic purposes, one of which is personnel research. Personnel research involves an analysis of employee actions and/or attitudes to determine any current or potential employee problems. Frequently, personnel or OD specialists conduct research to diagnose the cause of such problems as high turnover or absentee rates. Diagnostic tools used include interviews, surveys, and secondary data (e.g., records).

General Motors has had a systematic personnel research program for a number of years, with research focusing on differences in leader behavior, organizational climate, and organization structure among plants with good performance and plants performing poorly. General Motors' present research program is used as an intervention technique for organizational change. Its strategies involve both long- and short-range studies along with continuous monitoring.[9] In short-range research, specific problems at specific locations (e.g., employee turnover) are addressed. Longer-range research may examine a more general problem such as declining productivity throughout the company. For example, results of long-range research suggested that the majority of turnover occurred in the first four weeks of employment. Also, early job experiences were found to affect absenteeism rates of those retained. Further research showed that new hires who received individual orientations to their jobs and who were assigned to an above-average (in performance) operator for training were less likely to be absent

Figure 21-5

Organization Development Process

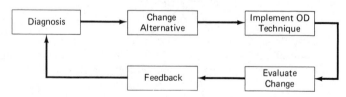

from work. These results led to changes in how newly-hired employees were handled.[10]

Some organizations will not have systematic personnel research programs. In these instances, managers may have to diagnose situations on their own. As such they may use many of the same tools used by personnel researchers. These tools include interviews, surveys, and unobtrusive measures such as records on turnover, absentee rates, and employee performance.

Interviews should be conducted by persons skilled in interviewing techniques. Diagnostic interviews designed to determine problems or causes of problems may be particularly sensitive. As a result, a skilled interviewer is required to obtain the necessary information carefully without intimidating the employee. A major problem with interviews is that they are not anonymous.

Surveys have two major advantages over interviews. First, they may allow the respondent anonymity. Second, a larger sample of employees may be obtained at less cost than with personal interviews. A number of different surveys may be used depending on the type of information desired. Surveys exist for measuring job satisfaction (e.g., Job Descriptive Index), organization climate (e.g., Organization Climate Index), and job design (e.g., Job Diagnostic Survey). Other surveys may be designed and tailored to the organization's particular needs.

The least disruptive diagnostic device is an unobtrusive measure such as records. Records may include turnover rates, accident rates, absentee rates, and performance measures. Managers should monitor these closely to spot potential problems quickly. Usually, unobtrusive measures can be used to identify problems, but further diagnosis is necessary to determine the causes of the problem.

Wayne Smith described several diagnostic tools used at Phillips. Among these were employee surveys, minineeds analysis in training programs, and manager observation. He also noted that his company sometimes uses an outside consultant for diagnosis of problems.

CHANGE ALTERNATIVES.   Once the problem and cause(s) of the problem have been diagnosed, the manager and/or OD specialist can develop possible alternatives for change. The goal of the change is to correct or resolve the problem. Thus the change alternatives generated should be ones that will help reach this goal.

Although there are organizations and consultants willing to sell "ready-made" alternatives for change, managers must be careful that (1) they fit the problem under study and (2) they will actually solve the problem. Too often, these ready-made programs are sold as cure-alls and may not, in actuality, fit the problem. Several OD techniques are discussed later in this chapter.

IMPLEMENT OD TECHNIQUE.   Once the change alternatives are generated, they must be evaluated and the best alternatives chosen. The alternative chosen is the one that will best solve the problem. Implementing this change is important for success. Implementation depends on the organization development technique chosen (e.g., team building, job enrichment, survey feedback).

The change implementation should be planned. Additionally, implementation of the change should be managed by someone with expertise in the OD technique being utilized. Thus, if team building were chosen to solve a particular problem and bring about a desired change, only someone well versed in team building should implement this strategy. If not, the change may fail and the problem may worsen.

EVALUATE CHANGE.   Once the change process has been completed, results of the change should be evaluated. Evaluation should occur after a reasonable time period from completion of the program. Evaluation is important to ensure that the goals of the change process were achieved. Although there are several approaches that a manager may use for evaluation, the approach must be appropriate for the change goals. One approach is to use a survey, say, to measure job satisfaction before the program and again at some point after the program is implemented. If the goal is to improve job satisfaction, differences, if any, in the overall job satisfaction of the target group could be identified. If this approach is used, a control group not involved in the change program should be used. This group would also be administered the survey before the program and after to see if other factors may be affecting changes in job satisfaction. If no changes in job satisfaction for the control group are observed, but the group participating in the change program has improvement in job satisfaction, the change may be attributed more confidently to the change program. If the objectives are not achieved, then new steps must be designed to attempt the change again.

FEEDBACK.   Feedback on the evaluation should go to all interested parties, such as the group manager, personnel department, and other managers involved in the change. Feedback is necessary so that future changes can be implemented effectively. Once feedback has occurred, diagnosis begins anew because organization development is a systematic and continuing process.

OD TECHNIQUES

Organization development is a systematic process, but the primary elements of OD are the techniques or strategies used to achieve change. There are many OD techniques. The focus here is on those techniques used most often by personnel or OD specialists. Many of these OD techniques stress organizational processes, structures, or both to achieve change. The techniques include sensitivity training, team building, process consultation, survey feedback, management by objectives, job enrichment, autonomous work groups, and structural changes.

Sensitivity Training

Sensitivity training has changed much from its inception in the 1940s as it grew in popularity with the development of the National Training Laboratories (NTL). Sensitivity training is also sometimes referred to as T-groups, laboratory training, and encounter groups. Its objectives include:

1. Understanding oneself in interpersonal and group situations.
2. Increasing understanding and sensitivity to the behavior of others.
3. Increasing one's awareness of group processes.
4. Improving diagnostic skills in interpersonal and intergroup situations.[11]

Sensitivity training: a group process whereby individuals become more sensitive to their personal environment, improve their understanding of the behavior of others and the group process, and learn to apply behavioral diagnostic skills.

Three different variations of groups are used in sensitivity training. First is the stranger group whose members do not know each other prior to the training. Second is the cousin group whose members work in the same organization but not necessarily in the same department. Third is the family group composed of members from the same department who work together regularly. Each of these groups may be handled differently for optimum results.[12]

It is expected that managers who learn more about themselves and group processes can bring this knowledge back to their jobs and hence be more effective. Care must be taken with sensitivity training or T-groups, however. The groups should be led by an experienced and knowledgeable leader, as these groups deal with personally sensitive issues. Moreover, some persons may be advised not to participate if they are insecure or easily threatened.

Team Building

Team building, intergroup and intragroup, has its roots in sensitivity training. Intergroup team building includes two or more separate groups that have to work together to achieve a common purpose; intragroup team building is designed for members of one work group. These groups may be permanent or temporary and existing or new.

Team building: a process designed to improve the functioning of one or more work groups so that its members are better able to achieve their objectives.

Most team building focuses on interpersonal or intragroup relations and the management of conflict, its purpose being to enhance coordination of activities and to make the group a functioning "team." The results of team-building activities may range from minor changes in team operations, for example, more group meetings, to changes in team members' behaviors and changes in group structure.[13] Team building is utilized to prevent conflict and/or increase leadership and cohesiveness of a group.

Often, team-building activities require the use of a third party who directs the group. The first step for team building is a diagnostic meeting to ascertain needs of the group. Once the needs are identified, team-building activities may focus on task accomplishment (decision making, problem solving, goal setting), building effective interpersonal relationships (peer and leader-member relations), understanding group processes, and/or analyzing group member roles as appropriate to satisfy the needs.[14]

One study of team building with forty separate cousin and stranger teams developed several conclusions:

Participants reported a greater awareness of the need to work together to solve problems.

Participants reported learning conflict resolution techniques such as open communication styles.

There was a greater use of group decision making in the organization for problem solving.

In general, there was more open communication in the organization.

There was a greater willingness to listen to others' viewpoints and compromise if necessary.

Managers delegated responsibility more readily than before.

The groups discussed problems and conflicts more openly.

There was greater warmth between supervisors of different sections and greater use of the open-door policy in the organization.[15]

One of the authors helped to implement a team building program with a group of managers within a department in a major corporation. Serious conflict between the department manager and his five subordinate supervisors was discovered. In fact, it was so bad that four of the five supervisors were searching for other jobs. To begin the team-building program, the third party (author) interviewed each of the parties individually to ascertain the problems. Next a diagnostic meeting (as described earlier) was held to define the problems of the group. The conflict within the group became readily apparent as well as the reasons for it. The major reasons were as follows:

1. The department manager was young and had been promoted over several of his supervisors, which bred resentment.
2. The department manager ran departmental meetings in a directive manner, allowing little input from the supervisors. Several of the supervisors had ten or more years of experience than the department manager.
3. The department manager sometimes went around the supervisors giving orders to their employees without their knowledge.
4. In general, poor communication existed between the department manager and his supervisors.

Several group meetings ensued with the third party as leader and group members discussing the problems and means of resolution. Eventually, the group agreed on solutions and implemented them. Communication improved and conflict was minimized.

Process Consultation

Process consultation is based on the use of a skilled third party or consultant from either inside or outside the organization.

> **Process consultation:** an approach to OD that uses a third party to work with organization members and groups to learn more about social processes in the work environment and to solve problems that arise from these processes.[16]

Some refer to this process as intervention because an outside party (consultant) intervenes in the processes of the organization.[17] The primary purpose of the consultant is to help diagnose any process-related problems and to help find solutions to those problems. However, the focus is often on diagnosis, with the solution left to the operating group.

A process consultant may analyze several areas of group activity. These include communication, functional roles of group members, decision-making processes used in the group, group norms, and leadership and authority in the group. The process consultant generally observes the group for a period of time and records significant behaviors and processes. The consultant is interested in the nature and style of communication used (verbal and nonverbal), the different roles of group members as they interact, and the process of identifying problems, making decisions, and implementing those decisions. Additionally, the consultant needs knowledge of the group's standards of behavior (e.g., freedom for group members to express ideas) and the nature of those standards (functional versus dysfunctional). Finally, the consultant can help the group to understand and deal with different leadership styles and/or help the leader to change to a more functional style.[18]

Although process consultation is practiced widely in organizations, little research has been done on its effectiveness. However, there is little doubt that group processes can either help or hinder the performance (e.g., mistrust in group, breakdown in communication, some group members not sharing their ideas for decisions). Thus, if handled properly and by a skilled process consultant, it can be a valuable OD tool.

Survey Feedback

Survey feedback is a method by which organization members respond to a survey and then receive tabulated data based on those responses. Assistance is provided in interpreting the survey results.[19]

Survey feedback: an OD technique in which survey results are used to solve existing problems or prevent them.

The normal methodology used in survey feedback is as follows:

1. Administer survey to organization members.
2. Analyze survey responses and tabulate results.
3. Feed back results to supervisors and subordinates on subordinates' responses.
4. Interpret results for organization members in terms of problems, potential problems, and/or changes needed.
5. Formulate and implement any changes necessary based on survey results (done by supervisors and subordinates together).

Survey feedback was used in a major health care organization shortly after the organization lost a union representation election and several key members of the top management team were replaced. The survey showed high dissatisfaction among the work force with regard to the compensation program, so the organization hired a consulting firm to analyze its compensation program. A number of other changes were implemented on a department-by-department basis according to the needs indicated by survey results.[20]

Although there is not an abundance of research to indicate the effectiveness of the survey feedback method, what does exist generally indicates positive results.[21] Additionally, research indicates that survey feedback is most effective in creating change when the survey results are negative instead of positive. Thus survey feedback would appear to be a more suitable OD technique when the organization or work group has major problems. It may not be as useful to organizations having few major problems but that have other reasons for change.[22]

Management by Objectives

Management by objectives (MBO) may be one of the most often used OD techniques.

Management by objectives: a process by which individual objectives are linked to organizational objectives through manager-subordinate discussions and negotiations.

This is a popular OD technique because it affects many managerial functions, among them planning, control, and performance appraisal. As a planning tool, objectives are set at the beginning of a period and activities required to reach those objectives are determined. As a control device, MBO permits a review and comparison of actual performance against objectives. As an appraisal tool, MBO is useful because managers and subordinates agree on performance-related job goals. Actual employee performance can be appraised against the mutually determined objectives.

The usual process involves a manager meeting with subordinates in which they jointly set performance objectives on the subordinate's job for a certain period. They also decide jointly what activities are needed to accomplish the objectives and how to measure objective achievement. Usually, the period for objectives is one year. Quarterly reviews are made to determine if the objectives are still realistic and to assess activities to date.

Two frequent criticisms of MBO are that (1) it involves too much paperwork and (2) it is difficult to set performance objectives on some jobs. Both criticisms are legitimate. MBO often does involve much paperwork, as mutually agreed-on objectives should be put in writing, quarterly reviews should be described in writing, and the final comparison of performance against objectives should be in written form. However, this is simply good management, ensuring proper communication and understanding of both parties, and protecting both parties. Also, it is more difficult to set objectives for some jobs than others. For example, it is difficult to set objectives for a research scientist. When end-result objectives are hard to develop, process objectives might be used. Rather than trying to specify what the end result will be, the process or method required to get there can be determined. Therefore, although the criticisms are legitimate, they should not limit the use of MBO.

If MBO is to be effective, objectives must be codetermined and not simply specified by the manager. MBO has several advantages over other systems:

1. Employees know what is expected of them.
2. Because of participation, employees are more committed to objective achievement.
3. Performance can be appraised more objectively.
4. Rewards can be tied to performance more easily.

Phillips Petroleum Company uses a modified form of MBO. Its system is referred to as Work Planning and Performance Review. The system is built around objectives and is designed to achieve the objectives noted. Appraisal of employee performance is based, at least in part, on achievement of objectives. Although it has not been an easy system to implement, officials at Phillips are pleased with its results.

Some proponents of MBO have coined the term "compensation by objectives" (CBO).[23] Basically, CBO is a more elaborate system for linking compensation rewards to performance using MBO as the base. When this is done, it is extremely important that the MBO system operate in the manner in which it was intended.

Job Enrichment

In Chapter 3, we discussed job design issues of which job enrichment is one. Job enrichment is an important OD technique as well. Like MBO, job enrichment has been popular and in frequent use.

Job enrichment: a process of redesigning a job to allow the employee more responsibility and autonomy in accomplishing job tasks.

In actuality, job design is the broader issue encompassing several different job restructuring techniques and thus should be considered an OD technique. However, our emphasis is on job enrichment because of its importance and popular use.

The issue of job design actually grew out of job enrichment. And the popularity of job enrichment and job design has grown out of the large number of repetitive and boring assembly-line jobs experienced in the United States and Europe. Because of these boring jobs, the work force has searched for ways in which to satisfy personal needs outside of the workplace. However, there is evidence that quality and quantity (in some cases) of work may have decreased (e.g., lower productivity in the United States). Several researchers proposed to "enrich" jobs, to place more challenge in the job, as an answer to this problem. Approximately 75 percent of job enrichment activities have been applied to blue-collar jobs.[24] It is broadly applicable to any type of job, however. The results of job enrichment applications have been mixed, primarily because it has been applied as a cure-all rather than as an OD technique should. It should only be used after diagnosis when it is determined that job enrichment will solve the problem.

Autonomous Work Groups

The development and use of autonomous work groups grew out of both job enrichment and the emphasis on quality of work life (Chapter 22).

> **Autonomous work groups:** a process whereby work groups are provided complete responsibility and freedom, within constraints, to perform group tasks.

Usually, individual job tasks expand considerably when autonomous work groups are formed. In addition, individuals experience more decision-making opportunities. When autonomous work groups are established, they are generally given a major task to accomplish, such as the complete assembly of an automobile. The work groups are then given the autonomy to determine the order of tasks and who will accomplish them within some set of reasonable constraints.

In one case, self-managed work teams were given responsibility for large segments of the production process. Seventy employees were organized into six work teams. On each shift there was a processing team and a packaging team. The processing team was responsible for unloading, storing materials, obtaining needed materials from storage, mixing, and then transforming mixture to a pet food product. The packaging team had to perform packaging, warehousing, and shipping duties. Each team had a large set of interdependent tasks, and assignments of employees to tasks were made by team consensus. Teams also solved manufacturing problems, covered for absent members, appointed team members to plant committees, screened and selected new employees, and counseled those who did not meet team standards. The work teams had considerable responsibility and autonomy.[25]

Autonomous work groups can be a powerful OD tool. Volvo used them, and although a plant using them cost 10 percent more to build and has only about one-third the production capacity as a conventional automobile assembly plant, quality of output is considerably higher and turnover and absenteeism are lower than at comparable plants. Volvo is changing most of its assembly-line plants to autonomous work groups.[26]

Structural Changes

There are a number of structural changes that may be made. For example, changing reporting relationships, changing design of the job, and developing autonomous work groups are all structural changes. However, the focus here is on structural arrangements designed to improve lateral relations.

Structural alternatives used to enhance lateral processes range from simple direct contact between two managers to the more complex matrix design. The following is a list of lateral structure approaches from simplest to the most complex:

Direct contact—two managers working together to solve a common problem.

Liaison role—a temporary coordinative position with the purpose of enhancing coordination between two departments.

Task forces—groups composed of members representing different departments with the purpose of solving specific problems affecting those departments. The task force disbands after the problem is solved.

Teams—permanent groups designed to solve continuing interdepartmental problems.

Integrating roles—permanent positions with the purpose of helping to coordinate various tasks. These positions usually report to the general manager.

Managerial linking roles—permanent positions whose role is to integrate major tasks. Incumbents are given decision-making authority and usually carry influence similar to a manager's role.

Matrix designs—complex structural arrangements whereby functional managers (e.g., finance, personnel) and project or product managers (e.g., product 1, product 2) have dual authority.[27]

The choice of one or more of these structural approaches should be based on the diagnosed problem or need. Matrix designs are not appropriate in all organizations. They often work best in highly complex situations where uncertainty is great.

Other OD Techniques

A few of the more prominent OD techniques not discussed so far are career planning and development, work time changes, and the job expectation technique.

Career planning and development has been implemented in many organizations in recent years.[28] Career planning and development has benefits for both the individual and the organization. It helps the individual to develop career goals and skills necessary to advance in his or her career. It helps the organization by having people prepared (with the proper skills) to undertake a new position when a vacancy occurs or when a new job is created. The process involves having employees communicate career goals, determine appropriate career paths, and develop plans for expanding skills (through training and on-the-job experience) that will enable the employee to move along the career path as desired.

Work time changes include two major variations: four-day workweek and flextime. The predominant workweek is five days, eight hours a day. In recent years, some organizations have changed to a four-day, nine-and-a-half or ten-hour-a-day workweek. The four-day or compressed workweek allows three-day weekends for leisure and more concentrated time away from work.

Flextime is a flexible employee work schedule. Under one form of flextime, all employees work a required number of hours in a day (e.g., eight hours a day) but may begin and end their workdays at other than normal times. For example, an organization may allow its employees to begin any time between 6:00 A.M. and 10:00 A.M. and leave work anytime from 3:00 P.M. to 7:00 P.M. A person who arrives at 7:00 A.M. may leave at 4:00 P.M., having worked eight hours (with a one-hour lunch). Other variations of flextime may allow employees to work less than eight hours in a day as long as they work forty hours a week. Flextime allows employees to adjust their work schedules to their life-style and family situations. Both flextime and the four-day workweek have their advantages, but they may not be appropriate for all jobs or all organizations (e.g., flextime often is not appropriate for assembly-line manufacturing jobs).

The job expectation technique (JET) aids in clarifying job understanding between a manager and his or her subordinates. JET is a variation of team building and focuses on clarifying roles, expectations, and responsibilities of managers and subordinates. It is particularly useful when a new team is formed, when diagnosis reveals role ambiguity or conflict among staff members, and when a new person joins an established work team.[29]

Although other OD techniques may be useful in specific situations, the most important have been noted. It must be emphasized that techniques should be used only when diagnosis indicates a particular need.

Wayne Smith described briefly several OD techniques at Phillips to include survey feedback, third-party interventions, training and development, and quality circles. The company also uses a modified MBO system for performance appraisal. Quality circles are a "hot" new OD technique whereby employees participate in decisions on how to improve productivity, product quality, and quality of the work environment.

Overview of Organization Development

Change is a continual process and, as such, organization development is not a one-time process but an ongoing one. Although the positive aspects of OD have been emphasized, planned change can have negative effects as well.[30] When organizations undergo change, they are vulnerable to power plays by special interest groups and individuals and to the use of politics for personal gain. These must be avoided to the extent possible.

There are always risks in any OD effort because selection and implementation of OD is more complex than most decisions made by managers. Further, there is little information on the parameters of success and failure.[31] Figure 21-6 shows a multitude of OD techniques. The selection and application of one or more of these techniques is not easy. In addition, there are structural limits on the use of OD. These occur primarily because many OD techniques focus on changing interpersonal relationships without consideration of the structure.[32] Thus both interpersonal relationships and structure should be considered in implementing organization development.

Although OD does present some risk (as well as many potential benefits), research is providing better information on which to base OD technique selection decisions. For example, one study examined the impact of five OD interventions on various types of work groups. Results indicated that each of the five OD techniques had differential effects on the various work group types.[33] Although preliminary, these results showed that OD techniques cannot be used as cure-alls for all groups. Second, OD must be applied on a contingency basis, only after thorough diagnosis.

SUMMARY

People and organizations face change and must adapt to it to remain healthy. Organizations face multiple pressures from change. Many come from a turbulent external environment. Included in these external change pressures are changing societal values, shortages of natural resources, government regulation, and greater interdependence

Figure 21-6

Organization Development Techniques

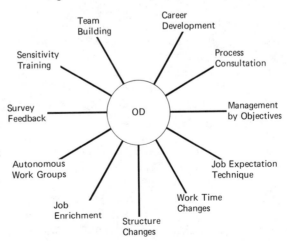

among the countries of the world. Internal change pressures come from employee demands and rapid changes in technology.

Although change is expected, it is natural for human beings to resist change—because of a fear of the unknown, feelings of insecurity, and inconvenience.

Resistance to change must be overcome if an organization is to grow and adapt as it should. Resistance may be overcome by applying the change process: unfreeze the forces that prevent change, implement the change, and refreeze the change.

Force-field analysis is effective in diagnosing the forces preventing change. There are two types of forces acting on a person to cause a certain type of behavior: driving forces and resisting forces. The supervisor may diagnose the forces acting on a person and attempt to increase driving forces or reduce resisting forces. Research shows that reducing resisting forces is the best way of unfreezing a person's behavior.

Individual development is the process by which individuals gain new skills, thereby increasing job performance. Organizations have a large investment in human assets, and it makes sense to increase the value of those assets through development. The process of individual development includes determining organizational and individual needs, designing and implementing an individual development plan, and evaluating results of the development program.

Organizational needs for individual development are usually identified through human resource planning described in Chapter 6. This process identifies the types and numbers of jobs that the organization will have in the future and hence identifies the required numbers and skill levels of employees.

Individual development needs are commonly identified in the performance appraisal process (Chapter 15). Other means of identifying these needs are career counseling and training needs surveys (Chapters 10 and 11). The development plan is designed to help satisfy the needs identified. Developmental techniques include supervisory coaching, on-the-job training, formal training programs, outside educational courses, and training videotapes. All development programs should be evaluated to ensure that the program objectives have been met.

Organization development is a planned, continuous process designed to increase organizational effectiveness by focusing on improving problem-solving skills, coping with environmental change, and changing organizational processes and structure. The five-stage OD process described includes (1) diagnosis, (2) consideration of change alternatives, (3) implementing the OD technique, (4) evaluating the change, and (5) feedback.

The first and perhaps the most important part of OD is diagnosis. Diagnostic tools include interviews, surveys, and unobtrusive measures such as turnover and absentee records.

Change alternatives should fit the problem under study and be able to solve it. OD specialists should avoid cure-all approaches. Once the appropriate alternative is chosen, it must be implemented. The change process noted earlier should be managed. Once a program is finished, it should be evaluated by one of several approaches. One of the most often used evaluation approaches is a survey administered before and after the program to see if change occurred. Of course, feedback on the evaluation should be given to all interested parties.

Other OD techniques include sensitivity training, team building, process consultation, survey feedback, management by objectives, job enrichment, autonomous work groups, and structural changes. Sensitivity training, which began in the 1940s, is a process designed to make individuals more sensitive to their personal environment, to improve understanding of behavior and group processes, and to apply behavioral diagnostic skills. Team building grew out of sensitivity training and is designed to improve the functioning and interrelationships in work groups. Process consultation is based on the use of a skilled third party to help group members learn more about social processes and to solve problems arising from these processes. Survey feedback uses survey results to prevent or solve problems. Management by objectives is a process by which individual objectives are linked to organizational objectives through manager-subordinate discussions and negotiations. Job enrichment is a job design alternative that allows the employee more responsibility and autonomy in accomplishing job tasks; it is not effective in all situations or with all groups of people. Autonomous work groups, which grew out of job enrichment, are work groups that are given complete responsibility and freedom, within constraints, to perform group tasks. There are numerous structural change alternatives. Those discussed involve lateral relations and include direct contact, liaison roles, task forces, teams, integrating roles, managerial linking roles, and matrix designs. Other OD techniques include career planning and development, work time changes, and the job expectation technique.

INTERVIEW WRAP-UP

Change pressures on Phillips include employee age distribution, projected growth trend, changing direction of company, growing international operations, increasing emphasis on productivity, changing technologies, changing employee expectations, diminishing worldwide conventional petroleum resources, the state of the U.S. economy, and interaction with numerous governments.

I think that Phillips would have problems (e.g., decline, loss of industry position) if it did not respond to the change pressures. Because of this, Phillips tries to diagnose and solve the problems it has. For example, it uses employee surveys, diagnostic instruments in training programs, manager observations, and outside consultants to help diagnose problems. Based on the diagnosed needs, Phillips makes use of several OD techniques, including survey feedback, third-party interventions, management development, quality circles, and management by objectives. Phillips is a progressive organization in responding to change pressures and using organization development effectively. —Wayne Smith, senior representative for management training and development, Phillips Petroleum Company.

WHAT MANAGERS SHOULD DO REGARDING
PERSONNEL MANAGEMENT ACTIVITIES

1. Managers should be aware of the change pressures and the need to react to them.
2. Managers should understand resistance to change and how to use the change process and force-field analysis to overcome resistance to implementing change.

3. The importance of individual development should be recognized. Managers must know how and when to design and implement individual development programs.

4. Managers should understand and recognize the value of organization development.

5. They should have an appreciation of the various OD techniques and use expert advice when implementing specific techniques.

REVIEW QUESTIONS

1. What are some of the internal and external change pressures faced by organizations?

2. Why do people naturally tend to resist change?

3. How can resistance to change be overcome?

4. In what ways are the change process and force-field analysis useful?

5. What is individual development and how does this concept apply to personnel management?

6. Why is diagnosis the most important step in the OD process?

7. In your estimation, what are the most important OD techniques? Why?

KEY CONCEPTS

Autonomous work groups
Career planning and development
Change
Change pressures
Diagnosis
Driving forces
Flextime
Force-field analysis
Four-day workweek
Individual development
Job enrichment
Job expectation technique

Lateral relations
Management by objectives
Organization development
Process consultation
Refreezing
Resistance to change
Resisting forces
Sensitivity training
Survey feedback
Team building
Unfreezing

CASE

THE HOSPITAL MOVE

Community General Hospital is one of three major hospitals in a city of about 200,000 residents. Community General's original building was erected in 1910 and has had a number of additions over the years. However, due to increasing pressures for new space, advanced equipment, and patient rooms, along with multiple repair needs, the hospital's administration and board decided that a new building was necessary. The hospital was healthy financially and could afford the debt of a new building.

The staff had heard rumors of the possible decision to move, but nothing was announced to them until a final decision was made. When the decision was made, Walter Nisson, the hospital administrator, sent the following memo to all staff members:

```
Date:    November 12, 1983

To:      All Staff

From:    Walter Nisson, Administrator

Subject: Community General Facility Relocation

As you know, our facility is old and in continuous need
of repairs.  Additionally, we have a shortage of space
for new equipment and patients.  Thus, the board has
decided to build a new facility.  The site for our new
location is 12th and Admiral.  I hope you are as
excited as we are in our continuing endeavor to provide
excellent health care to our community.
```

The memo was received with excitement from staff members. Many who had been working in cramped quarters were jubilant. However, after the initial excitement wore off, some grumbling was heard. Several nurses were unhappy because they had homes near the present location. The move was going to increase their commuting time. Moreover, there were rumors regarding which areas would receive larger space allocations and what new departments might be developed.

In fact, Walter had formed a space committee made up of doctors, technical staff, and administrative personnel to study space requirements. Sheila Walters, assistant administrator, recommended that the move was a good time to make some other changes they had been considering. They wanted to buy a new sophisticated body scanner that could help diagnose many health problems, particularly cancer. This would require a new department and new staff. Additionally, they wanted to improve their pediatrics staff and X-ray department. In both cases, Walter and Sheila felt that the first step was to replace the department heads. The chief pediatrics nurse (who was not popular with the staff nurses) had held the position for twelve years, and the manager of the X-ray department (who was well liked by his staff) had been in the position for five years. Neither change was going to be easy. They decided to make the changes at the time of the move.

As time progressed, the new building took shape. Eventually, it was completed and the move was planned. Sheila was given the task of informing both the chief pediatrics nurse and X-ray department manager of their reassignments to new nonsupervisory positions. The sessions went as well as possible considering the circumstances. These meetings occurred two weeks before the move. Walter and Sheila, along with Ruth Bastion, the personnel director, also met with both departments' staffs. In both meetings, the managerial changes met with considerable resistance. Some of the typical comments from both meetings are as follows:

"I don't even want to change hospital locations and now you dump a new untrained supervisor on us."

"Why make this change? He's doing a good job now. We are all treated fairly and try to do well for the hospital."

"Several of us heard about this last night, and we are thinking about quitting. We may not make the move to the new building."

"Who's our new department manager? What is his background? How do you know someone else can do a better job? Besides, don't you have faith in us?"

CASE QUESTIONS

1. What is wrong here?

2. Explain how the change process and force-field analysis could have been used in this case. Speculate as to some of the driving and resisting forces operating on these staff members.

3. Choose one or more OD techniques and describe how they might be used to solve the problem in these situations.

NOTES

[1]Information on pressures for change may be obtained from W. G. Bennis, *Changing Organizations* (New York: McGraw-Hill, 1966); E. F. Huse, *Organization Development and Change* (St. Paul, Minn.: West, 1980); R. D. Middlemist and M. A. Hitt, *Organizational Behavior: Applied Concepts* (Chicago: Science Research Associates, 1981).

[2]B. M. Bass, "Organizational Life in the 70s and Beyond," *Personnel Psychology,* 25 (1972), 19–30.
[3]Ibid.

[4]K. Lewin, *Field Theory in Social Science* (New York: Harper & Row, 1951).

[5]K. Lewin, "Quasistationary Social Equilibria and the Problem of Permanent Change," in *Organization Development: Values, Process and Technology,* eds. N. Margulies and A. R. Raia (New York: McGraw-Hill, 1972), pp. 65–70.

[6]L. A. Berger, "A DEW Line for Training and Development: The Needs Analysis Survey," *The Personnel Administrator,* 23 (1978), 51–56.

[7]Adapted from R. D. Middlemist and M. A. Hitt, *Organizational Behavior: Applied Concepts* (Chicago: Science Research Associates, 1981).

[8]B. P. Shin, "Organizational Change and Its External Environment in Relation to Selected Organizational Levels," *Management International Review,* 17 (1977), 45–50.

[9]H. C. Carlson, "Organizational Research and Organizational Change: GM's Approach," *Personnel,* 54 (1977), 11–22.

[10]Ibid.

[11]J. Campbell and M. Dunnette, "Effectiveness of T-Group Experiences in Managerial Training and Development," *Psychological Bulletin,* 70 (1968), 73–103.

[12]Huse, *Organization Development and Change,* p. 369.

[13]Ibid., p. 343

[14]W. L. French and C. H. Bell, Jr., *Organization Development* (Englewood Cliffs, N.J.: Prentice-Hall, 1978), pp. 118–119.

[15]T. H. Patten, Jr., and L. E. Dorey, "Long-Range Results of a Team Building OD Effort," *Public Personnel Management,* 6 (1977), 31–50.

[16]Adapted from E. Schein, *Process Consultation: Its Role in Organization Development* (Reading, Mass.: Addison-Wesley, 1969); French and Bell, *Organization Development.*

[17]C. Argyris, *Intervention Theory and Method* (Reading Mass.: Addison-Wesley, 1970).

[18]Huse, *Organization Development and Change,* pp. 332–337.

[19]R. J. Solomon, "An Examination of the Relationship Between a Survey Feedback O. D. Technique and the Work Environment," *Personnel Psychology,* 29 (1976), 583–594.

[20]J. F. Sullivan and T. J. Cotter, "Organization Development Efforts in a Major Health Care Organization," *Personnel,* 54 (1977), 32–41.

[21]D. G. Bowers, "O.D. Techniques and Their Results in 23 Organizations: The Michigan ICL Study," *Journal of Applied Behavioral Analysis,* 9 (1973), 21–43; L. D. Brown, "Research Action: Organizational Feedback, Understanding, and Change," *Journal of Applied Behavioral Analysis,* 8 (1972), 697–711; F. C. Mann, "Studying the Creating Change," in *The Planning of Change,* eds. W. Bennis, K. Benne, and R. Chin (New York: Holt, Rinehart and Winston, 1961) pp. 605–615; M. G. Miles, H. A. Hornstein, D. M. Callahan, P. H. Calder, and R. S. Schiavo, "The Consequences of Survey Feedback," in *The Planning of Change,* pp. 457–468.

[22]Solomon, "An Examination."

[23]T. H. Patten, Jr., "Linking Financial Rewards to Employee Performance: The Roles of OD and MBO," *Human Resource Management,* 15, (1976), 2–17.

[24]J. C. Taylor, "The Human Side of Work: The Socio-Technical Approach to Work System Design," *Personnel Review,* 4 (1975), 17–22

[25]R. E. Walton, "How to Counter Alienation in the Plant" in *Conceptual Foundations of Organizational Development,* eds. N. Margulies and A. P. Raia (New York: McGraw-Hill, 1978), pp. 356–373.

[26]R. J. Aldag and A. P. Brief, *Task Design and Employee Motivation* (Glenview, Ill.: Scott, Foresman, 1979).

[27]J. Galbraith, *Designing Complex Organizations* (Reading, Mass.: Addison-Wesley, 1973).

[28]J. Leach, "The Career Development Study as an OD Intervention," *Training and Development Journal,* 32 (1978), 34–38.

[29]Huse, *Organization Development and Change,* pp. 292–293.

[30]N. W. Biggart, "The Creative-Destructive Process of Organizational Change: The Case of the Post Office," *Administrative Science Quarterly,* 22 (1977), 410–426.

[31]B. M. Meglino and W. H. Mobley, "Minimizing Risk in Organization Development Interventions," *Personnel,* 54 (1977), 23–31.

[32]G. H. Rice, Jr., "Structural Limits on Organizational Development," *Human Resource Management,* 16 (1977), 9–13.

[33]D. G. Bowers and D. L. Hausser, "Work Group Types and Intervention Effects in Organizational Development," *Administrative Science Quarterly,* 22 (1977), 76–94.

QUALITY OF LIFE: WORK, LIVING, AND RETIRING

LEARNING OBJECTIVES

After reading this chapter, you should be able to:

1. Describe several elements of quality of life and define quality-of-work-life programs.
2. Discuss the four major problems that may be attacked by quality-of-work-life programs.
3. List several quality-of-work-life programs and explain the conditions necessary for their success.
4. Describe how older workers are affected by age discrimination.
5. Discuss the complexities involved in making retirement decisions.
6. Explain why the trend toward early retirement is changing.
7. Describe how to develop and implement an effective retirement counseling program.

Ray Carney is a newsman for KPNW AM and FM radio located in Eugene, Oregon. KPNW is one of the most powerful and most reputable stations in the Northwest. Ray has forty-one years of experience in the news media and has spent his last twelve years with KPNW. He received his bachelor's degree in 1945. Ray has considerable experience in his field. In the near future he will be thinking of retirement.

Interviewer: What are your feelings regarding the quality of your life?

Ray Carney: My own quality of life is high. The value of my investments has increased due to inflation, but my standard of living has not increased because of the recession. The broadcast industry has been good to me. Many people in the broadcast industry project an image of having "made it" but most have not. The public attaches success to them because of their public exposure. Unless they have made wise investments, few will be able to enjoy a high standard of living.

I have a nice home, all my children have finished school, I have a degree of material well-being (e.g., cars), and my wife and I have combined incomes and savings. In addition, I have good health, and my financial status is such that my wife and I may begin to plan for retirement in the next year.

Interviewer: How does your job affect your quality of life?

Ray Carney: My job has both positive and negative effects on the quality of my life. My press credentials provide many benefits, such as tickets to a variety of events, travel, meals, and accommodations. However, there are also nights without sleep and pressures that can present health hazards. Overall though, my job has more positive than negative effects. My affiliation with a prestigious radio station and the residuals from my job (such as a feeling of doing a job well) have contributed to a satisfying quality of life.

Interviewer: What are the best features of your company's retirement program?

Ray Carney: KPNW is a relatively new station and has no retirement program for employees. The company's fairness during my employment has made the lack of a retirement program more palatable. It is considering such a program, but it is too late to do me much good.

Several things are important to me in my retirement, for example, financial security and good health. Right now, I am concerned about the uncertainty in the social security program. I have news files full of tales of senior citizens who have lost their homes because of the inability to pay taxes or medical bills. I hope to avoid these problems.

At retirement, I plan to have a modest home on the shores of the Pacific Ocean where I can fish as much as I want. I also want to operate a small business to ensure a small income, but at my convenience.

As a contrast to the discussions with Ray Carney, we also interviewed Elise Dunphy, an employee of The Coca-Cola Company located in Atlanta, Georgia. Elise is a disbursing auditor in the corporate employee benefits department and has worked for The Coca-Cola Company for twelve years. Previous to that, she worked for a newspaper in Pennsylvania for twenty-two years. Elise started out as a cashier in the accounting department of The Coca-Cola Company in New York City.

Interviewer: What are your feelings regarding the quality of your life?

Elise Dunphy: I have been fortunate. I have always tried to do a good job, but my work at The Coca-Cola Company has been more rewarding than my previous work with the newspaper. The company is bigger, and has more benefits, and there is an opportunity to meet a wide range of people. I also like Atlanta. The people are friendly, and I have nice business associates. I have a comfortable quality of life.

Interviewer: What are the best features of your company's retirement program?

Elise Dunphy: The best feature of The Coca-Cola Company's retirement program is that employees do not have to contribute to it but receive retirement income. The program is based on a person's salary and number of years of service. In addition, the company voluntarily has provided improvements in retirement income.

In addition, the company allows retirees to have the same health plan as regular employees, but it is offset by Medicare. However, this plan will pick up some expenses that are not covered by Medicare, such as prescriptions and private-duty nurses.

I think about moving back to New York when I retire to be near my family. But I don't want to stop working entirely. I would like to have a part-time job, if possible. I have enjoyed my job and, in particular, working for The Coca-Cola Company.

INTRODUCTION

Both Ray Carney and Elise Dunphy seem to have an acceptable quality of life according to their own statements. Ray rates his quality of life as high, and Elise feels comfortable with hers. Both have worked for a number of years and are now examining the prospects of retiring. As we know, not everyone in the United States, and certainly not everyone in the world, feels that he or she has a high quality of life.

Quality of life and, in particular, quality of work life have become important issues in recent years to most people in the United States, Canada, and Europe. Quality of life is a broad term enveloping many areas of a person's life. Included would be one's social and work environments, physical living conditions, standard of living, personal pressures, availability of personal expression, and development and use of one's abilities, among other things. Quality of life is a complex issue, and it is decidedly personal. What Ray may see as important for a high quality of life may be unimportant for Elise, for instance. In fact, Ray's and Elise's personal situations vary considerably. One is married, the other is not; their jobs are considerably different; and they live in considerably different sections of the United States (Oregon and Georgia). However, both seem pleased with their personal lives.

In addition, both seem relatively pleased with the quality of their work lives. Elise says that her present job and work environment represent a considerable improvement over her work with the newspaper. Ray describes both positive (e.g., benefits of press privileges) and negative (e.g., pressures creating more stress) features of his job.

Unfortunately, many employees do not perceive that they have a high quality of work life. A task force on the quality of work life for the American Society of Training and Development established the following definition of quality-of-work-life programs:

Quality-of-work-life program: a process that enables organization members at all levels to participate actively in shaping the organization's work environment, methods, and outcomes. Its goals are to enhance the organization's effectiveness and improve the quality of life at work for employees.[1]

The quality-of-work-life issue has become important for several reasons, including the decline in productivity experienced by many U.S. businesses in recent years. The *1978 Economic Report to the President* stated that productivity was one of the most significant economic problems faced by the United States in many years.[2] Poor morale and job dissatisfaction are reasons advanced for the lack of productivity growth.

Another reason for current emphasis on quality of work life is the increasing turnover experienced by organizations in certain industries. High rates of employee turnover (employees leaving the organization) create many problems. When one person leaves an organization, another must be hired. The selection process is costly with advertising, interviewing, and paperwork processing costs. Additionally, there is *lost* productivity while a replacement is being sought and even after a new employee is hired until he or she is fully trained. Causes of voluntary turnover include boredom and monotony on the job and a poor work environment in general. Thus some turnover may be eliminated by improving the quality of work life.

Other reasons for focus on quality of work life include apathy among the general work force, sabotage of products, and employee strikes against companies. When employees are apathetic, quantity and quality of performance suffer. Sabotage has been an increasing problem among workers who are bored with routine and monotonous jobs. They may shoot rivets into spare tires or weld bottles into the gas tank to alleviate the boredom. Employees have also joined in strikes, some sanctioned by their union and others being wildcat, to improve their working conditions. Probably the most famous of these strikes occurred in the 1970s at the General Motors Lordstown, Ohio, plant. This strike focused attention on the frustration and alienation experienced by some employees regarding their working conditions. One final reason for quality-of-work-life programs is potential government involvement.

The federal government has become increasingly interested in the quality of work life for workers, as evidenced by the growing amount of legislation dealing with employees and their workplaces (e.g., the Occupational Safety and Health Act). Most organizations want to prevent the government's entry into this field if they can. Thus in the long run, potential government intervention may be a powerful impetus to the development of quality-of-work-life programs. When taken together, all these factors have provided strong impetus to the focus on and development of quality-of-work-life programs in organizations.

In this chapter, we examine the problems creating a need for quality-of-work-life improvements, means of implementing quality-of-work-life programs, and focus on quality of work life for older employees.

CURRENT PROBLEMS

Most of us work for several reasons, not the least of which is monetary reward. However, work fulfills several other needs, including personal development, self-esteem, and social relationships. If work does not satisfy these needs, we may become frustrated. In addition, we spend many of our active, waking hours at work. As such, work has a major impact and plays a central role in our lives. It affects our physical and mental health, our financial well-being, and our general satisfaction with life. There are several important problems that may be attacked with quality-of-work-life programs. These include job design, work environment, health and safety, and stress.

Job Design

The design of jobs has been the most critical issue addressed in quality-of-work-life programs. As noted earlier, many jobs are so routine that the work is boring and highly monotonous to most workers. In fact, most employees on these jobs are vastly overqualified. The jobs are highly specialized or, in some cases, overspecialized. We discussed the issues of job design in Chapter 3. However, we focus here on the employees' responses to their jobs. In many cases, employees on routine, boring jobs become frustrated and alienated. Nowhere is there a better example of this than along the automated assembly line.

In the early 1960s, Robert Blauner noted the increasing alienation among factory workers.[3] Blauner described alienation as being comprised of feelings of powerlessness, meaningless, isolation, and personal indifference or separation of self from the job. Blauner concluded that workers who have no power to change their jobs or work environment obtain no meaning or personal value from their jobs, cannot form social relationships on the job, and separate themselves from their jobs because of the lack of meaning. All these factors lead to alienation. This alienation produces discontent among the work force and is manifested in some of the behaviors described earlier (i.e., turnover, sabotage). Therefore, to change these behaviors and the workers' feelings toward their jobs, job design must be changed. Job redesign, then, is frequently the focus of quality-of-work-life programs.

It should be noted that neither Ray nor Elise seem to be experiencing frustration or alienation with their jobs. Ray noted some problems with his job, but they did not seem to be related to the job design. We know less about Elise's job, but she did describe the positive social contacts she makes on the job. So her job must not have many of the elements that lead to alienation.

Work Environment

The employees' work environment has an impact on the manner in which they respond to their work. This work environment includes the physical conditions—temperature (heat, cold), lighting, air quality (clean, fumes), work space, and so on—and general treatment—such as the pressure for production, relationships with supervisors and peers, and organizational policies.

Employees have often reacted negatively to poor working conditions. Employees at General Motors' Tarrytown, New York, plant, for example, reacted strongly to their original work situation. The pressure for production was strong. An employee had, on the average, only one and one-half minutes to complete his or her assigned task on each car (the high-speed line turned out fifty-six automobiles per hour). It seemed as if the job never ended. Work spaces were crowded, dirty, and noisy. First-line supervisors were seen as insensitive dictators. The workers tried to take out their frustrations on the supervisor, their union representative, and the job itself.[4]

Work environment, then, has a major impact on whether employees respond positively or negatively to their work. Quality-of-work-life programs must concern all aspects of employees' work environment.

Health and Safety

Health and safety for employees have become major issues in recent years, partly as a result of the Occupational Safety and Health Act and partly as a result of attention of recent studies linking personal health to job-related factors.

Safety has been emphasized in industry for a number of years. Accidents on the job are costly to organizations in several ways. First, accidents cause employees to miss work and thus reduce productivity. Second, most organizations are required to pay into a state insurance program called workmen's or workers' compensation, a funding mechanism designed to compensate employees who miss work due to job-related accidents. Higher accident rates cause the organization to pay higher rates. Finally, valuable, productive employees may be lost.

Health and safety are, of course, related matters. However, many health-related matters have gone untouched by organization safety programs. Safety programs are oriented to preventing accidents and have little to do with the employee's general health. Many recent studies suggest that certain elements (e.g., chemicals, asbestos) in physical work environments are carcinogens causing cancer. In addition, the nature of jobs and employee responses to them have been linked to heart disease and mental health problems.[5] Therefore, we must be concerned with both the employee's *physical* and *mental* health. Dissatisfaction with jobs and frustration with one's work environment may create personal stress that leads to physical and mental health problems and even to turnover and sabotage. The research now suggests that we are tampering with human life and a person's ability to cope with life. Organizations must react to provide satisfying and healthful jobs and work environments. If organizations do not respond, there is a high likelihood of government involvement.[6]

Stress

Stress is something that most of us recognize but know little about. Research has shown links between levels of job stress and a number of illnesses, such as heart disease, ulcers, arthritis, and strokes.[7]

We often associate stress with management and executive positions. Undoubtedly management positions are stressful. However, stress can occur with any person in any job at any level in the organization. Researchers have identified many types of situations that are stressful. Table 22-1 shows specific stress events associated with work.

Table 22-1

Stress Events Associated with Work in
Order of Stress Value

Rank Order of Stress Events
Fired from work
Retirement
Business readjustment
Change to a different line of work
Change in responsibilities at work
Outstanding personal achievement
Trouble with boss
Change in work hours or conditions
Vacation

Source: B. Weiner et al., *Discovering Psychology*
(Chicago: Science Research Associates, 1977),
p. 475.

The stress events noted in the table could affect anyone. In addition, people face stress events in everyday activities (marriage, death, divorce, obtaining a mortgage, health problems, arguments with spouse, moving to a new location, holiday celebrations, etc.). Stress may be related to personal illness. For example, one study found that over 50 percent of those people who experienced significant stress events in one year (e.g., several stressful events such as being fired from work, divorce, business readjustment) had a serious illness the following year. Thus stress can have significant adverse effects on a person's quality of life.

Stress can also adversely affect a person's quality of work life. A number of different work situations in addition to those shown in Table 22-1 contribute to increased stress. Some of these are:

Overly restrictive work rules.

Competition for scarce resources (salary increases, promotions).

Conflicting demands from supervisors, co-workers, and union leaders.

Ambiguous job descriptions and instructions.

Unreasonable expectations of performance exceeding employee capabilities.[8]

Although organizations cannot control the normal life events that cause stress, they have some control over stress events at work. They must attempt to ensure that stress at work is not unreasonable and that unnecessary stress does not occur.

A manager's job is one of the most stressful because of the increasing burdens and responsibilities placed on individuals in managerial positions. Many managers feel increased strain, anxiety, and tension when placed in situations that they have no power to change. For managers to deal with the increasing stress placed on their job, it has been suggested that they must have self-acceptance and a positive, stable self-concept.[9]

Therefore, quality-of-work-life programs may have to work with managers on their self-concept. Ray Carney is not a manager, but he has some stress on his job. His comments suggest his responses to stressful situations, such as lack of sleep at night, negatively affect his quality of life.

Some authors have argued that moderate stress at work may actually increase performance. However, excessive stress may decrease effectiveness on the job.[10] One recent study found much of the stress that occurs at work is dysfunctional, having negative effects on group performance.[11]

QUALITY-OF-WORK-LIFE PROGRAMS

As the need for improvements in the quality of work life increases, organizations have responded with quality-of-work-life programs.

The Programs

A number of different quality-of-work-life programs are being used. We review some of the more important ones.[12]

Flextime is one program that is growing in popularity. Flextime is a relatively simple but useful concept. Essentially, a system of flexible work hours is set up for employees as described in Chapter 21. For example, employees may choose to come to work any time from 6:00 A.M. to 10:00 A.M. and leave work any time from 2:30 P.M. to 6:30 P.M.(assuming a thirty-minute lunch break) after working a full eight hours. This allows employees to adjust their work schedules to their personal life-styles. However, flextime is not appropriate for all organizations or all employees. For example, the system might be difficult to implement with assembly-line employees.

Sociotechnical redesigns include physical and technical changes in the workplace. Thus the physical layout, the nature of the job, and even the social interactions are changed. An example of this type of change is the use of autonomous work teams. Volvo has redesigned the old assembly-line process and now uses a team of employees to assemble a complete automobile. The work is more stimulating and challenging, and Volvo claims that, although fewer cars are produced using this method, the quality of output is considerably improved.

Job enrichment is another program in common use that enhances autonomy and responsibility for performing the job. Research has shown that job enrichment is likely to be more successful with employees having a strong need for personal growth and development.[13] Therefore it may not be equally effective with all employees.

Other programs include the sharing of jobs to prevent layoffs or allowing individuals who prefer only part-time work to hold jobs. This approach may ease unemployment. Another program is aimed at allowing older workers to continue working but with reduced work time, that is, to retire gradually or to avoid retirement yet enjoy increased leisure time. Finally, some organizations allow employees to choose between full pay or increased leisure time. In this program, employees can choose to have greater leisure time at reduced levels of pay (e.g., an additional twenty-one days off during a year with a pay reduction of 10 percent).[14]

There are many variations of these currently popular programs. However, no program will succeed unless it is implemented properly.

Conditions for Success

Three common problems that must be prevented or overcome if the implementation of quality-of-work-life programs is to be successful are managerial attitudes, union influences, and the restrictiveness of industrial engineering.[15] In each case, changes may have to be made to have a successful quality-of-work-life program.

Many quality-of-work-life programs emphasize worker participation in decisions and allowance of increasing autonomy to do the job. As such, managers must have or adopt favorable attitudes toward worker participation and autonomy. Unions sometimes view quality-of-work-life programs suspiciously, as a means to speed up production. Management and unions must cooperate on quality-of-work-life programs, and unions must be shown the value of the program to the employees. Industrial engineering has the objective of increasing the efficiency of employee performance. Major changes in work design involve major changes in work standards and methods of work. Thus industrial engineers must be shown the value of such a program. In addition, the program should include an evaluation of the results to ensure that desired objectives were achieved.[16]

In summary, the conditions for successful implementation of quality-of-life programs include the following:

1. Managerial personnel must be committed to an open, participative style of operation, sharing information and opportunities with employees and sincerely desiring their inputs.
2. Employees must be provided with opportunities to advance their careers.
3. Managers must be trained to operate in a less directive and more collaborative style.
4. Status barriers between managers and workers must be eliminated to promote trust and open communication.
5. Employees should receive frequent feedback on their performance along with recognition and other positive rewards for a job well done.
6. The objective of personnel selection should be to choose those who can be motivated to perform excellently.
7. The quality-of-work-life program must be evaluated, reinforcing the positive outcomes and changing the negative outcomes.[17]

Quality-of-Work-Life Example

In 1970 the General Motors automobile assembly plant in Tarrytown, New York, had one of the poorest labor relations and production records in the company. However, within seven years it became one of the company's best producing plants. It did so by implementing a quality-of-work-life program. The effort was a cooperative one between union and management, born of frustration and desperation.

The company decided to stop assembling trucks at Tarrytown and change the entire layout of the plant. In two departments, it was decided to obtain the workers' ideas regarding needed changes. Although suspicious, employees provided ideas and supervisors were pleased with them. The changes were made efficiently, and the plant met its production schedule deadlines. Employee involvement was then implemented in the complete rearrangement of another major area in the plant. It also was successful, and the next year a new car model was added to the plant's assembly operations.

This was followed by a labor agreement in which the union and management committed themselves to establishing formal mechanisms to improve the quality of work life for employees. General Motors had been promoting organization development programs that were having some effect on their managers. There was no union involvement in these programs, however, so more action was necessary.

The management at the Tarrytown plant hired an outside consultant who worked with both union and management personnel. He conducted joint problem-solving training sessions for managers and employees alike. Soon employees began developing solutions to all sorts of problems. After several major changes at the plant (layoffs and employee recalls), in 1977 it was decided to launch a plantwide quality-of-work-life program. The purpose of the program was to obtain employee involvement and participation. Three thousand employees were trained in problem-solving methods and were encouraged to participate in decisions.

The results were good. Absenteeism went from $7\frac{1}{2}$ percent to slightly over 2 percent. Grievances went from 2,000 seven years earlier to only 32 at the end of December 1978. Production had improved dramatically.[18]

Currently, General Motors has hundreds of quality-of-work-life projects underway, including a quality-of-work-life survey it administers to employees to spot problem areas. Based on the outcomes of the survey, management attempts to develop programs to solve the problems. The survey can be used to evaluate efforts also. Each year, all key General Motors' executives meet to discuss new and innovative quality-of-work-life programs in their divisions. They train plant management and staff to emphasize quality of work life. They send internal consultants to start programs at new plants. As a result of some of these programs, they have no time clocks in some plants and work teams make large numbers of important decisions. Not all programs have been successful (some early failures were experienced because of poor implementation). However, the majority of results are positive, and the future for these programs looks bright.[19]

Some authors have suggested that government should get involved to promote improved quality of work life. Research has shown that many employees who are dissatisfied with their jobs are interested in changing jobs for more satisfying employment. In addition, these employees are willing to relocate within the state and retrain if necessary.[20] Government could stimulate job changes such as these by supporting geographic relocation, providing more information on the labor market and needs for certain employee skills, and establishing job retraining programs. Organizations offering a higher quality of work life would be rewarded with an abundant supply of trained personnel; organizations with a poorer quality of work life would be under pressure to improve if they are to retain an effective work force.[21]

All quality-of-work-life programs are dependent on the managers' and employees' values. In fact, the shift in values among the younger workers toward self-realization is one of the major reasons for quality-of-work-life programs.[22] Research has found that values affect behavior and decisions of managers regardless of the country in which they live. We should note that quality-of-work-life programs may vary by country because of different values.[23]

OLDER WORKERS AND QUALITY OF WORK LIFE

Approximately 27 percent of all those who are unemployed and 40 percent of the long-term unemployed are forty-five years of age or older. In the middle 1960s, the secretary of labor reported that approximately 50 percent of all job openings in the private sector were barred to applicants over fifty-five years of age. In addition, 25 percent were barred to applicants over forty-five years of age.[24] Significant job discrimination continues today.

The Age Discrimination in Employment Act of 1967 (as amended in 1978) prohibits discrimination against individuals forty years of age or older up to age seventy. However, many people in this age group are banned from employment in certain jobs because of their age. Despite the federal government's efforts, however, older workers' quality of work life and quality of life in general will suffer until age discrimination can be eliminated.

Retirement

Retirement has become an important issue in recent years. Early retirement programs flourished in the 1960s and 1970s. The amendment to the 1967 act raising the mandatory retirement age to seventy has created a whole new series of questions, particularly with the forced early retirement programs instituted in some organizations.

For years the "magical" retirement age was sixty-five. This practice began with Otto von Bismarck, who in 1889 adopted the modern world's first comprehensive program of social insurance. However, he did so only because of strong pressure and, in his own words, to avoid socialism. His Old Age and Survivors Pension Act made it necessary to decide when "old" age actually began. Bismarck set the age at sixty-five knowing full well that life expectancy in Germany at the time was only forty-five. Thus, by his own design, few workers would benefit from his program. Most programs in other countries have adopted the arbitrary age of sixty-five without question.[25]

The new retirement law has developed new questions for older workers. When the mandatory retirement age was raised to seventy, most predicted that it would have little change on the retirement patterns of older workers. For example, one survey showed that 70 percent of the workers retire before reaching age sixty-five.[26] One of the main arguments for raising the retirement age to seventy was so that large numbers of productive workers would stay on the job, thereby reducing public and private expenditures for retirement benefits. However, the data indicate that many people, given a choice, retire early and have little desire to re-enter the work force.[27] One study found that no more than 12 percent of retirees would be able to or would like to return to work.[28]

The decision of when to retire involves an assessment of a number of important factors:

Comparative economic incentive to retire or continue work.

Health needs, benefit coverage available, and cost of benefits.

Financial resources available to supplement income from pension plans and social security.

General type of employment available to older persons.

Quality of life desired and possible in retirement (psychological and social needs).

Probable life span.[29]

Thus, the decision to retire is a complex one for each person. Each of the factors listed is important. Each person may assign a different weight to each factor. Both Ray and Elise are looking forward to retirement for example.

Continuing Employment

Recent studies, however, indicate that employees desire to stay on the job. One such study indicated that over 50 percent of the surveyed employees desired to continue working past age sixty-five. In addition, a majority of recent retires stated that they wished to continue working rather than being forced to retire. It was concluded that the trend toward early retirement may be changing. A new trend of postponing retirement may be emerging.[30] The reasons for these changes are complex. Many people who have retired early have had economic difficulties due, in part, to the high rates of inflation experienced in recent years.[31] Economic difficulties are interrelated with quality of life. A recent survey revealed that 42 percent of retirees felt their incomes provide a less than adequate standard of living. In addition, many workers have little confidence that the social security system will be able to pay them the benefits to which they are entitled.[32]

Closer examination of retirees provides more information on why some people desire to retire and/or retire early. The results of one study indicate the primary reason for retirement is that of health. Those who do retire early tend to be those with health problems.[33] In addition, research indicates that those with health problems are affected more by job attributes than are those without health problems and that people in undesirable jobs are more likely to retire than are those in desirable jobs.[34] Further, early retirees reported that their jobs allowed less autonomy, skill variety, opportunity to interact with others, and intrinsic satisfaction than did those who did not retire early. Therefore, the quality of work life may affect a person's decision to retire. The retirement decision made by these people seems to have been an attempt to pursue more challenging and personally rewarding activities. These people, then, were trying to enrich the quality of their lives.[35]

People who continue to work after normal retirement age are healthier and have fewer financial problems. In addition, they tend to dislike retirement, draw their friends from work, and make firm plans to continue employment. These people have a strong interest in work and likely have jobs that are interesting and challenging to them.[36]

Both Ray Carney and Elise Dunphy stated that they expected to continue working after retirement. Ray has no pension plan where he works but seems to have made wise investments and has had the benefits of a two-income marriage. Elise has had only one income but feels she has an excellent retirement program provided by her company. Thus both look forward to a comfortable retirement period.

Retirement Counseling

The new retirement law, changing trends in retirement patterns, high inflation rates, a questionable social security program, and the impact of quality of work life and quality of life in general make retirement counseling highly complex but also increasingly important. Currently, over 20 million people are over age sixty-five, and by the year 2000, it is expected that 25 percent of the American population will be over sixty-five years of age. Currently many of these people live in poverty and substandard housing. Their retirement income has been seriously eroded. In addition, age discrimination in employment makes it difficult for these persons to supplement their incomes. Thus retirement counseling and preparation for retirement is sorely needed.

Retirement must be *managed.* Employees should know all the options available, develop proper attitudes, and understand fully the effects of the aging process. Proper preparation requires that one begin ten to fifteen years prior to retirement. Counseling should encourage self-direction and reduce the level of threat to a minimum.

A complete retirement counseling program covers six important subject areas: (1) finances (retirement income, tax considerations, budgeting, and investing), (2) health (medicare, insurance coverage, facts on aging, pharmaceuticals), (3) legal rights and responsibilities (writing wills, selling property, avoiding swindlers), (4) leisure time (hobbies, community services, second careers, educational opportunities, travel), (5) housing (selection of retirement locations, climate considerations, location of children and relatives and real estate arrangements), and (6) family relationships (spouse, children, friends, and loneliness, idleness, and deteriorating health).[37]

The means for implementing retirement counseling programs are also important. One useful approach is to establish an advisory board with several members ranging in age from fifty to seventy. Also included on the board should be at least a few individuals who are retired. This board can provide guidance and ensure that it covers legitimate and important concerns for those approaching retirement. In addition, the first stages of counseling should begin between the ages of fifty-five and sixty.

Ray Carney and Elise Dunphy do not tell us if their respective companies have retirement counseling programs. Based on the information provided, it is unlikely that Ray's company has any such program. On the other hand, Elise's company may have such a program with the seemingly other good retirement benefits it provides.

Quality of Life

Maintaining one's quality of life seems to be an important issue today for most people looking at retirement. For those with high incomes, retirement may allow greater freedom and add more meaning to their lives. Persons with low incomes can only look forward to more work, lessened opportunities, and no more freedom of time.

For many, however, interests and values shift with a desire for a different lifestyle. These people may desire more autonomy in living their own lives, choosing the work they desire to do, and choosing their own work hours, leisure activities, and employment.[38]

Research suggests that retirees' overall life satisfaction is associated with a positive view of themselves and the belief that they can control the factors that affect them. Good health seems to be quite important to a retiree's view of quality of life. Income does not seem to be as important above a certain level. A general positive attitude toward the previous job and toward retirement aids in retirees' life satisfaction. Retirees are more satisfied when they have prepared for retirement both financially and in activities after retirement. If one is forced to retire, general life satisfaction tends to decrease.[39]

Ray Carney feels that he has a high overall quality of life and expects, because of his investments and the operation of his small business during retirement, to have a high quality of life in retirement. He also noted that good health and a good job have helped lead to a high quality of life. He seems to have control of his life and is preparing well for retirement.

Unfortunately, older workers still have problems on the job and have trouble obtaining employment because of age stereotypes (e.g., older workers are perceived as being less capable of being creative and of changing their work methods). Research has shown that managerial judgments of the performance capacity of older workers are influenced by age stereotypes.[40] Therefore stereotypes must be avoided and/or overcome before older workers can be afforded equal opportunity in the job market and before we can expect to raise the general quality of life of older citizens. Both Ray Carney and Elise Dunphy are fortunate and seem to have the opportunity of having a relatively good quality of life currently and in the future, after retirement.

SUMMARY

Quality of life and quality of work life have become important issues in recent years. Quality of life includes one's social and work environments, living conditions, standard of living, amount of experienced stress, and so on. Quality of work life focuses on the work environment. A quality-of-work-life program is designed to increase organization effectiveness by allowing organization members to participate in decisions regarding work environment and work methods. Organizations have begun implementing quality-of-work-life programs because of decreasing worker productivity and increasing employee turnover and to prevent government intervention, along with other reasons.

Some of the job-related problems that may be attacked with quality-of-work-life programs include job design, work environment, health and safety, and stress. Many jobs have become so routine that they are boring and represent no challenge to the employee. Workers have become alienated because of these jobs and have reacted negatively. Jobs are then redesigned to change workers' feelings toward their jobs.

Employees react negatively to poor working conditions (both physical and psychological). Quality-of-work-life programs must take into account all elements of the employees' work environment. The government has become increasingly concerned with health and safety on the job. Organizations seem to have emphasized employee safety over health. However, the nature of jobs and employees' responses to them have been linked to physical and mental ailments. One major health problem is stress. When the level of stress is high, a person has a strong likelihood of developing a major illness. A number of job-related factors can cause stress. Quality-of-work-life programs must be concerned with physical and mental health and job-related stress.

Some of the quality-of-work-life programs are flextime and sociotechnical work designs. In flextime, a set of flexible work hours is developed (e.g., come to work between 6:00 A.M. and 10:00 A.M. and leave work from 2:30 P.M. to 6:30 P.M., after eight hours of work). Sociotechnical work designs include physical and technical changes in the workplace. Physical layout, nature of the job, and social interactions may change.

For quality-of-work-life programs to be successful, managerial attitudes and union influences must be appropriate, and industrial engineering must be flexible. Thus managers should be committed to open employee participation and reward employees for their efforts through frequent feedback, and elimination of status barriers between management and the workers.

Older workers are becoming an important force in our society. It is estimated that over 25 percent of our population will be sixty-five and older by the year 2000. However, currently many older workers face job discrimination because of their age, and many retired workers have low quality of life.

The retirement age of sixty-five was set arbitrarily in the late 1880s and has been adopted by most countries in the Western world. The United States has now raised the retirement age to seventy. Retirement decisions are complex, but the necessity of better incomes and the desire to be productive may keep many older workers on the job. Research shows that most people who retire early have health problems. People who continue to work after normal retirement age tend to be healthier and have fewer financial problems. They tend also to have a strong interest in work.

Organizations have the responsibility to prepare employees for retirement with effective retirement counseling programs. Retirement counseling should begin ten to fifteen years prior to retirement. Retirement should be managed. Effective retirement counseling programs should include finances, health, legal rights and responsibilities, leisure time, housing, and family relationships.

The quality of people's lives is affected by the quality of their work life and the view they have of themselves. Positive attitudes toward the job, themselves, and retirement enhance a retiree's life satisfaction.

INTERVIEW WRAP-UP

Ray Carney and Elise Dunphy work in significantly different jobs in significantly different industries. They live thousands of miles from each other, one near the West Coast, another in the hub city of the South. Yet both, for different reasons, feel they have a reasonably good quality of life at present. In addition, each is planning for and looking forward to retirement. Ray's company has no retirement program and Elise's has a comprehensive retirement program. However, both are planning to have a reasonable quality of life during retirement, Ray with his investments, Elise with her retirement program, and both supplementing their incomes with, at least, part-time work. Ray and Elise are fortunate when compared to the many older employees who have trouble finding work and/or have lowered quality of life in old age.

WHAT MANAGERS SHOULD DO REGARDING PERSONNEL MANAGEMENT ACTIVITIES

1. Managers should be concerned with employees' quality of work life. They should diagnose problems (e.g., causes of turnover) and/or take actions (e.g., redesign jobs) to prevent problems.

2. Implementing successful quality of work life requires that managers develop the proper attitudes and manage union and industrial engineering influences well. They must also develop an open and receptive work environment.

3. Managers must particularly be concerned with job design, physical and mental work environment, employee health and safety, and job-related stress. They should try to design rewarding, challenging jobs, develop a positive, healthful, and safe work environment, and attempt to control the amount of stress to which employees are exposed.

4. Managers should be particularly concerned about the plight of older workers. They should be careful to avoid age discrimination and not to develop age stereotypes. Managers must also help prepare employees for retirement.

5. Managers should be concerned with employees' overall quality of life while working and after retirement.

REVIEW QUESTIONS

1. What is the relationship between quality of life and quality of work life and why are they important?

2. How can quality-of-work-life programs help to solve job design and work environment problems?

3. How can quality-of-work-life programs help to solve health, safety, and stress problems on the job?

4. What must a manager do to ensure the success of quality-of-work-life programs?

5. In what way does discrimination affect older workers' quality of life?

6. What is involved in a retirement decision and how will the new law raising the retirement age affect workers and companies?

7. How does retirement affect quality of life and why is retirement counseling important?

KEY CONCEPTS

Age discrimination

Age Discrimination in Employment Act

Flextime

Health and safety

Job design

Job enrichment

Quality of life

Quality of work life

Retirement

Retirement counseling

Sociotechnical redesigns

Stress

Work environment

CASE

THE YOUNG WILDCATTERS AND THE OLD SCABS

Veronica Whitmore and Billy Young worked in the paint department of Wilson's Furniture Manufacturers, located in the northeastern United States. Janie Hill and Sam Moore worked in the packing department. They were taking a coffee break in the company cafeteria.

"Boy, I caught a five-pound bass last weekend. It was one of the best fishing trips I've had in a long time."

"Yeah, I can hardly wait until we get another three-day weekend and we can be out on the lake again."

"Well, I don't know about you guys, but I can hardly wait to get out of this place each evening. I'm going bananas on this job. All I do is stuff card tables and chairs into packing boxes and stack them for the forklift to come move them to the warehouse.''

"How would you like our job? All we do is spray-paint chair and table legs all day. Generally, it's the same color for a whole week. The only change is the colors once in a while. And the smell back there is awful.''

"It gets boring but we relieve the boredom some.''

"How do you do that?''

"We mix the colors in different spray guns and paint stripes and other designs on the furniture. Can you imagine the buyers' faces when they get home expecting a green set of chairs and open the package to find them in psychodelic colors?''

"Well, we are one up on you; we can't paint the tables or chairs but we can pack them backwards and upside down. We can also pack them so that the whole box must be torn apart to get the furniture out. Can you see these customers spending thirty minutes trying to get their new table and chairs out of the box? Also, we occasionally carve the initials of someone we don't like on the table top or seats.''

"Yeah, but all of this stuff is getting old. I don't think I can take this job much longer. I've complained to our union steward, but he says we can use it to get more money in the next contract.''

"Hell, I don't want more money! I want a decent job,'' Billy said as he pounded his fist on the table.

Veronica said, "Calm down, Billy. If we really want a better job, we have to do something about it.''

"What?''

"Well, since we've talked to our supervisor and our union reps and got no action, we've got to do something so those higher level managers will listen to us.''

At this point, Janie jumped back into the conversation. "They won't listen to us. You think we can walk through those carpeted halls, through the fancy doors, and get an appointment? No, we can't!''

"I wasn't talking about that—I'm talking about a strike.''

"The union will never go along with us.''

"I know it. But we don't need their approval. We can get enough people in a wildcat strike so they can't do anything.''

"I'm game.''

"So am I.''

Finally, Janie agreed and they plotted their strategy. The strike was to begin the next day promptly at 8:00 A.M. They spread the word all that afternoon.

The next morning about 25 percent of the employees joined them. By the end of the third day, almost two-thirds of the plant work force had joined in the strike. Production at the plant was only 25 percent of normal, and plant management was worried. The union was no help. The company decided to hire new workers in place of the strikers. Management knew it wouldn't be easy, because most "good'' workers were employed. Therefore, it was decided to focus on older workers, particularly those who had retired early and had remained in the community. After a media blitz (television, radio, and newspaper advertising for workers, a number of applicants responded, mostly older persons, male and female alike. There was little choice. Almost any person who was physically able was hired.

Of course, the strikers resented these "scabs." They called them names and tried to block their way into the plant. At the end of the first week of the strike, production was starting to increase slightly.

Veronica, Sam, Billy, and Janie were huddled with several other workers outside the gates Monday morning, plotting their new strategy, when Veronica saw her father coming through the gates.

"Father, what are you doing here?"

"I'm going to work, Veronica."

"But, Father, you are hurting us. You are a scab."

"I don't care. I've been living on my pension for three years, and Mom and I can hardly make it. I've tried to find work, but they all tell me I'm just too old. You young people don't know how good you have it. We have pride and we have to eat, too, when we get old. I'm going to work. I hope you stay on strike a long time."

Veronica didn't know what to say. She and her father both had tears in their eyes as they looked at each other.

CASE QUESTIONS

1. What is (are) the problem(s) in this case?

2. Is Veronica or her father right? Why?

3. Could quality-of-work-life programs be used to help solve the problem(s) in this situation. Explain.

NOTES

[1] D. J. Skrovan, "A Brief Report from the ASTD Quality of Work Life Task Force," *Training and Development Journal,* 34 (1980), 29.

[2] E. M. Glasner, "Productivity Gains Through Worklife Improvement," *Personnel,* 57 (1980), 71–77.

[3] R. Blauner, *Alienation and Freedom: The Factory Worker and His Industry* (Chicago: University of Chicago Press, 1964).

[4] R. H. Guest, "Quality of Work Life—Learning from Tarrytown," *Harvard Business Review,* 57 (1979), 76–87.

[5] *Work in America,* report of a Special Task Force to the Secretary of Health, Education and Welfare (Cambridge, Mass.: MIT Press, 1973); T. J. Keaveny, R. E. Allen, and J. H. Jackson, "An Alternative to Legislating the Quality of Work Life," *The Personnel Administrator,* 24 (1979), 60–64.

[6] Keaveny et al., "An Alternative to Legislating."

[7] *Work in America.*

[8] R. D. Middlemist and M. A. Hitt, *Organizational Behavior: Applied Concepts* (Chicago: Science Research Associates, 1981).

[9] K. R. Student, "Changing Values and Management Stress," *Personnel,* 54 (1977), 48–55.

[10] R. J. Burke, "Occupational Stresses and Job Satisfaction," *The Journal of Social Psychology,* 100

(1976), 235–244; H. Selye, *The Stress of Life* (New York: McGraw-Hill, 1967); F. C. Shontz, *The Psychological Aspects of Physical Illness and Disability* (New York: Macmillan, 1975).

[11]R. D. Allen, M. A. Hitt, and C. R. Greer, "Occupational Stress and Perceived Organizational Effectiveness in Formal Groups: An Examination of Stress Level and Stress Type," *Personnel Psychology,* 35 (1982), 359–370.

[12]G. W. Bohlander, "Implementing Quality-of-Work Programs: Recognizing the Barriers," *MSU Business Topics,* 27 (1979), 33–40.

[13]M. A. Hitt and D. R. Cash "Task Technology, Individual Differences and Satisfaction," *Review of Business and Economic Research,* 17 (1982), 28–36.

[14]M. McCarthy, "Trends in the Development of Alternative Work Patterns," *The Personnel Administrator,* 22 (1979) 25–33.

[15]Bohlander, "Implementing Quality-of-Work Programs."

[16]Ibid.

[17]Glasner, "Productivity Gains."

[18]Guest, "Quality of Work Life."

[19]E. C. Miller, "GM's Quality of Work Life Efforts . . . An Interview with Howard C. Carlson," *Personnel,* 55 (1978), 22–23.

[20]Keaveney et al., "An Alternative to Legislating."

[21]Ibid.

[22]S. Ronen, "Personal Values: A Basis for Work Motivational Set and Work Attitude," *Organizational Behavior and Human Performance,* 21 (1978), 80–107.

[23]G. W. England and R. Lee, "The Relationship Between Managerial Values and Managerial Success in the United States, Japan, India and Australia," *Journal of Applied Psychology,* 59 (1974), 411–419.

[24]S. A. Williams, "Age Discrimination: Involuntary Retirement Under the Age Discrimination in Employment Act," *Labor Law Journal,* 29 (1978), 391–408.

[25]"Retirement at 65: An Arbitrary Cut-off That Started with Three Men," *Dun's Review,* 110 (1977), 31–32.

[26]"Study Says Companies Unruffled by Mandatory Retirement Age Law," *National Underwriters,* 83 (1979), 24, 33.

[27]L. T. Smedley, "The Impact of Raising the Mandatory Retirement Age: A Brief Assessment," *Labor Law Journal,* 30 (1979), 470–476.

[28]D. K. Motley, "Availability of Retired Persons for Work: Findings from the Retirement History Study" *Social Security Bulletin,* 41 (1978), 18–28.

[29]F. H. Cassell, "The Increasing Complexity of Retirement Decisions," *MSU Business Topics,* 27 (1979), 15–24.

[30]J. Perham, "Retirement Revolution Brewing," *Dun's Review,* 113 (1979), 96–97, 100.

[31]R. M. Yaffe, "Changing Retirement Patterns: Their Effect on Employee Benefits," *The Personnel Administrator,* 24 (1979), 29–33; J. Schonbak, "Changing Demographics: The Effect on Pensions," *Pension World,* 16 (1980), 54–56.

[32]"New Survey Reveals Attitudes Toward Retirement," *The Personnel Administrator,* 24 (1979), 16.

[33]J. F. Quinn, "Microeconomic Determinants of Early Retirement: A Cross-Sectional View of White Married Men," *The Journal of Human Resources,* 12 (1977), 329–346.

[34]J. F. Quinn, "Job Characteristics and Early Retirement," *Industrial Relations,* 17 (1978), 315–323.

[35]N. Schmitt, B. W. Coyle, J. Rauschenberger, and J. K. White, "Comparison of Early Retirees and Nonretirees," *Personnel Psychology,* 32 (1979), 327–340.

[36]"Work After Retirement: Some Psychological Factors," *Social Security Bulletin,* 38 (1975), 36–38.

[37]T.L. Lamberson, "Realities of Retirement Point to Need for Corporate Counseling Programs," *Risk Management,* 25 (1978) 28–31.

[38]Cassell, "The Increasing Complexity of Retirement Decisions."

[39]N. Schmitt, J. K. White, B. W. Coyle, and J. Rauschenberger, "Retirement and Life Satisfaction," *Academy of Management Journal,* 22 (1979), 282–291.

[40]Ibid.

PERSONNEL MANAGEMENT AND THE FUTURE

LEARNING OBJECTIVES

After reading this chapter, you should be able to:

1. Describe the impacts of technology on work in the future.
2. Discuss five trends that will influence the future shape of organizations.
3. Describe four forces that influence the development of individual attitudes toward work and organizations.
4. Explain some of the major challenges that personnel managers will face in the future.

INTRODUCTION

We have seen a number of dynamic changes in society in the past ten or fifteen years. During this brief period, humans have traveled repeatedly to the moon and back, government has grown increasingly involved in the lives of people, and computers have vastly increased our capabilities to process data. Furthermore, we have witnessed major changes in people, their attitudes, beliefs, abilities, and goals during the same period. These changes have ranged from deep personal involvements in consumer issues, war demonstrations, civil rights, and feminist and abortion alliances to an emerging trend away from such involvements and the growth of the "moral majority."

Such rapid and drastic changes seem to preclude predicting the future, but effective organizations must undertake this chore. Without accurate forecasts, the ability of organizations to plan for and meet future needs is limited. To stay in business, to compete effectively, or to provide essential services, the organizations must anticipate the issues, challenges, and opportunities they will face tomorrow. This is as true for the management and use of human resources as it is for financial and physical resources.

The purpose of this final chapter is to examine some of the issues, challenges, and opportunities that personnel managers expect to face in the future. We look at these issues as they deal with the three central elements of personnel management: the organization, jobs, and people. The same basic logic espoused throughout this book applies to dealing with the future. Effective personnel management, in the future, will still depend on the relationships among these three central elements. However, changes in the elements will affect the manner in which personnel activities should be carried out. With this understanding, the examination of expected issues, challenges, and opportunities may yield effective planning for personnel activities in the future.

THE CHANGING NATURE OF WORK

Robots! The word titillates the imagination and, for most people, evokes images of *Star Wars* and two of its fanciful characters, R_2D_2 and C3PO. Few of us realize, however, that the world of *Star Wars* is not so different from some of the realities taking shape in our industrialized society.

For example, robot sales in the United States during 1980 increased by 50 percent and many experts predict a 35 percent growth rate through 1990.[1] Others project that robotic automation will result in huge labor reductions in jobs in selected industries, for example, a projected 30 percent reduction in jobs in the insurance and banking industries by 1990.[2] General Motors and General Dynamics are but two of the many organizations that have ambitious plans for the use of automated robots in tomorrow's jobs.

It is expected that General Motors will invest $200 million by 1983 to convert fourteen assembly lines to high-technology production, including 800 robots that will weld the bodies of new cars. By 1990, an additional $1 billion will add 13,000 more robots to assemble small parts, load and unload machines, paint and perform a variety of jobs that now belong to people. General Motors' management feels the robots are not only cheaper in a wage-inflated market, but they are superior in quality and dependability.[3] General Dynamics uses similar robotic technology in manufacturing F-16 fighter jets. There, robots select tool bits from a rack, drill a set of holes to tolerances of .005 inch, and machine the perimeters of 250 various parts. The robot makes twenty-four to thirty parts an hour with a zero rate of rejections, whereas a human spoils 10 percent of the six parts he or she can make in an hour.[4]

Work, be it a carpenter's job, a banker's job, or a teacher's, is something nearly everyone has done in the past and will continue to do in the future. Society values work; it has always constituted a major force in people's lives. However, the time is close at hand when work will undergo substantial changes, both in its importance in forming societal values and in its very shape or nature. As one author has stated,

> The shape work can take is decided by the available technology, adjusted to the social structure of the time, and then fitted into the prevailing values. It is because our technologies and social structures are changing that I see changes coming in the shape of our work, changes that will, in turn, change the central thrust of our society.[5]

According to this view, one should look at the nature of work as it is decided by the available technology and then adjusted to the prevailing social structure and values. Thus, although one may not be able to forecast the *precise* nature of a job, say, bank teller, in ten years, one can understand the forces that will cause it to change and the *general* nature of those changes in work.

Available Technology

As we have suggested, robotic technology is rapidly changing the nature of work. Some of the major changes that will result from robotic and other new technologies are:

1. Some 20 percent of the labor force in final assembly of automobiles will be replaced by automation by 1985.
2. Vision systems will allow robots to select parts scrambled in a parts bin by 1985.
3. Approximately fifty percent of the labor force in small-component assembly will be replaced by automation by 1988.[6]

Furthermore, robots and other technologies (e.g., computers, microelectronics) will soon take over most hazardous and unpleasant jobs such as in the production of toxic fuels. Also, they will perform a great many skilled jobs such as lathe operator, welder, and quality control inspector. In addition to the obvious consequences (fewer jobs, reduced workweeks, etc.), technological developments may likely stratify "people jobs" into two categories: those who are managerial, professional, or highly skilled and those who are at the entry level. Midlevel jobs will be performed largely by technological creations. The stratification of jobs will inhibit upward mobility and perhaps frustrate large numbers of entry-level workers.[7]

Social Influences

Although technology will be the first influence on the nature of work in the future, social structure and values will give work its final shape; that is, individual attitudes toward technologically shifted jobs will finally determine what those jobs must be. Furthermore, social values, such as work ethics, will serve as constraints to work in the future; that is, technologically altered jobs must be acceptable within the then prevailing sets of social attitudes and values. One major futurist sees four changes in jobs that will result from new or emerging attitudes and values:

1. An increasing number of people will be paid according to contract, that is, by fee rather than by wages. Thus many more people will work for a variety of organizations, performing job services for which they are paid fees. This means the work will be done at the worker's own pace, and in his or her own way.
2. Partially as a result of increasing energy costs, and partially due to the decreasing importance of organizations to individual lives, work will be performed increasingly in homes. Computer technology will provide work information to those who perform their tasks in their homes and send their finished products to the organization.
3. As they gain control over their work (due to contract and "at home" work), people will begin to accept lower-paying jobs that they enjoy.
4. More people will work in maintenance and repair jobs. These jobs will fit with the longer life cycle of products and the ecological attitudes (return to "quality life") and values of society.[8]

THE CHANGING NATURE OF ORGANIZATIONS

Work and organizations have been nearly synonymous since the 1800s. The process of industrialization required that jobs be contained within the confines of organizations or, if you prefer, that organizations be developed around the boundaries of work. Because of their close relationship, it is reasonable to expect that changes in the nature of work will be accompanied by changes in organizations.

Some changes in organizations are more obvious than others, such as the continuing growth in their size and the internationalization of industry. Other changes reflect the changes seen in the nature of work itself, such as the movement of the actual workplace away from the organization. Beyond these obvious and work-related changes, however, a number of other trends will influence the shape of organizations in the future. While we cannot anticipate all these changes, five seem especially relevant to personnel activities in organizations.

Declining Productivity

U.S. productivity growth has been declining and may continue to decline in the next several years. The decline is due to many factors, including governmental regulations, the movement to a service society, and reduced rate of capital investment. If this trend continues, as predicted by many, the organization's ability to provide employees with financial rewards will decrease.[9] Also, organizations will be forced to change many jobs to enhance efficiency and productivity, changes such as robotics or "at home" and contracted work.

Managerial Changes

The steady increase in the numbers of blacks, women, and other minorities, coupled with the previous bulge in young white male employees may result in severe crowding in the lower ranks of management. This trend is seen already, although the crowding is not yet so severe.

For example, by 1978 females constituted 23.4 percent of the managerial force and the number of black professionals increased from 4.8 percent to 11.7 percent.[10] All of this promises severe competition within organizations for higher-level managerial positions and considerable frustration among younger managers. Organizations will place increasing emphasis on the formal education of aspiring managers. Many of these people are, and will be, trained for six or more years beyond high school (e.g., master's and doctoral degrees) to think critically and creatively. They will bring new values and new procedures to organizations.

Skilled Personnel Needs

Organizations will continue to develop technology, especially technologies of energy, production, transportation, and communication. These techniques will demand high technological skills and the investment of billions of dollars. The size of these invest-ments and projects will place unprecedented demands on the labor market for skilled technological workers. Organizations will go beyond the local labor market to find these employees, seeking them in the international, as well as national, labor force.[11] Thus organizations are also influenced to become multinational in makeup because of their increasing reliance on technological skills.

Company Directors

Society is increasingly demanding a voice in public affairs. In the 1970s, this demand took the form of extreme activism (militance, demonstrations), but more recently the movement has become more subtle. In an effort to placate minority activists in the 1970s, several organizations placed minority members on their boards of directors. In the early days of this phenomenon, organizations were motivated by activist and gov-ernmental pressures. More recently, however, they have discovered that the new compositions of the directing boards can yield highly effective and socially relevant decisions.

The next change in U.S. organizations' boards of directors may likely be the inclusion of workers. Worker representation on boards of directors is largely a European concept, where it has been especially successful. Thus far, U.S. labor unions have resisted employee representation on boards of directors, perhaps feeling that such representation would threaten union security. However, given the changes in technology, advancing education of workers, and other forces, some change in the structure of boards of directors to include worker input may occur.[12]

The Role of Government

The relationships between organizations and government is always subject to political influence. That is, the administration in 1982 promises less interference in business than did the administration in 1978. Despite the protests of one or another politician, some observers predict that government will continue to play an increasing role in the policy setting and operations of organizations. Equal employment opportunity, occupational safety and health, environmental protection, and other issues must be faced by organizations, and it is unlikely that government, under any administration, will step back from its commitments.[13]

THE CHANGING NATURE OF PEOPLE

Our society has always been one of high stress. Stress is created by the drive for progress and improved conditions of living. With the expected continuation of social problems (inflation, urban pollution, etc.) and rapid changes in work and organizations, it is likely that we will continue to live with considerable stress. One of the major causes of change in people is the stress they experience.[14]

Although we cannot speculate on all the specifics regarding changes that will occur in people, we do know that such changes are inevitable. For purposes of our discussion, we would like to address two general types of changes that will have substantial impact on organizations in the future: changes in the composition of the labor force and attitudinal and value change forces.

The Labor Force

Intermediate projections by the Bureau of Labor Statistics provide some interesting looks at the future. Based on its most recent forecasts, the total labor force will grow to 115.0 million in 1985 and 122.4 million in 1990. Interestingly, more than two-thirds of this growth will be accounted for by women. Furthermore, most of this growth will be in the "prime age" group (twenty-five to fifty-four), which reflects a growing trend by older workers to retire earlier and for younger people to delay their entrance into the work force.[15]

The business education of both blacks and women is expected to continue to rise. In 1970, 41,000 blacks and 204,000 women were enrolled in business colleges. By 1978, these figures had increased to 221,000 and 819,000, respectively. This reflects a major change in the labor force composition, namely, the removal of large numbers of unskilled workers that may need to be replaced. One source of replacement is expected to be the Mexican labor force. Some forecasts predict that there may be as many as 15 million to 30 million Mexican laborers filling unskilled jobs in the United States by the year 2000.[16]

Attitude and Value Changes

A review of public opinion surveys indicates that societal attitudes toward business have become increasingly negative during the 1960s and 1970s. For example, a recent survey showed that only 3 percent of people surveyed trusted business executives.[17] This rather central attitude obviously will affect the relationship between employees and organizations in the future. Attitudes such as these raise two important questions. First, what forces influence the development of attitudes toward work and organizations? Second, what are some of the other attitudes and values that will influence workers in the future?

To begin, it is important to understand that work-related attitudes and values begin to form even as early as five or six years of age. In this development, four factors seem to influence young people's attitudes toward organizations:

1. The family—attitudes held by parents toward their employers.
2. Job experiences—especially for high school students who hold part-time jobs.
3. Mass media—news reports, editorials, and the like.
4. School—attitudes held and advanced by teachers and classmates.[18]

Of these four factors, the two most important are family and job experiences. Thus negative attitudes that parents acquire are often passed on to their children, even before the children are exposed to an actual work setting. Furthermore, since high school children usually accept menial and uninteresting tasks as part-time jobs, negative attitudes would likely be reinforced. This conclusion is especially significant, given current attitudes like the lack of trust in business executives.

Other important attitudes and values that will affect organizations in the future are

1. Sexual revolution—greater acceptance of nontraditional practices (homosexuality, intergeneration mating). Marriage will still be the ideal value in sexual relationships.
2. A decrease in one-worker households, which are expected to decline from 43 percent (1960) to 14 percent of all households in 1990. It will be more socially acceptable, and even expected, that mothers pursue careers and that fathers perform household duties.

3. Expectations that, by the turn of the century, society will hold a leisure ethic rather than a work ethic. Satisfaction and meaning in life will come from leisure rather than organization or work.[19]

4. A continued commitment by people to finding a life-style first and then a job to support it. This is the reverse of the job-life-style relationship that existed earlier.[20]

PERSONNEL MANAGEMENT CHALLENGES AND OPPORTUNITIES

Changes in the nature of work, organizations, and people will precipitate significant challenges and present varied opportunities for managers of human resources. Advancing technology, revised organization structures, and emerging values must be met by progressive and flexible personnel management activities. Discontinuous change, characterized by the silicon chip, high energy prices, and the two-career family, will require imaginative management of people, organizations, and jobs. The human resource manager must stay abreast of technological developments and a myriad of new governmental regulations and operate within the framework of social attitudes to help maintain organizational effectiveness.

From our review of the forecasts in the area of work, organizations, and people, it appears that there will be several challenges that personnel managers will face in the near future as well as some interesting opportunities in human resource management:

1. A decline in the rate of young people entering the labor force, coupled with increasing demand in jobs of little attraction (low wages, low challenge, etc.), will require personnel managers to tap previously unemployed marginal workers. Robotics is too expensive to replace all unskilled jobs, but these jobs will be the lowest paid, least interesting, and most limited in promotion opportunities.

2. Two-career families will present a variety of challenges for personnel managers. Flextime, job-sharing, and child care centers are likely to become more widespread in industry as solutions to personal problems for these families. Organizations will also need to explore solutions to the problems that relocation presents in these families.[21]

3. Equal employment rights will continue to be a major social force with which organizations must deal. However, the emphasis that was first on ethnic minorities and then on females is likely to shift to older (aged) workers in the mid-1980s. This reflects the changing composition in the work force. Preretirement counseling, career counseling, and retraining programs will likely be personnel activities that become important in this regard.[22]

4. Declining productivity in the United States is one of our society's most serious problems. Personnel managers must find viable ways in which to motivate an entire work force at a time when work is losing the central place in individual values. It may be that new means of enriching jobs can be devel-

oped. Flextime, MBO, and quality circles are current approaches that may lead the way to new motivational methods.[23]

5. Advancing technology will require that human resource managers perfect training, education, and development programs. The emphasis on education in the future will make education an activity for all ages, and training will become a lifelong activity.

SUMMARY

In the future, a major change will occur in the relationship among jobs, organizations, and people. It seems that our society faces the task of redefining basic concepts of work, education, leisure, and retirement. Robotics, computerization, miniaturization, and other technological advances will drastically alter the nature of work as we know it. These changes will be reinforced by simultaneous influences in the general society. Some forecasters feel that work will increasingly take place in individuals' homes and that payment will be in contracted fees as opposed to wages.

Organizations themselves will also be fundamentally different in the future. Further internationalization is likely to occur, especially in the face of declining productivity in the United States. We also expect to find more blacks and women in professional and managerial positions. Although demand for some types of employees will decline, the tremendous investments in technology will create unprecedented demands for skilled technological workers. Organizations may also find that the composition of their boards of directors includes worker representation and that they will be increasingly subjected to governmental regulation.

While the composition of the labor force is expected to change, reflecting population trends, attitude and value changes of people are more difficult to anticipate. As we examine available evidence, it appears that family influences and early job experiences are influential in forming work-related attitudes and values. Because society has become somewhat less positive toward work and organizations, managers will have difficulty maintaining effectiveness during technological and organizational changes.

These emerging trends suggest that the management of human resources will become increasingly challenging in the future. Personnel management will become increasingly important as it provides the leadership role in adapting organizations to the challenges of the future.

REVIEW QUESTIONS

1. What are two specific ways in which jobs may be changed by technology or social developments?

2. Five major factors affecting organizational change were described in the text. Which factor do you feel is most significant? Why?

3. Social attitudes and values have always undergone change. What are the forces that tend to precipitate these changes, and how do you expect them to affect future attitudes toward work and organizations?

4. The future promises to be very challenging in terms of personnel management. Describe what you feel to be the most important challenge and recommend some solutions.

KEY CONCEPTS

Attitudes	Quality circles
Boards of directors	Robotics
Flextime	Sexual revolution
Future	Technology
Job sharing	Two-career family
Leisure ethic	Values
Productivity	

CASE

A DISABILITY QUALIFICATION

The year 2001 was not a vintage one for Jacob Asher. In February, he celebrated two major events, both of which depressed him. First, he turned forty-eight years old, and then, three days later, he celebrated his sixth year of unemployment. Actually, his birthday wouldn't have been so depressing had it not been for his unemployment status. While Jacob knew it was no great thing to be unemployed (nearly 30 percent of all people of working age were unemployed), he still had a residual work ethic and it bothered him. His unemployment benefits were reasonable, providing him with a decent standard of living, but he just hated the idleness.

Many of his friends felt the same way, but some of them had discovered, quite by accident (if you'll pardon the pun), an unusual way of gaining employment. Last year, Mary Wilson, who lived in the village, lost her left arm in a boating accident. Neither she nor her husband held full-time jobs, but Mary did have a job-sharing arrangement at Helpmate, Inc., a local manufacturer of robot workers. To make a long story short, Mary was fitted with an advanced technology prosthetic arm. Within a month she found that she had increased tactile sense in her fingers and greater strength and flexibility in her arm and was able to repeat simple gestures precisely and for extremely long periods of time. It was almost as if she had become part robot herself. Not only did she retain her employment status, but she was promoted to a very intricate task position, which required the kinds of skills she had accidentally acquired. She now was one of the 10 percent of people who worked a full thirty-five hour week.

Two months later, her husband John had elective surgery on his left arm, replacing it with a similar prosthetic device, and Helpmate put him to work alongside his wife. Since then three other people in the village had taken the same path to meaningful employment. Then, in August, Jacob celebrated his third major event of the year when he awoke in the recovery room and looked down to admire his new prosthetic arm. Except for sensitivity, strength, and flexibility, you couldn't tell it from the other one.

CASE QUESTIONS

1. What would be some problems in adjusting to a leisure ethic if you still had a work ethic orientation?

2. What factors in this case have the greatest likelihood of coming true in the year 2001? Why?

NOTES

[1]J. Dodd, "Robots: The New 'Steel Collar' Workers," *Personnel Journal,* 60 (1981), 688–695.

[2]"Automation Blues," *Management Review,* 70 (1981), 54–55.

[3]"GM's Ambitious Plans to Employ Robots," *Business Week,* March 16, 1981, p. 31.

[4]J. Dodd, "Robots," p. 691.

[5]C. Handy, "The Changing Shape of Work," *Organizational Dynamics,* 9 (1980), 27.

[6]J. Dodd, "Robots," pp. 688–695.

[7]Ibid.

[8]C. Handy, "The Changing Shape of Work," pp. 26–34.

[9]A. M. Morrison and M. E. Kranz, "The Shape of Performance Appraisal in the Coming Decade," *Personnel,* 58 (1981), 12–22.

[10]R. J. Erickson, "The Changing Workplace and Workforce," *Training and Development Journal,* 34 (1980), 62–65.

[11]R. A. Hennigar, "People Management in the 1980's: A CEO's View," *Personnel Journal,* 59 (1980), 898–903.

[12]Ibid., pp. 898–903.

[13]Morrison and Kranz, "The Shape of Performance Appraisal," pp. 12–22.

[14]J. M. Ivancevich and M. T. Matteson, "Optimizing Human Resources: A Case for Preventive Health and Stress Management," *Organizational Dynamics,* 9 (1980), 5–25.

[15]H. N. Fullerton, Jr., "The 1995 Labor Force: A First Look," *Monthly Labor Review,* 103 (1980), 11–21.

[16]G. S. Odiorne, "Training to Be Ready for the '90's," *Training and Development Journal,* 34 (1980), 12–20.

[17]A. Mikalachki, "Managing Human Resources in the 1980's," *Business Quarterly,* 45 (1980), 32–37.

[18]Ibid.

[19]D. L. Lunda, "Personnel Management: What's Ahead?" *Personnel Administrator,* 26 (1981), 51–60.

[20]Odiorne, "Training to Be Ready," pp. 12–20.

[21]Lunda, "Personnel Management," pp.51–60.

[22]T. L. Leap, W. H. Holley, Jr., and H. S. Feild, "Equal Employment Opportunity and Its Implications for Personnel Practices in the 1980's," *Labor Law Journal,* 31 (1980), 669–682.

[23]L. E. This, "Critical Issues Confronting Managers in the '80's," *Training and Development Journal,* 34 (1980), 14–17.

GLOSSARY

ACCIDENT AND DISABILITY INSURANCE: A program designed to compensate employees for wage losses because of nonjob-related accidents or illness.

ACCIDENT RECORD SYSTEM: Record of statistics and pertinent information involving accidents and health of all employees.

ACHIEVEMENT TEST: A test that measures abilities, skills, or knowledge that has been acquired through training or job experience.

ADVERSE IMPACT: A substantially different rate of selection in hiring, promotion, or other employment decisions that works to the disadvantage of members of a race, sex, or ethnic group. A substantially different rate is less than ⅕ or 80% of the selection rate for the group with the highest selection rate.

AFFIRMATIVE ACTION PROGRAM: A set of specific and result-oriented procedures—in recruiting, hiring, upgrading, and other personnel practices—that are taken for the purpose of eliminating the effects of past discrimination and preventing further discrimination.

AGE DISCRIMINATION IN EMPLOYMENT ACT OF 1967: A federal law that applies to all employers with twenty or more regular employees and prohibits discrimination against those in age groups over 40 but less than 70.

AGENCY SHOP: Requires the employee to pay dues but membership in the union is not required.

AMERICAN ARBITRATION ASSOCIATION (AAA): An organization that provides arbitrators to settle labor relations disputes.

APPLICANT FLOW: Records that detail demographics of the stream of applicants, job offers, reasons why an applicant was not offered a job, names of interviewers, and names of individuals making hiring decisions.

APPRENTICESHIP: A combined on-the-job, off-the-job training approach in which the trainee agrees to work for a salary below that for fully qualified employees in exchange for a specified amount of formal training by the organization.

APTITUDE TEST: Tests designed to measure an applicant's mental or intellectual abilities (cognitive) or physical abilities (motor).

ARBITRATION: A procedure in which a neutral third party hears evidence and rules on grievances arising in a collective bargaining relationship.

ASSESSMENT: Measurements to determine what skills, knowledge, or attitudes are required by the job and possessed by the employee.

ASSESSMENT CENTER: A process by which individuals participate in skill-based exercises and their skills to perform certain activities are assessed.

ASSESSMENT OF EMPLOYEE ABILITIES: Measurements to determine what skills, knowledge, or attitudes new employees have at the time of the selection process; or to determine what skills, knowledge, or attitudes incumbent employees have learned.

ASSESSMENT OF JOB REQUIREMENTS: Measurements to determine what skills, knowledge, or attitudes are necessary for unique job situations.

ATTITUDINAL STRUCTURING: The process by which the relationship between the parties is changed so that positive outcomes can take place.

AUTONOMOUS WORK TEAMS OR GROUPS: Groups of employees assigned to perform a natural unit of work who are given the responsibility to manage their own work, acquire required materials, set the timing of tasks, assign tasks, and control employee efforts.

AUTONOMY: The amount of discretion allowed the employee on the job.

BARGAINING ORDER: The NLRB orders the employer to bargain with the union when an employer commits a flagrantly unfair labor practice during election proceedings.

BARGAINING UNIT: A group of employees represented by a union and covered by a collective bargaining agreement.

BEHAVIORAL CRITERIA: Measures of trainee behaviors on the job.

BEHAVIORALLY ANCHORED RATING SCALES (BARS): A form of performance appraisal that identifies specific employee behaviors on job dimensions by job category. These scales are then anchored with behavior that can be expected or is typical of an employee performing at a given level. Employee performance is then rated on these scales.

BLUE-CIRCLE RATE: Jobs below the minimum of their salary range which should be raised to the minimum of their range as soon as possible.

BONA FIDE OCCUPATIONAL QUALIFICATION (BFOQ): Hiring practices that permit the consideration of certain qualifications (i.e., age, religion, or national origin) that are necessary in the performance of the job.

BONUS: An extra amount of compensation paid when performance exceeds certain predetermined levels.

CAREER: Sequence or series of job and work-related activities over a person's lifetime.

CAREER COUNSELING: A process that examines an employee's skills, special talents, interests, and personality in order to determine the specific sequence of jobs the employee should undertake.

CAREER DEVELOPMENT: The process of planning the series of possible jobs one may hold in the organization over time and developing strategies designed to provide necessary job skills as the opportunities arise.

CAREER OPPORTUNITIES IN PERSONNEL: Personnel recruiter/interviewer, job analyst, salary and wage specialist, EEO counselor, training specialist, employee benefits administrator, occupational safety specialist, labor relations officer, testing design specialist, personnel researcher, human resource and organizational planner.

CAREER PATHS: A series of jobs representing potential progression tracks that employees may follow.

CAREER PLANNING: The process of identifying individual career objectives and plans to aid the individual in achieving them.

CHANGE: Modification of an existing situation, structure, and/or behavior.

CHANGE PRESSURES (External): Changing society values, shortages of natural resources, government regulations, and interdependence among countries.

CHANGE PRESSURES (Internal): Employees, technological developments, production systems, jobs, and work techniques.

CIVIL RIGHTS ACT OF 1964 (as amended by the Equal Employment Opportunity Act of 1972): Prevents discrimination in employment on the basis of race, color, religion, sex or national origin and applies to private sector employers having at least 15 employees each day for twenty weeks of one year; unions, employment agencies, educational institutions, and state and local government.

CLASSICAL CONDITIONING: Theory advanced in late 1800s by Pavlov that deals with the stimulus-response relationship in learning theory.

CLASSIFICATION METHOD: This method of job evaluation places groups of jobs into job grades or classes. Jobs in the same grade receive the same pay.

CLASSROOM INSTRUCTION: The process used in education whereby individuals are trained in a room at the same period of time each week.

CLOSED SHOP: Requires that an individual must be a union member before being hired.

COACHING: The assignment of a specific person to act as either an instructor or resource person for the trainee.

CODETERMINATION: A process whereby employees are represented on boards of directors and on boards concerned with the day-to-day management of the company.

COEFFICIENT ALPHA: Measures the correlation among test items after making an adjustment for the length of the test (number of items).

COMPANY UNION: Unions that the employer controls through placement of managerial representatives as union officers, by contributing financial support, or other means.

COMPENSATION: The total of all direct and indirect pay received by an employee.

COMPUTER SIMULATION: A human resource forecasting technique that is used to predict the effects of changes in personnel policies and the effects of other factors; personnel policies are varied to determine the impact of the changes on the future supply of human resources or determine how much various personnel policies must be changed in order to obtain desired outcomes.

CONCILIATION AGREEMENT: Agreements between the government and employers concerning discrimination; not enforceable by the courts.

CONCURRENT VALIDITY: A criterion-based validity on which the validity of a selection tool is determined on the basis of data obtained from current employees.

CONSENT DECREE: Judgments issued by the EEOC and enforceable by the federal courts.

CONSISTENCY IN DISCIPLINE: Consistent enforcement and administration of discipline.

CONSTRUCT VALIDITY: A demonstration that (a) a test (selection procedure) measures a construct (something believed to be an underlying human trait or characteristic, such as honesty), and (b) the construct is important for successful job performance. This is usually examined by correlating the test results with a valid measure of the same construct.

CONTENT VALIDITY: A demonstration that the content of a selection procedure is representative of important aspects of performance on the job.

CONTINUOUS PAY SCHEDULES: The employee receives a fixed dollar amount per unit produced.

CONTRAST EFFECT: An effect in the interviewing process in which the impact of preceding applicants affects the interviewer's evaluation of the current applicant.

CONTROLLING ACTIVITIES: A managerial process in which reviewing, measuring, and evaluating performance for the purpose of correcting problems and achieving goals is performed.

CORRECTIVE DISCIPLINE (constructive): Actions taken to correct or change an employee's behavior by rewarding and praising proper actions.

COST OF LIVING ADJUSTMENT (COLA): Increase in wage or salary which is based on increases in the Consumer Price Index.

CRAFT UNION: An organization of workers along craft or skill lines.

CRITERION RELATED VALIDITY: A statistical demonstration of a relationship between scores on a selection procedure and job performance of a sample of workers.

CRITICAL INCIDENTS: Incidents that represent outstanding and poor work behaviors for each job category and are used in assessing employee job performance.

CRITICAL INCIDENT TECHNIQUE (CIT): A method of job analysis that involves obtaining records of behaviors that have led to effective or ineffective job performance (critical incidents).

DAVIS BACON ACT: A federal law requiring all firms involved in construction of federal projects over $2,000 in value to pay prevailing wage rates.

DECERTIFICATION: Occurs when employees vote against the union continuing to represent them in their relations with their employer.

DELPHI PROCEDURE: A human resource forecasting technique that draws on the judgment of experts to estimate demand.

DIAGNOSIS: First step in the OD process to determine the cause of an existing problem or to predict future problems.

DIFFERENTIAL VALIDITY: Separate validation of selection tools for various demographic groups.

DIRECT COMPENSATION: Payment for employee performance in terms of productivity or amount of time worked.

DIRECTING ACTIVITIES: A managerial process of guiding employees, supervising their activities, and leading them to effective performance.

DISCIPLINE: Action taken against employees when their behavior does not conform to the rules of the organization.

DISTRIBUTIVE BARGAINING: A pure conflict process in which one party wins and the other loses.

DRIVE: A state of arousal.

DRIVING FORCES: Factors that direct an employee to make a particular decision or to follow a certain behavior.

DUE PROCESS: Following procedural requirements in actions taken by the employer that concern the employees.

EDUCATION: Systematic acquisition of skills, knowledge, and attitudes that have broad or general applicability in one's total social environment.

ELECTION UNIT: The voting unit of nonsupervisory employees who tend basically to have common working conditions.

EMPLOYEE OBSOLESCENCE: When an employee's skills are no longer appropriate for the job requirements, many times because of rapid advancement of technology and knowledge requirements.

EMPLOYEES: Human resources; people who perform the tasks and achieve the goals essential to the efficient operation of the organization.

EMPLOYEE SELF-RECORDING: This method of job analysis requires employees to provide descriptions of each task performed on their jobs.

EMPLOYEE VALUE: Values attached to how well the employee does the work based on the actual qualifications held by the employee and the actual level of performance achieved by the employee.

EQUAL EMPLOYMENT OPPORTUNITY ACT OF 1972: This act gave the EEOC the ability to take cases directly to the court system.

EQUAL EMPLOYMENT OPPORTUNITY COMMISSION (EEOC): An agency established to administer the provisions of the Civil Rights Act of 1964 (as amended by the EEO Act of 1972).

EQUAL PAY ACT: A 1963 amendment to the Fair Labor Standards Act that prohibits sex discrimination in rates of pay.

EQUITY: When the ratio of rewards to investments for one person is equal to the ratio of rewards to investments for another person in a similar situation (often a coworker).

ESSAYS: A form of performance appraisal in which the supervisor describes employee performance in an essay format.

EXCLUSIVE REPRESENTATION: Only one union can be the bargaining agent for the employees in one bargaining unit.

EXECUTIVE INCENTIVE COMPENSATION: A plan in which cash and/or stock is given to executives on the basis of the performance of the company or the major unit that an executive manages.

EXECUTIVE ORDER 11246: Covers federal contractors involved in interstate commerce having contracts in excess of $10,000 and prohibits discrimination against individuals during employment on the basis of race, color, religion, sex, or national origin.

EXPECTANCY: A person's assessment of the subjective probability of attaining a particular outcome.

EXPONENTIAL SMOOTHING: A human resource forecasting technique that predicts demand on the basis of past demand through an experience-based process.

EXTINCTION: Withholding reinforcement, decreasing the strength or likelihood of a response.

FACE VALIDITY: A type of validity that exists when a test looks like it would measure the factors that need to be measured.

FACTOR COMPARISON SYSTEM: This method of job evaluation ranks each job acording to key jobs and their rankings on such factors as mental effort, physical effort, skill, responsibility, and working conditions.

FAIR LABOR STANDARDS ACT: Defines minimum wage and overtime pay provisions for employees, outlaws child labor, requires time and one-half for overtime.

FEATHERBEDDING: "Make-work" requirements, the performance of unnecessary work or overmanning for the amount of work required.

FEDERAL MEDIATION AND CONCILIATION SERVICE (FMCS): A governmental organization that provides mediators and lists of arbitrators to settle labor relations disputes.

FEEDBACK: The process of providing information to employees regarding their performance on job tasks.

FLEXTIME: A flexible employee work schedule whereby all employees work a required number of hours in a day or week but may begin and end their work days at other than normal times.

FORCE FIELD ANALYSIS: A method used to diagnose the forces acting on a person such that he or she behaves in a certain way.

FOUR-DAY WORK WEEK: Four-day work week with $9\frac{1}{2}$ to 10-hour days as opposed to five-day work week with eight hours a day. Also called the compressed work week.

FUNCTIONAL AUTHORITY: Authority that carries throughout the organization; usually carries no disciplinary or reward power relative to other units and is constrained to only those decisions involving the specialized function; not limited to the manager's own unit.

GENERAL ELECTRIC V GILBERT: General Electric was accused of sex discrimination because its disability benefits plan contained no provision for providing benefits to women who were temporarily disabled as a result of pregnancy. The court ruled that GE did not discriminate, because pregnancy is a special disability; however, as a result of this case, Title VII of the Civil Rights Act was amended so that pregnancy was to be included in fringe benefit plans as a disability.

GENERALIZATION/TRANSFER: The extent to which learned responses to a specific stimuli in one specific setting will carry over to similar stimuli in other settings.

GOAL CLARITY: Clear and specific goals.

GOAL DIFFICULTY: The extent to which goals can or cannot be achieved.

GOAL GRADIENT: The time span between the individual's behavior and the reinforcer.

GOAL PROGRAMMING: A human resource forecasting technique that is a variation of linear programming.

GOAL SETTING: Developing goals to be achieved in task performance.

GOOD FAITH BARGAINING: A process that requires parties to conduct negotiations according to an "auction model," in which counter proposals are offered.

GRIEVANCE: A charge that a provision of a labor agreement or contract has been violated.

GRIEVANCE ARBITRATION: Arbitration over a grievance that the contract has been violated.

HALO EFFECT: When interviewers or supervisors allow their evaluation of the applicant on one dimension to affect their evaluation of other dimensions.

HEURISTIC (RULE OF THUMB): A human resource forecasting technique that uses past operating policies, simple rules, or decision processes to convert activity levels into human resource requirements.

HOLIDAYS: A fringe benefit whereby employees do not have to work on specified days and receive their normal pay.

HOT CARGO AGREEMENT: Employer agrees not to process or handle materials made by an employer with whom the union has a dispute.

HUMAN RESOURCE INVENTORY: A system that provides the organization with information on its current employees. It allows matching of an individual's experience, education, and preference with a task or function to be performed.

HUMAN RESOURCE PLANNING: The managerial process of determining the supply and demand for human resources and making plans for dealing with shortages and surpluses of such resources.

ILLEGAL BARGAINING ISSUE: An issue that cannot be bargained by either party (i.e., closed shop).

IN-BASKET EXERCISE: A selection tool where applicants are presented with a series of memos, letters, reports, messages, etc., in order to measure their administrative planning skills.

INCENTIVES: Financial rewards that prompt employees to achieve some specified job performance or other goal desired by the organization.

INCOMES POLICIES: Wage and price controls established by the government.

INDIVIDUAL DEVELOPMENT: The process by which individuals gain new skills, thereby increasing performance on the job.

INDIVIDUAL PRESENTATIONS: A selection tool designed to measure an applicant's communication skills, persuasiveness, and composure under stress.

INDUSTRIAL UNION: A union of workers that does not organize along skill lines, but instead organizes on a plant-wide basis.

INDUSTRY OR COMPANY-SPECIFIC GAMES: A selection instrument that evaluates an applicant's decision-making and analytical skills; also used as a management development aid.

INSTRUMENTAL CONDITIONING: A type of conditioning in which responses are reinforced with positive consequences, but not reinforced with negative consequences.

INTEGRATIVE BARGAINING: A problem-solving process in which there is open identification of parties' needs and maximum information sharing in order that both parties may have the potential to win.

INTEREST ARBITRATION: Arbitration over the terms of a new contract.

INTERVIEWING (JOB ANALYSIS): The method of job analysis in which the job analyst questions an employee with regard to the employees' tasks, duties, and responsibilities.

INTERVIEWS: A process in which a person asks another person a series of questions and evaluates the answers. It is a universally employed selection process for managerial and professional personnel.

INTRAORGANIZATIONAL BARGAINING: Used to resolve conflict within the parties' own organizations.

INTRINSIC REWARD: Internal rewards associated with the performance of the task.

JOB: A specific arrangement of tasks, duties, and responsibilities that must be performed in order for the organization to achieve its goals.

JOB ANALYSIS: A systematic process for gathering information about a job.

JOB DESCRIPTION: Written summaries of the basic tasks, duties, and responsibilities of jobs.

JOB DESIGN: The arrangement of task contents in order to satisfy both organizational and human requirements.

JOB ENLARGEMENT: The process increasing the number of tasks in a job by adding tasks related to those currently performed and usually requiring a greater variety of skills.

JOB ENRICHMENT: The process of changing the job to allow employees more discretion over their work and increased involvement in planning, decision making and controlling activities related to the job's tasks.

JOB ENVIRONMENT: Unique job situations (tasks, duties, responsibilities) that require certain skills, rules, knowledge, and attitudes.

JOB EVALUATION: The process by which the worth of jobs to the organization is assessed relative to all other jobs in the organization.

JOB EXPECTATION TECHNIQUE: A variation of the team building process that focuses on clarifying roles, expectations, and responsibilities of managers and subordinates.

JOB INSTRUCTION TRAINING: A set of coordinated procedures for conducting on-the-job training, developed by the War Manpower Commission during World War II.

JOB ROTATION: The process of having an employee perform several different jobs, moving from one to the other in some prearranged logical sequence over some period of time.

JOB SAFETY ANALYSIS: A process of identifying job hazards during job analysis.

JOB SATISFACTION: An attitude a person holds about his or her job.

JOB SECURITY: Contract provisions such as the union shop, seniority, and so on that preserve the union's status and the members' jobs.

JOB SHARING: A program in which two people share one job. Usually each works one-half time, with mutually agreed-on work schedules.

JOB SPECIALIZATION: The process of breaking work down into smaller sets of related tasks.

JOB SPECIFICATIONS: Written summaries of the skills, background, and qualifications necessary for an employee to perform the job in a satisfactory manner.

JOB STANDARDS: The expected performance for each job duty described in the job description.

JOB VALUE: Values attached to the kind of work one does based on the minimum qualification factors required by the job and minimum effort factors demanded by the job.

KNOWLEDGE OF RESULTS: The process of feeding back information on the effectiveness of responses.

LABOR AGREEMENT: Contract between the company and union regarding employees' conditions of employment and work resulting from collective bargaining between the two parties.

LABORATORY CONDITIONS: Consists of detailed rules governing the conduct of employers and unions so that an atmosphere free from coercive influences exists in the period leading up to the representation election.

LABOR MANAGEMENT RELATIONS ACT OF 1947: Also known as the Taft-Hartley Act. This Act added a series of union unfair labor practices.

LABOR MANAGEMENT REPORTING AND DISCLOSURE ACT OF 1959: Also called the Landrum Griffin Act. Regulates the investments and handling of union funds and other internal operations.

LABOR MARKET: The available collection of people who possess the skills required to perform any particular job.

LATERAL RELATIONS: Horizontal relations between two or more units in an organization.

LEADER BEHAVIOR DESCRIPTION QUESTIONNAIRE (LBDQ): An instrument administered to a manager's subordinates in order to obtain a measure of the manager's behavior (sometimes used in selection).

LEADERLESS GROUP DISCUSSIONS: A selection tool whereby a group of applicants is given a topic to discuss and asked to reach a decision. This process enables the assessors to observe communication skills, ability to channel a discussion toward an objective, facilitating arrival at group consensus, meeting deadlines, and interpersonal interaction skills of the assessees.

LEADERSHIP OPINION QUESTIONNAIRE (LOQ): An instrument designed to measure a manager's inclination toward employing initiating structure and consideration behaviors (sometimes used in selection).

LEARNING: The process by which new behaviors are acquired. Behavior change occurs, new behaviors are practiced, and permanency of the change is established.

LEARNING CRITERIA: Measures of training that pertain to facts, information, and other conceptual understanding.

LEISURE ETHIC: A social value in which leisure activity is given high priority.

LIFE INSURANCE: A program that provides payment of benefits upon the death of the employee to the survivors of the deceased.

LINEAR PROGRAMMING: A human resource forecasting technique that is used to predict supply. The forecaster can determine promotion policies, turnover rates, etc., that will enable the organization to achieve its manning goals at various ranks or levels. Utilizes data on promotions, proportion of persons promoted, assignment of persons not promoted, retirement, turnover rates, and other variables.

LINE AUTHORITY: Authority that includes primary decision rights and the right to discipline and reward subordinates; is limited in scope to those immediate subordinates in the manager's unit.

LINE ORGANIZATION STRUCTURE: Emphasizes the line authority throughout the organization; has no staff or functional positions.

LOGIC: Finding valid or justifiable relationships between one idea, or set of ideas, and another.

MANAGEMENT BY OBJECTIVES (MBO): A goal setting process whereby managers work with their employees to establish objectives for employee tasks and then evaluate employees' performance on the basis of goal achievement.

MANAGEMENT DEVELOPMENT: A process whereby employees can develop the "extra" skills necessary to undertake managerial jobs or improve performance in current managerial jobs.

MANAGEMENT GAMES: A selection tool that assesses an applicant's organization, leadership, and interpersonal communication skills.

MANAGEMENT POSITION DESCRIPTION QUESTIONNAIRE (MP DQ): A standard job analysis questionnaire that has been found to be extremely reliable and valid.

MANDATORY BARGAINING ISSUE: An issue that must be bargained collectively by both parties if either party brings it up. These issues include wages, hours, and conditions of employment.

MARKET VALUE: A value determined by conducting wage surveys, and added to job value and employee value, in order to obtain the final compensation for an employee.

MARKOV MODELS: A human resource forecasting technique that predicts internal supply. It is a probabilistic technique that uses historical data on personnel movements to derive probabilities for similar moves in the future.

MATRIX ORGANIZATION STRUCTURE: A structure that emphasizes line, staff and functional authority, and imposes dual lines of authority for subordinates; most complex organization structure.

MEDICAL INSURANCE: A benefit that provides payment of hospitalization costs and doctors' surgical fees.

MERIT PAY SYSTEM: A system whereby employees' pay increases are based on employee performance on the job.

MINER SENTENCE COMPLETION SCALE: A personality and leadership test that measures managerial motivation and is used as a selection tool.

MODELING: Vicariously learning by observing another person demonstrate the behavior and seeing the stimuli and reinforcers that apply.

MOTIVATION: Willful desire to direct one's effort (behavior) toward achieving given goals.

MOTIVATION TEST: Tests that may measure an applicant's personal interests, preferences, or desires to perform a job.

NATIONAL INSTITUTE OF OCCUPATIONAL SAFETY AND HEALTH: This agency's primary duties include conducting research into occupational hazards and conducting educational training programs on safety and health.

NATIONAL LABOR RELATIONS ACT OF 1935: Also referred to as Wagner Act. This law created the NLRB and gave employees the protected right to join and form unions and to engage in collective bargaining. The act does not cover agricultural laborers, domestic servants, employers' children and spouses, independent contractors, supervisors and managers, government employees, and railroad and airline employees.

NATIONAL LABOR RELATIONS BOARD (NLRB): NLRB created by the National Labor Relations Act (NLRA) of 1935 to administer the law in the area of labor relations.

NEED FOR ACHIEVEMENT: A motivational concept developed by McClelland in the late 1950s, in which the need for achievement is thought to affect one's motivation to perform elements of a task.

NEED HIERARCHY: Motivational theory proposed by Maslow in the 1940s that addresses issues related to the activation of willful desire to fulfill unsatisfied needs. These needs are arranged in hierarchical order from physiological (lowest) to self-actualization (highest), and each lower need is prepotent over higher order needs.

OBSERVATION (JOB ANALYSIS): This method of job analysis requires a trained job analyst to observe and record the tasks performed on a specific job over some period of time. It is used for jobs with tasks that take a short time to complete and are primarily physical in nature.

OCCUPATIONAL SAFETY AND HEALTH ACT OF 1970: The act created mandatory standards of safety and health such that even the most recalcitrant employer would take steps to protect the health and well-being of its employees.

OCCUPATIONAL SAFETY AND HEALTH ADMINISTRATION (OSHA): The agency created by the Occupational Safety and Health Act to develop and enforce safety and health standards.

OCCUPATIONAL SAFETY AND HEALTH REVIEW COMMISSION: A group that acts as a court rendering judgments in disputed enforcement actions between OSHA and employers or employees.

OFFICE OF FEDERAL CONTRACT COMPLIANCE PROGRAMS (OFCCP): This agency enforces EEO requirements with regard to federal contracts;

has power to bar employers who discriminate in employment from further contracts, or terminate contracts with the government.

OFF-THE-JOB TRAINING: Training conducted away from the actual work setting.

ON-THE-JOB TRAINING: A process whereby the employee reports to what will be his or her job setting and, with some form of guidance, begins to perform the task, learning while doing so.

ORGANIZATION: A social institution, composed of logically arranged task activities and persons with established patterns of interactions, having been developed to achieve specific goals.

ORGANIZATIONAL OR RECOGNITIONAL PICKETING: Picketing directed at causing an employer to recognize and bargain with the union.

ORGANIZATIONAL PAY LEVEL: The general level at which an organization wishes to compensate its employees, based on nature of the labor market, economic factors, unions, federal and state laws, job requirements, and other factors.

ORGANIZATION DEVELOPMENT: A planned, continuous process designed to increase organizational effectiveness by focusing on improving problem-solving skills, coping with environmental change, and changing organizational processes and structure.

ORGANIZING ACTIVITIES: A managerial process in which there is the creation of specializations and departmental units and creation of coordination so that necessary operations can be conducted effectively.

ORIENTATION: A systematic organization strategy for helping new employees form their expectations and become socialized into the organization.

PAID SICK LEAVE: A benefit that allows employees to stay at home when they are ill, without loss of pay.

PARALLEL FORMS RELIABILITY: A type of reliability in which two versions of a test are correlated. They theoretically ask the same questions in differently worded or differently constructed items.

PARTICIPATION: The process by which individuals jointly make decisions. Participation in goal setting causes increased productivity.

PENSIONS: Funds that employees and/or employers contribute are invested by the firm, and the employee receives the benefit of the funds plus investment earnings upon retirement.

PERFORMANCE APPRAISAL: An assessment of employee work behavior, with the general purpose of determining the degree of employee effectiveness on the job.

PERFORMANCE COACHING: The process whereby a supervisor helps employees to learn and apply job-related skills and abilities.

PERFORMANCE COUNSELING: Helping employees to deal with important career or personal issues.

PERSONNEL DEPARTMENT: A portion of the organization that coordinates human resource planning, recruitment and selection, wage and salary administration, training and labor relations. Activities may also include problem-solving, consultation with operating managers, participation in designing and implementing corporate policy, evaluation and development of mid- and top-level managers and contribution to the design of organizational structures and objectives.

PERSONNEL MANAGEMENT: The integration and coordination of human resources in order to move effectively toward desired objectives.

PERSONNEL MANAGER: A person in the organization who recruits, interviews, and selects employees; provides a channel for communication and counseling for all employees; and tries to create the most effective working ambience for employees.

PIECE-RATE PLANS: A pay plan that pays individuals a certain amount for each unit produced.

PLANNING ACTIVITIES: A managerial process that consists of forecasting and anticipating future events, and preparing the organization to deal with them effectively.

POINT SYSTEM: The most common method of job evaluation, in which general job factor categories are chosen, compensable job factors are developed and weighted, job factors are broken down into degrees, and point values are assigned to each degree.

POSITION ANALYSIS QUESTIONNAIRE (PAQ): A job analysis questionnaire that contains 194 job elements. Managers respond to a 5-point response mode, rating the degree to which each job element appears in the job. The job elements cover six major areas: information input, mediation processes, work output, interpersonal activities, work situation, and job context. It is designed to assign jobs equitably to appropriate salary ranges based on job content.

PREDICTIVE VALIDITY: A criterion-based approach in which test scores that are correlated with performance criteria are used to justify the predictive ability of a selection test.

PRIMACY EFFECT: When the first information received in an interview is weighted more heavily in the evaluation of the applicant.

PROCESS CONSULTATION: An approach to OD that uses a third party to work with organization members and groups to learn more about social processes in the work environment and to solve problems that arise from these processes.

PRODUCTIVITY: Real output per worker hour.

PRODUCTIVITY BARGAINING: Attempts to eliminate restrictive work rules and practices or obtain changes in job duties or jurisdictions that have detracted from efficiency.

PRODUCTIVITY-BASED COMPENSATION: Salary or wage received by the employee that is based on the productivity level of the employee.

PROFESSIONAL EMPLOYEES: Employees whose job requirements change frequently as a result of developing technology and who have a large range and variety of tasks, duties, and responsibilities.

PROFIT SHARING: The company makes a contribution to an employee or the employee's retirement plan based on each year's profits.

PROGRAMMED INSTRUCTION: Learning materials that are organized in a sequential fashion such that correct understanding of one set of materials must be indicated before the trainee can progress to the next set.

PROGRESSIVE DISCIPLINE: A system of discipline whereby a sequence of punishments is given, each one slightly more severe than the previous one. The goal is to change behavior and to use maximum punishment only as a last resort.

PSYCHOMETRIC PROPERTIES: Reliability and validity.

PUNISHMENT: Consequences (negative) that decrease the likelihood of repeating a specific behavior.

QUALITY CIRCLES: Voluntary groups of employees and managers that meet regularly to discuss, analyze, and propose solutions to product quality problems.

QUALITY OF LIFE: One's social and work environments, physical living conditions, standard of living, personal pressures, and opportunities for personal expression, development and use of one's abilities.

QUALITY OF WORK LIFE: A process that enables organization members at all levels to participate actively in shaping the organization's work environment, methods, and outcomes. Its goals are to enhance the organization's effectiveness and improve the quality of life at work for employees.

QUESTIONNAIRES (JOB ANALYSIS): Surveys are distributed to and completed by employees (e.g., PAQ, TAS, MPDQ). This method of job analysis is less costly and less time consuming.

RANKING METHOD: A job evaluation method that requires that jobs be arranged in order of their value or merit to the organization from highest to lowest.

RATER BIAS: When supervisors allow their values, beliefs, and/or prejudices to affect the manner in which they appraise employee performance.

RATER PATTERNS: When raters use only a narrow range of a rating scale on a consistent basis in the rating of employee performance.

RATING SCALES: A form of performance appraisal that lists personal and/or behavioral traits on which employees can be assessed.

REACTION CRITERIA: Measures of the trainer's or trainees' reactions or impressions about a training program.

REALISTIC JOB PREVIEW: A recruitment procedure in which the applicant may observe the performance of the job or actually perform the work.

RECENCY EFFECT: When the most recent information received in an interview is weighted more heavily in the evaluation of the applicant.

RECRUITMENT: The process of locating the people in the labor market whose skill combination is closest to the organization's requirements.

RED-CIRCLE RATE: Pay rates above a salary range that cannot be increased because they are above the evaluated level.

REFERENCES: Persons or employers who may be contacted for an evaluation of an applicant's ability and/or work history. Their use may have more credibility for managerial and professional personnel because the hiring employer may be familiar with the reference.

REFREEZING: Reinforcing change in order to make it permanent; third and final step in change process.

REGENTS OF THE UNIVERSITY OF CALIFORNIA V BAKKE: Bakke, a white male who was denied admission to the University of California medical school at Davis, claimed discrimination because lesser qualified minorities were admitted as part of the university's affirmative action program. The court ruled that Bakke was to be admitted. However, the university policies were not struck down.

REGRESSION ANALYSIS: A statistical technique useful in human resource forecasting of demand. Personnel levels (dependent variable) are regressed on one or more predictor variables (independent variables) to determine which factors vary closely with personnel levels.

REHABILITATION ACT OF 1973: Covers federal contractors involved in interstate commerce having contracts in excess of $2,500 and prohibits discrimination in hiring practices against handicapped individuals.

REINFORCEMENT: Any result, or event following a response, that acts to maintain the strength of the response to similar future stimuli.

RELIABILITY: When an instrument or procedure obtains consistent results with repeated administrations.

REPLACEMENT CHART: A human resource forecasting technique that graphically portrays supply and demand; enables the organization to determine if the supply of potential replacements will be adequate for expected vacancies or whether there is an oversupply of qualified replacements with no likely vacancies in the near future.

REPRESENTATION ELECTIONS: A process which allows employees to determine, through a secret ballot vote, whether their unit will be represented by a union.

RESISTANCE TO CHANGE: Employees' or managers' fears of the unknown or feelings of insecurity and inconvenience cause them to attempt to prevent modification of existing situations.

RESISTING FORCES: Factors that restrain an employee from making a particular decision or following a certain behavior.

RESPONSE: What one does in reacting to a stimulus.

RESULTS CRITERIA: Criteria for evaluating the training that pertains to the actual achievement of organizationally desired objectives or results.

RETIREMENT: The point in one's life at which a person ceases active employment in his or her chosen career.

RETIREMENT COUNSELING: Discussions in which plans or preparations are made for retirement covering such topics as finances, health, legal rights and responsibilities, leisure time, housing, and family relations.

RIGHTS ARBITRATION: See grievance arbitration.

ROBOTICS: A process whereby robots are used to perform production operations and/or other simple, routine tasks.

SALARY: Direct pay for performing a certain job that is not tied to the amount of hours worked.

SCANLON PLAN: A program in which cost savings or profits from efficiency increases and/or productivity increases are shared with employees on a mutually agreed upon and predetermined basis.

SECONDARY BOYCOTT: A boycott by the union that puts pressure on a neutral third party uninvolved in the primary dispute.

SELECTION MEASUREMENTS: Primary—measures of the presence of skills actually held by applicants (skill tests). Secondary—indirect measures of skills actually held by applicants (intelligence, personality, achievement, and aptitude tests).

SELECTION PROCESS: A process intended to find individuals whose skills are closest to those required for the job.

SELECTION RATIO: The ratio of hires to applicants.

SELECTION STRATEGY: A process whereby information obtained from different selection tools is utilized in the decision of whether or not to hire an applicant.

SENIORITY PAY SYSTEM: A system in which employees' progression through the salary/wage ranges is based on length of service.

SENSITIVITY TRAINING: A process in which a group of individuals works together for several days with the purpose of building self-awareness, understanding of group processes, and greater sensitivity to interpersonal relationships.

SEXUAL REVOLUTION: A time period in the United States in which the social values regarding sexual behavior changed.

SIMILAR TO ME EFFECT: The job applicant is evaluated favorably because his or her characteristics are similar to those of the interviewer.

SITUATIONALLY SPECIFIC REQUIREMENTS: Requirements for hiring managers. Their behavior is likely to be strongly affected by situational, as opposed to strictly individual, difference variables.

SKILLS INVENTORY: An information system containing data on employees' important skills and career goals.

SKILL VARIETY: A number of different tasks requiring diverse skills are included in a job.

SOCIALIZATION: Process of integrating the individual's values, abilities, behaviors, and social knowledge with those of the organization.

SOCIAL SECURITY: A federally mandated benefit for many employees designed to provide retirement income based on employer and employee contributions.

SOCIOTECHNICAL REDESIGNS: Physical and technical changes in the workplace based on social and/or technological requirements.

SPECIFICATION OF TRAINING NEEDS: The process whereby assessment of job requirements is compared to the assessment of individual abilities, to determine training needs.

SPLIT HALF RELIABILITY: A type of reliability that is assessed by correlating the responses on the two halves of a test.

STAFF AUTHORITY: Advisory or counseling service available to others who need periodic assistance in a specialized activity.

STAFFING ACTIVITIES: A managerial process in which the selection and training of needed employees is performed.

STIMULUS: An event or object that elicits a particular response or behavior.

STOCK OPTIONS: A program whereby executives are provided options to purchase company stock at some future date at a set price.

STOCK PURCHASE PLANS: Employees are encouraged to buy company stock, with the purchase being subsidized by the company.

STRESS: A force that acts on a person, creating physiological and emotional strain.

STRIKE: A work stoppage initiated by a union because of a disagreement between the union and management.

SUCCESSIVE APPROXIMATION: The schedule or sequence in which complex behaviors are best learned by beginning with the simplest basic behavior, then adding the next most simple behavior, and so on, until the entire complex sequence has been learned.

SUPERVISORY ANALYSIS (JOB ANALYSIS): This method of job analysis requires supervisors to record the activities, tasks, duties, and responsibilities of the jobs over which they have authority.

SUPERVISORY ESTIMATES: A human resource forecasting process used to predict demand. Supervisors project the personnel that their units will require in the future on the basis of experience and intuition.

SUPPLEMENTAL COMPENSATION: Some additional amount of compensation to be received for which the employee is not required to exert additional time or effort.

SUPPLEMENTAL UNEMPLOYMENT BENEFITS: A benefit program designed to provide normal wages or some major percentage thereof to employees who are laid off by the company for a temporary period.

SURVEY FEEDBACK: An OD technique in which survey results are used to solve existing problems or prevent them.

SYNTHETIC VALIDITY: Combining tests that have been shown to predict performance on similar task components in other jobs or other organizations.

TASK ABILITIES SCALE (TAS): A standard job analysis questionnaire that has been found to be extremely reliable and valid.

TASK IDENTITY: The degree to which successfully completed tasks can be determined and the degree to which one performing those tasks can associate with the end product.

TASK SIGNIFICANCE: The degree to which the job tasks have an impact on others both inside and/or outside the organization.

TEAM BUILDING: A process designed to improve the functioning of one or more work groups so that they are better able to achieve their objectives.

TEST-RETEST RELIABILITY: A type of reliability that correlates individuals' scores on two separate administrations of the same test.

TIME-BASED COMPENSATION: Salary or wage received by the employee that is based on the amount of time worked.

TRAINING: Systematic acquisition of skills, knowledge, and attitudes that have specific or narrow applicability to a limited set of situations in a specific job environment.

TRANSITION PROBABILITY: The probability of various moves in the organization, which are derived by determining the proportion of individuals in a position at the start of a time period who remain in that position at the end of the period, as well as the proportion who moved to other positions or out of the organization.

TWO-CAREER FAMILY: A family in which the husband and wife are both employed outside the home, with each pursuing a career.

TWO-FACTOR CONCEPT: A motivational theory developed by Herzberg in the late 1950s in which employee attitudes toward the job are influenced by motivators (factors contained within a person's job) or hygienes (conditions under which the job is performed).

UNDERUTILIZATION: The proportion of minorities and/or females in various jobs is lower than the proportion of such individuals in the applicable labor market.

UNEMPLOYMENT INSURANCE: A program that provides income to individuals who have lost a job through no fault of their own (while they search for a job); period of payment ranges from twenty-six to fifty-two weeks.

UNFAIR LABOR PRACTICES: Behaviors by employers or unions that interfere with employees' rights to engage in collective bargaining.

UNFREEZING: Preparing people to accept change; step 1 in change process.

UNION SHOP: Employer is required by the union to terminate employees who refuse to join the union within thirty days or who have not been paying union dues; illegal in right-to-work states.

UNITED STEELWORKERS OF AMERICA V WEBER: Kaiser and the steelworkers union agreed that Kaiser should undertake a training program to enable blacks to learn a skilled craft. In addition, separate seniority lists for blacks and whites were used to correct past discrimination practices. Weber claimed he had been denied admission to the training program on the basis of racial discrimination, because blacks and females with less seniority were admitted. Court ruled in favor of the company.

UNREALISTIC EXPECTATIONS: Inflated employee expectations about a new job.

VACATIONS: A fringe benefit whereby employees receive time away from work and receive their normal pay.

VALENCE: Anticipated value of an expected outcome—if such outcome does, in fact, occur.

VALIDITY: When a test or tool (e.g., for selection) measures what it is expected to measure.

VARIABLE PAY SCHEDULES: The employee usually receives a higher dollar amount per unit produced than a continuous pay schedule; however, the timing of the payment varies.

VARYING STANDARDS: Perceptions of performance standards may be different among supervisors.

VESTIBULE TRAINING: Training that occurs on a special site, usually on the organization's premises, away from the actual work setting, but using equipment and procedures similar to those used at the work setting.

VIETNAM ERA VETERANS READJUSTMENT ASSISTANCE ACT OF 1974: Covers federal contractors involved in interstate commerce having contracts in excess of $10,000 and prohibits discrimination against qualified disabled veterans of the Vietnam era.

VOLUNTARY BARGAINING ISSUE: An issue that requires no bargaining if either party declines to bargain.

WAGE AND SALARY SURVEY: A survey designed to obtain data on compensation practices and actual compensation paid to jobs similar to those in the focal organization.

WAGE RANGES: The minimum and maximum wages paid for jobs in several wage or salary grades.

WAGES: Direct pay for performing a certain job that is tied directly to the hours of time worked.

WALSH HEALY ACT: A federal law requiring all firms involved in construction of federal projects over $10,000 in value to pay prevailing local area wage rates.

WEIGHTED APPLICATION BLANK: Application blanks that provide a numerical score on each item reflecting an indication of the job applicant's likelihood of succeeding on the job.

WORK ENVIRONMENT: Physical conditions under which employees must work and the general treatment they receive.

WORKER'S COMPENSATION: A program that provides cash benefits for injuries sustained on the job.

WORK SAMPLE: Performance testing in which an applicant performs a real or simulated portion of the work that will be performed on the job.

WORK SIMPLIFICATION: The process of deleting those elements of a job that are least demanding of human skills and those that are unnecessary to task accomplishment.

INDEXES

SUBJECT INDEX

AUTHOR INDEX

544